Vitalizing Nature in the Enlightenment

Vitalizing Nature in the Enlightenment

PETER HANNS REILL

University of California Press
BERKELEY   LOS ANGELES   LONDON

University of California Press
Berkeley and Los Angeles, California

University of California Press, Ltd.
London, England

© 2005 by the Regents of the University of California

Library of Congress Cataloging-in-Publication Data

Reill, Peter Hanns.
   Vitalizing nature in the Enlightenment / Peter Hanns Reill.
   p. cm.
   Includes bibliographical references and index.
   ISBN 0-520-24135-5 (acid-free paper)
   1. Vitalism   2. Science—History—18th century.   I. Title.

Q175.32.V65R45   2005
509'.4'09033—dc22   2004023034

Manufactured in the United States of America
14 13 12 11 10 09 08 07 06 05
10 9 8 7 6 5 4 3 2 1

Printed on Ecobook 50 containing a minimum 50% post-consumer waste, processed chlorine free. The balance contains virgin pulp, including 25% Forest Stewardship Council Certified for no old growth tree cutting, processed either TCF or ECF. The sheet is acid-free and meets the minimum requirements of ANSI/NISO Z39.48-1992 (R 1997) (Permanence of Paper).

For Ellen and Dominique

Contents

Acknowledgments		ix
INTRODUCTION		1
PROLOGUE: THE HUMBOLDT BROTHERS CONFRONT NATURE'S SUBLIMITY		17
The Primordial Scene		17
Nature's Ambiguity		25
The Problem Posed		28
1. STORMING "THE TEMPLE OF ERROR": BUFFON, THE *HISTORIE NATURELLE*, AND THE MIDCENTURY ORIGINS OF ENLIGHTENMENT VITALISM		33
Natural Philosophy and the Mathematical Description of Nature		33
Toward a Redefinition of Organic Matter		42
System, Method, and Understanding		47
Preformation, Epigenesis, and the Historization of Nature		56
2. LEARNING TO "READ THE BOOK OF NATURE": VITALIZING CHEMISTRY IN THE LATE ENLIGHTENMENT		71
Creating a New Language of Chemistry		71
The Grammar and Vocabulary of the New Language of Chemistry		77
Chemistry, Heat, and Life		91
Enlightenment Vitalism and the Chemical Revolution		101
3. "WITHIN THE CIRCLE OF ORGANIZED LIFE"		119
Between Mechanism and Animism		119
Organization, Conjunction, Sympathy, and Nature's Economy		135
Elaborating the Vital Economy's Activities		143

4. THE METAMORPHOSES OF CHANGE 159
Generation, Reproduction, and the Economy of Nature 159
Death, Dying, and Resurrection 171
Ontogeny and Phylogeny in Enlightenment Vitalism 182

5. FROM ENLIGHTENMENT VITALISM TO
ROMANTIC *NATURPHILOSOPHIE* 199
Romantic *Naturphilosophie:* A New "Daring Adventure of Reason" 199
"Geometria est Historia": Toward a New *Universal Mathesis* 203
"Nature Is Visible Mind, Mind Invisible Nature":
From Harmony to Identity 209
"Being Itself Is Activity": From Change to Process 214
The Scientific Construction of Gender in the Late Enlightenment
and Romantic *Naturphilosophie* 220

EPILOGUE: FROM THE FOOT OF CHIMBORAZO TO THE
FLATLANDS OF EUROPE 237
Alexander von Humboldt's Dilemma 237
Reprise: What Is Enlightenment? What Isn't Enlightenment? 251

Notes 257
Bibliography 327
Index 367

Acknowledgments

This study has been a long time in gestation. It has required me to master many new areas of expertise, and it has forced me to try to free myself from traditional interpretations of the Enlightenment, whether positive or negative. In this book I have endeavored to reconstruct a way of knowing that was unique to mid- to late-eighteenth-century thinkers, neither "modern" nor "proto-Romantic," but fascinating because of the questions it raised and the types of answers it proposed. In my efforts to understand this form of Enlightenment thought, I was aided by advice and discussions with friends, colleagues, and students. Among them were Ivan Berend, Horst Blanke, Hans Erich Bödeker, Richard Bowler, William Clark, Lorraine Daston, Kimberly Garmoe, Carlo Ginzburg, Michael Hagner, Leeann Hansen, Georg Iggers, Jonathan Knudsen, Kirstie McClure, Hans Medick, Miriam Meijer, Kris Pangburn, Peter Park, John Pocock, Richard Popkin, Theodore Porter, Alisa Schulwies Reich, Jörn Rüsen, David Sabean, Michael Sauter, Jürgen Schlumbohm, Peter Schumann, Pamela Smith, Mary Terrall, Anne-Charlott Trepp, Robert Westman, and Norton Wise. I am indebted to Daniel Gordon, Roy Porter, Philip Sloan, and John Zammito, who painstakingly read the entire manuscript and provided me with invaluable help in shaping my arguments. I am also grateful to Stan Holwitz at the University of California Press, who encouraged me to submit my manuscript to the press, and to Randy Heyman and Mary Severance who have ushered its way through the publication process. David Anderson has done a marvelous job of text editing.

Much of my research and writing was carried out in Göttingen, at the "Niedersächsische Staats- und Universitätsbibliothek Göttingen," and at the Max-Planck-Institut-für-Geschichte. The Institute has been my second home for many years, providing me exciting intellectual stimulation and, over the last fifteen years, a refuge from the administrative tasks that have engaged much of my time. I owe a great debt to its former director, Rudolf Vierhaus, who has served as a discerning critic and an enthusiastic mentor and supporter. I am also thankful to his successor, Hartmut Lehmann, who has continued to encourage my work in the spirit of his predecessor. The initial phases of my research were funded by grants from the Guggenheim Foundation, the Fulbright-Hayes Commission, and the Wissenschaftskolleg zu Berlin.

Some of the arguments made in this volume have appeared in modified form in the following articles: "Anthropology, Nature and History in the Late Enlightenment: The Case of Friedrich Schiller," in *Schiller als Historiker*, edited by Otto Dann, Norbert Oellers, and Ernst Osterkamp (Stuttgart: Metzler, 1995); "Analogy, Comparison, and Active Living Forces: Late Enlightenment Responses to the Skeptical Critique of Causal Analysis," in *The Skeptical Tradition around 1800: Skepticism in Philosophy, Science, and Society*, edited by Johan Van der Zande and Richard Popkin (Dordrecht: Kluwer, 1998); "Death, Dying and Resurrection in Late Enlightenment Science and Culture," in *Wissenschaft als kulturelle Praxis, 1750–1900*, edited by Hans Erich Bödeker, Peter Hanns Reill, and Jürgen Schlumbohm (Göttingen: Vandenhoeck & Ruprecht, 1999); "Religion, Theology and the Hermetic Imagination in the Late German Enlightenment: The Case of Johann Salomo Semler," in *Antike Weisheit und kulturelle Praxis: Hermetismus in der frühen Neuzeit*, edited by Anne-Charlott Trepp and Hartmut Lehmann (Göttingen: Vandenhoeck & Ruprecht, 2001); "Vitalizing Nature and Naturalizing the Humanities in the Late Eighteenth Century," in *Studies in Eighteenth-Century Culture*, vol. 28, edited by Julie Candler Hayes and Timothy Erwin (Baltimore: Johns Hopkins University Press, 1999).

Finally, I would like to thank my spouse, Ellen Judy Wilson, and my daughter, Dominique, for their support, tolerance, patience, and good humor as I sought to combine my research and writing interests with those of administration and teaching, often to the detriment of a normal family life.

Los Angeles, 2003

Introduction

The initial impulse for this study arose from debates generated by my book on the rise of historicism in Germany during the Enlightenment, *The German Enlightenment and the Rise of Historicism*. In this earlier study I argued that the shift from a static to a dynamic worldview, central to modernity and usually called historicism, was conceptualized in the Enlightenment by Enlightenment thinkers. To make this shift clearer, I drew a distinction between Enlightenment historicism and Romantic historicism, each having its own agenda and methodological assumptions, but united by the larger view that history offers the basic mode to understand humanity. In my opinion this conceptual shift had been too narrowly associated with the "German historicist" form pioneered by Ranke and his followers and often mistakenly interpreted as a rebellion against the Enlightenment. I also suggested that the solutions Enlightened historicists offered to conceiving history were in many ways more compatible with the type of historical thought developed since the middle of the twentieth century than those advanced by "German historicism."

Although I still stand by the general outlines of this argument, I have since realized that I didn't go far enough in making my case. While rejecting traditional interpretations of the rise of historicism, I was still influenced by the German historicist assumption that posited a radical differentiation between the natural sciences *(Naturwissenschaften)* and the humanistic ones *(Geisteswissenschaften)*. According to this vision, "true" historical understanding can occur only when historians shake off any attempt to emulate the natural sciences. I assumed that the mid- to late Enlightenment thinkers I investigated had begun to draw this distinction. Stimulated by the discussions my book generated in Germany, however, I was forced to look more closely at the general outlines of Enlightenment thought, which led me to reevaluate the basic relation between "science" and history in the Enlightenment. I realized that Enlightenment thinkers never conceived of separating the humanities from the study of nature. For them, nature served as the basic model informing all human activities, the grand analogue upon which existence was grounded. Hence, I decided to undertake a more thorough study of the way in which Enlightenment and late Enlightenment thinkers conceived of nature and how this view guided their ideas of human interaction and change over time.

My original question was simple. Were mid- to late Enlightenment thinkers totally immersed in a mechanist view of nature that appeared to block the emergence of a dynamic worldview? If not, what type of natural knowledge did they develop capable of authorizing a new, dynamic concept of interaction and development encompassing the whole of living nature? Answering these questions proved difficult, and over time compelling, because of the emergence of contemporary postmodern critiques of the Enlightenment. In many ways these critiques seemed to rehearse those originally framed by the founders of Romantic German historicism and later reinforced by post–World War II intellectuals such as Theodor Adorno and Max Horkheimer.

In 1946 Horkheimer claimed in an essay that "the collapse of a large part of the intellectual foundation of our civilization is to a certain extent the result of technical and scientific progress."[1] Horkheimer located the origins of this demise—whose process he characterized as "the self-destructive tendency of Reason"—in the Enlightenment. This line of analysis, further elaborated by Horkheimer and Adorno in the *Dialectic of Enlightenment*, was later expanded and amplified by many commentators: postmodernists who rebel against the so-called hegemony of enlightenment rationality and analyze the knowledge-power dyad that gave rise to the intrusive panopticon of modern social control, some feminists who decry the Enlightenment's supposed elevation of universality over distinctness, and a cohort of philosophers of science, such as Stephen Toulmin, who seek to uncover Modernity's dangerous and outmoded hidden agenda by searching out the political and social forces that led to its inception. Despite the vast differences separating these critics, the indictment is clear: the Enlightenment in its fascination with science and universalizing reason sired such movements as gender and racial discrimination, colonialism, and totalitarianism.

For many students of the Enlightenment there seems to be a radical breach between the central signifiers in this critique and what they perceive. Clearly the major focus in these attacks is the Enlightenment's supposed worship of science, reason, and universality, of a form of power/knowledge based on control of both the physical and social realms that invariably is characterized in the singular as "the Enlightenment project." And we all know what that term suggests: the triumph in and by the Enlightenment of a mathematically based science, founded upon certain essential presuppositions concerning matter, method, and explanation whose reign has lasted until today. Stephen Toulmin described this macrohistorical movement as follows: "In choosing the goals of modernity, an intellectual and practical agenda that . . . focused on the seventeenth-century pursuit of mathematical exactitude and logical rigor, intellectual certainty and moral purity, Europe set itself on a cultural and political road that has led both to its most striking technical successes and to its deepest human failures."[2] These failures are often ascribed to the rise of instrumental rationality, to a new regime of strict discipline, scrutiny, and control, and to "the refashioning of cultural geographies and their associated anthropologies"[3] that directed the "Enlightenment project."

Yet when one begins to query what really was implied beneath this all-powerful engine of cultural and social change, the picture becomes much more hazy, complicating and confusing the new master narratives that are now being forged, and opening, I believe, fascinating new ways to evaluate the so-called Enlightenment project. This is especially true for the study of how nature was interpreted in the Enlightenment and how those interpretations were deployed in discourses dealing with human activities. For it has become increasingly clear that in the Enlightenment "nature was the principle that unified all narratives: the history of human society, as much as the history of the earth and stars, was a narrative about nature."[4] Hence it is essential to understand how nature was viewed, understood, spoken, and written about if one wishes to understand the question "What is Enlightenment?"

This study attempts to investigate one way in which nature was apprehended in the Enlightenment. It questions the notion of a unified Enlightenment project informed and driven by a language of nature founded upon mechanist natural philosophy, which reduced nature to a mechanism and humans to machines or automata. This attempt to disentangle some of the strands making up the Enlightenment is not in itself new. Already in the 1970s and 1980s, leading historians of science such as Roy Porter, Jacques Roger, Simon Schaffer, Robert Schofield, Steven Shapin, and Philip Sloan, to name but a few, called for a rethinking of how eighteenth-century science should be conceived. In 1980 Shapin characterized these new insights in a multiauthored volume entitled *The Ferment of Knowledge*, designed to take stock of existing historiography and point research in new directions.

Shapin says there, "We now have a developing perspective which points out the existence of a number of species of natural knowledge, and a number of opposed Enlightenments."[5]

Shapin's agenda has not been fully realized. Today different "Enlightenments" are analyzed most often by reference to specific social and cultural conditioners, generally producing concrete national, regional, local, or even disciplinary varieties. The editors of *The Sciences in Enlightened Europe*, a volume designed to demonstrate the direction in which the new history of science is now headed, reveal the shift in emphasis that has occurred over the past twenty years. They describe their approach as one that avoids the "thrall" of "positivism" and "mere anatomical dissection and microhistory": "These studies take as their topic one or another aspect of the construction of cultural unity in eighteenth-century Europe. By investigating the mechanisms of this construction, they provide us with a variegated geography of the Enlightenment and perhaps also permit us to recuperate a sense of the period as a whole."[6]

Thus the volume announces its goal of combining local, national, and disciplinary studies within a larger unified framework. However, this "recuperation" contradicts Shapin's original statement concerning opposing Enlightenments. The larger categories proposed there appear to have been forged by instruments taken directly from Foucault's toolbox; as a result, we encounter generalizations closely allied to those originally proposed by Horkheimer and Adorno in which discipline, control, dehumanization, and colonial exploitation emerge as dominant themes characterizing the Enlightenment as a whole.[7] There are exceptions to this interpretive stance in the volume, of course.[8] But, if its introduction represents the direction in which the study of Enlightenment science is going, then the task of tracing the existence of conflicting Enlightenment languages of nature that crossed national and regional barriers and represented a different take on essential questions seems to have disappeared from the research agenda of historians of eighteenth-century science. Nevertheless, I believe such languages existed, even if they had their own local dialects, which generated great internal conflicts. The following study is my attempt to reconstruct one of these Enlightenment languages of nature. If successful, I hope it will contribute to a redrawing of the Enlightenment's intellectual map.

· · ·

Not all historians of eighteenth-century natural philosophy accept the proposition that the Enlightenment can be reduced to "uniform reason ... defined by processes of classification and exclusion," to "a system of measure and disciplines."[9] This is especially the case for those who do not view the age as an integral totality, who are willing to acknowledge major intellectual, social, and cultural shifts occurring within the period.[10] It is usually conceded that during the first half of the Enlightenment, roughly from the late 1680s to the 1740s, mechanical natural philosophy became dominant, aided by the increasingly widespread acceptance of Newtonian science. During this period the central project of natural philosophy had been to incorporate the methods and assumptions of formal mathematical reasoning into explanations for natural phenomena. The overriding impulse was to transform contingent knowledge into certain truth, to reduce the manifold appearances of nature to simple principles. Leading proponents of the mechanical philosophy of nature proposed a new definition of matter, established methodological and explanatory procedures to incorporate this definition into a viable vision of science, and evolved an epistemology that authorized these procedures. Matter's essence was streamlined and simplified: it was defined as homogeneous, extended, hard, impenetrable, movable, and inert. The result, in Horkheimer's words, was that "Nature lost every vestige of vital independent existence, all value of its own. It became dead matter—a heap of things."[11]

By the middle of the eighteenth century, however, some of the core assumptions of this language of nature were no longer considered satisfying or self-evident. For many younger intellectuals, mechanism's very success made it suspect, for the brave new world of seventeenth-century mechanism, sometimes embodied in what is called "the radical Enlightenment,"[12] was very easily adapted during the early eighteenth century to serve as a support for the status quo—for political absolutism, religious orthodoxy, and established social hierarchies. Joined to that was an increasing crisis of assent, expressed in a wave of midcentury skepticism directed against the spirit of systems, against a one-sided reliance upon abstract reasoning in constructing a coherent picture of reality. For leading thinkers of the high and late Enlightenment,[13] deductive philosophy was deemed incapable of accounting for nature's vast variety. A strong skeptical critique, formulated most forcibly by David Hume but reflected in various degrees by thinkers as diverse as Georges-Louis Leclerc, comte de Buffon, Jean Le Rond d'Alembert, Marie-Jean-Antoine Caritat, Marquis de Condorcet, Denis Diderot, and Pierre-Louis Moreau de Maupertuis opened the way for a new approach to constructing nature.[14]

The mid-eighteenth-century skeptical critique of hypothetical thinking elevated the contingent over the coherent. It became a commonplace that all human knowledge was extremely constricted, because of its reliance upon sense impressions and because of its limited scope. If humans were endowed with reason, its power to pierce the veil of the unknown was circumscribed. At the same time, many late Enlightenment thinkers surrendered the idea that nature's operations could be comprehended under the rubric of a few simple, all-encompassing laws. Variety and similarity replaced uniformity and identity as the terms most associated with nature's products. Not only was nature seen as complex, it also was considered to be in continuous movement, in which old forms of existence are replaced by new ones.[15] In short, nature had a history. This triple movement—the limiting of reason's competence, producing a wide-ranging epistemological modesty; the expansion of nature's complexity; and the historization of nature—set a new agenda for Enlightenment natural philosophers. To paraphrase Hume, they were required to rethink the meaning of the terms "*power, force, energy* and *connexion*."[16] In late-eighteenth-century terms, the new science was to be a science of facts, observation, and controlled inference.

Generally, one can discern two broad mid-to-late-eighteenth-century strategies designed to satisfy the objections raised by the skeptical critique of reductive rationalism and uniformity. The first, and best known, was formulated by neomechanists such as D'Alembert, Condorcet, Joseph-Louis comte de Lagrange, and Pierre-Simon Laplace. Although retaining the mechanists' definition of matter as inert, they limited mathematics' role in describing nature to an instrument of discovery instead of considering it a model of reality. In so doing, they put aside those debates concerning the ultimate composition of matter (was it made up of atoms, monads, or immaterial points) or the mathematical definition of force (the *vis viva* controversy) that had animated early-eighteenth-century thinkers. Rather, they developed the mathematics of probability as the surest guide to direct observational reason, while maintaining an epistemological modesty concerning the truth claims of these activities.[17]

The second response to the skeptical critique was proposed by a loose group of thinkers, less frequently studied though extremely numerous, whom I call, for want of a better term, Enlightenment vitalists. Their interests usually centered on the fields of natural history, chemistry, the life sciences, medicine, and their interconnections. Unlike the neomechanists, they sought to reformulate the concept of matter, along with those of force, power, and connection in their construction of a natural philosophy that respected natural variety, dynamic change, and the epistemological consequences of skepticism. Their "reaction against the mechanical philosophy of the seventeenth century" served as a "powerful stimulus to the search for fresh vocabularies and methods with which to approach entities self-evidently more complex than automata."[18]

The general outlines of this language of nature that I will elaborate in this study can be summed up as follows. For the vitalists, the basic failure of mechanism was its inability to account for the existence of living matter. Mechanists had posited a radical separation between mind and matter that only God's intervention could heal, either as the universal occasion for all phenomena or as the creator of a preestablished harmony between mind and matter. This mind-body dichotomy was, according to Stephen Toulmin, the "chief girder in the framework of Modernity, to which all the other parts were connected."[19] Enlightenment vitalists sought to bridge or dissolve this dichotomy by positing the existence in living matter of active or self-activating forces, which had a teleological character. Living matter was seen as containing an immanent principle of self-movement or self-organization whose sources lay in active powers, which resided in matter itself. Thus, we encounter natural philosophers vitalizing the world with living forces such as elective affinities, vital principles, sympathies, and formative drives, reminiscent of the living world of the Renaissance. Rather than considering nature to be Horkheimer's "heap of things," Enlightenment vitalists envisioned it as a teeming interaction of active forces vitalizing matter, revolving around each other in a developmental dance.

The reintroduction into nature of goal-directed living forces led Enlightenment vitalists to reassess the basic methodological and analytic categories of natural philosophic investigation and explanation. The new conception of matter dissolved the strict distinction between observer and observed, since both were related within a much larger conjunction of living matter. Relation, *rapport*, *Verwandschaft*, cooperation of forces, and reciprocal interaction replaced aggregation and strict causal relations as defining principles of matter. Identity and noncontradiction were replaced with degrees of relation and similarity. The world of living matter consisted of a circle of relations, which, looking at it from the human vantage point, radiated out to touch all forms of living matter, uniting them in sympathetic interactions. Living matter's constituent parts formed a "synergy" in which each conjoined particle was influenced by the other and the *habitus* in which it existed.[20] By emphasizing the centrality of interconnection, Enlightenment vitalists modified the concept of cause and effect. In the world of living nature, each constituent part of an organized body was both cause and effect of the other parts, all symbiotically linked through the universal power of sympathy. Enlightenment vitalists explained change using the concept of goal, making it the efficient cause of development. An explanation for something's existence took the form of a narrative modeled upon the concept of stage-like development or epigenesis, in which a body evolves through steps from a point of creation. Unique creation and true qualitative transformation formed part of the vitalists' vision of living nature.[21]

These shifts in natural philosophic assumptions challenged Enlightenment vitalists to construct an epistemology capable of justifying and validating them. True to the skeptical critique of causation and forces, vitalists agreed that active life forces could not be seen directly, nor could they be measured. They were "occult powers" in the traditional sense of the term. At best they were announced by outward signs, whose meaning could be grasped only indirectly. In this language of nature the topos of locating real reality as something that lurked within a body played a crucial role. That which was immediately observable was considered superficial. Understanding entailed a progressive descent into the depths of observed reality, using signs as markers to chart the way. Thus, Enlightenment vitalists reintroduced the idea of semiotics as one of the methods to decipher the secrets of nature.

The basic epistemological problem was to understand the meaning of these signs and to perceive the interaction of the individual yet linked active forces, powers, and energies without collapsing one into the other. To resolve this problem Enlightenment vitalists called for a form of understanding that combined the individualized elements of nature's variety into a harmonic conjunction that recognized both nature's unity and diversity. The methods adopted to implement this program were analogical reasoning and comparative analysis. Analogical reasoning became the functional replacement for mathematical analysis. With it one could discover similar properties or tendencies between dissimilar things that approximated natural laws without dissolving the particular in the general. The fascination for analogies was strengthened by a general preference for functional analysis, subordinating actual outward form to inner activity. Comparative analysis reinforced the concentration upon analogical reasoning. It allowed one to consider nature as composed of systems having their own character and dynamics, yet demonstrating similarities not revealed by the consideration of form. The major task of comparison was to chart similarities and differences and mediate between them, finding analogies that were not immediately apparent.[22]

In pursuing this program founded upon analogical reasoning and comparative analysis, a further epistemological problem arose. If nature was unity in diversity, how could one choose which element to emphasize? When should one concentrate upon the concrete singularity, and when should one cultivate generalizing approaches? The proposed answer was to do both at once, allowing the interaction between them to produce a higher form of understanding than provided by simple observation or discursive, formal logic. This type of understanding was called divination, intuition, or *Anschauung*. Its operation was based on the image of mediation or harmony, of continually moving back and forth from one to the other, letting each nourish and modify the other. In this movement, however, understanding passed through a third, hidden and informing, agent that was, in effect, the ground upon which all reality rested. In eighteenth-century vitalist language, this hidden middle element, opaque, unseeable, yet essential, was called by such terms as the "internal mould," "prototype," *Urtyp*, or *Haupttypus*. Some writers used the image of a magnetic field to give it visual representation. It was constituted by the magnetic poles and yet united them without submerging them in a reductive unity. The area of its greatest effect was the middle, where the field encompassed the largest area.

This harmonic view of reality formed the core and essence of the late Enlightenment vitalists' vision of nature and humanity, differentiating it from early-eighteenth-century mechanism and later Romanticism. It accounted for its fascination with extremes—boundaries and limits—and their hoped for mediations, what Ludmilla Jordanova called "bridging concepts."[23] It was not a dualistic vision of nature and humanity, for real reality always lay between extremes. Harmony, the joining of opposites within an expanded middle generated by reciprocal interaction, served as the norm and desired end of each natural process, though that dynamic was continually in motion, leading to ever-changing harmonic combinations. Living nature became the place where freedom and determinism merged. Its description invoked images and metaphors either drawn from the moral sphere or directly applicable to it. Horkheimer had claimed that the "the inner logic of science itself tends towards the idea of one truth which is completely opposed to the recognition of such entities as the soul and the individual."[24] The natural philosophy envisioned by Enlightenment vitalists sought to reintroduce entities such as active energy (soul in a highly secularized form) and individuality into the inner core of scientific thinking.

· · ·

By labeling this language of nature "Enlightenment Vitalism," I am aware that I am creating a synthetic type not usually recognized in Enlightenment historiography. At best, the term "vitalism" has been reserved for a group of medical thinkers usually associated with the medical schools of Montpellier and Edinburgh, and with some midcentury chemists seen as followers of Georg Stahl. My claims are much stronger. I wish to show that the language of nature summarized above far transcended disciplinary boundaries, that its appeal was great, and that its terms, metaphors, and explanatory strategies easily translated into many spheres of human thought and activity. Further, I will show that these translations reciprocally interacted, leading to continual exchange and reformulation. Thus certain central Enlightenment vitalist categories such as sympathy, sensibility, or habit could migrate and take root in other spheres of human thought and culture and then move back, enhanced by their contact with those intellectual realms and cultural concerns. In this book I concentrate upon the specifics of how this language was constructed, with reference to natural phenomena and the types of mediations sought between them. I hope to show in a later study how this language of nature was translated into what we now call the humanistic and social sciences.

I have constructed "Enlightenment Vitalism," as with all synthetic categories in historical analysis, by generalizing from the writings of a number of major and minor participants who wrestled with questions accounting for life in its various manifestations or who described physical processes they thought central to its understanding. I have focused upon three interlocking areas of linguistic exchange—natural history, chemistry, and the life sciences, including medicine. I could have expanded my research to other areas, geology, for example, but I believe this expansion would not alter my main points, though it certainly would enhance them. I chose to limit my focus simply for reasons of convenience.

I begin my analysis of Enlightenment Vitalism with Buffon. I do not claim him to be "the founder" of vitalism, but see him as one who emerged as an iconic figure in its elaboration. His magnificent prose, the scope of his natural historical project, and the position he occupied as head of the *Jardin du Roi* in Paris enabled Buffon to set the agenda for many of the important discussions that would shape this new language of nature, though his specific formulations would be contested as frequently as adopted. In the three chapters that follow, I first focus upon chemistry, which as revised in the last half of the eighteenth century along parallel lines to natural history provided a new model for understanding "dead matter" and offered valuable analogies to comprehending living matter. The two chapters that follow deal directly with living matter. The first probes eighteenth-century vitalist formulations accounting for organization, conjunction, and sympathy, all incorporated into the image of a "vital economy of nature." The second discusses the "historization of nature" by focusing upon the issues of birth, death, and the relationship between ontogeny and phylogeny. In these sections I mobilize thinkers from diverse intellectual backgrounds, reflecting the lack of strict disciplinary boundaries during the eighteenth century. Chemists trained as doctors, doctors who taught moral philosophy, moral philosophers who pondered the secrets of generation, polymaths who wrote poetry and studied comparative anatomy, amateur and professional natural historians bent upon collecting as many new specimens as possible, mathematicians who wrote about chemistry and chemists who wrote about mathematics, theologians, civil servants, diplomats, and educated lay persons—all were fascinated by the need to establish a new vocabulary to account for living nature.

Thus, I treat Enlightenment Vitalism as a "real" type, not an ideal one, similar in its explanatory claims to other "real typologies" such as "mechanism" and "organicism." As with all such historical generalizations, this is not an exact definition. Its boundaries were sometimes fuzzy and its members often enemies, emphasizing some elements of the language while minimizing others. Still, I believe the people I place under this category knew that their disputes were carried out within the boundaries of an evolving language of nature that had a different vocabulary and grammar than the language of mechanism they were attempting to supplant or at least to modify and enhance.

But why call it Enlightenment Vitalism? Let me begin with vitalism. One simple reason to use the term is that it was an eighteenth-century neologism created to distinguish its goals from that of mechanism and animism. But more importantly, I use this term to draw a differentiation between vitalism and organicism. Readers in the twenty-first century may be tempted to consider vitalism as a variant of organicism. Intellectual historians and historians of science have often considered organicism and mechanism as the only two possible models for envisioning the order of things. Thus, for example, many historians of the life sciences trace the development of this field as being driven forward by the battle between these two "irreconcilable spirits," a process that is supposed to generate, increasingly, sophisticated formulations of the science's problems and methods, ultimately leading to scientific progress.[25] These two antithetical forms are considered binary opposites. Any intermediate formulations are often referred to as "transitional," that is, as inconsistent, contradictory, and unsuccessful attempts to aspire to one of the two opposed forms. Their lack of coherence is ascribed to residues of earlier modes of thought.

Such an analytic procedure may be valid and applicable for the works of authors who unintentionally mixed forms they designed to exclude, such as Robert Boyle's proclamation of a mechanical philosophy that still bristled with hermetic assumptions. However, adopting such an explanatory strategy for authors who consciously strove to mediate between different positions distorts their meanings. Here the authors' stated intentions are sacrificed at the altar of typological purity. This has been true for the case of late-eighteenth-century vitalists.[26] Enlightenment Vitalism may have been "transitional" in the most formal historical sense, namely, that it consciously shared things with what it criticized and inevitably contributed elements to what came after. But it was neither unintentionally mechanistic nor unconsciously "proto-organic" or "proto-Romantic."[27] It offered a unique formulation of the order of things that cannot be explained by the usual mechanistic, organic, or transitional explanatory categories of intellectual history. As such, it represented a specific and consciously constituted language of nature, based on the imperative to mediate between extremes in which harmony functioned as its overriding metaphor. Its creators consciously sought to retain elements of mechanism and animism (the closest eighteenth-century equivalent of organicism) but placed them in a new context. In some cases modern historians of science have recognized this in their analyses and in the terms they use to describe their subjects. Thus, for example, Jordanova discusses important late-eighteenth-century "bridging concepts" that "gave rise to productive ambiguity," while Timothy Lenoir would reify one such ambiguity in his characterization of late-eighteenth- and early-nineteenth-century German biology, calling it "teleo-mechanism."[28]

I add the term "Enlightenment" to underline my argument that the specific form of vitalism I am discussing was unique to the period. It formed part of the Enlightenment's intellectual terrain and should not be automatically equated to later movements that appropriated that name, such as the early-twentieth-century vitalisms of Henri Bergson in France or Hans Driesch in Germany. These latter movements are often associated with conservative if not right-wing politics, with a yearning to return to simpler times and a very strong critique of modernity. The same type of analysis has been applied—wrongfully, I contend—to many late-eighteenth-century thinkers who criticized mechanism using the language of Enlightenment vitalism. (Herder is the most obvious example.) Yet, as I try to show, Enlightenment vitalism was not politically conservative, though some of its proponents may have been. Rather, it employed the images of consent and cooperation; it spoke of the assembly of forces and their free play; its image of organization excluded a single directing power or "royal" force. As such it often contained liberal and sometimes revolutionary overtones, as the thought of some of its speakers such as Diderot, Rousseau, Joseph Priestley, Georg Foster, Benjamin

Constant, and Wilhelm and Alexander von Humboldt demonstrates. In short, I argue that Enlightenment Vitalism constituted a language whose chief modifiers, metaphors, and connecting terms had their own internal coherence, a coherence that disappeared as the language was supplanted by other languages of nature, rendering its forms incomprehensible to later ages.

Although I don't trace the degree to which this language was accepted in the late Enlightenment, I assume its framers spoke to a large constituency of Europe's educated elite. Their works were addressed to a variety of audiences, including the practicing anatomist and physiologist, the university student, the civil servant, the well-read bourgeois, and the enormous host of amateur naturalists who, spanning the social scale, avidly collected samples from all of nature's realms. This language of nature was packaged and disseminated by what Martin Gierl calls the Enlightenment's knowledge factory, its products consisting of a plethora of compilations ranging from handbooks, encyclopedias, and learned journals to daily newspapers and moral weeklies.[29] In these compilations excerpts from texts and review articles would be reproduced again and again, moving from one publication to another with hardly any changes, their compilers showing no qualms about what we now call plagiarism. To know what Buffon or Albrecht von Haller or Jean Barthez or Johann Friedrich Blumenbach believed did not require one either to have read these authors directly or to have owned their books: the compilations and reviews sufficed. These formal products of knowledge exchange were supplemented by an intensive correspondence network, which supported a still flourishing Republic of Letters. The products of these expanding mediums of communication were discussed in many different sites: academies, university lecture halls, reading clubs, secret societies, societies devoted to improvement, salons, coffee houses—in sum, in all of the Enlightened institutions that modern research is now investigating.

I close my analysis with a discussion of how the language of Enlightenment Vitalism unraveled. In so doing, I contrast Enlightenment Vitalism to Romantic *Naturphilosophie*. The latter is also a generalized type, constructed from my reading of many of the major German thinkers associated with this movement. I concentrate upon the core of thinkers who shaped its language, Friedrich Schelling, Lorenz Oken, and their allies, though I give Oken special attention because of his long and successful career as a *Naturphilosoph*. For today's readers, especially in the Anglo-Saxon world, this language of nature is almost incomprehensible, yet it swept the German universities during the first decades of the nineteenth century and attracted a strong but less numerous following in France, England, and Scotland. Its fellow travelers are said to have included Étienne Geoffroy Saint-Hilaire, André-Marie-Constant Duméril, and Étienne Serres in France, and Robert Knox, Peter Mark Roget, Martin Barry, William Carpenter, John Goodsir, and Richard Owen in Scotland and England.[30]

Naturphilosophie is often considered the logical culmination of positions staked out by the people I call Enlightenment vitalists, who are often interpreted as either enemies of the Enlightenment or as thinkers who overcame it. Rather than seeing *Naturphilosophie* as vitalism's logical conclusion, I interpret it as its negation, as a thoroughgoing critique of the epistemological, methodological, and linguistic assumptions that undergirded Enlightenment Vitalism. *Naturphilosophie's* major thrust was to dissolve the dichotomies that supported the mediations central to Enlightenment Vitalism. Its founders sought to evolve a science of the mind that accounted for the universe's birth and development, to return to a vision of nature based upon timeless universals in which phenomenal reality was to be explained by reference to primordial forms, in short, to escape from the horror of the contingent into the *ur*-world of absolutes. In this sense Romantic *Naturphilosophie* marks a major break with the Enlightenment in all its forms. But that does not make it a Foucaultian episteme shift. Certainly it is not one Foucault would recognize as belonging to the world of "positivities" he believed defined modernity. *Naturphilosophie* constituted a new post-Revolutionary language of nature that stood in sharp contrast to other evolving and contending languages of nature in the nineteenth century, positivism being the most prominent. Their collective triumph during the first third of the century spelled the doom of Enlightenment Vitalism's knowledge claims. Its parts were rent asunder and reconstituted in new configurations, leading over time to the nineteenth-century separation of the natural from the social and humanistic sciences, made most evident in the German philosophical distinction between the *Natur-* and *Geisteswissenschaften*.

This book begins with a prologue and ends with an epilogue. The prologue looks to the end of my narrative, the epilogue to the beginning of the book. In both I focus upon the thought of Wilhelm and Alexander von Humboldt, two figures who have occupied a central position in the discussion defining what the Enlightenment was and wasn't. In using them to "bookend" the study, I am trying to show how the concept of Enlightenment Vitalism might help us rethink the way in which we interpret the intellectual history of the period. Every synthetic historical category should perform useful intellectual work, highlighting things not seen and differentiating between others that might have been joined. In the case of Enlightenment Vitalism, if my reconstruction makes sense, then I believe it performs several tasks. It enables us to abandon explanatory categories such as pre- or proto-Romanticism, based upon a teleological reading of texts, by recognizing the regnant discussion of life and organization central to the Enlightenment. It allows us to better perceive the uniqueness of Enlightened thought, giving us pause before we make it our immediate contemporary, of associating it automatically with "modernity." It uncovers the importance of large-scale thought patterns that disciplinary studies have hidden or localized. It allows us to reevaluate the intentions of intellectuals such as the Humboldt brothers or Herder, who have been cast as major opponents of the Enlightenment project, questioning thereby the general concept of the "Counter-Enlightenment." On the broadest level it makes the idea of a single "Enlightenment project" problematic, without surrendering the idea of the existence of large transnational discursive realms within the Enlightenment's domain.

In my view Enlightenment Vitalism was a relatively coherent movement distinguished by a set of basic assumptions, often later considered contradictory, held together by a unique epistemological position based on the imperative to mediate between extremes. It constituted one of the basic languages of nature and humanity available to Enlightenment thinkers. In this sense Enlightenment Vitalism had its own linguistic and intellectual form, shaped by crucial questions that confronted thinkers of the last half of the eighteenth century.

What is fascinating about these questions is that they again speak to issues we are now facing: how does one define life and death, what is matter, to what extent is morality natural or artificial? Its assertion of the intimate link between humans and nature and its celebration of nature's creativity and sublimity speak directly to our need to rethink the issue of humankind's role within the environment and relationship to it. Its elevation of reciprocal interrelationship and cooperation, validated by the free play of nature's forces, coincides with our attempts to rethink causal explanations in nature and global interaction among humans. Its view of gender and discussions of race still resonate with today's discussion of these topics. Finally its attempt to formulate a new logic of complementarity, linked to its epistemological modesty and supported by a concern with semiotics and language, provides a model of knowledge that speaks to contemporary endeavors to escape from absolute solutions and maintain the search for knowledge without surrendering to skepticism. In all of these, Enlightenment Vitalism shares many elements usually seen as characteristic of postmodernity. In fact, once the image of the "Enlightenment project" is abandoned and replaced by a true appreciation of the high and late Enlightenment, of which Enlightenment Vitalism formed a part, the Enlightenment may well emerge as an age much more in tune with our concerns than is usually conceived. The questions they posed are still relevant, though their answers may not be; in fact, some answers easily appear weird and non-self-evident,[31] reminding us of the distance that separates us from the Enlightenment. Yet their basic epistemological temper still serves as a challenge, relevant today as it was then. For these reasons I hope this work will be judged as an attempt to help us answer anew the question: What is Enlightenment?

Prologue

The Humboldt Brothers Confront Nature's Sublimity

THE PRIMORDIAL SCENE

Wilhelm and Alexander von Humboldt occupy a unique place in German intellectual history. Ranked among the age's most important luminaries, they often have been seen as embodiments of contradictory but complementary visions of knowledge *(Wissenschaft)*. Wilhelm is considered the theoretician who broke Enlightenment natural science's spell on the cultural sciences *(Geisteswissenschaften)*, thereby laying the foundations for the rise of modern historicism. Alexander is usually acclaimed as the person whose exacting empiricism inspired the tremendous flowering of German natural science during the nineteenth century. For many German intellectuals the Humboldt brothers symbolized the split between the natural and humanistic sciences, a separation often considered essential for their respective developments. This dichotomy is symbolically expressed at the entrance to the Humboldt University in Berlin, where busts of Alexander and Wilhelm face each other as if to define the common goals of *Wissenschaft* while announcing their own independent and unique missions.

Certainly the brothers appeared to be opposites. Alexander, a born courtier, mingled easily in society, combining wit with learning without being boring or offensive. He was as comfortable in the salons and academies of Paris, where he spent many of his most productive years, as he was in Latin America's provincial towns and cities, or in Berlin, where he lived during the last years of his life. Wilhelm, equally as cosmopolitan as his brother and an extremely successful diplomat and statesman, was considered a loner— distant and tight-lipped, a master manipulator. After a fling at "self-cultivation," Wilhelm spent a good part of his mature life first in the service of the Prussian state and then as a semi-recluse in his villa at Tegel outside

/ *Prologue*

Berlin. Alexander never married; he was probably homosexual, although there is no concrete evidence. Wilhelm, on the other hand, was compulsively heterosexual. Throughout his open yet successful marriage, he remained a frequent and treasured client of the major European brothels.

Whatever their differences, the brothers devoted themselves primarily to the life of the intellect, although pursuing diverging paths in their scholarly careers. Alexander was a prolific writer, producing three important scientific works before his famous voyage; after his return he published, with his friend Bonpland, thirty volumes devoted to their South American trip. He followed this with a report on his travels to Russia and capped his career with his famous attempt to summarize contemporary knowledge in the four-volume *Cosmos*.

Wilhelm, in sharp contrast, had a great deal of trouble finishing any project he started. The vast majority of his projects remained torsos or fragments of larger programs that never were completed. His most famous early work, *On the Limits of State Action*, was not published during his lifetime. His essay on history, "On the Historian's Task," probably the most important early-nineteenth-century essay on the nature of historical understanding, was an occasional piece. Only his linguistic studies—his study on the Basque language and his analysis of the Kawi language (also published posthumously)—were full length and complete.

Yet, despite their considerable differences, both brothers employed a common symbolic and metaphorical language—what Alexander called a *Bildersprache*—in all of their work, founded upon a shared vision of nature and the processes of perception. Their common language of nature has not been reconstructed; in fact, those too eager to place Wilhelm and Alexander within artificially established disciplinary canons and movements or who believe in the universal distinction between the *Natur-* and *Geisteswissenschaften* have ignored their shared interests. It is time, I believe, to suspend these canons in order to see if Wilhelm and Alexander's shared vision can shed new light upon the dynamics of late-eighteenth- and early-nineteenth-century culture and thought. To pursue this inquiry, it is necessary not only to reconstruct their specific language of nature, but also to reflect upon its sources, dispersion, and meaning. In other words, it is necessary to reassess the period in which the Humboldts grew up with a new set of assumptions.

. . .

The Humboldts' shared language of nature emerged most clearly when Wilhelm or Alexander probed larger issues of meaning, nature, and existence, usually evoked by a confrontation with "sublime" vistas of nature's power and magnificence. Wilhelm experienced one such moment in 1799 when traveling to Spain from Paris, where he had been observing the new political order created by the French Revolution. As a rule, Wilhelm von Humboldt was never an easy writer to read. Destined, he believed, to be a critical rather than a creative thinker, Wilhelm composed works that appeared to be cold, impersonal, emotionless—"bright as the December sun,"[1] to render what he observed crystalline in its clarity. But occasionally he broke with his self-imposed restraint and hinted at "inner feelings" that often "robbed him of his repose,"[2] allowing them to run unreined by the sense of order and limits Wilhelm so greatly admired. This happened for a brief moment on his trip to Spain when he visited the town of St. Jean-de-Luz.

The view from the town, pressed on one side against the forbidding cliffs of the Pyrenees and on the other open to the relentless, roiling sea of the Bay of Bayonne, released in Humboldt a flow of near mythic associations. In the space of a few pages he dashed down a vision of nature that recounted primordial beginnings;[3] he felt, he later wrote, as "though he were witness to the first acts of creation."[4] Because of this strongly visceral reaction to a natural scene, his essay serves as an entry into a discussion of images central to Wilhelm's vision of nature and reality.

He began by describing St. Jean-de-Luz, a town divided by an arm of the sea, both halves connected by a wooden bridge. Because of the sea's potential for violence, a stone quay had been built during Louis XIV's reign to restrain the waters. Since the Revolution everything had been neglected, and the sea now threatened to break down the barriers and destroy the town. This observation with its contrast between civil order and political revolution, suggesting Humboldt's Parisian experiences, was the preface to a more general consideration of the forces of destruction, as reflected by the images of the mountains and the sea: "Never has the dead and raw mass of creation presented itself to me so overpoweringly, never has the germ of life in nature appeared to me so weak and powerless as here between the Pyrenees and the Ocean." The barren Pyrenees presented a picture of "everlasting inertia, of a mass pressing down forever on its own center of gravity, threatening to collapse upon itself." The mountains appeared so compressed and compacted that they seemed to "suffocate" the "free play of life." The sea, on the other hand, generated the opposite feeling. It offered Humboldt the frightening specter of untrammeled anarchic movement that endangered the entire globe with destruction. To Humboldt, "blind laws" ruled both the mountains' silent, dead mass and the sea's forever active, chaotic movement.

Yet, despite this apparently hopeless interplay between stasis and chaos in nature, something new took place: "Miraculously, a plant twists itself out of a rock's cleft; clinging to the harsh bluffs, living organization maintains itself in the midst of desolation; the formative drive *[Trieb der Bildung]* leaps from it like the spark hidden in the stone."[5]

For Humboldt, contemplating this scene of primordial creation unleashed his "thought, fantasy, and feeling." On the one hand, we "experience the feeling of human impotence and of our sinking into insignificance before these powerful elements." On the other, we are driven to wonder at the natural law that imposes equilibrium between the forces of dead mass and chaotic movement threatening universal destruction. Through this "secret move," this "revolution," grandiose nature inseparably chains us to her. She inspires in us "a feeling of gentle melancholy *[sanfte Schwermuth]*, from which we have as little desire to escape as we do from her gaze." In this gaze the resolution of the battle between life and lifelessness played a central role. Each element may be driven on by its own powers but is also bound in "harmony and concord, an eternal fate whose internal connection is hidden from us by an impenetrable veil."[6] The poetic act, which combines intuition *(Anschauung)* and reason informed by precise empirical study and creative imagination, can, however, at least point to nature's underlying harmony. Such a poetic act constitutes the highest form of knowledge, joining the study of physical nature with the study of the moral, linking blind forces to life drives.[7]

Here, *in nuce*, Wilhelm presented a characterization of nature, a concept of natural development, a view of aesthetics, a theory of science and understanding, and a political conviction in immediate, concrete form. The governing theme linking all of these elements is a yearning for the creation of harmony, for the mediation between conflicting extremes. It is a complex vision arising out of the idea that polar confrontation can be resolved, producing a harmonic conjunction, which is in turn constantly reshaped as the forces of nature revolve around each other in a dance of development.

Three years later Alexander von Humboldt confronted an even more imposing sublime natural phenomenon—the towering mass of Mount Chimborazo in Ecuador. Considered at the time to be the highest mountain in the world at 6,544 meters, Humboldt scaled it to 5,850 meters, one thousand meters higher than any other European had climbed.[8] At Mount Chimborazo's base Humboldt composed the first draft of his *Essai sur la géographie des plantes; accompagné d'un tableau physique des régions équinoxiales* (later translated in German as *Ideen zu einer Geographie der Pflanzen nebst einem Naturgemälde der Tropenländer*) and sketched out his immensely popular *Ansichten der Natur*, both published after his return to Europe.[9] Although much longer than Wilhelm's musings at St. Jean-du-Luc, partly due to the vast accompanying arsenal of exact measurements, Alexander's two writings offered a similar statement of faith about the workings of nature and how humans perceive them.

In the *Essai* and *Ansichten*, Alexander von Humboldt's basic goal was to present a "picture" of nature that the reader could apprehend with "one look": that is, he sought to combine the tools of exact analysis with poetic description to reveal the "secret play" of nature's powers *(Kräfte)* that continually created new harmonic conjunctions. Nature's manifold variety, discovered only through laborious observation and measurement, was formed and governed by the cooperation *(Zusammenwirken)* of nature's powers: "In the great chain of cause and effect no piece of matter, no activity should be observed in isolation. This equilibrium, which rules in the middle, below the perturbations of seemingly battling elements, results from the free play of dynamic powers *[Kräfte]*."[10] Three sets of principles governed this cooperation or "play" of nature's powers. The first principle, which was expressed in the contemporary language of chemical affinity, assumed continual interchanges between matter founded upon desire or loathing, attraction or repulsion. Humboldt had previously expressed this idea in an earlier essay written for Friedrich Schiller's journal *Das Horen* that he included in the *Ansichten*: "Already in the darkest chaos, matter either joined together or was separated because it was attracted by friendship or repelled by animosity."[11] The second principle asserted that the forces of life or the organic powers *(organische Kräfte)* were universally present, "even ready to animate the dead cliff," for, "wherever the gaze of the investigator penetrates, life or the germ of life is dispersed."[12] The third principle stated that all interactions or developments within living matter are limited by definite boundaries, determined by still unknown laws.[13] Because bodily structures had outer limits, living matter was regulated by the action of the life force *(Lebenskraft)* and thus achieves a temporary equilibrium between the interacting forces. The life force suspends the "democritic friendship and animosity of the atoms; it joins material substances that in dead nature eternally flee from each other and separates those that would have continually sought each other out."[14]

In his description of the "play" of conflicting powers resulting in harmonic creation and re-creation, Alexander used the same metaphors as Wilhelm but did not feel compelled to invoke the *Ur*-beginning of life symbolized by the single plant springing from the dead mass of the mountain. His explorations of the tropics close to the equator convinced Alexander that he had returned to a scene that closely approximated the youth of the world. In the tropics nature's powers worked undiminished, her profusion and grandeur unaffected by seasonal variations of the sun's intensity. Nowhere was nature's regularity more evident, nor its creative power more obvious. These powers were not alien or separate from human life. Quite the contrary: Humboldt believed in a universal, intimate connection between the human and the physical world, which was often blurred by "civilization." In the tropics that connection was unmistakable and omnipresent: "Nowhere does nature penetrate us more with the feeling for her greatness, nowhere does she speak to us more powerfully as in the tropical world. . . . The remembrance of a distant, richly endowed land, the vision of a free, powerful vegetation refreshes and reinforces the spirit, as though, oppressed by the present, the forward-striving spirit delights itself gladly on the youth of humanity and in its simple greatness."[15]

Alexander saw no radical separation between the natural and human worlds; they were joined in our "most inner, receptive faculty" where "everything stands in a secret, ancient, intercourse with the spiritual life of humans."[16] The imaginative reconstruction of experiences that affirm these connections validates natural observation. In fact, such reconstructions give a truer sense of the majesty and power of nature in the tropics than the observation of "the sickly plants forced into our greenhouses . . . which offer us a distorted and incomplete picture of the magnificence of tropical vegetation." The "active fantasy of the poet and painter" compensates for this loss: "The magic of the imitative arts transposes Europeans to the most distant parts of the earth. He who has the active feeling for this magic, whose spirit is cultivated enough to embrace nature in all its activities, creates for himself, as it were, in the loneliness of a desolate heath an inner world; accompanying the natural investigator, navigating through sea and air, on mountain tops and in subterranean caves, he takes possession of what the natural investigator discovered."[17] These portrayals transcend the mere description of outward phenomena; they provide us with true insight that makes us more attuned to changes over time, whether in the past or the future: "The knowledge of the inner, secret play of natural powers allows us to dare to draw conclusions about the future and to determine in advance the return of major events. In this manner, the insight into the world organism creates a spiritual pleasure and an inner freedom that in the midst of destiny's blows cannot be destroyed by an external power."[18]

Alexander von Humboldt presented his readers with a message built upon a seemingly contradictory set of assumptions. On the one hand, he elevated the importance of strict quantitative measurement of everything subject to periodic change to the status of physical law, while on the other hand, he emphasized the significance of subjective interaction between the human observer and physical world as a kind of insight or knowledge. It was this tension between the two assumptions that provided the parameters for an expanded vision of nature and, by analogy, of humanity, all of which could be recaptured only through an act of intuitive representation. Nature, human nature, and human history were locked in a close embrace.

. . .

These short works by Wilhelm and Alexander von Humboldt reveal that the brothers shared certain fundamental assumptions concerning nature, its relationship to humanity, the processes of perceiving reality, and the most effective means of representing these perceptions. For both Wilhelm and Alexander, nature's activity could best be comprehended in the interaction between powers resident in matter. What we perceive in nature is the product of a struggle of forces symbolized by two sets of hierarchically ordered dichotomies: the first, the tension between mass and movement, the second, between life and lifelessness. Wilhelm described the first in the tension between the sea and mountains at St. Jean de-Luz, physical entities whose overpowering presence obliterated all nuanced ideas, filling the observer with "horror" at their destructive powers. For Alexander nature also operated within the boundaries set by chaos and inaction. In his "Life Force or the Rhodian Genius," Alexander characterized matter in a sexually charged language as either being at rest or wildly coupling and recoupling when a suitor disturbed that rest.[19]

By introducing the concepts of "life forces" or "formative drive," the Humboldt brothers elevated the matter/motion dichotomy to another, higher plane. For Wilhelm and Alexander, life was the primary phenomenon of nature, everywhere present, an insight Wilhelm symbolized by the plant springing "miraculously" from the barren cliff. Both brothers considered life forces to be substantially different than the "blind," "sterile" ones of lifeless nature, as was made clear by their designation of the formative force with the anthropomorphic term *drive* (Bildungs*trieb*). Alexander also compared the life force's essence to a ruler's active gaze, whose "eyes were the symbol of the life force, which animates [*beseelt*] every germ of organic creation."[20] All of these images convey the idea of telos rather than mechanical balance. But the telos was not determined. The Humboldts modified the normal association of final goal by introducing the possibility of spontaneous ("miraculous") activity, usually encapsulated in the term "miracle of creation." For both Wilhelm and Alexander, a critical feature of animated nature was that its goal-directness was never totally predictable because of the possibility of new creation arising from the "secret play" of life forces.

The central dichotomy between life and lifelessness in the Humboldts' language incorporated and elevated the mass-motion dichotomy. Although inertia and chaos pertained to the lifeless world, the tension between mass and motion served as the most concrete analogy for comprehending the more complicated interplay between life and lifelessness. The struggle between mass (form) and movement (freedom) in the lifeless world played itself out in an elemental manner, while the struggle between the two contraries of lifelessness (form) and life (freedom) was directed toward a goal by the activity of the formative force or the *Bildungstrieb*. With mass and motion, equilibrium is neither active nor productive because no qualitative change results, only the release of energy, which quickly dissipates. No qualitative change results from the interaction, only an explosion of uncontrolled lust that is then stilled.[21] In the struggles between lifelessness and life, the resulting harmony could be progressive or regressive, entailing a transfiguration that the Humboldts called "revolutionary": that is, it brought forward something new.

Analogous rules governed both movements in spite of their differences. Through them, everything was interrelated. Nothing exists in and of itself, as Alexander recognized when he observed that "no earthly thing is to be found anywhere in simplicity, in a pure, virgin condition."[22] Any logical distinction that reified the separation of these linked pairs—such as experiments designed by chemists to separate basic elements—were "artificial." At best they served as heuristics that enable us to better appreciate the secret play of nature's forces, which create harmonic relationships between apparently isolated elements. Wilhelm's image of the plant that springs from the rock presupposes that the plant can exist only in the soil and be nourished by water. Life exists and is made possible because it harmonizes the threatening powers of mass (the soil) and motion (water), proclaiming its existence within the limits of material power. Thus, for both brothers the extremes of the dichotomies were linked; they were at opposite ends of a continuum.[23]

In Wilhelm's complex vision, every set of oppositions—mass/movement, life/lifelessness, form/freedom, male/female, to name a few—had its own existence and was related as well by transposition and analogy to the others. Inner drive is juxtaposed to outer force, goal to blindness, freedom and spontaneity to fate, organization to aggregation, vitalism to mechanism. Their interaction ensured the unity and diversity that nature. Most importantly, the play of forces found in nature als and characterized human development: "The influence of world upon the moral, the mysterious intertwining and interaction of the sensible and the nonsensible, imparts to the study of nature, when one raises it to a high plateau, its own, often ignored, appeal."[24] This close interconnection between the spiritual and the physical in the Humboldts' conception of nature broke down the strict distinction between matter and spirit, a central feature of early-eighteenth-century mechanism, suggesting a model whose forces "animated" physical nature and at the same time "naturalized" the spiritual and moral universe. As Jordanova remarked, this language of nature "was a deliberate attempt to formulate a common language for mind and body so that different levels of organic complexity could be dealt with in the same explanatory framework."[25] Developmental harmony, driven on by the play of forces, was the goal to which living nature, history, and human understanding inevitably strive.

NATURE'S AMBIGUITY

It would be tempting to interpret the Humboldts' vision as a form of dialectical reasoning or one of Romantic *Naturphilosophie*. Certainly it has many points in common with both, such as its emphasis upon conflict between opposites driving development, its assumption that development is goal-directed, and its establishment of the fundamental importance of the opposition between inertia and movement. But to draw this conclusion and transform the Humboldts into either proto-Hegelians or disciples of Schelling would be, I believe, a mistake. For it would overlook their exposition's most radical element.

One of the Humboldts' central assumptions, which they continually emphasized, was that it was impossible to pierce the "impenetrable veil of nature," to discover through reason a unity behind harmony. Here they proposed a theory of understanding challenging the universal applicability of binary systems of logic, of which *Naturphilosophie* and the dialectic are forms. Binary systems assume that the distance between signified and signifier can be collapsed, that reason can look at the world and it would look back reasonably. Such a binary system has, according to Foucault, "no intermediary element, no opacity intervening between the sign and its content." Wilhelm and Alexander, however, assumed the existence of an opacity between sign and content. They proclaimed a ternary system of signs "containing the significant, the signified, and the 'conjuncture.'"[26]

/ *Prologue*

The Humboldt's position seems to return to a way of thinking about nature that had been dominant before the Scientific Revolution of the late seventeenth century or before what Foucault defined as the "Classical Age." They consciously appropriated forms of thought from such diverse sources as Paracelsian chemistry, hermetic philosophy, and animistic medicine, which early-eighteenth-century advocates of mechanical natural philosophy had all but abolished from serious scientific discourse. In short, Wilhelm and Alexander attempted to formulate a way in which nature could be comprehended and explained without relying on reductive systems founded upon discursive logic. For this reason, they eschewed clear-cut analytical categories. Their language of nature is shot through with ambiguity and paradox, just as their analysis shifts abruptly from one realm to another to describe their conception of harmonic mediation that could not be couched in mechanistic terms.

A modern comparison may help to clarify this position. In many ways the Humboldts' activity parallels Gaston Bachelard's attempt to evolve a new way of understanding science. In *The New Scientific Spirit*, Bachelard labeled his position a "dialectical" one, yet modified it by drawing a distinction between the "crude dialectic of traditional philosophy" and his approach where "the poles between which it moves are less extreme, less heterogeneous": "Unlike traditional dialectics reconciling contradictory points of view does not do away with the dualism that is inscribed in the history of science itself, in every conceivable approach to the teaching of science, and indeed in the very structure of thought." He concluded by elevating the principle of ambiguity to a central category: "What I am proposing, therefore, is a new way of looking at ambiguity, a view sufficiently supple to comprehend the recent teachings of science. The philosophy of science is, I believe, in need of genuinely new principles. One such principle is the idea that the characters of things may be essentially complementary, a sharp departure from the tacit (philosophical) belief that being always connotes unity.... What would be needed, then, would be an ontology of complementarity less sharply dialectical than the metaphysics of the contradictory."[27]

As a rule, paradox and ambiguity are considered skepticism's chief tools, powerfully destructive, but not especially useful for constructing positive models of knowledge. Neither Wilhelm nor Alexander regarded themselves as skeptics, merely content to tear down false premises. This is quite evident in Alexander's sketches penned at the foot of Mount Chimborazo. His project of presenting a "natural painting" of the tropics juxtaposed strict quantitative analysis of factors such as altitude, mean temperature, barometric pressure, refraction of the sun's rays, humidity, air composition, and color of the sky with an effusive rendition of nature's powers and goals, as well as analogies to human history, all offered in the interests of a generalizing science that would consciously avoid reducing these elements into one over-arching scheme.

Not only did Alexander attempt to unite quantification with poetic description; he also desired to mediate between the two conflicting models of plant classification associated with the names of Linneaus and Buffon. The first, the so-called artificial one, focused upon one set of criteria to classify a plant; the second, designated as natural, sought to place the plant in a family within its complete environment.[28] Alexander proposed that there was a connection between the two, what he called *Hauptformen*, or general structural characteristics, that guided and regulated development. How these forms operated and why was beyond human comprehension, but they were for him that third, mediating conjuncture tying the signifier with the signified. By following this strategy of attempting to ascertain connections between unrelated elements, Alexander was certain that the resulting insights would advance science, for the person interested in considering "nature in its interconnections and as a whole" would discover many important insights and comparisons. Alexander could not specify the means or the method by which the investigator of nature might succeed in harmonizing opposing elements, an undertaking as difficult as diagramming the secret play of nature's powers. They both operated mysteriously, by a sort of "magic."

Wilhelm also combined modes of apprehension when he portrayed the images conjured up at St. Jean-de-Luz, and how his spirit reached harmonic resolution. The analog of dead mass sparked feelings of impotence and fear. These were replaced by joy tinged with terror when he contemplated the sea's chaotic motion, finally to be resolved into feelings of gentle melancholy. The noun Humboldt chose to capture this harmonic resolution—*sanfte Schwermuth*—was a beautifully concrete representation of the two original competing emotions (*Schwere* = heaviness, *Mut* = spirit, daring) in a creative oxymoron modified by *sanfte*, or tender, giving the whole process a positive tone.

The Humboldts' feeling of dissatisfaction with the present emerged in these representations of harmonic conjunction in nature and spirit. Their language is charged with tension, ambivalence, and yearning: ambivalence about the present and yearning for simpler times that were closer to life's origins. Wilhelm's evocation of the quay's imminent collapse betrayed his fear of future political catastrophe, while Alexander's claim that turning to

history would create a sense of inner freedom independent of
l power was consistent with his negative vision of the present. But
se of free activity and the existence of the formative drive mediated
these feelings of ambivalence and yearning. Thus, though at first frightened by the prospect, Wilhelm's meditation ended on the note of gentle melancholy rather than desperation. And Alexander, who regarded the history of our "separated [entzweiten] race as a 'bleak picture' " still, hoped for a better future, thanks to the exercise of knowledge gained about the true, inner workings of nature.[29] Yearning laden with remorse was not reaction in the Humboldts' view, but rather, to use one of their favorite terms, a "revolution," or a turning around in the hope of harmonizing thought and action more fully. Wilhelm yearned for a "restoration" of the sciences, for a new synthesis that would reunite the physical and moral sciences, which had been rent asunder since the triumph of mechanical natural philosophy. But he had no desire to abolish the mechanical sciences, nor did he question their validity, even though he was convinced that reliance on them would rob life and nature of their inner meaning. He believed his brother, Alexander, would be the new Bacon to pioneer this revolution, in which a new, "mysterious" harmony would arise from the remoralization of nature and the naturalization of the moral world.[30]

THE PROBLEM POSED

In Wilhelm von Humboldt's free-floating associations concerning human creations, nature continually served as his primary guide and model. When confronted with a primal experience, he employed what I would call a "language of nature" to frame and formulate his speculations.[31] For the late eighteenth century, this was not an unusual response, for the vast majority of the period's intellectuals accepted the imperative that life mirrored and ought to be modeled upon nature. Further, most assumed that "natural philosophy," or what we today call science, however defined, offered the vehicle to explicate nature. Thus, the language of nature a thinker adopted had far-ranging consequences, determining how one perceived "the order of things." It provided the means to define "reality," as well as to interpret, explain, and represent it.

At first glance the only thing seemingly unusual about the language of nature that the Humboldts employed was that it was not the one usually associated with the supposed dominant "scientific" culture of the late Enlightenment. In traditional views the Enlightenment is defined as the moral, political, and aesthetic expression of mechanistic rationalism. Its guiding principles were order, reason, and the search for universal laws, embodied in the metaphors of the clock, the balance, and the machine. According to this framework, any eighteenth-century critique of mechanism, especially of Newtonian mechanism, was formulated by rebels against the Enlightenment, representatives of what Isaiah Berlin has called the "Counter-Enlightenment," or what Antoine Faivre and Rolf Christian Zimmermann characterize as the last remnants of the hermetic mystical tradition.[32]

Based on this reading of eighteenth-century cultural and intellectual history, those who used antimechanistic or non-Newtonian languages of nature have often been seen as representing either old-fashioned religious conservatives, wild-eyed religious enthusiasts, or a new, young group of "proto-Romantics," outsiders attacking the Enlightenment establishment. Since many of the better-known critics of mechanist assumptions were German, this interpretation lends support to the notion that the German revolt against the West constituted the first step in the direction of the *Sonderweg*, a move that proved disastrous for both Germany and its neighbors. If this interpretation were correct, then the traditional characterization of Wilhelm and Alexander von Humboldt as major critics of the Enlightenment would seem quite valid. In fact, it would even modify conventional interpretations that date Wilhelm's turn away from the Enlightenment to the period in his life when he composed his most famous work, "On the Historian's Task," which many take as the theoretical starting point for German historicism.[33] Crucial to this interpretation is the assumption that in most ages there is a dominant language of nature, and that in the Enlightenment an antimechanistic language of nature was opposed to its goals and to its science. This assumption, however, is no longer tenable.

Recent studies of the history of Enlightenment science suggest that these wide-ranging explanations have hidden more than they revealed. Many scholars in France, Great Britain, the United States, Germany, and Italy question the concept that a universal mechanism characterized Enlightenment thought.[34] More importantly, they have raised some serious doubts about the traditionally accepted social and political implications of eighteenth-century mechanism and its critics.[35] As Jordanova has argued "there is no one privileged language of nature at any one time, but competing ones, claiming to offer a convincing and accurate picture of the natural world."[36] It is becoming increasingly clear that from the mid-eighteenth-century onward, a large sector of Europe's educated elite were attracted to alternatives to mechanism, even of the Newtonian variety, and that these new visions of nature and science were by no means antithetical to a liberal or

adical political philosophy. In other words, a powerful counterdis-
to mechanism was being created within and not against the general
:s of Enlightened scientific thought, a competing language of nature
that did not deny the Enlightenment's basic values. Steven Shapin characterized this new shift as follows: "we now have a developing perspective
which points out the existence of a number of species of natural knowledge,
and a number of opposed Enlightenments."[37]

Were the Humboldts drawing upon one of these other Enlightenment
discourses? If so, what does that tell us about the Humboldts' endeavors and,
in turn, of the intellectual history of the late eighteenth century? These
questions, to date, have not been posed in these terms, although an increasing number of studies are now appearing that investigate the nuances
between different national Enlightenment traditions and probe specific
problem areas using the methods of the new cultural history.[38] Still, this
summary of the Humboldts' thinking suggests a possible line of investigation, which I intend to follow in this study.

Certainly the degree of assuredness Wilhelm demonstrated in portray-
ing his reactions to the visage of St. Jean-de-Luz suggests that he was not
struggling to construct a new language of nature. For if he had been, he
would have had to explain himself much more precisely. Wilhelm's description of the feelings St. Jean-de-Luz awakened was a spontaneous meditation, which suggests that he regarded much of what he said as self-evident.
Alexander's extensive "portraits" of the tropics corroborate this. He certainly was aware that his undertaking was unique in scope and thorough-
ness, but he considered it as an extension of visions of nature proposed by
thinkers such as Buffon, Georg Forster, Captain Cook, and Benedict Saussure, among many others. Simply said, the Humboldt brothers not only
thought these forms of expression "natural," that is, self-evident, but they
also assumed them to be equally comprehensible to many of the people to
whom they addressed their writings, an audience that included the general
educated public.

The task, then, is to understand the language of nature the Humboldts
spoke and its larger implications. Such a study requires that we discern the
patterns of associated concepts, images, metaphors, and symbolic forms
that constitute this language, that we establish the context in which the
language was formed, discover the language's central areas of inquiry, and
describe the epistemological field that supported its truth claims. In short,
it is imperative to look at how this language was created and used, to investigate its various dialects, and to chart its internal contradictions.

To accomplish this task it is necessary to turn back to the period when this new language of nature was first articulated and captured the imagination of a significant and growing sector of Europe's intelligentsia. By most contemporary accounts and increasingly by the testimony of modern researchers in specific disciplines,[39] Enlightenment Vitalism's first formulations can be dated to the mid-eighteenth century. Georg Forster, the famous naturalist and a close friend of both Wilhelm and Alexander, wrote in 1786 that "the sciences of his time, especially botany, chemistry and physics, looked totally different than they had fifty years earlier. Then they were overly systematized, too formalized." The attack upon overformalization, what came to be called the spirit of systems, in the mid-eighteenth century can be associated with a number of important thinkers, among them Pierre-Louis Moreau de Maupertuis, Robert Whytt, William Cullen, Charles Bonnet, Théophile Bordeu, and Charles Secondat baron de Montesquieu. However, the person most often cited as the one who "strove against all systematic projections,"[40] who broke the spell of system, was Buffon. The appearance in 1749 of Buffon's first three volumes of the *Historie naturelle* marks the symbolic starting point for the widespread development of this new language of nature.

1 Storming "the Temple of Error"

Buffon, the Histoire naturelle, *and the Midcentury Origins of Enlightenment Vitalism*

NATURAL PHILOSOPHY AND THE MATHEMATICAL
DESCRIPTION OF NATURE

The publication of the first three volumes of Buffon's *Histoire naturelle, générale et particulière* in 1749 marked a significant moment in both eighteenth-century intellectual history and the history of book publishing. Along with Montesquieu's *L'esprit des lois,* (1748) and the *Encyclopédie,* which began its publication career in 1751, the *Histoire naturelle* announced a new approach to nature, knowledge, human nature, and society. All three works proposed a new language of nature that reached a very broad sector of Europe's educated reading public, summarizing and clarifying positions advanced by some of Europe's most daring writers on medicine, physiology, chemistry, natural philosophy, and natural history. Of the three texts, Buffon's most forcefully expressed this revised language of nature; its scope was more extensive than Montesquieu's, yet less discursive than the *Encyclopédie*'s. Like the first, it presented a cogent argument organized around a set number of interrelated problems; like the second, it offered an introductory statement of goal and method that itself became a classic. Buffon's focus was sharp, and his language impressively eloquent. By the time Buffon finished, the *Histoire naturelle* comprised thirty-six volumes. It had been reprinted, abridged, and translated into almost every European language. In France the *Histoire naturelle* became regarded as a work of classical literature. By 1780 it was the third most commonly owned book in France and the most popular one in natural history.[1] As Emma Spary reminds historians, Buffon, though "scarcely known today," "was a name which to many defined what 'natural history' was for over a century, from 1749 . . . until the 1860's."[2]

The *Histoire*, as most classics, became the intellectual property of Europe and the Americas. Conscious, half-conscious, and unconscious citations, paraphrases, and recapitulations of Buffon's positions can be discovered in an amazing spectrum of late-eighteenth-century writers.[3] Even when they differed strongly with Buffon's positions, most addressed the problems he had posed. In this crucible of discussion and debate, Buffon became a symbol for a radically new way of picturing and describing nature, for he seriously challenged some of the basic assumptions of mechanism, still dominant when the *Histoire naturelle* appeared,[4] although increasingly under attack. To understand the depth of Buffon's critique, it is necessary to look briefly at mechanism's language of nature.

Mechanism, or the mechanical philosophy of nature, is, at best, a vague concept, suggesting certain common characteristics, without providing hard and fast definitions. The term seems to have been popularized by Robert Boyle, soon becoming the appellation that described thinkers such as Descartes, Gassendi, Leibniz, Newton, Boerhaave, and Linneaus, to name but a few of the more prominent systematizers who had established or extended its principles. Although one would be hard put to place all of these intellectuals into a single category, they did share a number of basic assumptions. Mechanism's major thrust consisted of three interrelated goals: it proposed a new definition of matter, established methodological and explanatory procedures to incorporate this definition into a viable vision of natural philosophy, and evolved an epistemology that authorized these procedures. The first was directed against both the Aristotelian tradition, which still ruled in the universities, and the popular and radical subculture of hermeticism and natural magic, which appeared to pose a threat to the established order. Although quite different, both Aristotelianism and hermeticism assumed matter to be animated, endowed with qualities, appetites, sympathies, and desires. Mechanical natural philosophy excluded these from matter's essential realm, deeming them, at best, accidental qualities, produced by something more basic.

According to the mechanists, the "two catholic principles" of extension and impressed motion characterized matter.[5] It was homogeneous, extended, hard, impenetrable, movable, but not self-moving, and endowed with inertia. Observable differences in matter could be explained by variations in shape, size, or the motions of matter's particles. Since matter was no longer defined as driven by internal principles of self-activity, only an outside agent or force acting upon matter produced motion. Whether at rest or in motion, matter remained in that state until something else intervened. Leibniz made this clear: "Whatever takes place in matter arises in accordance with laws of change from the preceding condition of matter. And this is what those who say that everything corporeal can be explained mechanically hold, or ought to hold."[6] Hence, in an analysis of motion, the relations of cause and effect were considered to be directly proportional and that a fixed relation between them could be established.

With this simplified definition of matter, mechanical natural philosophers were able to evolve a convincing new research program and explanatory strategy capable of further elaboration. Natural philosophy's goal was to establish a comprehensive system of measure and order, a universal *mathesis*. As Foucault described it, the "relations between things are indeed conceived in the form of order and measurement, but with this fundamental imbalance, that it is always possible to reduce problems of measurement to problems of order. So that the relation of all knowledge to the *mathesis* is posited as the possibility of establishing an ordered succession between things, even non-measurable ones."[7] This indeed is true. Order could be constructed without measurement. But though nonmeasurable things may be ordered, the overriding imperative of mechanical natural philosophy was to transform as much knowledge as possible into a form that approached the mathematical. Almost all mechanists would have agreed with Galileo's dictum that "the book of nature is written in the language of mathematics."[8] This form did not necessarily require direct measurement or quantification,[9] but rather the reduction of things to fixed, logically coherent principles inspired by mathematics' simplicity and elegance.

Mathematics, in this sense, became the privileged language of natural philosophy. More than that, it was assumed to be its ideal form of exposition. Knowledge was arranged within a hierarchy established by the degree to which it was susceptible to description according to mathematical principles. Thus, for the mechanists "'mathematics' was applied to the general exercise of reason."[10] Despite the considerable differences between the better-known mechanical natural philosophers, they all aspired to a mathematical explanation of the universe, which they regarded as the only procedure that could establish certain, self-evident knowledge. Mathematics became, in Spinoza's phrase, the eye of natural philosophy: it was to be the core for a new language of exposition, a symbolic universe where every sign had but one meaning and a definite, invariable relation to the signified. A mathematical description of reality was seen as the way to escape the perceived horrors of contingent, and hence, unsure knowledge. The mechanical philosophy offered a haven for many late-seventeenth-century thinkers seeking intellectual and emotional security in a world marked by chaos, unrest, and revolution. The images conjured up by mechanical natural philosophy reinforced the desire for absolute certainty, imposed authority, and impartial rule. Mathematics seemed the surest solvent to dissolve the ideological disputes that had thrown seventeenth-century Europe into an orgy of partisan bloodletting.

Descartes most clearly articulated this project, designed to establish incontrovertible truth through a new epistemology grounded upon the radical distinctions between mind and matter and between the observer and observed. Mechanism bifurcated the world. A law unto itself governed each of the poles of mind and matter. Leibniz asserted this idea in his critique of Georg Stahl's medical philosophy, which assumed a direct interaction between mind and matter:

> Thus I have shown that for actions of (perhaps all?) bodies not only a material but also a formal principle is required, which I have elsewhere called a first entelechy, from whose manifestations what we call form arises. I have moreover shown that the material principle is bound up with the laws of mathematics, such as "the whole is greater than the part,' and 'equals to a third are equal to each other." So also the formal principle is bound up with the laws of metaphysics such as "the effect is not more potent than the cause' and 'nothing finite acts without undergoing a reaction."[11]

Despite the considerable differences separating the adherents of the mechanical philosophy of nature, none denied Cartesian dualism.[12] Only when nature could be considered as the "radically other" could it be treated as pure object, freed from the moral universe of human agency.

In mechanism's language of nature, things were either identical or different. It denied any intervening or mediating connections, thereby establishing a direct relationship between the name and the named, the sign and the significant. This epistemology transformed signs, once hieroglyphs of active matter, into arbitrary, yet specific, symbols that could be ordered and manipulated by sovereign human reason, freed, by definition, from the contingencies of matter. This binary system of signs abolished the earlier interpretive figures of affinity, analogy, and resemblance: "The whole domain of the sign is divided between the certain and the probable: that is to say, there can no longer be an unknown sign, a mute mark."[13] Accordingly, analysis replaced "divination" or "intuition." Analysis breaks down an entity into its constituent parts, ascertains the relationship between those, and then reconstitutes them, divested of the extraneous, into a system resembling a mechanism. It is well known that the machine became the dominant metaphor to characterize nature during the first half of the eighteenth century. For mechanists, the world machine was, "composed of inert bodies, moved by physical necessity, indifferent to the existence of thinking beings,"[14] a model they regarded as clear, simple and comprehensible.[15]

. . .

By the middle of the eighteenth century, however, some younger intellectuals considered mechanism's basic assumptions as neither satisfying nor self-evident. For them, mechanism's very success made it suspect, for its principles had been adapted to support political absolutism, religious orthodoxy, and established social hierarchies.[16] As Margaret Jacob has argued, "the great mechanical philosophers of the seventeenth century, from Descartes through Newton and Leibniz . . . labored to use these new explanations of the natural order to emphasize the dependence of the created world on the will and power of the Creator. In short they lent their support to the established Christian churches of their various societies, and often to the maintenance of established monarchical authority."[17] By the mid-eighteenth century, mechanism's metaphysical dualism and its theology had hardened into a series of platitudes. In France it often became associated with the political system created by Louis XIV.[18]

The reaction against mechanical-mathematical natural philosophy and its associated forms in intellectual, political, and social discourse generated a larger crisis of assent concerning the "spirit of systems." It found expression in a thoroughgoing skepticism against the overreliance upon abstract reasoning in the construction of a coherent picture of reality. For many thinkers of the mid-eighteenth century, deductive philosophers were incapable of accounting for nature's vast variety, which Hume criticized in the opening paragraph of his essay on "the skeptic":

> There is one mistake, to which they [speculative thinkers] seem liable, almost without exception; they confine too much their principles, and make no account of that vast variety, which nature has so much affected in all her operations. When a philosopher has once laid hold of a favorite principle, which perhaps accounts for many natural effects, he extends the same principle over the whole creation, and reduces to it every phenomenon, though by the most violent and absurd reasoning. Our own mind being narrow and contracted, we cannot extend our conception to the variety and extent of nature; but imagine, that she is as much bounded in her operations, as we are in our speculation.[19]

The mid-eighteenth-century skeptical critique of hypothetical thought elevated the contingent over the coherent, because all human knowledge was by necessity constricted given its reliance upon sense impressions and its limited scope. Humans were endowed with reason, but its ability to pierce the veil of the unknown was greatly circumscribed. As a result of this view, many mid-eighteenth-century thinkers surrendered the idea that a few simple, all-encompassing rules could fully account for nature's operations. As Hume made clear in his *Enquiry Concerning Human Nature*, variety replaced uniformity and similarity identity in perceiving nature's operations. He denied all concepts of inherent identities, arguing that things appear to be identical only because we have been accustomed by habit to consider them so: "But there is nothing in a number of instances, different from every single instance, which is supposed to be exactly similar; except only, that after a repetition of similar instances, the mind is carried by habit, upon the appearance of one event, to expect its usual attendant, and to believe, that it will exist."[20]

Midcentury skeptics like Hume saw nature as complex, but also in movement. As an anonymous French author stated, "the world is a theater of continual revolutions,"[21] in which new forms of existence replace old ones. By limiting reason's competence, reasserting nature's complexity, and historicizing nature's operations, Enlightenment natural philosophers proposed a new agenda, requiring them, to paraphrase Hume, to rethink the meaning of the terms "*power, force, energy* and *connexion.*"[22]

Hume's skeptical analysis of causation was but one instance, though perhaps the most radical, of the reevaluation of mechanical natural philosophy. Buffon's attack upon some of mechanical natural philosophy's fundamental principles was more forthright and certainly more accessible. Buffon offered his critique in the *premier discours*, "De la manière d'etudier & de traiter l'Histoire Naturelle," to the first volume of the *Histoire naturelle*. This introductory chapter proposed an alternative to Descartes's *Discours de la méthode*, in which Buffon sought to forge a new language of nature based upon a skeptical attack against hypothetical reason. A master literary craftsman and an exceptional translator, Buffon consistently resorted to the analogy of language in his discussions of the essence and function of natural philosophy. According to Buffon, natural philosophy was itself a language: it named things, connected the *nomina propria* through grammatical form to generate meaning. For Buffon, knowledge was indivisible from its mode of communication, so he consciously placed the problem of language formation and of philosophic explanation and method within the ambit of rhetoric, that is, in its traditional meaning of giving sensate expression to true things. In so doing, Buffon hoped to escape from mechanical philosophy's conception of language as "purely arbitrary." It "had become more difficult than the science itself."[23] Buffon strove to evolve a language of nature that avoided artificiality, abstraction, and mere enumeration. He wished to return to an older idea of natural language, which expressed intuitive, experimental insights about nature reintegrating humans into its scope.[24] To do so Buffon rehabilitated naturalists dismissed by the mechanists—Pliny, Hippocrates, Aristotle, and possibly (though I can't prove that) the hermetic writers of the seventeenth century. In short he revived popular traditions in order to reintroduce the concept of living nature into natural philosophic discourse. By taking up this project, Buffon attempted to dissolve or at least modulate the strict Cartesian separation between mind and matter, between observer and observed.[25] As in the Renaissance language of nature, to which he was drawn, Buffon regarded the human as "the center upon which relations are concentrated and from which they are once again reflected."[26]

In the *Premier discourse*, Buffon questioned the two prominent modes of natural philosophic explanation and method, founded upon the distinction between the observed and observer, which were vying for supremacy: simple empiricism and mathematical mechanism. Both, in his eyes, were arbitrary, and hence artificial, languages of nature because neither could mediate between word and form or between the particular and the general that to Buffon constituted real knowledge. In empiricism, words took precedence over form and reduced linguistic order to alphabetical arrangement. Its practitioners were word collectors;[27] its ideal form of representation was the dictionary. In mathematical mechanism, on the other hand, form overshadowed words, reducing them to one-dimensional symbols: its advocates were framers of hypotheses, its ideal form of representation demonstrations, empty syllogisms.

Buffon disposed of the first mode of natural philosophic explanation with sarcastic, surgical precision. Like antiquarians, the "word collectors," or "nomenclateurs" mindlessly compiled mountains of facts. Buffon condemned virtually all books written "a hundred or two hundred years ago for saying too much and having nothing to say." For example, he criticized Aldrovandus for "a fault or an excess that one can find in almost all books written one or two hundred years ago, and that the German savants still have today; it's this useless quantity of erudition with which they purposely inflate their works, so that the subject that they are treating is drowned in a quantity of foreign matters on which they reason with much indulgence and dwell on with so little consideration for their readers that they seem to have forgotten what they had to say to you, and only recount what others have already said."[28]

Buffon's second task, that of providing an alternative to the language of mathematical mechanism, proved far more difficult. On first reading, it seemingly undermined the foundations of late-seventeenth-century natural philosophy, for he denied mathematics' prime position in generating natural knowledge. Buffon sought to show that mathematics could not reveal the "secrets of nature," that any edifice of knowledge erected upon mathematical-mechanistic principles was a "temple of error."[29] Buffon's critique drew a distinction between abstract and physical truths. Abstract truths were products of human ratiocination, imaginary creations arrived at independently of careful observations. Mathematical proofs belonged to this category; they were its prototype. Founded upon arbitrarily accepted logical principles, they could in turn generate only equally arbitrary but more complex principles. To maintain consistency, anything that logically disagreed with the first principle had to be excluded. Buffon considered a mathematical proof sterile, incapable of affirming anything other than its starting point. Thus mathematical systems were hermetically sealed, closed to the realities of observable nature.[30] They were, according to Adam Ferguson who adopted Buffon's critique, "a species of disguised tautology, in which a subject repeated in the form of a predicate is affirmed to itself."[31]

Physical truths in contradistinction were based on actual occurrences. They were not merely constructs of human reason susceptible to endless manipulation because "they do not depend on us."[32] Natural philosophy, according to Buffon, was the description and understanding of real things that have taken place in the world: "In Mathematics, one supposes; in the physical sciences one poses a question and establishes truth. The former deals with definitions, the latter with facts. One moves from definition to definition in the abstract sciences, and from observation to observation in the real sciences; in the first, one finds self-evidence, in the second, certainty."[33] For Buffon, historical description replaced mathematical demonstration in a true natural philosophical explanation. His "overriding concern . . . was to achieve some kind of immanent, connected understanding of phenomena."[34]

Buffon stood late-seventeenth-century mechanical-mathematical natural philosophy on its head, reversing its intellectual priorities. According to leading late-seventeenth- and early-eighteenth-century mechanists, history was the lowest form of knowledge, being nothing more than knowledge of individual facts. Whatever order imposed on them was, at best, pragmatic, as history dealt only with the contingent. Since history could not banish contradiction, mechanists deemed it incapable of certainty. History was acknowledged as a form of understanding, but it ranked low in the hierarchy of knowledge because it could provide only contingent knowledge. Although knowing facts was sometimes deemed the starting point for sound natural philosophy, those facts had to be reordered by the universal *mathesis* under whose rule contradiction vanished before the piercing rays of human reason. History became the handmaiden for discursive logic and mathematical analysis, the appointed sovereigns of human understanding. For Buffon what was real was contingent. Grand mathematical descriptions, self-evident logical systems were delusions. Thus, he elevated history from the lowest form of understanding to a primary one. As Philip Sloan remarked, "Physical truth conceived of as the *successional ordering* of empirical events in series becomes in Buffon's thought a veritable ontological foundation for knowledge of the natural world."[35] Buffon admitted the contingent, the individual, and the unique into the inner sanctum of natural philosophy, thereby changing the relation of the sciences to one another.

When Buffon demoted the principle of noncontradiction, essential to mechanical natural philosophy, to a secondary function, he redefined the way in which one considered the relation of the general to the particular. By questioning the principle of noncontradiction in natural philosophy, he denied the imperative to discover identities in nature, reducing mathematics' role as secondary in the search for truth. He assigned it the task of assisting in the process of accurate observation. Mathematics became an essential tool for the naturalist who needed to answer questions of "how much and how strong."[36] As a practical craft it could be useful in establishing probabilities, which Buffon himself used extensively.[37] In this sense Buffon participated in the late-eighteenth-century turn to probabilistic reason, pioneered by his opponents in the Academy of Sciences, d'Alembert and Condorcet. As Lorraine Daston remarks, they were part of the "postpyrrhonist tradition," derived from Marin Mersenne and others. Hume, on the other hand, advocated "a rejuvenated skepticism against the mathematicized moderation" represented by d'Alembert and Condorcet.[38] Buffon's views stood closer to Hume's than to Condorcet's. Buffon affirmed that mathematics could not reveal the order of things. In his view, there were just two categories of positive knowledge, both directed to investigating the contingent: the history of nature and the history of civil society:

> Sensible people, however, will always feel that the only true science is the knowledge of facts . . . ; facts are to sciences as experience is to civil life. One could, therefore, divide all the sciences in two principal classes that would contain all that is necessary for man to know; the first is Civil History, and the other, Natural History, both founded on facts that are often important and always agreeable to know. The first is the study for Statesmen, the second for Philosophers; and although the utility of the latter is perhaps not as clear as that of the former, one can

be assured, however, that Natural History is the source of other physical sciences & the mother of all truths.[39]

Historical knowledge, whether directed toward nature or human society, displaced mathematics as the primary form of understanding.

TOWARD A REDEFINITION OF ORGANIC MATTER

Buffon's critique of the mathematical method and his championship of historical understanding were parts of his many-pronged assault on mechanical natural philosophy. When he assailed mechanism's definition of matter, its concept of method, and its basic epistemology, he recategorized what mechanists considered primary, essential, and self-evident as secondary, superficial, and hypothetical. In so doing, Buffon reintroduced concepts that had constituted part of the Aristotelian and hermetic worldview dismissed by the mechanical philosophers of nature. By vitalizing and remoralizing nature, Buffon proposed a way of understanding in which the ancient procedures of analogical thinking, comparison, and divination might be rehabilitated and heal the breach between mind and matter.

Buffon's treatment of matter is typical of his attack on mechanistic philosophy. Buffon never denied that the mechanistic description of matter had led to important discoveries, for this would have been a reactionary move no cosmopolitan thinker who shared the Enlightenment's critique of encrusted tradition and blind authority would have made. By the time Buffon wrote, most intellectuals accepted the Newtonian descriptions of planetary motion.[40] The challenge was twofold: (1) to give proper credit to mechanism's achievements, but to demonstrate at the same time that those methods were limited to certain clearly defined spheres; and (2) to devise new definitions and methods for phenomenal areas that mechanism could not explain adequately. One of these areas was the definition of matter's primary attributes: "The idea of reducing the explication of all phenomena to mechanical principles is assuredly grand and beautiful. This step is the boldest that one could make in philosophy, and it's Descartes who did it. But this idea is only a plan, and is this plan well founded? Even if it is, do we have the means to execute it? Are these mechanical principles the extent of matter—its impenetrability, its movement, its external appearance, its divisibility, the communication of movement by the means of impulsion, by the action of springs, etc.?"[41] Buffon answered with a resounding No. These attributes were only things that our limited senses could easily apprehend. They were superficial, secondary surface phenomena rather than primary attributes. Instead of concerning ourselves with such phenomena, we should attempt to penetrate beneath the surface to the inner nature of a body.

With this argument, Buffon reintroduced the complex Renaissance and hermetic topos of the inner/outer relationship, which mechanism had conflated. His goal was to relate the visible outer form to its invisible, deeper, and more important foundation. In his natural history Buffon elevated the ideas of internal relations and functions to a prime position, breaking with what Foucault defined as the hallmark of the "Classical *episteme,*" its concern "with surfaces and lines, not [with] functions or invisible tissues."[42] To make his point that natural philosophy had to discover the reality of things below their external characteristics, Buffon suggested that matter might have many more attributes than the mechanists were willing to allow: "Should we not believe that these qualities that we take for principles are nothing other than ways of seeing? And could we not think that if our senses were different than they are, we would recognize in matter qualities that are very different from those we just enumerated? Only wanting to admit to matter the qualities that we know it to have seems to me a vain and unfounded pretension."[43] Buffon used the analogy of gravity as an example of secret forces. He defined it as a basic property of matter, a penetrating force that works "internally," not on the surface.[44] Having redefined Newton's most famous discovery as an analogue to a living force, Buffon used this concept as a Trojan horse in his attack on mechanism. What would we see if our senses were indeed capable of penetrating to the core of reality? We would perceive living or organic matter as primary and inorganic or "dead matter" as secondary. The mechanists had mistakenly concentrated upon dead matter as primary, regarding the body as an aggregate of simple, elementary inert particles of various shapes. But for Buffon, one primary fact seemed obvious: such a construction could not account for life. He countered that simple informed observation revealed organized matter to be "joined and animated" *(vivant, animé).* Life was not a "metaphysical principle" as the Cartesians and Leibnizians maintained, "but is a physical property of matter." With this statement Buffon undercut Cartesian duality.[45] He was not afraid to draw its consequences.

If matter were animated, then animation should be considered seriously in any general inquiry into matter's composition. What were its attributes? The first was conjunction, because an organized body was not an aggregation of simple identical particles. Buffon insisted that all of nature was interconnected: "In nature, on the contrary, the abstract does not exist, nothing is simple and everything is composite."[46] Buffon argued that instead of beginning with the simple and aggregating those parts into a complex entity that is the sum of its parts, one should start with the notion that "the ideas that we communally have of the simple and the composite are abstract ideas, and cannot apply to the composition of works of Nature. When we want to reduce all beings to elements of a regular shape, or to prismatic, cubic or globulous particles, we are putting what is only in our imagination in the place of what really is.... We can assume and believe that an organized being is composed of similar organic parts, just as we can suppose that a cube is composed of other cubes."[47]

These similar parts consisted of what Buffon called "organic molecules," a concept that has perplexed many of Buffon's commentators. Jacques Roger interpreted the organic molecule as Buffon's attempt to retain a form of atomism without falling into mechanism. If Roger is correct, then Buffon "remained a prisoner of the mechanical images that he vainly tried to exorcise."[48] He is, in this view, an amphibian in an age of transition. I would like to propose another possibility. Buffon's retention of certain mechanist principles may have been a conscious attempt to mediate between the existing concepts of reality derived from the postulates of Cartesian duality and the older ideas of an animated nature, not an internal contradiction but a concerted plan to rewrite the history of nature. Buffon's synthesis may represent what Gaston Bachelard referred to as a "new way of looking at ambiguity" in which complementarity could not be collapsed into unity.[49] As Buffon maintained that if everything in nature was composite, then understanding should also be composed of at least two juxtaposed elements, an image he proclaimed in his definition of the ideal natural historian: "The love of the study of Nature supposes two seemingly opposite qualities of the mind: the wide-ranging views of an ardent mind that embraces everything with one glance, and the detail-oriented laboring instinct that concentrates only on one element."[50] This merging of opposites, held together in tension, without elevating one over the other is characteristic of Buffon's whole approach, signaled in the *Histoire naturelle*'s subtitle, as well as in the numerous paradoxical terms he coined to explicate his vision. Buffon was a master of the creative paradox. The organic molecule was such a paradox: it was matter and energy, the "extended middle" in which reality could be located.[51] In this sense it resembled Cudworth's "plastic natures," Grew's "vital bodies," and van Helmont's idea of the "archaeus." But the organic molecule could never be observed directly because of its opacity. As the middle term linking the signified and significant, it could be portrayed only by ambiguity or paradox.

Because of this assumption, Buffon found it impossible to define the organic molecule beyond describing it as living and composite, a prototype of larger, more complicated organic bodies. Nature demonstrated differences of degree, not of kind, in the progression from organic molecule to organized body. An organized body was a conjunction of symbiotically related parts; thus it would be impossible to isolate or subtract a single element from the whole without changing substantially the relations between the remaining parts. Buffon conceived of an organized body as a set of relations or *rapports* existing between mutually interdependent parts.[52] The *rapports* between the parts constituted the whole, creating a unique organism. He denied the homogeneity of matter by emphasizing the elemental nature of conjunction. Each type of matter had its own unique quality, not reducible to more basic atomic particles. For Buffon, individuality was a brute fact. Yet he considered all individual entities linked in a complex world of *rapports*. Each living individual or animal "is a center where everything is related, a point where the entire universe is reflected, a world in miniature."[53]

The second basic attribute of organic matter was its ability to reproduce. Each individual species, from the polyp to the lofty elm tree, had the power to generate its own kind with a minimum of effort. To illustrate this point, Buffon conducted a thought experiment to show how much organic matter could be produced from one elm seed if allowed to grow, and all of its seeds and their seeds as well. One seed weighing less than a "hundredth part of an ounce" would generate a thousand cubic miles of organic material in 110 years. In another thirty years, it would have produced a "billion" cubic miles of organic material. And 150 years later, the face of the globe would be "transformed in organic material of one specific kind." The same thought experiment could be conducted for any other organic body with the same result; after an X amount of time, one form of matter would populate the world. Of course, this could never happen, because living nature's economy sets specific limits to organic matter's increase. Buffon's thought experiment demonstrated, he believed, "that nature's principle goal is indeed to produce organized bodies."[54]

Given these circumstances, natural philosophy should focus upon the organic, as "the most ordinary work of nature, and apparently the one, which costs the least."[55] Nature was essentially alive: hence the categories of life should govern natural philosophic inquiry. Buffon actually considered the distinction between organic and inorganic misleading, preferring the contrast between living and dead matter.[56] Like Aristotle and the hermetic philosophers, Buffon vivified much of nature, without denying the existence of dead matter. He simply reduced inert matter to a special case. As long as it described only the motions of dead matter or cases where matter could be treated for practical purposes as dead, mechanism's methodological and explanatory principles were appropriate. Thus, Buffon recognized the applicability of mathematical methods to celestial mechanics and optics, but to little else, since everything else was too complicated, too "material."[57]

Organic matter's third attribute was that it was animated by active forces, operating beneath its surface that formed and conjoined matter. Buffon justified the existence of such hidden forces by invoking the analogies of gravity, chemical affinities and magnetism, which by definition could not be seen directly. But unlike their physical analogues, organic forces could not be measured or defined mathematically, because of conjunction: "It is thus evident that we will never have any clear idea of these penetrating forces, nor about the way that they act; but at the same time, it is no less certain that they do exist, that it is because of them that most of Nature's effects take place."[58] Although he did not employ the term in the *Premier discours*, Buffon, for all practical purposes, reintroduced the concept of occult force into nature. At first glance this is not surprising, for Newton himself had once defined gravity as an occult force, that is, a phenomenon whose cause could not be known. But Newton believed that gravity could be described mathematically, transforming an occult force into a law of motion. This saved the phenomenon. Buffon's dismissal of mathematics' ability to generate physical laws restricted the Newtonian solution to a special case, not applicable to living nature. Instead, Buffon's "penetrating forces" were occult qualities in the older sense; they were associated with certain forms of things.[59]

Newton had dismissed the notion of individual occult forces: "to tell us that every Species of Things is endowed with an occult specifick Quality by which it acts and produces manifest Effects is to tell us nothing." Buffon disagreed and proposed the existence of such a force that was *both* general and particular. It existed throughout organized matter, yet produced different effects in individual species. He called it the *moule intérieur*, which the mathematician Kästner rendered in German as *innerliche Form*, and Buffon's English translators called the "internal mould," or the "general mould of things." Buffon's formulation established a rhetorical strategy that used Newtonian vocabulary but transformed its general meaning. He correctly invoked Newton in abandoning the search for ultimate causes and concentrating upon phenomenological explanations yet challenged the assumption that "occult" qualities could be transformed through mathematics into general laws of motion. Buffon employed paradox to explain his concept of the *moule intérieur*. It appears, he said, to "join two contradictory terms." "One, the idea of form," applied "only to surfaces." The other, "inner" or "internal," was usually applied to mass. This seeming paradox joining the inner with the outer combined two apparently opposed concepts in order to create a mediated thought form that generated a heightened awareness of a conjunction defying strict geometric expression. Buffon's *moule intérieur* became the physical symbol of the "extended middle," a formulation designed to transcend binary forms of argumentation.

Buffon was aware of the difficulties raised by his definition of the term *moule intérieur* and had a response ready for his detractors: "The opposition is only in the words." He added, "when it is necessary to represent ideas that have not yet been expressed, we are sometimes obliged to use terms that seem to be contradictory."[60] Here, I believe, Buffon was concealing what he really thought, for it is possible that certain things cannot be expressed clearly, that, in mirroring nature they must be linguistically paradoxical. Simple definitions destroyed linked opposites, which in nature operated as complementarities. Buffon believed nature to be "a perpetually living work.... The springs that she uses are living forces, which space and time can only measure and limit without ever destroying: forces that balance one another, merge, and oppose each other without ever destroying one another."[61] A language of nature must be able to capture these opposing, merging and balancing forces, without destroying any of them linguistically by reducing them to a false unity. Only by emphasizing these contradictions can nature be represented as it actually is. The term *moule intérieur* certainly met these representational requirements. The *moule intérieur* acted as matter's organizing agent. All organized bodies had a *moule intérieur*; each was specific to its species, according to a unique plan generated when the species first appeared. For this reason, all living things were similar yet different, and therefore could not be described by methods of mechanical natural philosophy. Here Buffon clearly explicated the theme of mediation that was to become essential to the interpretive impulse of Enlightenment Vitalism.

SYSTEM, METHOD, AND UNDERSTANDING

Buffon formulated a new concept of a scientific system to validate his redefinition of natural history. This was essential because most eighteenth-century thinkers believed that natural philosophy had to anchored upon systematic analysis, an idea encapsulated by Adam Ferguson when he proclaimed that "the love of science and the love of system are the same."[62] Buffon advanced his idea of scientific system most clearly in his critique of Linnaeus's taxonomy. As a result, it has often been interpreted within the circumscribed sphere of the debate about taxonomic procedures, much to Buffon's disadvantage. However, modern commentators such as Jacques Roger and Philip Sloan have now placed the controversy within a larger interpretive context.[63] As Sloan observed, "Buffon's opposition to Linnaeus was of an entirely different order. Rather than dealing with specific taxonomic issues, it concentrated instead on a general philosophical critique of the root assumptions underlying virtually all the taxonomic work of the time."[64] Because Buffon associated these assumptions with mechanism, his critique of Linnaeus and other structural taxonomists reflected Buffon's desire to define an order of things that reflected natural order rather than an arbitrary approach.

For Buffon, the chief flaw of the Linnaean system lay in its high level of abstraction. Linnaeus had arbitrarily defined certain physical characteristics as elemental and designated the rest irrelevant for the purposes of classification. Moreover, Linnaeus "discovered" those primary attributes through observation of surface phenomena alone. According to Buffon, this error in procedure betrayed the fact that Linnaeus misunderstood "how Nature works, which is always by nuances." It never could be described adequately according to formal principles: "It is easy to see that the great fault in all of this is a Metaphysical error . . . in wanting to judge a whole by only one of its parts: a very obvious error, and one that is surprisingly found everywhere; for almost all of the classifiers have employed only a part, such as teeth, claws, or talons, to classify animals, and leaves or flowers to categorize plants, instead of using all of the parts, looking for the differences and similarities in the entire individual thing."[65] Only when one represented these similarities and differences was the creation of a "natural system" possible.

A natural system described a body as it actually was (in its functions and its relationship to the environment) and its history. Buffon called on his fellow naturalists to model their procedures upon the first great classifiers, Pliny and Aristotle. The challenge was to join structure and process, what today we would call the synchronic and diachronic, into a unified field of explanation. Buffon described this activity as follows:

> The exact description and a faithful history of each thing is . . . the only goal that one should at first propose to oneself. In the description one must consider the form, size, weight, colors, postures during rest and

movement, the position of the parts, their relationships to e
their shapes, their actions and all the exterior functions; if c
to all of this the display of the interior parts, the descriptio
all the more complete. . . . History must follow description
uniquely depend on the relationships that natural things have be..
each other and with us: the history of an animal must be not the history of the individual animal, but of the entire species of these animals; it must include their reproduction, the length of gestation and of the birthing process, the number of offspring, the care given by the fathers and the mothers, the type of education, their instincts, where they live, their food and the manner in which they procure it, their morals, their ruses, their hunting, and finally the services that they can render us, and all the utility and commodities that we can get from them.[66]

Buffon designed this concept of system to avoid the reductionism of mechanical systems by emphasizing conjunction over aggregation.[67] Each composite individual, however, also belonged to a species, which was best defined as "a chain of successive existences of individuals, which reproduce and interbreed among themselves." Species "exist only in considering Nature in the succession of time, and in the constant destruction and renewal of beings."[68] These species resembled each other in varying degrees, thus creating a finely graded sequence from the most complex to the most simple within living nature. For this reason Buffon's classification began with man and proceeded downward, with each species defined by the ability of its individuals to produce fertile offspring.

Buffon's use of terms such as "gradations" and "chain of existence" suggests that he accepted the notion of the Great Chain of Being. In fact, his theory of species classification negated the concept of unbroken continuity upon which the Great Chain of Being was predicated. There are breaks in nature, minute though they may be, which were ensured by the universal and invariable law of fertile reproduction.[69] Discontinuity is a general principle of nature. No matter how similar an ape and a human may be, they were of a different species because they could not produce fertile offspring. The gap between them was unbridgeable, a concept totally at odds with the idea of continuity. By denying the reality of the Great Chain of Being, Buffon introduced another basic question central to Enlightenment Vitalism's development, whether there could be well-demarcated differences within a species. Today we use the word "race" to characterize these differences and though the word was available to Buffon and his peers, it had a variety of connotations. For eighteenth-century thinkers the simple question was whether what we call "race" was an ontological or merely a heuristic category. Buffon hardly used the term, preferring "variety" because he saw no hard and fast markers separating individuals from one another within a species. Skin color, bone structure, stature, and prominent features were so minutely varied that they blended into one another. As Jacques Roger remarked, in Buffon "individual differences therefore blur racial differences."[70] Although Buffon may have denied an unbroken continuity between species, he established instead a form of chain of being within species by replacing a vertical continuity over species with a horizontal one within species. As the anthropological discussions of the late eighteenth century developed, the difference between those using the terms "variety" and "race" would become increasingly sharper, exacerbated by the unresolved battle between naturalists concerned with "charting relations among existing forms" and those focusing upon temporal succession and transformation.[71]

If varieties were not fixed categories created by God in the beginning, then Buffon was obliged to account for differentiation within species. He offered two sets of interrelated explanations. Because no individual resembles another exactly, the matings between individuals produced over time an almost infinite number of variations. When individual characteristics are combined, they generate new combinations, which in turn are passed down to offspring, and the cycle continues. The larger the number of individuals, the greater the variations within a species. If females can mate freely, the greater the possible variations.[72] Buffon applied this explanation chiefly for plants or animals that had remained in their place of origin and had not become domesticated. Once animals moved or were domesticated then other forces triggered variation: climate, food, mores, and time. The mechanism was simple. If the offspring were raised in a place different from their "natural homeland," they would be susceptible to the influences of food and climate, which would modify its *moule intérior*. These modifications, though not immediately apparent, were transmitted to the offspring and over time would become more pronounced.[73] Buffon called variations caused by changes in diet or in the environment "degenerations" from the individual's natural form. For him, degenerate organisms were smaller and less hardy than the originals, a position that enraged Thomas Jefferson, who believed that a different environment such as the New World could revitalize older species, making them stronger and larger.

What applied to species moved from their original environment applied equally well to domesticated plants and animals, which were very well adapted to certain functions, but totally dependent upon man for their continual existence. Domesticated species carried the "stigma of slavery,"[74] because they had lost some of their original nobility. When humans imposed their will upon these captive animals, they reduced the stock of available males, diminishing thereby the diversity and the vitality of the species. Humans tended to favor those characteristics in the plants and animals that made it impossible for them to survive without human care and cultivation, and, as a result, deformed and weakened the species as a whole.

Because variety could be caused by forces, natural and imposed, internal and external, these forces were the agents of organic change, making nature "a perpetually living work, a constantly active worker."[75] Behind the teeming panorama of creation and destruction, of change and transformation, Buffon discerned a hidden force that held everything together, exempting nature from the rule of chaos or chance. He outlined a fragmentary notion of this in the article on the horse in the fourth volume of the *Histoire naturelle*:

> There is in nature a general prototype of each species on which every individual is modeled, but which seems, in becoming a reality, to alter itself or perfect itself through circumstances. . . . The first animal, the first horse, for example, was the exterior model and the *moule intérieur* on which all horses that are born, all that exist, and all those that will be born are formed; but this model, of which we only know copies, was able to alter or perfect itself in communicating its form and multiplying itself.[76]

Thus, species have some sort of primitive model, determining both exterior and internal features, a blueprint for all subsequent appearances. But Buffon went even further. In the article on the ass, he suggested that perhaps an even more general "original design" *(un dessein primitif et général, un premier dessein)* existed for the whole animal kingdom: "Without speaking of the organs of digestion, circulation and generation, which are part of all animals, and without which the animal would stop being an animal and could neither survive nor reproduce, there is an incredible similarity in the very parts that contribute most to the variety of the exterior shape, which necessarily reminds us of an original design according to which all seems to have been conceived."[77] Here Buffon attempted to probe the very essence of living matter, seeking in some deep way to combine the general and the particular without submerging one in the other. As we shall see in later chapters, this image of a primitive design will resonate in the works of such diverse thinkers as Robinet, Herder, Goethe, and Alexander von Humboldt.

Not only did Buffon's concept of system attempt to reformulate the relationship between the general and the particular; it also served to transform the traditional mechanistic definition of cause and effect. In a system such as Buffon's, which was built upon the concepts of *rapport*, of the *moule intérieur,* prototype, and original design, it was difficult to designate cause and effect because each element of an "organized" body could be both cause and effect of the other parts. Within this system, neither external physical contact nor chronology could serve as a model to structure causal analysis. The topos of internal forces operating within certain limits allowed one to envision an intellectual hierarchy of different causal moments, each possessing different time spans. In this definition the three primary attributes of living matter—conjunction, reproduction, and penetrating force—guided Buffon's thought and provided it with its internal consistency. Certainly the program he proposed was ambitious, and it proved extremely appealing for many of his generation and even more to the two generations that followed. It attracted those who were weary of mechanism's rage for calculation and troubled by its seeming disregard for human uniqueness, moral qualities, environmental conditioning, and purposive change over time. It received further affirmation because it saw nature in terms that paralleled Montesquieu's model for the study of nations. Like an organized body, the nation's spirit could be defined only by considering it as a whole, formed by a complex set of interacting elements. Contemporaries who were attracted to either Montesquieu or Buffon usually found the other sympathetic as well.

It is sometimes forgotten that Buffon's proposal was far more ambitious and radical than Montsequieu's. Not only did Buffon apply this mode of analysis to humans; he treated nature the same way, integrating humanity within its study. But even more importantly, Buffon attempted through the formulation of the *moule intérieur,* the prototype, and the original design to introduce a mode of thinking that could not be considered causal in any traditional way. More than anyone else of his generation, Buffon led the way to the reanimation and remoralization of nature, thereby establishing possibilities for the naturalization of the moral sciences, initiating what Philip Sloan has called "the Buffonian Revolution."[78]

. . .

Buffon's critique of mechanical natural philosophy, together with his definitions of matter, system, and the relationship between place, climate, diachronic change, and organic organization, demanded a new set of principles that would guarantee the legitimacy of this new language of nature. Buffon, aware of his critique's wider implications, outlined an analytic and explanatory structure designed to generate new forms of knowledge. Believing that true knowledge was the knowledge of relations, not of essence or cause, the natural philosopher had to begin by observing relationships humans could

perceive clearly, because the human was "the midpoi[ ]
tions met: "One judges the objects of Natural Histo[r]
tions they have with man. Those, which are the mo[st]
to him, will take the first rank. . . . Then he will co[n]
which while not so familiar to him, inhabit the s[ame]
climates."[79] Buffon's theory of understanding was founde[d]
controlled regression from the known to the unknown, from the co[mplex]
the less complex, and from experienced and intuited human relations to the related but dissimilar relations of other organic beings. He considered his system "the most natural of all," and "preferable to the most highly refined and elaborate taxonomic methods,"[80] precisely because he had rooted his epistemology in relations that we could reexperience.

This argument had a proviso that humans could not become detached observers of natural processes. Buffon remarked that

> The first truth that emerges from this sober examination of Nature, is a truth perhaps humbling to man. This truth is that he ought to range himself in the class of the animals, which he resembles in all of his material aspects. Even their instincts will appear to man more certain than his own reason, and their industry more admirable than his arts. Then, examining successively and by order the various objects that compose the Universe, and placing himself at the head of all created beings, he will see with astonishment that one can descend by almost imperceptible degrees from the most perfect creature to the most unorganized matter, from the most organized animal to the most inert matter.[81]

This assertion undercut the mechanist epistemological basis for a universal natural philosophy by closing the breach between mind and matter, man and animal. It also seemed to imply an even more drastic restriction of natural philosophy's truth claims, for it made the contingent the prime area of inquiry. For Buffon this apparent loss was a gain. By accepting this principle, humans would attain a type of understanding that was both more certain and "deeper," because it would go beyond the concentration upon what he considered superficial surface phenomena. There are striking parallels between Buffon's vision of a new science and that of Vico's, even though both began with different premises. They transformed what the mechanical philosophers of nature had considered a mistaken premise—that humans were immersed in a natural world from which they cannot escape—and made it into a virtue, believing that humans were better able to understand this world because they are a part of it, in fact, the most complete part because humans can reflect upon their experiences through the

Storming "the Temple of Error"

 of language. But Buffon's formulation was more radical than "*Verum = Factum.*" Vico limited his type of knowledge to human tory, whereas Buffon extended it to all living nature, which, in his view had a history similar to that of humanity.

How, then was this new science to be instituted, what was its epistemological justification? Given Buffon's belief in the compound nature of living matter along with the "fact" that humans were embedded in nature, he argued that the binary distinction between identity and nonidentity did not exist. Ideas were not clear and distinct, but rather related to each other through a series of gradations that could be discovered only by comparison. By taking this stand, Buffon not only attacked Descartes's idea of innate ideas, he also rejected Locke's belief that the mind was capable of forming clear and distinct ideas by immediate perception.[82] Buffon once again reconciled two contradictory views. Although nominally a Lockean, he was critical of Locke's belief that limited forms of direct, self-evident knowledge were possible as he was of Descartes's belief in the attainability of self-evident knowledge through reason. For Buffon, every idea resulted from a comparison of things, neither of which was independent or self-evident: "For upon reflection, one will note that the first idea always is itself a comparison. For example, the concept of the size of an object or of its distance necessarily entails a comparison to a measure of size or distance."[83]

To make his point, Buffon offered a counterfactual proposition. Let us imagine, he suggested, a person who was stricken by total amnesia, or a person who awoke from a long sleep only to discover he was absolutely ignorant of the surrounding world. Let us place this person in a field where animals, birds, fish, plants, and stones appear to his view: "At first, this man will distinguish nothing and confuse everything; but let's let his ideas strengthen little by little through repeated sensations of the same objects. Soon he will form a general idea about living matter, he will distinguish it easily from inanimate matter, and soon thereafter he will be able to distinguish living matter from vegetative matter very well, and naturally he will arrive at the first great division, *Animal*, *Vegetable*, and *Mineral*."[84] From there Buffon went on to describe how his mythical "sleeper" reconstructed the world around him through the reciprocal process of particularizing and generalizing from experience, following thereby a course that paralleled that of nature and, therefore, was true. Buffon's point was that the "natural method" of close observation and comparison was based upon the compar- rities and differences, of resemblances, not of defining identity tity. For him, resemblance became the foundation upon which y system was to be constructed. However, Buffon warned his readers, resemblances can be established only if the whole is considered, that is, the individual's "form, size, external characteristics, its various parts including their number and arrangement, and its substance."[85]

Comparative knowledge may be certain because it followed nature's order, but it had limitations. In Buffon's view, all human understanding was rooted in existence: from this midpoint of shared human experience it proceeded outwards to less similar organized bodies becoming less certain as it went. To make this point, Buffon replaced the unilinear image of working from the human downward with one moving outwards from the center in many directions: "Moreover, if one pays attention, one will see very well that our general ideas, only composed of particular ideas, are relative to a continuous scale of objects, of which we see only the middle parts clearly, and of which the extremities disappear in the distance and always escape our perception more and more, so that we can only ever grasp the general idea of things, and thus we must not believe that our ideas, however general they might be, comprise the particular ideas of all existing and possible things."[86] This middle realm of certain knowledge was not a static, self-enclosed segment in the order of things. Comparing unknown individualities to known ones and then drawing generalizations from this procedure enabled the natural philosopher to expand knowledge. Buffon's vision of scientific activity was open-ended and provided a theoretical basis for deepening our vision of the natural world as long as the comparative method was based upon an appropriate logic of generalization.

For this reason, Buffon preferred analogical reasoning to discursive logic. Analogical reasoning, he believed, allowed the natural philosopher to discover similar tendencies in dissimilar things without dissolving the particular in the general and obscuring nature's actual operations: "This goal is the most important one . . . to combine observations, to generalize about facts, to tie them together by the force of analogy, and to try to arrive at this high degree of knowledge where we can judge that particular effects depend on more general effects, where we can compare Nature with herself in her great operations, and from where we can finally blaze the paths that will permit us to perfect the different parts of Physics."[87] The search for this higher understanding committed the natural philosopher to a close investigation of empirical phenomena and to the cultivation of creative imagination. Analogical reasoning, ever active, not clearly defined, yet always productive, would encourage interaction between observation and imagination and generate a form of understanding superior to discursive reasoning. He called this type of understanding divination or intuition, and regarded it as a form of mediation that resulted in the heightened ability to perceive simultaneously form and force, structure and process, to discern the resemblances between sign and significant, and to mediate between the particular and the general. Its ideal form was divine knowledge to which humans could aspire but never reach.

In this theoretical and methodological assault on mechanical natural philosophy, Buffon united elements of mechanism with ideas formulated in the period preceding the "Scientific Revolution," including active hidden powers, elective affinities, the centrality of resemblance, the doctrine of signatures, analogical reasoning, juxtaposition, and divination. At the same time Buffon cleansed them of their most objectionable qualities, limiting their application by insisting upon the primacy of careful, repeated, and precise observation. The methods of the natural philosopher were to recapitulate the manner in which Buffon's mythical "sleeper" rediscovered the world or the way in which the "herdsman" acquired his practical knowledge. Buffon attempted what Wilhelm von Humboldt later would establish as a theoretical necessity for the continued expansion of all "languages of science." They were to nourish themselves periodically by returning to the language of practical understanding, what Humboldt called the "language of speaking." They had to return to their roots in history and culture in order to move forward with greater "force, radiance, and beauty."[88] In this partial return Buffon reasserted the living aspect of nature in a dynamic vision of reality.

PREFORMATION, EPIGENESIS, AND THE HISTORIZATION OF NATURE

Buffon's image of a living nature led him to address one of the central problems of the time, that of animal generation. Through his efforts and those of his friend Maupertuis, the question of generation became one of the most contested issues of the late Enlightenment, revealing in its own way the crucial tensions of the period. During the first half of the eighteenth century the prevailing theory of generation was "divine preformation," its cognates being "evolution," "development" and "Entwicklung," a concept intimately bound to the mechanist vision of nature, which also served to support traditional "physicotheology." Accepted by most of the leading thinkers of the time and popularized by countless religious writers, divine preformation assumed that God had created all living things at the beginning of time and then encased these minutely fully formed entities in seeds or *germes*, either in the ovaries or in the sperm depending upon whether one favored ovarian or spermist preformation. George Cheyne described the spermist position as follows: "Now, since there is no necessity to think *God Almighty* is confin'd to a new Creation, in every *Generation* of an *Animal*, and that these *Animals* themselves are conspicuous in all Male Seeds hitherto examined, it is plain that they must have been all created at once; and lodged in the Loyns of the Original pair of all the *Species* of *Animals*."[89] In divine preformation, birth and development entailed no qualitative difference. The fully formed fetus lay wrapped up like a ball of string in its encasement. When awakened through the mechanism of sexual intercourse, which served primarily as a stimulus, its limbs unfolded and got bigger until it was ready to emerge from the womb. Bernard Nieuwentyt described this process in his immensely popular *The Religious Philosopher:* "This however is sure enough . . . that all living Creatures whatever proceed from a *Stamin* or Principle, in which the Limbs and Members of the Body are folded and wound as it were in a Ball of Thread; which by the Operation of adventitious Matter and Humours are filled up and unfolded, till the Structure of all the Parts have the Magnitude of a full grown Body."[90]

For the modern reader, the universal popularity of divine preformation during the late seventeenth and early eighteenth century boggles the mind. Why were some of the finest minds of the period attracted to it?[91] A simple starting point is that preformation offered a way to attack Aristotelian and hermetic natural philosophy. Both proclaimed life to be generated by a living force or "virtue" that animated matter, brought homogeneous parts together, and then directed formation through a series of steps. Harvey, for example, adopted this Aristotelian explanatory strategy in his *De generatione animalium* (1651). According to him, all life originated in "eggs," which he considered primary matter, an undifferentiated beginning. When a power or "contagion" activated this "primordium," blood, the first form of living matter, was produced. When it appeared, it took on the qualities of living matter; it moved in a spontaneous manner and demonstrated signs of sensation. From this "leaping point," there soon followed the formation of the heart, the lungs, and then the liver and brain.[92] Similarly, the active power resident in the egg sparked the successive stages of formation until the whole creature was shaped. Once fully formed and grown, the adult creature supplied either the matter or the contagion that led to the generation of new, similar creatures, the female providing the matter, the male the power. Harvey coined the term "epigenesis" to characterize this process.[93]

Mechanists rejected such an explanation of generation. The positing of active powers and creative leaps in nature not only seemed to support miraculous creation, which they rejected, but also could serve to justify the chaos, turmoil, revolution, and popular dissent that characterized seventeenth-century society. Rejecting new creation, leaps in nature, and hidden forces, mechanical philosophers of nature "regarded the formation of all individual things as a process by which suitable preexisting particles are fitted together,"[94] a view consistent with the renewed interest in Platonic, Pythagorean, and Augustinian traditions that were nourishing the religious sensibilities of the age. Augustine's statement "Deus creavit omnia simul" (God created everything at the same time) struck a chord among mechanists and religious reformers alike.[95] Matter was indestructible, and so were God's creations and His order of things, made material at the beginning of time.

The concept of divine preformation, which dates to around 1670, combined two theories. The first, derived from botany, argued that plants were fully formed in the seed or *germe* of a plant. The second, asserting the preexistence of *germes*, was grafted onto the first. Malebranche, inspired by Swammerdam's supposed discovery of a fully formed moth in a silkworm, articulated the idea in his *De la recherche de la verité* (1674–75): "Perhaps all the bodies of men and animals born until the end of times were created at the creation of the world, which is to say that the females of the first animals may have been created containing all the animals of the same species that they have begotten and that are to be begotten in the future."[96] At first divine preformation was ovist, supported by a number of "discoveries," such as Redi's hypothesis that maggots in meat were hatched from flies' eggs, Malpighi's claim that fertilized eggs contained tiny embryos, and de Graaf's announcement that a rabbit's ovary had female eggs. The ovist position was challenged by Leeuwenhoeck's discovery of spermatozoa. Spermists or animaliculists argued that the preformed *germes* were found in the male. For those who saw the male as the nobler, more active of the species, this was a far more satisfying solution, even though ovism was preferable to orthodox religious thinkers because it accounted more easily for the virgin birth. Both animaliculists and ovists struggled mightily to discredit each other even though they shared the same basic assumptions, namely, that all creatures were divinely preformed, that the preformation took place in only one of the sexes, that sexual activity incited but did not cause generation, and finally that nothing new under the sun could appear, so there could be no new creation.

Once the idea of divinely preformed *germes* had been proposed, thinkers of various intellectual persuasions quickly adopted it because it addressed many scientific and extra-scientific interests. As a scientific theory, it offered a radically simple answer to the questions of continuity, resemblance, and ontogeny, while also apparently confirming the mechanistic definitions of matter as passive and indestructible. It supported the mechanist idea of God as supreme architect who could not err. It is no surprise that the divines of almost all major Christian sects in Europe, with the possible exception of the Pietists, who believed in spiritual "rebirth" and "leaps" embraced preformation. That the concept could be so readily transformed into a religious message convinced many to accept it. Thus, mechanical natural philosophy proved to be one of the strongest pillars supporting the Biblical account of creation, even though it has often been pictured as the opening wedge in the secularization of European thought. It also supported the doctrines of predestination and the bondage of the will central to Calvinism, doctrines making strong inroads in all of the Christian sects, including post-Tridentine Catholicism.

In addition, the theory of divine preformation was consistent with the argument from design to prove God's existence, invoked by thinkers such as Boyle and the Abbé Pluche who saw God's majesty and power in all things great and small as well as by the physicotheologians, many of them earnest Anglican and Lutheran clergymen in England and Germany, who turned out enormous tomes on subjects such as the sex life of the snail or the theology of the snowflake to prove God's unerring design. The argument from design, which became one of the eighteenth century's most common theological and moral topoi, achieved the status of a self-evident truth, partly because of its "modern," scientific quality.[97] With respect to its theory of generation, mechanical philosophy came quickly to religion's support and the concept's popularization for religious consumption was quick and fairly complete.

The doctrine of divine preformation was also adapted in the social and political realm, serving as the support for the idea of God as all-knowing creator and sole mover of passive matter and for its earthly parallel in the "absolute" monarch. According to this view, the monarch imposed order on the state and served as the fountainhead from which all power and authority flowed. As the embodiment of reason, it was the monarch's duty to clarify these lines of transmission, introducing the natural rule of order that was simple, streamlined, and effective. Divine preformation's concept of a fixed, static universe, in which there were no leaps in nature or new births lent further credence to the idea that "man's duty is to discover and to obey preordained laws."[98] By denying the possibility of substantive change, preformation suggested that a political and social structure founded upon distinctions of birth paralleled nature's hierarchical order of creation. Regardless of their intentions, the mechanical philosophers of nature forged a powerful language, readily appropriated by apologists to justify the prerogatives of absolute monarchs and late-seventeenth-century religious leaders.

Preformation also provided what could be called the logical predisposition that made the late-seventeenth-century mechanical philosophy of nature so convincing to the majority of its adherents—perhaps the most abstract, but by no means least important of its nonscientific applications. Simply stated, preformation addressed the debate waged about God's mode of action, whether He was all volition, personally directing each phenomenological event in nature, or whether He was all logos, the essence of absolute wisdom and hence the designer of a world that was "perfect," the most complete of all possible and conceivable worlds. The formal and abstract side of the debate raged unabated from the 1670s till the middle of the eighteenth century without any conclusive resolution. The more popular side of the debate never took this extreme form; rather, it was a relative question. At that time there were very few devout Christians who would have believed that God could not intervene in the world He had created if He so wished. If He could not, then it would be impossible to explain miracles. On the other hand, there were also very few who would choose a purely willful God, a continual busybody, pulling every string, demonstrating incompetence as well as irrationality. This is a point Mme. du Chatelet emphasized: "If the possibility of things depended on his volition, then it would be necessary to say that God had been without understanding while his volition was occupied in creating the possibles."[99] If that were so, then every event would be a miracle, in effect making God's special miracles impossible to define. However one judges the formal outcome of the Newton-Leibniz controversy, it is safe to say that on the popular level Leibniz had the better of the argument. In its simplest terms, Leibniz argued that mind cannot move matter. If that were true, as the mechanists believed, then God established the movements of mind and matter at the creation. As Leibniz expressed it: "Thus the basis of this concord [between mind and matter] must be sought in God; and not as if He were newly producing it and disturbing the laws of things (as the proponents of occasional causes will have it) but because in the beginning He gave perceptions to the soul, as well as movements to the body, so coordinated that the soul is the essential representative of the body and the body the essential instrument of the soul."[100]

Leibniz advanced this formulation of the preestablished harmony in a critique of Georg Stahl's medical philosophy, which argued that the soul could indeed effect changes on matter. For Leibniz, this assertion raised the specter of "falling back upon a miracle," or an "occult force," instead of a rational explanation: "But if in truth an intelligible explanation is to be sought in the nature of the thing it will come from what is clearly apprehended in the thing, namely, from form and motion existing in matter."[101] Such an intelligible explanation would be possible only if divine intelligence instituted eternal relations between things. For Leibniz, the entire system was predicated upon preformation, "for the success of the whole system is due to divine preformation."[102] The majority of the mechanist philosophers, whatever their differences, would have agreed with Leibniz's statement. To attack preformation was to attack mechanism at its heart. Moreover, to attack the doctrine was to call into question the whole edifice of overlapping motives that has led to its formulation, ensured its acceptance, and undergirded its credibility.

. . .

By the time Buffon raised the issue of animal generation, a corpus of works questioning the presuppositions of divine preformation already existed. Among them were a few holdouts who had refused to accept the idea of a passive nature even during the strongest tide of mechanistic philosophy at the end of the seventeenth century and the beginning of the eighteenth. In England, for example, a small group of academics held on to the idea of an active nature, including the Cambridge don Robert Greene.[103] The most persistent critics of the mechanists were the animists, of whom Stahl was the most prominent. He attracted a small but vociferous group of followers, chiefly in Germany and Great Britain, most of them radical evangelists. In France the medical school at Montpellier accepted animism in the 1740s. In Scotland, Edinburgh's medical men turned to animism at about the time Buffon was composing the *Histoire naturelle*. But these were minority voices that did not play an influential role in shaping scientific discourse until after Buffon's *Histoire naturelle* began to appear.

Buffon's critique drew its nourishment from a variety of sources, from Leibniz in particular. Although Leibniz insisted upon the absolute theoretical necessity for divine preformation, his definition of the organic machine could be, when abstracted from its philosophical base, reinterpreted in a manner consistent with the idea of living matter.

Leibniz had characterized animals as "nature's machines, living organic bodies, which are in fact machines of divine invention purposefully designed for a definite kind of function.... Furthermore they have that splendid feature of a divine machine, surpassing those that we can make, in that they can protect and perpetuate themselves."[104] This image of "living machines" provided the basis for La Mettrie's attack upon a strict constructionist definition of organization in *Man the Machine*. Other midcentury intellectuals began entertaining the idea of a living and active nature. Trembly's discovery of the freshwater hydra or polyp's reproductive powers provided empirical evidence to support this idea.[105] Proponents of divine preformation could not explain how the polyp, when cut into sections, could form a new, complete animal from each of the sections. Did God foresee which polyps would be cut in pieces and provide them with extra *germes* at the beginning of time? To pose the question virtually pointed to its absurdity. Trembly's polyps also led to the revival of the idea of spontaneous generation, which John Turberville Needham, Buffon's close friend, claimed to have observed in microscopic animals. In addition to these new data from experiments, nagging questions abounded about "monstrous" births, hybridization, and the resemblance between parents and offspring.[106]

These discussions set the stage for Maupertuis's *Vénus physique* (1745), one of the first successful attempts to revive the theory of epigenesis. The work, published anonymously and employing the language of the salon rather than that of the academy,[107] became the rage of Paris. Buffon claimed that it "contained more philosophical concepts about generation than scores of heavy tomes."[108] By 1751 it had gone through six printings.[109] Its success can be explained by Maupertuis's skill in retaining epigenesis' general outlines, while explicating its details in a new erotically tinged natural philosophic vocabulary, refurbishing it with analogies drawn from gravity, chemical affinity, and veiled sexual allusions. Maupertuis argued that generation was the product of a chemical combination of male and female fluids composed of organic particles drawn from and imprinted upon by each part of the body. Attractive force joined the constituent particles according to the material's overall proportion of fluids from each donor, as well as by the specific proportions of matter from each donor's body parts. Maupertuis's explanation could account for gender, as well as degrees of resemblance between offspring and donors. "Monstrous" births resulted either from the incomplete combination of fluids or from a disproportionate number of particles from one body part suppressing particles from another. As a result, Maupertuis reversed the focus of reproduction from anatomy to generation, effecting "a veritable reversal of perspective."[110] Buffon considered Maupertuis "the first writer who once again approached the truth, from which one had strayed more than ever before by positing the existence of eggs and through the discovery of animalicules."[111] Buffon also pointed to the direction further investigation should take. He believed naturalists had to return to conceptions formulated when humans were less estranged from nature and less inclined to rely upon abstract reason. As the proponent of historical reasoning, Buffon accused his predecessors of reversing rather than advancing the progress of knowledge by neglecting the achievements of the earlier past.

Buffon's indictment betrays his deep ambivalence about the present, of what purported to be "new" or of recent origin. For Buffon anything not firmly attached to its roots was a "degeneration," an incorrect or incomplete appearance. This was true for both animal species and species of knowledge. If natural history was to advance, naturalists had to find a truer generational model, propounded when humans could still observe without being blinded by hypothetical reasoning. They should reattach themselves to it in order to reestablish knowledge's "natural progression." For Buffon, as with Jean Jacques Rousseau, his fervent admirer,[112] knowledge of nature's history and the history of natural philosophy was crucial in evaluating where we have gone wrong and how to correct the direction for future investigations. History in this sense served a threefold function. It was liberating, allowing the natural philosopher to slough off the accretions of false development. It was conservative, insofar as it warned against placing too much trust in ahistorical forms of reasoning and falling too easily prey to contemporary intellectual fashions. And it served as a tool of scientific authorization and legitimization, distinguishing between "correct" and "incorrect" research methods and goals by bringing current research activities back into harmony with the achievements of the true founders of the discipline.

Buffon underscored the importance of historical analysis by prefacing his detailed description of animal reproduction with a historical critique of contemporary theories. In so doing, he ran into the problem of discovering the older traditions to which one should return. Unlike the hypothetical case of his "sleeper," who instinctively constructed a natural system, history suggested that humans tended very quickly to replace correct observation with abstract hypothesis. The Greeks offered a paradigmatic example, to which Buffon continuously turned. For him, Greek history presented clear analogues to the present. Thus, mechanism and its philosophical excesses had its proponents in ancient times as well as their opponents. Buffon's analysis juxtaposed two opposing Greek philosophical systems, which he mediated by turning to a third, nonphilosophical one. Plato and Pythagoras represented the first, negative pole in the Greek natural philosophy. They had forgotten "that we are not disembodied spirits," but rather "bound to matter," and ruled by our sense perceptions, not by abstract ideas. Plato was bad enough. A "painter of ideas" who had blithely soared into the realm of abstraction, he virtually sacrificed his humanity on the altar of reason. His philosophy was "empty," a "desert of speculations," despite his lofty intentions. Pythagorean philosophy, a reification of Plato's, was even worse. It was founded upon two principles, "one false, the other a mere supposition."[113] The first claimed that numbers represented nature's true relations, power, and essence, collapsing the signifier and the signified into an identity. The second assumed the reality of arguments from final causes or design. Buffon's critique of the first need not be reiterated, but his attack on teleological reasoning is interesting, for it is often assumed to be central to vitalist and organic models.

When Buffon was writing, arguments from final cause were usually employed to support a static, hierarchically constructed universe. Although originally attacked by leading mechanists, Leibniz reintroduced the argument of final causes through the idea of sufficient reason, which Christian Wolff expanded to support an elaborate philosophy of being.[114] Sufficient reason became the prime intellectual tool supporting physicotheology, combining the argument from design with the assumption that everything was made for humanity's benefit. It was this form of teleological reasoning, which Buffon mocked as saying "that there is light because we have eyes, that there are sounds because we have ears, or to say that we have ears and eyes because there is light and sound."[115] For Buffon, this explanatory procedure betrayed the highest degree of human hubris imaginable. It also provided the theoretical support for the idea of divine preformation. Buffon dismissed the idea of sufficient reason, arguing that it was not grounded in human desire nor in nature. It portrayed "arbitrary connections" and "abstract moral ideas."[116] Teleological arguments were relevant only if the idea of final goal could be historicized, placed in time as an end to which a thing strives.

After dismissing the Platonic-Pythagorean paradigm, Buffon turned to the other famous classical model of human reproduction, the Aristotelian. Basically, Buffon admired Aristotle: "Aristotle, who was as great a philosopher as Plato and a much better naturalist [*physicien*], instead of loosing himself in the land of hypotheses, on the contrary depends upon observations, collects facts, and speaks a more understandable language."[117] Aristotle's works reflected Buffon's basic principles of research and explanation: collection, comparison, and simplicity of expression. Buffon also agreed with Aristotle's championing of epigenesis. Still, Buffon detected a serious error in Aristotle's reasoning. Aristotle defined matter merely as something "demonstrating the ability to be formed," which led him to conclude that the formative principle must come from outside of matter, from an active principle or "contagion." According to Aristotle the female merely provided the matter for regeneration. The male principle was the active agent that animated female matter. Aristotle and his followers, from Averroës to Harvey, had portrayed the female as material and passive, the male principle as immaterial and active. To dematerialize one gender, Buffon argued, was to fall into the error of the dualists, separating mind from body. To deactivate matter, even for one gender, was to make the mistake of the mechanists. To do both, assuming thereby that only one sex played a qualitatively significant role in animal reproduction, was to lay the groundwork for the concept of divine preformation. Although Aristotle was better than Plato, he too had made the mistake of being taken in by speculative philosophy. He too worshipped in the temple of error.

Having demonstrated the deficiencies of the two major Greek philosophical traditions with regard to reproduction, Buffon turned to an earlier, nonphilosopher, Hippocrates, whom he regarded as the Greek embodiment of his "sleeper." According to Buffon, Hippocrates had offered a relatively true account of animal reproduction, though it was in some respects blurred and in others too complex. Hippocrates had argued that generation resulted from the of mixing active male and female fluids, which contained elements drawn from all body parts joined in a form based upon the relative power and proportion of the fluids. The action of heat and cold generated life, and the "fruit" developed in stages. For Buffon, Hippocrates had blazed a path that could lead to a correct understanding of animal reproduction: "This system is less obscure and more reasonable than that of Aristotle, because Hippocrates seeks to explain particular things using particular reasons, and he borrows only one general principle from the philosophy of his time: that hotness and coldness create spirits, and these spirits have the power to order and arrange matter. He saw reproduction more as a Doctor than as a Philosopher. Aristotle explained it more as a Metaphysician than as a Naturalist; this is why the faults in Aristotle's system are general and obvious errors."[118]

By juxtaposing Hippocrates with Plato and Aristotle, Buffon could accomplish four goals. First, he reiterated the dangers posed by abstract philosophy to the advance of natural history. Second, he pointed to a significant scientific tradition that was aphilosophic, motivated by the pragmatic need to observe life carefully. Buffon rehabilitated the physician as the prototype of the true natural philosopher in a manner strikingly similar to Carlo Ginzburg's recent distinction between the interpreters of signs (hunters, physicians, detectives, historians) and abstract thinkers (astrologers, philosophers, and theoretical scientists). The physician was necessarily concerned with careful observation, comparison, and judgment, employing what Ginzburg has called the "conjectural paradigm," which, Ginzburg, echoing Buffon, associated with Hippocratic medicine.[119] In late-eighteenth-century France, Great Britain, and Germany, vitalists called for a return to practical concerns and to "common" wisdom, which in the life sciences harkened back to Hippocrates.[120] Third, Buffon was able to criticize both system builders and Aristotelians, while acknowledging their specific contributions by using Hippocrates as a control. Thus, he recognized Harvey's importance while rejecting his formulations derived from Aristotelian metaphysics. Similarly, he praised late-seventeenth-century mechanists such as Malpighi and de Graaf, who had made significant observational advances, while denying their explanatory systems. He recognized Descartes's "two seeds" theory in the formation of the human fetus but rejected the manner in which Descartes explained the fetus's development. As James Larson made clear, "Descartes . . . had correctly championed the mixture of seminal fluids as the source of organic formation. But he had gone on to argue that purely mechanical causes formed body parts, views accepted by no one."[121] Thus, Buffon freely abstracted elements from various systems of thought without committing himself to any. Fourth, Buffon could retain Hippocrates's general system but also correct its mistakes, thus ensuring his vision of instituting progressive science.

To update Hippocrates's account of generation, Buffon extrapolated elements from modern theory to explain how the fluids mixed, how and why the parts were arranged, and how formation proceeded. Buffon's "modernized" Hippocrates (or "vitalized" Descartes) set the parameters for the late-eighteenth-century debate concerning generation. Working from the conviction that animal reproduction resulted from the mixing of male and female seminal fluids, Buffon assumed, as had Maupertuis, that each of the seminal fluids contained continually active organic particles drawn from all parts of the body. Although composed of the same vital substance, animal particles were shaped or encoded by the part of the body where they had originated. Thus, the seminal fluids contained "excerpts of all parts of the human body."[122] When the male and female fluids mixed, particles from each of the respective donors combined to form a new creature, similar to the parents, yet constituting a unique conjunction by combining their elements in varying proportions.

This hypothesis immediately raised a number of questions. Why, for example, do head particles combine only with head particles, especially if they were made up of the same vital substance? Why did they combine in the same relation to one another as they had in the parents? More importantly, why was the mixing of male and female fluids necessary to produce an offspring if both sexes had full complements of organic particles? Could the "excerpts" be joined in one sex alone? The last question was the most critical and difficult. An affirmative answer would support rather than deny preformation.

To answer these queries, Buffon roamed freely through contemporary natural philosophy, synthesizing elements into an explanatory field that the Enlightenment Vitalists would develop further. He began with the Newtonian idea of penetrating power, joined it to the antimechanist concept of elective affinity, and rounded it off by linking these to the phenomenon of polar interaction from magnetism. Not only did his synthesis help establish the discursive matrix of Enlightenment Vitalism, it also attested to a renewed midcentury interest in chemistry, contributing further to its rehabilitation; for Buffon had defined reproduction as a chemical process in which something new was created by the "internal bonding" of elements from two fluids.

Traditionally Chemistry had employed sexually charged metaphors to explain the process of chemical combination, establishing a linguistic linkage between chemistry and life. Buffon returned to that topos, making chemistry essential for explaining generation because it dealt with internal joining. In Buffon's view, penetrating force and polar reaction created the conditions for chemical bonding to occur. Buffon's account of generation runs roughly as follows. Organic particles constantly move about randomly in the body's seminal fluids, and the body continually recycles them, making it impossible for the particles to combine. Therefore, complex animals cannot reproduce asexually. For combination to occur, Buffon argued, the random motion had to be halted, the particles focused upon a "point of combination," a "living point," or a "sphere of attraction," some fixed point that holds the particles still, enabling the forces of elective affinity between similar particles to engage, allowing particles to seek out their similarly encoded particles and rush to conjoin. But what stops this random motion? To solve this puzzle, Buffon turned to polar reaction. In a single body all of the encoded particles pass by each other with little obstruction. In the sexual mixing of male and female fluids this is also true with one exception, namely, between the particles encoded by the respective donors' sexual organs. When these two opposites come into close proximity, their opposing forces, acting like poles in a magnet, create the living point, halting random motion close to it and slowing it down in its immediate vicinity. Once motion is halted, the encoded particles closest to the point, now directed by elective affinity, rush to the center and to each other. Organization occurs in a split second, something arising where there was nothing before.

But what happens to the excess organic particles unfortunate enough not to have been caught in the force field of the sphere of attraction? Buffon introduced another occult penetrating force to answer that question. If the new formation's constituent particles were drawn to the vital point by attraction, the newly formed creature would be endowed with a force working outwards from its center, sufficiently strong to cancel the remaining particles' originally encoded message and reorganize them into the placenta and the amniotic sac, thereby providing the new creature with nourishment and protection. Thus nature is neither wasteful nor does it do anything in vain. This force's action assures the process of formation, affirms the unitary nature of organic matter, and demonstrates the self-regulating action of the animal economy.

Buffon's explanation for generation offered an alternative that mediated between Malpighi and de Graaf's preformationist claim that the egg contained the fully formed animal, Descartes's two seeds theory and Harvey's concept of epigenesis. By emphasizing the sudden and almost miraculous generation of a new creature, Buffon denied any form of preformationism. But, Buffon also took issue with Harvey, who believed creation began with the heart and the vitalization of blood and proceeded slowly by degrees until an animal was formed. Buffon opted for a modified form of spontaneous generation, claiming "that those who believed that the heart was first formed have erred, the same applies to those who gave preference to the blood: everything emerges at once."[123] Although not fully formed, this new creation was in essence an animal, though in very rough outline. Epigenesis did not lead to the creation of an animal, but rather to the formation and refinement of its specific parts. Buffon's imaginative vision of reproduction provides an extremely vivid material example of what I call the idea of the extended middle in which creativity is achieved through the juxtaposition of extremes. In the case of generation, the two opposed forces of sexual polarization do not interact dialectically. Rather, the tension between them makes creativity possible by opening up a space within which it occurs. Here Buffon reified the rhetorical figure of juxtaposition, transforming it into a physical principle, a law of nature that informed, mirrored, and authorized the type of thinking he considered central to the acquisition of knowledge about nature.[124]

. . .

To Buffon's contemporaries the *Histoire naturelle* clarified and gave direction to the shift in natural philosophic sensibilities taking place in France, Great Britain, and Germany during the late 1740s and afterwards. His work became so influential partly because of Buffon's position as head of Europe's premier institution for the study of natural history, the "Jardin des Plantes."[125] But its message conveyed in a magnificent prose that portrayed scientific concerns in the popular style of the salon,[126] also spoke directly to emerging intellectual concerns that far transcended the conflicting Parisian interests of the academy and salon. Buffon succeeded in placing many specific issues within a larger matrix of interrelated assumptions that was disseminated, elaborated upon, expanded, and modified. This discursive matrix, which I call Enlightenment Vitalism, came to characterize an important sector of late Enlightenment natural philosophic thought and practice. By its very popularity it also served as a challenge to contending traditions, at times subtly influencing them, at others forcing them to counter its claims with more precise formulations of their own. Buffon's general legacy to Enlightenment Vitalism's subsequent development can be characterized as follows.

He emphasized the primacy of living over inanimate matter, asserted the existence of inner, active forces as central agents in nature, envisioned a world of new creation and leaps in nature, and proclaimed the ineffable quality of individuality and the manifold variety of nature. He called for new forms of natural philosophic explanation in which the mind-body duality was blurred and based it on the principles of comparison, resemblance, affinity, analogical reasoning, and divination. And he argued that only through the creation of a natural system could one truly aspire to understand nature's forces, to penetrate beneath the veil of surface phenomena to the core of reality.

But above all, Buffon proclaimed an order of things that elevated dynamic relations and qualitative change over time. He revitalized and historicized nature without denying the existence of a comprehensible order.[127] For many late-eighteenth-century thinkers, this vision of the order of things and the natural philosophic assumptions and procedures that accompanied it was appealing both because of the internal logic of the vision and because of its ability to speak directly to analogous issues concerning human freedom, and the social and political order. Adam Ferguson made this linkage explicit:

> Our notion of order in civil society is frequently false: it is taken from the analogy of subjects inanimate and dead; we consider commotion and action as contrary to its nature; we think it consistent only with obedience, secrecy, and the silent passing of affairs through the hands of a few: The good order of stones in a wall, is their being properly fixed in places for which they are hewn; were they to stir the building

must fall: but the order of men in society, is their being placed where they are properly qualified to act. The first is a fabric made of dead and inanimate parts, the second is made of living and active members. When we seek in society for the order of mere inaction and tranquility, we forget the nature of our subject, and find the order of slaves, not of free men.[128]

For both "internal" and "external" reasons, this new language of nature for which Buffon served as an icon spread quickly, usually following lines of least resistance. It was developed in those fields of knowledge most poorly served by mechanism and less dependent upon atomism and then moved into the harder sciences, effecting physics itself. This change can be most clearly seen in the areas of chemistry, in the life sciences and in medicine. As Robert Schofield remarked, "few areas were more prolific in ingenious mechanistic speculation than physiology and chemistry. With the shift in intellectual climate, in none was the flight from mechanism more explicit and complete."[129]

2 Learning to "Read the Book of Nature"

Vitalizing Chemistry in the Late Enlightenment

CREATING A NEW LANGUAGE OF CHEMISTRY

In 1777 the eminent Swedish naturalist Torbern Olof Bergman evaluated what he considered the major forms of natural philosophy in an introduction to Carl Wilhelm Scheele's path-breaking *A Dissertation on Air and Fire*. Bergman ranked the forms of natural philosophy in a tripartite order of increasing importance. It began with Linneaen natural history, which directed one's attention to surface phenomena and taught one to recognize external characteristics in order to classify them. The second, higher stage, was the study of physics, that body of knowledge acquired when one investigated the universal properties of matter (extension, impenetrability, and inertia). The third and highest was chemistry, which dealt with basic elements, their compounds, and their reciprocal relations: "The first teaches us the Book of Nature's alphabet, the second how to spell, and the third how to read it clearly. The first two, therefore, were auxiliaries that lead us to the last, which is the real goal."[1]

A contemporary admirer of Bergman, the German mathematician Wencelaus Johann Karsten elaborated upon this theme in 1786 and related it to early-eighteenth-century discussions concerning matter: "Earlier, when one spoke about the elemental properties of matter, one introduced the question of its divisibility. . . . This idea generated a host of treatises that appeared very learned but were, in fact, totally useless." Karsten then listed these "useless" questions. They included "whether matter was infinitely divisible or divisible only down to a minute point, whether this indivisible point could be considered as totally simple (without for͏͏ or whether one should accept very minute indivisible particˈ these points be called monads, atoms, physical points or whatͰ could call them." Thus, Karsten continued, "one occupied oneself with these and similar questions as if one didn't know better."[2] Karsten believed the contemporary natural philosophers knew better. They are "indifferent to the questions of whether matter can be divided to infinity or to a minuscule point." Instead of these theoretical considerations, they know "other types of divisibility, or better said, other types of decompositions of physical matter into non-identical elemental matter. This type of matter belongs to reality."[3] In 1789 Johann Samuel Gehler confirmed these views in his highly influential scientific dictionary, the *Physikalisches Wörterbuch*. Writing about the theory of heat, he declared that explanations based on "mechanical systems" were insufficient: "To correctly order these phenomena and bring them under specific laws, one had to speak the language of the chemists."[4]

Had a leading natural philosopher of the first four decades of the eighteenth century been transported forward in time and presented with these declarations, that naturalist would probably have considered them weakminded.[5] For, until the midcentury, they described neither dominant chemical theory nor the relations between the natural sciences. It was then common to treat chemistry as an adjunct to the mechanical philosophy of nature. From Boyle to Boerhaave, chemical phenomena were explained by reference to the general principles of imparted motion, vibration, impact, mass, and shape, all of which were related to the existence of Karsten's "minute bits of matter." To cite a few examples, heat was considered the result of friction or increased vibration between atoms, acidity the effect of sharply shaped secondary particles, and liquidity of spherical ones. Chemical reactions were explained by changes of particle shape due to collisions between two opposed bodies.[6] The subsumption of chemistry under the general categories of the mechanical laws of matter and motion had dethroned it from the preeminent position it had once occupied in Renaissance and Early Modern natural philosophy.[7] It became a minor speck on natural philosophy's firmament. The leading texts on natural philosophy written during the first forty years of the eighteenth century attested to this altered role. In them chemistry received scant attention, though these texts were "deemed complete."[8] Of all the great early-eighteenth-century writers of general texts, only Boerhaave considered chemistry seriously. And, as we shall see later, his deep concern with chemistry led him to introduce concepts that inadvertently began to undermine the mechanistic philosophy to which he subscribed.[9]

What happened during these forty or so years to induce respected naturalists to propose such a radical reordering of scientific priorities? Certainly it had nothing to do with a failure of physics. Physics had not lost its explanatory precision, especially in the privileged areas of mechanics, hydraulics, optics, and celestial mechanics. In these it handled what Charles Gillispie called "the theoretical physicist's exacting instrument of abstraction and mathematicization" with great and increasing skill.[10] When Bergman, Karsten, and Gehler wrote their pieces, there was no shortage of people with advanced mathematical skills or with a consuming interest in natural philosophy. Quite the contrary: there were a larger number of people with advanced mathematical skills than at any previous time in early modern European history, and the interest in natural philosophy, at least among the educated, was at a high pitch. Still, Karsten, a professor of mathematics, would proclaim, rehearsing Buffon's position, that "mathematical theorems along with their proofs do not belong in natural philosophy [*Naturlehre*]; when writers employ them to teach physics instead of mathematics, it entails the introduction of alien principles [*Sätze*]. By this," he continued, "I don't mean that one shouldn't apply mathematical principles in physics. That is something quite different from when one weaves such a principle or principles into the explication of physics as though they belonged to the system of physics."[11] What was true for physics was even truer for chemistry. Since it dealt with immediate matter, its methods and explanatory procedures were increasingly judged to be far superior than any discipline modeled upon mathematics. Bergman provided one answer to justify this reordering of priorities: chemistry focused upon "elements, compounds, and their relations." He clarified this definition by using the rhetorical topos of descending from the surface to the core, from immediately perceived and sensed reality to something hidden and invisible, something essential but that could be seen only through a glass darkly. Extension and appearance were no longer the operational parameters for Bergman's vision of natural philosophy. What once was primary, he made secondary.

In this conception, all of the central categories of mechanism were shunted aside. Elements or "simple substances" replaced atoms as the basic core of matter, defined as bodies "capable of no further reduction."[12] The decomposition of compounds substituted for the idea of the divisibility or indivisibility of homogeneous atomic matter. Relations between active or activated material substances replaced the action and reaction of abstract forces. In this theoretical and practical reorientation of natural philosophy the central explanatory features and most of the lexical items of the mechanical philosophy of nature were dropped, ignored, or, if used, drastically redefined. A new language of nature was being formed, which some modern investigators have called the "compositional revolution" in chemistry.[13] This new language had many elective affinities with the one Buffon forged in natural history, often attested to by naturalists in both areas.[14] It mobilized the same rhetorical figures: a preference for observable reality over hypothetical-mathematical reasoning, an affirmation of nature's manifold variety over homogeneity, a concern with the particular over reductive systems, a concentration on complex composition over aggregation, and a turn to explanations based upon internal attractions or affinities.

The development of this new language of chemistry in the last half of the eighteenth century has often been overlooked or minimized by the tendency to concentrate upon the "revolution" Lavoisier achieved at the end of the century. By focusing on the replacement of the phlogiston theory with the oxidation theory of combustion, eighteenth-century chemistry (often called Stahlist) could be considered the scientific equivalent of the ancien régime, an antiquated, irrational system crying out for reformation, but changed only by the coup de grace that Lavoisier, the "first self-conscious revolutionary in science," administered.[15] This is a tidy scheme, for it associates scientific advance with political change, confirms the "whiggish" idea of scientific progress effected by great thinkers, and makes a serious discussion of what is called Stahlian chemistry unnecessary.

Yet this story conceals more than it reveals. Its basic fault lies in its defective evaluation of Stahlian chemistry. First, by categorizing it as the dominant form of eighteenth-century chemistry, it overlooks the late acceptance of Stahlian ideas. Second, it overemphasizes the centrality of phlogiston to the system and assumes a constant and unchanging body of Stahlian chemical thought and practice. Third, what is called "Stahlist" chemistry was not a fixed approach, but was an elaboration of a way of looking at chemistry that went far beyond Stahl's own premises and ideas.[16] In reality, "Stahlian" chemistry became popular only after the midcentury critique of mechanism. As the young Franz von Baader argued, it thrived only with the attack upon the *Methodo scientifico-mathematica* with its ideas of "mechanical vibration, collision and pressure."[17] In this new formulation, phlogiston constituted but one part of a "more general approach to the whole of chemistry,"[18] which was capable of extensive revision and development, sometimes leading to conclusions well beyond Stahl's original formulations. The chemical thought conveniently labeled Stahlist was a specific expression of a larger reshuffling of scientific and cultural priorities that took place during the last half of the century at various centers of chemical practice. The cultural and social environment in which each was formed shaped these "local" traditions,[19] but taken together they still revealed broad areas of agreement, attesting to a shared language of chemistry. This language and set of practices provided Lavoisier with the practical and linguistic tools that enabled him to develop and propose his chemical theories. Without wishing to demonstrate these points by attempting a survey of the history of late-eighteenth-century chemistry, I would like to discuss the first three points made above to focus on the grammar and vocabulary of this new language of chemistry and its linkage with Buffon's project for reforming the study of nature. Then, in order to discuss Lavoisier and the Chemical Revolution, I will deal with a central issue in the elaboration of this language, the question of heat. It serves, I believe, as the functional and logical equivalent to the question of animal reproduction in the life sciences, and it formed the link between the physical and life sciences.

. . .

The creation of this new language of chemistry followed a three-stage pattern, paralleling the path Buffon had employed to evolve his vision of natural history. The first entailed the rehabilitation of an older tradition to counter the claims of mechanism. The second strove to carve out a unique explanatory and methodological field that differentiated chemistry from physics without directly challenging the principles upon which physics was constructed, establishing thereby a new grammar and vocabulary for chemistry. The third involved the reordering of scientific priorities, defining mechanical physics as less important or, in some radical instances, as ancillary to chemical knowledge.

When searching for an older tradition to authorize chemistry's reformulation, mid-eighteenth-century chemists turned to Stahl, whose ideas quickly replaced those of mechanism.[20] People sympathetic to Buffon found Stahl a kindred spirit in the attack against the ruling but tired intellectual establishment. In Stahl's work one could discover most of the basic themes Buffon had announced. Stahl indicted mechanism for the same two errors Buffon had cited. On the one hand, it "licks the surface of things while leaving the nucleus intact."[21] On the other, it indulged in useless and "amusing mathematical speculations."[22] Mechanism also erred, Stahl claimed, in its definition of matter, at least the matter with which the chemist was concerned. It was useless, he argued, to consider bodies as aggregates of minute homogeneous, elementary particles.[23] In the phenomenal world matter is always conjoined: "Nowhere in nature do there exist elementary bodies which our senses are able to perceive. Everything which we see, taste, feel, or touch is mixed, compounded [composé]."[24] Perceptible matter was heterogeneous. Stahl argued that only basic elements existed in the perceptible world. Each had its own quality or essence. These elements combined with other elements and with combinations of elements in a variety of ways, forming a complex gradation of species that could be classified according to degrees of resemblance or similarity.[25]

Stahl's antimechanism, his definition of matter, his emphasis upon resemblance, similarity, and heterogeneity, and his call for a type of "natural" classification proved extremely congenial to those favorable to Buffon's message. These positions formed the basis for what Robert Siegfried, Betty Jo Dobbs, and Jerry B. Gough consider the essence of the "Stahlian Revolution" in chemistry: its emphasis upon composition.[26] Stahl's attraction for later thinkers lay in his attempt to formulate a nonmechanistic theory of chemical combination that sought to account for the complexity and seeming capriciousness of chemical reactions. In it he joined his theory of the elements to the Paraclesian idea of elective affinity. Using his five "base" elements (air, water, vitrifiable earth, phlogistic or sulphurous earth, and metallic earth), Stahl argued for the existence of an equal number of basic chemical phenomena or unified processes that were dominated by these elements. These were founded on the inherent principles of acidity, alkalinity, vitrifiability, combustibility, and metalicity, respectively. These principles accounted for the processes of acidation, alkalization, vitrification, combustion, and metalization. Thus, beneath or informing each acid or form of combustion, an acid principle or combustion principle (phlogiston) could be postulated explaining the general process without denying its uniqueness.[27]

In the process of combustion, for example, the principle (phlogiston) formed the "nourishment" necessary for combustion to occur. When burning or calcination took place, another substance fed upon the nourishment until it was satiated and its appetite stilled. The principle departed the original combustible substance and entered the devouring substance in proportion to its appetite, generating heat in the process. Combustion and calcination, therefore, were examples of the same general chemical process, framed in the language of nourishment and reproduction. The degree of attraction existing between the principle of combustion (phlogiston), the combustible substance, and the substance with which it combines explained the process's variation. The greater the attraction between the principle of combustion and the new body, the greater the reaction, the more heat generated, the more complete the burning.

Sympathy, *rapport*, or elective affinity constituted Stahl's central explanatory concept. Drawn from premechanistic theories of natural philosophy, especially from van Helmont and Paracelsus, the idea of elective affinity or *Wahlverwandschaft* incorporated the ideas of resemblance, analogy, and sympathy into a unified "law" of chemical reaction. According to Stahl, elements, though heterogeneous, were not isolated. They were related to each other through varying degrees intensity. This also held for the immense number of individual compounds. They were composed of elements that possessed a set of desires and aversions to combine with or repel other elements from other compounds. When these compounds were brought together under certain conditions, these inherent desires asserted themselves, generating a chemical reaction.

In Stahl's view, the closeness of relation determined the intensity of affinity. Like attracts like (the German term *Wahlverwandschaft* retained this original meaning even after the concept was changed). According to the early Stahlists, in complex chemical reactions the constituent parts of a compound were drawn from the original compound to more similar parts of another element or compound. Unlike the mechanists who viewed chemical reactions in terms of collisions between opposing forces of different shapes, sizes, and mass, the proponents of elective affinity couched their explanations of chemical change in the language of generation, reproduction, and relationship. These midcentury chemical reformers chose the same metonymies and metaphors as had Buffon to characterize their endeavors. Chemistry pierced the outer shell to probe the mysteries of nature: it revealed the "intimate" union between elements. In the case of the reaction between acids and bases, the grand effervescence produced was seen as the result of similar parts, propelled by their inherent principles, rushing to embrace each other, breaking down earlier combinations and forming new ones.

THE GRAMMAR AND VOCABULARY OF THE NEW LANGUAGE OF CHEMISTRY

By the 1760s, a majority of chemists had adopted the general outlines of Stahl's chemical philosophy, without necessarily accepting its particulars. This loose consensus was founded upon an operational definition of chemistry joining the reciprocal procedures of analysis and synthesis. Through the decomposition and recomposition of bodies the chemical investigator acquired an understanding of the "intimate union" of substances. Macquer provided this description in 1749: "Separate the different substances which enter into the composition of a body, examine each one in particular, discover their properties and analogies, decompose them again as far as is possible, compare them and combine them with other substances, and then join them together again in order to make the original compound appear replete with all of its properties."[28] Forty years later Lavoisier, Macquer's major opponent, defined chemistry's operational procedures in similar, though clearer terms: "Chemistry affords two general methods of determining the constituent principles of bodies, the method of analysis and that of synthesis . . . and in general it ought to be considered as a principle in chemical science never to rest satisfied without both these species of proofs."[29] This definition virtually paraphrased ones provided earlier by Scheele and Bergman. Similar statements can be found in the methodological pronouncements of virtually every leading chemist of the last half of the eighteenth century.[30] Clearly, despite the many disputes among these chemists, they all agreed upon chemistry's ideal investigative procedures. By the 1780s, the imperative to combine "analysis" and "synthesis" had become part of the larger vocabulary of accepted investigative practice, transcending specific chemical problems.[31] Wilhelm von Humboldt championed this idea in a letter written to a friend in 1788, elevating the chemical method into a universal way to discover truth: "Nothing stands isolated in nature, for everything is combined, everything forms a whole, but with a thousand different and manifold sides. The researcher must first decompose and look at each part singly and for itself and then consider it as part of a whole. But here, as often happens, he cannot stop. He has to combine them together again, re-create the whole as it earlier appeared before his eyes."[32]

Not only did late-eighteenth-century natural philosophers adopt this operational definition of chemistry; they concurred in accepting the following propositions derived from their conception of chemical combination, decomposition, and recombination: (1) Different bodies "intermix, and unite so intimately as to be inseparable by mere mechanical means."[33] Mechanistic explanations could not account for the "internal fusions" of chemical combinations. (2) Chemical processes took place between substances of different kinds with different qualities, forming substances with equally unique properties. (3) Compounded or "mixed" substances can be decomposed only to a certain point, producing a limited number of heterogeneous "base" elements or "principles." (4) The law of elective affinity directed and regulated the processes of chemical combination and recombination. These four interlocking assumptions derived in part from Stahl, constituted what could be called the grammar of the language of late-eighteenth-century chemistry. But within this general grammatical form, important lexical changes were effected that gave this endeavor a specific character, differentiating it almost as much from Stahl's original propositions as from the immediately preceding mechanical philosophy against which it was formulated.

The most significant changes dealt with the manner in which matter and the relation between it and force was conceived. Probably the most striking shift in mid- to late-eighteenth-century natural philosophy incorporated the desire to resubstantialize the universe, which derived either from a return to Aristotle or to the development of Newton's idea of a universal aether, announced in the *Optics*.[34] In contradistinction to what is considered the classical "Newtonian" perspective, namely, a world consisting of vast, empty spaces infrequently inhabited by tiny specks of hard impenetrable matter held in place by invisible forces acting at a distance, the newly substantialized world of the late eighteenth century was completely filled by material substances. They ranged from immediately perceptible substances to a host of "fine," "delicate," invisible, and subtle fluids, whose presence could be "divined" only through observing their effects. As Robert Schofield has demonstrated, justification for this vision could be culled from Newton's revised edition of his Queries to the *Optics*.[35] In it, Newton postulated the idea of a universal aether binding the world together. But late-eighteenth-century naturalists, while piously citing Newton, creatively reinterpreted the idea of a subtle fluid so that Newton's original intentions were often disregarded or even lost.

According to Newton, aether was a universal, homogeneous subtle fluid that served as the carrier or transmitter of force. It was, as all matter, passive and ultimately reducible to an aggregation of particles. During the last half of the century, naturalists replaced universal aether with different, individual fluids, each imbued with unique properties and characteristics. Although admitting the possibility that these fluids might be manifestations of a more basic aethereal fluid, late-eighteenth-century natural philosophers usually refused to reduce these phenomena to an identity until such an identity could be demonstrated. If united at all, these fluids were joined in the unknowable realm of the extended middle. Until this realm could divined, each of the subtle fluids must be assumed to be a different form of matter.[36] Baader voiced this opinion in his study of what was called the matter of heat *(Wärmestoff)*. After mentioning some of the individual subtle fluids then believed to have existed, he concluded: "And perhaps our successors or we will discover the universal-ruling principle in all of these [fluids]. . . . Till then, however, we should separate with words what in nature is truly separated according to different characteristics. For, as long as experiments actually do not prove the connection of these manifold substances, then one must, as did *Fontana*, consider them as distinct from each other (and in so far, as simple). Where the effects are different, so too must the causes and, even more so, the names be different."[37] Over time, the number of fluids was expanded to account for all observed phenomena, a subtle fluid created for every new effect discovered.[38]

The introduction of these fluids was not merely a pragmatic attempt to account for new phenomena: it marked an important shift in perceptions and associations then taking place. Penetrability, solubility, and "intimate," internal combination overshadowed visions of impenetrability, collision, transferred motion, and the primacy of form in the mental economy of late-eighteenth-century intellectuals. To them, nature looked radically different than it had for the proponents of mechanical natural philosophy. This conceptual shift in which matter was considered essentially fluid rather than solid engendered two important consequences. First, since, as Baader exclaimed, "we know of no bodily stuff *[Körperstoff]* that is absolutely unmeltable or fire-proof,"[39] the question of change of state came to occupy an important role in chemical analysis and explanation. For many natural philosophers, the change from solid to liquid entailed the penetration of the solid by an active, subtle fluid that energized the solid, releasing it from its cold imprisonment. Accordingly, change of state could be seen as analogous to regeneration or metamorphosis in the animal realm.[40] Second, change of state did not take place uniformly, but in leaps: it proceeded at different rates and at different temperatures for each type of substance. It was seen as a phenomenon explicable only by reference to the specific qualities of the unique substantial species undergoing these changes. Thus, the late-eighteenth-century emphasis upon individuality and manifold variety and its questioning of the Great Chain of Being appeared proven by the most basic properties of matter.

The belief in matter's essential "fluidity" supported chemistry's claims to superiority over mechanical physics. Chemical reactions were fluid reactions. The two operational "paths" of chemistry, analysis and synthesis along the "wet" or "dry" routes, both assumed the central importance of the action of a "biting" or "devouring" fluid. In the first, one either mixed two or more fluids or mixed a fluid with a solid. In the second, heat was used as the tool effecting transformation. However, since "matter of heat," "elemental fire," "phlogiston," or "caloric" (depending upon which theory one used) was considered a highly active, penetrating fluid, the dry path formed an explanatory analogue to the wet, though more complicated, because "matter of heat" acted as a mediating force and as a solvent. The description of both types of reactions employed the language of reaction, penetration, combination, and exchange, entailing the attendant creation of a new substance with qualities differing from those of the combining ones. Since it appeared that the most basic physical phenomena involved the action or interaction of fluids or "potential" fluids, the explanatory terms associated with liquidity were elevated to metonynomic meanings far transcending the specific boundaries of chemistry.

A redefinition of the relation between matter and forces accompanied the turn to a substantialized universe. In the Cartesian and Leibnizian systems, which also assumed a substance-filled universe, matter was never active, never an *agens*. It served as a medium, transmitter, carrier, or analogue (in Leibniz's preestablished harmony) of a force. Late-eighteenth-century naturalists rejected this position and reactivated matter, ascribing to it the anthropomorphic properties of striving, aversion, sympathy, penetration, and, sometimes by inference, copulation. But in so doing, they did not return blindly to the doctrines of earlier animism. For earlier animists, including Stahl, the living or animated principle that guided nature had its own existence, independent of and superior to matter. Modeled after the idea of the Holy Spirit or the rational soul, the *animus* (Stahl's term) or *archaeus* (Paracelsus and van Helmont) differed from the mechanist's definition of spirit or reason only by its ability to move matter. Thus, in Stahl's medical philosophy the *anima* acted as an inner principle of movement regulating bodily functions, analogous to the eternal soul or psyche. In the same way, I believe, his basic chemical "principles" were analogous to the *anima*, though partaking even more of matter than the former. Although moving matter, they were clearly not material. They appear to hover above the substances, which they direct.

For mid-to-late-eighteenth-century natural philosophers, the separation of principle, power, or force from substance appeared a contradiction in terms. Matter, not disembodied principles or qualities, reacted with matter to produce effects. This is a crucial element in the attempt Enlightenment vitalists made to mediate between mechanism and animism. In Stahlian chemistry the distinction between principle and matter could still be discerned. One could still see the existence of principles in new combinations. It was assumed, for example, that when two things combine, the new combination would express a qualitative mean between both principles. Thus, when one knew the nature of the compound, one could predict which constituents formed it. Fourcroy described this assumption as follows: "Stahl and his partisans have alleged that compounds always participate in the properties of the bodies that compose them, and that the compounds bear the mean of the properties of their principles. They have pushed this idea to the point of believing that it is possible to determine from the properties of the compound the nature of those substances that entered into its composition."[41]

Late-eighteenth-century naturalists assumed matter and power to be linked, incapable of being mechanically discerned, for matter's effects were "expressions of power."[42] As the Göttingen philosopher Michael Hißmann claimed, "the proposition that force and substance are one is true in the strictest sense."[43] Baader expressed this conviction in simple terms. Active power independent of substance "is the same as a spirit without body." It is "truly an empty spectre."[44] Substantalized force was "a striving, an inclination, a drive *[Nisus]*."[45] Late-eighteenth-century naturalists, when accepting the linkage between active, striving force and substance, envisioned nature as continually in movement, never static, never at rest, always forming and reforming itself through combination, dissolution, and new combination. For that reason late-eighteenth-century chemical writers and practitioners had no problem accepting that a compound might differ radically from its original constituents, that no determinate relation existed between constituents and compound.[46] As d'Holbach proclaimed, "everything in the universe is in movement. The essence of nature is its activity. Look attentively at its parts, there is not a single one which enjoys absolute rest."[47]

. . .

The image of continuously active matter experiencing countless transformations presented late Enlightenment naturalists with a basic problem. How could one discern regularity beneath this seeming chaos? They believed the solution lay in developing the concept of elective affinities, which would enable one to order phenomena without slighting their basic uniqueness. The first task in this endeavor was to differentiate elective affinity from gravity, or universal attraction. Bergman offered a typical solution, drawing a distinction similar to the one Buffon had used. Gravity explained the actions of dematerialized matter working over vast distances with great speeds. It presented a specific case, where mass could be centered at points, forces expressed by vectors, and friction forgotten. Elective affinity, however, dealt with perceptible matter and proximate attraction *(attraction prochaine)*.[48] It pertained to real, substantialized matter. Only elective affinity addressed the questions of "specific physics," rendering it capable of accounting for "internal union," in which formed substances were more than merely the sum of their constituent parts or principles.[49] As they developed their ideas of elective affinities, late Enlightenment naturalists focused upon two projects. The first sought to determine which affinities were the most intense and productive of substantial change. The second dealt with the question of whether affinity relations could be considered constant. In their elaboration these naturalists modified or rejected positions earlier laid down by Stahl.

When Stahl discussed elective affinities or *rapports*, he assumed the intensity of affinity to be determined by the closeness of relation. Identity constituted the strongest elective affinity. The intensity diminished as the relationship became increasingly distant. Here he took relation in its literal meaning, perhaps unconsciously mirroring the ideal of family and patronage traditions in Early Modern Europe. *Like attracts like*. From the midcentury on, identity and close similarity became increasingly relegated to a special and not very exciting class of elective affinity. Macquer devoted little space to it, Bergman even less. The latter's description of identity attraction—he termed it "homogeneous attraction"—illustrates how unimportant it had become: "All homogeneous substances tend to reunite, which always results in an augmentation of mass, without the nature of the substance experiencing the least change. That effect is called the *attraction of aggregation*."[50] Obviously Bergman considered this form of attraction inconsequential, a judgment reinforced by his use of the mechanistic term "aggregation." By the time of his writing, chemists increasingly associated qualitative combinations with "heterogeneous attraction," which presented a panorama of complex couplings, dissolutions, and intricate exchanges between compound substances. Bergman defined this type of elective affinity as follows: "Heterogeneous substances scramble to join and to abandon each other and form new combinations among themselves: the change that happens to them has more relation to their quality than to their quantity. It is what we name *attraction of composition*."[51] Bergman, as Macquer before him, proposed a general typology to deal with the forms of composite attraction. According to him, there were two types of composite chemical affinity: "single elective attraction," which occurred when a simple substance combined with a constituent of a compound, setting a substance of the original compound free, and "double elective attraction," in which two compounds reacted with each other, exchanging constituent parts and forming new compounds. In all, the probabilities of combination were immense and increased by such phenomena as change aided by a catalyst (called by Macquer *affinitas adjuta* and the Germans *vermittelnde Verwandschaft*).[52]

During the late eighteenth century the tables of affinity grew in size and complexity. Bergman's were based on over thirty thousand individual experiments.[53] The 1783 edition of his *Traité des affinités chymiques* contained fifty-nine columns of elective affinity discovered by the wet route and forty-three by the dry, both recorded in a complex symbolic system designed to illustrate the reaction. Despite the tables' complexity, it was obvious to even the most casual reader of late-eighteenth-century chemical theory that many of the attractions involved substances of radically different natures. Thus, the emphasis upon heterogeneous attraction often was translated into a fascination for the attraction of opposites or polar attraction. *Opposites attract.* Elective affinity not only affirmed the universal nature of attraction, it also assumed the possibility, as Macquer argued, that all substances had the potential ability to combine with each other. A certain degree of affinity existed between the most disparate of entities. There was no such thing as an impossible combination.[54]

In this fluid and dynamic universe hard and fast boundaries were blurred, and new combinatorial vistas opened. Most chemical researchers believed that the paths these substances took in their couplings and uncouplings could be charted and their relative intensities someday measured.[55] However, the causes that drew elements together could only be divined. As Bergman exclaimed, "It is idle to ask what nature is able to accomplish, for this truly lies in complete obscurity; instead we should learn from experiment what nature actually does."[56] Late-eighteenth-century naturalists assumed that the ultimate causes for attraction lay hidden in the depths of nature, closed to the direct perception of human understanding. This theme is central to Enlightenment Vitalism and explains its reliance upon phenomenology and instrumentalism in scientific explanation and in its continual invocation of the idea of occult qualities. According to late-eighteenth-century chemists, chemical knowledge was probable knowledge. In their search to make this type of knowledge understandable, many eighteenth-century thinkers assumed that the ties of chemical attraction were analogous to those of human sympathy. Just as all substances could be combined under correct conditions, so could sympathy unite the most diverse of natures. Given the tendency to see humans as a part of nature directed by similar laws and the parallel tendency to vitalize nature, ascribing active powers to physical occurrences, the language of human relations and chemical reactions were easily interchanged.

The doctrine of elective affinity reinforced late-eighteenth-century assumptions of what the basic forces of nature were. Increasingly the affective terms of affinity, attraction, sympathy, and reproduction were linked together in a linguistic figure uniting nature with humanity through one of the most basic of anthropomorphic analogies. The young Franz Baader offered a vivid representation of these associations: "Love is the universal bond that ties and intertwines every substance *[Wesen]* in the universe to and with each other. One can call it universal gravity, attraction, cohesion, affinity, ... etc. mere words, if one will, that certainly cannot explain everything: but, how could they?—Enough, the universal striving of all parts of matter to mutually combine is attraction.... Without affinity there is no whole, no world, not even an imaginable one; without it our globe would be a desolate, eternally dead chaos, a mash *[Brei]* without structure and form, that is, a non-thing."[57] But how constant was the affinity, how eternal the love?

This was the second central issue proponents of elective affinity sought to resolve. When the French chemist Geoffroy first composed his tables of *rapports* at the beginning of the century, he had assumed a constant and invariable order of relations to exist between substances. As Bergman remarked, Geoffrey "imagined he could see at one glance the series of elective attractions." This belief was sustained by his assumption of constant laws.[58] Geoffrey's language of nature though differing in many respects from the mechanists' structured the linguistic field in a similar manner. Nature was ordered and that order was transparent; relations were clear and could be arranged according to a simple scale of invariable gradations, providing one used the correct method to establish these relations. Geoffrey's specific chemical assumptions, however, were closer to those of genealogy than geometry: his tables fulfilled a function analogous to the genealogical charts tracing degrees of nobility that were so treasured at the beginning of the century.

During the last half of the century this simple, fixed, and transparent world was dissolved as chemical experimenters, impelled by the new dynamic-fluid language of nature, demonstrated a wild profusion of possible combinations and recombinations, including partial ones and combinations effected by mediating marriage brokers. Macquer, who is credited with rehabilitating Geoffroy, also began the process that undermined Geoffroy's assumption of constant relations. Macquer's *Élemens* and his two subsequent dictionaries focused on complicated attractions *(affinitatis complicatae)* in which he discerned sets of different types of affinity, not of simple elective attraction. In the last edition of his *Chemical Dictionary* (1766) he had expanded his original six forms of chemical affinity to seven, most of which had no counterpart in Geoffroy's work. At the same time, researchers and experimenters throughout Europe were discovering ever more anomalies to the principle of constant relations of attraction.

By 1775 there were so many exceptions to the rule that Buffon would complain in the first volume of his *Supplement* to the *Historie naturelle* that there were almost as many "little laws of affinity" as there were possible mixtures.[59] In the same year Bergman published the first edition of his *Disquitio de attractionibus,* proposing a solution designed to save the concept of elective attraction without denying the variations that had been observed. His solution bears a striking resemblance to that proffered by Buffon in his treatment of species, varieties, and family. Faced with the contending claims that chemical combination could better be explained either by reference to the conditions under which the reaction took place or by the assertion that it was determined by the inherent qualities of the chemical species,[60] Bergman joined the two without subsuming one under the other. Both the nature of the species and the conditions under which the reaction takes place determined affinity relations. Or to translate this solution to the realm of animal reproduction, organism and habitat together participated in the creation of a variety. In both cases the two terms defining the relation (species and condition) could not be separated.[61] Once Bergman became convinced that no constant laws of affinity existed, he sought to discern factors conditioning affinity relations. In addition to the two major routes of chemical combination—the wet and the dry—he listed six basic variables:

1. Changes in temperature alter affinity relations.
2. Double elective attractions can create intermediary relations.
3. Graduated changes of a substance can produce different types of attraction on each level.
4. The degree of solubility effects specific affinities.
5. The joining of three materials can produce enhanced or diminished affinities.
6. An excessive amount of one material can alter the affinity relation.[62]

Thus, almost all of the environmental conditions in which a chemical relationship takes place can alter and direct the specific form of the product.

Lavoisier's friend and ally Berthollet carried the natural historical approach to chemistry to its logical conclusion. He expanded upon the assumptions of the mutual interaction between substance and condition, species and habitat, and in the process introduced so many conditioning principles that rendered the project of designing a workable table of natural affinities almost impossible.[63] Berthollet had always considered elective attraction the basic principle of chemical explanation. He also was aware that not all elective attractions reached perfect saturation or achieved complete exchange. The idea itself was not original. For naturalists such as Bergman, Scheele, and Lavoisier, each affinity relation could proceed in steps of saturation levels, each step producing different qualities.[64] However, they were more interested in the nature of the general reaction than in the "anomalies" fixing the reaction at a specific point in the saturation process. Berthollet focused his attention upon these anomalies to chart affinity relations more accurately than before.

Berthollet's experience as a scientific member of Napoleon's Egyptian expedition stimulated this desire. Berthollet became fascinated by the fact that the shores around Lake Natron had a seemingly limitless supply of sodium carbonate. The question was where it came from. Berthollet knew that the soil in the area was rich in salt and that the hills were even richer in limestone. He reached the obvious conclusion that a double elective affinity between the salt and limestone produced the sodium carbonate. The only problem was that this never happened under normal conditions. The elective affinity between the two substances was usually too weak to produce exchange. Therefore, Berthollet concluded that the specific reaction must have been made possible by unique conditioning factors. He argued that the specific factors were the high temperatures of the region, the enormous preponderance of limestone, and the slow trickling of the salt solution through the limestone. These enhanced the weak elective affinity between salt and limestone and produced a substance that under different conditions would not have appeared. From there Berthollet expanded his researches and published his findings in his two major studies, *Recherches sur les lois d'affinité* (1801) and *Essai de statique chemique* (1803), in which he adopted Bergman's categories and added the powers of cohesion, elasticity, effervescence, the tendency toward crystallization, and the effect of the solvent. More significantly, he introduced the idea of polar opposition, which had acquired great importance in the last third of the century, into the very definition of the power of elective attraction.

Berthollet's approach virtually transformed chemistry into a form of natural history, whereby the chemist had to deal with each reaction both as a type, illustrating a general law, and as a specific event in which individual conditions play a major role.[65] Not only was the chemical universe made up of many unique individuals whose number was being multiplied enormously through chemical research, but the individuals themselves were influenced directly by the conditions under which they were formed and existed. Thus, as in natural history, chemical genera, species, and varieties could be grasped only through a procedure combining diachronic and synchronic understanding. This explanatory model was similar to Buffon's definition of a natural system, one that differed radically from "arbitrary," hypothetical modes of classification. Its imperative to locate phenomena within a natural classificatory order had become an integral part of late-eighteenth-century scientific discourse, motivating chemists as well as natural historians. As the German chemist Erxleben declared in 1773, the "natural method" was the 'philosopher's stone of the naturalists."[66] This is a point Mi Gyung Kim emphasized in her excellent dissertation on nineteenth-century organic chemistry, namely, that natural history, not physics, offered late-eighteenth- and early-nineteenth-century chemists its most fruitful models: "Even a brief glance at the literature of organic chemistry in the period indicates that it was rather natural history that provided chemistry with the bulk of its language, and moreover, with a *method* that proved to be so productive. . . . The concern for 'natural classification' functioned as the most productive mode of theorization in organic chemistry."[67]

This general late-eighteenth-century concern with representing the natural order of things was also central to Lavoisier's desire to reformulate chemistry's language: "To those bodies which are formed by the union of several substances we gave new names, compounded in such a manner as the nature of the substances directed; but as the number of double combinations is already very considerable, the only method by which we could avoid confusion was to divide them into classes. In the *natural order of ideas*, the name of the class or genus is that which expresses a quality common to a great number of individuals: the name species, on the contrary, expresses a *quality* peculiar to certain individuals only."[68] But here Lavoisier merely asserted what had become a commonly felt desire among late-eighteenth-century antimechanist naturalists, the need to reformulate the language of nature upon nonartifical grounds, usually inspired by "natural-historical concerns."[69] Lavoisier and Bergman, as Buffon and Condillac before them, assumed that the natural order of things could and should be represented by the natural order of ideas. Science was "nothing more than a language well arranged."[70] This new language was a language of signs, what Alexander von Humboldt called a *Bildersprache*, a point made clear by Bergman when he remarked that "in order to comprehend at one stroke the effect of three substances mixed together, I have devised a manner of representing them with signs."[71] To understand the type of semiotics proposed, one must remember that the concept of "comprehending at one glance" *(apercevoir tout-d'un coup, coup d'oeil, Anschauung)* was considered the equivalent of intuition or divination. Such knowledge joined the diachronic and synchronic in a single, seeable picture, a *Naturgemälde*. As Hélène Metzger remarked, the concept of elective affinities itself was based on the idea that one could "divine" or "penetrate" the infinite gradations of unseen "intimate" attractions.[72]

. . .

The type of explanation Berthollet proposed for chemical reactions posed a definite problem for late Enlightenment naturalists. Since the possibilities of potential combination were virtually limitless, many felt that some simpler ordering principles regulating chemical combination existed. They discerned two interrelated ones that provided them with a base from which to avoid what could become an anarchic vision of reality. The first derived directly from the definition of matter as substantialized active force and of the universe as completely matter-filled. Given these propositions, some naturalists considered chemical combination to be governed by the principle of the conservation of matter *and* of active force. Matter could not be created nor destroyed, though it was capable of many modifications. Force could not be annihilated, though individual forces could be enhanced or diminished.[73] They derived the second principle directly from the first, namely, that nature could be interpreted as constituted by an "economy" or "living circulation." In the "economy of nature" every change of state, of force, or modification of matter led to the formation of a new equilibrium or harmony. In this context they joined the image of the balance to the idea of harmony. The balance served as both a concrete instrument for investigation and a symbol for nature's economy. As Bernadette Bensaude-Vincent contended, "the balance was not simply a mix of abstract and concrete. We can better understand it as having served as a sort of processing unit that connected terms of the most diverse nature by rendering them commensurable. . . . It was a universal mediator, a principle of continuity. In this sense it fits into Michel Serre's category of 'quasi-object,' an object that circulates, passes through, connects, mediates, and finally creates the consensus that welds a collective, culture or community."[74]

The combination of the concept of active force with the economy of nature transformed the early-eighteenth-century images of static equilibrium and preestablished harmony.[75] The new "economy of nature" was in constant motion involving the interplay between active and less active forces, between positive and negative charges, between living and brute matter, and between the creation and destruction of forms. Many late-eighteenth-century naturalists equated an achieved, static equilibrium with stagnation and death.[76] Baader described this vision as follows: "The continual movement of nature, her living circulation *sweeps* everything away in her current and *deposits* it again, *dissolves* everything in invisible mediums and makes the invisible visible again through *precipitation*, *destroys* forms and *shapes [bildet]* forms again. This beneficent, economic circle, which, in this immensely great workshop, does not pass anything by unused or unformed, surely presents for the tranquil, reflective observer the most stimulating, sublimest spectacle."[77] Within this ever-moving sublime spectacle, harmony or equilibrium was neither its beginning point nor its constant condition. Rather, harmony or equilibrium formed the goal toward which nature was striving: "The first principle of all continual transformations is the necessary, restless striving toward equilibrium. From it all life and destruction transpire." Or more simply said, "as the striving to equilibrium is a general law of nature in the distribution of mechanical forces, so a similar process takes place in the combination of chemical substances and powers, namely, *respective saturation*."[78] Since nature was never at rest, the sought for harmonic resolution constantly changed. It like matter itself was fluid. Harmony entailed a real interaction between substantialized forces leading to new creation. In this language of nature, what is, is temporary—a momentary equilibrium within an ever-changing series of newly forming configurations. It could not be encompassed under the continuous category of the Great Chain of Being.

Working from this assumption it was easy, almost natural to consider the achievement of harmony as the result of the mediation between two or more different and opposed forces. Polar confrontation and harmonic conjunction increasingly became the operational explanatory categories deployed to account for the shifting world of natural phenomena. Increasingly naturalists defined bodies as composites of antagonistic substances. John Elliot expressed this view in an essay on animal heat: "It seems, therefore, as if all bodies are constituted from two types of contradictory types of substances."[79] Many drew support for this position from Buffon's idea that "population equilibrium is achieved from the oscillation between abundance and scarcity, between a species' capacity and destructive forces"[80] from the physical theories of electricity and magnetism, and from the physiological ones of sensibility and irritability. As Horst Thomé wrote, "the task of the vitalist conception was to mediate between antinomies."[81]

Nobody pursued this vision of polarity and harmonic mediation (the extended middle between the extremes) with greater intensity than Goethe in his scientific writings. Whether in his physiological works, his use of chemical ideas, or his theory of colors, this same theme is announced and developed with single-minded determination and imagination.[82] Thus, in the *Theory of Colors* he would characterize "living nature" and its "economy" as follows:

> With light, poise and counterpoise, Nature oscillates within her prescribed limits, yet thus arise all the varieties and conditions of the phenomena which are presented to us in time and space. Infinitely various are the means by which we become acquainted with these general movements and tendencies: now as a simple repulsion and attraction, now as an unsparkling and vanishing light, as undulation in the air, as commotion in matter, as oxydation and deoxydation; but always, uniting or separating, the great purpose is found to be to excite and promote existence in some form or other.[83]

Polar opposition, harmonic conjunction, elective affinity, and dynamic transformation, joined together, constituted a language of nature that elevated chemistry to a place of central importance for the physical sciences.

CHEMISTRY, HEAT, AND LIFE

In their reaction against the mechanical philosophy of nature, late-eighteenth-century chemical writers desired to reinvigorate their subject by returning to older, premechanistic models of explanation drawn from such diverse sources as Aristotle, Paracelsus, van Helmont, and especially Stahl. These traditions, however, were also to be purged of their "excesses" and made modern. In pursuing this program of revival and reformulation, late-eighteenth-century chemical writers accepted the idea of the existence of a limited number of elements, bases, or basic substances, of which chemical compounds were composed and over time expanded these to include a host of "simple substances," impervious to chemical reduction. At first, at midcentury, the tendency among the chemical reformers was to adopt what Scheele called the "peripatetic" definition of elements, which posited the four elements of earth, water, air, and fire.[84] Among these basic "elements," the one that most captured the attention of late-eighteenth-century natural philosophers was fire or heat.

The reasons for fire or heat's central importance were many, but three appear crucial. Two of them can be considered strategic, related to the definition and scope of inquiries into natural phenomena. The third was essential, based upon the idea of what constituted the core of physical reality and activity. First, of all the postulated elements, fire or heat had during the first half of the century appeared the most amenable to explications invoking the two central categories of mechanical philosophy, matter and motion. The other three elements were usually comprehended under the categories of form or extension, being, respectively, a solid, a liquid, and a gas. Mechanists had defined fire/heat as a *condition*, the direct result of matter in motion, produced by friction, vibration, or collision. Hence, its redefinition was of central importance for any elaboration of an antimechanistic philosophy of nature.

Second, as a phenomenon heat was not directly perceptible. When not accompanied by flames, it lay "hidden" from view and proved impossible to weigh. Even its measurement presented great difficulties, as the late-eighteenth-century concern with thermometry testifies. The relation between quantity of heat, intensity of heat, and perceptible or "sensible" heat remained undecided until the discoveries of Black, Wilcke, and Irvine clarified them. Thus the question arose whether one could explain a "hidden," "invisible" thing using the normal transparent categories of mechanical natural philosophy. At issue was the problem of representation and what was to be represented. As mentioned above, semiotics became a major issue in late-eighteenth-century scientific discourse, and its most intensive area of discussion in chemistry concerned the nature and effects of heat.

Finally, the question of heat proved so appealing to late-eighteenth-century chemical writers, many of whom were also medically trained, because of the intimate associations of heat with life, activity, and transformation. Heat was, in one way or another, linked to animal existence. But it also seemed to generate strong and violent movements and effects: it produced fusion, energetic effervescences, combustion, and expansion: it functioned as a central agent in chemical reactions and proved necessary in effecting change of state. Wherever greater activity was found, an increase in heat was discernible. Hence, heat became associated with the increasingly positive images of energy and liberation and, by extension to other realms, with those of imagination, liberty, patriotism, sympathy, and love. To focus on heat simultaneously raised questions dealing with the definitions of matter, method, activity, representation, and ultimately life.

When chemical writers proposed a return to an animated world based upon "purified" Aristotelian and Paracelsian traditions, they reconceptualized the concept of heat. Instead of seeing it as a condition, they argued that it was a substance whose effects could be explained by the laws of chemical reaction.[85] Hermann Boerhaave had already modified the stark juxtaposition between condition and substance in the 1730s in his immensely influential text *The Elements of Chemistry*.[86] Boerhaave, a convinced Newtonian mechanist, attempted to reduce phenomena to the categories of extension, motion, friction, vibration, and expansion and contraction. He appeared so successful that Fontenelle in his *éloge* praised Boerhaave for having reduced chemistry "to a simple, clear and intelligible branch of physics."[87] For Boerhaave, heat or fire occupied a prime position in chemical analysis; yet heat resisted the simple mechanistic reduction to which he had striven. Mechanism could not explain heat transfer, change of state, or heat retention. To account for these phenomena, Boerhaave argued that heat was an extremely subtle substance, which he called "elementary fire." Its action could be understood by its ability to penetrate the spaces between corpuscles in matter, expanding them and through friction generate heat. Coldness arose from the loss of this substance, which resulted in reduced friction and loss of heat.

By postulating a distinct substance of heat, Boerhaave introduced the Trojan horse of substantialized force into chemistry. It reinforced the neo-Aristotelian line of argument that became typical for antimechanists whose major target became Boerhaave himself.[88] Boerhaave assumed matter of heat to be extremely subtle; though everywhere present, it could not be weighed nor contained. Yet Boerhaave continued to explain the action of this substance by mechanical effects, which, in theory, were the same for all substances. Friction produced measurable heat, and heat capacity and density governed heat transfer. He considered heat distribution uniform, dependent upon unit volume (instead of unit mass as many other mechanists had argued). There was nothing unique about elementary fire except its degree of subtleness (a simple mechanical principle), which accounted for its ability to penetrate other substances. Matter of heat was in essence no different from Newton's description of aether. Late-eighteenth-century chemists sympathetic to the goals of Enlightenment Vitalism thought of heat as a true element, imbued with its own properties and character and governed by the laws of elective affinity. It could not be subsumed under the idea of a universal aether. Only when one was ready to adopt this position was it possible to "see" phenomena concerning heat, combustion, and respiration in a new light and to evolve a different language to account for their existence. This perceptual and linguistic shift, accompanied by a corresponding methodological program marked the beginning of the chemical revolution.

This perceptual and linguistic shift can be illustrated in the way mechanists such as Boerhaave and Fahrenheit and antimechanists such as Black and Wilcke approached the problem of heat distribution. Although performing similar experiments using instruments of comparable accuracy and attaining in some cases the same results, their conclusions were radically opposed. Differing basic assumptions concerning matter and heat determined their respective explanatory strategies. Boerhaave and Fahrenheit both believed heat to be distributed uniformly and directly proportional to the bodies' volume. In this view, when two different substances of equal volume with different temperatures were mixed, the resulting temperature would be equidistant between the two initial temperatures. To demonstrate this, they mixed equal volumes of water and mercury of unequal temperatures. However, the results did not correspond to their assumptions. No matter how they varied the experiment, they discovered that when equal volumes of water and mercury were mixed, the resulting temperature was always closer to the original temperature of the water. Only when three parts of mercury were mixed with two parts of water did the resulting temperature fall exactly between the two initial temperatures. This result should have led them to deny the idea of uniform heat distribution and to formulate some notion of specific heat.[89] It didn't. Boerhaave's faith in mechanism did not allow him to entertain the idea of unequal heat distribution. Rather, he believed these experiments confirmed his original theory.[90] He desired to demonstrate that heat was distributed uniformly according to volume rather than to mass, as some mechanists believed. Since two-thirds was closer to one than the ratio of one-thirteenth predicted by the proponents of equal distribution according to mass,[91] Boerhaave rested his case. He found what he was looking for and looked no further. He did not seem to have been disturbed by the assertion that two-thirds equals one, probably because he expected more precise experiments to come closer to the postulated identity. So much for "crucial experiments."

Black, however, was not satisfied. Neither was Wilcke in Sweden, who worked along lines similar to Black's without knowing of his experiments. Both could accept the differential between the heat-retaining capabilities of water and mercury because they were ready to forgo the mechanistic assumption of matter's uniformity and affirm the idea that each substance possessed unique, specific qualities. Both also assumed heat to be an elementary substance different from the mechanistic definition of a universal aether.[92] Matter of heat actively reacted with other individual substances according to the chemical law of elective affinity. According to Baader, heat "loves and is loved, fuses and is fused, is swept away or held back."[93] For chemists attracted to Enlightenment Vitalism, asserting that different substances have different heat capacities presented no theoretical problem. In fact, the existence of these varying capacities reinforced their vitalist views. "Each material," Baader said, paraphrasing Wilcke, "takes up, holds or transmits matter of heat according to its peculiarly unique, though specific and fixed, attractions, laws and proportions."[94] Working from this proposition, Black, Wilcke, and others sought to determine the specific heats of various substances, composing charts analogous to the classificatory tables of elective affinities and animal species.

Black and Wilcke's formulation of the idea of specific heat led to their researches into latent heat. The two theories were united in their minds because both theories transcended mechanical models of explanation and questioned their application to chemistry: "This knowledge was . . . important in legitimizing" their "chemical approach" to heat.[95] As in the case of specific heat, Black and Wilcke were led to their researches by an observation made by Fahrenheit and recorded by Boerhaave, namely, that water, when absolutely still, could be cooled below the freezing point. However, when shaken, it immediately freezes and the temperature rises to 32 degrees. Fascinated by this phenomenon, both devised elegant and imaginative experiments to investigate the question of melting and freezing and then of the general process of change of state.[96] They concluded that change of state required the transfer of substantial quantities of heat not registered on the thermometer. This "hidden" or "latent" heat lay concealed until released and converted into sensible heat. Thus snow or ice absorbed a great quantity of heat, while remaining at the same temperature until they melted. In a similar manner Black and Wilcke discovered the existence of latent heat in vaporization. Water when heated reaches its boiling temperature in a certain amount of time with the addition of a given quantity of heat. It remains at that temperature for a much longer time until all of the water vaporizes. In the process of vaporization water receives five times the quantity of heat required to bring it to its boiling point. Hence, in producing steam, 790 degrees Fahrenheit of heat are generated when matter of heat combined with water to form steam.

The discovery of latent heat had wide-ranging implications going beyond the restricted circle of chemical analysis. On one level, it provided definite physical proof for questioning the idea of continuous change and the existence of the Great Chain of Being. The relationship between temperature change and heat flow proved to be discontinuous. Change of state involving radical expansion or diminution more resembled the process of metamorphosis. Increasingly, this process of discontinuous change was seen as necessary for the preservation of nature's economy.[97] On another level, the theory of latent heat provided definite support for the concept of the conservation of substance-force and the regular functioning of the economy of nature. Since quantity of heat, defined as an active substance, was conserved,[98] it followed that the quantity of substantialized force also was conserved. With each shift in the metamorphosis of substances the tendency was to achieve a new equilibrium of temperature or harmony until another transformation occurred. Thus, the analysis of latent heat reaffirmed the vitalist assumption that nature's economy was dynamic, consisting of step-like transformations leading to new harmonic resolutions.

Finally, the methodological assumptions Black and Wilcke employed supported by the experiments they designed raised the question of representation or semiotics to a central place in scientific discourse. Both Black and Wilcke were guided by the conviction that the immediately visible or sensible did not always reveal the essential aspects of a natural phenomenon. Often what can be seen and directly measured was superficial, hiding rather than illuminating reality's inner core.[99] Outward phenomena were, as Goethe exclaimed, "indications by which" the chemist "may detect the more secret properties of material things."[100] To attempt to draw a direct binary relation between sensible measurement and internal reality, similar to the identity between sign and signified in "classical" grammar, could lead to grave errors. This inner/outer, hidden/transparent juxtaposition, which constituted one of the prefiguring topoi of Enlightenment Vitalism, enabled Black and Wilcke to abandon the early-eighteenth-century concentration upon temperature as the primary measure of heat.

The shift from a concentration upon external phenomena to internal ones is striking. For Boerhaave and Fahrenheit, temperature proved the only reliable measure of heat. For late Enlightenment chemists, it represented merely the measure of the "sensible," external manifestations of heat. It failed to account for heat's internal combinations, which were considered crucial. Since Black and Wilcke believed heat to be an active, subtle fluid that reacted "internally" with other substances, they deemed internal combinations primary. Heat's activities were hidden from sight, not capable of being registered by a simple measuring instrument. Working from this assumption, Black and Wilcke distinguished clearly between quantity of heat and temperature, "between what we sometimes describe as the *extensive* and *intensive* measures of heat."[101] Without denying the importance of temperature as a measure of *something*, they denied that it measured quantity of heat. In their quest to measure quantity of heat, Black and Wilcke tried to establish a relation between sensible and insensible heat, to construct a system of external signs revealing internal activity. In other words, they proposed a semiotics of heat. This semiotics was founded upon a dynamic model incorporating temperature change over time. They used time as the means to modify and enhance temperature to arrive at the elusive and hidden figure for relative quantity of heat. This solution consciously strove to mediate between static and dynamic models of analysis.

It serves as an analogue to Buffon's attempts to fuse the synchronic with the diachronic.

. . .

No subject of inquiry was more productive in demonstrating nature's variety than heat research. And no area of the physical sciences was considered more important. Some histories of science have tended to downplay the importance of heat in the mental universe of late-eighteenth-century natural philosophers, preferring instead to consider pneumatic chemistry as the thread tying eighteenth-century chemical research to the Chemical Revolution. To do so, however, ignores the stated intentions of late-eighteenth-century natural philosophers. It concentrates upon what subsequently appeared to be the most interesting part of their work. Black offers a case in point. Although traditionally considered the founder of modern British pneumatic chemistry, his most recent interpreters have shown that he was basically a "heat theorist."[102] All of Black's experiments, including those with magnesia alba that led to his discovery of "fixed air" (carbon dioxide), were driven by his desire to investigate heat's combinations with other bodies.[103] Black recorded his fascination for heat in a notebook entry that Adam Ferguson quoted in his biography of Black. In it heat virtually takes on properties analogous to vital force in natural history:

> Heat is in nature the principle of fluidity and evaporation, though, in producing these effects, it is latent in respect to the thermometer, or any sensation of ours; and as matter, otherwise quiescent, becomes voluble and volatile in liquid and vapor, heat may be considered in nature as the great principle of chemical movement and life. . . . [W]e must consider it not as an accident in bodies, but as a separate and specific existence, not less so than light or electric matter; and though agreeing with these in some of its effects, in its nature possibly different from either.[104]

This observation illustrates two interlocking assumptions about physical reality that were to play a critical role in the development of late-eighteenth-century chemical-physical theory. The first affirmed the primary existence of heat as an active, substantialized agent in both chemical and vital processes. It suggests the hidden vitalist core of late-eighteenth-century chemical reasoning. The second pointed to the existence of other possible elements or principles beyond the traditional "peripatetic" definitions of elementary matter. This second aspect highlights the turn late-eighteenth-century chemical-physical research took from its initial mid-eighteenth-century neo-Aristotelian formulations that led to the concept of simple substance.[105] Increasingly, "matter of heat" was elevated to a primary position, while the other three "principles" were shown to be either compounds or mixtures. Their displacement led, at the same time, to the discovery of new "simple substances," discovered and defined according to analytical instrumentalist procedures.

The dethroning of the three other principles had already begun with the distinctions Stahl and Macquer had drawn between types of elementary earth. Soon thereafter, air fell victim before the onslaught of chemical analysis. Black's experiments with magnesia alba suggested that air was not uniform, but rather a mixture of various gases, one of which was "fixed air." Cavendish soon added another primary gas, "inflammable air" (hydrogen), often equated with phlogiston. In the early 1770s Scheele and Priestley discovered "fire-air" or "dephlogisticated air" (oxygen) and "corrupted" or "mephitic" air (nitrogen). By the early 1780s most chemists viewed air as a "collection of elastic fluids which compose our atmosphere."[106] It was also evident that some of these elastic fluids seemed intimately connected to the generation of heat. Water became the next casualty in the destruction of the peripatetic principles. It lost its elemental status when Lavoisier, who originally believed water to have been "l'agent favori de la nature,"[107] conducted his experiments on combustion, discovering water to be a compound of oxygen and hydrogen.

Only matter of heat remained untouched, and no one arose to contest its elementary existence,[108] though the manner in which it was defined and the supposed modes of its operation became a critical issue in chemical-physical discourse. This difficulty can be explained by the postulated dual nature of active elements (as opposed to simple substances), typical of late-eighteenth-century thought. Active elements were considered both as visible, existing in the pure state—that is free—and as "hidden," joined in an intimate union with other substances that veiled their presence. Macquer defined the element of heat in such a manner: "Chemists consider fire, just like other elements, from two very different points of view: that is, as really entering, as a principle or as a constituent part, into the composition of an infinity of bodies; and as being free, pure, forming part of no compound, but as having a very marked and very strong action on all the bodies of nature, and singularly as a very powerful agent in all operations in chemistry."[109] This dual character of heat made it imperative to understand how it appeared and disappeared, how it was at one moment transparent as sensible heat, and at another, "fixed" or latent in the depths of matter. The attempts to probe its nature guided late-eighteenth-century chemical research and led to the advances made in pneumatic chemistry and to the redefinition of what constituted active elements and irreducible substances.

The intimate connection between heat theory and pneumatic chemistry is clearly evident in Scheele's researches. In his most important publication, *Chemische Abhandlung von der Luft und dem Feuer*, Scheele defined his project as an attempt to propose a "theory of fire." To do so, however, required an investigation of air.[110] In Scheele's view the atmosphere consisted "of two very different kinds of air. The one is called *corrupted air*, because it is very dangerous and fatal . . . ; it constitutes the greatest part of our atmosphere. The other is called *pure air, fire air*. This kind of air is salutary, supports respiration, and consequently the circulation; without it we could form no distinct idea, either of fire or how it is kindled."[111] What fire was and how it was kindled were the questions Scheele sought to answer.

Scheele came to the conclusion that matter of heat (which he called phlogiston), warmth, and fire were not identical. Phlogiston or matter of heat was a simple element—an active substantialized principle. It had the ability to penetrate all bodies. As a substance it had weight, but it could not be weighed.[112] Its penetrating powers made it impossible to isolate. No retort, no container could imprison it. Given this penetrating power, phlogiston was omnipresent. It filled the spaces between the harder parts of all matter, making it the cause of extension, and it was one of two opposing substantialized forces that operated in polar confrontation to maintain nature's economy.[113] Matter of heat's expansive powers counteracted the forces of cohesion within bodies. Hence, matter of heat was hidden or latent in all bodies; no material substance was totally bereft of it.

Warmth resulted from the release of matter of heat from a body. It could be generated through friction, warming, and chemically, through the combination of phlogiston with fire-air (oxygen). Scheele considered friction a mechanical operation and therefore not of great interest. Warming also posed no great problem. It loosened the bonds of cohesion, allowing matter of heat increased movement.[114] However, when warming took place in the presence of oxygen, then the phenomenon of fire-heat occurred. This Scheele considered a chemical reaction creating new compounds with distinct characteristics. The intense elective affinity between oxygen and phlogiston induced phlogiston to depart from the combustible material and to combine with oxygen to form a new substance: "When pure air meets phlogiston uncombined, it unites with it, leaves the corrupted air, disappears, if I may say, before our eyes."[115]

As in many chemical combinations, fire-heat took various forms depending upon the ratio between the phlogiston and oxygen in the new combination.[116] This observation led Scheele to construct a scale demonstrating the possible combinations of oxygen and phlogiston beginning with simple heat, moving on to radiant heat in which more phlogiston was available, and ending, through the increase of the amount of phlogiston, with the production of fire accompanied by light. Even with the appearance of fire, gradations of fire existed, signified by light's colors. Different colors were the products of varying combinations of phlogiston with oxygen.[117]

Thus, according to Scheele, entities often treated as elements such as sensible heat, light, air, and color were really chemical compounds.[118] These were capable of further reduction. Things that could not be reduced he termed "elements." However, Scheele complicated this scheme by speaking of "elemental principles" that could not be known in their pure state, either by direct observation or by the indirect observation of their effects. They functioned as formative principles and appear to be analogous to Buffon's concept of the *moule intérieur,* Monstesquieu's political principles, or Goethe's idea of the *Urtyp* proposed in his study of plants and of color. For Scheele the most prominent of these formative principles was the acid principle. Here he seemed to have accepted Johann F. Meyer's idea of an *acidum pingue,* a "protean substance," almost an *Ur*-acid, "closely related to fire and light" that "was the 'universal primitive acid' of which all acids were modifications."[119] According to Scheele, who considered oxygen a simple acidic substance, acids showed the greatest affection for phlogiston. The tendency of any substance to burn, that is, to surrender its phlogiston to oxygen, was connected to its acidic qualities.[120] For Scheele an intimate tie linked heat generation, acidification, and calcination.

As Scheele's work illustrates, by the late eighteenth century the term "element" could be understood in three possible and sometimes conflicting ways. The first corresponded to the manner in which one defined phlogiston as matter of heat. It was considered an extremely subtle fluid, which sometimes acted as a universal active agent or solvent. At other times it was seen as the burnable substance consumed or transferred in chemical reactions. In either instance it could neither be seen nor weighed. It was subtle enough to penetrate everything else but could be known only by its measurable effects. The second concept of an element, a lingering echo of Stahl's theory, pertained to "principles" or genera such as acidity and alkalinity, which could never be isolated in and of themselves: the characteristics of the genus's individual members affirmed their existence. The third consisted of elements defined instrumentally, as bodies that resisted further chemical decomposition. As a rule, when these substances were invoked, the word "element" was modified by the term "simple substance."[121]

During the last third of the century, great strides were made in identifying and discovering members of the last two categories. Scheele alone is said to have isolated and described over seventy new substances, including acids such citric acid, prussic acid, boric acid, and lactic acid, and basic elements such as molybdenum and tungsten. In theory, however, the latter two cases of elemental matter could also be considered compounds since they were joined in varying degrees with matter of heat. Thus, all chemical reactions were to be understood as the result of a complex elective affinity involving, in one way or another, the exchange of heat. To quote the young Baader, there was no such thing as a "virgin" element.[122] Heat, however designated, reigned over terrestrial life. It was, as Baader proclaimed, "the first *agens* that awakened dead nature and vitalized it; it was the first stimulating force, the pulse of creation . . . the incubating, life-fecundating spirit." For him, heat was the *Weltseele*.[123] However one characterized it, heat appeared to most late-eighteenth-century intellectuals "as the great principle of chemical movement and life."

ENLIGHTENMENT VITALISM AND THE CHEMICAL REVOLUTION

One of the "master narratives" of the history of science centers on the Chemical Revolution of the late eighteenth century. Lavoisier himself forged the original emplotment of the standard story. Never one to minimize his achievements, Lavoisier described them as a revolution in chemical thought. Until recently a majority of historians of science have concurred. In their dramatic recounting of this revolution they have tended to consider the dispute between "antiphlogistonists" and the "phlogistonists" as a titanic struggle between two opposing camps of chemical thought, two paradigms of scientific explanation, essentially incommensurable with each other. On the one side stood Lavoisier and his allies, outsiders storming chemistry's Bastille: on the other, the doomed defenders of the outmoded ancien régime. In this battle the major forces opposing revolution were, according to Lavoisier's own testimony, older German chemists, still locked in the embrace of Stahl's ideas; his allies came from physicists and younger scientists. In traditional accounts the revolution created a radically different understanding of chemistry accompanied by a new language and set of investigative procedures, all of which reenthroned mechanism as the dominant model of chemical explanation and brought chemistry back into the sacred space of the mathematical physical sciences. It was, as one recent commentator has called it, "a revolution into science."[124] According to

Thomas Kuhn, Lavoisier "after discovering oxygen . . . worked in a different world."[125]

Recently some historians of chemistry have questioned the traditional outlines of this narrative, revising both the more traditional and the Kuhnian explanations.[126] Some minimize the importance of phlogiston in pre-Lavoisierian chemistry, others call for a thorough reevaluation of the supposed breach between "Stahlian" chemistry and Lavoisier's proposed model, while still others point to traditions such as Swedish and German mineralogy where non-Stahlian approaches were evolved that were central to the new chemistry. Even the content of Lavoisier's use of the term "revolution," at least as he initially used it, has been reinterpreted. According to Bernadotte Bensaude-Vincent, "The notion of revolution underlying his earlier writings, with its connotations of a return to past experiments and positions was thus closer to the astronomical meaning of the word 'revolution' as applied to celestial bodies, than to the modern sense of the word."[127] What many of these revisionists do not realize is that the counternarrative they are offering also had an eighteenth-century counterpart. Although Lavoisier's framing of the chemical revolution has often received the imprimatur of the history of science, it was not the only contemporary attempt to place his work within a larger story founded upon the two poles of continuity and rupture.

The young Franz Baader, one of Lavoisier's most ardent German supporters, provided such an alternative interpretation in his work on "matter of heat." Baader's narrative and the historical connections he drew reversed those of Lavoisier's. While Lavoisier seemingly emphasized rupture and disjunction, Baader stressed continuity. He located Lavoisier's achievement within a tradition established at the mid-eighteenth century. While many historians of science see Lavoisier's work as the triumph of mechanism, Baader interpreted it as the crucial stage in the destruction of a mechanist worldview. According to Baader, Lavoisier's work affirmed and refined the basic lines of chemical argument proclaimed by such critics of mechanism as Bergman, Black, Wilcke, Priestley, and Scheele.[128] For Baader, Lavoisier's antiphlogistic theory simply clarified the essential nature of "matter of heat" to which the others had contributed. The "chemical revolution" that Baader described was anything but the reintroduction of mechanist methods and assumptions into chemistry. Rather, it signified the latest and most advanced stage in the development of a new, antimechanist language of nature. Rupture there had been, but in Baader's eyes it had occurred at the midcentury, not at its end.

Today very few historians of science know or care about Franz von Baader, yet this early work offered an extremely interesting interpretation based upon a sure grasp of the most recent chemical research carried out in France, England, Germany, Sweden, and Italy. In fact, it was so "up to date" that it served as a source for writers of major German dictionaries and encyclopedias of science and chemistry published in the 1780s and 1790s. Further, Baader, though thoroughly committed to both antimechanism and the "new" chemistry, was not overly blinded by nationalistic assumptions. He, unlike some of his German contemporaries,[129] willingly gave the French their due, but also argued that they had overlooked the achievements of Black and other British writers as well as the German, Swedish, and Italian practitioners of the science.

The traditional accounts of the "Chemical Revolution" have often been based upon a tendency to read only what remains of Lavoisier's formulations back into his original program. Disturbing elements such as his theory of caloric are often glossed over or dismissed as mere remnants of older conceptual patterns, irrelevant to the major thrust of his thought.[130] Yet there is no valid intellectual reason to assume this to be the case. Lavoisier was extremely careful in his use of language and terms, so those that he employed should be integrated into an analysis of his intentions. When this is done, when one looks at the structure of Lavoisier's thought and the language of nature he employed in explicating it, his "revolution" emerges less as a rejection than a brilliant reordering of the lexical elements within an already accepted linguistic field. Lavoisier simplified its constituent parts, removed many internal contradictions, and streamlined its arguments. In so doing he strengthened, rather than weakened or destroyed, the model's explanatory procedures. In sum, Lavoisier formulated his theories within this language of nature, which gave them their internal coherence.

To justify this assertion I would like to emphasize two features I consider central. The first is based upon a reading of Lavoisier's chemical theories as I believe he presented them: it includes the "warts" of caloric, "generating" principles, and oxygen as a universal acidifying agent that later commentators have sometimes omitted, disparaged, or minimized. I suggest that though Lavoisier changed substantially the way one came to think and speak about the process of combustion and calcination, he affirmed and strengthened the central elements of the language of nature I have described above. They included the acceptance of active substantialized force, the importance of elective affinity, the tripartite distinction between "elements," the assumption of the conservation of substance-force, the belief in a dynamic economy of nature, and the concern with evolving a "natural" system of classification influenced by natural history and grounded upon the idea of symbolic representation.

The second feature deals with the reception of Lavoisier's thought by members of the evolving community of "professional" chemists and natural scientists. Here I shall look at the treatment accorded his ideas by some of his critics and admirers and compare it to discussions of works that proposed theories lying outside of the ambit of "accepted" chemical arguments and procedures. I hope to demonstrate thereby that though Lavoisier's theories were indeed controversial, especially for a group of established German chemists, they were taken seriously, discussed, and criticized along the lines of inquiry he proposed. In other words, a shared set of assumptions and a general language of nature that allowed Lavoisier's critics and admirers to dispute with one another without being dismissed out of hand linked these discussions. In short, a chasm of incommensurability did not separate Lavosier from his opponents. The acknowledged members of the chemical community understood the basic outlines of Lavoisier's new chemical language, though many realized that to adopt it meant accepting all of Lavoisier's specific principles, which many were reluctant to do for reasons that often went far beyond the specific scientific issues raised.

. . .

Lavoisier's formulation of a new explanation for the process of combustion and calcination constitutes the central episode in most accounts of the Chemical Revolution. Indeed, this achievement along with his new nomenclature was the most challenging and controversial part of his chemical doctrine. What is often overlooked in these accounts is the general manner in which Lavoisier framed his arguments and the language he used to justify them. Rather than obliterating the ideas associated with "phlogiston," Lavoisier decomposed the term, isolated its specific elements, reified them into individual entities, and reintroduced these into a more coherent logic of chemical explanation. Within the context in which it was formulated, Lavoisier's chemical theories served to affirm a vitalist and dynamic vision of chemical reaction in a manner more consistent than originally proposed by the so-called Stahlians.

When Lavoisier grappled with the concept of phlogiston, it had acquired during the thirty years after Macquer's first publication a web of meanings that were eminently self-contradictory. To simplify the existing situation, it can be said that three different types of explanatory procedures governed phlogiston's definition. The first derived directly from Stahl's definition, supplemented by the discovery of pure or fire air. Phlogiston was the "burnable substance." It was consumed in the act of burning, leaving the pure substance behind, often combining in the process with "pure air" to form heat and "fixed air." In this interpretation phlogiston was a real substance having extension and weight, theoretically capable of being weighed or measured. The second definition of phlogiston seems to be directly opposed to the first. Instead of being the substance burned, it was identified with the effect of combustion, the generation of heat. In this guise phlogiston was the highly subtle "matter of heat" that could not be weighed because it could not be contained. It appeared in two forms, either fixed or free. Devices designed to discover quantity of heat and the thermometer provided its only measure. Finally, in a third, though related, definition phlogiston assumed the guise of the "principle" of heat, the active agent that caused burning to take place.

Depending upon one's predilection, phlogiston could be seen as cause, effect, and/or agent of the generation of heat. The concept combined the contradictory qualities of being passive or active, heavy or without weight, localized or omnipresent. Because of these contradictions, no single mode of observation and measurement could be considered crucial in assaying its character; it was impossible to choose between caliometrics, thermometrics, or gravimetrics, for each measured different and contradictory properties of this supposed substance. Lavoisier was correct in observing that phlogiston by his time was "a veritable Proteus, which changes its form every minute."[131]

Lavoisier, endowed with a sure logical sense and great experimental intuition, unraveled the puzzle surrounding phlogiston. He isolated each of these concepts and assigned them either to a specific substance, a type of substance or a chemical process. Phlogiston disappeared from sight, its individual qualities being retained and displaced to one of Lavoisier's categories of *active elements, base* or *radical, caloric,* and *generating principles.* Each of these constructions performed one or more of the linguistic and explanatory functions originally associated with phlogiston.

The most obvious case of retention and displacement can be found in Lavoisier's general explanation for chemical reaction (of which combustion was an example). Here he incorporated and internalized the language employing the explanatory schema of a generating principle acting upon a base to produce a new entity. All chemical or "internal reactions," from the simplest to the most complex, follow this pattern. Thus, "acids, for example are compounded of two substances, of the order of those which we consider as simple; the one constitutes acidity, and is common to all acids. . . . The other is peculiar to each acid and distinguishes it from the rest." Combinations between "simple substances" often proceeded in gradations, depending upon the proportions of the substances involved. Again acids offer an example: "But in the greatest number of acids, the two constituent elements, the acidifying principle and that which it acidifies, may exist in different proportions, constituting all the possible points of equilibrium or saturation."[132]

While Lavoisier retained the prefiguring language of a reaction between a principle and a base, he reversed the orthodox Stahlian order, assigning universal active properties to the principle, making it an analogue to the active principle in living organisms. The active principle combines with a substance instead of being drawn away from it, being consumed or liberated by an alien body. In the case of combustion Lavoisier argued that the active principle combined with the base to form a more complex entity; it impregnates it, producing heat, and "begets" a new species. Combustion involved a synthesis rather than a reduction. This new formulation of the relations between principle and base, including Lavoisier's descriptive language drawn from the process of generation, strengthened the message of vital creativity: if phlogiston was a prisoner waiting to be released, oxygen was a wooer striving to conjoin. It would be interesting to speculate on the connotations of this shift: certainly it is known that Stahl was a devout Pietist who believed that regeneration and freedom came from outside, from God's grace that led to spiritual liberation. The soul was like phlogiston, drawn away from its normal association by a more appealing outside force. Lavoisier was Stahl's opposite, probably one of the most self-directed people among his contemporaries and thoroughly committed to a secular, activist policy of political regeneration. For him activity implied formation. Whatever their personal and/or political differences, their evaluation of action varied greatly, though both positions were proposed within the general complex of antimechanistic chemistry.

Lavoisier made his commitment to active principles clear in his attempts to mint a new chemical nomenclature, in which he consciously employed the language of activity and fecundity: a principle generates something. The changing designations for oxygen illustrates Lavoisier's desire to incorporate this view within the core of chemical thinking. At first, Lavoisier believed oxygen's major role was as the active agent generating combustion. He originally named it "vital air," a term recommended to him by Turgot. The term was, as we shall later see, highly suggestive, for it paralleled the then popular concept of *principe vital* proposed by French vitalists such as Barthez.[133] Through the most obvious of analogies, it clearly suggested the existence of an active principle of chemical combination. Later Lavoisier changed his mind, coming to the conclusion that oxygen's primary function was acidification. Accordingly, he assigned this "element" the name "oxygen," literally meaning begetter or generator of acids.[134] Given the regnant discussion of the time over preformation and epigenesis, the decision to include the root *gen* in oxygen's name indicates the hidden linkages between the new chemistry and vitalism. In the same manner Lavoisier postulated the existence of two other active elements, hydrogen (begetter of water) and azoyte (bringer of death—nitrogen). All three emphasized the active role of these universal principles in constituting the universe, even if negatively in the case of azoyte.

When Lavoisier formally defined an element, he adopted the antimechanist language of his eighteenth-century contemporaries. But, because of his close association with the neomechanist Laplace, he expressed this position in a highly diplomatic manner, acknowledging the existence of atoms, yet refusing to discuss them: "I shall only add ... that if by the term elements we mean to express those simple and individual atoms of which matter is composed, it is extremely probable we know nothing at all about them; but, if we apply the term *elements* or *principles of bodies*, to express our idea of the last point which analysis is capable of reaching, we must admit, as elements, all the substances into which we are not capable, by any means, to reduce bodies by decomposition."[135] This sounds clear enough. But Lavoisier, along with his contemporaries, did not consistently adhere to this definition. He went on to distinguish between three different types of elements or simple substances. The first class consisted of simple substances or principles belonging to all kingdoms of nature. The second category contained primary elemental bases (e.g., sulfur, phosphorus, charcoal, and the metals), and the third consisted of substances found to be impervious to reduction.

In the first category Lavoisier discerned five basic "elements" (light, caloric, oxygen, hydrogen, and azoyte). Their universal distribution made it logically essential to consider them as active inciters of change in other substances. The interesting issue here is why Lavoisier felt compelled to consider azoyte active. One answer may be that he did not desire to ascribe the passive qualities of Stahlian phlogiston to an element.[136] Therefore, appearances notwithstanding, azoyte had to be classified as a principle or active element. Its activity was negative or retarding. The assumption that azoyte possessed negative active power was reinforced by the increasing late-eighteenth-century fascination with polar confrontation and its role in establishing the limits within which the extended middle could appear. In this view, as Goethe expressed it, all elementary phenomena exhibit themselves "by separation and contrast, by commixture and union, by augmentation and neutralization, by communication and dissolution."[137] Thus it seemed logical that the polar confrontation between oxygen and azoyte occurred in the atmosphere, the medium in which life takes place. The interaction between oxygen and azoyte furthered the goal toward which chemical reaction strove, namely, saturation, equilibrium, "or mutual union with each other."[138]

Since the principles of acid generation, water generation, and death inducement were associated with "elements," we still recognize, later commentators have tended to ignore or minimize Lavoisier's consciously coined language of activity, principles, and bases. More often than not, these terms have been treated as metaphors rather than metonymies, despite Lavoisier's own testimony that he sought to construct a chemical language that represented "nature" and its relations. We find it more difficult to dismiss the reality of principles in Lavoisier's description of complex reactions involving compounds rather than simple substances. Here a class of substances functions as the active principle while another is acted upon. In this analogical progression from simple to complex, the principle passes from association with a specific substance to association with a genus.

Lavoisier illustrated this shift in his discussion of the activity of acids. When acids unite with other substances to form neutral salts, the acids function "as the true *salifying* principles, and the substances with which they unite to form neutral salts may be called *salifiable* base."[139] With each increase in the complexity of chemical reaction, the principle appears to liberate itself from an association with a specific element, implicitly affirming its independent existence. Thus, not only did Lavoisier adopt chemistry's language of active agents and principles, but he made the former more concrete and the latter more ubiquitous and consistent as well.

In Lavoisier's eyes elective affinities governed all chemical reactions, from the simplest to the most complex.[140] For him, the physical universe was teeming with continuous combinations and reductions. Although no new basic matter could be created (impossible in a totally substantialized world), a vast number of new material combinations, each with their own character, were being formed and reformed. Even when a limited number of simple substances were involved, the diversity was immense. Such was the case in the "animal and vegetable kingdoms." All of their oxides and acids

> are formed by means of a small number of simple elements, or at least
> of such as hitherto been susceptible of decomposition, by means of
> combination with oxygen; these are azoyte, sulphur, phosphorus, char-

coal, hydrogen and the muriatic radical. We may justly admire the simplicity of means employed by nature to multiply qualities and forms, whether by combining three or four acidifiable bases in different proportions or by altering the dose of oxygen employed for oxidating or acidifying them.[141]

These changes were instigated by the "addition of a very slight force," sufficient "to destroy the equilibrium of their connection." Once the connection was disturbed, the process of reformulation "continues until completed."[142] In other words, in contradistinction to mechanistic concepts of cause and effect, the energy of the new reaction far exceeded the original "slight" force necessary to induce it. The problem with such a position was to account for the source of the reaction's original impulse without evoking an external agent such as the hand of God. To give his vision coherence, Lavoisier had to introduce an agent eternally active and universally present. Before he launched his attack on the specter of phlogiston, phlogiston had fulfilled that role in some of its shifting guises. Lavoisier abstracted one of these and elevated it to central importance. The agent that partook in all reactions, stimulating the release of energy was "matter of heat," which Lavoisier renamed caloric.

Caloric had all of the qualities Scheele ascribed to phlogiston minus the burden of serving as the base consumed in combustion. As such, caloric was a "real material substance or very subtle fluid" that "penetrates through the pores of all known substances." It was the universal solvent, the cause for extension (effectively combating the forces of attraction to create an *equilibrium*), and the determiner of the physical state or "states of existence" of a substance. According to Lavoisier, caloric appeared in two forms. As free caloric it passed from one body to another. In this form caloric could never be isolated since, as "we live in a system to which caloric has a very strong adhesion, it follows that we are never able to obtain it in the state of absolute freedom." In this form caloric had the same qualities as those occult forces that late-eighteenth-century vitalists saw everywhere in the world: "We can only come at the knowledge of its properties by effects which are fleeting and with difficulty ascertainable."[143]

In its liberated form caloric acted as the agent inciting the innumerable chemical reactions constituting the economy of nature. Heat exchange served as the basis of universal activity. To be liberated, however, caloric first had to have been fixed, or imprisoned. Its second state, what Lavoisier called "combined caloric," "is that which is fixed in bodies by affinity or elective attraction, so as to form part of the substance of the body, even part of its solidity." Given this definition, it is obvious that Lavoisier retained all of the specific characteristics formerly ascribed to "matter of heat." It also meant that, strictly speaking, no pure element existed in nature; caloric was everywhere and every substance contained caloric with which it was chemically "fixed" in varying quantities, not just mechanically aggregated.[144] According to late-eighteenth-century terminology, the chemical reactions Lavoisier discerned could be defined as complex affinity relations, that is, relations affecting three or more substances. The case of oxidation is typical.

In modern terminology oxygen combines with another substance to form a compound. The two reactants are considered active substances, though the conditions for their combination may have been made possible by the application of heat. For Lavoisier the case was much more complex. What we usually consider oxygen was, for him, the aeriform compound of oxygen base with active caloric; thus oxygen gas was, as were all other gases, a compound form. The substance with which oxygen reacted was also fixed with caloric. The reaction that resulted involved the oxygen base of the aeriform compound and its fixed caloric with the elementary base of another element with its caloric, supplemented by the caloric added to initiate the reaction. As a rule, this reaction involved the transformation of oxygen from a gas to a liquid or solid form.[145] The permutations for such reactions, all based upon a minimum of three participants (oxygen base + caloric, other base + caloric + inciting caloric) of varying intensities and proclivities, are mind boggling. Lavoisier described them as follows. In any chemical equation "we must take into consideration the nature of the elements which enter into composition, the different affinities which the particles of these elements exert upon each other, and the affinity which caloric possesses with them."[146] Rather than undermining the logic of elective affinities, Lavoisier placed elective affinities on an even sounder footing than before.

Not only was caloric necessary to preserve the logic of elective affinities, its introduction and definition enabled Lavoisier to bring order into the experimental and explanatory procedures of Enlightenment chemical vitalism, where a confusion between weight, quantity of heat, and energy still reigned. By limiting caloric's definition to the properties assigned to matter of heat, he was able to isolate its activities, integrate its analysis into a self-contained system, design an instrument (ice calorimeter) to measure its action, and thus eliminate the problem of accounting for quantity of heat in explaining chemical reaction.

Lavoisier did not directly face the question of whether caloric was weightless or not; instead he excluded questions of caloric's weight from discussions about the relation between the weight of the combining substances and their end products, because of caloric's universal penetrating powers.[147] In experimental terms these powers made it impossible to weigh caloric, rendering it instrumentally weightless. Measurement of quantity of heat had to be related to caloric's activities, not to any single state of equilibrium, that is, to heat exchange, change of state, and heat capacity: its fleeting activity could be charted only by calorimetry and thermometry. These became the symbolic registers of caloric's activity. If caloric's weight could be discounted, then gravimetrics could be employed to investigate chemical reactions, indicating the exchanges that occurred between reactants and their products. All of them could be contained, isolated, and weighed. This sharpening of caloric's definition and its isolation into a system represented solely by heat exchange measurable by the calorimeter established the basis for Lavoisier's famous assertion of the conservation of the quantity of matter:

> We may lay it down as an incontestable axiom that, in all the operations of art and nature, nothing is created; an equal quantity of matter exists both before and after the experiment; the quality and quantity of the elements remain precisely the same and nothing takes place beyond the changes and modifications in the combinations of these elements. Upon this principle the whole art of performing chemical experiments depends. We must always suppose an exact equality between the elements of the body examined and those of the product of its analysis.[148]

According to Baader, who considered Lavoisier's theories the clearest expression of the antimechanist position, Lavoisier's treatment of caloric was the "best" and most "illuminating" because it explained "all appearances easily and without distortion."[149]

. . .

Thomas Kuhn considered Lavoisier's chemical theory a classic example of a scientific revolution, a paradigm shift separating two incommensurable visions of science. If this were true, then one would expect a basic misunderstanding to have existed between Lavoisier and his "Stahlian" critics. However, when one looks at contemporary reviews and discussions of his work, especially in Germany where the greatest opposition to Lavoisier occurred, the picture of a confrontation between contending and incommensurable paradigms loses its power. In the German commentaries Lavoisier appears as a highly respected member of the "scientific" establishment who employed accepted practices and methods to propose a major revision concerning the processes of combustion and calcination and then evolved a new chemical nomenclature incorporating these revisions. As was the case with most English chemists, the majority of German chemists did not agree with Lavoisier's chemical revision, either in its specifics or more importantly because of its lexical reforms.[150] But these chemists took them seriously, gathered evidence to attack or support them, and certainly did not consign them to the categories of the misguided, heretical, or simply outrageous.

Karl Hufbauer has written an excellent study of the German resistance to Lavoisier's theories and their subsequent acceptance within the emerging chemical establishment;[151] there is no need to repeat what he said. However, I would like to supplement his portrayal in two ways: first by mentioning briefly the rhetorical strategy Lavoisier's early German proponents employed in his support, and then by comparing the way the "phlogistonists" dealt with Lavoisier and with other chemical theories with which they disagreed.

What is interesting about Lavoisier's early German supporters is that they came from the camp most strongly committed to Enlightenment Vitalism. The most famous of these was Johann Friedrich Blumenbach, whose vision of a dynamic universe driven by active powers will be discussed in the next two chapters. His former mentor and then colleague Georg Lichtenberg seconded him. As Lavoisier had asserted, most of his German allies were younger men, virtually all of whom considered Lavoisier's theories a clear affirmation of antimechanism in the physical sciences. Among them were Georg Forster, Samuel Thomas Sömmerring, Alexander von Humboldt, Wilhelm von Humboldt, Joachim Brandis, Friedrich Schlegel, Novalis (trained as a geologist), Lorenz Oken, and Friedrich Schelling (though the manner in which the last three adopted the new chemistry was highly eccentric, as I shall show in the last chapter). The most important book defending Lavoisier written in Germany in the 1780s was Baader's work on the matter of heat, to which I have often referred. Surprisingly, if one accepts the assumption of incommensurability, Baader's championship of Lavoisier's interpretation and experiments did not harm the book's reception. Quite the contrary, it was cited by many contemporary German commentators and used extensively in their discussions of heat, even when they rejected Lavoisier's specific theories. Thus, Johann Samuel Gehler, who until 1790 opposed Lavoisier, paraphrased Baader in the *Physikalisches Wörterbuch* in his articles on heat, written before 1790. For many "professional" chemists, such as Gehler, and educated laymen, such as Wilhelm von Humboldt, Lavoisier played a central role in developing an ongoing project—the progressive development of an antimechanistic science of chemistry.

This attitude is made evident in the writings of one of Lavoisier's more respected opponents, the Göttingen professor Johann Friedrich Gmelin, who wrote most of the reviews in the *Göttingen Gelehrte Anzeige* on chemistry, mineralogy, geology, and their related disciplines. As such, his views, along with those of his colleagues and fellow reviewers Abraham Gotthelf Kästner and Lichtenberg, were extremely influential. This influence was strengthened by Gmelin's position at Germany's leading university and as an author of a successful textbook on chemistry. The major theme that runs through all of Gmelin's chemical writings is his commitment to ensuring chemistry's development as a professional discipline, endowed with accepted explanatory terms and common experimental and verification procedures. To further this project he and like-minded colleagues adopted a rhetorical strategy that attacked unprofessional or "unscientific" procedures on the one side and on the other, though admitting differences within the emerging chemical community, emphasized the progressive nature of the chemical enterprise.

In this endeavor Gmelin always treated Lavoisier and his supporters as respected members of the chemical establishment, their doctrines given a fair hearing, and their achievements praised. Thus, in the discussion of Lavoisier and Laplace's experiments on water, the *Göttingen Gelehrte Anzeigen* provided a good summary of their theories and the experiments they designed to test them. The only judgments Gmelin ventured concerned the design of the experiments, and Gmelin praised them, calling them imaginative *(sinnreiche)* and beautiful.[152] Gmelin continued in this vein in the introduction to his text *Grundriss der Chemie* (1789), in which he presented a "historical" account of chemistry's development to authorize the methods of which he approved and attack those that he believed had led chemistry astray. Gmelin's chief villains were the "alchemists" and the "mechanists." Only recently, Gmelin argued, had chemists overcome these dangers, because one now questioned "nature through diligent and careful experimentation and observation." Gmelin attributed the creation of this new mentality to the "fortunate endeavors of French chemists . . . the discoveries of British chemists . . . the industriousness of the Germans . . . and the great Swedish chemists." Among the French worthies he cited were "Macquer, de Morveau, Lavoisier, Rouelle, La Metherie, Bertholet, and Fourcroy." In short, he accorded both phlogistonists and antiphlogistonists membership in the select circle of those "who have raised chemistry to the position it now occupies."[153]

Gmelin's cautious evaluation of Lavoisier's work becomes evident in his treatment of three of the major areas of contention between the antiphlogistonists and the phlogistonists: (1) the definition of the burnable substance, (2) the role of oxygen or the base of pure air in acidification, and (3) the project of establishing a new chemical nomenclature. In the first case, Gmelin recognized the importance of clarifying the concept of the burnable substance. For this reason he welcomed Lavoisier's critique as central to the endeavor but could not follow him all the way. Lavoisier, according to Gmelin, "correctly" attacked "those who saw the burnable substance as merely the combined condition of the essence of fire *[Feuerwesens]*." But Gmelin could not accept Lavoisier's critique of those who saw it as the weightless substance "that in burning passes through all containers," as well as those who consider it a "substance with weight that combines with dephlogisticated air [oxygen] to produce fixed air."[154] In the second case, that relating to oxygen and acidification, Gmelin simply could not accept the proposition that "pure air" (oxygen) was the principle of all acids, a position he shared with Berthollet.[155]

Gemlin was also ambivalent about the new chemical nomenclature Lavoisier and his allies had proposed. His review of this undertaking alternated between praise and skepticism concerning its practicality. "All chemists," Gmelin wrote, "owe the authors their gratitude, for here the authors provide a key without whose use their excellent writings would be as incomprehensible as those of Paracelsus and his students." With these muted words of praise, Gmelin then asked if new technical words *(Kunstwörter)* were really necessary. It had often been the case, he claimed, "that the introduction of new terms seldom are successful in a science where older ones, even though not totally applicable, still exist." Here Gmelin voiced a feeling that lay at the heart of Priestley's opposition to Lavoisier's new nomenclature. For Priestley the new language was a bald assertion of power over the chemical community, which treated it "as incapable of independent judgement." It reflected, in Cavendish's view, the "present rage of name-making." Jan Golinski summed up this English opposition to the new language: "Behind these objections lay the view, articulated prominently by Priestley, that language should be the common currency of a community devoted to purely factual discourse. A language framed to serve a particular theory, such as that of the French chemists, would be inappropriate for use in such a setting."[156] Gmelin was milder in his opposition. He did not go further than issue a warning about the efficacy of newly constructed languages in natural philosophy. The rest of his review offered examples of how the new nomenclature operated.

. . .

The circumspection Gmelin and others like him showed to Lavoisier was not evident in their reviews of chemical works deemed outside the pale of professional chemical research, that is, outside the linguistic matrix of antimechanist chemistry that enabled discussion and dissent to proceed. Gmelin and his compatriots were especially harsh on three types of chemical works that can be categorized as follows: (1) Revived hermeticism, (2) philosophic or theoretical chemistry, and (3) for lack of a better term, idiosyncratic attempts to propose new-old universal chemical explanations, an activity that proliferated during the last half of the century. All three seemed to share certain elements in common with the new principles of chemistry. Therefore, its proponents felt the need to draw as sharp a distinction as they possibly could between these works and their own endeavors.

With the late-eighteenth-century rehabilitation of premechanistic models of reasoning, it appeared that the floodgates were opened for the reappearance of hermeticism and uncontrolled speculation. Christian Gottlob Heyne, the renowned classicist, director of Göttingen's Academy of the Sciences, and Georg Forster's father-in-law, remarked on the seemingly strange resurgence of these modes of reasoning in the late eighteenth century: "Enlightenment, progress in science, chemistry, and medicine, along with historical narratives are the only weapons by which magical nonsense can be battled effectively. Thus, it is remarkable that in an era where such Enlightenment is more widely spread than ever, this dangerous plant has not only spread its roots, but has also sprouted new branches."[157] The members of the chemical community attempted to stamp out this dangerous growth through unremitting critique.

The reaction engendered by Johann Salomo Semler's campaign to resurrect hermetic chemistry and place it at the pinnacle of all scientific activity can be seen as typical. The major theological goal of Semler's, one of the most progressive German theologians of the late Enlightenment, was to define Christianity as a religion driven by an inner force; it strove to achieve what was *actu primo* in its original formulation through the process of polar confrontation between form (established, dogmatic religion) and force (inner spirit). For eighteenth-century Protestant theologians this was an extremely liberating message, and Semler became a herald for a nondogmatic, humanistic, and progressive Protestantism. However, it appears, at least to me, that Semler's religious views were very closely linked to his scientific assumptions.[158] These were formed through his extensive reading of hermetic and seventeenth-century Rosicrucian writings.

In the 1780s Semler published his scientific theories in a number of works, the most important being *Von ächter hermetischer Arznei* (Of True Hermetic Medicine).[159] Here he drew the distinction between inner spirit and outer form, this time applied to chemistry. Outer chemistry was the established chemistry of the period. Inner chemistry, the true hermetic chemistry, was concerned with secret active substances, invisible and unknown to man and still *actu primo*, which were silently working and progressing through nature. These could be harnessed to produce a "universal salt" capable of curing all diseases. For late Enlightenment natural philosophers, Semler's evocation of unknown, active powers joined to the assertion of the existence of a secret language that only adepts could comprehend came dangerously close to the world of the Renaissance magus. It appeared dangerous to the new chemistry because it shared some of the same sources. Karsten and Gmelin responded. Karsten wrote a major work designed to demolish the faulty structure erected by Semler.[160] Gmelin supported Karsten in long and positive reviews designed to destroy this dangerous form of *"Schwärmerey."*[161]

This was not the only type of *Schwärmerei* that appeared to threaten the middle course of "healthy philosophy," founded upon what Sergio Moravia has called "observational reason."[162] Alongside the *Schwärmerei* of the spirit there appeared a *Schwärmerei* of the intellect, which rationally constructed a picture of nature without bothering to question her. Both forms of *Schwärmerei* seemed to share common traits: they relegated normal observation to a low place in the hierarchy of scientific inquiry and assumed that it was possible for a few adepts to pierce the veil of nature and reveal nature's unity. In both, the realm of the extended middle was to be abandoned in favor of a philosophy of pure intuition or of identity. The attempts at formulating a rational philosophy of chemistry appeared to Gmelin to announce the return of hypothetical-speculative reasoning that could only lead science astray. His review of Johann Melchoir Beseke's Kantian-inspired *Entwurf eines Systems der transcendental Chemie* (1787) reveals this stance. Beseke had built his chemical system upon Kant's assumption of universal polar confrontation between expansive and contractive forces. Beseke postulated two essential chemical forces, elementary earth (which he called phlogiston) and elementary fire. These interacted and were directed by a primary motor *(Primus Motor)* to produce normal observable phenomena. As he sought to elaborate this system, Beseke introduced a host of complex theoretical principles that approximated Descartes's theory of vortices. With more than a hint of sarcasm, Gmelin remarked that "the author's intentions of raising the chemist above empiricism and accustoming him to abstraction may be well meant."[163] But his intentions were wrong. During the rest of the review Gmelin showed how none of Beseke's formulations accorded with the experimental results reached by normal chemists. After ticking off all of the difficulties, Gmelin concluded: "You may judge for yourself if he . . . is really the carrier of the torch of a healthy philosophy."[164]

The third group of rejected chemical writers, whom I call the idiosyncratic systematizers, proposed elements found in the other two and supplemented them with isolated and sometimes bizarre observations. The number of such books that appeared during the late eighteenth century were legion, composed by local school teachers, obscure clerics, self-educated philosophers, medical practitioners, pharmacists, and sometimes charlatans. They point to the existence of a "Grub Street" scientific style with many filiations to people such as Mesmer, St. Germain, Cagliastro, and Casanova and testify, in their own way, to the intellectual ferment produced by the Enlightenment revitalization of nature.

Authors of such works offered a potpourri of hermetic thoughts and older nonmechanistic theories joined to observations often inspired by new discoveries in electricity and magnetism. Sometimes, as was the case with the Viennese schoolteacher Carl Schneider, the result just affirmed the chemical theory that had become popular at the midcentury. Other authors were more innovative and informed, though their theories still failed to pass muster. One example should suffice. The Parisian chemist Sage proposed in his *Analyse chimique et concordance des trois règnes* (1786) a "new way of seeing, where others had failed." What M. Sage saw, Gmelin reported, was that "fire-acid" constituted the *Ur*-substance of the universe. Its concentration and passage between combined substances explained all natural phenomena. Sage illustrated this theory with many bizarre examples; for example, he explained the death of a young man by the rapid passage of fire acid through his body occasioned by his eating fifty unripe plums for breakfast. Gmelin, in his review, commented that he had nothing against seeing where others had failed to see, providing what was seen bore the "stamp of truth" and was supported by accepted chemical proofs.[165] Throughout their writings, members of the scientific establishment voiced extreme concern about the proliferation of popular chemical theories. They were clear to differentiate between those who belonged to their self-defined group and those who didn't. Clearly they considered Lavoisier's theories, methods, and explanatory procedures as part and parcel of normal science. Although sometimes novel, they did not endanger the way one spoke about chemistry or practiced it.

In an article entitled "What Are Scientific Revolutions?" Thomas Kuhn looked back upon his original distinction between normal science and scientific revolution, expanded upon it, and modified his original exposition, concentrating this time upon the relationship between language, representation, and nature.[166] In his view scientific revolutions can be characterized as follows: (1) They are holistic; they create a large number of interrelated generalizations that cannot be explained by piecemeal development. (2) They involve a change of the way words and phrases "attach to nature." They alter "not only the criteria by which terms attach to nature, but also, massively, the sets of objects or situations to which those terms attach." (3) They entail "a change in several of the taxonomic categories prerequisite to scientific descriptions and generalization." (4) They produce a major change of metaphor, analogy, or model; that is, the basic juxtapositions one used to bring things together in a pattern of understanding and recognition were irredeemably transformed. (5) "These metaphorlike juxtapositions" that are changed "are central to the process by which scientific language is acquired."[167]

These criteria go very far in establishing an analogy between science and language, in seeing scientific revolution as entailing a major shift in the use, acquisition, and signification of language. I have tried to frame my argument within a similar explanatory model. By looking at the grammar and vocabulary of late-eighteenth-century chemistry and the contours of chemical discussion, I argue that Lavoisier's chemistry—as originally conceived—did not entail a *massive* alteration of the set of objects or situations attached to nature; that it did not destroy the basic metaphors, models, or analogies upon which late Enlightenment chemistry was constructed; and that it did not involve a holistic change of deep-seated fundamental generalizations. In many cases practicing chemists combined elements of both traditions, meaning that some saw "the phlogistic and the antiphlogistic theories as methodologically equal." As Anders Lundgren concluded with respect to Sweden, "there is good reason to suspect that many chemists did not consider the overthrow of the phlogiston theory to be of outstanding importance in the development of their science."[168] Whatever the changes chemistry underwent in the late eighteenth century, they were not revolutionary in the larger sense of the word, but rather elaborations of a language whose first formation can be traced to the midcentury critique of mechanism.

3 "Within the Circle of Organized Life"

BETWEEN MECHANISM AND ANIMISM

In 1775 the French physician Pierre Roussel sketched the recent history of the life sciences in his popular book *Système physique et moral de la femme*.[1] Sounding a theme analogous to that voiced by contemporary chemists, Roussel announced that the life sciences had been revolutionized in the mid-eighteenth century. Mechanism, whose "shaky edifice was already threatening to collapse," had been dethroned. The leaders of this "learned revolution" were physicians from Montpellier and Paris who challenged "the power of established authority." They accomplished for medicine what Buffon had achieved in natural history and Montesquieu in philosophy. Mechanism's "prattle," its "exaggerated," "empty," and "contradictory" explanations, had been destroyed by reviving the ancient concept that life and morality could not be separated.[2]

Three years later Jean Barthez also called for a renewal of physiology and attacked mechanistic explanations in his *Nouveaux éléments de la science de l'homme*.[3] But unlike Roussel, Barthez also heaped scorn upon another physiological "sect," whose theories Barthez considered equally wanting. They were the animists, who, though successful in refuting the mechanists, had replicated their errors on a different plane. The animists, as the mechanists, sought simplistic answers to complex problems. The animists had reduced the cause of physiological phenomena to the actions of the conscious soul, an explanation based upon nonscientific notions propounded by "metaphysicians and theologians." Both sects were reductionist. They had failed to see that "an extreme simplicity of ends and an enormous variety of means characterized nature's operations."[4] Only when a third "sect" appeared at the midcentury were the conditions for physiology's reformation made possible. This sect, the *solidistes*, had attempted to mediate between animism and mechanism. Inspired by some of van Helmont's doctrines, it ascribed a specific life to every organ, independent of both mechanistic laws and the conscious direction of the soul.[5]

At the end of the century, Charles Louis Dumas recapitulated these themes and elaborated upon them in his *Principes de physiologie, ou introduction à la science expériméntal, philosophique et médicale de l'homme vivant*. Dumas agreed that a "revolution" in physiology had been inaugurated in France at the middle of the century. Although Dumas's interpretation of the immediate past supported those of Roussel and Barthez, he presented a more complex story. First, Dumas extended the geographic scope of the revolution to include most of Europe. He cited parallel endeavors in Scotland, England, Germany, and Italy. Second, Dumas also asserted that the mid-eighteenth-century revolution consisted of more than a rejection of mechanism. It also questioned animism, mechanism's early-eighteenth-century alternative. The revolution's core consisted in the need to mediate between the twin "metaphysical" mistakes of "materialism" and "spiritualism." A "third class of physiologists" standing "between them" undertook this task, one that "did not derive all of the manifestations of life from either matter or the soul. Rather, it derived them from a capacity, lying in the middle of both. This capacity differentiated itself from one and the other through specific characteristics; it ruled, directed and ordered all of life's activities. The material body did not determine it, nor was it animated and enlightened by spiritual activity or by the intellectual powers of essential rationality." Among physiologists, the first class comprised the "mechanists," the second the "animists and Stahlians," and the third the "vitalists."[6]

Dumas's characterization documents the shift in basic assumptions that occurred in the loose conjunction of disciplines referred to as the "life sciences." And Dumas's description of this endeavor clearly identified the central tropes of this reformulation. Its overriding imperative was to discover a middle path between the dictates of mechanism and animism, entailing the positing of a capacity lying between the extremes of mind and body where real reality was located, and proposing a new theory of matter, activated by vital forces or principles. It also asserted that a moral regeneration would accompany the reconstitution of the life sciences. All were seen as complimentary constituents directing the shift in late-eighteenth-century physiological, anatomical, and medical thought and practice.

This realignment proceeded along lines parallel to Buffon's restructuring of natural history and repeated in late-eighteenth-century chemistry. It followed a similar three-stage pattern. The first rehabilitated an "ancient" tradition to counter the claims of mechanism. The second defined a unique explanatory and methodological field differentiating the life sciences from chemistry and physics, forging a new grammar and vocabulary for the life sciences. The third reordered scientific priorities, considering mechanical physics as less important, chemistry and electricity as important supporting players, and the life sciences as the core disciplines for understanding living nature, establishing thereby an independent disciplinary matrix for the life sciences.

. . .

At midcentury, the primary tactical objective for leading life scientists was to discredit mechanism. For, as in chemistry, mechanism had become the dominant explanatory pattern for physiological and medical phenomena during the previous seventy-five years. This first stage of the attack rehabilitated ancient traditions closely associated with animism to counter some of mechanism's more radical claims. In implementing these tactics, Enlightenment vitalists also reinterpreted the revived animist propositions, minimizing their spiritualistic, idealistic, rationalistic, and more blatantly hermetic components.

In the early Enlightenment, mechanical physiologists, physicians, and anatomists had portrayed the living body as a vast and complicated aggregate of levers, pulleys, pumps, and hydraulic tubes. Beguiled by advances made in mechanical-mathematical physics, convinced of matter's passivity and of the separation of mind and body, and desirous of establishing transparent, self-evident relations between effect and cause, these physiologists elevated the symbol of the dead animal machine to the status of an incontrovertible physical and physiological reality. Simple mechanics and hydraulics provided the explanatory principles that made the functioning of the living body comprehensible. Boerhaave systematized these basic assumptions in his two immensely influential works, the *Institutiones medicae* and the *Aphorismi de cognoscendi et curendis*. The *Aphorisms* expanded and enriched with commentaries by Boerhaave's prize student Gerhard van Swieten became the eighteenth century's bible of medical mechanism. It served in many places as the primary vehicle of instruction well into the 1780s, especially since the learning of medicine during much of the eighteenth century was based more on oral instruction than on clinical practice or theoretical research.[7] Medical mechanism remained a worthy and powerful opponent throughout the period. For that reason, the attack on mechanism played a continuing role in the reformulation of the life sciences. Given the *Aphorisms*' widespread use and Leiden's prominent role in the training of Europe's and America's physicians and chemists during the first half of the century,[8] Boerhaave and the Leiden "school" became a primary focus and symbol for mechanism's critique.

The most vocal and concerted midcentury assault against medical mechanism came from two centers of medical training, Montpellier and Edinburgh. Since I have already alluded to Montpellier's role in this "revolution," I would like to turn briefly to Edinburgh to illustrate this process. At Edinburgh some of the first critiques of medical mechanism originated from people trained personally by Boerhaave or directly according to his principles. This paradox is striking because Edinburgh's medical school was modeled upon Leiden's, though it later eclipsed it. Founded in 1726, Edinburgh first slavishly imitated its more famous predecessor. However, during the late 1740s, it developed its own approach, which, by the mid-1760s, reached its fruition. From then, as Christopher Lawrence remarked, "it is possible to speak of an authentic Scottish medical school, characterized both by its institutional structure and its intellectual coherence."[9] A rejection of medical mechanism informed that intellectual coherence. Physicians such as Alexander Monro, *secundus*, Robert Whytt, and William Cullen replaced the Boerhaavian-Leiden approach with a consciously constructed vitalism.[10]

William Cullen's work illustrates this shift. He launched a direct attack upon both Boerhaave's chemical and medical mechanistic assumptions.[11] Cullen's lectures on medicine, later revised and published as the *First Lines of the Practice of Physic*, became one of the most important late-eighteenth-century correctives to Boerhaave's approach. In it Cullen rejected the mechanistic concept of dead matter and offered a system founded upon the existence of active, directional forces in nature. Cullen argued that the body, rather than being a passive receiver of impressions, could generate active forces capable of combating internal threats and even of transcending them. The "reactions of the body" were radically different than simple mechanical action and reaction. Cullen also advanced an epistemological ideal calling for combining close empirical observation with systematic reflection, which he associated with Bacon,[12] and he strove to evolve a nosological system for the natural classification of diseases. In short, Cullen presented ideas in both his medical and chemical works that paralleled Buffon's major interests. Cullen's lectures certainly had an effect. When first held, they engendered outrage. As Lester King remarked, Cullen "was assailed as 'a Paracelsus, a Van Helmont, a whimsical innovator,' and his doctrines were disparaged."[13] In fact, Cullen's critique was considered so outrageous that Edinburgh's provost warned him "that his behaviour was likely to hurt both himself and the university."[14]

"Within the Circle of Organized Life"

These negative associations employed to discredit Cullen's doc revealing on two counts. They point to the seriousness of the conceptual shift and demonstrate, though inadvertently, the dyn that shift. To be a (whimsical) innovator was bad enough; but to invoke the theories of Paracelsus and van Helmont appeared to invite a flight from the present back to the shadowy world of Renaissance and early modern animism and down to the ideas of folk medicine. Although designed to disparage, the linkage of the revolt against mechanism with a type of animist philosophy prevalent before mechanism's dominance and still evident in popular belief contained a kernel of truth. As was the case with Buffon and the mid-eighteenth-century chemists, the first lines of attack against established mechanist positions were launched with ammunition and ideas drawn from the adversaries the mechanists themselves had attacked. In the life sciences as in natural history and chemistry, a creative reinterpretation of the past guided this innovation and reformulation. In the life sciences Hippocrates emerged as the ancient source most frequently mustered to counter mechanism. His views were supplemented by positions drawn from Aristotle, Paracelsus, and van Helmont. But the person considered the modern equivalent of Hippocrates and also his reviver was Georg Stahl. Late-eighteenth-century life scientists interpreted classical, Renaissance, and early modern animism through the lens of Stahl's pronouncements, reground, however, to satisfy the demands of their age. So altered, Stahl acquired a startling popularity in the last half of the eighteenth century, emerging as a prophet before his time.

For the majority of early-eighteenth-century life scientists Stahl had appeared hopelessly out of date. To them, his theories had appeal only for the pious and superstitious, for Stahl's theories ran counter to dominant academic medical practice and theory. A review written in 1751 by Albrecht von Haller of a book by an obscure German Stahlian offers an insight into the way the early-eighteenth-century medical elite evaluated Stahl's theories:

> If the Hr. author steps forward to lead the Stahlian army and ascribes to this sect an advantage over mechanical physicians in the successful healing of disease just because Stahlians pay attention to the soul, then I would like to present the author with this single observation. Both a Stahlian and a mechanical physician can be a person with great intelligence and excellent talents. . . . But both sects do not compete with the same weapons. If the Stahlian, out of obstinate superstition, wishes to heal a fever without using cinchona bark *[Fieberrinde]*, if he shuns and demeans the use of opium, of repeated bleedings, of camphor and of other effective remedies, then he appears in comparison to the mechanical physician as did the half-naked, half-armed German attempting to

do battle with the fully armed fighting Roman. The courage of both can be the same. No matter, the better arms will invariably triumph.[15]

Clearly, established medicine associated itself with the Roman legions, surrogates for order, control, and dominance. Their victory appeared assured.

French and Scottish vitalists were the first to initiate the process of transforming Stahl from a poorly armed barbarian to a triumphant Arminius. His enhanced reputation then spread throughout the rest of Europe. By 1775 Roussel claimed that Stahl was the most reliable guide and the greatest of modern physicians. Dumas asserted that "all philosophic physicians" had adopted Stahl's teachings.[16] Pierre Jean Georges Cabanis agreed. In his historical work *Coup d'oeil sur les revolutions et sur la réforme de la médecine* (1804), Cabanis wrote Stahl a long éloge, describing him as "one of those extraordinary geniuses which nature brings forward from time to time to renew the sciences." Cabanis used Buffon's scientific ideal to describe Stahl's qualities, placing him in a pantheon occupied only by figures such as Hippocrates, Bacon, and Newton: "he possessed a rapid and vast *coup-d'oeil* capable of overseeing the whole" combined with "that patient observation which scrupulously pursues minute details."[17]

Blumenbach, probably Germany's most influential late-eighteenth-century life scientist, presents one of the most telling indications for Stahl's rehabilitation.[18] Blumenbach presented his clearest evaluation of Stahl in a journal he edited, *Die medicinische Bibliothek*. In each issue Blumenbach composed a short appreciation of the most important shapers of the medical discipline. The article on Stahl began with a simple, though decisive, statement: "without any doubt whatsoever, one of the greatest, deepest-thinking physicians the world has ever seen." Blumenbach then remarked that recognizing Stahl's genius had contemporary relevance because "the seeds he sowed many years ago, were finally bearing fruit, and . . . all of his most important principles, with certain corrections or limitations, have become the ruling ones in the enlightened parts of Europe."[19] Blumenbach's praise was significant not only because of his rising reputation, but also because he taught at Göttingen, which for years had stood under the dominating influence of Albrecht von Haller.[20] Certainly, if Stahlian ideas could conquer Haller's own fortress, then there was a chance for half-naked, poorly armed barbarians after all.

At first glance Stahl's late-eighteenth-century popularity appears hard to comprehend. Why Stahl? After all, his system incorporated many elements late eighteenth-century writers abhorred. Stahl was an ardent Pietist whose writings seemed to reek of the obscure, "the mystical and the e also was an atrocious stylist, who "veiled his . . . system in the cloak of a dark and externally dry presentation."[21] And though Stahl criticized mechanism harshly, there were others in the first half of the century—doctors, apothecaries, surgeons, faith healers—who had refused to accept mechanist assumptions, were not Pietists, and probably wrote clearer prose. The simple answer is that Stahl's theories became important because of the specific form his opposition to mechanism took: late-eighteenth-century thinkers could read into these theories what appeared central to their own concerns. His writings became an important vehicle because it could be steered in many directions.

Stahl's injunction to return to the origins of physiological and medical thought, to go back to simpler times before the excesses of speculative reasoning and luxurious living had dimmed men's minds, signaled one theme that spoke to many late-eighteenth-century thinkers. "We must," Stahl announced, "observe the core of classical traditions about the organic act; in so doing, we will discover that the classical traditions are far superior to modern mechanistic speculations."[22] Buffon had proclaimed the same message, one repeated by many others, especially those not totally enamored with the way the modern world had developed. It accorded with the growing late-eighteenth-century fascination for classical, republican, and primitive traditions (including popular medieval and Renaissance ones). Stahl called for a return to Hippocrates, supplemented by the study of Aristotle, Paracelsus, and van Helmont to rejuvenate medical studies. All of these authors but especially Hippocratus, Stahl claimed, offered a clearer idea of the nature and function of the animal economy than had modern mechanists. Stahl saw it as his purpose to resurrect and modernize the doctrines of the ancients and their followers.

In so doing, Stahl drew a sharp distinction between a "mechanical Body" *(corpus mechanicum)* and a living system. This argument became central to late-eighteenth-century Enlightenment Vitalism. A living system, which constituted an "*oecononia vitae,* had its own laws, its own goals, its uses and effects."[23] Its mode of action surpassed physical-mechanistic necessity, transcending simple passive action and reaction. The mechanists made the mistake of conflating life with mechanical reaction: "necessity was too closely connected to passive contingency *[Contingentia passiva]*." "A higher principle" with its own self-prescribed goal governed matter. Goal or telos constituted, Stahl argued, an integral part of the "living economy" of nature. It assumed the existence of an active moral principle, a "*Principium moraliter activum,*" which Stahl associated with the conscious human will.[24] The rational soul constituted the principles controlling the organic body. It directly and consciously guided all of the body's movements; though one sees only the outward accompanying conditions, the soul is the single true cause of everything that takes place in the body. According to Stahl, the soul regulated the flow of liquids, established the relations between its solid and liquid parts, accounted for its form, and prevented the body from decomposing, even though its constituent materials had a strong tendency toward putrefaction. In all, the soul established "a beautiful harmony" between all of the body's parts.

In his exposition Stahl employed two explanatory figures later eighteenth-century vitalists adopted and expanded. The first defined harmony as generated by an active force. Unlike Leibniz's harmonic ideal where spirit and body followed separate though parallel tracks, Stahl assumed a real exchange between them in which the principle directed matter. The second deployed the inner/outer topos, considering the hidden, nonseeable as the real, the immediately observable merely a representation of the real. The external sign lost its transparent nature, now requiring an act of interpretation to give it meaning. Hence, the path to understanding reality called for a mode of perception that transcended abstract rationalism and simple empiricism. One had to go beyond the obvious to approach the inner core of reality.

The similarity between the observed and the observer made such an approach possible. Since humans were endowed with souls, they could sympathetically understand the operation of the soul in other bodies. This process, which Stahl called "synergy"—the merging of two energies— required humans first to understand themselves. Knowledge of the living economy of nature began with self-investigation. These assumptions led Stahl to propose the following corollaries concerning the relationship between soul and body: (1) The soul constructs the body, nourishes it, and acts within it to achieve the goal of harmony. (2) Basic defects in the soul lead to basic defects in the body. (3) Cures must be guided by an understanding of the soul. (4) No one can understand living sentiments *(Gefühlsleben)* who does not understand his own.[25] If external signs suggest inner activity, it followed that bodily form represented the soul's "characteristics" *(Wesenszüge)*. These combined with the passions constituted the temperament. Stahl defined temperaments as the set of "reciprocal relations between a body's solid and fluid parts."[26] The intensity and nature of the "passions of the soul" gave the temperaments their specific shape, form, and character. Returning to the ancients, Stahl argued for the existence of four basic temperaments (analogues in the living world to chemistry's simple principles) and a multitude of combined ones *(zusam-*

mengesetzte Temperamenten) (analogues to chemical compositions).[27] Each expressed a specific character type susceptible to certain diseases.

Obviously, there was nothing novel in advancing a theory of temperaments. However, in Stahl's explication of this theory he concentrated on two points that later Enlightenment vitalists accepted as crucial. In the first Stahl strove to mediate between the poles of nature and nurture in explaining a temperament's origins. In the second he sought to link voluntarism to analyze habit's role in directing human activity. Stahl considered temperaments as products of both inherited and acquired traits. The "passions of the soul" were not irremediably fixed. They could be modified, changed, or redirected by an act of will: the change could be made lasting through habitual retraining (this "voluntarism" constituted a central feature in Pietistic thought as well as its concern with forming new habits to cement one's regeneration in Christ). Hence, habit emerged in Stahl's thought as the second nature of living organisms; habits were almost as powerful as inherited characteristics. For example, a dominant passion could be driven to a secondary or even a tertiary position by the power of an opposing habit. This was possible because passions were always goal-directed. They expressed a wish, a desire for a vague *(vorschwebende)*, anticipated fulfillment. By modifying either the passion's object of desire or by introducing habits that countered the original desire, a person's characterological and nosological system could be altered. Habit could become a vehicle for physical and spiritual improvement. Stahl's medical doctrines placed a great emphasis upon the centrality of the soul and little upon mechanical cures, making the physician more a soul-healer and psychologist than the cutter, bleeder, purger, and opium dispenser favored by the mechanists.

But it wasn't the soul-healing side of Stahl's doctrines that made his theories so attractive to mid-eighteenth-century antimechanists. The points they found important were Stahl's new epistemology, his theory of matter, his concentration upon active forces or principles, his joining of spirit and body, his attitude to the tension between nature and nurture, and his voluntarism, all of which they emphasized and expanded upon. At the same time, they ignored or modified other important features of Stahl's medical doctrines, especially those closely related to religion or to his desire to reduce all phenomena to the rational soul's direction. These modifications took different forms depending upon the culture in which they were proposed. Although life scientists throughout Europe hailed Stahl, no single unified Stahlian theory reigned supreme. This can be illustrated by the attempts to explain the animal economy in the mid-eighteenth century by three representative life scientists from Scotland, Germany/Switzerland, and France, who in their own way became founders of Enlightenment Vitalism.

. . .

In Scotland late Enlightenment physiologists who investigated the animal economy focused their attentions upon the priority of the central nervous system in directing the activities of an organized body.[28] Robert Whytt (1714–66), one of the first and most interesting Scottish antimechanists, addressed this issue in *An Essay on the Vital and other Involuntary Motions of Animals* (1751; 2nd ed., 1763). He dealt with those areas of the animal economy that mechanists and animists had the most difficulty explaining: involuntary and semivoluntary animal motion. For mechanists these human functions—for example, the beating of the heart, the digestive system, the circulation of blood, and the stimulation of the genitalia—were "automatic" activities, not explicable by mind and therefore necessarily produced "by virtue" of their "mechanical construction."[29] Stahl had reversed this explanation and ascribed all animal motion to the action of a "rational agent" of the soul. Whytt sought a middle ground between Stahl and the mechanists, though he tended more to Stahl than to Descartes and Boerhaave.

Whytt proposed three central arguments in his text. The first stated that the animal system could not be comprehended under the idea of a machine. He employed the concepts of "organic conjunction" and "active forces" to justify this position.[30] He demonstrated this by citing examples showing the insufficiency of the mechanical concept of cause and effect to explain muscle contraction. Muscles, when touched, contract with a force much greater than the original cause. They continue to contract and relax following a pulsating pattern well after the original cause had disappeared. Simply said, the effect was not directly proportional to the original causal force. Whytt concluded that a different type of force caused these motions, which he called "the energy of the mind" or the "sentient principle," distinguishing it clearly from Stahl's more religiously charged term, the rational soul.

Whytt focused his second argument on Stahl's claim that the conscious, rational mind "presided over, regulated, and continued" vital motion. He did this by denying that reason and consciousness were the defining characteristics of mind. Although functions of the mind, they were not primary. Sensation constituted vital matter's basic property, whereby mind receives a stimulus, processes it, and then reacts accordingly. This takes place, as a rule, without the active intervention of reason. Since "there are actions, towards the performing of which" are "in no ways determined by reason," the "mind is not a free but a necessary agent."[31] This may sound Lockean, but Whytt refused to accept the mechanical implications often ascribed to Locke. Mind possessed its own "energy," producing effects greater than the received stimulus: hence, the disparity between cause and effect. Whytt replaced the concept of cause and effect with that of stimulus and what we would call "reflex action." He considered the animal economy to be a perpetuum mobile because of the ability of "a cause producing an effect greater than itself, but also an effect increasing by degrees . . . of its own accord."[32]

Whytt's third argument asserted that the "energy" of the central nervous system directed all animal motion. Here he had to overcome two hurdles. First, no single common place had been discovered where all nerve endings met. Since no physical contact existed between all of the nerves, many contemporary thinkers found it difficult to conceive of directed motion. Second, no clear proof existed that nerves controlled muscle contraction. He answered the first by pointing to the existence of "sympathetic reactions" between parts of the body that had no direct contact with each other and whose nerves did not "terminate precisely in the same part of the brain."[33] He claimed that only the existence of a principle of energy binding the brain, spinal chord, and nerves could account for this sympathy.[34]

Whytt also used the concept of sympathy to overcome the second hurdle: "Muscles are excited into action by a stimulus affecting a remote part with which they have no immediate connection, or so much as even a communication by means of nerves, unless it be that general one subsisting between all parts, as their nerves are derived from the same brain."[35] Thus, nerves and muscles being of the same essence participated in a larger combination guided by a ruling principle. To support this position Whytt drew upon a general proposition that had very little to do with muscles or nerves. Arguing that nature did nothing in vain, that it always chose the simplest solution, it would be wrong to ascribe to muscles any particular power not controlled by a more general force. With a grand rhetorical flourish, he rested his argument with the following assertion:

> But if it be imagined that he [the all-wise AUTHOR of nature] has given to animal fibres a power of sensation, and of generating motion, without superadding or uniting to them an active PRINCIPLE, as the SUBJECT and CAUSE of these, we presume to say, that a supposition of this kind ought by no means to be admitted; since, to affirm that matter can, of itself, by any modification of its parts, be rendered capable of sensation, or of generating motion, is not less absurd than to ascribe to it a power of thinking.[36]

A year after the publication of the first edition of Whytt's book, Germany's most eminent life scientist, the Swiss-born Albrecht von Haller, read a paper before the Royal Society of Sciences in Göttingen entitled "Von den empfindlichen und reizbaren Teilen des menschlichen Körpers" (A Dissertation on the Sensible and Irritable Parts of Animals) that proclaimed precisely what Whytt considered absurd. Published in 1753 it became one of the most influential scientific tracts of the last half of the century.

Unlike Whytt, it would be hard to consider Haller an avowed antimechanist. One of Boerhaave's prize students, he had invested much of his emotional and intellectual energy in propagating and refining mechanistic physiology. As a devout Calvinist, Haller found the mechanistic belief in an all-powerful creator continually directing a world machine otherwise destined to run down theologically persuasive. These religious beliefs also made him one of the most ardent defenders of the theory of divine preformation. Yet, whatever Haller's personal opinions, this little work led to the materialist assumptions Whytt had feared. It also established a precedent for one of the major forms of physiological thinking evolved by late-eighteenth-century vitalists. Haller argued for the existence of two different and opposed types of powers residing in the organized body, calling them "sensibility" and "irritability," which he defined as follows: "I call that part of the human body irritable which becomes shorter upon being touched; very irritable if it contracts upon a slight touch. . . . I call that a sensible part of the human body, which upon being touched transmits the impressions of it to the soul." These two powers were contained in different types of matter and were opposed: "the most irritable parts are not at all sensible, and vice versa, the most sensible are not irritable."[37] Thus, nerves were capable only of sensibility, muscles of irritability. Through many gory experiments upon living animals, Haller established which types or organized matter belonged to each category. "The internal membranes of the stomach, intestines, bladder, uterus, vagina, and womb" were sensible, while "the viscera, . . . viz. the lungs, liver, spleen, and kidneys had very little sensation."[38] The heart possessed the greatest degree of irritability. Haller adamantly differentiated irritability from the traditional mechanical forces, introducing in his physiology the specter of vital force.

Unintentionally Haller helped undermine medical mechanism in a manner similar to Boerhaave's introduction of substantialized matter in chemistry. Irritability was a force "different from all the other known properties of bodies and is new. For it depends neither on weight, nor upon attraction, nor upon elasticity. It has its seat only in soft fibers. With their hardening, this power disappears."[39] In effect, Haller proposed a view in which different force systems worked within the animal body propelled by powers that defied both simple mechanical explanations and Whytt's emphasis upon the reign of the central nervous system. While Whytt argued for spiritual centralization, Haller envisioned a decentralization of active powers within the animal economy.

At the same time that Haller and Whytt were locked in the battle about whether irritability and sensibility were separate vital forces, Théophile Bordeu (1722–76), a younger French physician, offered a different take upon Stahlian theory. Bordeu had been trained at Montpellier, the stronghold of Hippocratic medicine and the place where Stahl and van Helmont were first revived in eighteenth-century France.[40] With this background, Bordeu understandably demonstrated a strong preference for earlier animist writers, though he rejected animism as a doctrine. As was the case with Whytt, he wished to mediate between animism and mechanism and therefore added a good dose of mechanism to his explications. His theories stood between Whytt's and Haller's, confirming and denying them both. Bordeu affirmed Whytt's emphasis upon the importance of the central nervous system, yet he went much further in derationalizing it, almost dethroning mind from its position as its absolute ruler. Although opposed to Haller, whom he considered a rival and adversary,[41] Bordeu affirmed and intensified van Helmont's position of postulating individual centers of life and activity within the living body.

In Bordeu's version of vitalism, the central nervous system, which carried and transmitted sensations, was essential to life. Sensitivity (the communication of an impression) and sentiments (the response to the impression) were intimately related. Without stimulus, there could be no response. Hence, the nervous system held the animal economy together, linking each part in a functioning system. According to Dumas, Bordeu compared "the sensible or nervous system . . . to an insect whose claws penetrate all living parts."[42] The image is striking. On one level, it reveals Bordeu's fascination for animist forms of thought. On another, it demonstrates his desire to mediate between the centralized vision of Whytt and the separatism of Haller. The tentacles of the nervous system were embedded within living organic tissue, yet they did not vivify organic tissue, for each type of organic tissue, each organ had its own "specific life," its own "taste" *(gout)*, or "appropriate sentiments" *(sentiment propre)*.

Bordeu, though connecting stimulus and response, did not collapse one into the other. Sensibility, a general principle, did not determine individual response. Outside impressions were conveyed to a specific organ, which

"Within the Circle of Organized Life"

according to its own unique nature and function, its own ntiment," its own "spontaneous activity." To borrow a phrase ne could say that sensibility proposed and the sentiments dise formulations indicate Bordeu's desire to mediate between the d the specific and between nature and nurture, arguing that though the animal economy could not be explained without the use of general principles, the principles were inadequate to account for all its actions. The animal economy consisted of unity in diversity, where the sum of individual lives operating together in constant reciprocal action and reaction constituted the animal economy.

Working from this basic vitalist assumption, Bordeu constructed an elaborate picture of the animal economy's unity and diversity. He revealed his desire to combine animist insights with mechanistic explanatory devices. In his discussion of the nervous system, for example, Bordeu pictured the nerves' "arms" as fibers, which translated sensations through vibration or oscillation. When stimulated they vibrated back and forth, resulting in "a species of peristaltic movement." Its oscillations were "like a flux and reflux." The system functioned as a complex stringed instrument capable of producing an almost infinite number of overtones as the fibers of different lengths and widths vibrated in sympathy with one another.

Unlike animists who equated soul with mind and mechanists who had difficulty joining both, but usually placed the seat of sensations near the head, Bordeu adopted van Helmont's theory that the greatest source of animal sensations were in the middle region of the body *(la région moyenne du corps)*. This middle region encompassed the heart, stomach, diaphragm, genitalia, and entrails. It operated as the "principle center" of a body's movements, "a base of sensibility, too long unrecognized by those who do ordinary physiology."[43] In ascribing prime position to the body's central region in the animal economy, Bordeu both reified the language of mediation, making it a physiological principle, and returned to forms of thought regnant during Rabelais's time. By focusing upon the epigastric center and emphasizing its great influence upon the soul,[44] he effectively exorcised the rationalist and religious roots from Stahl's original formulations.

In addition to singling out fibers as central to the animal economy, Bordeu also underscored the importance of a substance he called the *mucus tissue (le tissue muqueux)* or the cellular organ in the economy's functioning. It served as the base material from which all organs originated. From it each organ derived its own specific sentiments, which Bordeu called "irritability." Differing with Haller, Bordeu considered irritability a modification of sensibility, unique to specific organic matter; it was "an activity, a virtue, a property, a particular disposition" of an organ.[45] Whatever the nature of this cellular matter or mucous membrane, it formed the bridge between different organs, allowing an even greater increase in sympathetic effects and consent between the organizations' parts. Thus, according to Bordeu, the animal economy was a complex conjunction of nerve and muscle fibers and cellular matter, all imbued with sensibility and specific life. Their continual action and interaction created the conditions for sympathetic effects and for consensus. Working together all of the parts contributed to maintain the general good of the whole, which was harmony or good health.

Although Bordeu hardly used political metaphors to describe the animal economy, his famous image of the beehive, borrowed by Diderot in *D'Alembert's Dream*, did indeed suggest a political vision of living nature, one in which the general and the particular merge to form an ever-changing harmony or rapport between the individual-yet-connected parts. The comparison was based upon the informing figures of conjunction, sympathy, consensus, activity, and harmony. The living body subsisted without need of a single dominating center or director. Taken to its logical conclusion, Bordeu presented a republican vision of the animal economy's functioning:

> In order to perceive the particular action of each part of a living body, we compare it to a swarm of bees, assembled in a cluster and hanging from a tree like a bunch of grapes. One cannot consider wrong what a celebrated ancient author said of the organs of the lower abdomen: it was an *animal in animali*. Each part is, so to speak, certainly not an animal, but a species of an independent machine, which in its own way contributes to the general life of the body. Thus, to pursue the comparison of the cluster of bees, it is a whole stuck to a tree branch by the action of many bees who must act together in order to stay fast; there are some who are attached to the first ones and so forth; all cooperate to form a solid enough body; each one, however, has, in addition, its specific action. A single one who stops or acts too vigorously, will throw the whole mass askew. At the moment when they will all conspire to embrace each other mutually, according both to the order and proportions required, they will compose a whole, which will exist until they are disturbed. The application [of the comparison] is easy; the organs of the body are linked with each other; they each have their distinct sphere and their action; the relations of these actions, the harmony that results from them, make health.[46]

As the above comparison between Whytt, Haller, and Bordeu illustrates, mid-eighteenth-century critics of mechanism and animism differed considerably about their specific interpretations of life. At the same time they also shared a number of basic assumptions that lay at the core of the developing language of Enlightenment Vitalism. All sought to delineate the characteristics of a "living system" that differed radically from a "dead," mechanistic one. They called this living system an "organization" or an "organized body," defined as driven by goal-directed active powers. Unlike the "blind" forces of mechanism, vital powers could "see," could aspire to an end, and hence were analogous to moral forces. Organized bodies were both structured and imbued with powers of transformation. The late-eighteenth-century concept of organization included the idea of mediation between the extremes of the fluid and fixed. August Wilhelm Schlegel's definition clearly summed up this position: "The concept of organization necessarily assumes a middle condition between liquidity and solidity; for the first is without form *[Gestaltlos]*, the second completely formed. The organized continually forms itself."[47]

To apprehend the animal economy required joining the analytic categories of conjunction and development. Their respective analyses formed the grand topics of late-eighteenth-century physiological, anatomical, and medical research and debate. The first topic called for an analysis of the complex living system, in terms of both the interrelationships between its parts and the relation between the living body and the habitat in which it subsisted, for each organized body fulfilled the needs of existence in a special manner equipped with unique instruments. The medium of conjunction was space (both internal and external), its object of inquiry reciprocal relations or *rapports*, and its temporal focus the synchronic. The second topic sought to account for the creation, development, reproduction, and possible transformation of the organized body, to consider what Blumenbach called "the different epochs or revolutions of its existence."[48] Its medium was time, its object of inquiry directional forces, and its analytic procedures directed to the diachronic.

While pursuing both analytic operations, sometimes individually, sometimes simultaneously, late-eighteenth-century life scientists sought to mediate between them, hoping in the process to divine the extended middle, the "middle condition" in which they were joined. This attempt produced creative insight but also divisive disputes, often generated by the desire to elevate one side of the equation over the other, sometimes exacerbated by veiled and not so veiled sociopolitical and religious disagreement. For simplicity's sake, I propose to deal with each category separately, devoting the rest of this chapter to the concept of organization and the next to the idea of development. In doing so, however, I wish to emphasize that both operations were guided by basic prefiguring assumptions uniting them within a specific discursive field.

ORGANIZATION, CONJUNCTION, SYMPATHY, AND NATURE'S ECONOMY

The sharp distinction Whytt and Bordeu drew between the "animal economy" and normal mechanical aggregation became a self-evident proposition central to Enlightenment Vitalism, reinforcing, I believe, the manner in which "economy" and "economics" were radically revised in the same period. The distinction between organization and mechanism, though sometimes veiled by paradoxical terms such as "animal machine" or "living machine,"[49] supported the assumption that the methods and explanatory devices evolved to account for "dead matter" were insufficient for living bodies. Enlightenment vitalists would not deny that the body could be seen as a collection of tubes, levers, pumps, and fluids, all of which in their action or movement obeyed the laws of mechanics and hydraulics. But, if mechanism could, for example, explain the pumping action of the heart, it was incapable of saying why the heart continually kept pumping without running down. They would also agree that the body could be seen as a complicated chemical laboratory, constantly breaking down and forming new materials through the action of elective affinities. However, they added that the affinity relations common to a living body were different from those of dead ones. Living force generated chemical reactions, which replenished the body, and hindered putrefaction and the body's breakdown.[50]

Enlightenment vitalists argued that, unlike physical, mechanical, and normal chemical effects, physiological activities demonstrated no immediately visible cause. Vital bodies were, to use the language of the time, self-organizing. For that reason, when investigating living matter vitalists considered the following as true: (1) No simple and unvarying relationship between physiological cause and effect could be established. (2) The true connections between living parts could not be clearly discerned. (3) Relations between cause and effect varied radically from those of mechanical action and reaction, for physiological effects often far exceeded their immediate causes in terms of duration, intensity, and extent.

These observations led late Enlightenment life scientists to deny that the physical forces of impulsion and attraction explained physiological phenomena. Impulsion or transferred motion could not account for consensus, sympathy, and the disproportion between cause and effect. Its emphasis upon sequential change also made it impossible to deal with the simultaneous reaction of different, physically unconnected organs to a single stimulus. Attraction, though capable of explaining action at a distance, required a center to which the attractive power strove, a middle point being either at the center of the world or at the center of the body. Vitalists ruled out the first because of the complexity of physiological reactions, the second by "the observation" that the body had many centers.[51] Vitalists defined the animal economy as a system consisting of animated matter organized around individual centers of life that worked together through mutual reciprocity, sympathy, and consensus. This assumption supported the derationalization and decentralization of the living system. Even when invoking the concept of a living principle, Enlightenment vitalists carefully disassociated it from the activities of the "thinking soul," that is, from the rationalistic explanatory models of Stahl and early-eighteenth-century animists.

Vitalists employed the term "organization" to make the intended mediating position between mechanism and animism clear. In contradistinction to mechanism, the concept of organization emphasized the importance of interconnection and reciprocal relations or *rapports*. Unlike animism (and modern organicism), it refused to postulate the existence of a single directing "royal" agency or ontologically determinate rational spirit. Enlightenment vitalists rejected scientific explanations based upon a philosophy of identity, which postulated the existence of a uniformly distributed informing essence, making the part merely a reflector of the whole, a microcosm of the macrocosm.

Their treatment of interconnection, defined as the essence of an organized body, took two forms, the first with respect to all other bodies in the world, the second with respect to the parts of the individual body. Charles Bonnet in his voluminous writings concentrated upon the first. Although late Enlightenment vitalists would reject many of Bonnet's positions, his passionate espousal of universal interconnection reverberated throughout the century and into the next.[52] "Everything in the world's edifice," Bonnet proclaimed, "is systematic. Everything is in connection, in relation, in combination and precise conjunction." But though interconnected, the world, especially the organized world, was composed of a myriad of different systems, each linked yet unique. The sum of these systems constituted "the universal system." Yet within it, "every thing has its own effect, its own sphere determined by the order that thing has in the world."[53] According to Bonnet, the connections between the parts of each system and of the individual systems to the universal system were not immediately perceptible. They were linked by "secret rapports," which we can judge only by "a sort of intuition," not be mere *raisonnement*.[54]

This definition challenged the concept of system predominant in the late seventeenth and early eighteenth centuries. In seventeenth-century philosophy a system suggested a hierarchical ordering of concepts and phenomena guided by an informing *ratio* and made comprehensible by the application of formal logic. It assumed an analogy between human and divine reason, authorizing the belief that the former could mirror adequately the order of the latter. In contrast, late Enlightenment vitalists defined a system as a contingent connection of facts, discovered and illuminated by intuition and divination, not by the methods of abstract, hypothetical reasoning. In this sense Buffon's general definition of a natural system became the desired goal of vitalist life scientists, though most naturalists accepted some artificial systems as useful heuristics. They considered interconnection as naturally given, existing outside and above the ordering power of human reason. As Buffon had argued so eloquently, nature presented a conjunction between unity and diversity that could not be encompassed by the principles of discursive logic. It constituted a relationship between brute facts—what Barthez called *faites-principes*—that defied the attempts of "speculative-hypothetical" philosophers to order these facts according to their whims. Thus a new concept of "systematics" was forged in the mid- to late eighteenth century, which John E. Lesch defined as "the classification of objects into groups according to degrees of identity and difference." He concluded that the "systematic model formed a major modality of late Enlightenment thought," whether it arose "as the result of a diffusion of the model from one or a few sources—most probably natural history—or as the synchronous expressions of an underlying disposition."[55]

It is important to emphasize that both Buffon and Bonnet—major opponents on the question of generation—employed the same language to characterize systematic interconnection. This consent testifies to its increasing acceptance in the last half of the century, which Dumas expressed in his definition of the interrelation between humans and the universe: "The human stands in the center of nature and is at the same time the object of all of its actions. The human—internally linked with all the beings of the universe, which constitutes an order of things where everything changes and through which change is conserved—must live within ever newer and newer forms of being. This person cannot be examined and presented by us as existing alone and separated from the rest of the remaining world."[56]

. . .

The definition of universal interconnection and the continued call to formulate a natural system led vitalists to consider the connection between the parts of a single organized body. Blumenbach defined this interconnection in its broadest terms: "This whole collective assemblage of all the faculties and laws ... by which the functions of the human body are performed and regulated from the opening, to the closing pulse of life, is called *human nature*, or the *nature of man;* from whence arose the name *physiology*."[57] Goethe elaborated upon this idea using terms similar to Blumenbach's: "Each living thing is not a singularity, but a majority; even when it appears to us as an individual, it still remains an assembly of living independent essences."[58] Dumas carried this definition further when he defined a living body as a "living aggregate." It consisted of "the total sum of the movements and appearances of the organs which depends on their mutual action and reaction; it was the compound of all specific qualities, all active, living forces, which arise from the parts of a living thing."[59] These definitions clearly point to the mediating imperative of Enlightenment Vitalism. The deployment of the terms "sum," "assembly," or "aggregate" still suggests elements of mechanism. They signaled the rejection of a single, universal organizing principle, logos, soul, or spirit that constituted the living body. Life was not, for Enlightenment vitalists, a uniform attribute of all parts of the body. Further, these vitalists also refused to consider the question of whether the animating principles of an organized body could exist independently of the matter they animated. The question was impossible to answer and, hence, deemed irrelevant.

This skepticism concerning the ability to discern life's cause led Enlightenment vitalists to reintroduce the idea of occult qualities into their work. How conjunction occurred and why, they considered a mystery. Goethe's description of the organized system attested to this belief concerning the mysterious juncture of individual elements constituting the whole. Many vitalists resorted to the language of miraculous creation, believing the act of combination simultaneously vitalized the parts and the whole. The animating agent became the *act of combination* itself, not some previously existing spirit or externally active agent. In the mysterious combination that constituted an organized body each individual part "loses its specific life in order to live with the whole and to contribute its own part to the total sum of life. These are the points upon which all distinctions between dead and living bodies are founded."[60] This is a difficult concept to define clearly. It focused upon the question of how an aggregate is transformed into a collective body, a question Rousseau posed in the *Contrat social*, probably inspired by Buffon and Bordeu. Their answers were the same. Each part of the body surrenders its own freedom in order to win back an enhanced freedom.[61] The act of surrender simultaneously creates and is impelled by the idea of the whole. In the newly formed entity each part retained a type of individuality and freedom unknown in simple mechanical aggregative systems.

Given this special dynamic, the relations within the "assemblage of essences" were considered to be of a special kind, different from those suggested by the words sum, majority, assembly, aggregate, and collection. Reciprocal relation excluded linear causation and simple aggregation as ordering and explanatory principles. Reciprocal relation became one of the principle definitions of an organized body. According to the German naturalist Christoph Girtanner, "organized bodies are such bodies in which everything is connected to everything as ends and means. Everything that is contained in an organized body is related to everything else as ends and means."[62] Reciprocal interconnection negated the attempt to answer the riddle of which came first, the vitalizing principle or the vitalized parts. Rather, each living element, which in combination constituted the living body and drew its life from it, was locked in a symbiotic embrace with every other element. Together they formed what Barthez, borrowing Stahl's term, called a synergy.[63] Blumenbach referred to this concourse as the "circle of relations between active forces." Within this circle the "whole routine of action and reaction corresponds with such exactness and definitude, as to constitute a perfect and harmonious equilibrium."[64] The summing activities of a living body—its constituting act and its means for maintenance and growth—transcended the simple addition of discrete elements. In living matter, harmony, and equilibrium were not static concepts.

In juxtaposition to the language of arithmetic aggregation, the vocabulary of ends and means and of surrender and regain introduced a counterdiscourse into science built upon the analogy of morality and choice. As in the other seemingly paradoxical juncture made between the opposing conceptual pairs of machine and animal (animal machine, living machine), this linguistic combination (e.g., living aggregate) can be viewed as a deliberately constructed oxymoron, as an attempt to introduce complementarity directly into the concrete definition of phenomena that constituted a linguistic field including elements from the opposed elements, which embodied Enlightenment Vitalism's mediating ideal. It linked the discourse of summation with that of reciprocal relations and authorized the assumption that each individual in a living system played the role of an active participant, while retaining its own unique specific life.

. . .

A central issue raised by this vitalist conception of connection revolved around the questions of how individuals acted in concert and what form connections between them took. Late-eighteenth-century vitalists denied the adequacy of mechanist and animist concepts of connection. Mechanists postulated the necessity of actual physical contact to account for connection. Simultaneous interaction among unconnected distant parts appeared to them as a hermetic fantasy. Animism explained connection by the activities of the conscious soul, which ruled the body in a manner approximating the most exaggerated claims of late-seventeenth-century apologists for absolute rule. To escape from the restrictions of these two models, both equally formal and rationalistic, Enlightenment vitalists resurrected the ancient idea, still regnant in eighteenth-century folk tradition, of sympathy or consensus to account for connection and interaction between organs within the circle of organization. The concepts of sympathy and consensus enabled late Enlightenment life scientists to account for action at a distance and simultaneous reaction in widely dispersed parts of the organized body. They predicated their argument upon the existence of vital, internal forces, principles, or energies that formed living analogues to chemistry's elective affinities and gravity in dead matter, constructing, thereby, a hierarchy of "occult qualities," each differentiated by the matter they controlled or animated. The more complex the reactions, the more active and "free" the occult force.

Barthez in his *Nouveaux éléments de la science de l'homme* (1778) underscored the central role of sympathetic reactions. In it he launched a major critique of the reductive assumptions of mechanism and animism, proposing in their stead an elaborate and complex system founded upon the analysis of the dynamic relations between dual manifestations of an essential vital principle. He based his renovation of physiology or what he also called the *science de l'homme* (he used the two terms interchangeably) upon the assumption that "the great and governing view of the *science de l'homme* is the consideration of an essential being, animated by vital forces whose action is subject to the primordial laws of sympathy and synergy."[65] Synergy and sympathy were as basic to living matter as gravity to dead matter. They constituted essential types of reactions within the circle of organization, symbolized by the terms "concourse" and "affection." Barthez defined synergy as a regular concourse of forces working together to keep the organized body running. Synergies governed stable processes. Because this concourse controlled generic phenomena, it existed independently of the specific sympathies of an organ or organs.[66] While accounting for normal functioning or regularly occurring phenomena, synergies did not explain how the organized body responded to the ever-changing world in which the body subsisted. Sympathetic reactions fulfilled this task and were, for him, more important than synergies. Barthez spent a major part of his discussion charting the various types of sympathies he believed could be discerned in organized matter. Concentrating upon sympathies would, he argued, change the way in which many important phenomena in the animal economy were viewed. Their most striking characteristic seemed to be their inconstancy and unpredictability: "The sympathy between two organs is not always reciprocal" and "is never perpetual."[67]

Central to this position was Barthez's refusal to draw a radical distinction between irritability and sensibility, seeing the former as a special case of the latter. Each organ would act with varying intensities when stimulated in a specific way due to its degree of sensibility. The universal existence of a differentiated sensitivity in all organs accounted for the primordial phenomenon of sympathy, for only similar things demonstrated affections for one another. Sympathetic reactions depended upon the degree of mutual "affection" between organs, the response one organ could evoke from another, and the conditions under which that response was generated. As in the language of chemistry, but even more so, Enlightenment vitalists described sympathy using the metaphoric language of human affection, attraction, and even love.

Thus, sympathies could be considered analogues to elective affinities. In fact, for Barthez and most Enlightenment vitalists, the terms were often interchanged. For example, Blumenbach assumed a strong "native sympathy" between similar parts *(partes similares)* in nature and described this sympathy "as a particular law of affinity," in which elements possessing "reciprocal and kindred propensities" are attracted.[68] And Lichtenberg considered the organized body to be a "generalized sphere of affinity," *(gemeinschaftliche Affinitätsspähre)*.[69] However, vitalists did not consider sympathies and elective affinities to be identical; they elevated sympathies to a higher plane of nondeterministic affective action than elective affinities. While elective affinities always tended toward equilibrium, vital sympathies sometimes did not; they could result in an enhancement of vital energy. To borrow the language of Adam Smith, Barthez's slightly older contemporary, who considered sympathy essential to the moral economy, sympathies acted as the hidden hand guiding the specific functions and reactions of an organized body.

Given the nondeterminate yet creative qualities of sympathetic affections, late-eighteenth-century physiologists believed sympathies resisted reduction to simple lawlike relations. The brute facts of sympathetic affections could, at best, be classified according to how they manifested themselves. Their appearance could be observed, the reason for that appearance only divined. Barthez discerned four types of sympathies, which he further ranged into two related pairs. He characterized the first pair according to the manner in which sympathetic organs were connected and differentiated, the second according to their degree of specificity and their type of action. In the first pair connection was direct, mediated, or analogous. In direct and mediated connection sympathetic organs were either physically linked or were tied together by a third element, usually cellular material. Irritation of one organ passed immediately to the other linked organs over physical lines of communication, however, not in direct proportion to the original stimulus, nor in sequential order since sympathetic reactions were both simultaneous and reciprocal. The organs' nature determined their reactions, their degree of sensitivity, and the types of affections they experienced. Thus, though similar to mechanistic concepts, the direct/mediated sympathetic system still demonstrated qualities unknown in mechanistic explanations. The cardiovascular system served as the classic example of such a linkage.

Barthez explained the second type of connection, classified as analogous sympathies, by similarity in either function or structure. The closer the structural resemblance of organs within a functional system, the stronger their affective sympathy. Although Barthez considered function and structure related, he emphasized function over structure,[70] a choice he made clear in his second pairing of sympathetic reactions. In it Barthez distinguished between "active forces," which produce more general sympathies and "radical forces" with particular sympathies, a language anticipating the one Lavoisier employed in chemistry. The general vital principle governed active forces that it "sets into action at every moment in all organs," irrespective of whether the source of the sympathetic stimulus is external or internal. Radical forces directed the active forces of individual organs toward specific ends. The radical forces were able to augment, modify, diminish, and even override or redirect the general acting forces.[71] By so doing, they established new sympathetic relations of momentary intensity to react to changes within the circle of organization.

In all, the sum total of active and radical forces constituted a system in which complex conjunctions were formed between synergies and between general and particular sympathies as the organized body responded creatively to external and internal stimuli. Barthez like all Enlightenment vitalists refused to speculate upon the origin or nature of the vital principle, assigning it to the category of occult forces. Although arguing for its unitary nature, he marshaled the language of aggregation to define its qualities, asserting that the sum of active and radical forces constituted its activities: "The ensemble or rather the aggregate of the sums of these two sorts of forces constitute what I call the complete system [*système entier*] of the forces of the vital principle."[72]

ELABORATING THE VITAL ECONOMY'S ACTIVITIES

By the late 1770s and early 1780s, a majority of leading life scientists had reached the conclusion that it was imperative to formulate a comprehensive language of nature to account for organized matter's existence and activities. Central elements of that language had been forged in the dispute between mechanists, animists, *solidistes*, and vitalists. A general consensus had been reached concerning this new language's basic structure. Most life scientists accepted the proposition that interconnection and reciprocal interaction distinguished a vital body from a "dead" one. They believed that inherent active forces directed living matter. They agreed that these forces suspended normal affinity relations in order to maintain the functioning of the animal economy. They recognized the crucial role supposedly played by sympathy and synergy in the vital economy. And they accepted the idea that the occult forces directing vital matter could never be perceived directly, hence the necessity for evolving a semiotics of the living body. In explaining these concepts, they applied a metaphoric language implementing figures drawn from the world of human relations, especially ones associated with generation, love, and morality. Still, major differences emerged within this linguistic field, becoming more apparent as the battle against mechanism appeared to be successful. One of the most important centered upon the definition of vital forces and principles. Two general approaches were proposed, usually associated with two of Vitalism's most renowned representatives, Barthez and Blumenbach.

As we have seen, Barthez postulated the existence of a universal active vital principle, which he patterned upon Paracelsus's idea of the *Archeus*.[73] He defined it as an aggregate of active forces that regulated and directed the primordial laws of sympathy and synergy. It served as the first and final cause for the functioning of the organized body. Barthez interpreted the activities of the organized body as the result of the interaction between individual and compound forces of various intensities and duration. He considered all vital movements as compounds composed of at least two interacting forces, usually treated as opposites. Thus, for example, when Barthez dealt with circulation, he explained its action as the result of the competition between a unique *force circulatoire* and a *force anticirculatoire*. In working out his system, Barthez aspired to delineate an "algebra" of active forces, in which the specific unknown forces could be assigned arbitrary names, similar to the unknowns x, y, and z employed in algebra. He sought to reduce each movement of the organized body to a force diagram. Since there existed an enormous number of unique bodily movements, it followed than a much greater number of active forces existed, though all were controlled by the vital principle. Barthez envisioned the animal economy as a dynamic equilibrium called forth by the play of a vast number of opposing forces, a view he portrayed with imagination in his *Nouvelle méchanique*. Although these forces regulated matter, they did not, in Barthez's theory, inhabit matter. The relations between different organs could be seen as "produced by a sort of preestablished harmony."[74] Unlike the *solidistes*, who associated specific forces with specific organs, Barthez concentrated upon the force dynamics of bodily activity. In effect, he focused his concern on individualities and their resolution into overarching generalities; he was less concerned with establishing middle-level generalities.

Blumenbach, on the other hand, directed his efforts to defining such middle-level generalities, accounting for their operation by a limited number of active powers, locating these powers within matter, and differentiating between their competence and mode of operation. If, for Barthez, forces and principles appeared to hover *over* matter, for Blumenbach, powers, energies, and drives resided *within* matter. Specific powers "animated," or "impregnated," differentiated matter. Since "observation" showed that organized matter's species were limited, so too must be the number of active powers. For this reason, Blumenbach could accept neither Barthez's proliferation of opposing individual forces nor his insistence upon the real existence of an overarching, active vital principle. The first seemed to destroy the unity and simplicity of scientific explanation—forces could be multiplied at will. The second neglected the real variety of nature. It relegated organization to the control of a single cause that despite Barthez's protestations seemed, for Blumenbach, to resemble too much the soul of the animists or the *ratio* of the mechanists. Finally, it also suggested an analogy to the direct rule of an all-powerful monarch, serving thereby as an implicit defense of absolutism, a position that corresponded to Barthez's political views but not to Blumenbach's.[75]

Blumenbach's analysis of vital powers reflected his desire to begin with simple phenomena and to proceed to the more complex without bringing them all under the rule of a single, "royal" authority. He followed this pattern in his two popular compendia, the *Anfangsgründe der Physiologie* and his *Handbuch der vergleichende Anatomie*. Blumenbach described his goals in an anonymous review he wrote of his own *Anfangsgründe der Physiologie*: "He [Blumenbach] has constantly looked first at the *solidum vivum*, then has differentiated precisely between the different kinds of life forces, whose confusion and multiplication has led to so many of the most dangerous mistakes in medical practice. . . . He looks at the various kinds of consensus of the parts and deals with the particular functions according to the usual four classes."[76] Blumenbach postulated the existence of five active energies. He began with simple "contractibility," the equivalent of Bordeu's *vis cellulosa*, and then proceeded to "the irritability of Haller," which "resides" in muscle fibers only. Sensibility occupied the third rung in Blumenbach's ladder of vital forces. It "resides solely in the nervous medulla, communicating with the sensorium."[77] He called it the *vis nervea*. These three energies showed how Blumenbach joined the basic ideas of Haller, Bordeu, and Whytt. They represent conclusions that, in the 1770s, had become generally accepted in Germany, Great Britain, Italy, and parts of France. Blumenbach considered these energies as "common or general vital energies, because they exist . . . in almost all . . . parts of the body, which the ancients called therefore *similares*."[78] He differentiated them according to the matter they inhabited and vitalized. Contractibility could be discovered in all organized matter, irritability in much, and sensibility only in the living matter of higher life forms.[79]

The final two energies Blumenbach defined were more controversial and, therefore, more closely associated with his own attempts to formulate a science of life. Blumenbach's fourth power functioned as a wild card enabling him to introduce the element of indeterminacy into his system. He described it as follows: "There exists . . . the *vita propria* or *specific life* under which denomination I mean to arrange such powers as belong to certain particular parts of the body, destined for the performance of peculiar functions, and which cannot with any propriety be referred to either of the classes of *common energies*."[80] Here Blumenbach borrowed directly from van Helmont, Bordeu, and the *solidistes*. Blumenbach appropriated the idea to preserve the reality of individuality within the circle of organization without denying common or joint action. Each organ in the living body, because of its specific role in a functional system, had its own unique character, its own inherent life force. Thus, to cite one of Blumenbach's favorite examples, the action of the uterus can be understood only by reference to its own *vita propria*. No concurrence of common or general forces, no mechanistic principles, and certainly no invocation of the action of a self-conscious soul could explain what occurs there.

Blumenbach's introduction of the concept of the *vita propria* seemed to break from his methodological movement from the simple to complex. All parts of an organized body possessed a *vita propria*. In the simplest body, the *vita propria* and the animal were identical. Only in complex animals did the number of *vita propria* expand, increasing with the increase in the body's organs and functional tasks the organs performed. By making such an argument, it might appear that Blumenbach was guilty of the same thing he had accused Barthez of doing, namely, of multiplying living forces to a dangerous degree. There is, however, an important difference. According to Blumenbach, the *vita propria* was intimately joined to a specific form of organized matter. He considered force and matter as inextricably linked. As did contemporary chemists, Blumenbach substantialized force. Each form of matter possessed its own character. It could not be further reduced to pairs of conflicting forces. The uterus acted, Blumenbach claimed, because it was a uterus, not because uterine action resulted from the reaction between positive and negative uterine forces. Blumenbach justified this position with an analytic language borrowed from contemporary philosophy:

> Inferring synthetically, or *a priori* . . . it is not repugnant to sound induction to conclude, that parts differing from others in texture, in arrangement, and particularity in function, must also be furnished by nature with peculiar properties and powers, adapted to the performance of such specific action.
> But reasoning analytically, or *a posteriori*, we are likewise taught by accurate observations made on nature herself, that there are certain parts of the body, particularly some of the viscera, which perform motions so very singular, as cannot by any means be supposed to arise from either one or other of the common energies . . . but must be referred to a *vita propria*, or specific energies of their own.[81]

Specific life guaranteed nature's unity in diversity.

The last vital energy Blumenbach invoked became the one that made him famous. He called it the *Bildungstrieb* or *nisus formativus* and characterized it as follows: "The fifth and last energy . . . is the *nisus formativus*, or formative propensity, which should be considered as the efficient cause of the whole process of *generation* (taken in so extensive a latitude as to include both *nutrition* and *re-production* as modifications of itself)."[82] Blumenbach considered the *Bildungstrieb* present in all organized matter. In fact, of all the energies Blumenbach enumerated, the *Bildungstrieb* came closest to a universal energy existing in organized matter. It regulated change over time and accounted for the dynamic nature of living matter. Its importance for framing the way Enlightenment vitalists dealt with generation, growth, and development can hardly be overstated. I will discuss it in the next chapter, dealing with change over time.

In Blumenbach's attempt to classify the operations of living forces, the four general energies he isolated became the starting point for comprehending a complex organized body, the fifth energy, the *vita propria* allowed for manifold variation within specific species, types, and individuals. For most Enlightenment vitalists, the sympathetic and syngergistic relations between individual organs constituted only one part of the complicated interchanges of an organized body. They realized that certain organs worked together within a larger system designed to perform specific functions. Thus, as Lavoisier had expanded his vision from single chemical interactions to larger chemical ones (e.g. from acids to acidification), so too did Enlightenment life scientists turn their attention to systemic functional analysis. In addition to dealing with individual vital energies, they ascribed vital functions and activities to "composite" systems within the vital economy.

Blumenbach's discussion of the "four classes" of functions mirrored vitalist thought of the late 1770s. The four he discerned were (1) *vital functions*, basic to all living things; (2) *animal functions*, whose job was to maintain "an uninterrupted commerce and intercourse between the body and the various faculties of the mind," a class that included the two great subdivisions, sensation and "muscular motion"; (3) *natural functions:* nutrition and the reproduction of existing matter; and (4) *genital functions*, "which are destined for . . . the propagation of the species."[83] However, as physiological investigation and observation proceeded, Enlightenment vitalists expanded the number of functional systems within the organized body, each centered about a specific group of organs. Thus, for example, Dumas listed seven systems: (1) the skeletal or foundational system, (2) the muscular or irritable system, (3) the nervous or sensible system, (4) the vascular or heat-generating system, (5) the intestinal or replenishment system, (6) the lymphatic, glandular, or absorption and retentional system, and (7) the sexual or reproductive system.[84] No matter how one grouped these varied activities, Enlightenment vitalists assumed that the functions they discerned could be compared across species and genera. These systems functioned analogically, though the specifics of the reactions depended upon the constitution of the organized body under consideration. It became an accepted proposition that all organized bodies were equipped to do their job in unique and different ways. Life's activities depended upon a dynamic interchange between organs, solids, fluids, powers, and functional systems.

· · ·

Of all the body's functional systems, the one that proved the most important and the most difficult to discern was that directed by "sensibility." For it became the focus for one's attempt to understand how ideas were generated, to define the relationship between sensibility and consciousness, and, on the most elevated level, to comprehend human nature. This system comprised organs tied together by immediate connections, by analogous (sympathetic) ones, and even by connections considered more mysterious. It included the "organs of the *cerebrum*, the *cerebellum*, and their appendage the *medulla spiralis*, together with the nerves that originate from these sources." This system could be further subdivided into two classes, "namely, the *Sensorium* and *Nerves*."[85] For the majority of Enlightenment vitalists, the nervous system became a primary area of inquiry and reflection in physiology, comparative anatomy, psychology, and physical anthropology. Its analysis emerged as one of the most contested areas within Enlightenment vitalism.

Enlightenment vitalists considered the nervous system critically important because of its mediating role in linking body and mind.[86] Its analysis formed part of the larger mind/body problem that had exercised many of the greatest thinkers of the late seventeenth and the early eighteenth century and played a central role in vitalism's attack on mechanism. In approaching their study, vitalist life scientists were convinced that they were better able to explain the phenomenon than earlier, speculative philosophers because their arguments were founded upon physiological "facts." As the Berlin physician Marcus Herz and the young Friedrich Schiller (then aspiring to become a doctor of medicine) argued, the time had come to free experiential psychology *(Erfahrungs-Psychologie)* and "philosophical physiology" from metaphysics and make it a science.[87]

In this quest, all Enlightenment vitalists assumed an intimate union existed between mind and matter, effected either through the agency of sympathy, animated fluids, active powers, and/or some combination of them. Although not all vitalists would locate sensibility solely within the nervous system,[88] the majority did.

Blumenbach, accepting this proposition, defined the nervous system as "a complete system . . . beautifully constructed, which . . . serves as the medium of communication and mutual intercourse between the body and mind."[89] Such a definition blurred the strict mechanist mind/body distinction without accepting the mind-dominance alternative of the animists. But how the nerves mediated between sense impression and idea formation proved extremely difficult to comprehend. To arrive at an answer, Vitalists concentrated on three analytic questions: How did sense organs process stimuli? How were they communicated to the sensorium or brain? And how did the sensorium translate them into ideas?

Understanding the operation of the sense organs, initial receivers of external impressions, posed a protean challenge. As Blumenbach remarked, "no other class belonging to the animal economy, is subjected to such an astonishing variety in different individuals, as that of the external senses." For that reason, the analysis of the "instruments of sensation" had generated countless disputes.[90] Blumenbach located one source for these disputes in the mistaken propensity to draw generalized explanations using analogies drawn from humans. It had been assumed "that animals that have a tongue must therefore be able to taste with it, or, to take an opposite example, that animals without a nose cannot smell."[91] But such was not the case. There were many animals, for example, birds, whose tongues had other uses than for tasting, and there were animals, especially insects, that could smell but had no noses. Blumenbach warned against confounding the instrument with the work being done, the structure with the function.

Marcus Herz saw another difficulty to be overcome in analyzing the sense organs. Too often life scientists concentrated upon one sense, usually sight, and used it as a model to explain the others. Seeing served as the model for all sense impressions. But, Herz argued, seeing depended upon the unique construction of the sight organs and their mode of operation. Each sense organ received stimuli in different ways, hence "conclusions drawn from the analogy of the eye are certainly not binding."[92] Enlightenment vitalists attempted to overcome these difficulties by ascribing a unique organization, mode of operation, and form of apprehension to each sense organ. Each instrument had its own unique activity and form designed to process incoming information according to the internal needs of the species. The vitalists focused upon functional analogies, minimizing the importance of homologies and structural analogies between different organs.

Given the imperative to abandon structural identities in favor of functional similarity, many vitalist life scientists ascribed active powers to the instruments of sensation, modifying thereby the simple mechanist image in which stimuli were seen as passing directly and unprocessed to the sensorium. As an example, John Elliot argued that the organs of hearing possessed their own internal tonal scale, their own possible harmonies. Hearing entailed a sympathetic reaction between external sound and the inherent sounds of the ear.[93] Bonnet believed the same applied to all sensations: "Colors are in us; they are certain modifications of our soul, and it is the same with all of our perceptions and sensations. Sound, smell, taste are as little in the objects as color. All of these relations have their source in the differences between the tools by which the soul judges things."[94] Already in dealing with external sense impression, the vitalist concentration upon internal forces and functional systems modified the earlier ideas of mechanical impression and reception, rejecting direct translation from outer stimulation to inner sense.

After the sense organs processed the first impressions, they communicated them to the nerves whose task was to "convey and announce," the impressions "like active heralds to the sensorium and there give rise to perception."[95] How was this accomplished? Four alternative answers were debated by the late 1770s. The first, inspired by the mechanists, argued that a fine fluid translated the impressions to the brain, acting as a simple conduit. The second answer, formulated by the *solidistes*, saw nerves as analogues to strings in an instrument. When struck they would vibrate creating sympathetic vibrations in the sensorium, a similar, though much grander, stringed instrument. The third solution drew upon the idea of the existence of differentiated subtle fluids,[96] which translated the message to the medium. The fourth solution ascribed the transmission to a basic force, a *vis nervie*[97] or *Nervenkraft*, that linked the brain and the nerves by "unique, unknown and special laws, which totally diverge from already known laws" and are derived from their nature.[98]

Over time, Enlightenment vitalists increasingly tended toward the fourth solution, chipping away at the remaining elements of mechanism that invoked matter in motion, in favor of one concentrating upon the activities of substantialized force. Friedrich Schiller's and Marcus Herz's attempts to explain the mind-body relation are indicative of this development. Schiller addressed the question of the transmission of impressions through the nerves in his first medical dissertation, *The Philosophy of Physiology* (1779), which the medical faculty at the Stuttgart Karlsschule rejected because of Schiller's disrespect for traditional authorities, especially Haller.[99] In it, Schiller judged the first three solutions as insufficient to explain the complexity of sense transmission. While providing well-argued reasons why each explanation failed, Schiller's basic rhetorical approach feigned skepticism, questioning whether any answer could be posited: "I am in a field where many a medical and metaphysical *Don Quixote* has entered the lists and is still riding furiously to and fro. Should I disturb the spirits of the dead and buried, or arouse the sensitive souls of the intellectually dead with old objections, or produce a new theory and perform the role of a *deus ex machina*? I shall do none of these things."[100] But what was left to do after such a statement? Either desist from providing an explanation, which is not what Schiller desired, or enter the lists whether he liked it or not. This he did with élan, his pretensions to skepticism serving merely as a cover for an asserted attack.

Schiller turned to active force for his solution. He began his discussion of force by raising the question that had separated Leibniz and Newton concerning God's power, namely, whether God is all cognition or all will.

Both answers were, for Schiller, inadequate. The first elevated necessity, saw no relation between mind and matter except that of a preestablished harmony, and thereby denied human freedom and human happiness: "Freedom and moral education would be phantoms. Happiness a dream." The second allowed spirit to act on matter, but in so doing elevated chance and by extension miraculous intervention. But "miracles betray a blemish in the design of the world."[101]

What then is the answer? Schiller suggested one: "There must be a force at work that mediates between mind and matter and unites them. A force, which can be altered by matter and which can alter the mind. This would be a force which is spiritual on the one hand and material on the other, an entity that is penetrable on the one hand and impenetrable on the other." After posing the possibility, Schiller asked whether such a force was rationally conceivable and answered, "Of course not!" But that did not close the question, it just pointed to rationalism's weakness. For "brute facts" affirmed what reason denied: "Be that as it may, a force in fact exists between matter . . . and mind. This force is quite distinct from the world and the mind. If I remove it, the world can have no effect on the mind. And yet the mind still exists, and the object still exists. Its disappearance has created a rift between world and mind. Its presence illuminates, awakens, animates everything about it—I shall call it the transmutative force."[102] Schiller located this force in the nerves. It served as the concrete and symbolic substance mediating between sense impressions and idea formation. It conveyed its message to mind because it resided "in an infinitely subtle, simple and mobile substance, which flows through the nerve, its channel, and which I call not elemental fire, nor light, nor ether, not electrical or magnetic matter, but nerve spirit *[Nervengeist]*."[103] Thus the force makes changes in the nerve spirit, which effects the sensorium. Still, for Schiller, the fluid quality of the nerve spirit played a role in the transmission of ideas through its back and forth movement. The specter of mechanism still hovered over his theory.

Herz followed a similar explanatory strategy in his important work, *Versuch über den Schwindel* (1786; 2nd ed., 1788), but went farther in deleting mechanistic overtones. Herz also argued for the "mutual connection between mind and body," considered the nerves crucial in the transmission of ideas,[104] and believed nerve fluid the physical mediator between sense organs and the sensorium. Although Herz introduced substantialized matter as a mediating link, he divested it of any effect founded upon movement or collision. Instead, Herz employed analogies taken from elective affinities and especially from magnetic force relations. He compared what happened in the nerve fluid to the result of holding the opposite poles of two magnets at a given distance. They constituted a specific attractive drive *(Anziehungstrieb)* that could not be destroyed by any movement. This attractive drive locked organs and sensorium together in a constant and reciprocal force field.[105] Increasingly, Enlightenment vitalists turned to images of substantialized force or drive to explain phenomena in the vital economy, enshrining their desire to mediate between extremes through the medium of the extended middle, represented by the merging of forces with fluids.

This fusion of force with fluid could take extreme and sometimes bizarre forms. The renowned comparative anatomist Samuel Thomas Sömmerring offers such an example in the attempt he made to define and locate the "organ of the soul." Sömmerring, an anatomist, concentrated upon spatial analysis and therefore sought to locate the place from which animal life received direction. He very well knew the difficulties associated with such an undertaking. Like Whytt before him, Sömmerring recognized that no single location had been discovered where all nerve endings met. But that did not deter him, for he believed researchers had failed because they looked at the wrong thing. They concentrated upon the solid parts of the brain, seeking structures resembling normal organs. Sömmerring argued that the brain area housed a cavity around which all of the system's activities seemed to revolve and that a liquid *(acqua Venticulorum Cerebri)* filled this cavity, forming the common element uniting all nerve endings. He then raised the question whether liquids could be animated, answered it in the affirmative, and drew the conclusion that the organ of the soul must reside in the animated liquid of the brain.[106] This was a bold step, for even those anatomists and physiologists who accepted the existence of animated fluids did not believe animated fluids could be organs. Sömmerring countered that the "soul" required a fluid organ, since a solid, rigid mass could never register the subtle movements of the nerves or nerve fluid. A fluid organ became the reified expression of the physical mediation between mind and body, an anatomical representation of the extended middle: "The uniting middle substance [vereinigende Mittelding], medium uniens, consequently would be the fluid of the brain cavity."[107]

Sömmerring dedicated the *Organ of the Soul* to Kant and filled it with references to Kant's work. Kant, however, did not receive it with enthusiasm. He questioned whether an organ could be a fluid, whether fluids could be animated, and if so, whether this specific fluid was animated. His conclusion: the fluid of the brain's cavity was ordinary water! Sömmerring's suggestion and Kant's response illustrates some of the tensions within Enlightenment Vitalism generated by the inherent structural difficulties of joining contradictories without subsuming them in an overarching unity. Their dispute led to a heated discussion focusing upon the question of whether fluids could be animated (all accepted the proposition that solids could be animated) and if so, which ones. In the exchange of letters and reviews, Goethe provided the wisest answer, defending the major assumptions of Enlightened Vitalism, while invoking its epistemological modesty to warn against pushing its assumptions too far. Goethe chided Sömmerring for his choice of title and method: the first disturbs physiologists and philosophers alike; the second awakens mistrust in anyone wary of a-priori reasoning. Why, he asked, talk about the a-priori question of whether the "liquid in the brain cavity contains the general sensorium, since no one can know anything a-priori about either the brain's cavity or its liquid." Why raise questions about the possibility of a fluid being animated, especially when the term was misleading: Sömmerring should have employed the more modest term *belebt* (vivified or vitalized). Finally Goethe questioned Sömmerring's use of the term "soul": "You should also, *meo voto*, have not mentioned the soul; the philosopher knows nothing about it, and the physiologists should not even think about it." In short, Sömmerring should have left the philosophers out of the picture.[108] Goethe's final piece of advice reflected the self-image Enlightenment vitalists had forged for themselves as antispeculative students of facts and real phenomena: "why should we empiricists and realists not learn our limits *[Kreis]* and understand our advantages? At the most, we should perhaps listen to the philosophers when they criticize the powers of understanding with which we necessarily must apprehend substances."[109]

Life scientists unwilling to accept the existence of an organ of the soul, a *sensorium commune*, defined the sensorium as an intricate functional system in which the brain played, at most, a supporting role. Blumenbach made this clear when he asserted it incorrect to single out any part of the nervous system as "the very seat, and royal court (as it were) of the mind."[110] The sensorium consisted of a conjunction of energies and energy centers, each cooperating to make the system work. The system's activities were further complicated because it was involved in a sympathetic feedback system of amazing intensity and variety, making its activities even more difficult to comprehend. This "extensive and diversified consent of the *nervous system*" explained how the passions of the mind or the imagination could affect the human body.[111] The nervous system functioned as all vital ones. Although too mysterious to be fully understood, its operation depended upon an assumed affinity between the mind's faculties (perception, attention, memory, imagination, will, and reason), vital energies, and the overarching effects of the great animal functional systems.

. . .

The images of consent and sympathy linking all forces of nature, including reciprocal relations between an organized body and its outside stimulus, emerged as central tropes in Enlightenment Vitalism's language of nature. Its ambitious joining of all aspects of life in an explanatory structure denying identity and causal relations also engendered an enormous number of disputes within this discursive field, as the above discussions concerning vital forces and the sensorium illustrate. The same occurred when vitalists applied these tropes to defining individual uniqueness. To comprehend this category, Enlightenment vitalists reinvigorated the ancient doctrine of the temperaments, because they believed that living bodies, though different in form, structure, and origin, demonstrated similar functional activities, which varied among individuals within the same species. Each individual possessed its own degree of "irritability," dependent upon the individual specimen's "degree of perfection and energy."[112]

Leading Enlightenment vitalists considered life a primordial phenomenon existing between the parameters of maximum and minimum life, *vita maxima* and *vita minima*. The two extremes defined the outer reaches of the circle of organization for each species. Within this circle life manifested itself in varying degrees of intensities of irritability, which could be classified according to the individual's degree of activity or indolence. This endeavor paralleled the classificatory procedures of affinity chemistry and the medical-pathological ones of nosology. Late-eighteenth-century life scientists referred to life's activities as the temperaments, a term sometimes reserved for humans, though over time extended to all other organized bodies, including plants.

The theory of the temperaments is ancient, stretching back at least to Galen. It had played an important role in medical practice and theory, at least, until the advent of mechanistic medicine, which relegated it to the category of a secondary characteristic. Although demeaned by leading mechanistic theorists, it did not totally disappear from Europe's intellectual landscape. Stahl and other early-eighteenth-century animists held on to it, and it lived on in folk medicine and folklore virtually untouched by the new mechanist theories. The antimechanistic physicians and medical theorists, drawing intellectual nourishment from the ancients and Stahl, revived it at midcentury. Although most late-eighteenth-century medical theorists adopted the theory of temperaments, a crucial question was whether temperaments were ontologically real or just heuristic devices enabling one to introduce order to account for the vast variety of individuals within a living species. The controversy replicated the battle waged by contemporary chemists concerning the degree to which affinity relations were fixed or variable.

The most convinced proponents of the theory of temperaments were the "neo-Stahlians," physicians of Montpellier and their sympathizers, who in this instance propounded a simplified version of Stahl's position. They defined temperaments as ontologically real. Temperaments existed in nature independently of the observer, for they expressed the relations between a body's solid and fluid parts. As a rule, most late-eighteenth-century neo-Stahlians postulated four primary temperaments (analogues to Stahl's primary chemical principles): the phlegmatic, the sanguineous, the choleric, and the melancholic, though a few medical writers tried to expand that number to introduce more variations, including, in one case, a "peasant" or "donkey like-temperament."[113] Neo-Stahlian theory treated temperaments as reifications of material relations. Certain outward signs announced the internal essence constituting an individual. Thus, for example, Roussel characterized the sanguineous temperament, which he believed dominant in females, as follows: "The sanguine temperament requires solid parts of a porous, sponge-like type and a not overly concentrated blood, which could circulate freely. One can recognize this temperament by a portly, full form, fleshy limbs, and a rosy skin color."[114]

But temperaments were more than the physical attributes announced by external bodily signs. Every temperament had its own "moral character," its own set of "passions." Each formed a self-contained entity joining the physical and the moral. This assumption authorized the creation of a semiotics of the soul. Roussel provided a typical Stahlian definition of this juncture between the body and morality: "The moral character peculiar to each temperament is derived from the degree of ease which the fluids have in their circulation and therefore are determined according to the degree of regularity in which life activities take place. If they proceed easily, then the soul experiences a certain calm and security, which can clearly be discerned in all of the moral manifestations of the individual. One sees how those who have a sanguine temperament, that is, where all of the bodily activities transpire in the easiest manner, have a very jovial, resolute, and free character."[115] Neo-Stahlians provided similar descriptions of the other temperaments. For example, the moral signs of "mistrust and timidity" characterized the melancholic temperament, generated "because the cellular texture . . . had broad and large openings" and "the blood and the fluids were thick and tough."[116]

According to Stahl these physical-moral relations, though initially fixed, could be altered through the action of the conscious rational soul (a type of physical rebirth accompanying a spiritual one). Later theorists excluded the action of the soul and saw the four categories as defining the real relations between the solid and the liquid, the static and the dynamic, the physical and the moral. The neo-Stahlian approach shorn of its religious overtones undergirded the search for a formalistic semiotics of the soul, for assuming a strict and invariable connection between outer and inner reality, between physical characteristics and moral nature. It found its most exaggerated expression in the late eighteenth century's fascination for physiognomy.

Opponents to this essentialist approach considered temperaments as nothing more than a useful heuristic. Neither anatomy nor the simple relation between solid and liquid parts of the body shaped human character. Rather, the interaction between living forces within the organism and between individual will and the outside world accounted for moral and physical character.[117] Kant propounded this position in his *Anthropologie*, where he juxtaposed what nature gives us (a temperament) and what we make of ourselves (a character), framed in a language drawn equally from Enlightenment and Pietistic assumptions, and employing the metaphors of "rebirth" and "revolution":

> The person who is conscious of the character in his mode of thinking does not have that character by nature, but must always acquire it. One may also take it for granted that the establishment of character is similar to a kind of rebirth, a certain solemn resolution, which the person himself makes. This resolution and the moment at which the transformation took place remain unforgettable for him, like the beginning of a new epoch. This stability and persistence in principles can generally not be effected by education, examples, and instruction by degrees, but it can only be done by an explosion, which suddenly occurs as a consequence of our disgust at the unsteady condition of instinct. Perhaps there will be a few who have attempted this revolution before their thirtieth year, and fewer still who have established it before their fortieth year.[118]

In redefining the temperaments in this manner, Kant joined those critical of postulating static, determined character traits founded upon the idea of fixed temperaments or characteristics, a position Blumenbach employed in his discussion of human variety.[119] They expanded the definition of temperaments to include active energies and their attendant functional activities that regulated and guided the animal economy: "The constitution of the temperaments depends, not only on the proportion and mixture of the constituent parts of the blood, but also on the peculiar vigor of the vital energies ... and likewise on the consequent variety in the mode of the reciprocal action and reaction of the body and the mind on each other."[120] When they introduced the agency of function, energy, and reciprocal interaction in shaping and modifying temperaments, Blumenbach and Metzger did the same for the theory of sentiments as Bergman and Berthollet had done for the idea of elective chemical affinity. They dissolved the hard and fast boundaries that separated, defined, and classified the temperaments.

According to Blumenbach, the "varieties of temperaments were literally infinite and can never be reduced to any certain and definitive class."[121] Metzger expressed the same idea: "Therefore, one can postulate two, four, eight, twelve temperaments; no matter, one is required to admit an infinite number of subcategories."[122] In short, while Metzger and Blumenbach denied the existence of the Great Chain of Being connecting species (each species was unique to itself), they argued as had Buffon before them for a form of infinite gradation or continuity within species. An infinity of possible combinations existed within the limits assigned to any living species. Both Metzger and Blumenbach negated any theory grounded upon hard and fast distinctions in character or temperament. Still, for both the concept of temperament proved useful, providing one recognized its purely heuristic and instrumentalist function. When this was done, "we may," Blumenbach remarked, "give our assent with sufficient propriety to the common mode of arrangement."[123]

But Blumenbach weakened this affirmation by introducing another observation that further modified the original theory. Not only could one speak of different temperaments existing among individuals, one could also discern a progressive change in temperamental structure within specific individuals: "Thus, in the tender age of infancy the *phlegmatic* temperament chiefly prevails. This, in youth, is exchanged for the *sanguineous*. The *choleric* marks the period of adulthood. And the *melancholic* is the temperament of old age."[124] Blumenbach not only relativized the concept of temperaments, he temporalized it, adding an even greater indeterminacy to its application: "The variety in the existing degrees of the same, and in the mixtures of different temperaments, is so unbounded, as to afford an open and a very extensive field of speculation to such as would wish to amuse themselves with tracing out, and establishing, on this subject, more minute combinations, or divisions and orders."[125] Whatever amusement one had in charting this "unbounded" field—an implicit critique of Linnaean over classification and Lavater's physiognomic reductionism—Blumenbach made it clear that a full understanding of the vital economy could not focus solely upon the relations existing within the circle of organization. This assumption, which most Enlightenment vitalists shared to a greater or lesser extent, led to the interest in investigating the organization's development, arguing that all living entities were part of an eternally dynamic universe, involving both interchange and transformation. As John E. Larson made clear in his discussion of the eighteenth-century naturalist Peter Simon Pallas, the question of linking the two axes around which the life sciences were organized was central: "Pallas . . . was preoccupied from the beginning of his career by the dual axes along which the objects of his study were located: the axis of simultaneity, where his contemporaries charted relations among coexisting forms, and the axes of succession, where as Buffon had suggested, the repetitions and variations of form were located."[126] This second axis, the fascination with diachronic development joined to the concern for vital interconnection, forms the second core element defining Enlightenment Vitalism's language of nature.

4 The Metamorphoses of Change

GENERATION, REPRODUCTION, AND THE ECONOMY OF NATURE

Organic interconnection constituted a basic pillar supporting Enlightenment Vitalism. It accounted for self-organization and complex interaction, and employed the metaphors of affinity, synergy, and sympathy that were proposed at midcentury but worked out extensively after the 1760s.[1] However, if left standing alone, this vision of nature's economy easily could have been reduced to one espousing the static, mechanistic images of balance and equilibrium and mobilized to legitimate the status quo in religious, political, or social terms. To counter these dangers, Enlightenment vitalists evolved a theory of change over time to complement and modify their discussion of the circle of organization. It emphasized new creation, sharp breaks, and directional change. From the mid-eighteenth century to the end of the Enlightenment, natural historians, physiologists, comparative anatomists, and physicians forged new explanations to account for the creation and cessation of life, the development of individual life forms, and the history of species, processes governed by the universal principle of qualitative transformation.[2]

The first theme they focused upon was generation, crucial to understanding how life began and what it was. When Buffon and Maupertuis resurrected epigenesis in the middle of the century, they initiated a conflict between epigenesists and preformationists that raged unabated for decades. The battle was long and bitter, partly because it was fought over the same fund of empirical data,[3] but more importantly because it spoke to crucial religious, political, and social questions. Epigenesis threatened established authority, questioning foundations established to worship God and vener-

160 / *The Metamorphoses of Change*

ate social hierarchies. At the midcentury, preformation offered the most impressive testimony to God's majesty and greatness, transcending or even supplementing scriptural interpretations. John C. Cook, an English physicotheologian, expressed this view in 1762 on how we should look at creation:

> But when he comes to look back on the Beginning of Things, and takes a thorough View of his own long and hidden Pre-existence, ever since the Creation; . . . he will be struck with fresh Wonder, and be lost in deep Adoration and Amazement; till, by laying his Hand on his Mouth, and Humility to his Heart, at last must acknowledge that great is our God indeed. . . . I say again, if we nicely behold ourselves while yet in Miniature, floating at first in our first Parent's Loins . . . how can we sufficiently love, serve, and adore his supreme Majesty, the Maker of Heavens and Earth, and of all Animals therein also? For he, in a literal Sense, *made us, and we not ourselves;* much less our Parents; and we are thence emphatically *his People, and the Sheep of his Pasture*.[4]

Kant, never desirous of being a sheep God's pasture, serves as a witness to the fact that during the 1750s and early 1760s no self-evident solution to the problem of generation had been reached. In *Der einzig mögliche Beweisgrund zu einer Demonstration des Daseyn Gottes* (1763), Kant proposed a new form of physicotheology that avoided the pitfalls of the normal conservative physicotheology yet still affirmed the Supreme Being's dignity. Focusing upon the questions raised by the Leibniz-Newtonian debate concerning God's essence, Kant attempted to mediate between the two original positions (God as will, God as logos). He accepted the proposition that the Supreme Being freely chose to create the existing world but added that God instituted basic laws that operated independently in nature. This enabled a person to explain physical phenomena mechanistically, in the sense that God did not directly dictate them. Kant had little difficulty diagramming the mechanical forces of nature, describing how, following Maupertuis's law of least action, the principles of matter, reciprocal interaction, and the laws of motion accounted for the vast multiplicity of the physical world.

The world of living nature presented Kant with a greater problem; he considered it absurd to explain living nature with simple mechanical laws. But he also could not choose between the two contending explanations, preformation, "where every individual is directly constructed by God (therefore making its origins supernatural), and whose propagation proceeds by 'development,'" or epigenesis, where "some individuals of the plant and animal kingdom . . . are endowed with a capacity, . . . enabling them to generate their own kind (not just to develop them) according to regular natural laws." In 1763 Kant announced that the "answer . . . has yet to be decided," for he considered both Buffon's and Maupertuis's explanations and those of the preformationists "arbitrary speculations";[5] they were neither science nor sound philosophy.

In 1790 Kant returned to the question of living matter's generation in his *Critique of Judgment*. Once again he asserted the impossibility of explaining organization in mechanical terms, stating that no one "can hope to understand the generation of even a blade of grass by mere mechanical causes."[6] He also characterized preformation or "evolution" and epigenesis or "genetic preformation" in the same manner as he had in 1763. He used the same images including a veiled reference to Buffon's internal mold and Maupertuis's "law of least action."[7] Yet this time Kant made his preference clear, opting for epigenesis as the only rational explanation for generation because it "considers nature . . . as self-generating, not merely as developed." In epigenesis "everything, except the most minimal expenditure of the supernatural, is derived from the first beginnings of nature, without, however, attempting to determine its first beginnings."[8] Obviously something had happened within the span of twenty-seven years to convince Kant that epigenesis provided the only reasonable answer to the question of generation.

For many a modern reader, the real question concerning Kant's two texts might be why didn't he opt for epigenesis in 1763? Why did he wait until the end of the eighteenth century to assert the epigenicist position? One answer is that when Kant first posed the question, Albrecht von Haller and Charles Bonnet, two of the age's most renowned naturalists, had initiated a major counteroffensive challenging all of epigenesis's claims. They received support from other leading naturalists such as Lazzaro Spallanzani and Jean Senebier. That Haller and Bonnet, often hailed as pioneers in forming the new language of vitalism, emerged as spokesmen for divine preformation illustrates the tensions accompanying the language's construction.

. . .

Albrecht von Haller initiated the counterattack on epigenesis after a short flirtation with it when Buffon's *Histoire* first appeared.[9] Tormented by the belief that epigenesis led directly to "materialism," which he equated with atheism, Haller sought religious and scientific refuge in preformation. He felt especially uneasy about the theological implications raised by posing the existence of formative force (a force operating according to its own volition). If such things existed there was no need for God's active intervention in the world. Haller denied formative force's existence, arguing that all forces acted "blindly," that is, in a constant and simple manner, precluding an ability to form differentiated organized matter. To prove this position, Haller undertook a serious investigation of animal reproduction, leading him to a supposed discovery that he and Bonnet considered equal to the "discovery" of irritability. Haller concentrated his studies on the reproduction of chickens. In 1758 he read a paper before the Göttingen Academy of Sciences announcing a "conclusive proof " *(argumentum crucis)* for ovist preformation (now referred to as the membrane-continuity proof). Haller claimed that "he found that the membrane of the yolk of an incubated egg was a continuation of the membrane of the chick's intestines and that its blood vessels . . . were a continuation of the chick's. Since the egg yolk and its membrane existed in the hen previous to impregnation so too must the embryo, though it was too small to be discovered by our eyes."[10] In addition to its minute size, Haller argued that the preformed embryo was liquid and transparent, making it impossible to observe, proposing therefore that an organized body could be liquid well before Sömmerring.

Although reaffirming ovist preformation, Haller imaginatively altered its traditional argument by asserting that the preformed embryo did not possess the exact form of an adult chicken. Rather, its organs were wrapped around each other in the egg, waiting to exfoliate. When fertilization took place, the semen stimulated the heart, which because of its high degree of irritability immediately began to beat, initiating the process of development, which proceeded mechanically. The heart pumping fluids through the transparent, preformed embryo induced some of its parts to solidify and become visible earlier than others. Development included a twofold process: the shift from transparency to visibility and the expansion and reordering of the embryo's parts. With this highly sophisticated modification of traditional preformationist views, Haller accounted for the normally observed stages of embryonic development without accepting the reality of epigensis.[11] For this reason, he argued, mere observation of the developmental process could never settle the question of generation; only crucial observations such as the membrane tie counted.

Bonnet took up Haller's argument and used it to launch an attack against the "systems founded upon *épigénèse,* especially those of MM. Buffon and Needham," who "lost themselves in the night of conjecture," preferring "romances to history." Bonnet directed his diatribes to those who failed to see "that the yolk is the intestines of the chick."[12] To bring light back into natural history, Bonnet used the "torch of philosophy" to formulate a physicotheology organized around the major themes of divine providence and the Great Chain of Being. Bonnet's position and the responses it elicited allow us to diagram the development of Enlightenment

Vitalism's language of nature concerning change over time, revealing the fault lines that developed between a religiously inspired antimechanism, focusing primarily upon organic interconnection and a more secular version of antimechanism, emphasizing the reality of qualitative, nondeterminate change within organic bodies.

According to Bonnet, Haller's discovery of the membrane continuation theory didn't merely explain the chick's development: it proved both universal preformation and the "pre-existence of the organic whole." It demonstrated "order and purpose," resulting in an infinite harmonic connection attesting to the knowledge and power of "an effecting will," which "brought forth this cosmic structure and still maintains it. That will was God and shall be God. What He wished, He still wishes." Bonnet joined Newton to Leibniz, asserting that a combined mind and will created and maintains the universe: "The object of power was also the object of wisdom."[13] In his argument Bonnet combined the two concepts of divine purpose or teleology generated during the heated discussions that had raged throughout the late seventeenth and early eighteenth centuries. The first and oldest referred to the final cause or end of things, typical of Aristotelian thought. Final ends were qualities in the making, the end point toward which a body strove, defining its "natural state," an asymmetrical process, often illustrated by the example of the acorn and the oak. Although the oak may be contained in the acorn, the acorn naturally develops into an oak, not vice versa.[14] In this form telos could contain "progressive" or "revolutionary" moments. Telos's second definition emphasized function, judging something by the role it occupied in the world order, most clearly expressed by the idea of sufficient reason. A thing's function is its purpose, attesting to divine wisdom where nothing is created in vain, proclaiming that whatever is, is right in this best of all possible worlds.

Bonnet wove both explanations together, abrogating any possibility of qualitative change over time. Divine will and logic had created an infinitely interconnected world constituting a spatio-temporal unity: "This unbounded system of conterminously existing and successively following things is not less a single unity in succession as in construction." Bonnet supported his uniting of the two ideas of divine purpose by affirming the existence of the Great Chain of Being. Everything was interconnected, constituting a harmony from which "springs the subordination of things and their connection to space and time." No space could be unfilled, no leap in nature possible, for "nature does not tolerate a leap; everything proceeds in nature by gradations and at the same time through shadings. If there were an empty space between two things, then what reason could account for the transition from the one to the other? For that reason no substance exists that does not have ones below and above it, which approach it through some characteristics and separate it through others."[15] According to Bonnet and naturalists such as Antoine-Laurent de Jussieu who shared this view, "natura non facit saltus."[16]

Bonnet's idea of the Great Chain of Being differed substantially from the "ladders of organization" invoked by many Enlightenment vitalists. A ladder implied a series of defined steps tracing the progress or regression of organized bodies, where each step was independent, not a "shading." Buffon's definition of species provided such a model, where the ability to produce fruitful offspring served as an unbridgeable barrier separating species, no matter how they might resemble each other. Bonnet elevated shadings. He considered species to be merely a heuristic category helpful to satisfy our need to know.[17] Bonnet sought to demonstrate nature's fixed interconnections in his *Contemplation de la nature*, where he ranged over nature's whole spectrum, arguing for infinitive overlap.

But he encountered a host of problems when he dealt with animal reproduction, which forced him to formulate a theory of preformation whose major points came very close to epigenesis. He called his theory "palingenesis" and believed it answered the major objections epigenesists had raised about preformation, namely, that it failed to account for abnormal births (monstrosities), for resemblance between parents and offspring, for hybrids, and for the reproduction of simple animals like polyps. Although Bonnet retained some elements of divine preformation such as the idea of encasement *(emboîtment)*, he introduced important modifications, the most significant being Haller's claim that the preexistent germ did not resemble the finished product, its parts being "disarrayed" in the egg.[18] Thus, Bonnet assumed some sort of internal shaping in the "developmental process." He used the disparity between disarrayed parts and final product to account for abnormal births. Since the difference between the original disarray and the end product was great, mistakes, wrong turns, and one-sided expansion or contraction appeared possible.[19] Bonnet also redefined the role of male semen, elevating it to a nourishing fluid rather than a mere stimulant. It penetrated the germ, effecting great changes within the embryo.[20] In this way he believed he could account for the resemblance between parents and children.

Bonnet's reinterpretation of the seminal fluid's activities brought him very close to Buffon's description of the mutual exchange between male and female agents in the process of generation. According to Bonnet, semen united with the germ in an actual physical union, stimulating some of the preformed organs to grow faster than others, causing distinct growth patterns and emerging characteristics in the embryo's final form. As Buffon had, he also defined semen as a composite of all the parts of the male organism. Still, Bonnet refused to accord it any active agency: "The seminal fluid did not create anything; it can alter only that which is already present. It does not generate the chick, which already was present before fertilization. Growth is the result of nourishment, which results from the incorporation of the seminal fluid in various parts of the germ."[21] Bonnet's treatment of semen illustrates his desire to include elements of indeterminacy into his explanations for differentiated development. His discursive practices undermined his original theories of telos, necessity, and purpose because of his need to frame his position in a modern language acceptable to his readers. He defined the preexistent and preformed germ so vaguely that it could easily be understood metaphorically (e.g., as a tendency or predisposition within a substance), its preformation demonstrated very little form, and the embryo's development seemed much more precarious and open to influence from the male seminal fluid than traditional ovarian preformationists had postulated or would accept.

. . .

When Bonnet composed his last great synthetic work, the *Paligénése philosophique* in 1769, the tide against preformation had grown to major proportions, though there still remained a committed core of supporters throughout Europe.[22] However, epigenesis's acceptance varied greatly. It occurred more quickly in France and Great Britain, largely due to the influence of "philosophic physicians" who advocated a return to Hippocrates's principles.[23] By the early 1770s the Hippocratic explanation had won over a majority of leading physicians in France and Great Britain. Roussel offers a typical example, adopting Hippocrates's theory and adding to it the idea of active forces. Each of the combining male and female genital fluids possessed a unique capacity *(genie)* or degree of activity. Their mixture generated a new organism endowed with an active principle, the *faculté generatrice*, which directed its general development. The quantity, quality, and intensity of the genital fluids determined the organism's gender, form, and character. The stronger the female fluid's *genie*, the more the child resembled the mother and vice versa. The overall strength of one of the mixing fluids accounted for the child's gender, yet its specific characteristics depended upon the localized strength of one or other of the fluids. When fertilization took place, the fetus's formation did not occur at once but passed through a steplike process instigated by and guided by the *faculté generatrice*. What was true in the womb was equally true once birth took place: "The history of animal life consists of a series of successive transitions. Each segment of life is characterized by its own unique natural drives."[24] This order of development is generally the same for all members of the species, varying only in duration and specification.

In Germany acceptance of epigenesis proved more difficult, not achieved until after Haller's death in 1778. Johann Friedrich Blumenbach, originally an ovarian preformationist, played the central role in sealing its victory. In 1779 he tentatively expressed doubts about the adequacy of preformationism in the first edition of his *Handbuch der Naturgeschichte*.[25] A year later he made his conversion to epigenesis official when he read a paper before the Göttingen Academy of Sciences entitled *Über den Bildungstrieb (Nisus formativus) und seinen Einfluß auf die Generation und Reproduction*, which propounded an aggressive and fully worked out critique of every aspect of the preformationist position.[26] That essay, expanded, translated, and reprinted many times over the last two decades of the century, became a core text defining Enlightenment Vitalism's vision of generation, reproduction, and change over time. Blumenbach supplemented it by analogous discussions of generation in his popular and influential texts on physiology, osteology, comparative anatomy, and natural history, by his anonymous reviews in the *Göttingische Gelehrten Anzeige* (including reviews of his own books), and by his activities as editor of his journal, *Die medicinische Bibliothek*, which he used to castigate preformationists and assemble an international network of those sympathetic to his views.[27] More than anything else, his interpretation induced Kant to do what he had not been willing in 1763, to choose epigenesis over preformation.[28] What was true for Kant applied to many thinkers of the late eighteenth century. In their view Blumenbach applied the coup de grace to preformation. For that reason his theory deserves further analysis.

. . .

Blumenbach was not the first German to attack preformation. Before him Caspar Friedrich Wolff and Joseph Gottlieb Kölreuter strove to establish epigenesis against Haller's authority. Wolff took on Haller directly, choosing the forming chick as the battleground for their dispute, arguing that an essential force *(vis essentiales)* constituted "the sufficient principle of all vegetation [development] both in plants and in animals."[29] Matching observation for observation with Haller, Wolff asserted epigenesis's validity not only because it corresponded to his observations, but also because of its philosophical superiority. It allowed for a greater degree of natural variety and envisioned nature as infinitely active while still acknowledging a supreme being.[30] Despite Wolff's assertion of the existence of a living, eternal, ever-changing nature, his specific formulation failed to convince many Enlightenment vitalists, primarily because of his definition of essential force. Unlike Buffon's internal mold or Roussel's *faculté generatrice*, the essential force did not form things. Rather, it functioned as a simple power called into being at fertilization that propelled nourishing fluids through matter. For both preformationists and epigenesists, Wolff's essential power appeared "blind," not capable of shaping differentiated matter; therefore it could easily be considered a simple mechanical force.[31]

Kölreuter presented an oblique, though perhaps more damaging, critique expressed in his experiments on hybridization (called bastardization at the time).[32] Preformationists had great difficulty explaining hybrids, usually invoking outside influences upon the preformed germ to account for their existence. Kölreuter believed he could destroy the preformationist position if he were able to transmute one type of plant into another by numerous hybridizations. He undertook this project, experimenting upon two types of tobacco plants, the *Nicotiana paniculata* and the *Nicotiana rustica*, producing bastards of each and then cross-pollinating these hybrids (which supposedly were sterile) with the pollen of the original male and female parents arriving at ever more hybrids, until he succeeded in transmuting a *Nicotiana rustica* into a *Nicotiana paniculata* and a *Nicotiana paniculata* into *Nicotiana rustica*. Kölreuter's belief in the sexuality of plants guided his efforts, which he explained by invoking Hippocrates's theory that fertilization results from the mixture of male and female fluids and joined it to a language employing hidden forces, mediation, and internal bonding.[33] This led Kölreuter to draw an analogy between propagation and chemical combination, which he then extended to alchemy, comparing his achievement to alchemical transmutation. Here Kölreuter followed a path most Enlightenment vitalists dared not follow. Kölreuter equated the transmutation of plants with that of metals because both, he believed, were generated by the combination of masculine and feminine fluids, seeds, or principles. He ascribed alchemy's failure to the mistaken desire to affect transmutations in one step rather than by degrees as he had done.[34] For Kölreuter, alchemy's message reinforced vitalism's. Transmutation aided by art could be carried out in all of the realms of nature, attesting to its vital dynamism and demonstrating preformation's poverty.[35]

Kölreuter's experiments should have played a major role in dethroning preformation. They didn't. Very few naturalists took notice of them, perhaps because of Kölreuter's hermetic ideas or his reluctance to attack Haller and Bonnet directly. The contrary was true for Blumenbach. His essay on the *Bildungstrieb* is filled with devastating attacks upon the theory of *embôitment*, directed at Haller, Spallanzani, and especially Bonnet. Blumenbach observed with sarcastic delight that the most adventurous theory of *embôitment* was presented by a "famous Genevan," who

> has given us a history of organized bodies before their fructification. In it he informs us that: 1) we are all older than we believe; 2) all humans in the world are the same age, the grandfather not a day older than his newly born grandson; 3) this respectable age of all humans, who now live on the earth, is about six thousand years. He also expresses the opinion . . . that we along with Cain and Abel and the other two hundred million people that according to general calculations have gone before us have lain fallow since shortly after the first creation, in a sense still incognito and sleep-intoxicated, but not totally without movement. During the fifty-seven centuries that passed until our turn came to be stimulated, awakened and developed, we gradually grew. At the time of Cain's sister we could move a bit more than her mother, and so we received with every new development of our ancestors, a roomier lodging, and that was nice, then we could stretch out more and more until our turn came."[36]

Blumenbach's sarcastic dismissal of Bonnet's position runs like a red thread through the whole work.

By 1780 Blumenbach considered divine preformation a "quixotic romance."[37] Even its strongest proof, the membrane continuity theory proved nothing. Assume, Blumenbach proposed, that the observation was correct, namely, that a continuation of the skin and blood vessels of the chick with the yolk exists—and that was a big assumption since it is almost impossible to prove. Does it follow that since they now coexist after impregnation they coexisted before it? He answered with a resounding No. Upon reflection, Blumenbach asked, how could we all have been so naive as to accord so much weight to such an argument?[38]

In his rejection of preformation, Blumenbach did not blindly accept the Hippocratic view but sought to reconceptualize it, expanding it to encompass the phenomena of generation, nutrition, growth, and reproduction (the organism's ability to replace lost tissue and in some cases lost parts). He concluded that a single force, the *Bildungstrieb* or *nisus formatives*, governed these activities. It was "a peculiar power perpetually active, perpetually efficacious, the immediate destination of which is, first, to mould the bodies in which it resides into their native and specific forms by the mysterious process of *generation*, to preserve them afterwards from destruction by the ceaseless function of *nutrition,* and, in case of accidental mutilation, to restore their parts again, as far as consistent with the regular establishments of nature, by the process of *reproduction.*"[39] Blumenbach compared the *Bildungstrieb* to gravity and attraction, considering them all occult forces, whose "existence and reality ... are deduced from actual observations made on the constant and universal occurrence of certain physical phenomena."[40]

Blumenbach claimed his formulation was superior to other postulated forces of generation because it brought a number of life forces under a single rubric. Its action did not disappear with birth but existed throughout the life of an organized body; it inhered in matter and focused only on one set of functionally related phenomena. But its major advantage over other vitalist alternatives was that it successfully mediated between the "two principles ... that one had assumed could not be joined, the teleological and the mechanical."[41] Blumenbach's idea of the *Bildungstrieb* presents a prime example of the joining of opposites characteristic of Enlightenment Vitalism. He clearly recognized the necessity of redefining both mechanism and teleology as they applied to the life sciences.[42] The teleological principle encompassed both the purposive function of an organ and the general direction of development. The mechanical referred to the general construction of the body, to what Blumenbach called the normal type or normal schemata *(Normaltypus, Normalschema)* of a species. In many parts of the body the teleological and mechanical overlapped, but for others it didn't. Thus, for example, in chickens the *bursa Fabricii* played a purposive role in the cock but was only "a mechanical rudiment" in the hen. Or for humans, female breasts were purposive (i.e., teleological) while in "men they appear as rudiments, formed according to the mechanical principle."[43] Similar rudiments could be found in other animal species, all attesting to the dual operations of the *Bildungstrieb.*

By locating the *Bildungstrieb* within matter Blumenbach considered the goal to which the *Bildungstrieb* directed matter as ordered yet not predetermined. He reintroduced contingency and development as central scientific explanatory concepts. Change did not proceed automatically, it was dictated by the interaction between the organized body and the world in which it subsisted, where the *Bildungstrieb* responded to every challenge, either from the environment or from accident, compensating for any possible deviation. This applied for hybrids, "monsters," and "degenerations" from a type. Hence, Blumenbach established the "law of compensation" as a central element in his explanatory strategies, though such adjustments took place within proscribed limits.[44] Blumenbach brought accidental change within the purview of regular or "progressive" development. Each case of adaptation followed a pattern analogous to normal development directed by the *Bildungstrieb*. In this case Blumenbach like Sömmerring sought to "discover and present the succession of steps and natural order in the malformations of our bodies. Nature is admirably instructive even in its detours."[45] Blumenbach helped to translate "monstrosities to a field of scientific investigation. . . . As a result, bodily deviations became a constitutive part of the life sciences."[46]

Whether change proceeded normally or analogously, the progressions were not, Blumenbach believed, continuous. Qualitative transformation consisted of a series of "revolutions" in which the outward form changed drastically, followed by a gradual development in the newly formed shape. A continuous interplay between free creation and regular development occurred. The critical transition periods were marked by "astonishing revolutions in almost the whole economy of the system."[47] Blumenbach often turned to the image of metamorphosis to characterize these revolutions, especially when discussing the development of the fetus: "One can say that the chick in the egg succeeds in achieving its complete form through a kind of metamorphosis, and that with reference to individual viscera as well as to its total formation."[48] Blumenbach supported his position by reference to Lyonet's researches upon the metamorphosis of the butterfly from the caterpillar: "The most recognized judge in this question, Mr. Lyonet assures us that the internal construction of the butterfly is absolutely different than it had as a caterpillar."[49] The reality of metamorphosis further confirmed Blumenbach's opposition to the Great Chain of Being: "One cannot be more fervently positive of something than I am of the enormous chasm which nature has fixed between living and dead creatures, between organized and unorganized bodies; despite my respect for the shrewdness with which the defenders of the chain of being or the continuity of nature have constructed their ladders, I cannot see how in treating the transition from the realm of organization to the unorganized they are able to succeed without positing a really daring leap."[50] Leaps in nature do occur, attesting to nature's continual activity.

By the 1780s a large number of European intellectuals subscribed to the idea of a world in continual movement presenting a "theater of continual revolutions," in which old forms of existence are replaced by new ones. Most Enlightenment thinkers, however, thought these changes had "an invariable natural order to them,"[51] tending toward a goal. The acceptance of epigenesis supported these beliefs. In it final goal had been historicized and teleology redefined as a process of temporal adaptation effected by an active drive. Neither goal nor process was considered a given, but rather as a tendency to which an organization aspired. Many late-eighteenth-century intellectuals consciously integrated these assumptions in their work, employing a "genetic model" to narrate dynamic transformation, conceiving it as a steplike process (either positive or negative) with each step possessing its own unique character.

In such narratives "progressive" development began with generation and ended with the death or the destruction of the organized body. Not only did the first of these capture the imagination of late Enlightenment thinkers, but increasingly the question of death and its definition assumed an important place in their thoughts and anxieties. It too fueled an important debate revolving around the concepts of the process of dying, the real definition of death, and the possibility of bringing someone back to life or awakening that person from the dead. This new discourse of death, dying, and resurrection was fought out in the life sciences but was driven by important social-political imperatives. It forms an integral part of the discourse of Enlightenment Vitalism.

DEATH, DYING, AND RESURRECTION

Death is always with us, serving as both the opposite of life and as that, which defines it. Together life and death are the grand boundaries around which human hopes and expectations in this world and perhaps in the next are forged. As a rule, in most ages one of these two boundaries receives prime consideration, the other pushed into the peripheries of consciousness and of cultural life. It is usually assumed that during the Enlightenment the rich symbolic and emotional language of death forged over previous centuries was repressed, almost dismissed as a concept with significant cultural or symbolic meaning. Death seemed little more than the necessary yet regretful final event in the more important drama of developing one's full human potential in this world. Rather than function as the gateway to salvation or perdition, death, at best, either ensured one's posterity or obscurity, or it was, as Mendelssohn and Lessing argued, a transition in the development of a spiritual monad.[52] In many ways this characterization is true; for during a good part of the century death was seen as unproblematic, simply the end of a life, either extinguished through natural or accidental causes. Its signs were clear and simple. The animal machine stopped functioning, its springs and levers no longer operated, its hydraulics were halted. Movement, the sign of action and, therefore, of life, ceased. Yet following the midcentury critique of mechanism and the emergence of Enlightenment Vitalism, the whole question of death and dying acquired a new set of assumptions and doubts, generating in certain sectors acute anxieties and fears about what death was, how it could be infallibly determined, whether it was possible to bring the dead back to life or even to generate life where there had been none.

The locus of this debate lay not in the fact of death but in the definition of actual death and the understanding of its relationship to the process of dying. It was intensified by the fear of being prematurely consigned to the ranks of the dead, exacerbated by the hopes that those deemed dead could be brought back to life, and sometimes darkened by the consequences such a generation might entail. In this discourse of death the most terrifying anxiety was that of being buried alive, the most optimistic hope that of saving many who otherwise would have been condemned to an early and horrible demise. Thus, the three terms, death, dying, and resurrection, were closely linked in a new discourse of dying during the late Enlightenment that earlier would have been incomprehensible and unthinkable.

Two interlocking concepts drawn from the vitalist definition of life fueled the new doubts concerning death. The epigenetic description of life's "progress" constituted the first, the belief in the existence of active occult forces operating internally in matter's core the second. Vitalists working from these defined life as a primordial phenomenon defying exact determination. No measuring device could penetrate its core; no sure signs discovered announcing its disappearance. Life existed between the parameters of maximum and minimum life, *vita maxima* and *vita minima*, the boundaries within which life progressed in varying degrees of activity or intensities of irritability.

These assumptions shaped the new discourse of death. Physicians viewed death's progress as approximating that of life's, creation working in the opposite direction:

> Human death is not a sudden transformation, not the work of a moment; rather it is a step-by-step transition from the condition of active life to the constrained, or *Scheintod,* culminating in absolute death, or the total loss of all life forces. It is an ancient but still a very injurious prejudice to believe that inner life halts when outer life does, or, in other words, that the causes disappear with the effects. A glance at the rise of life provides a striking illumination. So sure is it that the human passes by stages from imperfect to complete life; so sure is the heart the first pulsating point in which life stirred and acted and radiated out to form and animate the other organs before any other part existed; so is it equally sure that this step-like process is followed in reverse order

with the disappearance of life. It retreats from the outer parts to the inner, actual life organs and becomes concentrated in the heart where it endures the longest.[53]

Once the obvious signs became impossible to read, vitalist physicians believed the body had entered a middle stage *(Mittelzustand, état intermédiaire)*,[54] which could last for a while, where it was possible that the active forces, reduced to their inner core might be able to recoup their powers and reawaken, leading to a revivification of the body, basically to a rebirth. Christian Hufeland, one of the leading medical men of the period, stated this belief clearly: "The physical life power of our bodies has, for us, a totally unknown source, which maintains it. As long as this source is not injured, the human can, if his organs are in good condition, retain for a long time the ability to reawaken to life *(wiederaufzuleben)*."[55]

For this reason, vitalist physicians expressed strong doubts about the reliability of the traditional "outward" signs determining death. By the end of the century it had become an article of medical and educated belief that death was very difficult to differentiate from dying, that great differences existed between the really dead and the apparently dead *(Scheintode)*. No longer did one associate death with the stopping of the animal machine's mechanisms, including the most radical, that of severing a head from the body. As Christian Hufeland, paraphrasing Herz, wrote: "The borderline between life and death appears by far not as certain and determined as one normally believed and as one should expect according to the traditional concepts of life and death. There exists between life and death a condition, which cannot be called life, but also which in no way can be termed death; a condition, in which our senses are not only unable to detect any trace of life, but in which the life force actually doesn't live and has no effects or influence upon the body with which it is united."[56] Because it was virtually impossible to differentiate between death and apparent death, which was this in-between condition, one had to be very cautious in using the traditional signs signifying death. Hufeland cast doubt on all of them, arguing that they were deceptive *(betrüglich)*.[57] There was only one sure sign of death, namely, "the general putrefaction of a corpse. This putrefaction alone is able to give us absolute assurance that not only are all the connections between the life force and the machine terminated *[aufgehoben]*, but also that the body's organization itself is destroyed, making re-animation *[Wiederbelebung]* impossible."[58]

Although not as radical as Hufeland, many of the dictionary and encyclopedia articles on death written at the end of the eighteenth century and the beginning of the nineteenth mirrored Hufeland's skepticism about relying upon outward signs to measure death. The entry in the *Encyclopedia: or a Dictionary of Arts and Sciences* published in Philadelphia in 1798 is typical; in fact the same paragraph was repeated verbatim in at least two later encyclopedias: "The signs of death are in many cases very uncertain. If we consult what Winslow or Bruchier have said on this subject, we shall be convinced, that between life and death the shade is so very undistinguishable, that all the powers of art can scarcely determine where the one ends and the other begins." The *Americana Encyclopedia* of 1830 agreed with Hufeland: "The commencement of putrefaction . . . affords the first certain evidence of death."[59]

Hufeland and many Enlightenment vitalists came to this conclusion because they believed the most obvious distinguishing feature of animated matter was its capacity to suspend normal chemical affinities, substituting new ones enabling the body to rejuvenate itself and defy putrefaction. Alexander von Humboldt adopted this position in his highly evocative essay entitled "Die Lebenskraft oder der rhodische Genius: Eine Erzählung." He used the metaphor of a ruler's active gaze to symbolize life force animating an organized body's elements. Once that gaze was obliterated, the elements separated, entering into a wild flurry of uncontrolled couplings until normal elective affinities were reestablished, instituting a stable, dead, mechanical harmony.[60]

The assertion that death's only sure sign was general putrefaction created problems for medical researchers. Johann Metzger observed that if this were true, dissecting a corpse could constitute an act of murder. Although agreeing with Hufeland about the existence of *Scheintod*, he argued that death occurred before the onset of putrefaction: "Surely there is an intermediary period where the organized body maintains its original integrity after the life force is extinguished and the spark of putrefaction appears."[61] John Hunter raised similar issues, distinguishing between "a suspension of the actions of life," when the body still possesses life force and "absolute death."[62] He discerned a number of signs indicating death, some contradictory, yet when taken together served as an indication that the shift from suspended life to death had occurred. Yet both Metzger and Hunter could not offer a satisfactory alternative to putrefaction using the language of Enlightenment Vitalism. Thus, Hunter called his own observational principles in doubt when he claimed "that so long as the animal retains the susceptibility of impression, though deprived of the action of life, it will, most probably, retain the power of action when impressed; therefore the action may frequently be suspended, and yet recoverable: but when the susceptibility of impression is destroyed, the action ceases to be recoverable."[63]

Given such assumptions it is easy to understand the fear of being buried alive. Marcus Herz set the mood when he described this death in his attack upon contemporary Jewish burial practices: "it is the most painful, excruciating death that we can cause! I don't know of a more hideous one. The death that a criminal endures at the public place of execution is a trifle, is nothing in comparison to awakening in the grave." He then painted a picture of the physical sufferings endured by those who awoke in the grave: "And the physical martyrdom of this death! The deadly anxiety, the suffocating, the restrictions in the chest accompanied by choking, the blood streaming to the head, the convulsive trembling of the whole body, the hopeless straining of the muscles to push away the oppressive burden, the stench of the neighboring corpses! Can one think of anything more abominable?"[64] For an age well aware of the suffering normally inflicted in public executions, this was indeed a powerful statement, revealing a deeply felt fear, made even more poignant by the carnage accompanying the wars of the French Revolution and the Napoleonic era, in which thousands of young men were unceremoniously buried immediately after battle, many of whom, contemporary theory assumed, might have been buried alive.[65]

It is also easy to understand the other side of the new discourse on death, namely, the optimism generated by the belief that people who appear dead may be brought back to life, that life could actually be restored or even created. Herz and others claimed that more people died in a year through premature burial than through suicide. Others thought that almost a quarter of those deemed dead had the chance of being brought back to life. Especially susceptible to reanimation were those who drowned, were struck by lightning, were frozen or hanged. For those who experienced more "normal" forms of dying, vitalists proposed numerous categories to identify persons more likely to be *Scheintod* than really dead. Hufeland, for example, provided an extensive list of those more likely to be *Scheintod* and those more likely to be really dead, where the category *Scheintod* far exceeded that of the really dead. He argued that the determining factor was the person's degree of irritability or *Reizbarkeit*, which led Hufeland to conclude that women were more susceptible to *Scheintod* then men.[66] The young Frankenstein in Mary Shelley's novel, which utilized this language of death and reanimation, expressed the most optimistic side of this belief: "Life and death appeared to me ideal bounds, which I should first break through, and pour a torrent of light into our dark world. . . . I thought, that if I could bestow animation upon lifeless matter, I might in process of time (although I now found it impossible) renew life where death had apparently devoted the body to corruption."[67]

. . .

The difficulties vitalists faced in defining death were manifested in three contemporary debates. The first focused upon the possibility of saving victims of drowning, electrocution, or accidental hanging. Its scope was European, in which the hope of defying death was transformed into a program of public and private action. The second arose in Germany and East Central Europe, revolving around a dispute concerning Jewish burial practices. The French Revolution, especially the Terror, generated the third, which dealt with the efficacy and effects of the guillotine, the Terror's most feared symbol.

The new discourse of death raised peoples' hopes that victims of accidental death such as drowning, whose bodily functions had been halted unnaturally, could be brought back to life. John Hunter wrote a long essay delineating how victims of drowning, whose "action of life was suspended," could be revived. He offered a number of prescriptions to accomplish this, based on conserving life force and stimulating the major sympathetic systems to reawaken life. His practical solutions called for blowing air into the lungs to restart the heart, applying heat to the body, and administering medicines to activate both the heart and lungs. Under no circumstance, however, did Hunter recommend bleeding or purging, procedures "which . . . weakens the animal principle and life itself."[68] Hufeland was even more sanguine in his expectations that drowned people could be revived, even after they had been submerged for an hour or more. His remedies were similar to Hunter's with one great exception, the letting of blood, which Hufeland said had to be done quickly if it was to be effective.[69]

The image of resurrecting people who have "almost the exact likeness of death" acquired great symbolic and metaphorical power in the last half of the eighteenth century and the beginning of the nineteenth. Goethe provided an example of this in the final chapter of *Wilhelm Meisters Wanderjahre*. In it Wilhelm Meister's son Felix falls from a precipice into a raging river. He is pulled out by boatmen but appears dead. Goethe described his condition and continued the story: "Apparently lifeless *[Entseelt scheinend]* lay the graceful youth in the boat. After quick deliberations, the able men directed the boat to a sandbar . . . . Landing, the body brought on shore, the first order of business was undressing and drying it. But still no sign of life to be seen, the beautiful flower collapsed in their arms. Wilhelm immediately grabbed the lancet and opened the artery in the arm; the blood sprang out in rich spurts, tracing a spiral path to the ground. Life returned again."[70] In this description Goethe deliberately used the language of resurrection, not the more modest term of saving a person from drowning. Felix initially showed no signs of life, yet was *wiederbelebt*, reversing death, symbolized by the spiral movement of the blood (for Goethe spiral movement characterized life and growth) as it leapt from Felix's opened artery.

If the attempts to reawaken the apparent dead from drowning spoke to the positive expectations of Enlightenment Vitalism's new discourse of life and death, the controversy over Jewish burial practices reveals a more ambiguous blend of hope and fear, tinged with overtones of religious and perhaps ethnic tension. The dispute arose in the 1780s and 1790s. Leaders of the Jewish Enlightenment, the *Haskala*, attacked the traditional practice of burying a body four hours after death unless sundown intervened, in which case the body was buried at dawn. Moses Mendelssohn and especially Marcus Herz launched a major campaign against this "delusion," opposed to "healthy understanding" and against which "humanity is roused to indignation."[71] Herz argued that such practices made his coreligionists into murderers, for, he proclaimed, it had been conclusively proven that most methods of ascertaining death were inconclusive. Since antiquity there had been innumerable cases of people apparently dead being brought back to life.[72] In fact, according to Herz's testimony, he himself had witnessed such a case of a supposedly dead young Jewish woman being revived after the postponement of her burial because of the arrival of dusk.

Along with his medical arguments, Herz also raised all of the themes now associated with the conflicts between Enlightenment and traditional religion, or between advocating assimilation and maintaining one's religious identity. According to Herz, the Talmudic defenders of early burials were locked in a medieval system that had no knowledge of modern science; they had put too much authority upon Scripture, which they misread, and, locked in their world of primitive superstition, had failed to recognize the true demands of humanity.[73] For these reasons their authority was nonexistent, their power that of the cunning manipulating the unenlightened. Since the leaders of the Jewish Enlightenment thought they were fighting for humanity, they did not hesitate to call for state assistance in their battle against darkness, hoping that if the rabbis could not be convinced of their errors, the state would intervene to forbid the practice of early burial.

The literature on Jewish burial laws is not large, and that which exists has been framed within the larger question of discussing the consequences of assimilation, and implicitly upon the role played by assimilation in leading to the Holocaust. Earlier scholars, writing before the Holocaust, had sided with the reformers, but today some younger scholars, interpreting the dispute as a battle between state and community for the control of Jewish bodies, side with the Rabbis against the *Haskala*, seen as unwitting apprentices to extending German state control over Jewish lives.[74] No matter which position one takes in this discussion, the most immediate context, namely, what defined death and life, has been virtually ignored. It has been turned into a problem in Jewish history rather than considered part of a larger issue concerning cultural assumptions focusing upon life and death.

But that was not the case at the time. The fear of being buried alive fueled the whole controversy, and the Jewish practice of very early burial seemed a blatant invitation to massacre countless people who were only *Scheintod*. It is interesting that at the time virtually none of the participants in the debate denied the possibility of being buried alive. The rabbinical defenders of early burial simply asserted the adequacy of their methods to ascertain absolute death, including holding a mirror or a very light feather before the nose, or placing a bowl of water on the chest of the deceased. Their opponents ridiculed these signs, claiming that, at best, they could detect suspension of life's actions, not indicate life's disappearance. Those with medical training defending the Jewish practice denied that a person, though still possessing a spark of life, could be reawakened. In this scenario the person expired quietly in the grave without any great trauma, a regrettable, but rare, occurrence.

The linkage of trauma and pain with death was central to the discussion concerning death and dying generated by the introduction of the guillotine as an instrument of execution. Death by mechanical decapitation was originally touted as a humane solution to the necessity of the death penalty, being quick, sure, the least painful,[75] and democratic, ensuring an execution without the horrors associated with executions of the ancien régime. Yet during the terror some leading naturalists contested the original justifications for the "national razor." Samuel Thomas Sömmerring was the first to deny its supposed humaneness and was quickly seconded by the French physicians Sue and Oelsner.[76] Sömmerring and his supporters argued that mechanical decapitation was the most painful of tortures. Despite its apparent speed, its effect was horrible because the separated head still was fully alive and experienced excruciating pain. To justify this, Sömmerring contended that the head was the seat of sensations and sentiments. When decapitation occurs, the *"sentiments,* the *personality,* the *self* remained alive for a period of time"* in the severed head.[77] The guillotine because of its speed left a living head convulsing with pain, of which it was fully conscious and would remain so for an extended period of time. It could, Sömmerring claimed, remain active enough for a quarter of an hour to move the face muscles, but even when the capacity to move disappeared the ability to think persisted. And even if the time were much shorter, Oelsner remarked, since the whole brain was still alive, each second would seem like an eternity.[78] The famous episode of the head of Charlotte Corday supposedly blushing when struck by the executioner seemed to provide these critics with a vivid example, demonstrating the prolongation of the "moral principle" in the head. Not only did the brain retain consciousness in the severed head, the pain immediately accompanying the execution was the most powerful imaginable, for as the blade fell, it crushed the most sensitive parts of the body, the nerves coming together in the brain and the spinal chord. In short, despite appearances, "medical facts, not vain speculation,"[79] proved beyond a doubt that execution by the guillotine constituted the most horrible and painful death imaginable.

It is interesting that Sömmerring's opponents did not contest the assumption that the severed body parts still possessed life force; they just denied that consciousness persisted, which meant that pain could no longer be felt. Of course, that the guillotine had become the symbol of the Revolution intensified the debate. Oelsner's comment on Sömmerring's letter bristled with indignation concerning the circumstances surrounding the death. For many, the guillotine's mechanical nature set the tone for the mechanization of death, robbing death of any honor or dignity. In France, unlike areas such as Switzerland and Germany where the death penalty had hardly been used for over thirty years, the victims were degraded before their deaths: a victim's hands were tied, the hair cut, he or she presented to the ridiculing gaze of the public, executed in the nude, and then dragged by a *charrette* like a vile cadaver to the public dumping ground. For a nation that liked to associate itself with ancient republics or even Greek gods, such a practice appeared simply shameful to its critics.[80]

This consciousness of dehumanization was made more poignant by the feeling that decapitation cut short a life too abruptly, robbing the process of dying of its drama and importance. Sue pursued this point, though he used medical theory to frame it. Arguing that the body consisted of three life systems, located in the brain, the heart, and the reproductive organs, he contended that life and good health required a harmony between them. A peaceful death takes place when all three centers expire together in harmony. However, if one of these *foyers de vitalité* is suddenly extinguished, the resulting death is horrible, for each *foyer* has a conception of the death, due to the *rapports* of the living machine of the other parts.[81] All three authors did not condemn outright the death penalty, but were opposed to any form of violent execution. Oelsner opted for poison, using Socrates as his model; Sömmerring thought hanging more humane, believing it induced a sleep very quickly, which dulled the sensations; Sue favored asphyxiation, again thinking it led first to a sleeplike trance and then to death.

As in the case of Jewish burial practices, the discussion about the guillotine incorporated many levels of symbolic meanings rooted in issues concerning politics, life and death, and the nature of the "body politic." The whole discussion expressed, as Ludmilla Jordanova remarked, "a fundamental anxiety about the process of death which gripped the entire nation, and which provided a set of powerful images for European literature."[82] On the one hand, the guillotine's critics used it as a symbol to attack the Terror and the Revolution. On the other, the debate marks the further extension of the critique of capital punishment, rejecting ideas that it was allowable if "transformed" into a simple and painless practice.

. . .

The fear of being buried alive or the hope for resurrection led medical proponents of this new discourse of death to propose practical solutions to avoid what they considered a horrendous waste of human life. Typical solutions consisted of building warehouses for the dead *(Leichenhäuser),* where all who "supposedly" died would be kept under ideal conditions, overseen by a watchman, until the "dead" awoke or putrefaction occurred; of forming family contracts that under penalty of law made sure that not only was the body transported to a *Leichenhaus,* but that the watchman would also be watched by the contracting members; of legally requiring all people including Jews to wait at least three days before they buried their dead; of designing elaborate apparatuses to detect the existence of "inner life"—the most popular being portable galvanic machines that tested the irritability of the supposedly dead body; of erecting contraptions designed to warn people if someone already buried awoke from the dead (e.g., running a line through the earth for air, and rigging all of the extremities to strings that were attached to bells above ground to chime if any movement took place), and of instituting a major program of building and staffing humane and life-saving associations (e.g., the London Humane Association, Amsterdam Humane Association, *Hamburger Rettungsanstalten*) to save drowned persons and others dying from accidental causes such as freezing, drowning, hanging, or being struck by lightning.[83] Thus, many various life-saving societies as well as the institution of the morgue all stem from these initial fears that those who were merely *Scheintod* would be deemed really dead and thereby condemned to a horrible death.

The practical applications of this new discourse of death raises the question of its cultural and political consequences. Since Foucault's linkage of the dyad between power and knowledge, it has become commonplace to associate every change in scientific sensibility that took place in the Enlightenment and thereafter with an increasing tendency to subject the individual to control and regulation, to make them objects of the all-seeing eye of organized power. In one sense the measures taken to still the anxieties of this new discourse on death seem to confirm Foucault's position. Not only do we encounter a "panopticon" of the living, this gaze is now extended to the dead in the form of *Leichenhäuser*, panoptica of the dead, in which the watchers are themselves watched. Accompanying these activities, the state, at least in Germany, sought to regulate burial practices, not only in terms of when a body could be buried, but also setting certain standards about how the body was to be handled before burial. It encouraged the implementation of public health measures (to increase life), supported the establishment of local life-saving organizations, and financially and materially assisted in the development of scientific disciplines such as pathology and forensic medicine, which sought to decipher the signs of death. In all of these activities the linkage of knowledge and power certainly enabled the state to intrude upon and regulate new areas of social and cultural life.

A second part of Foucault's linkage of knowledge with power assumes that the creators of a new scientific discourse themselves profit in power and prestige from this activity. The psychologist who could recognize insanity and perhaps "cure" it, the penologist who constructed elaborate structures to "rehabilitate" his charges are the types Foucault has immortalized in his searing critiques of the origins of modernity. All participated in effecting a large-scale displacement of power from traditional sources to the more arcane realms of expert opinion. Does this apply to the new discourse of death? Not that I can see. It was not designed to empower a newly emerging group of "experts" who could decide with certainty who was or was not dead. It did, however, seek to discredit older authorities who believed had fool proof methods of ascertaining death—for instance, the rabbis in the debate about Jewish burial practices. Within this discursive model the only person who could certify death was the dying subject. No expert, no profession was able to say whether this or that person was dead. Only the ultimate proof of death, general putrefaction, was certain. Nature became the judge.[84]

This modest stance reveals, I believe, one of the basic elements of late Enlightenment thought, namely, its project of evolving a form of knowledge mediating between absolutes. Enlightened thinkers propounded a vision of reality constructed upon the images of mediation and harmonic conjuncture employing ambiguity and paradox as positive tools of apprehension. Terms such as *Scheintod* or middle stage *(Mittelzustand, état intermédiaire)* illustrate this discursive practice. Hence, in the late Enlightenment the same life-affirming elements of the early Enlightenment were still present, complicated, however, by the lack of clear signposts defining death. In its definition of death, it revealed its ambivalence toward all absolute answers, a position soon destroyed by the totalizing solutions of nineteenth-century scientism, positivism and Romantic *Naturphilosophie*. In this sense the late Enlightenment's perception of death affirms its general stance toward life, understanding, and reality.

ONTOGENY AND PHYLOGENY
IN ENLIGHTENMENT VITALISM

In their meditations on rupture and continuity in nature's economy, Enlightenment vitalists confronted the issues of whether species change, whether different life forms developed progressively from the simplest to the most complex, and whether a unifying pattern linked all living phenomena. Buffon had initiated the debate by his discussion of species differentiation, degeneration, varieties, and prototypes (see Chapter 1). He presented a vision elevating graduated qualitative change within a vital economy informed by "a primitive and general design" or "general prototype." He also suggested the existence of a genetic relationship between species, implying a theory of descent.[85]

Buffon's ideas of gradation and of the relation of the individual to the whole did not go uncontested. Defenders of continuity and universal interconnection arose to offer alternative interpretations. One of the most vocal and interesting was the Genevan Jean-Baptiste Robinet, a friend of Bonnet's, who shared many of his views. Robinet presented his arguments supporting preformation and continuity in his two major works, *De la nature* (4 vols., 1761–66) and *Vue philosophique de la gradation naturelle des formes d'être, ou les essais de la nature qui apprend a faire l'homme* (1768). As had Bonnet, Robinet denied the distinction between living and dead nature, treating all matter as animated and organized.[86] He maintained that the generation of all matter, from the simple stone to the most complex animal, occurred through the intermixing of male and female "semen" or seeds *(semences)*, all having "their own manner of sensibility" *(façon de sentir)*.[87] Every existing substance was composed of "germes" created by God at the beginning of time, leading Robinet to deny the possibility of new creation. However, though no new *germes* could be created, Robinet believed the preexisting *germes* capable of combining in an infinite number of ways.

No matter how they combined, the resulting product mirrored in its own way a universal "prototype" or "primitive design," defined as a "model representing being reduced to its minimal terms." Robinet's prototype, though borrowing Buffon's term, came much closer to the alchemists' Archaeus; it served as the unalterable principle "which realized itself in matter." Robinet discerned a basic truth in nature's constant transformations: "One finds in a stone and in a plant the same essential principles of life as in the human machine. The only difference consists in the combination of the principles, in the number, proportion, order, and form of the organs."[88]

Although these combinations were virtually infinite, nature did not act randomly. A definite plan guided her "secret operations," charting the movement from the simplest substance to its culmination in the human being, the *telos* toward which all development strove. In his *Vue philosophique de la gradation naturelle des formes d'être,* Robinet demonstrated how each form "announced" the human, describing rocks that resembled a heart, a brain, diverse fragments of a skull. He pictured more complex "fossils" as approximating human visages, with eyes peering at the reader, while others took the form of the female vagina or the male penis. With each increase in a substance's complexity, the resemblance to humans became stronger, most clearly demonstrated in the progression from monkey to ape to the human. Robinet supported this view of gradation by affirming the theory of continuity, where each physical manifestation of the prototype was intimately related to the form immediately above and below it. The Chain of Being had no missing links. For this reason Robinet argued for the existence of intermediary beings such as mermaids, mermen, and fauns, of which he provided illustrations. Robinet's interpretation, though seemingly naive and strongly reminiscent of earlier alchemical traditions, could also be read as a major plea for considering nature in constant movement, where organized bodies were transformed in a never ending round of new creation. This is the way Diderot interpreted Robinet, whose writings helped shape Diderot's mature musings on development and the relations between species in the ladder of organization.

Diderot had been an early ally of Buffon, but as his creative imagination increasingly spun out new variations on the vitalist theme, he came to espouse a more radical monist, materialist position. Not only did he deny the mind/body duality, he became increasingly critical of the vitalist search for a mediating position. Diderot elaborated this position in his masterpiece *D'Alembert's Dream*, written around 1769 but not published until 1830 in mutilated form. It illustrates the radical implications one could draw from the theory of continuity shorn of its connection with preformation and located within a materialist version of reality. Diderot expressed his opposition to preformation clearly, asserting it "flew in the face of experience and logic."[89] In so doing, he opted for epigenesis, which he illustrated by an account of how D'Alembert emerged from a vital point resulting from the mixture of male and female fluids and aided by the processes of nourishment and assimilation and evolved into the great mathematician. There was nothing very radical about this given the time he wrote it, at least not in Paris; but Diderot's modifications to the standard epigenetic account were. He radicalized it by denying the fixity of species, advancing the idea of the uniformity of matter, and affirming the ideas of continuity and universal connection; in the process he suggested a theory of recapitulation.

Diderot's denial of the fixity of species differed substantially from Robinet's. Diderot made explicit what was merely a possibility in Robinet by envisioning a world in which species go through actual physical transformations rather than serving as individual signs of that which will become. Further, Diderot denied unilinear change, emphasizing transformations in all directions. Hence we have no way of knowing what members of one species looked like in the past nor what they will become in the future: "Some earthworm squirming about in a dung heap is perhaps on his way to becoming a large animal, while some huge beast, who now amazes us by his size, is perhaps on his way to becoming a worm. In other words, he may be only a momentary and unique product of this earth."[90] Diderot supported this vision of change with a theory of matter. He assumed matter to be uniform and active, distancing himself from mechanists and vitalists. He also avoided the animist position, which posited the existence of a universal principle animating all matter, which logically would require one to assert that rocks could think or feel. He did this by drawing a distinction between the degree of feeling forms of matter exhibited, illustrating it by an analogy between kinetic and potential energy.[91] Matter, like energy, possessed different levels of activity, one visibly active, the other latently active. Diderot drew no hard and fast boundaries separating them. Active matter could be transformed into latent matter and vice versa.

Matter's convertibility authorized Diderot's claim for constant transformation in nature's economy. To this he added the principle of universal connection and continuity. He has the dreaming D'Alembert first assert the proposition: "All beings participate in the existence of all other beings; consequently every species . . . all nature is perpetually in flux. . . . Every animal is more or less human; every mineral is more or less vegetable; every plant is more or less animal. . . . Then will you not agree that in nature everything is bound up with everything else, and that it is impossible that there should be any gap in the chain of beings?"[92] The good doctor Bordeu confirmed this position, illustrating interconnection with a number of examples, including the swarm of bees cited earlier. Although Diderot offered a vision of nature's interconnection as absolute as Robinet's, he drew radically different conclusions. Diderot presented a picture of constant movement up and down the chain of being. The only teleological explanation he offered was that nature given enough time must bring forth everything that is possible.

What propelled these changes, if not preformed and preordained by God? For Diderot, nature's activities essentially were chemical reactions, a position mirroring chemistry's reemergence in the midcentury: "Eat, digest, distill in a closed vessel, and you have the whole art of making man." But chemical reaction could not explain transformation of form. Diderot added two other explanations to his arsenal. As did many of his contemporaries, he adopted a theory of challenge and response: "The original shape of a creature changes and develops in response to necessity and habitual use."[93] To this, he introduced the influence of heredity. Some traits could be inherited and even held latent for a generation or two and then reappear. Thus, a "freak" of nature might be the parent of a "normal" child, but the original abnormality could "leap over several generations" and reappear. All of these shifts "must be sought in the bundle of threads. And variations within the bundles of a single species account for all the individual freaks produced by the species."[94]

In whatever manner these mutations occurred, Diderot suggested that all creatures rehearsed the history of natural development that preceded them. It was absurd, he argued, to believe the beginnings of any creature had a relation to their final form. Rather animals in their epigenesis go through stages. At an early stage they are "nothing but a soft, fibrous, shapeless, wormlike substance, more comparable to the bulb or root of a plant than to an animal."[95] Later they acquire characteristics reminiscent of sea creatures. Thus, in Dr. Bordeu's imaginative description of Mll. De l'Espinasse's evolution he used analogies drawn from the sea to describe her postplant stage: "Your eyes (handsome as they are now) were no more like eyes than the tip of a sea anemone's claw is like the sea anemone. But then each of the strands in the bundle of threads began to change—solely as the result of nutrition and conformity with the special structure of each—into a particular organ."[96] From there Bordeu went on to show how sensation was formed and finally how the specific structure of an animal came into being.

Diderot never carried these ruminations further to construct a recapitulation theory, assuming individuals replicated the history of living things. But he was able to play with these concepts because he joined epigenesis and extreme materialism to the ideas of continuity and uniformity. Diderot constructed a vision of endless natural transmutations far more radical than anything advocated by the major proponents of Enlightenment Vitalism. He collapsed all of their mediating assumptions into an identity founded upon the physical questions of how fibers were positioned and fermentation proceeded.

. . .

Very few Enlightenment vitalists would have subscribed to Diderot's radical materialism and animation of the world, for they firmly believed in the chasm separating dead from living matter. Yet, mirroring Diderot and Robinet, they too sought to integrate individual life forms within larger categories, including all of living matter or significant segments of it. Increasingly naturalists and educated laymen considered humans and higher animals as either variations or complicated elaborations of these basic types. They adopted the principle that some universal elements linked all living creations within a common development scheme. Johann Gottfried Herder expressed this vision in the *Ideen zur Philosophie der Geschichte der Menschheit* (1784), his attempt to compose a "pure natural history of human powers, actions, and drives in space and time."[97]

To include Herder in an analysis of the formation of an Enlightenment language of nature might appear misplaced on two accounts. First, as a rule, Herder is not considered someone who commanded the natural philosophy of his era. He is often portrayed as someone congenitally immune to scientific reasoning, an intuitive and poetic soul alienated by scientific discourse.[98] Second and more important, Herder has been considered a major figure in what Isaiah Berlin has characterized as the Counter-Enlightenment.[99] If either were correct, it would make Herder one of the Enlightenment's major critics, not a participant in the discursive field I am trying to map. But I consider both reservations unconvincing. Herder's supposed antipathy toward the Enlightenment was more an antipathy toward mechanical natural philosophy and Wolffian German school philosophy. It cannot be traced to his preference for the "irrational" or to a mentality incapable of understanding the direction contemporary science was taking, and most certainly not to a rejection of the Enlightenment. Herder was antimechanist, not anti-Enlightenment. His reading of the leading thinkers of the time—Kant, Tetens, Lambert, Rousseau, Buffon, and Hume, among others—intensified his dissatisfaction with mechanism. These authors led Herder to probe the language of Enlightenment Vitalism, providing him with further substantiation of his initial doubts. By the time he wrote the *Ideen,* Herder had mastered this new language of nature extremely well. His knowledge of contemporary chemical theory, the life sciences, and natural history was encyclopedic.[100] He admired the same ancient and modern natural philosophers resurrected by Enlightenment vitalists: Hippocrates, Aristotle, Harvey, Bacon, and Stahl (with the necessary homage to Newton). And he rehearsed the same arguments about their superiority over the newer (mechanical) philosophers. Contemporary critics of mechanism had eschewed hypotheses and looked only at nature's facts: "theirs is the oldest philosophy of the world as it probably is the most modern."[101]

Although Herder cannot be seen as an innovator in framing Vitalism's language of nature, he commanded its grammar and syntax to such an extent that the *Ideen* can be seen as one of the most consequential and thorough-going late-eighteenth-century experiments employing this language to explicate human history. In the process Herder formulated a number of fascinating suggestions concerning the unity of nature, including ones that related to the question of ontogeny and phylogeny, which then were picked up by leading natural philosophers and integrated into their researches. For this reason alone, Herder deserves a place in the discussion of the question of the relationship between ontogeny and phylogeny.

Herder founded his conception of human history upon the proposition that history's laws were analogous to those of nature where "all existence is the same, founded upon the same laws."[102] But he drew a distinction between the laws and the matter they regulated. Mechanical laws dealt with dead matter, vital laws with living matter. Thus, for Herder, to treat animals as though they were machines would be a "sin against nature,"[103] for living matter demonstrated directional movement, each step calling forth a different conjuncture of forces and matter: "In the creation of our earth a sequence of ascending forms and forces prevail. We see the form of organization ascend, from a stone to a crystal, from crystals to the metals, from these to plant creations, from the plants to animals, and from these to humans. Along with them the forces and drives *[Kräfte und Triebe]* of creation become differentiated until finally all unite in the form *[Gestalt]* of the human, to the extent that the human can contain them."[104] Robinet could easily have made this statement, but Herder differed with him in one respect. Herder, in the *Ideen*, vehemently rejected preformation and the Great Chain of Being, believing preformation, which excluded free activity from nature's realm, questioned God's existence.[105] Herder advanced a theory of discontinuous change, though he still posited the existence of a ladder of organization linking the simplest substance to the most complex organization. Each rung constituted a unique configuration of joined matter and powers. As had the Enlightenment vitalists, Herder dissolved the Cartesian duality between mind and matter but did not draw an identity between them: "Force and an organ indeed are intimately joined, but are not one and the same. The material for our bodies was there, but without form and life, until it was formed and animated by the organic forces."[106]

Herder modified the image of organization's ladder by introducing the idea of nature's constant permutations, for "nothing in nature stands still, everything strives and moves forward."[107] Herder envisioned linear change driven by "forward striving forces" increasing in number with each stage. Each creature in this process borrows something from what had preceded it, a signature linking both. Herder underscored this assumption when he asked and answered the question "Why do we and all other animals have calcium in our bones? Because it was one of the last transitions *[Übergänge]* of rude earth formation, which, according to its internal form, could be of service to a living organization in its skeletal structure. So it is with every other constituent part of our body."[108] The human was, in effect, a composite of all the types of things that have existed: "His blood and his many named components are a compendium of the world: calcium and earth, salts and acids, oil and water, forces of vegetation, irritability and sensation are organically united and intermingled with each other in him."[109]

Herder carried this conclusion further, using it to authorize a recapitulation theory, where each individual passes through the stages that preceded and led to its species formation. Humans as the highest form of life therefore recapitulated organization's history: "It appears that the child in the mother's womb must go through all of the conditions, which fell to an earthly creature. It swims in water; it lies with an open mouth; its jaw is large, before it can be covered with a lip, which forms relatively late. As soon as it comes into the world, it gasps for air and sucking is its unlearned first accomplishment. The whole work of digestion and nourishment, of hunger and thirst, goes forward instinctively, or because of still dark drives."[110] More than anyone before him, Herder clearly announced a close connection between ontogeny and phylogeny. In fact, his position appears to anticipate what Ernst Haeckel termed the basic biological law, namely, that ontogeny recapitulates phylogeny. But despite appearances, a wide intellectual gulf separated Herder from Haeckel. Haeckel had directed his research and writing to explaining the descent of species, employing the language of linear causation. He rejected the existence of vital forces and vehemently denounced any explanation reeking of final ends. Herder, an advocate of Enlightenment Vitalism, eschewed causal analysis in favor of analogical reasoning, postulated active forces, and believed in final ends. For Herder, nature's ladder consisted of a series of variations around a common theme rather than a tightly linked chain.

In essence, Herder attempted to join two models of change in his theory of recapitulation, linear development and analogical recapitulations of a basic plan. He expressed the linear element in the statement quoted above and repeated it in the following rhetorical question: "Could we have viewed the first period of creation—how one realm of nature was built upon another—what a progression of forward striving forces would be shown in every development!" At the same time he argued that living creatures bore "a certain unity of structure,"[111] explicable only by the existence of what he called the *Haupttypus* (principal type), *Hauptform* (principal form), or prototype. To support this contention, Herder cited the bone structure in land animals, where eyes, head, rump, hands, and feet were similar: "Even the most noble members of these are formed according to a single prototype and, as it were, only infinitely varied."[112] Herder did not consider the prototype an exact blueprint for all organization, discoverable by looking at a single example. Nature varied the specifics enormously, enlarging parts in one, minimizing them in another, hiding them here and revealing them there.[113] Still, a dynamic harmony operated in all of nature's activities.

Were these two visions of change contradictory? The answer would be yes if one evaluated them according to the dictates of binary logic. They neither give a satisfactory causal explanation nor do they establish an adequate identity relation. But this is precisely the point, for Herder did not strive for such explanations. Herder's logic combined comparison, analogy, and mediation to chart what he considered a new way to perceive the relations between contraries. The history of nature and of humanity demonstrated the interaction between regular development and revolutionary eruption; they attested to the harmonic mediations between matter and force, law and creation, immobility and chaos, determinism and freedom, all linked in a "mysterious connection."

Herder called this connection "harmony," which he envisioned as a marriage of extremes founded upon force and matter. Increasing the number of interacting forces and widening the distance between the extremes limiting active forces could intensify harmony, resulting in an expanded middle realm in which life was experienced. Progress, therefore, entailed an increase in activity, an intensification of complexity, accompanied by a heightening of consensus among all of the interacting parts. Herder, as had Wilhelm von Humboldt after him, condemned one-sidedness, leading him to invest the term "middle"—which he associated with concepts *(Mittelbegriff)*, creations *(Mittelgeschöpf)*, class *(Mittelstand)*, and place *(Mittelstrich der Erde)*—with symbolic importance, signifying a privileged site linking freedom with stability.

If progress consisted in the intensification of force and the complication of connections rather than in the continuous generation or degeneration of creatures, passing from earthworms to elephants or vice versa, then Herder's ladder of organization could be interpreted as a diagram charting nature's experiments with possible combinations of force, matter, and form. For Herder, no direct physical cause could account for the leaps in organization's ladder. One species does not emerge from another, no matter how many variations may take place within a single species. Herder remained true to Buffon, as he made clear in his judgment concerning the late-eighteenth-century discussion about the relationship between apes and humans. Herder clearly affirmed that "apes and humans were never one and the same species." At the same time, he acknowledged the infinite variations within a species, demanding that the term "race" be abolished from scientific discourse: "Colors lose themselves in each other . . . and on the whole, everything is just a shading of the same great picture, which is dispersed through all spaces and times of the earth." In a rhetorical sweep, he concluded, "But you, human, honor your self. Neither the Pongo nor the Longimanus [eighteenth-century terms for the great apes] is your brother, but certainly the native American and the black is. He you should not oppress, not murder, not steal from; for he is a human as are you."[114]

The human, according to Herder, occupied the highest rung on the ladder of organization, the "middle creature," joining all of nature's contending forces in an intensive harmony. Although this claim sounds imperialistic, this was not Herder's intention. Unlike proponents of the Great Chain of Being or of sufficient reason, Herder rejected the assumption that humans were the world's sovereigns or that it had been created for their enjoyment and exploitation. Each rung in the ladder had its own dignity, self-sufficiency, and right to existence. That which placed humans at the top of the ladder, the intensity of their harmonic relations, also functioned as the motor of their development, capable of producing the most debased of creatures, yet also having as its highest expression the drive toward humanity *(Humanität)*. There is no self-complacency in Herder's rhetoric and certainly very little hint of Eurocentrism.

For Herder this middle position also made human knowledge possible. Precisely because humans were nature's compendium, the results of controlled observations directed by intuitive imagination allowed humans to understand nature's inner workings. Because of the linkage of all organized creatures within a nexus of spiritual and material relations, Herder argued that all great scientific thinkers had used analogies, which he equated with poetic imagination, to achieve their breakthroughs. Newton, Leibniz, and Buffon had arrived at "their great and daring discoveries through a new picture, an analogy, a striking similarity."[115] Thus, nature, which "progressed" through analogical transmutations, could be apprehended only by analogies. Here Herder closed the circle linking nature and knowledge, giving coherence to his vision, which we, living in a different mental universe, often have difficulty apprehending. The same applies to Herder's explication of the relationship between ontogeny and philogeny. It is familiar yet strange: familiar because he raised the issue, strange because he didn't pose the question we would expect. As Roselyn Rey observed, Herder, though discussing the connection between ontogeny and phylogeny, never directly addressed the issue of ontogenesis.[116] For him it probably was a nonissue.

. . .

Although Herder did not raise the question of ontogenesis, it soon emerged as important, inducing some of the leading naturalists to incorporate it in their discussions of species and change over time. Carl Friedrich Kielmeyer offered one of the first and most original solutions, which he framed in the language of Enlightenment Vitalism. Kielmeyer, virtually ignored during the last half of the nineteenth century and well into the twentieth,[117] is now considered one of the most important physiological thinkers of the late eighteenth century. His rehabilitation has sparked a debate over where he should be located within the intellectual currents of his era. Some consider Kielmeyer a Romantic, others a Kantian "transcendental *Naturphilosoph*," while others, taking a fallback position, describe him as a transitional figure between Enlightenment and Romanticism.[118]

In my opinion Kielmeyer can best be interpreted as an authentic representative of Enlightenment Vitalism, closely allied with Blumenbach, influenced by Herder, ambivalent about Kant's definition of science, and far from being either a *Naturphilosoph* or a Romantic. In his writings and lectures Kielmeyer deployed all of the elements constituting the language of

Enlightenment Vitalism to chart nature's progress and "acquire a closer knowledge of life's active forces."[119] He used analogical reasoning and comparative analysis to achieve this goal, arguing that all natural phenomena had to be studied diachronically seeking to answer "How is it, how was it, and how will it become?"[120] Kielmeyer's great ambition was to compose a general history and theory of development, a project never completed. He did, however, publish some of his views in his *Ueber die Verhältniße der organische Kräfte unter einander in der Reihe der verschiedenen Organisationen, die Geseze und Folge dieser Verhältniße* (Concerning the Relations of Organic Forces with Each Other in the Succession of Various Organized Bodies and the Laws and Results of These Relations). For some commentators this brief study constitutes one of the most important scientific documents of the era.[121]

In it Kielmeyer posed three related questions: (1) What forces are united in individuals? (2) What relations do these forces have with each other in different species, and how do these relations change in the succession of organized bodies? (3) How can the changes and continuities in species be grounded in the causes and effects of these forces?[122] To answer the first, Kielmeyer turned to a standard vitalist trope. He postulated the existence of five interacting forces that "demonstrate a permanence of effects under otherwise constant conditions,"[123] a definition virtually replicating those for occult force provided by Barthez and Blumenbach. The five forces were (1) sensibility, (2) irritability, (3) reproduction, (4) the force of secretion, and (5) the force of propulsion.[124] Each influenced the body through its own "law" regulating some phenomena but not all. Only when they operated in concert did they come close to accounting for nature's infinite variety.

As an example of how these laws worked singly and in concert, Kielmeyer discussed the first three forces of sensibility, irritability, and reproduction, propounding laws for each, but warning that vital laws, which narrated sequential change, differed from mechanical ones, which established fixed relations. Thus, a vital law cast in the linguistic form x increases *as* y decreases should not be read as a simple inverse relation. Rather, the German *wie* (as) should be thought of as *während* (during).[125] He discerned four basic laws pertaining to these forces: (1) "The variety of possible sensations in the series of organic forms decreases as the fineness and discrimination of the remaining senses within a limited domain increases." (2) "Irritability (measured by the permanence of its expression) increases as the speed, frequency, or diversity of these expressions and/or the multiplicity of sensations decreases." (3) "The force of reproduction (measured by the number of new individuals generated at a specific place) increases ... as the size of the procreated individuals decreases." (4) "The more the reproductive force is expressed in the number of new individuals produced at a specific place, the smaller are the new individual's bodies, the simpler is their body, the shorter the time required for them to be formed in their parent's bodies, and the shorter the force's duration."[126]

In explicating these laws, Kielmeyer sought to avoid the implication that the sequences he established were simple linear accounts of decline. Rather, as had other Enlightenment vitalists, he made the idea of compensation central to his explication. Thus, for example, in the case of the senses, when one of the senses disappears and the variety of sensations are reduced, "a free space is won for the others, and there where a less developed one stands, the other appears better perfected."[127] Not only did compensation work within each law, it determined how Kielmeyer thought these laws interacted, explaining the general order of nature but also accounting for its diversity.

The five forces interacted to shape organized bodies, where the assertion of one or two resulted in diminution of the others. Kielmeyer illustrated this dynamic by the interplay between sensibility, irritability, and reproduction, arguing that sensibility diminished when the other two forces asserted themselves, and how irritability would weaken with an increase of reproductive force. He defined the process as follows: "The more all modes of reproduction's expressions are united in one organism, the sooner is sensibility excluded and the sooner does irritability weaken. . . . The more one force is heightened, the more others were weakened. Sensibility and the reproductive force are the least compatible. Further, the more one of these forces is developed on one side, the more it is neglected on the other side."[128]

This process was regulated by compensation, harmony, and mediation, concepts that Kielmeyer believed universally applicable to all levels of organized life, from the individual to the species. This led him to clearly formulate the idea that ontogeny recapitulates phylogeny:

> The simplicity of these laws, which result in products that cascade forth in an unbelievable diversity, must become even more evident when one considers that just these laws, according to which the forces are divided among different organized bodies, are also exactly the same laws according to which these forces are distributed among individuals of the same species and even within the same individuals in different developmental stages. Both the human and the bird are plant-like in their earliest stage; the reproductive force is highly active in them. Later, their irritability arises in the fluid element in which they then live; even the hearts of these animals are indestructibly irritable; only later does one sense organ after another appear, almost in exactly the order, from the lowest

up, as they come into view in the succession of organized bodies; what once was irritability develops in the end into the ability to perceive [*Vorstellungsfähigkeit*], or at least into its invisible immediate material organ.[129]

In constructing these overarching patterns, Kielmeyer raised analogical thought to its highest degree, seeing in all living bodies the same sets of progressions, though taking many different forms. Kielmeyer assumed the existence of some basic pattern, similar to Herder's *Haupttypus*, around which the various forces interact to produce nature's infinite variety.

The question was how did development take place. Kielmeyer denied the continuous linear development of species or individuals and affirmed the real existence of species, assuming definite boundaries between them. For example, the development of a plant does not demonstrate a "continuous line." There are "intervals" between the gradations in the plant's transformations. The same is true in the succession of species. Kielmeyer proposed that not only did leaps take place but also the largest were between the most complicated species: "The more complex and compounded [*zusammengesetzt*] the organization, the greater will be the chasm that separates it from its nearest and most similar species." Thus, appearances to the contrary, the human, "as the last link stands so far distanced from all the others."[130] How did these transformations occur? Kielmeyer could not propose a simple answer, for he believed the generation of the succession of species has "been different in different times." He discerned two different types of species development. The first was "original," produced by nature at specific moments in time and then subject to variation due to climate and nourishment, though he also recognized that in some of these species, "perhaps all of their *primitive parents* have totally died out." The second he called "transmuted states of development," whereby some species "seem to arise from others as the butterfly does from the caterpillar. Initially they were stages of development" and then became "sanctioned as permanent species."[131] In theory, at least, three types of species could exist at any given time after the beginning of life: transmuted species, primitive species including their variations, and species somehow analogous to but not identical to their extinct parents. Thus, though Kielmeyer considered species to be real, they were neither fixed nor immutable. The complex world of living matter witnessed the birth of new species, the disappearance of existing species, and the prolonged survival of others. All of this took place within a dynamic equilibrium established by the interplay between the creative and destructive forces of nature. Given these possibilities and their myriad combinations, Kielmeyer believed no simple, uniform developmental pattern accounted for species change and permanence.[132]

Instead of offering a single model for the descent of species, Kielmeyer, envisioned a more complex picture in which no single organism recapitulates the total phylogeny of living nature. Rather, organisms go through stages analogous to one another, modified by compensation. Within the world of living organization, Kielmeyer discerned certain combinations of forces and organs forming specific types centered on a set of predominant organs, what he called an "organ system." A combination of interacting forces put pressures on each of these systems, producing innumerable variations and a certain number of species transmutations, which the observer could order serially. Yet though each animal and species in all the systems undergoes change over time, Kielmeyer believed that "many of the species in each system developed simultaneously, though analogically."[133] Kielmeyer's position, drawing upon Enlightenment Vitalism, offers an interesting contrast to theories later developed by Cuvier and Lamarck concerning species and development over time. They illustrate how, at the turn of the century, the mediated elements of Enlightenment Vitalism were slowly being uncoupled, the harmonies dissolved, the unconscious discursive bonds joining what later would appear as contradictory loosened, leading to different, contending, and exclusive explanatory patterns.

. . .

Cuvier and Lamarck both were formed in the discursive universe of Enlightenment Vitalism. Originally they believed in vital powers, the radical separation of living and dead matter, the real existence of species as defined by Buffon's reproduction law, and the centrality of analogical reasoning.[134] However, by the first decade of the new century, propelled by their increasingly bitter dispute concerning species and species development, they began to unravel the mediations between dynamic development and structural analysis characteristic of Enlightenment Vitalism. Each concentrated on one side of the mediation to the exclusion of the other.

Cuvier provided a radical interpretation of discontinuous change founded upon structural analysis that offered a very modern defense for the fixity of species. Unlike earlier defenders of the fixity of species, he did not deny that major changes had occurred in the natural history of the world. Quite the contrary, he argued that the world had experienced cataclysmic transformations, resulting in the destruction of species, whose only traces could be found in fossil evidence. Still, Cuvier tenaciously held the conviction that a species could not transmute or metamorphize into a new species. How did he resolve this seeming contradiction between immutability and revolutionary change? He did it by radicalizing the idea of revolutionary change, making it the agent for species destruction and new generation. In his pioneering studies on paleontology, Cuvier accepted fossil evidence showing that many species that once had lived no longer can be found on the earth. He reasoned that momentous historical catastrophes had caused their disappearance, destroying them at one blow and generalized this belief into a universal history of nature marked off by hermetically sealed periods. Each period had its own allotment of fixed species either created anew (probably through an act of spontaneous generation) after the disastrous revolution or populated by older species from other parts of the world spared from the cataclysmic change. Thus, he denied all connections between seemingly analogous species from different cataclysmic time periods. No matter how similar they appeared, they were totally different. (Of course, the only real proof for that assertion, given Cuvier's definition of species, could neither be substantiated nor disproved, namely, the successful mating of the two to produce fruitful offspring.) He supported this contention by referring to organic interconnection, to the functional integrity of the living organism.[135] Since all parts in an animal were interrelated, it was unthinkable, he maintained, to see a gradual change in one part without a corresponding change in the others. Simple, incremental addition slowly leading to new configurations defied the laws of organization and the economy of nature. For Cuvier, species change was either radical or nonexistent.

Cuvier historicized universal natural history to save the concept of the fixity of species by opting for a radical concept of discontinuous change. Natural history could be seen as a series of single episodes, each self-sufficient, independent of what came before and after, dramatic moments bereft of teleological emplotment. Depending on the extent and severity of these calamitous events, species either were obliterated or over time migrated to different parts of the world. Those that migrated remained the same, though subject to environmentally induced variations. New species arose to take the place of those obliterated.

Lamarck also historicized natural history, but in the direction of continuous change and teleological emplotment. Lamarck attempted to solve two interrelated questions. The first asked whether species do change, the second whether different forms of life "were progressively developed from the simplest to the most complex."[136] The first related directly to Cuvier's formulations, the second to Lamarck's desire to evolve a natural system of classification. In answering both questions, Lamarck provided a modernized version of the Great Chain of Being, set directly into historical time and accompanied by causal explanations for the gradual transformation of one form of organized matter into another. He founded it upon a general principle of movement, namely, that there was a "constant tendency for the volume of all organic bodies to increase and for the dimensions of their parts to extend up to a limit determined by life itself."[137] In mid-eighteenth-century language this law encompassed what had been understood as "development," namely, simple growth and expansion and associated with preformation. Lamarck had to show how "normal" development could lead to transmutations without accepting Cuvier's proposition of radical transformation.

To counter Cuvier, Lamarck argued that the difference between fossil evidence and present phenomena could be explained by the gradual transformation of previous forms over time into present ones. Lamarck did not deny that ancient fossils differed demonstrably from present forms, but he refused to see this difference as implying species destruction. This led him to deny the reality of species, returning to Daubenton's contention that the individual constituted the only real natural category. If one realized that everything over time changes by imperceptible degrees and no hard and fast blocks of living reality such as species exist, then the slow transformation of forms (recorded in fossil remains) into today's world of organization should come as no surprise. Lamarck supplemented this assertion by proposing a linear ladder of organization linking the simplest living organism through a series of progressions to the most complex. However, unlike later "evolutionists," he assumed this linear development capable of repetition because of spontaneous generation. The simplest organism generated today could, over time, travel a similar course as those formed in the past.

On a formal level this approach seems very close to Robinet's. But a vast conceptual breach separated them, for Lamarck—as virtually any major late Enlightenment thinker—rejected divine preformation. For this reason Lamarck had to account for ontogenesis. He offered a causal explanation based upon environmental challenge and organic response supported by the assertion that acquired characteristics can be inherited. Lamarck's theory of challenge and response offered nothing new. It had been a staple of vitalist thought since the revival of Hippocratic medicine. Vitalists had also often used the idea of the inheritability of acquired characteristics to explain certain phenomena, for example, skin pigmentation in humans. Lamarck, however, intensified this explanatory trope, arguing that the use or nonuse of certain organs and limbs led to qualitative organic change, which could be "preserved in the reproductive process and transmitted to the next generation."[138] These incrementally acquired characteristics led over time to major transformations in organic form, seemingly separating the original parent from the offspring. Lamarck turned Cuvier on his head. Where Cuvier believed in large-scale extinctions and new creation, Lamarck argued that hardly a species had ever disappeared; it has just been transformed over time.

Although differing in their definitions of species change, Cuvier, Lamarck, and Kielmeyer still employed a vocabulary largely derived from Enlightenment Vitalism. All conceived of a world exhibiting qualitative dynamic transformation, spontaneous creation, and organic interconnection unique to living matter. They believed the environment played a role in effecting change, on either a micro- or macrolevel. Although they did not agree upon the degree to which forces could be used to account for transformation, they all, to greater or lesser degree, assumed the existence of active, substantialized force. And all of them adamantly asserted the Buffonian ideal that progress in natural philosophy could be achieved only through intense and careful observation guided by a scientific imagination striving to embrace everything in one glance. In this sense they still spoke the language of Enlightenment Vitalism, even while its internal tensions were building, making it a target for a new language of nature formulated primarily in Germany, though quickly spreading to Great Britain and France. Its formulators called this language *Naturphilosophie*, announcing their intention to slack away what they considered a mishmash of divergent views in favor of a new, unified philosophy of nature. Although sometimes seen as the logical development of Enlightenment Vitalism, *Naturphilosophie* differed radically from it, advancing opposed methods, explanatory strategies, and conclusions. Without wishing to gloss over the obvious continuities between *Naturphilosophie* and Enlightenment Vitalism, I believe it imperative to distinguish between them in order to clarify the nature of the Enlightenment and to test the usual assumptions concerning its relation to the origins of modernity. This is the task I have chosen to undertake in the following chapter.

5 From Enlightenment Vitalism to Romantic *Naturphilosophie*

ROMANTIC *NATURPHILOSOPHIE:* A NEW "DARING ADVENTURE OF REASON"

Until recently scholars, especially historians of science, have treated Romantic *Naturphilosophie* with disdain, if not contempt. However, the emergence of postmodernism has led to its reevaluation. Postmodernism's critique of the Enlightenment, its attack upon instrumental reason, and its apprehensions concerning the dangers of scientism and technical progress appear to recapitulate themes announced by the *Naturphilosophen*.[1] Many scholars now consider *Naturphilosophie* an important corrective to what Max Horkheimer called "the self-destructive tendency of Reason," whose origins he located in the Enlightenment.[2] In this guise some contemporary critics characterize *Naturphilosophie* as an attempt to reestablish our ties with nature, to recapture the subjective and unconscious realms of human existence, to curtail the mechanization of the world picture, and to reestablish a harmony between nature and humanity.[3] Those working from this revised interpretation who trace *Naturphilosophie*'s immediate history locate its origins in the writings of the vitalists discussed in the preceding chapters. Considered the predecessors of *Naturphilosopie*, they are often excluded from the normal definition of the Enlightenment and subsumed under categories such as "proto-Romanticism," or "Counter-Enlightenment," designed to announce what will emerge rather than what had been. In such a teleological interpretation, the *Naturphilosophen* completed what "proto-Romantics" such as Buffon and "Counter-Enlighteners" such as Herder had begun. When dealt with at all, eighteenth-century vitalism is shorn of its ties to the Enlightenment "project" and treated as an episode in the prehistory of Romantic *Naturphilosophie*.

There is no doubt that Romantic *Naturphilosophie* could not have been constructed without concepts generated by Enlightenment vitalists. But in its goals, assumptions, and conclusions, Romantic *Naturphilosophie* differed radically from Enlightenment Vitalism. The *Naturphilosophen* proposed an intellectual, moral, and scientific agenda that stood in stark contrast to Enlightenment Vitalism. Thus, Romantic *Naturphilosophie* can indeed be considered a revolt against the Enlightenment, but not the type of revolt usually described. Its uniqueness lay not in the rejection of instrumental reason, in the attack upon mechanism, or in the concentration upon living nature, positions already staked out during the last half of the eighteenth century by Enlightenment thinkers. Rather, Romantic *Naturphilosophie* attempted to evolve a different language of nature, accompanied by new definitions of matter, reality, scientific method, and epistemology that contradicted those proposed by Enlightenment vitalists. In short, as Nicholas Jardine has suggested, the *Naturphilosophen* asked totally different questions than did their Enlightenment predecessors and came up with answers that varied radically from those previously posed.[4]

The chasm separating Enlightenment vitalists and the *Naturphilosophen* can be illustrated by an exchange of letters between Cuvier and Kielmeyer in 1807. Cuvier had asked Kielmeyer to comment upon contemporary trends in German natural philosophy, which had been passionately conveyed to Cuvier by Christian H. Pfaff, a recent convert to *Naturphilosophie*. Pfaff had joined a loose group of intellectuals, most of them born in the 1770s or later, dedicated to restructuring the manner in which nature and reality should be conceived. For them, Kant had laid the groundwork for this project in his *Metaphysical Foundations of Natural Science* and the *Critique of Judgment*, which they believed Fichte had sharpened and refined, though not adequately enough when applied to nature. They considered it their task to extend, simplify, correct, and complete what Kant and Fichte had begun. They were led in this undertaking by Friedrich Wilhelm Schelling and seconded by people such as Lorenz Oken, Carl von Eschenmayer, Andreas Röschlaub, Gustav Carus, Novalis (Friedrich von Hardenberg), Jacob Wagner, Pfaff, and many others, including in his own unique way, Hegel. As this abbreviated list suggests, a significant number of the most gifted young people in Germany were drawn to *Naturphilosophie*, though not all, as the counterexamples of Hufeland and the Humboldt brothers testify.

Cuvier, then secretary of the "Academie des Sciences," was well aware of the fissures threatening to rent the scientific community. The reports he had received from Pfaff convinced him that German *Naturphilosophie* posed a threat to what he considered normal science. In order to combat it, he wished to understand its essence, which led him to turn to his friend Kielmeyer. Cuvier asked Kielmeyer two questions that had emerged as central in his correspondence with Pfaff. The first: can one derive an explanation for the outside world through an a priori consideration of the human spirit? The second: to what degree could this explanation account for nature's manifestations? Kielmeyer's answer, entitled "On Kant and German *Naturphilosophie,*" reveals the difficulties the new system posed for late Enlightenment vitalists.

Kielmeyer located the connection between Kant and the *Naturphilosophen* in Kant's definition of matter. Kant had denied the reality of extension, considering it a product of sensory, subjective experience, constituted by the interaction between the two essential forces of attraction and repulsion. Kant claimed that "matter occupies space through active forces and not because of its mere existence."[5] He considered space and its attributes merely external appearances, whose understanding he relegated to practical wisdom, not pure science, which, according to him, focused upon rational principles derived from the activity of the mind. With one blow, Kant denied the mechanists' idea of atoms and the vitalists' concept of substantialized force.[6] Kielmeyer rejected Kant's reduction of matter to force, considering it purely a priori, and therefore not capable of accounting for nature's variety.[7] But Kielmeyer did not consider Kant a *Naturphilosoph*. Kielmeyer was correct. Kant had not attempted to explain the sensate world through an a priori consideration of the human spirit. Although he reduced extension to force, Kant refused to speculate upon the origins of basic forces, arguing "they can just be assumed."[8] Here Kant remained true to the Enlightenment's epistemological modesty, recognizing reason's limits, which must be respected.[9]

Although Kielmeyer did not mention this, Kant was equally wary about constructing a narrative explaining life's origins. In the appendix to the second part of the *Critique of Judgment,* Kant reflected upon the desire of the "archaeologist of nature to explain how the great family of living creatures ... arose." Kant did not say such an undertaking was opposed to reason; in fact, "a few of the most acute naturalists" had experimented with it. Still, Kant termed it "a daring adventure of reason" *(ein gewagtes Abenteuer der Vernunft),* for which no empirical proof could be found.[10] Kant considered such adventures highly suspect, certainly not part of the sober, critical study of philosophy or of nature.

The *Naturphilosophen* elevated this "daring adventure of reason" into a fundamental imperative. They replaced the Enlightenment's open, skeptical, and sometimes ambivalent stance with a totalizing vision. The stress of decades of warfare, of social and emotional uncertainty, and of a loss of faith in the complex aspirations of the late Enlightenment, symbolized by the failure of the French Revolution, led many young men and women to yearn for absolute answers that relegated the mundane world to an epiphenomenon, asserting, in its place, spirit as the true essence of reality. The new adventure of reason sought to unite what Enlightenment vitalists had sundered. The *Naturphilosophen* desired to recapture on a different level the universal vision that had animated the philosophies of Pythagoras, Plato, Plotinius, and Leibniz—most of them, with the possible exception of Leibniz,[11] proclaimed enemies of late Enlightenment natural philosophy. They sought to unite spirit and matter into a uniform whole, devoid of leaps in nature, empty space, and the distinctions between living and dead matter. They launched a full-scale attack upon any form of mechanism used to explain natural phenomena and attempted to narrate the history of the universe, considered as a living entity developing itself according to inherent principles. The Romantic *Naturphilosophen* constructed a new "creation myth," formulated in the language of the most "advanced" contemporary "sciences" of the time—the disciplines central to Enlightenment vitalism—yet aspiring to transcend the explanatory limits that had been imposed upon them.[12] In these endeavors the *Naturphilosophen* sacrificed epistemological modesty at the altar of certainty, raising reflective introspection to the status of universal truths of nature, spirit, and humanity.[13]

Kielmeyer judged *Naturphilosophie*'s assumptions as misplaced, rehearsing the same type of critique vitalists had made a half century earlier when they attacked "the spirit of systems." The mind could never overcome its own limitations and soar to the heights of pure knowledge to which the heirs of Pythagoras and Plato aspired. Thus, Kielmeyer contended that whatever valuable discoveries the *Naturphilosophen* made had nothing to do with the philosophy undergirding them. They were either due to serendipity or to the genius of the individual discoverer. After reviewing *Naturphilosophie*'s German career, Kielmeyer "gladly agreed" with Cuvier "that these investigations of natural knowledge, undertaken primarily by younger persons, have, in Germany, produced more damage than benefits."[14]

The *Naturphilosophen* dismissed such critiques as the last cries of those "stuck in the rubbish dump of sensory reflection."[15] For them observation's role in science remained secondary. Oken, who though not as creative as Schelling was probably the most influential *Naturphilosoph* of his time, expressed this conviction, using a gendered language I will discuss later:

"The observation of nature is the mother of *Naturphilosophie*, not its father. As the male generates only himself in a woman, so is *Naturphilosophie* eternally its own creator within the female [i.e., observation]."[16] Observation was merely the matter upon which the active spirit operated to generate its true self. The *Naturphilosophen* desired to go beyond the goals of the Enlightenment vitalists, who tried to harmonize the contending activities of precise observation and imaginative reconstruction. They attempted to reinvigorate science through philosophy, creating in the process a new cultural synthesis capable of reintroducing meaning into a world seemingly gone sour.

"GEOMETRIA EST HISTORIA": TOWARD A NEW *UNIVERSAL MATHESIS*

Although there were almost as many variations of *Naturphilosophie* as there were interpreters, a number of common themes emerged as central to the *naturphilosophic* project, giving it a certain unity despite its theoretical multiplicity. Lorenz Oken announced one of them in a work written to accompany his lectures, a theme he repeated in numerous works written between 1805 and 1809.[17] In his *Abriss der Naturphilosophie*, Oken chose as the work's motto the Pythagorean statement "Geometria est Historia," which he elaborated as follows: "There is only one certainty [*Gewissheit*] and that is the mathematical. The *mathesis* itself, however, is just the spiritual expression of that which one finds materially presented in nature. If we understood all of the modifications of the *mathesis*, we would then know all the symbols of nature and with them the modifications of nature itself. The modifications of both are endless, but in this exchange of mathematical forms certain basic figures are established, which remain unmoved, and around which all other forms gather as mere derivatives."[18] Here Oken expressed the *naturphilosophic* conviction that all sciences had to be modeled upon one and the same unitary form, providing them with essential explanatory categories. The *Naturphilosophen* justified this claim by asserting nature's unity, which when accepted and applied to science, Schelling claimed, would obliterate the "antithesis between mechanism and organicism, which has so long impeded the progress of science."[19] For Schelling and the other *Naturphilosophen*, all "natural operations must be derived *a priori* in order to recognize the possibility of a specific differentiation of each part of matter."[20]

The two related assumptions of the uniformity of nature and the identity between matter and spirit informed the complicated and seemingly bizarre explanations the *Naturphilosophen* formulated, which make their texts so difficult to comprehend. At times it appears these authors inhabited an alien intellectual terrain whose topography cannot be discerned without the assistance of a trained native guide.[21] Still, their overriding imperative is clear. The *Naturphilosophen* strove to reduce the variety of observed reality to simple, universal principles.[22] They proceeded by elevating proof over description, structure over empirical evidence, where "phenomena [the material] must totally disappear and just the laws [the formal] remain." These laws were to be "evident and certain."[23] The terms *evident* and *certain*, associated with the procedures of a priori thinking, and simplification, leading to the production of formal knowledge clearly testify to the desire to construct a universal *mathesis* based upon a mathematical model.

The *Naturphilosophen* announced the theme of mathematizing natural philosophy with fugal consistency. Johann Jakob Wagner said it simply: "There is no understanding [*Erkenntniß*] other than mathematics.... Don't all things live in numbers and figures and can understanding be anything other than the image of the thing?"[24] Oken defined mathematics as form "suspended above matter," referring to form as "etherealized [*vergeisigte*] matter." And Novalis considered differential calculus to be "the universal method that enables one to reduce the irregular to the regular" because of the "preestablished harmony" between it and matter.[25] These definitions, and they can be multiplied many times, all point to fundamental assumptions separating the *Naturphilosophen* from Enlightenment vitalists. The most obvious was the *naturphilosophic* quest to dematerialize the universe, reducing it to a system of signs independent of the signified.[26] They considered mathematical number and figure the purest examples of such a transparent language. As Wagner remarked, they "represent what is truly universal in every idea.... Mathematics is the true *a priori*."[27]

The *Naturphilosophen* turned to past philosophers to authorize their project of mathematizing and dematerializing the universe, adopting the rhetorical strategy the vitalists had employed against the mechanists, except invoking different authorities, namely, those the vitalists had condemned. Those most cited were Pythagoras, Plato, Plotinus, and Leibniz, sometimes accompanied by Paracelsus and the Kabbala. The *Naturphilosophen* accorded prime place to Pythagoras among the ancients and Leibniz among the moderns. This choice was obvious, for as John Neubauer has demonstrated, the *Naturphilosophen* consciously took up the seventeenth-century goal of constructing a universal *mathesis*, guided by reason, whose task was to order, control, and reign over the everyday flotsam and jetsam of material and empirical reality. This was a brave new world, enjoining the philosopher-mathematician-naturalists to comprehend what their immediate predecessors deemed incomprehensible, namely, the essence of life and its origins. Schelling threw down the gauntlet when he announced: "It is an old delusion that organization and life cannot be explained by natural principles. Does that mean as much to say that the first origin of organic nature is inexplicable, if so then this improvable assertion serves no purpose except to dampen the spirit [Muth] of the investigator."[28] Schelling showed no signs of a dampened spirit. He advanced an epistemologically aggressive program, highlighted by the assertive call to comprehend all of nature philosophically, for "to philosophize about nature means to *create* nature."[29] Schelling and his many admirers staked out a new claim for power and authority founded upon their invocation of the liberating force of absolute reason.

If mathematics provided the key to unlock nature's secrets, for us, it appears few *Naturphilosophen* knew how to use it. Their writings demonstrate no evidence of sophisticated mathematical reasoning. How can one account for this dichotomy between epistemological assertion and explanatory practice? In previous chapters I drew a distinction between mathematization and quantification, the former directed to reducing qualities to symbols to deduce laws from first principles, the latter to using quantification as a tool to explore the "facts" of nature. Mechanists mathematized, believing mathematical logic and nature's language identical. Late Enlightenment naturalists quantified, believing it impossible to establish an identity between reality and abstract symbols. The *Naturphilosophen* returned to the mechanist ideal, but with one major proviso, namely, that mathematics had first to be philosophized. They considered it necessary to recapture mathematics' essence and meaning, which they believed both mechanists and vitalists had ignored. Wagner presented a typical argument. After praising mathematics as a science of pure forms, he added that "since Pythagoras it no longer has recognized its essence [Wesen]; it has lost its highest value and richest meaning through the opinion that it should be separated from philosophy.... This science must return to its mother's womb if it wishes to embrace the nature of things with productive power."[30]

According to the *Naturphilosophen*, a vast chasm separated "higher mathematics" from normal mathematical practice. The *Naturphilosophen* felt surrounded by "calculators," quantifiers, people whose receptivity to the "magical world of characters" has been replaced "by a totally deadened fantasy."[31] For them this tendency found its clearest expression in France: "The French have given up thinking a long time ago and are now, since their political transformation, almost only calculators, experimenters, *raisonneure*, and undisciplined declaimers." Even Lavoisier had not escaped this contamination. Although the *Naturphilosophen* welcomed the new chemistry, it did not provide, as it stood, "an insight into inner nature. It is nothing more than a fact established through the strict application of calculation, one to which *Naturphilosophie* must first supply its meaning and importance."[32] The *Naturphilosophen* wished to reanimate that fantasy in order to recapture mathematics' pure ideas.

This program, designed to slough off existing research agendas, raised the *naturphilosophic* enterprise far above the mundane one Enlightenment vitalists had proposed. Novalis illustrates both this shift in assumptions and the types of knowledge claims the *Naturphilosphen* made. He had learned much of his philosophy from reading Dietrich Tiedemann's excellent six-volume *Geist der spekulative Philosophie*.[33] Tiedemann, a product of the Göttingen philosophical and philological tradition, composed the work to warn his readers of the dangers of speculation, castigating any philosopher succumbing to the charms of Plato, Pythagoras, Plotinus or "Theosophy." Tiedemann ranked Leibniz among them, for, Leibniz had assumed God to be the ultimate mathematician. According to Tiedemann, Leibniz believed that "when God calculates, a world arises *[cum Deus calculat: fit mundus]*." The perplexed Tiedemann, asked: "What could that mean but that all substances are thoughts of God ... that His modes are nothing but powers, that they exist as though they were ideas of reason *[Vorstellungen im Verstande]*? ... So it also follows that through the intellectualization of all substances there is no other way to explain their generation then: they are nothing but ideas, they must also be generated as are ideas."[34] What Tiedemann found disconcerting, Novalis considered exciting. He made it his task to look at the world from a universal vantage point and diagram the combinatorics of its matterless forms.[35] He and his fellow *Naturphilosophen* believed that since substances were generated in the same manner as were ideas, the principles of "higher mathematics" would enable them to rethink God's thoughts.

. . .

Lorenz Oken attempted to demonstrate how higher mathematics could achieve this goal in his *Lehrbuch der Naturphilosophie*, published in 1809 and dedicated to "his friends Schelling and Steffens." Oken asserted that mathematics' basic idea was "that zero equals zero," that is, zero was the base to which everything could be reduced. He called zero the "Nothing," the spiritualized core of all mathematics, where "the reality of mathematical multiplicity" originates.[36] Since the "Nothing" or zero was spiritual, it also constituted the core of reality, but its "allness" *(Allheit)* was not reality itself. Reality occurred with the ideal's extension, generating numbers, arising from what Oken described as "the emergence of the idea from itself, a manifestation as a singularity; every process of the idea becoming real *[Realwerden]* is a process of becoming finite *[Endlichwerden]*." Oken further argued that each "real" manifestation of the idea in numbers simply expresses the idea in a different form. Idea and reality are the same. In both, "there is an infinity; in reality there is an infinity of single forms, in the ideal, however, there is a single boundless form, here *an* eternity, there *an* infinity."[37]

In this argument Oken emphasized the nonmateriality of the zero, which he equated with the absolute, of the *Monas* (defined as inseparable, numberless, eternal, without any designation of time or space),[38] and of the *Monas*'s extended manifestations (numbers and individualities). Reality did not entail the generation of something that at one time did not exist and then appeared in time. Rather, it was the idea extending itself, where the first stage posited the basic duality of positive (+) and negative (−). Everything else in the real world derived from this initial positing. The essence of mathematics and of reality was contained in the ideas of the positive and negative: "Numbers are merely an act of the two ideas, where (+) according to its essence is nothing but a mere positing, a mere affirmation; the (−) is merely a denial *[aufheben]* of this affirmation, a negation." But Oken emphasized that all affirmations and negations passed through the zero, positive being the zero affirmed (= +o), negative the zero negated (= −o). The first step in the process of becoming real *[Realwerden]* entailed the positive affirmation of a number (+1), which "is a postulated absolute."[39] This affirmation results in reality and is directly aligned with the zero, accounting for the quality of infinite singularity. This being the case, what role did negation play in the process of becoming real? Were negative numbers also real? Seemingly not. For Oken, the perceptible world was a world of positivities. Negation occupied a secondary position in this process, a retarding one, hindering it and therefore making positivities perceptible. As such, negation partook both of the original positing (serving as its denial) and of the zero. The negation brought the affirmation back to zero, ensuring its appearance and containing its dissolution.

Oken sought to prove three points central to Romantic *Naturphilosophie* in this argument. The first denied the real existence of individualities (substances, matter, atoms, elements) in nature. They arose as a result of the play between the affirmations and negations through the *Monas*: "Nothing exists but the *Nothing*, nothing but the absolute, nothing but the eternal; all individual existence is nothing but an illusionary existence [*Trugexistenz*]."[40] For this reason, the *Naturphilosophen* denied that nature could be considered a product, something finished. Rather, it was an expression, as Schelling said, of the "active unconditional." To philosophize about nature required one to "animate it with freedom," an activity allowing us to understand nature's free development *(Entwicklung)*.[41] This led to the second point, the rejection of causal explanation, for causality assumed a temporal process in which things act upon things. Since all temporary manifestations of the process of becoming real were rooted in the *Nothing*, things cannot act upon each other. A -1 and a $+1$ are opposed ideas; they do not interact. The denial of the real existence of individuals and of causality led to the third proposition. If there were no causal connections between the *Monas*'s affirmations and negations, there would be no way to establish any temporal sequence in the process. This implied that in the process of becoming real the positive and negative appeared simultaneously: "The self-appearance of the absolute is not a mere appearance of the (+), but of the (+) and (−) at the same time, for 0 is not equal to plus (+), but rather is equal to plus/minus (0 = +/−)."[42]

Still, though Oken and the other *Naturphilosophen* affirmed simultaneous appearance, their language often suggested the opposite, which has led many to interpret the *naturphilosophic* concept of *process* in a manner counter to what I believe were their intentions. Oken's characterization of the process of becoming real offers a case in point. Linguistically it appears to describe a temporal progress, beginning with an affirmation, leading to a negation and then resulting in a resolution or a return to the zero. His claim that the negation included qualities of the affirmation (and not vice versa), strengthened by using the term *aufgehoben*,[43] reinforces this view. But Oken was aware of these linguistic difficulties and sought to counter them on two levels. On one he sought to modify the words' meanings by adding numerous modifiers drawn from analogies, comparisons, and an extremely rich metaphoric language. On the other, he transferred his analysis to the universal. He contended the absolute's self-appearance expressed God's universal consciousness. Since God is eternal, so is His self-consciousness, which includes the positive and negative joined to the zero as its definition (God's formula = + 0 −). Therefore, affirmation and negation have existed and will exist for all time. In other texts Oken spoke of the world's creation, using a language very similar to what we would call a big bang theory. No matter which version he used, God and His attributes existed or came into being simultaneously.

It is obvious in this case that Oken could not craft a language capable of expressing his ideas adequately. This applied as well to the other *Naturphilosophen*, who struggled to convey their insights largely with the grammar and words of an alien language of nature. Thus, they created terms such as the "process of becoming real" in a metaphorical manner, not to describe temporal succession but rather formal, one-dimensional relations. Oken's use of the term "process" reflected his desire to represent an eternal set of primary relations expressed in many possible variations, all replicating, however, the initial tension between (+), zero, and (−). These relations were fixed ratios, as Schelling would claim.[44] Oken's equation of God as the eternal embodiment of this linked, yet separated trias led him to draw a conclusion the skeptical Tiedemann had predicted, expressed forcefully in a language that found its echoes in Ranke's musing on historiography: "God's ideas and the creation of the world are the same. All things are nothing but images, thoughts, ideas of God. . . . Everything that we see are thoughts of God; we only see God thinking, or more, since we are also nothing other than thoughts of God, so we recognize only the succession of God's thoughts." In Oken's opinion, *Naturphilosophie*'s highest task, then, "was to seek out the forms in which God thinks."[45]

"NATURE IS VISIBLE MIND, MIND INVISIBLE NATURE": FROM HARMONY TO IDENTITY

Perhaps the most significant difference separating Enlightenment Vitalism from Romantic *Naturphilosophie* can be found in their contrasting epistemological tempers—fundamental attitudes toward what can be known, why it can be known, and how. The *Naturphilosophen* shunted aside the late Enlightenment's epistemological modesty, branding it timid and sterile, replacing it with an epistemological aggressiveness staking out bold new claims to power and knowledge. Novalis embodied this new temper. Unlike late Enlightenment thinkers, Novalis no longer disdained nor feared hypotheses: "Hypotheses were nets; only he who wishes to catch something casts them." Earlier fishing expeditions, feigning no hypotheses, had proven fruitless. Both "skepticism" as well as "ordinary empiricism have not done even the minimum for the expansion of science *[Wissenschaft]*."[46] But what assumptions enabled these young intellectuals to believe they could fish the waters of natural philosophy safely and successfully and thereby effect an explosion in knowledge and understanding? Carl von Eschenmayer provided a typical answer: "Study yourself and you certainly will find her [nature]."[47] At first glance this appears to repeat a typical Enlightenment trope. From Buffon through Hume, Rousseau, Blumenbach, Herder, and Kant, late Enlightenment thinkers argued that humans, being part of living nature, could acquire an intimate understanding of it through self-reflection, and vice versa, by examining living nature, humans could better understand themselves. But in this quest they emphasized the harmony between both, limited strictly the degree of knowledge one could obtain, and usually excluded acquiring knowledge of dead matter through this epistemological procedure. The *Naturphilosophen* obliterated all of these reservations. Human reason and nature's processes were one. As Wagner defined it, "That which [the human] forms through consciousness is only a higher stage of that which nature unconsciously develops outside of him; indeed the identity is so thorough that the free intellect in all of its conscious activities can only *reproduce* what nature unconsciously *produces*."[48] Or to put it more succinctly using Schelling's words, "Nature [is] visible mind, mind invisible nature."[49]

In arguing for the strict identity between mind and nature, the *Naturphilosophen* collapsed the distinction between them, denying Enlightenment Vitalism's mediating logic. But the collapse did not mean that one could choose either the path of observational reason or the method of a priori analysis to uncover nature's secrets. Turning to observation inevitably condemned one to wallow in a morass of contradictory and confusing results because of nature's infinite phenomenal multiplicity. Thus, the only true path to discovering truth lay in investigating mind. Self-reflective consciousness directed toward nature produced self-evident knowledge. Of course, once this knowledge was divined, one then could query nature through experiment. According to all of the *Naturphilosophen, constructing* reality followed a one-way street illuminated by the light of theory:[50] "He who does not have a correct theory, cannot possibly have correct experiences. . . . The fact, is, in itself, nothing."[51] Nature, defined as thought in appearance, followed the same pattern essential to thought. Since thought was an activity that discriminated, it cannot appear except through contradiction. This applied as well for nature once it emerges from its wholeness, its "absolute indifference." Nature expressed this duality through polar opposition, which, according to Schelling, "establishes the condition by which an infinity can be represented in the finite, that is, by which nature is at all possible."[52] Not only was duality the source of all finite appearances, but it was incapable of further reduction as well: "This antithesis is simply postulated. It is not capable of being empirically derived. Its origin is to be found in the original duality of our spirit, which constructs a finite product through opposed activities."[53] The *Naturphilosophen* populated the phenomenal world with bipolar oppositions, supposedly recapitulating the *Ur*-polarity, drastically revising the content of the "normal" sciences from which they borrowed some of their individual concepts. Chemistry provides a striking example.

Modern research has shown that the "new" chemistry occupied a central role in *naturphilosophical* thought.[54] It provided the *Naturphilosophen* with crucial metaphors and with a model explaining combination, leading Schelling to define life as a chemical process.[55] But when he said that, he did not mean that life could be reduced to the actual physical operations Lavoisier had described. Rather, as in mathematics, chemistry had to be enhanced by the law of polarities to produce a "philosophical chemistry." For this reason the *Naturphilosophen* dismissed Lavoisier's analysis of oxidation as one-sided. It had to be supplemented by a negative concept, which they called, using Stahlian terminology, "phlogistication," the "phlogistic process," "decombustion," or in Oken's case "deoxidation." They argued that in the chemical process two forms had to be present, a positive material (oxygen) and its negation (phlogiston). Phlogiston "exists not in itself, but only as opposition to oxygen and light, and expresses nothing else but a concept of reciprocal interaction.... Phlogiston is therefore no more nor less than the Negative of Oxygen."[56]

As was their wont, the *Naturphilosophen* generalized their definition of philosophical chemistry into a universal principle characterizing all phenomena, discovering oxidation and phlogistication everywhere in nature, accounting not only for "combustion and decombustion," but also for "the antithesis between the sun and the planets."[57] Chemistry therefore took on a totally new meaning. Oken, for example, spoke of a "universal chemistry" *(Weltchemismus)*, a uniform process that stretched from simple phenomena to the most cosmic, which he evoked in almost biblical language: "The brain deoxidizes itself..., seeing occurs; the sun deoxidizes itself, the air deoxidizes itself, the water deoxidizes itself, it becomes day."[58] The *Naturphilosophen* elevated philosophic chemistry, founded upon the principle of polarity, to an essential element of the language of nature. "Nature and chemistry," Schelling proclaimed, "are related to each other as language is to grammar."[59]

. . .

Although polar opposition constituted the essential prerequisite for thought, the *Naturphilosophen* did not construct their language of nature solely upon it. They believed in identity and unity, not in a Manichaean universe of pure opposition. Therefore, they claimed the existence of a linking element, joining the oppositions, partaking in them, yet preserving them. Schelling called this binding element the *Band* or *Cupola* and claimed this discovery constituted the greatest contribution he had made to comprehending thought and nature: "The ancients had already known or surmised that a contradiction, a duality lay at the core of matter. But that this duality is elevated *[aufgehoben]* to a third element and that it represents itself as a closed and self-identical triplicity is now in everyone's mouths since these investigations have lately suggested it."[60] The *Cupola* ensured identity in nature. As Nees von Esenbeck asserted, "polar oppositions take place in the unity and through it, namely, through the point of indifference *[Indifferenzpunct]* to which they are drawn."[61] The *Naturphilosophen* often used the image of the magnet to give this idea visual representation. In it the poles arose only because they were united through the indifferent middle. The poles existed in tandem and never interacted directly. The phenomenon of magnetism constituted for them a unity in triplicity. But, as in chemistry, once the *Naturphilosophen* decided that magnetism expressed a basic truth, they translated it into a universal. Schelling would ask, for example, doesn't "every body, as iron, have its own ore, i.e., its own body for which it is a magnet?" He answered in the affirmative and called for the general search for the magnet in each and every body. In this endeavor to universalize magnetism, the *Naturphilosophen* often dematerialized it. Along with physical magnetic bodies, "symperimagnetic" bodies, they posited "idiomagnetic"ones.[62] It was clear, Schelling stated, that there is not a single substance in nature that does not have a magnetic principle,[63] a position that explains why the *Naturphilosophen* were such avid supporters of animal magnetism during the first third of the nineteenth century.

In their writings the *Naturphilosophen* continually strove to demonstrate the linkage of polarities through the *Cupola,* proposing theories concerning nature's processes totally opposed to the era's normal science. Oken's explanation for the genesis of matter's first forms is typical. He argued that matter first arose through fixing aether's poles, constituting the first emanation out of the absolute *Nothing.* It produced the phenomenal forms of "light matter"*(Lichtstoff),* which was positive, and negative "heavy matter" *(Schwerstoff).* Matter's further elaborations were compositions of these two *Ur*-principles linked to the original aether from which they arose. In them, light matter, *Ur*-aether, and heavy matter combine to become first the sun, the planets, and the aether, then appear in a second manifestation as light, gravity, and heat, which in the terrestrial world turn into air, earth, and water.[64] Water served as the *Cupola* joining earth and air. With its appearance, Oken exclaimed, "the metamorphoses of the divinity *[Gottheit]* is consummated and completed, for no closer can the divided person appear than in this mating *[Begattung]*, no tighter can the dyadic circle close than in this point.... In water the two sexes of the divinity have wedded."[65]

The *naturphilosophic* assertion of nature's unity led its proponents to resurrect an ancient idea rejected by mechanists and Enlightenment vitalists alike, namely, that each individuality is a microcosm of an all-encompassing unity. According to Schelling, when the "copula affirms itself in a singularity, there is microcosm, organism, a complete representation of the universal life of substance in a specific life."[66] Oken took this idea to its logical and perhaps most bizarre conclusion when he sought to account for the phenomenon of consensus or sympathy between organs in a living animal, using the language of identity and micro-macro relations with wild abandon:

> If universal consensus is the identity between the consenting organs, so must it also be with the specific organs. The consenting organs are consequently necessary appearances of the self, as are the brain and the skin. That they are such makes it not difficult to prove a system of physiology, and everyone would comprehend that in all organs there is just a graduated repetition of the basic organ. He who believes that an organism consists of alien individualities joined together will never see two organs appear as capsule and corolla; for him [the idea of] sympathy is lost. He who is not capable of perceiving the stomach in the brain, the lungs in the kidneys, the thorax in the nose, the whole rump in the ear, the whole body in the sexual organs, the female sexual organs in the male's, can never feel how sympathy works.[67]

It should be clear from this that Oken and the other *Naturphilosophen* had staked out a vastly different intellectual terrain than the one inhabited by the Enlightenment vitalists. The vitalists did believe that "an organism consists of alien individualities joined together" through *rapports,* sympathy, and consensus. Each conjunction represented the interaction between active forces and between the body and the environment in which it existed. Their language elevated the centrality of human interchange, paralleling a political model envisioning independent participants reaching consensus within an "assembly of forces." The Romantic *Naturphilosophen,* confronted with the apparent failure of this model of the body politic, lost faith in all effects dependent upon the fickle interactions of postulated individualities, whether in the realm of everyday experience or especially in nature. They sought to discover permanence behind the facade of mere events. Their solution of dematerializing the body led them to change the meaning and content of each of the concepts they took from the dominant sciences of the late Enlightenment. We have seen how this applied to mathematics, chemistry, magnetism, and organic interconnection. This is especially clear in the manner in which the *Naturphilosophen* conceived of process.

"BEING ITSELF IS ACTIVITY": FROM CHANGE TO PROCESS

There are few historians who do not wince at some of the *naturphilosophic* scientific explanations, but there are many who believe the *Naturphilosophen* made an enormous contribution to shaping modernity through their dynamic vision of process.[68] Schelling, for example, is said to have been the first to explicate in "systematic form one of the most influential ideas in modern thinking: the idea that self-consciousness has to develop in stages from a point where it did not exist as such."[69] For many critics, the *Naturphilosophen* were leaders in effecting the early-nineteenth-century "episteme shift," which supposedly historicized nature, thought, and life.

Certainly the language the *Naturphilosophen* employed to describe nature appears to demonstrate their fixation with change. Schelling consciously called his philosophy a dynamic one, seeing its essence in the proposition that "nature is simply active," in "every one of its products there lies the drive [*Trieb*] toward an infinite development [*Entwicklung*]."[70] Nothing was permanent or static in nature: no fixed elements, no basic substances, and no unchanging relations. The idea of permanence was "a lie": "Every product that now seems *fixed* in nature, will exist only for a moment and then be involved in continuous evolution [*Evolution*], always changeable, only appearing transitionally and in vanishing."[71] Schelling equated nature's dynamism to an organism, whose essence was activity: "The whole of nature = an organization, therefore nothing in nature can arise that does not belong to this universal organism, or is subject to it; in short, nothing individual can exist in nature."[72] The law of duality within the trias ruled the universal organism, setting it in infinite motion.[73]

Schelling used Blumenbach's term *Bildungstrieb* to characterize organic process, but philosophized it, raising it to a single universal tendency in nature. It played itself out through the antagonism between expansion and cohesion, manifesting itself in ever-new forms. Although each new form appeared to be the result of chance, the *Trieb*'s direction was determined, for the *Bildungstrieb* represented the organism's "desire to be itself." The formative process proceeded through gradations, none of them fixed. Formation presented a continuity of infinite variations of the basic polar opposition, where differences could at best be expressed in the relative terms of more or less, in rising or sinking, or as a pulsation between two extreme points, in which one form flows into the other.[74] For Schelling, unlike Blumenbach, there were no leaps in nature. The chain of being was closed and complete: "The various gradations of development are nothing other than various steps of *Bildung*, or formation *[Gestaltung]*. Every individual product of nature goes through all possible formations until it reaches the point of its own retardation."[75]

From the above, it could be concluded that Schelling and the *Naturphilosophen* adopted some of the central concepts of Enlightenment Vitalism, transformed them by generalizing them, and in so doing constructed a language of nature elevating process as supreme. But the critical question here is what did the *Naturphilosophen* mean by the term "process"? Does it have the meaning we usually ascribe to it, and to what extent did it agree with the vitalists' concept of change? From what I have suggested about Oken's concept of process, I believe that the usual interpretation of the *Naturphilosophen* as pioneers in creating the modern idea of historical change misreads their intentions.

An insight into how the *Naturphilosophen* conceived of process can be gleaned from a comment Schelling made on how natural gradations should be understood: "The assertion however, that in reality the various organizations have formed themselves through a gradual development from each other is a misunderstanding of an idea that actually belongs in reason. Namely: all individual organizations taken together should be equivalent to a single product; this is conceivable only if nature has held before them the one and same *Urbild*."[76] If these gradations were not a "real genesis," what did they represent? Dietrich von Engelhard answered: "an ideal genesis, a change in the ideal foundation of nature."[77] Schelling underscored the process's ideal character when he denied that one form of matter (or one idea) could influence another directly.[78] Could one consider these gradations ideal types, abstractions of reality designed to clarify and illuminate the essentials of real development? As far as the evidence suggests, I doubt it. Although the concept of ideal types traces its origins to Max Weber, analogous constructions were used in the eighteenth century, represented by Montesquieu's typology of rule or, in the life sciences, the various ideas of

Haupttypus, prototype, and *Urtyp.* Eschenmayer explicitly rejected these eighteenth-century typological formulations in his discussion of nature's essential duality. This duality cannot be seen "as the relation between type *[Urtyp]* and antitype *[Gegentyp],* but as pure negative ideality opposed to pure positive reality."[79] In whatever manner ideal types are constructed, their final goal is to explain real relations. The *Naturphilosophen* denied the actual existence of real relations as Oken made clear: "After the universe was created, absolutely nothing more arises through analysis; for what could arise, since everything, what is, and can be, is."[80] At best, these statements suggest that process constituted a continual cycle of formation and disintegration revolving around the core of reality, the eternal trias. Schelling expressed this view when he claimed that "The distinctness of the stages at which we now see the organization fixed evidently presupposes a ratio of the original forces peculiar to each one; whence it follows that nature must have initiated anew each product that appears fixed to us."[81] Thus, as Jardine concluded from this statement, "it should be possible in principle to derive a priori the entire sequence of types of organization through which nature strives to reach the original ideal."[82]

In making this argument, the *Naturphilosophen* rejected linear change, whether in a positive or negative direction, itself a major departure from Enlightenment Vitalism. It is true the *Naturphilosophen* did invoke the term *Stufengang* tied to the idea of the Great Chain of Being linking the lowest to the highest to describe gradation, which seems to suggest linear progression. In this series *(Reihe),* Schelling established a hierarchy of three potencies *(Potenzen)* by which the trias was expressed. The first was the potency of matter and the universe defined by the interactions between repulsion, attraction, and gravity. The second, the potency of the inorganic, defined by the interactions of magnetism, electricity, and chemistry. The third, the potency of the organic, defined by the interactions of reproduction, irritability, and sensibility. Yet in explicating the potencies, Schelling and the other *Naturphilosophen* turned to metaphors grounded either upon pulsation—the continual moving from point to point and back again—or upon circular movement—of continual return to the original starting point. For Schelling, universal organic metamorphosis was marked "by a continual *return of nature into herself,* which is her essential character."[83]

Schelling, using a striking metaphor, spoke of the wheel of life, which rolled from one point to another, tracing a circle, returning to the point where it began, and beginning again its eternal journey.[84] It might appear then that the idea of a series, a *Reihe,* stood in stark contrast to either circular movement or pulsating processes. This disappears when we remember that Schelling and the other *Naturphilosophen* derived their image of a series from an infinitive mathematical series, not from a physical image of serial transformations. In mathematics a circle constitutes an infinite series. Each potency, therefore, was a circle within a circle replicating the original trias in its own sphere.

If Schelling sketched out the outlines of this argument, Oken made them explicit in his *Lehrbuch der Naturphilosophie*.[85] Oken argued that an isolated straight line cannot exist in nature. The only possible line, the *Ur*-line, was a radius, linking a center to a periphery. Oken called the difference between the center and the periphery the *Ur*-opposition; since everything was activity, the radius automatically traced out a sphere. Hence, the sphere was the most complete form in nature, the only one in which God could appear: "When God wishes to become real, He therefore must appear in the form of a sphere; for God no other form exists. The God in being is an infinite sphere." The sphere was nature's *Urform;* "the more spherical the form, the more perfect, the more God-like it is."[86] If the *Ur*-line was a radius, the *Ur*-surface was spherical.[87] Nature's essential sphericity ensured that all "movement is circular; everywhere there is no linear movement just as there is no straight surface." Essential circularity expressed in spatial terms as a sphere negated any form of progression, the "movement of the *Ur*-sphere cannot be progressive, for it fills everything."[88]

This obsession with the idea of return, an expression of a fundamental nostalgia so prevalent among the *Naturphilosophen,* explains their fascination for the *Ur* in other aspects of life—with mythology, ancient languages, original folk tales, Vedic religion, ancient Greek philosophy, the Middle Ages, and, for some, Roman Catholicism. By returning to the "mother's womb," to use Wagner's formula for reforming mathematics by harking back to Pythagoras, the *Naturphilosophen* expressed their dissatisfaction with the world as it had become and their hope for its general purification by recovering its original roots. Equating mechanism and normal science with the ravages wrought by the French Revolution, they hoped for the reemergence of the positive in life's essential polarity, for the appearance of organic understanding.

Images of return and circular process may deny linear development, but normally incorporate temporal progression within spatially defined limits. The question is whether the *Naturphilosophen* framed their vision of process in these terms. Despite the counterevidence of a number of temporal and spatial metaphors, I believe they detemporalized process, transforming it into a set of statically defined relations. Oken made the *naturphilosophic* separation of motion and process clear: "There is in the universe no original movement *[Bewegung]*, which in and through itself would be simply movement; instead all movement, including the *Ur*-movement, [exists] only through a process, not through a process of movement *[Bewegunsgprocess]*, for such a thing does not exist; rather it [exists] through an *Ur*-process, determined by the nature of the *Ur*-creation; only through and within this *Ur*-process is movement established. It is therefore the process before movement that must be investigated."[89] Movement in the normal sense of the word (as we might use it) at best constituted a phenomenal derivation of process, a secondary characteristic irrelevant to *naturphilosophic* investigation.

What then constituted "movement" in *naturphilosophic* terminology if not sequential change? Schelling defined it simply: "the movement of a thing is nothing other than the expression of its *Band* with other things."[90] He redefined movement as a relation determined by the manner in which the polar oppositions were united through the *Band*, or trias, namely, the specific ratios of the "original forces peculiar to each one." Oken made this clear in his explication of reality's rise through the initial appearance of the trias: "The positive idea is the first to appear, the negative the second, the combined the third, but not as if they appeared one after the other—this is impossible, for they appear conjointly (before all time)—or as if they were in different places, for they are everywhere, but rather only according to their disposition and their value. The three are one, and the One is three, because it is and because it must be, what is."[91] In short, the *Naturphilosophen* transmuted the language of succession into one expressing a relational hierarchy of values, constructed to differentiate between simultaneously existing appearances of reality's initial manifestation. They considered process as the total appearance of duality in triplicity, movement the specific expressions of the tension or the *Spannung* between the poles within any triadic combination. But all manifestations of reality simply replicated the *Ur*-polarity, differentiated only by the *Spannung* between the two poles and of the combined intensity of the united trias in each.

This is not an easy concept to explain, so perhaps an example will help illustrate the breach separating *Naturphilosophie* from the late Enlightenment. I turn again to Oken, this time to his explanation for the solar system. He considered the solar system an example of what he called a "centro-peripheral system" found everywhere in nature. It depended upon the *Spannung* between center and periphery, leading to the appearance of coagulated aether or, in this case, light (the first positive manifestation of aether). It had been created at a "single blow, and remained as it had become." Thus, the solar system's creation could never be comprehended mechanically, but rather "dynamically." It arose "through polarization according to eternal laws, according to the laws of light."[92] The dynamic polarization of light within the centro-peripheral system instantaneously produced the sun and the planets, the sun as the positive pole, the planets as the necessary negative pole. It also immediately established the other *Spannungen* between the universe's visible appearances, including comets and the moon. Oken was adamant in insisting that the moon could never have appeared after the earth's formation, nor could it have broken away from the earth at a moment in time. Its relation to the earth replicated the relation of suns to planets, all held in place through the strength of the bipolar *Spannung*.

The relative strength of the opposite poles in the *Spannung* determined the distances between planets and suns (Oken envisioned a universe filled with different solar systems not clustered around a "universal" central body—only God was central). If a sun, as active pole, is strong, then the planets will be further away from it. If the central pole is weak, then the planets will be closer. At the same time, the negative strength of the planets also determined their respective place in their solar system. The stronger the planet's "polar energy," the farther away it will be from its sun, for "the more alive *[lebendig]* the planet, the more eccentric its orbit must be, because it's opposition with light would be too great."[93] Thus the weakest planet was closest to the sun.

In this argument Oken totally reversed standard Newtonian physics. There was no such thing as a void, for the perceptible universe was nothing but the polarized modifications of the omnipresent universal aether, forever replicating the *Ur*-trias on various levels. The planets did not possess centrifugal force tending toward the tangent and countered by an attractive force originating from the sun: "The theory of attraction has no meaning. Attraction is a *Qualititas occulta,* an angel, which flies by the planets." Rather than being determined by physical attraction and repulsion, the planets moved "playfully around the sun," because they were alive, animated by the bipolar *Spannung*.[94] Working from this denial of mechanistic explanations, Oken rejected the possibility of physical interaction between aether's "coagulated" bodies. All were phenomena of the original *Spannung,* placed in a hierarchy of positions determined by their own polar energies. For this reason Oken denied the possibility that comets could ever collide with a planet. Such a fear was "ridiculous *[lächerlich],* just as is the hypothesis that a comet caused the deluge, or shifted the earth's axis. How can one imagine such a thing, even if one had no other insight into the planetary system than the knowledge of its regularity?"[95]

I undertook this excursion into Oken's solar theory to demonstrate that *Naturphilosophie*'s "dynamic" language of nature was not what many have claimed it to be. Rather than making process, as normally understood, central, they strove to eliminate or minimize the temporal and epistemological uncertainties of a fully historicized world. Perhaps Oken's dismissal of any likelihood that a comet could come crashing into the earth was symbolic of their fears and their hopes: their attempt to contain contingency and revolutionary transformation, their elevation of spirit above matter, a claim that empowered them as insightful interpreters of nature and meaning. The *naturphilosophic* vision of process stood in stark contrast to the language of change evolved by Enlightened vitalists. Rather than expanding upon the vitalists' concern with change over and through time, with leaps in nature and with the "real" interaction between vitalized bodies, the *Naturphilosophen* created a language of nature that dissolved change into pulsations within a strictly demarcated sphere, constructed process as repetition of a basic form in which each repetition had no contact with any other, and privileged the newly constituted hierarchies it had spawned. Nowhere is the hierarchic and dynamic-static element of their thought more clearly expressed than in the discourse the *Naturphilosophen* evolved to explain generation and gender relations.

THE SCIENTIFIC CONSTRUCTION OF GENDER IN THE LATE ENLIGHTENMENT AND ROMANTIC *NATURPHILOSOPHIE*

In the second and third editions of Johann Friedrich Blumenbach's essay on generation, *Ueber den Bildungstrieb* (1789, 1791), Blumenbach included an endpiece picturing two snakes sensuously entwined around each other. The lower half of their bodies were tightly wound around each other on the ground. Their upper halves moved toward an erect position where the circles became looser, ending in a grand sweep with their heads joined in a kiss. The diagram traced a spiral movement in which the last turn of the spiral expanded out to form two curved lines, each approximating Hogarth's line of beauty and together almost tracing the figure of a heart, the symbol of love.[96] The scene took place in a forest before a large rock from which plants sprung forth, the space framed by living vegetation. Both snakes were drawn without any marks or features to distinguish one from the other except for a difference in size. Blumenbach noted that the engraving presented "a decorous but, as naturalists know, very meaningful representation of the pleasure, which is a result of the *Bildungstrieb*."[97]

Enlightenment Vitalism to Naturphilosophie / 221

In 1805 the young *Naturphilosoph* Lorenz Oken published a work entitled *Die Zeugung* (Generation). It had a frontispiece that also pictured two snakes. Coiled tightly around each other as strands in a rope, the snakes formed a circle where each strand increased in size from tail to head. Rather than interacting with one another, each snake held its own tail in its mouth to complete its own circle. Each head pointed in a different direction, one facing upwards, the other horizontally. There were no flora and fauna in the picture. The engraving creates the impression of abstract one-dimensionality without any hint of sensuality or even of the mild eroticism suggested by Blumenbach's allusion to the *Bildungtrieb*'s pleasures.

The contrast between the two illustrations is dramatic and, in my opinion, not accidental. Given that Blumenbach's work was the most influential late-eighteenth-century German treatise on generation, it is more than probable that Oken conceived his frontispiece as a direct commentary to Blumenbach's endpiece. It served as a silent though effective critique of Blumenbach, who wielded considerable academic power, making him too dangerous to attack directly in print, especially since Oken was teaching at Blumenbach's university when *Die Zeugung* was published.[98] The two representations depict in striking form the difference between the gender constructions of late German Enlightenment vitalists and German Romantic *Naturphilosophen* and point to their radically opposite ideas of generation.

Generation occupied a central category in the intellectual economy of late Enlightenment thinkers. It mobilized a host of cultural, social, and political symbols and metaphors that spoke directly to central issues of Enlightenment culture. When the issue of generation first came to a head in the midcentury, the central disputes focused upon how creation took place, what defined a species, how one could represent change in and through time, to what extent hierarchies were natural and unchanging, and what was the connection between traditional Christian concepts and natural philosophy. In this phase of the discussion generation and gender were vaguely linked, and when done, gender played a bit part in the drama that captured the imagination of educated Europeans, who argued over preformation and epigenesis for philosophical, religious, and political reasons. There were indeed important gender implications raised by these disputes, but they did not loom as central. The type of specific interpretation one took within each of the contending models of generation could call forth different gender interpretations.[99]

Over the course of the last half of the century, however, gender, often interpreted in terms of sexuality, increasingly occupied a more important place within the competing discourses of generation. Rather than focus solely upon the process of either "development" (preformation) or epigenesis, one increasingly began to investigate the actors in this play, namely, the male and the female, and asked what separated and linked them. As the question was posed, the answers tended to lead to a physical differentiation between both sexes in which naturalistic narratives increasingly were mobilized to account for gender differentiation. In this sense, Thomas Laqueur's assertion that the eighteenth century invented the modern idea of sex, which served "as a new foundation for gender," is correct.[100] But though the language of sexuality increasingly served as the vehicle for expressing gender, it did not focus upon specific sexual organs as central in defining sexuality, a position made clear by Ludmilla Jordanova: "Naturalistic ways of thinking about gender did not locate sex differences in organs but in the interaction between a way of life and an organism considered as a totality."[101] This certainly applied to the Enlightenment vitalists. In their adoption of a Hippocratic explanation for generation (rather than an Aristotlean one, which Laqueur believes was the case), they located the causes of sexual differentiation in the relative powers of the mixing male and female fluids, both in determining the sex of the new individual and in shaping its particular features. And they fervently believed that this action was greatly influenced by the environment in which the organized body lived and by the "customs," "habits," or "morals" of the time. Enlightenment vitalists, as many eighteenth-century thinkers who considered nature and morality conjoined, assumed that the appearance of sexual differentiation (when that occurred was a matter of heated discussion) also signaled a "moral" differentiation between the genders. At first, the vitalists explained gender differentiation using the theory of temperaments, then turned to relative degrees of irritability, and finally concluded that it was a product of the interaction between vital forces. No matter which explanation they deployed, most vitalists modified it by subsuming sexual and gender difference within the unity of the human species, considering it a variable. As Jordanova argues, "It had become clear by the end of the eighteenth century that living things and their environment were continually interacting and changing each other in the process. This was true of sexuality, for, although sex roles were seen as being in some sense 'in nature,' because of the relationship to physical characteristics, they were also seen as mutable, just as physiology and anatomy in general were taken to be."[102] Complimentarity rather then incommensurability guided their thoughts about gender difference.

This was true for Blumenbach. The essay on the *Bildungstrieb* dealt primarily with generation. He wrote it to destroy the preformationist position, not to reduce humans to sexually defined objects. Sex played a minimal role in the work. When Blumenbach did evoke sexual difference, he did it to demonstrate the unity of the species shaped by the *Bildungstrieb*'s action of merging mechanism with teleology. He proposed two prominent examples illustrating this unity in diversity. The first was the *bursa Fabricii* in the cock, the second the human male's nipples. In the first, the *bursa* played a real role in generation, serving as an organ to attract the female to mate. In the second the male nipple was merely a mechanical remnant, serving no function, but reminding us of the unity of the human species. Blumenbach's idea of the *Bildungstrieb*, when applied to sexual difference and by extension to gender, offers a prime example of the imperative to mediate between opposites, central to the late Enlightenment's scientific and epistemological project. This imperative, along with the assumption that all humans were mixtures of masculine and feminine qualities, led to constructions of gender relations that tended more toward idealizations of androgyny than to incommensurable differentiation.

If one looks at the gendered world inhabited by many educated men and women in Germany during the late eighteenth century, this tendency toward androgynous attitudes becomes evident. Let me cite two examples. The first was the widespread shift in forms of address, expressions of emotion, and polite conventions between people of both sexes. The second, partly arising as a consequence of the first, entailed a loosening of taboos concerning male and female social and sexual conventions, which led many to question the traditionally accepted models of gender that had been forged during the early modern period and to propose new alternatives to them.

The first phenomenon has often been associated with such diverse movements as the rise of the modern idea of romantic love, the effects of the *Sturm und Drang*, the secularization of Pietistic models of religion, or the German rebellion against French classicism and aristocratic culture. However explained, there is no doubt that the last third of the century in Germany witnessed an intensification of emotion between individuals expressed in terms of intimacy with very strong erotic overtones. This is evident if one looks at the correspondence between friends during this period. The hetero- and homoerotic flavor of these letters is unmistakable. Expressions of love and affection were used as frequently between members of the same sex as between ones of the opposite sex, and often by the same correspondents writing to friends of either sex. This alone is indicative of the breakdown of normal gender relations, showing the narrowing of the distance between the two. Men addressed men as they addressed women in a language that for earlier generations would have seemed highly inappropriate and for later ones too intimate. At least this was true for those letters exchanged by intimates linked together in loose associations of friendship such as the *Tugendbund* to which Wilhelm von Humboldt and some of his closest male and female friends belonged.

This highly charged erotic-emotional universe also witnessed the emergence of a group of very impressive women whose personalities and learning placed them on an equal footing with the men with whom they socialized, corresponded, married, or had liaisons. These women provided physical proof for the general questioning of traditional gender relations. From Madame de Staël through the Berlin *salonnieres* such as Henriette Herz and Rachel Varnhagen, to the daughters of famous scholars and intellectuals, such as Brendel Veit (Mendelssohn's daughter), Caroline Michaelis, Dorothea Schlözer, and Therese Heyne, women such as these played an important role in shaping the cultural and emotional life of those growing up in the late Enlightenment. Taken together, the interactions between and among the sexes and the highly charged emotional environment in which they were played out appeared to threaten seriously the traditional rules governing gender relations.

One of the most powerful ideas evolved within this shifting world in which ambiguity appeared to reign was that the new person, whether male or female, should incorporate, as best as possible, the positive aspects of the other gender. Thus, categories of male and female, though increasingly constructed according to certain contrasting typologies, were seen as both the limits within which life was lived as well as one-sided exaggerations, which should be modified through interaction. The Enlightenment vitalists did not propose an essential physical and emotional equality between the sexes, as had some radical Cartesians a century earlier, but rather a reciprocity and mutual interchange between masculine and feminine qualities, the first representing activity, the other receptivity. Anne-Charlott Trepp recently characterized this ideal as "tender masculinity and self-reliant femininity" *(sanfte Männlichkeit und selbstständige Weiblichkeit).*[103]

Trepp's study shows how this behavioral ideal, incorporating terms that later would be considered oxymorons, directed the lives of *"bürgerliche"* men and women in late eighteenth and early-nineteenth-century Hamburg society. An analogous blending of the masculine and feminine can be seen in a letter written by Friedrich Gentz to Rahel Varnhagen in 1803, in which Gentz expressed both his love and admiration for her by reversing their sexual identifications, he becoming the female (receptive), she the male (productive), couched in the language of generation:

Do you know, my dearest, why our relationship has become so great and complete? I will tell you. You are *infinitely productive*, I am *infinitely receptive;* you are the great *man; I* am the first among all women who have ever lived.... My receptivity is totally without boundaries; your eternal, eternally active, eternally fruitful spirit (I mean not just mind, but soul, everything) met this unbounded receptivity, and so we gave birth to ideas, and to feelings, and to language, which have not been heard before. No mortal can surmise what we both know together.[104]

Earlier Wilhelm von Humboldt, then an intimate friend of Gentz, expressed similar ideas in an essay written in 1794 for Schiller's journal *Das Horen:* "On Sexual Differentiation and Its Influence on Organic Nature" *(Ueber den Geschlechtsunterschied und dessen Einfluss auf die organischen Natur).* It serves as a clear expression of the vitalists' attempt to differentiate yet merge gender categories and, more importantly, of the distance separating the vitalists' vision of gender from that of the Romantic *Naturphilosophen.*

Humboldt directed his attention to interpreting the process of artistic and poetic creation using categories drawn from the analogy of generation in the natural realm. He desired to go well beyond the "limited sphere" in which aesthetic discussion had been framed and "to transfer it to an immeasurable field." He undertook this project because he believed "physical nature and moral nature formed a great unity and the appearances in both accord to the same laws."[105] Humboldt took his model of natural generation directly from Blumenbach and the Enlightenment vitalists, considering life the instantaneous product of the interaction between living forces. It began with a living point of matter and through the action of the *Bildungstrieb* was epigenetically formed, then maintained, and compensated for when damaged. Life was based upon two necessary components, matter and formative force acting upon and through it. Generation resulted from the interaction between masculine and feminine forces, both of them active, yet working in different directions. Masculine forces were spontaneous, feminine ones receptive. Nature, forever alive, progressed through the continual reciprocal interaction *(Wechselwirkung)* of these opposed forces, which ensured the continuation of the species, led to its progress, and constituted nature's unity.[106]

What applied to generation in the physical world was also true by analogy for the spiritual. All creation, Humboldt asserted, had to be understood as the result of the active interchange between energetic masculine and energetic feminine forces. As in the physical world, each force worked initially in one direction. The masculine or generative force was more prone to "action," the feminine, more to "reaction," both equally active, though complementary. Masculine forces demonstrated more spontaneity: they tended to dissect, to destroy, and to isolate. They were more likely to be expressions of power. In the intellectual sphere masculine forces were analytic, led by cold reason. Feminine forces were receptive: they tended to assimilate, to collect, and to join. They were more likely to be expressions of profusion (*Fülle*). In the intellectual sphere they were synthetic, guided by warm fantasy. Thus Humboldt constructed a series of dyads that expressed the differences between masculine and feminine forces. The most prominent were active/receptive, form/matter, reason/imagination, light/warmth, hard/soft, and analytic/synthetic. He supplemented these by associating each power with a type of knowledge. The male principle directed the search for evident truth, the female for beauty. In the humanities philosophy and history constituted the two necessary ways for understanding the human condition, the first being masculine, the second feminine.[107]

For the modern reader these characterizations appear to announce the gender stereotypes later associated with the construction of "a biology of sexual differentiation," implying a direct linkage of psychological/intellectual categories with physical attributes, and some recent critics have interpreted them in this manner.[108] However, I believe that a careful reading of Humboldt's work when located within the parameters of Enlightenment Vitalism demonstrates the opposite. Unlike later writers, Humboldt refused to equate gender qualities with sexual difference. In only a few places in the text did he refer to the physical differences between men and women. Employing the accepted differentiation between the beautiful and the sublime, he noted that women more closely embodied the idea of beauty, men of power. But he modified the comparison, claiming such differences relative at best. He went even further, arguing that all clear distinctions such as those of active and receptive could never be isolated, considered as an absolute quality, a thing in itself. Every active force was receptive, every receptive force active, for "every pure separation contradicts the analogy of the laws of nature."[109]

This observation underscores Humboldt's message that the distinction between masculine and feminine forces cannot be interpreted as one between the active and the passive and has very little to do with sexual differentiation. Both forces were equally active, working, as he said, in different directions. The difference between them did not rest in ability or degree of activity: "In humans, spontaneity and receptivity reciprocally correspond to one another. The spontaneous spirit is also the most sensitive; the heart that is most receptive for every impression returns each with the most active energy. Thus, only the different direction distinguishes masculine from feminine power. The first, because of its spontaneity, begins with action *[Einwirkung]*, but then because of its receptivity absorbs the counteraction. The second operates in the opposite direction. It absorbs the thrust and returns it with spontaneity."[110] In this construction strong masculine forces required strong feminine forces for successful generation or creation and vice versa.

Humboldt's personal inclinations reinforced his theoretical formulations. Strong women attracted and fascinated him, whether they were intellectually powerful such as Caroline Dacheröden (his wife), Henriette Herz, Therese Heyne, and Madame de Staël, or physically powerful women, such as the ferry woman who awakened in him intense sadomasochistic sexual fantasies: "Between Duisburg and Crefeld one crosses the Rhine with a ferry. On the ferry, among the workers was a young woman, outwardly ugly, but strong, masculine, industrious. It is inconceivable how alluring such a sight of active physical power in women—especially from the lower orders—is for me."[111] Strong, energetic females and feminine forces were central to nature's plan. Humboldt therefore did not design his distinction between masculine and feminine forces as a hierarchy in which the masculine took primary place. Each force incorporated an element necessary to life's drama, each of equal worth. He made this clear in a footnote added to clarify his discussion of creation and genius. He argued that there were some works of genius in which masculine reason took precedence, others in which feminine fullness predominated. He illustrated this by four sets of geniuses, the first of each set being "feminine," the second "masculine." They were: "*Homer* and *Virgil, Ariosto* and *Dante, Thompson* and *Young, Plato* and *Aristotle.*"[112] Given Humboldt's tastes, this list did not demonstrate a preference for one or the other of the gendered categories. He chose, for example, the feminine Homer over the masculine Virgil and the masculine Aristotle over the feminine Plato.

Humboldt also illustrated this late-eighteenth-century ambivalence by his self-characterizations. In 1792, in a letter to his friend Brinckmann, Humboldt placed himself within the feminine sphere, invoking suggestions of fullness and receptivity: "I can or I must say in honesty that I have never striven to attain the heights. Actually I've concerned myself with the acquisition of the greatest possible number of objects of knowledge and feelings and this was hardly done intentionally."[113] He repeated this passage in 1816 in a short biographical fragment, adding further "feminine" characteristics, calling himself "pregnant with ideas" never brought to fruition. In it he said his highest goal was "to apprehend the world in its individuality and its totality," and complained of his inability to strictly separate "the individual from the general." It was the "profusion" *(Fülle)* of ideas that attracted him.[114] These descriptions contrasted sharply with those he later composed characterizing his intellect as "cold as the December sun," or declaring his abilities to be basically critical, which placed him in the masculine sphere. The contradictory self-evaluations Humboldt produced over his lifetime attest to the ambiguous blending of gender categories so characteristic of him and his contemporaries.[115]

Humboldt did not consider ambiguity a negative trait. Quite the contrary, it pointed to the type of creative harmonization between extremes to which Enlightenment vitalists strove. Humboldt's essay presented a paean to androgynous mediation. He provided an example of this in his footnote delineating masculine and feminine geniuses. He proposed the possibility of mediating between the hardness of reason and the fullness of fantasy, citing Sophocles, who stood midway between Aeschylus and Euripides. The image of androgynous mediation runs throughout the whole essay. He called for the necessary interaction of masculine and feminine powers, which should be maximized, to produce a higher union: "For only by combining the characteristics of the two sexes can perfection *[das Vollendete]* be generated."[116] Failure to join them could lead to destructive anarchy on one side and stifling stasis on the other, a theme rehearsing his reveries at St. Jean-de-Luz. If one-sidedness were to be avoided, then the masculine must bind its natural spontaneity to a strong law; the feminine, which represents the feeling of law, must animate itself from within through spontaneity. In short, Humboldt used the metaphors of merging, marriage, and love to describe how a higher harmony between individual masculine and feminine forces could be achieved, both in the realm of personal relations and in the products of genius.

Humboldt embedded this gender construction within a larger historical and theoretical framework, proclaiming the vitalist belief in purposive change effected through free activity. He supplemented this vision with ideas drawn from Schiller and Kant concerning the vocation of the human race and the tasks of reason. But Humboldt gave his own highly original spin to these ideas by recasting them in the language of gender. Only through the intensification and combination of masculine and feminine principles could the human attain the "ideal which reason has prescribed." The reconstruction of gender became the necessary condition for a leap in human consciousness and its progressive development. Humboldt announced this goal, utilizing an eroticized language with images vaguely evoking the endpiece to Blumenbach's *Bildungstrieb:* "This elevated vocation *[Bestimmung]* can be established only when the effects resulting from [the two forces operating freely] are entwined around each other; the inclination, which leads one to longingly approach the other, is *love*."[117]

. . .

If one turned directly from Humboldt's essay on sexual differentiation to Oken's *Die Zeugung*, it might appear as if they had been produced in two different eras. Yet only eleven years separated their publication. They offer striking proof of the idea that no age can be compartmentalized under simple rubrics, that, to use Ernst Bloch's phrase, there is always a noncontemporaniety of the contemporaneous. Humboldt was only twelve years older than Oken, yet those twelve years made a great difference. Oken's formative years stood under the shadow of the French Revolution, the Napoleonic wars, the defeat of Prussia, and the failure of the French Revolution to achieve the ideals to which most German intellectuals had at first been attracted. The ambiguities of life and nature that people such as Humboldt celebrated and believed offered the basis for social, political, and social improvement appeared to many of Oken's generation as dangerous, leading to chaos and uncertainty. This disillusionment drove them to search for certainty, which the new philosophy of nature would ensure.

The *Naturphilosophen*'s longing for certainty clearly spilled over in to the world of gender relations. In fact, they may have become concentrated there, revealing in a purer light the yearning for order, clarity, and hierarchy that, I believe, directed their thoughts and feelings. The ambiguous and highly charged sexual waters of the late Enlightenment, in which traditional boundaries were breached, became too difficult for them to navigate or to comprehend. Some members of the first generation of *Naturphilosophen*, people such as Schelling and the Schlegel brothers, had indeed been active players in this general scrambling of gender norms but pulled back once successfully married and established. The *Naturphilosophen* began to associate ambiguity, the blurring of boundaries, and the transmutation of gender categories with mechanism and materialism, which they believed had spawned the excesses of the French Revolution. Without saying it directly, they yearned to return to the older gender norms, authorized, however, with the most advanced instruments of natural philosophic reasoning.[118] In this they were similar to the people Laqueur analyzed, with one major difference. The *Naturphilosophen* did not "make sex," using it as a way to define gender; they made gender and used it to define sex.[119]

Oken wrote *Die Zeugung* to demonstrate *Naturphilosophie*'s validity when directed to the issues of gender and generation, vowing to put to rest all of the controversies that had arisen between preformationists, epigenesists, and believers in spontaneous generation *(generatio aequivoca)*. He started from the basic assumption proclaimed by Schelling that sexual differentiation constituted a universal principle in nature,[120] and developed it using the *naturphilosophic* principles of spontaneous creation made manifest through the appearance of polar duality. Employing the language of progression (though denying its reality) Oken proclaimed that matter first appeared in the form of what he called an infusions-animalcule *(Infusionsthier)* or a polyp. It embodied the positive male principle. As with all positive principles, the polyp-male represented a radial line, extending to infinity, constituting the essence of creation, found everywhere and always in the same quantity, though in different forms.[121]

All creation consisted in combinations of polyp-male *Ur*-matter. Complex organic forms were merely "a coalescing, a becoming one *[einswerden]* of all of these animalcules, which from then on lead no independent life, instead all are subordinated in the service of the higher organism." According to Oken, all creation occurs at once: "With the act of impregnation . . . the total embryo arises at once with one blow . . . ; it is not formed over time, which also means that one is not allowed to speak of a formation before impregnation."[122] In this formulation Oken denied both preformation and epigenesis and opted for a modified interpretation of spontaneous generation consisting of infinite polarizations of polyp-male *Ur*-matter. Since this *Ur*-matter constituted all natural products and was universally distributed, Oken came to the conclusion that it had to be sexless. It could not be otherwise, for if it had sex, all products of creation would have to be males. Thus, though all living forms arose from the male principle, pure masculinity was untainted by the appearance of sex. This led Oken to conclude that pan-spermism provided the only correct interpretation of generation. He considered pan-spermism "the oldest, most venerable idea in the history of natural philosophy; it began to make itself be felt at the moment when true philosophy awoke in Pythagoras." What applied to all of nature applied equally to humanity: "The total human race is nothing but a continually propagating male."[123]

Despite that claim Oken realized that animal propagation could not occur without the appearance of sex: therefore he had to account for its existence. According to Oken, sex arose from the necessary female negation of the polyp-male's affirmation. It took the form of a plant,[124] the opposite of the polyp-male. As with all negations, the plant-female contained an inner contradiction because it included its negated affirmation. Hence, according to Oken, the plant-female was a hybrid, the essential definition of universal sexuality: "The character of the plant is thus an inner duality. . . . This dissatisfaction of the plant with itself, this striving to seek a complement outside of itself on which it could hang, reveals itself as an internal duplicity, not in the numerical sense, but as a double-sidedness, as polarity. This duality is sex—the essential character of the plant is sex. It is thoroughly sex in the sense that it is a plant."[125] The plant-negation forced the radical line (polyp-male) back upon itself forming a circle. The circle expressed femininity's essence, embodied in the animal as the womb where spermatic material collected and polarized.

The animal represented the synthesis of polyp-male and plant-female, the former active, the latter passive. This synthesis, however, did not constitute a merging or interaction between the masculine and feminine as Humboldt and the Enlightenment vitalists would have described. Since the polyp and plant expressed opposite sides of a polarization process, they could not intermingle or interact.[126] Oken postulated a radical separation between male and female, modified by one important proviso. Since the female as negation incorporated male elements, the female was dependent upon the male, in fact, was defined in and through the male: "The ruling character of the animal in animality is separation of the sexes in two individuals. The masculine sex is independent from the female, because it is an infusions-animalcule. It is the first organism in nature. The female sex is dependent upon the male; it is the second organism, because it is a plant, a hybrid fixed in the form of femininity."[127]

Oken drew a number of startling conclusions from this reordering of sexual/gender categories. He resurrected what Laqueur called the single-sex model of gender, a position Laqueur considered virtually outmoded by the time Oken wrote. Oken's reasoning is, as usual, convoluted, but goes something as follows. Since the female is a hybrid and all living matter is polyp-male, there can be no such thing as a pure female sexual organ. The female organ can be nothing more than an imperfect variation of the male model. Therefore "the female genitalia, according to their nature demand the masculine form."[128] Given the universality of the masculine form, Oken also could not abide by Blumenbach's characterization of male nipples as useless mechanical reminders of the species' unity. Oken declared that nipples played a central role in the development of the fetus, serving as the vehicle through which the fetus received nourishment. The placenta's only role, he maintained, was to allow the fetus to breathe. Relieved and excited about this discovery, Oken concluded, "Finally one can no longer accuse the creator that he gave to the men useless nipples."[129]

Oken's desire to relate everything to the male also required him to explain female birth. As a pan-spermist, he denied the female any substantial role in the generation process except to provide the place where polarization occurred and to nourish the fetus. However, he added that the womb helped shape the new creature's form. Thus, in an animal, the polyp-male must reproduce himself in the female hybrid. This meant that the female had the tendency to transmute polyp-males into plant-females because the process took place in the womb. The production of males or females depended upon the female principle's power: "The more feminine the female, the more likely, everything else being equal, she would be to bring a girl into the world; the more masculine the female, the more likely a boy."[130]

In *Die Zeugung*, Oken sought to rewrite the story of generation in order to recast gender relations. Although he began with the same assumption as had Humboldt, namely, the universality of sexual differentiation, he reached radically different conclusions. Oken established an unbridgeable gulf separating males from females, denying the possibility of real interaction and constructing hierarchies based upon the essential polarity between polyp and plant. These he extended through all creation ranking, for example, worms and birds under the active polyp category, insects and fish under the passive one of plants. He even extended this separation to the individual body, considering the respiration system male, the lymph system female. The metamorphic language Oken deployed reinforced these strict hierarchies. He designated males as active, creative, self-sufficient, females as passive, imitative, dependent. No possibility of overlap existed between the dyads. The oxymoronic formulations of Enlightenment vitalism disappeared, condemned as major errors in correct scientific thinking, breaches in logic. Thus, Oken turned the vitalitists' positive image of mediation into the negative one of hybridization (the essential characteristic of femininity), making it inherently inferior to a pure form, the essence of masculinity. Oken's major theme that females can only live in and through males, which runs like a red thread through his work, testifies to the major shift in gender conceptions separating the *Naturphilosophen* from Enlightenment vitalists.

. . .

Upon reading Oken's *Die Zeugung*, one might come away with the impression that its apparently weird and idiosyncratic message could not truly represent the *Naturphilosophen*'s ideas on gender and generation. Yet the same ideas appear in other *naturphilosophic* writings, as evidenced by the work of a later *Naturphilosoph*, Carl Gustav Carus, whose career extended well in to the 1860s. Carus, educated as a physician, became a leading gynecologist, training scores of young men in this discipline who spread out over Germany, degree and forceps in hand empowered to treat women and, of course, to discourse about them.[131] Carus considered himself a moderate and pragmatic thinker, not an uncritical fan of Schelling and Oken, a view he published in 1861, when he stated that he had always maintained a degree of skepticism concerning the excesses of *Naturphilosophie*.[132] If that were the case, then Carus's narrative of gender, presented in a textbook on gynecology, the *Lehrbuch der Gynäkologie* published in 1820 and reprinted many times afterwards, offers a startling confirmation that Oken's position, despite its excesses, was highly appealing to and readily accepted even by the more skeptical *Naturphilosophen*.

The textbook purported to investigate "the teachings concerning the specifics of the female body, its construction, its life, its sicknesses and its respective dietetic and medical treatments."[133] But before Carus addressed these specific medical questions, he presented an introductory section dealing with the female as such. His overriding imperative was to confirm and even to strengthen the difference between the male and female adumbrated in Oken's work. Carus began by a discussion of the female's physical characteristics. The female body in comparison to the male's focused upon assimilation and reproduction: but more than that, it revealed incomplete development, making it similar to a child's body. He supplemented this linkage of the female with the child by relating the female's body to "lower species," or "incomplete organizations." The homology Carus preferred here was the fish, for Oken one of the prime embodiments of the female principle. To make his point even clearer, Carus also equated the female to the plant, which he also considered radically opposed to the animal.[134] The plant (fish)-female was directed to formation, maintenance, and metabolism, the animal-male to unity and freedom.[135] When Carus considered the female body, ranging from the rump to the brain, all he could detect, when compared to the male, was imperfection, childlike tendencies, and analogies to "less developed" species.

This excursion into the physical characteristics of the female served as a prelude to Carus's discussion of the female's psyche. Carus, as all of the *Naturphilosophen*, did not consider the body the determinant of the psyche, but rather the vessel of its spiritual principles. The psyche was both "the true mirror of the physical, but even more the ideal side of the organism itself."[136] Carus applied the same characteristics to the psyche as he had to the body. On all of the psyche's levels (*Gemüth, Geist*, and Will), Carus considered the female far less capable and active than the male. Although the female possessed greater sensibility, more lively feelings, and a more active fantasy than the male, these features could never be developed to serve as a counter-balance to male superiority. They were always verging on the brink of overexaggeration or of inactivity. Although the female was, Carus claimed, more sensitive to sounds, she lacked the ability to distinguish carefully between them, was incapable of acquiring a total tonal impression, and hence possessed very little true musical ability. The same pertained to the female's overly active fantasy and sensitivity; they got in the way of allowing her to produce great and elevated works of poetry and art. She had fantasy and sensitivity, but not the power of "creative fantasy," or of "deep feeling." Everything in her was superficial. Since, in Carus's judgment, the male embodied the rational principle, Carus judged the female as congenitally incapable of making any contributions to the sciences and the humanities. Being vegetative, the female also lacked the ability to act quickly, decisively, and arbitrarily. The only tasks Carus believed the female better able to carry out were small ones, requiring patience and quiet, such as taking care of children, the sick, and newly delivered children.

In the sexual and emotional sphere Carus argued that the female needed to attach herself to a stronger person to compensate for her own weakness and lack of energy. This was translated into a binding love for her husband and an even stronger love for her children *(Mutterliebe)*, feelings that already manifested themselves in the way little girls played with dolls. This desire also explained the explosions of hate and revenge of which she was capable if someone threatened child or husband or if she was betrayed in love. The desire to please finally lay at the heart of the female's fascination with housekeeping and her mania for ornaments, attire, and fashion *(Putzsucht)*.[137]

In the last section of this general discussion of woman's nature, Carus asked whether sexual and gender characteristics were inborn, a matter of education, or perhaps stages in the development of the human from the embryo through childhood to adulthood. Simply said, he asked whether women were born feminine, men born masculine. Carus acknowledged that some theorists, arguing for the unity of the human race, had posited the theory that the original embryo was of one sex and sexual differentiation occurred over time during epigenesis. Some even argued that the original sex was female and hence should serve as the norm against which men should be measured. Carus, true to his *naturphilosophic* assumptions, denied all such theories, for generation was nothing but the appearance of already formed dualities.[138] Generation did entail the constant transformation of matter; there was continual emergence, generation, and disappearance, but never "a new creation, which is unthinkable."[139]

For Carus and the other *Naturphilosophen*, gender illustrated the hierarchies enshrined in nature. Although everything was in movement, nothing new was created, everything pulsated within its own circumscribed sphere or circle. Each circle formed part of the infinitely graduated but continuous chain of being, in which no leaps could exist. All differences were analogues of the original difference, all reducible to a one-dimensional diagram charting abstract relations. The "realities" that the Enlightenment vitalists attempted to harmonize—time and space, matter and force, masculine and feminine, fact and imagination—the *Naturphilosophen* translated into expressions of the one, the *Monas*. They considered the man the highest and most perfect expression of this unity making *him* the most perfect expression of the duality in the trias. Man was the "highest of the animals in whom everything that is noble and capable found distributed in the rest of living things is united; in him all the seeds and fruits, all matter and forms of the earth and heavens, the *avulsio ätheris*, flow together as in a focus."[140]

. . .

It has often been claimed that the philosophy of the Enlightenment had raised the human being (often interpreted as the white, male European) to a dominant position over the rest of the living world. There may be something to such an accusation, but in comparison to the *Naturphilosophen*, the Enlightenment's claims were modest indeed. The *Naturphilosophen* consciously placed the male at the pinnacle of all creation. His reason, imagination, and willpower enabled him to lift nature's veil, using his self-reflective consciousness to recapture her origins and return to the womb from which he had sprung. This celebration of the male established the grounds for a type of instrumental reason far more dangerous than anything proposed by Enlightenment thinkers. *Naturphilosophie*'s audacity, its elevation of theoretical reason over epistemological modesty, its denial of active individual agency, and its static and hierarchical worldview did indeed constitute a rejection of the Enlightenment, but not the Enlightenment many postmodernists portray. This is the final irony. For a careful look at the late Enlightenment might reveal a way of thinking and doing that is much more sympathetic to postmodernism than Romanticism.

I have sought in this chapter to contrast the styles of thought and feeling separating Enlightenment Vitalism from Romantic *Naturphilosophie*. In so doing, I realize that I am going against the grain of normal interpretive practice. I contend that the during the late Enlightenment a significant number of intellectuals felt the need to vitalize nature in order to meet the problems that had been raised and not solved by mechanism's definition of matter as inert and the conclusions that this assumption supported. The imperative to redefine matter led the vitalists to recast the language of natural philosophic discourse, ranging from the definitions of the object one should study to the manner in which that study should proceed and the types of conclusions one could obtain. In this process the newly formed language revealed and explored central tensions of the social, political, and intellectual universe in which they were formulated. As Jordanova remarked, "Eighteenth-century savants were intensely conscious of the complexity of masculinity and femininity, and of the social, political, economic, and moral entailments of these concepts. They sought to bring this complexity within the domain of natural knowledge."[141] Their overriding goal was to mediate between opposites, to create a language of nature and society in which these mediations took concrete form, whether expressed in the dynamic between form and freedom, time and place, or living and dead matter. The modes of ambiguity and paradox were employed to suggest the inexplicable, yet essential need to blur boundaries, to see linkages where only contradictions had earlier been asserted. This position was extremely productive as long as one considered the social, political, and intellectual world open to transformation or even radical transmutation (metamorphosis). When the great experiment of radical transformation did take place in France during the Revolution and failed (at least in the eyes of German thinkers), the ambiguities of late Enlightenment thought were dismissed as signs of excess or weakness. *Naturphilosophie* emerged as the most clearly articulated critique of the late Enlightenment, of both late-eighteenth-century vitalism and neomechanism. For most commentators, this shift in intellectual styles has been seen as the beginnings of a modern, dynamic vision of nature and human history. Foucault proposed the most radical formulation of this idea in his early writings. However, the supposed *episteme* shift he described certainly does not characterize the German thinkers he used to justify it. They had structured their vision of what a new science could and should explain from the *Naturphilosophen*. Yet when one looks closely at the conceptual universe the *Naturphilosophen* proposed, it consciously returned to a way of constituting the order of things that corresponds to Foucault's characterization of the "classical" era of Leibniz, Descartes, and the Port Royal grammarians. This search for a new universal *mathesis*, for one-dimensional Pythagorean certainty in a world seemingly filled with chaos, found its clearest expressions in the new definitions of gender the *Naturphilosophen* forged. What is even more interesting is that these definitions outlived *Naturphilosophie* itself.

Epilogue
From the Foot of Chimborazo to the Flatlands of Europe

ALEXANDER VON HUMBOLDT'S DILEMMA

When Alexander von Humboldt departed Germany in 1798 for his expedition to South America, many thought he was destined to become one of the age's leading naturalists, someone who would reveal daring new insights about nature and its relations to humanity. Goethe, Georg Forster, Friedrich Jacobi, Lichtenberg, Blumenbach, Cuvier, Laplace, and countless others were fascinated by his intelligence, diligence, and dedication to uncovering the secrets of nature. He had published a number of important scientific treatises on a remarkable range of topics, including his two-volume study of the influence of galvanic electricity on muscles and nerves.[1] Alexander was conversant with all of the latest scientific theories and had already built up a network of contacts and correspondents throughout Europe. His elder brother Wilhelm shared this enthusiasm about Alexander's promise. As early as 1793 he considered Alexander the only person whom he knew either in person "or through history" who "could combine the study of physical nature with the moral, and finally show the true harmony of the universe as we know it."[2]

When Alexander and his traveling companion Bonpland returned to Europe in 1804, he seemed to have more than fulfilled these expectations. He was hailed as a hero, a person who combined the mind of a precise observer with the daring of an adventurer. Cuvier bore witness to these opinions in an unpublished review of the *Tableaux de la nature*, stressing the theme of Alexander's ability to harmonize conflicting scientific imperatives by blending observation with meditation: "When he presents his reader with the grand views of nature, he seems always to have reflected; when he brings together data, recalls and weighs his opinions, he seems never to have left the library; when he traces the sketch of his grand results, he seems to have given himself over ceaselessly to meditation."[3] Humboldt's scaling of Mount Chimborazo, instruments in hand, acquired mythic proportions, forging an image of the daring explorer-scientist that was to captivate the nineteenth-century imagination. Not only did Humboldt acquire a towering reputation, but as Mary Louise Pratt argues, he also "reinvented South America first and foremost as nature. Not the accessible, collectible, recognizable, categorizable nature of the Linnaeans, however but a dramatic, extraordinary nature, a spectacle capable of overwhelming human knowledge and understanding."[4]

But the scientific and intellectual world to which Humboldt returned had changed appreciably. Very quickly Humboldt discovered that, despite his fame, his language of nature no longer seemed self-evident, either to the young *Naturphilosophen* who during his absence had occupied important chairs in Germany's leading universities or, more surprising, to many of the leading scientists in Paris, some of them close allies. The Enlightenment vitalists' assumption of the reciprocal interaction between nature and humanity, their imperative to harmonize painstaking research with broad aesthetic synthesis, and their goal to mediate between extremes in order to perceive the "free play" of nature's forces no longer had the same appeal it enjoyed when Humboldt set sail for South America. Humboldt's basic operating assumptions increasingly were dismissed as either bent upon achieving an impossible universalism or as being hopelessly mired in simple-minded empiricism.

Humboldt was caught in a dilemma that led him to launch a two-pronged defense justifying the intellectual integrity of his grand undertaking. He virtually retraced the moves Buffon had taken to attack the proponents of mechanism and animism, of simple empiricism and deductive speculation. But unlike Buffon, whose strategy was founded upon proposing a new vision of nature, Humboldt's turned out to be a rear guard action, defending a position that many considered outmoded, naive, or impossible to implement. It was a brilliant defense, culminating in one of the great scientific syntheses of the midcentury, Humboldt's *Cosmos*. But it was unsuccessful, for the basic Enlightenment motives that held his work together and gave it meaning were over time deemed irrelevant. Humboldt shared Buffon's view of the natural philosopher as one who combines "two seemingly opposite qualities of the mind: the wide-ranging views of an ardent mind that embraces everything with one glance [*coup d'oeil*], and the detail-oriented laboring instinct that concentrates only on one element."[5] These two qualities, joined together in creative tension during the Enlightenment, during the first third of the nineteenth century were separated and constituted as alternative ways to understand nature and humanity. The *Naturphilosophen* had turned to the first, the French, in the first third of the nineteenth century, to the second.

. . .

Humboldt was aware of some of the problems he was to face upon his return, for his first efforts at justifying his position were already formulated at the foot of Chimborazo. There he sketched out the outlines of his *Ansichten der Natur,* designed specifically to appeal to a German audience and diffuse the appeal of the *Naturphilosophen.* Humboldt knew about the shifts that had taken place in Germany. He also realized that the *Naturphilosophen* were ambivalent toward his position. Although many acknowledged Humboldt's preexpedition works and his promise, these judgments were often expressed in disparaging tones, hinting that he was, at best, a gifted empiricist but could never aspire to true insight into the workings of nature. Johann Jacob Wagner considered him naive because of his commitment to quantification, and Heinrich Steffens later remarked that, before he got to know Humboldt personally, he was negatively disposed to him because of "some blind, enthusiastic expressions of the younger *Naturphilosophen.*"[6] That the University of Jena had emerged during his absence as the bastion of *Naturphilosophie* probably intensified Humboldt's desire to recapture his position in Germany. Jena and adjacent Weimar had been sites of many of his most intensive intellectual exchanges—with Goethe, Schiller, his brother, and the other thinkers who had been drawn there. Goethe, who was in charge of Weimar's educational system and hence controlled the University of Jena, shared Humboldt's vision of nature but now appeared to favor *Naturphilosophie.* He had appointed Schelling to a professorship in Jena in 1799, and when Schelling left in 1803, Goethe replaced him with Oken, though they later became involved in a battle over scientific and political issues, which led to Oken's dismissal in 1819.

Clearly, if Alexander was to reenter the German scientific world and reclaim his preexpedition eminence, he had to confront the challenge of *Naturphilosophie* but, given its popularity and Goethe's apparent support, not attack the *Naturphilosophen* directly. His strategy seems to have been to disarm the *Naturphilosophen* by praising their efforts and then to neutralize them by demonstrating the superiority of his own approach.[7] He followed this plan in the *Ansichten* and in the *Ideen zu einer Geographie der Pflanzen nebst einem Naturgemälde der Tropengeländer* (1807), in which

Alexander affirmed his commitment to "empirical research," to which he had devoted his whole life. He conceded that his work described things as they existed, linked to each other, and that he did not aspire to portray "them in their internal connections" by "penetrating to the nature of things." Humboldt also confessed that before his return he had thought it impossible to reduce "all natural appearances, all activity and pictures *[Gebilde]* of nature to the never ending battle between opposing basic forces of matter." Never admitting that he now had accepted such a view, he claimed that such a project was feasible and asserted "that he was not of the opinion that true *naturphilosophical* studies would endanger empirical investigations, as though empiricists and *Naturphilosophen* would repulse each other eternally as opposing poles." In this rhetorical exercise, cleverly deploying the *Naturphilosophen*'s own metaphoric language, Humboldt offered them a truce, yet also challenged them to recognize his own achievements. To make this more palatable, he hailed the appearance of *Naturphilosophie*, but for the same generic reason Oken had praised Blumenbach while denying all of Blumenbach's basic points. According to Humboldt, the *Naturphilosphen* had seconded his attempts to change science's language of representation *(Bildersprache)*. They had helped destroy atomism, that "one-sided mode of explanation that derived all of the differences in matter to merely the difference in expansion and density." They also, he added, could throw light upon the phenomena of organic life, warmth, light, electricity, and magnetism.[8] But, clearly, Humboldt considered *Naturphilosophie*'s rejection of atomism its most noteworthy achievement.

Humboldt's appraisal of *Naturphilosophie* was a smokescreen designed both to confuse the enemy and to condemn them with praise. For, no matter what Alexander said about his respect for the *Naturphilosophen* and how his work complemented theirs, he never sought to change the way he did and explained science, which became clearer in each of the works he published after the *Ideen*. Whatever bows he made to *Naturphilosophie* were modified by his use of the term "true" *(ächte) Naturphilosophie* (suggesting, of course, that there was also a false one), which served to challenge the *Naturphilosophen* to incorporate his insights or be consigned to the ranks of false philosophers of nature. Further, his thumbnail sketch of polar opposition, which replicated the *Naturphilosophen*'s basic operating assumption about how polar opposition functioned, stood in stark contrast to the way he described opposition. Alexander never conceived of opposition in terms of "eternal repulsion," but rather as the "cooperation" or the "congress of forces." If there was indeed a "true" natural philosophy, Alexander probably believed his researchers would serve as its beginning and foundation. He made this clear in his essay "Naturgemälde der Tröpenländer," which was published in the *Ansichten:* "I would like to flatter myself that even the *Naturphilosoph,* who reduces nature's manifoldness to the elemental action of a unitary matter, and who grounds the world organism in the never resolved battle of contradictory powers, must consider such a composition of facts essential. The empiricist counts and measures what phenomena directly present: the philosophy of nature's task is to comprehend all these together and to reduce them to principles."[9] Alexander, along his brother Wilhelm, was committed to a totally different project, designed to achieve different explanatory ends, and he saw his endeavors in a political light that stood in stark contrast to the *Naturphilosophen*. Two scientific, epistemological, and "moral" (to use their language) worlds confronted each other, with very little uniting them except the general dissatisfaction with the excesses of a mechanism that was already generally discredited, at least in the life sciences.

As the quotation indicates, this opposition is most clearly evident in their respective evaluations of the value of observation. But these differences should not be framed as a simple choice between theory and empiricism. Rather, they should be read as a basic disagreement about how one defined the relationship between nature and humanity, how one understood nature's processes, how one could best comprehend these actions, how certain this knowledge was and what ideological function it served. Humboldt's answer drew its nourishment from the basic principles of Enlightenment Vitalism, but he worked it out with the greatest degree of sophistication and methodological rigor, making him the greatest and probably the last of the Enlightenment vitalists.

Humboldt's belief in the intimate connection between man and nature stood at the heart of his whole endeavor. Humans are embedded in a complex interaction of forces that help shape them, for "the physical world is truly and vitally mirrored in the innermost, receptive mind *[Sinn]*."[10] But humans are not merely passive recipients of outside influences. Rather, human energies are awakened by the challenge of these forces, which both stimulate creative action and limit it at the same time. The whole formed a mysterious intercourse, a "cooperation of forces," which could be perceived only by careful attention to every interacting force, guided by the imperative to "comprehend nature in a single glance."[11] Thus the study of nature was central to the understanding of the moral world and to the greater harmony that united both.[12]

Since humans were deeply enmeshed in the interaction of countless natural forces, it was impossible for the mind to abstract itself from nature and comprehend it as rational object. Rather, natural knowledge could be won only by immersing oneself into nature's actions, by recording and seeing how nature inscribed its patterns upon the world and us. To accomplish this, the naturalist had to train the senses to observe and record the "free play" of natural forces, and to enhance the senses by the use of the finest and most varied instruments available. Humboldt firmly believed that scientific instruments were extensions of the naturalists' senses, recording devices that measured facts that spoke to the soul. The only way one could capture nature's language was to look at nature from every angle, measure every phenomenon, and then try to imagine them in interaction. Nature's secret language could be deciphered only by investigating "the confluence and interweaving of all physical forces."[13] This required a strict adherence to quantification, for only through measurement can one see nature in its operations. Already in 1792, Humboldt had expressed this view to his former mentor, Lichtenberg: "Every science, which is not capable of pure knowledge, can achieve only a degree of certainty to the extent that its concepts can be constructed. Any science to which quantitative reasoning can not be applied fluctuates."[14] By the time he set forth on his expedition, Humboldt was convinced that quantitative methods and instruments had been so improved that he was "in the position to measure extremely small quantities with precision; and it is no longer allowed, to ignore magnitudes, which earlier appeared indeterminable."[15]

Humboldt's commitment to quantification has often been interpreted as an innovative turn toward modern scientific methods and understanding. But such a view is misleading. For him quantification served as an exploratory tool, not an end in itself. He never believed that these measurements portrayed "reality." Rather, they served to control experiments and provide the naturalist with a symbolic language enabling one to grasp but never totally comprehend nature's dynamic quality. Michael Dettelbach made this point clear: "The hypsometric profiles or "tableaux physiques" that Humboldt invented were explicitly *not* representational, but abstract attempts to convey to the senses an otherwise only indirectly perceivable physical reality, nature's profound, dynamical, historical character. Humboldt's various graphic innovations were explicitly designed to sensibly register dynamic relations or immaterial entities."[16] Humboldt turned to quantification as a tool to help him "dissect," "decompose," or "analyze" nature. As did his brother Wilhelm, Alexander believed this was the first step in making "Nature speak its own, universal language."[17]

Humboldt's conception of quantification's use and its limits was guided by the same epistemological modesty characteristic of Enlightenment Vitalism. Throughout his life Humboldt expressed a great distrust for theorizers who believed it possible to acquire complete, objective knowledge about nature's origins and laws. In his work on galvinism, he called this "the delusion of completeness" *(die Wahn der Vollendung)*[18] and argued that all closed systems were disastrous for the advancement of science. At the end of his life in the introduction to his *Cosmos*, he reiterated the same theme: "The empirical element, the elements of contingency and indeterminacy, the unresolved, the unknown and unmeasured always remain and should forever make us modest and self-critical."[19] Rather than seeing it as a closed system, he linked the act of observation to the explanatory openness of the aphorism, a form beautifully developed by his teacher Lichtenberg, which Humboldt used in the title of his preexpedition work on chemistry.[20] Paraphrasing Bacon, Humboldt argued: "All forms of error can be reduced to the premature and peremptory reduction of knowledge to arts and methods, from which time the sciences are seldom improved. For as young men rarely grow in stature after their shape and limbs are formed, so knowledge, when it lies in aphorisms and observations, remains in a growing state. But when fashioned into methods though it may be further polished, illustrated, and fitted for use, it no longer increases in bulk and substance."[21] In true Enlightenment fashion Humboldt emphasized his commitment to a science of facts. But the discovery of the simple fact was not the goal to which he strove. Rather, facts had to be integrated into a larger whole, guided by the action of cultivated imagination, sympathetic understanding, and the use of analogical reasoning.

True natural philosophy was founded upon aesthetic appreciation, not upon the assumption that the mind's operation provided the model for nature. Thus, though science began with analysis, it ended with a creative, though not absolute, synthesis, using the evocative power of poetics. The breach between sign and signified could be bridged only through the activity of aesthetic understanding, a process his brother Wilhelm referred to in 1788 as *"beobachtende Verstand,"* stating that "observational understanding and the poetic power of imagination must stand together in a harmonic conjunction."[22] Wilhelm later elaborated upon this insight, using a language employing metaphors drawn from both chemistry and aesthetics: "Nothing stands isolated in nature, for everything is combined, everything forms a whole, but with a thousand different and manifold sides. The researcher must first decompose and look at each part singly and for itself and then consider it as part of a whole. But here, as often happens, he cannot stop. He has to combine them together again, recreate the whole as it earlier appeared before his eyes."[23] In "On the Historian's Task" he made the aesthetic element clearer, arguing that the connecting of events was founded upon "intuitive understanding." He concluded: "Even a simple depiction of nature cannot be merely an enumeration . . . ; there is also the breath of life in the whole and an inner character which speaks through it that can neither be measured nor merely described. Description of nature, too, will be subjected to the second method, which for such description is the representation of the form of both the universal and the individual existence of natural objects."[24]

This act of aesthetic recreation, in which one "saw" nature as a whole but in a new and different light, formed the goal of what Alexander called "terrestrial physics" or "general physics," which was to be guided by the "physiognomic eye." In a direct critique of *Naturphilosophie,* Alexander reiterated his brother's insight and directed it to the study of nature in general: "In the great interconnection of cause and effect, no substance, no activity can be examined in isolation. The equilibrium, which reigns *in the midst of the perturbations of supposedly conflicting elements,* is an equilibrium arising out of the free play of dynamic forces. A complete overview of nature, which is the highest goal of all physical studies, can be achieved only if no force, no form is ignored, which thereby will prepare a broad and promising fertile field for the *Philosophie der Natur.*"[25] For both Alexander and Wilhelm, one could till this field successfully only if one realized that nature was forever in movement, a movement in which real forces interacted within a complex nexus, whose discovery proceeded by considering the local detail as the starting point to arrive at the grand view.

Alexander's dispute with the *Naturphilosophen* centered on the manner in which a generalizing natural science could be constructed and what conclusions one could expect from it. Where Humboldt used the language of seeing to characterize his general physics, the *Naturphilosophen* turned to the logic of mind to describe their philosophy of nature. Alexander sought to provide his "viewers" with a living picture of nature's activities. He did this by charting isothermes, by publishing complex graphic representations such as his famous tableau of the equinox region in the *Essai sur la géographie des plantes,* and by deploying a descriptive language filled with the drama of his confrontations with nature's sublimity. Humboldt desired to offer a "view" of a three-dimensional universe in which layer after layer of life manifested itself, each called forth by subtle variations of temperature and climate, acting locally but only understood globally. The *Naturphilosophen* presented their readers with one-dimensional abstract charts diagramming the universal order, complemented by a language employing daring homologies with wild abandon. The *Naturphilosophen* promised absolute knowledge, Alexander approximate, momentary insights, ever capable of revision through new and better observations. Still, despite these enormous differences, both agreed that some form of generalizing science was necessary.

. . .

It was Alexander's quest for a "general physics" that some of his French colleagues came to distrust, leading them to question Humboldt's basic assumptions and methods. For many of his Parisian friends, the days of constructing universal sciences were over, proven by the excesses of the *Naturphilosophen* as reported to them by Cuvier and by the impossibility for one person to comprehend the wealth of facts provided by the enormous expansion of individual sciences. The air of dilettantism seemed to hang over Humboldt's work, leading many of the great figures of the time, including Berthollet, Laplace, and Ramond de Carbonniéres, to question his measurements and some of his conclusions.[26] Although Humboldt was greatly influenced by Laplace because of his commitment to precise measurements, Humboldt differed from his French colleagues about what measurements recorded. He saw measurements as *chiffres* that helped one to apprehend nature's hidden language. Laplace and his French colleagues tended toward a positivist position in which measurements recorded reality. In fact, some believed measurements "might actually themselves be the objects of positive scientific knowledge or theory."[27] This turn to a reductionist vision of scientific explanation transformed the Enlightenment's epistemologically moderate theory of probabilities into an aggressive, "objective" one.[28] Similar to the *Naturphilosophen*, French naturalists, led by Laplace and Lagrange, also assumed that absolute truth could be discovered, that nature could be described transparently, though with a radically different approach than advocated by the *Naturphilosophen*. The French sought to reduce "dynamics to statics and transformed mechanics into an algebraic analysis free of visual aids."[29] This movement was also driven by an increasing professionalization of the individual sciences, where each science constituted its own explanatory field and supported it by a system of patronage and power that ensured its independence. Humboldt's "general physics" threatened these newly created scientific preserves and did not follow the path of the new positivism.

Humboldt's defense against his positivist critics took two forms. The first was derived from a distinction he made between naturalists who cared only about single phenomena and those who were aware of the complex interconnection of things. Here he drew his inspiration from Georg Forster and Forster's idol Buffon. The second supported his position by grounding "general physics" in the existence of "basic types," a position well worked out in Enlightenment Vitalism by thinkers such as Buffon, Daubenton, Robinet, Herder, Goethe, and Kant.

Alexander first staked out these claims in the *Essai sur la géographie des plantes*, the introductory volume to his enormous publication project, which he later rendered in German as the *Ideen einer Geographie der Pflanzen*. Although these publications differed because of their intended audience, one designed to make his case to the French, the other to the Germans, they complemented each other. In both Humboldt expressly thanked his "friend Georg Forster" for giving him the first impulse for such a study.[30] In another text, published in the *Andenken*, Humboldt cited naturalists who were able to differentiate between "individual natural description" and "general description," or the "physiognomy of nature." Once again Forster occupied a prime place, followed by Buffon and Goethe, among others. Humboldt cited two Forster sources as central to his own development, Forster's "travels" and his *kleine Schriften*. The latter were published in 1790 and contained an essay Forster wrote in 1781 entitled "Ein Blick in das Ganze der Natur" (A Look at the Whole of Nature). In this essay Forster portrayed the dangers of specialization and professionalization, a position Humboldt took to heart: "One cuts the sciences into pieces. . . . Faculties arise and within them appear almost innumerable subdivisions and fields of study. Each individual part of human understanding acquires its own observer, who ignores the whole, who only dedicates himself to the part. Thus the beautiful soul departs the beautiful body, and each ossified member grows through internal fermentation to become its own kind of monster. Everyone treasures only the science he has chosen and appears to have forgotten that only when the sciences are combined with each other can human happiness be promoted." The result of such specialization, Forster proclaimed, would be the creation of an "empty twaddle *[Gewäsch]* of names, jargon, and systems."[31]

Humboldt drew a similar distinction between those who look at the whole and those simply preoccupied with a special discipline. According to Dettelbach, Humboldt used the term *nomenclateur*, a term of derision borrowed, I believe, from Buffon, to characterize the latter, and juxtaposed it to the *physicien*. Thus, in botany the *"botaniste nomenclateur"* was interested only in individual structures, which distinguish one species from another. This work was important, but only preliminary to that of the *"botaniste physicien,"* who focused upon large-scale relations and the geographical variations wrought by the congress of interacting forces, which point to the great laws operating in the world.[32] When contemplating the whole, the normal process of isolating simple variables and considering the rest of the system constant could not explain complex phenomena. Humboldt drew this distinction in his discussion of how the normal procedures of scientific analysis were inapplicable for understanding temperature and magnetism, an argument that demonstrates a close similarity to Buffon's idea of a "natural system":

> Temperature and magnetism are not like those phenomena which, derived from a single cause or central force, can be freed of the influence of disturbing causes by restricting attention to the mean results of a great number of observations, in which these foreign effects reciprocally counteract and destroy one another. The distribution of heat, like the declination and inclination of the compass needle or the intensity of magnetic force, is essentially conditioned by location, composition of the soil, by the proper ability of the earth's surface to radiate heat. One must beware of eliminating what is sought; one must not classify as foreign and disturbing causes those upon which the most important phenomena in the distribution and the more rapid or slow development of organic life essentially depend.[33]

The task of Humboldt's *physicien* or physiognomist was to obtain "a total impression of a region." The descriptive botanist "separates quantities of plant groups, which the *physiognomist* sees himself required to join together. Where the plants present themselves en masse, all of the outlines and distribution of leaves and the structures of stems and branches flow into each other. The painter (and precisely the artist's fine feelings for nature are applicable here) differentiates in the background of a landscape painting pine or palm trees from beeches, but not these from other deciduous trees."[34] Viewing nature en masse, "as a whole affords a pleasure [*Genuss, jouissance*], essentially different than that generated by the dissection of an organic body and the study of its admirable structure. Here the detail excites our curiosity, there the masses operate on our fantasy."[35]

If the artist's eye, which links things together and generates thereby an elevated *Genuss*,[36] was central to "general physics," what ensured the truth claims of these aesthetic "views" besides Humboldt's insistence upon precise measurement? Humboldt's answer paralleled Buffon's and Herder's. Behind the particular measurements and local phenomena, one could discern, though through a glass darkly, the outlines of basic types or *"Hauptformen"*: "When someone comprehends with one glance the various 'phanerogamic' species of plants . . . one recognizes within this enormous number specific *Hauptformen*, to which many can be reduced. In order to determine these types, upon which the individual beauty, the distribution, and grouping of the physiognomy of a region is dependent, one must not (as happens in other botanical systems working from other premises) concentrate on the smallest reproductive organs, perianths, and fruits, but only take into consideration how the vegetation's mass individualizes the total impression of a region."[37] The act of abstracting from local phenomena to view nature "with a single glance" *(coup d'oeil)* was authorized scientifically, Humboldt believed, through the secret play of nature's forces, which produces "stable, eternally recurring types."[38] In a statement evoking terms proposed by Buffon, Robinet, and Goethe, Humboldt announced what he considered one of the major goals of his science: "The geography of plants inquires whether, beneath the countless number of plants on the earth, specific *Urformen* can be discovered and whether the plants' specific differences can be considered as degenerations and variations of a prototype."[39] And, true to the dictates of Enlightened Vitalism, Humboldt considered analogical reasoning the major procedure enabling the sensitive naturalist to abstract from the local phenomenon and attain this view of the whole.[40] In a sense, that which was to be discovered—the recurring types—validated the endeavor, the whole process based upon the sensitivity and cultivation of the individual naturalist.

Given such a position, which for many of Humboldt's French counterparts reeked of metaphysical speculation or subjectivity, it is no surprise that many of his Parisian colleagues increasingly became critical of his work. For they were interested in evolving a positive scientific method and explanatory procedure that stood apart from the subjective investigator, that abstracted the "moral" from nature. Among the holders of power and position in the Parisian scientific community of first third of the century, only Cuvier continued to praise Humboldt, even though they never had a close friendship. But Cuvier was one of the last exponents of Enlightenment Vitalism and, like Humboldt, a man of two intellectual worlds, which he sought to combine. Thus on both sides of the Rhine Alexander increasingly became dismissed by professional scientists and academics as either a popularizing generalist or a misguided empiricist. Both critiques attest to the breakup of the conceptual and political imperatives that held Enlightenment Vitalism together and imparted meaning to Humboldt's ambitious project.

· · ·

Aesthetics played the crucial role in Alexander's concept of how "physiognomists" arrived at their generalizations. But here one should avoid mistaking eighteenth-century aesthetics with what it later became, namely, a discipline limited to the study and explication of literature and the fine arts. Enlightenment aesthetics dealt with the more general question of how sensations, especially those of fear, passion, and pleasure—often combined in the sublime—shaped human thought, feelings, and behavior. As such, aesthetics, psychology, physiology, and epistemology were closely intertwined. In this form aesthetics provided a logic of combination different from that offered by discursive logic or causal analysis. It joined form with energy, or as both Humboldt brothers defined it, form with freedom, resulting in a "harmonious" linking of contradictories.

This reciprocal intertwining, which Alexander sometimes referred to as equilibrium, was not the simple balancing of forces typical of a mechanistic system, but rather a dynamic equilibrium forever in movement, bounded by the limits of stasis and chaos. For both Alexander and Wilhelm, nature was continually progressing, which meant that its true understanding could be achieved only through knowing its history. And since the bonds linking humanity to nature were so close, natural history and human history followed a common path. In this sense the brothers developed Buffon's insight that all knowledge, whether of nature or humanity, was historical. Both brothers sought to find the "reflection of the past in the present."[41] Thus, as Dettlebach correctly observed, Alexander's approach "makes natural science thoroughly historical, that is, an embodiment of development, progress, and evolution: a product of internal and external causes acting in a temporal theater, the fixed points of which Humboldt has located with all the precision afforded by the current state of chronology and historical research."[42]

The same was true of Wilhelm's attempts to understand history and language, though very little research has been undertaken to show how the two brothers' "scientific" activities overlapped.[43] For Wilhelm, the human race was a "natural product," whose history had to be understood as the result of the cooperation of active forces, the most important being the "forces of generation, formation [Bildung], and inertia."[44] As with nature, the human race progressed guided by laws, similar to those Alexander discovered. In a homage to his brother's tableau of the Andean equinox region, Wilhelm declared in "On the Historian's Task": "All living forces, men as well as plants, nations as well as individuals, mankind as well as individual peoples, have in common certain qualities, kinds of development and natural laws. This is even true for products of the mind, such as literature, art, morals, or the outward form of society, insofar as they are based on continuous activity with a specific tradition. The same truth is evident

250 / *Epilogue*

in the step by step ascension to a peak and the gradual decline from it, or in the transition from a certain perfection to certain types of degeneracy, and so forth."[45] In a fragment written slightly earlier, in 1818, Wilhelm tied Alexander's idea of general physics directly to his concept of world history: "If one correctly, in my opinion, labels philosophy world history, then as applied here, it means its physics, if that term be not too daring. One should trace not world history's final cause, but its motive powers; world history should not narrate preceding events from which later ones arose. The forces themselves upon which both depend should be traced. What is necessary is a dissection of world history, a decomposition . . . in new, not already present components."[46] Wilhelm even argued that this new way of understanding world history required a "chemical mode of explanation." It would enable one to understand "the laws which direct it, the individual components of history, the activity of the forces and reagents which act on it and which receive their counter-thrust."[47]

These forays into world-historical physics were not reductionist, just as Alexander's explication of "general physics" was not. Both brothers shared the Enlightenment vitalist belief in the intertwining of determinism and freedom, of the "free play" of natural forces, and of the ultimate progress of human history propelled by the dynamic between nature and freedom. Natural development was not always predictable. Explosions of new creation, inexplicable yet sublime, resulted in revolutions that changed the world. Wilhelm compared these eruptions of creativity to those of volcanoes—again a veiled homage to his brother, who had opted for catastrophism rather than the slow process of global transformation Abraham Gottlob Werner had proposed: "When a crater collapses, a volcano arises, beauty or sublimity attaches to its form. When a nation appears, there lives in it spiritual form, fantasy, and the restful and sensitive tones of its language. Therefore in every destruction *[Untergang]* there is consolation, in every transformation *[Wechsel]* compensation."[48]

The study of nature didn't just serve to better understand this dynamic, it helped refresh the soul, preparing it for a new expansion of knowledge and freedom, despite the continual threat of falling back into barbarism. Both Alexander and Wilhelm saw their researches as supporting the Enlightenment's hope for a better world, achieved through acting in it, directed by understanding nature's operations. For Wilhelm, the cultivated person's goal was "to renew spiritual fertility, to reinforce living spiritual creations and to work against everything that was dead and mechanical. . . . And to the extent that this is possible to renew the world through mind and spirit."[49] For Alexander, general physics provided a means to reach this goal, leading "to an intellectual pleasure and a moral liberty, which can fortify us against destiny's blows."[50]

REPRISE: WHAT IS ENLIGHTENMENT? WHAT ISN'T ENLIGHTENMENT?

I begin and end this study with Wilhelm and Alexander von Humboldt for a number of reasons. The primary one is to challenge the manner in which the Enlightenment has been interpreted in contemporary historical and literary studies. I deliberately chose the Humboldts because they have played a central role in the complex accounts describing what the Enlightenment was not. In these accounts both brothers are portrayed as post-Enlightenment figures: Alexander, either the revolutionary creator of modern empirical science or the ultimate Romantic,[51] Wilhelm, the Romantic idealist who founded German anti-Enlightenment historicism.[52] Thus, to argue that they were not only Enlightenment thinkers, but also among its last and greatest representatives, offers an interpretation many will surely consider wrongheaded. And, indeed, it would be if we accept the standard account of the so-called Enlightenment project, propounded either by postmodernism or in Germany by a strange alliance between defenders of a historicist tradition and populist critics of intellectual history.

From whatever position these readings are drawn, they share many things. They define the Enlightenment in the singular, usually assuming it to be a philosophy of absolute reason. For postmodernists and followers of Horkheimer and Adorno, the Enlightenment supposedly advanced a project whose fine phrases served as an ideological cover for dangerous movements that it supposedly sired, movements such as rationalism, instrumentalism, scienticism, universalism, eurocentrism, masculinism, racism, colonialism, and totalitarianism, to name but a few. The Enlightenment constituted the embodiment of modernity, the enemy postmodernism promises to overcome. For contemporary admirers of German historicism, the Enlightenment functions as the ahistorical premodern, already overcome in early-nineteenth-century Germany by the "modern" historization of the world picture, though still holding a lease on life in the Anglo-Saxon world. All of these accounts assume the Enlightenment to be a uniform movement, embodying a single set of principles, which either set the stage for modernity or was radically replaced by a "paradigm" or "episteme" shift at the beginning of the nineteenth century. In whatever guise, as beginning or end, the "Enlightenment project" is deemed both deficient and dangerous. These stereotypes replicate in many ways those propounded by conservative critics in the nineteenth and early twentieth centuries, but with one major exception, namely, the thinker chosen as the symbolic representative for the movement. Before postmodernism, Voltaire and/or Rousseau occupied that position. Today it is Kant, whose answer to the question "Was ist Aufklärung" has led contemporaries to propose their definition of what it is or should have been or could not have been.

The answer I offer in this study differs from those that I have sketched above. Rather than accepting the proposition that there was a single Enlightenment deploying a uniform language of nature and society, I have attempted to decompose it (to use Wilhelm's and Alexander's vocabulary), seeing if this process might reveal the existence of other constellations of Enlightenment thought and practice. From my researches and reading I have become convinced that the midcentury marked a major shift in the Enlightenment's intellectual concerns, characterized by a skeptical questioning of early Enlightenment postulates used to explain nature and society. Directed against "the spirit of systems," against a one-sided reliance upon abstract reasoning, the skeptical critique led many thinkers to reformulate ideas central to the Enlightenment, especially those defining knowledge, nature, and humanity. The results of such a reconstruction were to historicize nature, limit reason's competence (producing thereby a wide-ranging epistemological modesty), and emphasize and contemplate nature's complexity (leading to a concentration upon contingency instead of coherence). Generally one can discern two broad late-eighteenth-century strategies designed to satisfy the objections raised by the skeptical critique. The first and best known was a form of "neomechanism," most clearly adumbrated by thinkers such as D'Alembert, Condorcet, and Laplace. The second is what I have called Enlightenment Vitalism.

I have chosen to reconstruct the latter, partly because it has been virtually ignored in standard histories of the Enlightenment. But this neglect is not a mere omission, something that adds to but doesn't change the standard view of the Enlightenment. If this reconstruction makes sense, it denies the content and validity of the so-called Enlightenment project, adding another reason to call for its redefinition or abandonment.[53] At the same time my reconstruction also questions the structural arguments of the early Foucault, most clearly presented in *The Order of Things*. Here all-encompassing *epistemes* determine, shape, and limit local language, incarcerating its speakers in an iron cage of which they are not aware and from which they cannot escape. The shift from one discourse to another, when it occurs, sweeps everyone with it, creating a void of linguistic incommensurability, which the historian or archaeologist cannot explain, only unearth.

Thus, for the "early" Foucault the characteristics I ascribe to Enlightenment Vitalism could not exist, for they correspond more closely to the modern rather the classical *episteme* in which, for him, the Enlightenment was embedded. Nor would the explanation I give for Romantic *Naturphilosophie* as the search for a universal *mathesis* founded on the principles of identity, continuity, and clearly defined hierarchies make sense in his conception of the modern order of things. In many ways *Naturphilosophie* had closer ties to the tabular "classical age" than to the irruption of the historical accompanied by the creation of "positivities" central to the *episteme* in which we are supposedly still living. Rather than viewing the age *en bloc*, I doubt that any age can be compartmentalized under simple rubrics. There are always competing social, cultural, and scientific languages, which in their interaction attest to the drama and importance of the issues they seek to encompass.

Although I question Foucault's portrayal of the Enlightenment, I do not wish to follow most postmodernists (and perhaps the "late" Foucault) in viewing the Enlightenment as the birth of modernity. As Dorinda Outram has rightly warned, we should be on guard about making "the Enlightenment our contemporary," for by so doing "we run the risk of approaching it simply as a mirror to ourselves, of sacrificing its specificity to the need to find projections of ourselves in the past."[54] Enlightenment Vitalism may have some filiations with what is called "modernity," but its unique conjunction of assumptions held together by the imperative to mediate between extremes, its vitalization of matter, and its naturalization of morality all run counter to standard definitions of modernity. This vitalist conjunction was sundered during the first decades of the nineteenth century, rendering the vitalists' efforts incomprehensible or contradictory to following generations, forcing them to either translate or transmute vitalist thought. The usual strategy in these reinterpretations was to isolate and concentrate on one side of the vitalist goal of combining "the wide-ranging views of an ardent mind that embraces everything with one glance, and the detail-oriented laboring instinct that concentrates only on one element."

Nowhere is this more evident than in the manner Alexander and Wilhelm von Humboldt have been treated. The dual fragmentation of Alexander's project that began in the nineteenth century has been replicated and expanded by contemporary critics. One side has focused upon Humboldt as the meticulous observer, the other on Humboldt as the essential Romantic. As an example of the first approach, Susan Faye Cannon considered Humboldt the revolutionary creator of a modern approach to the empirical sciences, which she labeled "Humboldtian science." Its hallmarks were a new insistence on accuracy, a sophisticated conception of the relationship between measurement and mathematical laws, and a "new set of conceptual tools: isomaps, graphs, theory of errors."[55] The other interpretation focuses upon Alexander's aesthetic, "Romantic" side. Mary Louise Pratt offers a striking example. Not only does she consider Alexander a Romantic par excellence, but she goes further than most critics, using Humboldt to interpret Romanticism rather than Romanticism to explain Humboldt: "To the extent that Humboldt 'is' a Romantic, Romanticism 'is' Humboldt; to the extent that something called Romanticism constitutes or 'explains' Humboldt's writings on America, those writings constitute or 'explain' that something." And "that something" Pratt invokes is a broad and hazy thing indeed. For her, Humboldt's "Romanticism" included Schiller, but also "another 'Romantic' line—Georg Forster and Bernardin de St. Pierre (two of Humboldt's personal idols), Volney, Chateaubriand, Stedman, Buffon, Le Vailliant, Captain Cook, and the Diderot of the 'Supplement to the Voyage of Bougainville.'"[56] Only recently have some contemporary historians sought to reconnect the empiricist and aesthetic elements of Alexander's project, leading some to conclude, to quote Dettelbach, that Alexander was "neither a naïve empiricist, nor a Romantic idealist." Rather, he was engaged "in an Enlightenment redefinition of the authority of the philosopher."[57]

The interpretation of Wilhelm's work has been more one-sided. Rather than seeing two Wilhelms—one the Romantic idealist, the other the fact-grubbing specialist—Wilhelm has emerged as the person who spearheaded the movement separating history from nature, thereby constituting history as an autonomous and independent field of study. In this guise Wilhelm could propose a close attention to individual *historical* facts, which had to be integrated into a comprehensive whole through empathetic understanding. In this standard interpretation, recently given new life by Ulrich Muhlack, Wilhelm's core assumption of man's essential rootedness in material nature is denied; his belief that the humanistic sciences had to be modeled upon the sciences of living nature ignored; his language, pregnant with the essential concepts and metaphors of Enlightenment Vitalism, reinterpreted; and his message transmuted into its opposite, namely, that history's task was to investigate the realm of human freedom, natural science's that of determinism, each having its own independent epistemological field, each designed to follow its own inherent truth claims independent of the other. History and natural science became equal but separate realms of knowledge.[58] According to this interpretation, the Wilhelm who wrote "On the Historian's Task" emerges as the Enlightenment's most significant early-nineteenth-century critic, the theoretical founder of German historicism.

All of these interpretations of "Was ist Auklärung" and those who were its enemies have served to hide or deny the existence of the broadly based late-eighteenth-century attempt to confront the problems of explaining life, matter, and humanity that I have sought to reconstruct in this study. The simplest way to exclude Enlightenment vitalists from a definition of the Enlightenment was to relegate them to other explanatory categories. Some of these exclusionary practices were founded upon a teleological approach to history or literature, others on the accepted definition of the Enlightenment as the embodiment of reason and mechanistic science, and still others shaped by the logic of specific disciplinary histories. In the first case the vitalists became either "proto-Romantics," or "transitional" figures in the movement from Enlightenment to Romanticism, thinkers who without realizing it prepared the ground for the Enlightenment's demise. The second case expands upon the first and turns these thinkers into conscious enemies of the Enlightenment. Because of their critique of mechanism many Enlightenment vitalists (Herder being the most prominent example) have been relegated to the category of the "Counter-Enlightenment." The third has to do with how most disciplinary histories are written. The history of biology presents an example, in which the efforts of "biological" thinkers are located in an explanatory model postulating the ontological existence of the discipline from antiquity to the present. The field's development is usually plotted as the result of an ever-recurring dialectic between organic and mechanistic explanations. Thus, though histories of eighteenth-century "biology" recognize the importance of vitalists such as Blumenbach, Barthez, and John and William Hunter, they are more likely to be treated as proponents of one side of the inherent dialectic than as spokesmen for a unique form of Enlightenment thought. It was this interpretive model that Foucault attacked with such brilliance in *The Order of Things*, dissolving all artificially constructed disciplinary continuities.

In opposition to these explanatory strategies, I argue that Enlightenment Vitalism was a relatively coherent movement distinguished by a set of basic assumptions, often later viewed as contradictory, held together by a unique epistemological position based on the imperative to mediate between extremes. In this sense it constituted one of the basic languages of nature and humanity available to Enlightenment thinkers. Only through a consideration of the total character of this movement do its unique characteristics emerge, characteristics that cannot be considered simply as transitional, oppositional, modern, or merely part of the history of a specific discipline. In this sense Enlightenment Vitalism had its own linguistic and intellectual form, shaped by crucial questions that confronted thinkers of the last half of the eighteenth century.

What is fascinating about these questions is that they speak to issues we are now facing again: how does one define life and death, what is matter, to what extent is morality natural or artificial? Enlightenment Vitalism's assertion of the intimate link between humans and nature and its celebration of nature's creativity and sublimity speak directly to our need to rethink the issue of humanity's role within and relationship to the environment. Its elevation of reciprocal interrelationship and cooperation, validated by the free play of nature's forces, coincides with our attempts to rethink causal explanations in nature and global interaction among humans. Its view of gender and discussions of race still resonate with today's discussion of these topics. Finally its attempt to formulate a new logic of complementarity, linked to its epistemological modesty and supported by a concern with semiotics and language, provides a model of knowledge that speaks to contemporary endeavors to escape from absolute solutions and maintain the search for knowledge without surrendering to skepticism. In all of these characteristics, Enlightenment Vitalism shares many elements usually seen as belonging to postmodernity. In fact, once the image of the "Enlightenment project" is abandoned and replaced by a true appreciation of the high and late Enlightenment, of which Enlightenment Vitalism formed a part, the Enlightenment may well emerge as an age much more in tune with our present-day concerns than is usually conceived. The questions posed by the vitalists are still relevant, though their answers may not be; in fact, some answers easily appear weird and non-self-evident,[59] reminding us of the distance that separates us from the Enlightenment. Yet their basic epistemological temper still serves as a challenge, relevant today as it was then, asking us to seek liberation in the face of uncertainty, recognizing skepticism but holding it at bay, and, while acknowledging humans' capacity for debasement, hoping that understanding nature and human nature will help us realize the best in ourselves. These traits also define the Enlightenment.

Notes

INTRODUCTION

1. Max Horkheimer, "Reason against Itself," in *What Is Enlightenment? Eighteenth-Century Answers and Twentieth-Century Questions*, ed. James Schmidt (Berkeley: University of California Press, 1996), p. 359.

2. Stephen Edelson Toulmin, *Cosmopolis: The Hidden Agenda of Modernity* (New York: Free Press, 1990), p. x.

3. "Introduction," in *The Sciences in Enlightened Europe*, ed. William Clark, Jan Golinski, and Simon Schaffer (Chicago: University of Chicago Press, 1999), p. 29.

4. Lorraine Daston, "Afterword: The Ethos of Enlightenment," in Clark et al., *The Sciences in Enlightened Europe*, p. 503.

5. *The Ferment of Knowledge: Studies in the Historiography of Eighteenth-Century Science*, ed. George S. Rousseau and Roy Porter (Cambridge: Cambridge University Press, 1980), pp. 111–12.

6. "Introduction," in Clark et al., *The Sciences in Enlightened Europe*, p. 20.

7. Lorraine Daston makes a similar point in her closing essay in this volume, "Afterword": "Distrust of the enlightened—of their tendency to conflate their own narrow interests with the dictates of universal nature, and to substitute rationalization for rationality—is as least as old as the Romantics, and was famously elaborated by Marx. It is still alive and kicking in this volume. With only a few exceptions, the authors of these essays regard the material claims of the enlightened to serve the commonweal with a skepticism that ranges from mild to vehement" (p. 496).

8. As in the majority of multiauthored volumes, the research and explanatory agendas of individual contributors sometimes vary from the program announced in the introduction or just partly converge and overlap with it. In this volume, composed of uniformly outstanding essays, the degree to which they agree with the general interpretations offered in the introduction runs from very strong to weak, if not in some cases to critical. In my opinion the

essay that most clearly and consequently explores the theses set forth in the introduction, demonstrating in its elaboration interpretive imagination and rhetorical flair, is Simon Schaffer's "Enlightened Automata." Needless to say, I don't always agree with his interpretations.

9. Clark et al., *Sciences in Enlightened Europe*, p. 22.

10. See, for example, the work of Ludmilla Jordanova, especially her excellent introduction to *Languages of Nature: Critical Essays on Science and Literature* (London: Free Association Books, 1986), pp. 10–47; her analysis of the eighteenth century in *Sexual Visions: Images of Gender in Science and Medicine between the Eighteenth and Twentieth Centuries* (New York: Harvester Wheatsheaf, 1989); and her essay "Sex and Gender" in *Inventing Human Science: Eighteenth-Century Domains*, ed. Christopher Fox, Roy Porter, and Robert Wokler (Berkeley: University of California Press, 1995), pp. 152–83.

11. Horkheimer, "Reason against Itself," p. 361.

12. On the radical Enlightenment see Margaret C. Jacob, *The Radical Enlightenment: Pantheists, Freemasons, and Republicans* (London: Allen and Unwin, 1981); Jonathan Israel, *Radical Enlightenment: Philosophy and the Making of Modernity* (Oxford: Oxford University Press, 2002).

13. Ever since the unity of the Enlightenment has been contested, its internal periodization has emerged as a problem. Terms like "early," "high," and "late" have been used to differentiate moments within the Enlightenment. I have just accepted the normal conventions here and use "high" and "late" to designate the period from ca. 1750 to ca. 1800. Some interpreters have taken a more radical stance, foremost among them being the practitioners of *"Begriffsgeschichte"* in Germany. In their scheme the major changes that led Europe to "modernity" occurred in what they call the *"Sattelzeit"* (saddle time), from ca. 1750 to 1850. The increasing tendency to speak of a "long eighteenth century" is leading in a similar direction, though at its most radical it doesn't go much past 1832.

14. For the importance of skepticism in the late eighteenth century see Johan van der Zande and Richard Popkin, eds. *The Skeptical Tradition around 1800* (Dordrecht: Kluwer, 1998).

15. "The world is a theater of continual revolutions": Anon., *Traité des extrêmes ou éléments de la science de la réalité* (Amsterdam, 1767), p. 232. The same position was proclaimed by August Ludwig Schlözer: "Der Erboden hat Revolutionen erlitten. Er ist nicht mehr, wie er aus der Hand des Schöpfers kam. Er ändert, verschönert, verschlimmert sich, wie das Menschengeschlecht, das ihn bewohnt": *Vorstellung seiner Universal-Historie* (Göttingen, 1772), p. 8.

16. David Hume, *The Philosophical Works*, ed. Thomas Hill Green and Thomas Hodge Grose, 4 vols. (Aalen: Scientia Verlag, 1992), vol. 4, p. 51. This is a reprint edition of the second edition (London, 1882–86).

17. For the rise of probability theory in the eighteenth century see Lorraine Daston, *Classical Probability in the Enlightenment* (Princeton: Princeton University Press, 1988).

18. Jordanova, *Languages of Nature*, p. 41.

19. Toulmin, *Cosmopolis*, p. 108.

20. The term "synergy" was coined by Georg Stahl and then used extensively by Paul-Joseph Barthez in his theory of vital physiology.

21. Kant was much more influenced by this explanatory model than is usually supposed. For an excellent discussion of the vitalistic influences on his philosophy see Wolfgang Krohn and Günther Küppers, "Die natürlichen Ursachen der Zwecke: Kants Ansätze der Selbstorganisation," *Selbstorganisation: Jahrbuch für Komplexität in den Natur-, Sozial- und Geisteswissenschaften* 3 (1992): 7–15.

22. See Jordanova, "Sex and Gender," p. 163, for an excellent discussion of the centrality of comparison in the late eighteenth century.

23. Jordanova, "Introduction," in *Languages of Nature*, p. 35.

24. Horkheimer, "Reason against Itself," p. 364.

25. This is the model Goethe used to explain the dispute between Cuvier and St. Hilaire, which he said replicated the differences between Buffon and Daubenton on a higher plane. Jacques Roger used a similar pattern in his pioneering work, *Les sciences de la vie dans la pensée francaise du XVIIIe siècle* (Paris: Armand Colin, 1971).

26. François Duchesneau offers a similar critique of traditional modes of dealing with vitalism in his article "Vitalism in Late Eighteenth-Century Physiology: The Cases of Barthez, Blumenbach and John Hunter," in *William Hunter and the Eighteenth-Century Medical World*, ed. William Frederick Bynum and Roy Porter (Cambridge: Cambridge University Press, 1985), pp. 259–60.

27. The use of the term "proto" is built upon a strong teleological analytic procedure that distorts the phenomenon under consideration by judging it in terms of its supposed filiation with something that came after it. In effect, it transposes a form of analysis into historical analysis that I believe is misleading. In this case it collapses similarity into identity, transposes terms to a different context, and often refuses to deal with the specific meanings and definitions of the specific terms.

28. Jordanova, *Languages of Nature*, p. 35; Timothy Lenoir, *The Strategy of Life: Teleology and Mechanics in Nineteenth-Century German Biology* (Chicago: University of Chicago Press, 1982).

29. Martin Gierl, "Compilation and the Production of Knowledge in the Early German Enlightenment," in *Wissenschaft als kulturelle Praxis, 1750–1900*, ed. Hans Erich Bödeker, Peter Hanns Reill, and Jürgen Schlumböhm (Göttingen: Vandenhoeck & Ruprecht, 1999), pp. 69–104. Although Gierl focuses upon Germany, his analysis could be transferred to other European lands with little difficulty. Gierl is pioneering a way to deal with the broadly based production and communication of knowledge. His book *Pietismus und Aufklärung: theologische Polemik und die Kommunikationsreform am Ende des 17. Jahrhunderts* (Göttingen: Vandenhoeck & Ruprecht, 1997) analyzes how Pietistic views were formed and generated through theological polemics.

30. Nicholas Jardine, *The Scenes of Inquiry: On the Reality of Questions in the Sciences*, 2nd ed. (Oxford: Clarendon Press, 2000), p. 50; Philip Rehbock,

260 / Notes

The Philosophical Naturalists: Themes in Early Nineteenth-Century British Biology (Madison: University of Wisconsin Press, 1983).

31. Lorraine Daston in her closing remarks to the volume *The Sciences in Enlightenment Europe* reminds readers of the distance that separates us from the Enlightenment, as does Dorinda Outram in her opening essay: "The very nature of their accounts [Daston uses physicotheology as an example] should compel closer reading by historians alert to the weirdness, the non-self-evidence of the Enlightenment" (p. 504).

PROLOGUE

1. Humboldt described his intellectual temperament to Schiller thus: "Ich bin fester als je überzeugt, daß, wenn ich irgend einen intellektuellen Beruf in der Welt habe, es der Kritik ist"; quoted by Siegfried A. Kaehler, *Wilhelm von Humboldt und der Staat: Ein Beitrag zur Geschichte deutscher Lebensgestaltung um 1800*, 2nd ed. (Göttingen: Vandenhoeck & Ruprecht, 1963), p. 11. The comments about Humboldt's impersonal, cold, and emotionless nature are legion. They range from Friedrich Schlegel's nasty characterization of one of Humboldt's writings as demonstrating a loss of manliness (Kaehler, p. 439, fn. 1) to Friedrich Gentz's less impassioned, though equally negative, evaluation: "By virtue of his intellect and fund of knowledge he is one of the superior men of our time. Cold, without passion, incapable of love and of hate, he toys with the world and with human beings as though it were a game"; quoted by Paul Robinson Sweet, *Wilhelm von Humboldt: A Biography*, 2 vols. (Columbus: Ohio State University Press, 1978–80), vol. 2, p. 161. The reference to the December sun was made by Humboldt in a poem describing himself in the following manner:

> Hell, wie Dezembersonne, sie mich nannten,
> weil sie in mir nicht an Gefühle glaubten;
> die mir so oft des Lebens Ruhe raubten,
> die innren Stürme sie in mir nicht kannten.

Wilhelm von Humboldt, *Gesammelte Schriften*, ed. Albert Leitzmann et al., 17 vols. (Berlin: B. Behr's Verlag, 1903–36), vol. 9, p. 428.

2. W. von Humboldt, *Gesammelte Schriften*, vol. 9, p. 428.

3. Sweet, in his excellent biography of Humboldt, notes briefly the importance of this trip. He remarked that it "is perhaps legitimate to wonder whether a certain ritual quality was . . . involved" (*Humboldt*, vol. 1, p. 233). However, Sweet never followed this point up. Excerpts of this piece were published in "Die Vasken, oder Bemerkungen auf einer Reise durch Biscaya und das französische Basquenland im Frühling des Jahres 1801," in *Gesammelte Schriften*, vol. 9. Humboldt must have thought highly of this piece since he reproduced it to describe a later trip. The whole essay was published posthumously and entitled "Cantabrica," in *Gesammelte Schriften*, vol. 3. Marianne Cowan has trans-

lated parts of it in her collection: *Humanist without Portfolio: An Anthology of the Writings of Wilhelm von Humboldt* (Detroit: Wayne State University Press, 1963), pp. 117–18.

4. Wilhelm von Humboldt, *Briefe an Christine Reinhard-Reimarus*, ed. Arndt Schreiber (Heidelberg: Lambert Schneider, 1956), pp. 83–85.

5. W. von Humboldt, *Gesammelte Schriften*, vol. 3, p. 115; vol. 13, p. 30.

6. W. von Humboldt, *Gesammelte Schriften*, vol. 3. pp. 115–17; vol. 13, pp. 30–31.

7. Humboldt to Brinkmann, 18 March 1793, in *Wilhelm von Humboldts Briefe an Karl Gustav von Brinkmann*, ed. Albert Leitzmann (Leipzig: Karl Heirsemann, 1939), pp. 60–61.

8. When Humboldt, Bonpland, and a native guide climbed to the height of 5,850 meters, they broke Saussure's record of 4,775 meters achieved on his ascent of Mount Blanc.

9. Alexander von Humboldt, *Essai sur la géographie des plantes; accompagné d'un tableau physique des régions équinoxiales* (Paris: Schoell, 1805–7). The book was supposed to appear in 1805, and the title page of the introduction and the *Tableau* bear that date. But because of the war, the text was published only in 1807. See also *Ideen zu einer Geographie der Pflanzen nebst einem Naturgemälde der Tropengeländer*, ed. Mauritz Dittrich, Ostwalds Klassiker der Exakten Wissenschaften 248 (Leipzig: Akademische Verlagsgesellschaft, 1960); and *Ansichten der Nature: erster und zweiter Band*, ed. Hanno Beck, in Alexander von Humboldt Studienausgabe, 7 vols. (Darmstadt: Wissenschaftliche Buchgesellschaft, 1987), vol. 5.

10. A. Humboldt, *Naturgemälde der Tropenländer*, p. 55. "In der großen Verkettung von Ursachen und Wirkungen darf kein Stoff, keine Thätigkeit isolirt betrachtet werden. Das Gleichgewicht, welches mitten unter den Perturbationen scheinbar streitender Elemente herrscht, dieß Gleichgewicht geht aus dem freyen Spiel dynamischer Kräfte hervor."

11. A. von Humboldt, "Die Lebenskraft oder der rhodische Genius, Eine Erzählung," in *Ansichten*, p. 321. "Schon im dunkeln Chaos häufte sich die Materie und mied sich, je nachdem Freundschaft oder Feindschaft sie anzog oder absteiß."

12. A. von Humboldt, "Ideen zu einer Physiognomik der Gewächse," in *Ansichten*, p. 178. "so sind die organischen Kräfte sogleich bereit den toten Fels zu beleben." A. von Humboldt, "Physiognomik der Gewächse," in *Ansichten*, p. 176. "Wohin der Blick des Naturforschers dringt, ist Leben oder Keim zum Leben verbreitet."

13. A. von Humboldt, "Physiognomik der Gewächse," in *Ansichten*, p. 185. "Die absolute Größe und der Grad der Entwicklung, welche die Organismen (Pflanzen- und Tierarten) erreichen, die zu einer Familie gehören, werden durch noch unerkannte Gesetze bedingt. In jeder der großen Abteilungen der Tierreiches, den Insekten, Crustaceen, Reptilien, Vögeln, Fischen oder Säugetieren, oszilliert die Dimension des Körperbaus zwischen gewissen äußersten Grenzen."

14. A. von Humboldt, "Lebenskraft oder rhodische Genius," in *Ansichten*, p. 322. "Sie [die Lebenskraft] kümmert sich nicht um die demokritische Freundschaft und Feindschaft der Atome; sie vereinigt Stoffe, die in der unbelebten Natur sich ewig fliehen, und trennt, was in dieser sich unaufhaltsam sucht."

15. A. von Humboldt, "Über die Wasserfälle des Orinoco bei Atures und Maipures," in *Ansichten*, p. 129. "Auf diesem Verkehr beruht der edlere Teil des Genusses, den die Natur gewährt. Nirgends durchdringt sie uns mehr mit dem Gefühl ihrer Größe, nirgends spricht sie uns mächtiger an als in der Tropenwelt. . . . Die Errinnerung an ein fernes, reichbegabtes Land, der Anblick eines freien, kraftvollen Pflanzenwuches erfrischt und stärkt das Gemüt, wie, von der Gegenwart bedrängt, der emporstrebende Geist sich gern des Jugendalters der Menschheit und ihrer einfachen Größe erfreut."

16. A. von Humboldt, "Wasserfälle," in *Ansichten*, p. 128. "Denn in dem innersten, empfänglichen Sinn spiegelt lebendig und wahr sich die physische Welt. . . . [A]lles steht in altem, geheimnisvollem Verkehr mit dem gemütlichen Leben des Menschen."

17. A. von Humboldt, *Ideen Geographie der Pflanzen*, p. 50. "Die krankenden Gewächse, welche Luxus oder Wißbegierde in unsere Triebhäuser einzwängt, erinnern uns nur an das, was wir entbehren: sie bieten ein verzerrtes, unvollkommenes Bild von der Pracht der Tropenvegetation dar. Aber in dem Reichthume und der Kultur der Sprache, in der regen Phantasie der Dichter und Maler, finden die Europäer einen befriedigenden Ersatz. Der Zauber nachahmender Künste versetzt sie in die fernsten Theile der Erde. Wessen Gefühl regsam für diesen Zauber, wessen Geist gebildet genug ist, um die Natur in allen ihren Thätigkeiten zu umfassen, der schafft sich in der Einsamkeit einer öden Heide gleichsam eine innere Welt: er eignet sich zu, was die Kühnheit des Naturforschers, Meer und Luft durchschiffend, auf dem Gipfel beeister Berge oder im Innern unterirdischer Höhlen, entdeckt hat."

18. A. von Humboldt, *Ideen Geographie der Pflanzen*, p. 50. "Hier sind wir auf dem Punkt gelangt, wo Kultur der Völker und Wissenschaft am unbestrittensten auf individuelle Glück einwirken. Durch sie leben wir zugleich in dem verflossenen und in dem gegenwärtigen Jahrhunderte. Um uns versammelnd was menschlicher Fleiß in den fernsten Erdstrichen aufgefunden, bleiben wir allen gleich nahe. Ja, die Kenntniß von dem innern, geheimen Spiele der Naturkräfte, läßt uns bey vielen selbst Schlüsse für die Zukunft wagen, und die Rückkehr großer Erscheinungen vorher bestimmen. So schafft Einsicht in den Weltorganismus einen geistigen Genuß, und eine innere Freyheit, die mitten unter den Schlägen des Schicksals von keiner äußern Macht zerstört werden kann."

19. A. von Humboldt, "Lebenskraft oder rhodische Genius," in *Ansichten*, p. 322. "In der toten anorganischen Materie ist träge Ruhe, so lange die Bande der Verwandtschaft nicht gelöst werden, so lange ein dritter Stoff nicht eindringt, um sich den vorigen beizugesellen. Aber auch diese Störung folgt dann wieder unfruchtbare Ruhe."

20. A. von Humboldt, "Lebenskraft oder rhodische Genius," in *Ansichten*, p. 322.

21. A. von Humboldt, "Lebenskraft oder rhodische Genius," in *Ansichten*, p. 322.

22. A. von Humboldt, "Lebenskraft oder rhodische Genius," in *Ansichten*, p. 322. "Kein irdischer Stoff . . . ist daher irgendwo in Einfachheit und reinem, jungfräulichem Zustande zu finden."

23. Jordanova, in her introduction to *Languages of Nature*, provides an excellent discussion of the various function opposing elements of boundaries and dichotomies can play (pp. 34–36).

24. A. von Humboldt, "Physiognomik der Gewächse," in *Ansichten*, p. 183. "Der Einfluß der physischen Welt auf die moralische, das geheimnisvolle Ineinanderwirken das Sinnlichen und Außersinnlichen gibt dem Naturstudium, wenn man es zu höheren Gesichtspunkten erhebt, einen eigenen, noch zu wenig erkannten Reiz."

25. Jordanova, "Naturalizing the Family: Literature and the Bio-medical Sciences in the Late Eighteenth Century," in *Languages of Nature*, p. 93.

26. Michel Foucault, *The Order of Things: An Archaeology of the Human Sciences* (New York: Pantheon Books, 1971), p. 42. Foucault denied the universal nature of binary logic but saw the emergence of the binary mode as central to "classicism" and still dominant today. Needless to say, the position I ascribe to Humboldt here would be impossible if one accepts Foucault's interpretation.

27. Gaston Bachelard, *The New Scientific Spirit*, trans. Arthur Goldhammer (Boston: Beacon Press, 1984), pp. 14–16. Jordanova also suggests something similar in her introduction to *Languages of Nature*, p. 36.

28. For a discussion of Humboldt's attempt to mediate between Linnaeus and Buffon see James Larson, *Interpreting Nature: The Science of Living Form from Linnaeus to Kant* (Baltimore: Johns Hopkins University Press, 1994), pp. 115–18.

29. A. von Humboldt, "Ueber die Steppen und Wüsten," in *Ansichten*, p. 19. "So bereitet der Mensch auf der untersten Stufe tierische Roheit, so im Scheinglanze seiner höheren Bildung sich stets ein mühevolles Leben. So verfolgt den Wanderer über den weiten Erdkreis, über Meer und Land, wie den Geschichtsforscher durch alle Jahrhunderte das einförmige, trostlose Bild des entzweiten Geschlechts. Darum versenkt, wer im ungeschlichteten Zwist der Völker nach geistiger Ruhe strebt, gern den Blick in das stille Leben der Pflanzen und in der heiligen Naturkraft inneres Wirken oder, hingegeben dem angestammten Triebe, der seit Jahrtausenden der Menschen Brust durchglüht, blickt er ahnungsvoll aufwärts zu den hohen Gestirnen, welche in ungestörtem Einklang die alte, ewige Bahn vollenden."

30. W. von Humboldt to Brinkmann, 18 March 1793, in *Humboldts Briefe an Brinkmann*, pp. 60–61. "Zu dieser Restauration [der Wissenschaften] ist der wichtigste Schritt Einheit in alles menschliche Streben zu bringen, zu zeigen, daß diese Einheit der Mensch ist, und zwar der innere Mensch, und den Menschen zu schildern, wie er auf alles außer ihm, und wie alles außer ihm auf ihm

wirkt, daraus den Zustand des Menschengeschlechts zu zeichnen, seine möglichen Revolutionen zu entwerfen, und die wirklichen, soviel möglich, zu erklären. Vor allem, was auf den Menschen einwirkt, ist das Hauptsächlichste eigentlich die physische Natur und diese Wirkung ist um so stärker, als ihre Ursachen uns unbekannt sind. Ueberhaupt ist die physische Natur eigentlich die wichtigere, da, was man sonst studiren mag, man eigentlich es mit Menschenwerk zu thun hat, bei dem Studium jener aber eigentlich der Gang des Schicksals, dem auch der Mensch selbst unterthan ist, offenbar wird." Humboldt thought his brother Alexander would be the one to do this, at least for the physical sciences: "Das Studium der physischen Natur nun mit dem der moralischen zu verknüpfen, und in das Universum, wie wir es erkennen, eigentlich erst die wahre Harmonie zu bringen, oder wenn dieß die Kräfte Eines Menschen übersteigen sollte, das Studium der physischen Natur so vorzubereiten, daß dieser zweite Schritt leicht werde, dazu, sage ich, hat mir unter allen Köpfen, die ich historisch und aus eigner Erfahrung in allen Zeiten kenne, nur mein Bruder fähig geschienen."

31. For a brief but insightful discussion of the concept of language of nature, see Jordanova, *Languages of Nature*, pp. 17–50.

32. Antoine Faivre and Rolf Christian Zimmermann, *Epochen der Naturmystik: Hermetische Tradition im wissenschaftlichen Fortschritt* (Berlin: Erich Schmidt Verlag, 1979), p. 23.

33. Georg Iggers presents this argument as follows: "With his essay 'On the Tasks of the Writer of History,' the philosophical theory of German historicism was complete. The break with the *Aufklärung* and *Humanitätsideal* was now very real"; *The German Conception of History: The National Tradition of Historical Thought from Herder to the Present* (Middeltown, Conn.: Wesleyan University Press, 1968), p. 62. In Iggers's later works on the Enlightenment's vision of history, he modified this position, locating the origins of much of early historicist thought in the Enlightenment.

34. Over the last twenty-five years or so an increasing number of studies have focused upon the emergence in the eighteenth century of ways of thought in various disciplines that were either critical of mechanism or implicitly rejected it because of the scientific and practical demands of the discipline. This is especially true for the areas of the life sciences, natural history, and medicine. Among the most important studies for the life sciences and natural history are Jacques Roger, *Les sciences de la vie dans la pensée française du XVIIIe siècle*, recently translated and abridged as *The Life Sciences in Eighteenth-Century French Thought*, ed. Keith Benson, trans. Robert Ellrich (Stanford: Stanford University Press, 1997); Colm Kiernan, *The Enlightenment and Science in Eighteenth-Century France*, Studies on Voltaire and the Eighteenth Century, ed. Theodore Besterman (Oxfordshire: Voltaire Foundation, 1973); Sergio Moravia, "From *Homme Machine* to *Homme Sensible*: Changing Eighteenth-Century Models of Man's Image," *Journal of the History of Ideas* 39 (1978): 45–60; Theodore M. Brown, "From Mechanism to Vitalism in Eighteenth-Century Physiology," *Journal of the History of Biology* 7 (1974): 179–216;

Richard W. Burkhardt, Jr., *The Spirit of System: Lamarck a*[...] *Biology* (Cambridge, Mass.: Harvard University Press, 1977); [...] neau, *La physiologie des lumières: empirisme, modèles et t*[...] tional Archives of the History of Ideas 95 (The Hague: M[...] Timothy Lenoir, "Generational Factors in the Origin of *Ron*[...] *philosophie," Journal of the History of Biology* 11 (1978): 57–100; [...] *egy of Life: Teleology and Mechanics in Nineteenth-Century German Biology* (London: Reidel, 1982); Philip Sloan, "Buffon, German Biology, and the Historical Interpretation of Biological Species," *British Journal for the History of Science* 12 (1979): 109–53; "From Logical Universals to Historical Individuals: Buffon's Idea of Biological Species," in *Histoire du concept d'espèce de la vie*, ed. Scott Atran (Paris: Foundation Singer-Polignac, 1985), pp. 101–40; "The Gaze of Natural History," in Fox et al., *Inventing Human Science*; James Larson, "The Most Confused Knot in the Doctrine of Reproduction," in *The Quantifying Spirit in the Eighteenth-Century*, ed. Tore Frängsmyr, John L. Heilbron, and Robin Rider (Berkeley: University of California Press, 1990), pp. 267–90, and *Interpreting Nature*; Mary Terrall, "Maupertuis and Eighteenth-Century Scientific Culture," Ph.D diss., University of California, Los Angeles, 1987, "Salon, Academy and Boudoir: Generation and Desire in Maupertuis's Science of Life," *Isis* 87 (1996): 217–29, and her definitive book-length study, *The Man Who Flattened the Earth: Maupertuis and the Sciences of the Enlightenment* (Chicago: University of Chicago Press, 2002). The volume of collected essays *Cultures of Natural History*, ed. Nicolas Jardine, James A. Secord, and Emma Spary (Cambridge: Cambridge University Press, 1996), does a fine job of showing the diversity of the natural historical endeavor in the eighteenth century. See also Miriam Meijer, *Race and Aesthetics in the Anthropology of Petrus Camper, 1772–1789* (Amsterdam: Rodopi, 1999); Nicholas Jardine, "Inner History: or How to End Enlightenment," in *The Sciences in Enlightened Europe*, pp. 477–94; Emma Spary, *Utopia's Garden: French Natural History from Old Regime to Revolution* (Chicago: University of Chicago Press, 2000), "Codes of Passion: Natural History Specimens as a Polite Language in Late Eighteenth-Century France," in *Wissenschaft als kulturelle Praxis, 1750-1900*, ed. Hans Erich Bödeker, Peter Hanns Reill, and Jürgen Schlumbohm (Göttingen: Vandenhoeck & Ruprecht, 1999), pp. 105–35, and "The 'Nature' of the Enlightenment," in *The Sciences of the Enlightenment*, pp. 272–304; Michael Hagner, "Vom Naturalien Kabinett zur Embriologie: Wandlungen des Monströsen und die Ordnung des Lebens," in *Der "falsche" Körper: Beiträge zu einer Geschichte der Monstrositäten*, ed. Michael Hagner (Göttingen: Wallstein, 1995), 73–107; "Enlightened Monsters," in *The Sciences in Enlightened Europe*, 175–217; Roger French, "Sickness and the Soul: Stahl, Hoffman and Sauvages on Pathology," in *The Medical Enlightenment of the Eighteenth Century*, ed. Andrew Cunningham and Roger French (Cambridge: Cambridge University Press, 1990), pp. 88–110; Julian Martin, "Sauvage's Nosology: Medical Enlightenment in Montpellier," in *Medical Enlightenment*, pp. 111–37; Thomas H. Broman, *The Transformation of German Medicine, 1750–1820* (Cambridge:

...mbridge University Press, 1996). Roy Porter has been one of the most indefatigable proponents of reinterpreting the Enlightenment's idea of nature. Among the many works he has written and edited see *The Ferment of Knowledge: Studies in the Historiography of Eighteenth-Century Science* ed. George S. Rousseau and Roy Porter (Cambridge: Cambridge University Press, 1980); Fox et al., *Inventing Human Science: Eighteenth-Century Domains*; Bynum et al., *William Hunter and the Eighteenth-Century Medical World*; *Patient's Progress: Doctors and Doctoring in Eighteenth-Century England*, ed. Dorothy Porter and Roy Porter (Cambridge: Polity Press, 1989); *The Enlightenment in National Context*, ed. Roy Porter and Mikulàs Teich (Cambridge: Cambridge University Press, 1981); "The Enlightenment in England," in *The Enlightenment in National Context*, pp. 1–18; *Languages of Psyche: Mind and Body in Enlightenment Thought*, ed. George Rousseau and Roy Porter (Berkeley: University of California Press, 1990); "Barely Touching: A Social Perspective on Mind and Body," in *Languages of Psyche*, pp. 45–80; *Mind-Forged Manacles: A History of Madness in England from the Restoration to the Regency* (London: Penguin Books, 1987); *The Cambridge History of Science*, vol. 4: *The Eighteenth Century*, ed. Roy Porter (Cambridge: Cambridge University Press, 2002). There are not as many studies that deal with antimechanistic views within the physical sciences. One of the most important and influential has been Robert Schofield, *Mechanism and Materialism: British Natural Philosophy in an Age of Reason* (Princeton: Princeton University Press, 1970).

 35. Charles Coulston Gillispie's "The *Encyclopédie* and the Jacobin Philosophy of Science" was a pioneering article that dealt with the rise of anti-Newtonianism in the late Enlightenment, which, though informed by a deep distaste for this type of thought, clearly related it to radical political strains; "The *Encyclopédie* and the Jacobin Philosophy of Science: A Study in Ideas and Consequences," in *Critical Problems in the History of Science*, ed. Marshall Clagett (Madison: University of Wisconsin Press, 1962). Margaret Jacob has probed the relations between radical politics and antimechanistic science, especially in *The Radical Enlightenment*; *Living the Enlightenment : Freemasonry and Politics in Eighteenth-Century Europe* (New York: Oxford University Press, 1991). In his excellent study of public science in Great Britain, Jan Golinski has traced out the intimate connections between radical politics and chemistry: *Science as Public Culture: Chemistry and Enlightenment in Britain: 1760–1820* (Cambridge: Cambridge University Press, 1992).

 36. Jordanova, *Languages of Nature*, p. 27.
 37. Porter, *The Ferment of Knowledge*, pp. 111–12.
 38. See Porter and Teich, *The Enlightenment in National Context*. *The Sciences in Enlightened Europe* attests to the increasing sophistication of analyzing the Enlightenment in its national contexts, presenting excellent studies of Enlightenment scientific thought and practice in France, England, Italy, the Netherlands, Sweden, and Prussia, along with essays on other more general topics. *The Ferment of Knowledge*, when it appeared in the early 1980s, attempted to both summarize the latest trends in the historiography of eighteenth-century

science and set an agenda for further research. It was successful in many ways, as demonstrated by the contributions to *The Sciences in Enlightenment Europe*, an impressive volume that had the same ambitions for the end of the twentieth century as did the *Ferment of Knowledge* when it was published. Although there are many challenging essays in *The Sciences in Enlightened Europe*, few if any try to realize the agenda set forth by Shapin as quoted above. When different "Enlightenments" are discussed, it is with reference to specific social and cultural conditioners, generally producing national or even regional varieties. When more general categories are proposed, they seem to be forged using tools taken directly from Foucault's "toolbox," often resulting in critiques closely allied to those originally proposed by Horkheimer and Adorno in which discipline, control, and dehumanization emerge as dominant themes in characterizing the Enlightenment as a whole. There are exceptions to these two analytic strains in the volume, of course, but very few attempts try to trace contesting Enlightenment languages of nature that crossed national and regional boundaries. Granted, these languages had their own local dialects, but I do believe they existed.

39. For an excellent analysis of the changes in the life sciences in France during the eighteenth century see Roger's *Les sciences de la vie*. Colm Kiernan has argued in a similar vein, asserting that "the thought of the Enlightenment is . . . a debate between proponents of the physical and of the life sciences, where, as the century advanced, victory passed to the latter"; *Enlightenment and Science in Eighteenth-Century France*, p. 14. Sergio Moravia has written an outstanding article discussing the change in concepts of human nature, "From *Homme Machine* to *Homme Sensible*." Arthur L. Donovan has investigated the contributions of the Scots Cullen and Black in his article "William Cullen and the Research Tradition of Eighteenth-Century Scottish Chemistry," in *The Origins and Nature of the Scottish Enlightenment: Essays*, ed. Roy Hutchinson Campbell and Andrew S. Skinner (Edinburgh: John Donald, 1982). He elaborates the same point in *Philosophical Chemistry in the Scottish Enlightenment: The Doctrines and Discoveries of William Cullen and Joseph Black* (Edinburgh: University Press, 1975). In his study of "animal heat," Everett Mendelsohn also describes the major shift in conceptualization concerning that subject that took place at the midcentury: *Heat and Life: The Development of the Theory of Animal Heat* (Cambridge, Mass.: Harvard University Press, 1964). John L. Heilbron also notes the change in mid-eighteenth-century visions of science, though he deplores them; see his *Electricity in the 17th and 18th Centuries: A Study of Early Modern Physics* (Berkeley: University of California Press, 1979). This theme is made even more forcefully in Frängsmyr et al., *The Quantifying Spirit in the* Eighteenth *Century*. Gary Hatfield also points to a major midcentury change in "Remaking the Science of Mind: Psychology as Natural Science," in *Inventing Science: Eighteenth-Century Domains*, pp. 201, 207.

40. Georg Forster, "Noch etwas über die Menschenrassen," in *Forsters Werke*. ed. Gerhard Steiner, 2 vols. (Berlin: Aufbau, 1968), vol. 1, p. 22.

1. STORMING "THE TEMPLE OF ERROR"

1. Daniel Mornet, "Les enseignements des bibliothèques privées (1750–1780)," *Revue d'Histoire Littéraire de la France* 17 (1910), p. 460.

2. Emma C. Spary, *Utopia's Garden: French Natural History from Old Regime to Revolution* (Chicago: University of Chicago Press, 2000), p. 12.

3. Spary in her essay "The 'Nature' of Enlightenment" convincingly shows how important natural history was for eighteenth-century culture and concludes: "Moreover Buffon, his opus, or his institutions were acknowledged in virtually every work on natural history published after 1749 that I have consulted. The *Histoire naturelle* was instrumental in promoting the view that natural history offered a privileged access into the natural foundations of human association, and a route to 'natural' development, both physical and moral"; *The Sciences in Enlightened Europe*, ed. William Clark, Jan V. Golinski, and Simon Schaffer (Chicago: University of Chicago Press, 1999), p. 296.

4. Montesquieu's work can be seen as proposing a logic of the social sciences that was opposed to mechanism. In the natural sciences, Buffon's friends Maupertuis and Needham had attacked mechanism, as had La Mettrie and Benoit de Maillet. For Maupertuis, Needham, and Benoit de Maillet, see Jacques Roger, *Les sciences de la vie dans la pensée française du XVIIIe siècle* (Paris: Armand Colin, 1971), pp. 457–526. For Maupertuis see the following works by Mary Terrall: "Maupertuis and Eighteenth-Century Scientific Culture"; "The Culture of Science in Frederick the Great's Berlin," *History of Science* 28 (1990): 333–64; "Representing the Earth's Shape: The Polemics Surrounding Maupertuis's Expedition to Lapland," *Isis* 83 (1992): 218–37; *The Man Who Flattened the Earth*. La Mettrie is often considered as the archetype of the mechanical philosophy of the Enlightenment. But though he employed the metaphor of "man the machine," he also transformed the idea of an "organic machine" so radically that it had little to do with traditional mechanist explanations. As Aram Vartanian notes, La Mettrie's "primary task was to vitalize the Cartesian 'dead mechanism' approach to biology. In order to lift the *homme machine* beyond the reach of animistic criticism, La Mettrie had first to show that purposive motion could be a property of organized matter as such, or, put differently, that the man-machine was automatic in a manner that no man-made machine, requiring direction from without, could truly duplicate"; *La Mettrie's L'Homme Machine: A Study in the Origins of an Idea* (Princeton: Princeton University Press, 1960), p. 19.

5. This is Boyle's phrase, quoted by Richard S. Westfall, *The Construction of Modern Science: Mechanisms and Mechanics* (Cambridge: Cambridge University Press, 1977), p. 66.

6. Lelland J. Rather and John B. Frerichs, eds., "The Leibniz-Stahl Controversy–I. Leibniz' Opening Objections to the *Theorie medica vera*," *Clio Medica* 3 (1968), p. 24.

7. Michel Foucault, *The Order of Things: An Archaeology of the Human Sciences* (New York: Pantheon Books, 1970), p. 57. I use Foucault's testimony

here for purposes with which he would not have agreed. He dismissed the emphasis upon mechanical natural philosophy as a key to understand the period. He included Buffon within the *episteme* of classical thought, supposedly dominant from the mid-seventeenth century to the end of the eighteenth century:

> But neither this endeavor (to mathematize empirical knowledge) nor the attempts of mechanism should be confused with the relation that all Classical knowledge, in its most general form, maintains with the *mathesis,* understood as a universal science of measurement and order. Under cover of the empty and obscurely incantatory phrases 'Cartesian influence' or 'Newtonian model,' our historians of ideas are in the habit of confusing these three things and defining Classical rationalism as the tendency to make nature mechanical and calculable. Others are slightly more perceptive, and go to a great deal of trouble to discover beneath this rationalism a play of 'contrary forces': the forces of nature and life refusing to let themselves be reduced either to algebra or to dynamics, and thus preserving, in the depths of Classicism itself, the natural resources of the non-rationalizable. These two forms of analysis are equally inadequate; for the fundamental element of the Classical *episteme* is neither the success or failure of mechanism, nor the right to mathematicize or the impossibility of mathematicizing nature, but rather a link with the *mathesis* which, until the end of the eighteenth century, remains constant and unaltered. (pp. 56–57)

I find his discussion of the type of thinking he calls classicism applicable only to the dominant scientific, philosophical, and social thought of the period ca. 1660–1750, not for what follows, and as the last chapter of this study argues, the idea of a universal *mathesis* became the battle cry of the *Naturphilosophen* against the Enlightenment.

8. Quoted by Tore Frängsmyr in "The Mathematical Philosophy," in Frängsmyr et al., *The Quantifying Spirit in the Eighteenth Century,* p. 28.

9. I believe there is a difference between quantification, measurement, and mathematization. Mathematization in the eighteenth century implied something much more consequential than quantification. To mathematize was to employ the model of mathematics as a guide to construct the phenomenal world. It carried over the rules of mathematics into logic, assuming that what exists is basically definable according to mathematical principles. Quantification, on the other hand, is a much hazier concept. It can be simply a tool of inquiry, answering such questions as how much or how many. It could be attached to a principle such as probability theory, which is a much weaker version than mathematization. These differentiations were at the heart of the contest between natural philosophers in the last half of the eighteenth century. Quantification very often became the tool used by empiricists to attack the

claims of the mathematizers. This difference is central for the authors in the volume *The Quantifying Spirit in the Eighteenth Century,* though they don't use the linguistic distinction I am making. All believe that a major shift in the way in which mathematics was used and conceived took place somewhere around 1760. John Heilbron characterized this latter movement as one imbued with "the quantifying spirit," which included "the passion to order and systematize as well as to measure and calculate" (p. 2). But this general definition was given a slightly different spin by Gunnar Broberg. Commenting upon the midcentury shift in assumptions, he concluded, "It might be possible to argue that such a shift reflects a general development during the second half of the century from a 'geometrical' to an 'arithmetical' mentality, when systems and stable structures mattered less than quick, irregular information" (p. 71). It is this type of shift that I wish to emphasize.

10. Frängsmyr, "The Mathematical Philosophy," in Frängsmyr et al., *The Quantifying Spirit in the Eighteenth Century,* p. 28.

11. Rather and Frerichs, "Leibniz-Stahl Controversy–I," p. 25.

12. Even Leibniz leaves the split intact, though he postulates the idea of the preestablished harmony in which mind and matter proceed along parallel paths; however, they never interact. This was made clear in his dispute with Stahl, who saw a direct connection between both. Leibniz claimed that "The system of preestablished harmony, which I first presented, preserves a parallelism between the body and soul. For although the primary source of all action is in the soul, just as that of passivity is in matter, nevertheless it must not be supposed that the soul through her innate operations of perception and appetite diverts even the smallest body from that body's proper mechanical laws, but rather that she operates in agreement with them, and that from the beginning God, in creating souls and bodies, so established all things that a series of movements in the body perfectly corresponds to a series of perceptions in the soul, and vice versa" (Rather and Frerichs, "The Leibniz-Stahl Controversy–I," p. 26).

13. Foucault, *The Order of Things,* p. 59.

14. Westfall, *The Construction of Modern Science,* p. 33.

15. John L. Heilbron, *Electricity in the 17th and 18th Centuries: A Study of Early Modern Physics* (Berkeley: University of California Press, 1979), pp. 42–43.

16. Margaret C. Jacob, *The Radical Enlightenment: Pantheists, Freemasons, and Republicans* (London: George Allen and Unwin, 1981); "Christianity and the Newtonian World View," in *God and Nature: Historical Essays on the Encounter between Christianity and Science,* ed. David C. Lindberg and Ronald L. Numbers (Berkeley: University of California Press, 1986), pp. 238–55; Aram Vartanian, *La Méttrie's l'Homme Machine.*

17. Jacob, *The Radical Enlightenment,* p. 31.

18. Vartanian, *L'Homme Machine,* p. 31; Robert Darnton, *The Forbidden Best-Sellers of Pre-Revolutionary France* (Princeton: Princeton University Press, 1995), p. 196.

19. David Hume, *The Philosophical Works*, ed. Thomas Hill Green and Thomas Hodge Grose, 4 vols. (London, 1883), vol. 3, pp. 213–14.

20. Hume, *Philosophical Works*, vol. 4, p. 62.

21. Anon., *Traité des extrêmes ou élements de la science de la réalité* (Amsterdam, 1768), p. 232.

22. Hume, *Philosophical Works*, vol. 4, p. 51.

23. George-Louis le Clerc Comte de Buffon, *Histoire naturelle, générale et particulière*, 36 vols. (Paris: L'Imprimerie royale, 1749), vol. 1, p. 13. Hereafter referred to as *Histoire naturelle*.

24. Buffon, *Histoire naturelle*, vol. 1, p. 7.

25. It is true that Buffon believed only humans had the "spark of reason," but as I shall argue later, Buffon placed humans within the class of animals, comparing their reason to animal instinct and human art to animal industry in a favorable light. According to Philip Sloan this move led to "a revolution in the human sciences"; Philip Sloan, "The Gaze of Natural History," in Fox et al., *Inventing Human Science: Eighteenth-Century Domains*, pp. 112–13.

26. Foucault, *The Order of Things*, p. 23.

27. Buffon, *De la manière d'étudier & de traiter L'Histoire Naturelle* (Paris: Bibliothèque Nationale, 1986), p. 28. Hereafter referred to as the *Premier discourse* to differentiate it from the original 1749 edition.

28. Buffon, *Histoire naturelle*, vol. 1, pp. 26–27.

29. Buffon, *Histoire naturelle*, vol. 2, p. 77.

30. Buffon, *Histoire naturelle*, vol. 1, p. 54; "it is enough to have proven that mathematical truths are merely truths of definition or, if you will, different expressions of the same thing, and they are only truths relative to these same definitions that we have discussed. For this reason, they have the advantage of always being exact and demonstrative, but also abstract, intellectual and arbitrary."

31. Adam Ferguson, *Principles of Moral and Political Science*, 2 vols. (Edinburgh, 1792), vol. 1, p. 79.

32. Buffon, *Histoire naturelle*, vol. 1, p. 54.

33. Buffon, *Histoire naturelle*, vol. 1, p. 55.

34. Sloan, "The Gaze of Natural History," p. 129.

35. Philip R. Sloan, "The Buffon-Linnaeus Controversy," *Isis* 67 (1976), p. 368.

36. Buffon, *Histoire naturelle*, vol. 2, pp. 31–32.

37. Buffon, *Histoire naturelle*, vol. 1, p. 62. In this point Buffon's program could coincide with the project associated with d'Alembert, Turgot, and especially Condorcet so admirably described by Keith Baker in his *Condorcet: From Natural Philosophy to Social Mathematics* (Chicago: University of Chicago Press, 1975). Buffon was not opposed to using quantitative data. For example, in his chapter on man, Buffon made extensive use of Dupré de Saint-Maur's statistical researches on human mortality.

38. Lorraine Daston, *Classical Probability in the Enlightenment* (Princeton: Princeton University Press, 1988), p. 283.

39. Buffon, *Histoire naturelle*, vol. 1, pp. 28–29.

40. As Roger Hahn noted, Newton's "three laws of motion had been given succinct mathematical expression in the handy language of the calculus by Leonard Euler. The concept of universal gravitation, though still occasionally challenged by die-hard Cartesians for metaphysical reasons, was proving to be a fruitful working hypothesis. . . . All mathematically inclined astronomers, theoreticians and observers alike, were working toward a common goal of developing the fine structure of the Newtonian paradigm for the solar system"; Roger Hahn, "Laplace and the Mechanistic Universe," in *God and Nature: Historical Essays on the Encounter between Christianity and Science*, ed. David C. Lindberg and Ronald L. Numbers (Berkeley: University of California Press, 1986), pp. 257–58.

41. Buffon, *Histoire naturelle*, vol. 2, pp. 50–51.

42. Foucault, *The Order of Things*, p. 137.

43. Buffon, *Histoire naturelle*, vol. 2, p. 51.

44. Buffon, *Histoire naturelle*, vol. 2, p. 34.

45. Buffon, *Histoire naturelle*, vol. 2, p. 17. Kästner, Buffon's German translator, hoped this remark would not lead to him being branded a heretic, saying that Buffon did not attempt to define the soul, but merely to say that one of the attributes of matter is to be animated; *Allgemeine Historie der Natur nach allen ihren besonderen Teilen abgehandelt. Mit einer Vorrede Herrn Doktor von Haller*, 3 vols. (Hamburg and Leipzig, 1750), vol. 2, p. 12. "Vivant et animé haben wohl nicht anders gegeben werden. Ich hoffe man wird den Herrn de Buffon wegen dieses Satzes nicht zum Ketzer machen. Er erklärt nicht die Seele selbst, sondern beseelt zu seyn für eine Eigenschaft der Materie."

46. Buffon, *Histoire naturelle*, vol. 2, p. 22.

47. Buffon, *Histoire naturelle*, vol. 2, pp. 23–24.

48. Jacques Roger, *Buffon: A Life in Natural History*, trans. Sarah Lucille Bonnefoi (Ithaca: Cornell University Press, 1997), p. 138.

49. Gaston Bachelard, *The New Scientific Spirit*, trans. Arthur Goldhammer (Boston: Beacon Press, 1985), p. 15.

50. Buffon, *Histoire naturelle*, vol. 1, p. 4.

51. Roger, *Les sciences de la vie*, p. 550. "Refusant de doter toutes les particules matérielles d'un psychisme élémentaire, mais ne se résignant pas malgré tout à confondre *actuellement* le vivant et l'inorganique, Buffon trouve dans ses molécules organiques vivantes un intermédiaire commode."

52. Buffon probably took the term *"rapport"* from Etienne François Geoffroy's important work on chemical affinity *Table des différents rapports observés en chimie entre différentes substances* (1718). In it, *rapport* described the relationships *(certains rapports)* that determine how chemical elements are conjoined.

53. Buffon, *Histoire naturelle*, vol. 2, p. 6. Kästner translated this into German as "ein einzelnes Thier ist ein Mittelpunct, auf den sich alles beziehet, ein Spiegel des ganzen Baues der Schöpfung, eine Welt im Kleinen"; *Historie der*

Natur, vol. 2, p. 5. Kästner noted the similarity to Leibniz and remarked, "Ich habe den Herrn de Buffon hier leibnizianisch reden lassen, weil ich un point ou tout l'universe se reflechit nicht anders zu geben wusste."

54. Buffon, *Histoire naturelle*, vol. 2, p. 39.

55. Buffon, *Histoire naturelle*, vol. 2, p. 39. In this discussion it is clear that Buffon borrowed heavily from Maupertuis's principle of least action. For an excellent short summary see Mary Terrall, "Metaphysics, Mathematics, and the Gendering of Science in Eighteenth-Century France," in *The Sciences in Enlightened Europe*, pp. 249–51.

56. Buffon, *Histoire naturelle*, vol. 2, p. 39.

57. Buffon, *Premier discourse*, pp. 70–72.

58. *Histoire naturelle*, vol. 2, p. 45.

59. Such a definition was provided by the Jesuit Duarte Madeira Arrais in 1650 when writing about magnetism, which he called a class of "occult super-elemental qualities. . . . These virtues are called 'occult' because, 'though manifest to the intellect, they are not apparent to the senses'. . . . They must be super-elemental because 'remarkable effects' like the attractions of . . . magnets, or the shock inflicted by electric eels, cannot arise from elemental qualities"; quoted by Heilbron, *Electricity*, p. 24.

60. Buffon, *Histoire naturelle*, vol. 2, p. 36.

61. *Historie naturelle*, vol. 2, pp. 36–37.

62. Ferguson, *Principles of Moral and Political Science*, vol. 1, p. 278. For an extended discussion of the post-Buffonian concept of system in the life sciences see James Larson, *Interpreting Nature: The Science of Living Form from Linnaeus to Kant* (Baltimore: Johns Hopkins University Press, 1994), pp. 28–60. John Lesch provides a fine discussion of system and systematics in the late eighteenth century in his article "Systematics and the Geometrical Spirit," in Frängsmyr et al., *The Quantifying Spirit in the Eighteenth Century*, pp. 73–112.

63. Both Roger and Sloan see Buffon as a leader in formulating a new scientific ideal. However, they differ strongly about the sources of Buffon's inspiration and the degree to which he altered his views over time. Roger saw Buffon as the central figure in proposing a new vitalistic vision of the life sciences that was elaborated by Diderot and the Montpellier school. However, he considered Buffon to have been a Lockean and argued that over time Buffon changed his views considerably, especially concerning the issues of the existence of classes, orders, and *genera*. Sloan is more radical in his conclusions. He denies the direct connection between Locke and Buffon and argues that Buffon was consistent in his formulations. Although I have been greatly influenced by Roger's writings, I believe Sloan's argument is more convincing.

64. Sloan, "Buffon-Linnaeus Controversy," p. 359. Also see his discussion in "The Gaze of Natural History," especially pp. 121–41.

65. Buffon, *Histoire naturelle*, vol. 1, p. 20.

66. Buffon, *Histoire naturelle*, vol. 1, pp. 29–30.

67. Buffon, *Histoire naturelle*, vol. 2, p. 20.

68. Quoted by Sloan, "Buffon-Linnaeus Controversy," p. 370.

69. Cuvier would argue the same point. In a letter to Pfaff in 1790 he chided his German correspondent as follows: "Warum findest Du denn so thöricht, daß Hunter den Wolf, Hund und Chakal als blosse Varietäten ansieht? Vielleicht hast Du den Begriff einer Speciei noch nicht recht festgesetzt (welches überhaupt sehr wenige Naturforscher gethan). Ich denke Folgendes darüber: Classen, Ordnungen, Genera sind blosse Abstractionen der Menschen, und Nichts dergleichen existiert in der Natur.... N.B. daß, ich dennoch vom Nutzen dieser Abstractionen überzeugt bin. Aber sind Species eine blosse Abstraction? Existiert nicht ein wahres, von der Natur allen Individius der Species eingeprägtes Verhältnis mit den übrigen? Denke nach! Du wirst finden, daß wir Specien heissen: alle Individua, die ursprünglich von einem einzigen Paare entweder wirklich abstammen oder wenigstens abstammen könnten,... Es bleibt in der That Nichts übrig als die Begattung, und ich behaupte, daß sei das einzig gewisse, aber auch das ganz untrügliche Kennzeichen sei, um eine Species zu erkennen. Alle übrigen sind nur Muthmassungen"; Georges Cuvier, *Briefe an Christoph Heinrich Pfaff aus den Jahren 1788 bis 1792*, ed. Wilhelm Friedrich Behn (Kiel, 1845), p. 172.

70. Roger, *Buffon*, p. 177.

71. Larson, *Interpreting Nature*, p. 60. Larson argued that one of the overriding concerns of the period was to "establish some equivalence between the different concerns of" these "two ordering principles."

72. Buffon, *Histoire naturelle*, vol. 7, p. 280.

73. Buffon, *Historie naturelle*, vol. 8, p. 154.

74. This was a very strong indictment indeed, for Buffon was totally opposed to the slave trade: "Humanity revolts against this odious treatment which greed has rendered customary"; quoted by Spary, *Utopia's Garden*, p. 116.

75. Buffon, *Histoire naturelle*, vol. 10, p. iii.

76. Buffon, *Histoire naturelle*, vol. 4, p. 249.

77. Buffon, *Historie naturelle*, vol. 4, p. 381.

78. Sloan, "The Gaze of Natural History," pp. 126–27.

79. Buffon, *Histoire naturelle*, vol. 1, p. 12.

80. Buffon, *Histoire naturelle*, vol. 1, p. 12.

81. Buffon, *Histoire naturelle*, vol. 1, pp. 13–14.

82. Sloan, "Buffon-Linnaeus Controversy," p. 363.

83. Buffon, *Histoire naturelle*, vol. 1, p. 32.

84. Buffon, *Histoire naturelle*, vol. 1, pp. 31–32.

85. Buffon, *Premier discourse*, p. 29.

86. Buffon, *Histoire naturelle*, vol. 1, p. 35.

87. Buffon, *Histoire naturelle*, vol. 1, pp. 50–51.

88. Wilhelm von Humboldt, "Ueber das vergleichende Sprachstudium," in *Gesammelte Schriften*, vol. 4, p. 30. "A nation that does not seek and find its mid-point [*Mittelpunkt*] in its poetry, philosophy, and history—all of which belong to the language of speaking—deprives itself of the beneficial counter-

thrust *[Rückwirkung]* of language. Through its own fault, that nation cannot nourish itself with the matter *[Stoff]* which alone can maintain its force, its radiance, and its beauty."

89. George Cheyne, *Philosophical Principles of Religion Natural and Reveal'd* (London, 1715), p. 321.

90. Bernard Nieuwentyt, *The Religious Philosopher: or the Right Use of Contemplating the Works of the Creator,* trans. Jean Theophilus Desaguliers, 5th ed., 2 vols. (London, 1724), vol. 1, p. 168. This work was originally written in Dutch and translated into the major European languages.

91. Both Jacques Roger and Émil Guyénot comment upon the fantastical nature of these concepts. In Roger's words: "La théorie de la préexistence des germes, qui envahit la pensée biologique à la fin du XVIIe siècle, offre à l'historien un étonnant spectacle, tant par son contenu même, que par la rapidité, l'étendue et la persistance de son succès, malgré les difficultés insoutenables qu'elle ne tarda pas à susciter"; *Les sciences de la vie,* 325. Guyénot is equally amazed: "La croyance à la préformation devait fatalement conduire à l'une des plus extraordinaires conceptions qu'ait engendrées le cerveau des savants"; *Les sciences de la vie aux XVIIe et XVIIIe siècles: l'idée d'évolution* (Paris: Albin Michel, 1941), p. 296.

92. Robert G. Frank, Jr., *Harvey and the Oxford Physiologists: Scientific Ideas and Social Interaction* (Berkeley: University of California Press, 1980), p. 38.

93. Westfall, *The Construction of Modern Science,* p. 98.

94. Westfall, *The Construction of Modern Science,* p. 88.

95. This is a point made by Roger from whom I also took Augustine's quote; *Les sciences de la vie,* p. 333. His article "The Mechanistic Conception of Life" in Lindberg and Numbers, *God and Nature,* summarizes the argument.

96. Quoted by Clara Pinto-Correia, *The Ovary of Eve: Egg and Sperm Preformation* (Chicago: University of Chicago Press, 1997), p. 19.

97. On Boyle's use of the argument from design see Roger, *Les sciences de la vie.* For physicotheology in general see Wolfgang Philipp, *Das Werden der Aufklärung in theologiegeschichtlicher Sicht,* Forschungen zur systematischen Theologie und Religionsphilosophie 3 (Göttingen: Vandenhoeck & Ruprecht, 1957).

98. Kiernan, *Enlightenment and Science,* p. 147.

99. Quoted by Iltis (Merchant), "Madam du Chatelet's Metaphysics and Mechanics," in *Studies in History and Philsopny of Science* 8 (1977), p. 33.

100. Quoted by Rather and Frerichs, "Leibniz-Stahl Controversy–I," p. 27.

101. Rather and Frerichs, "Leibniz-Stahl Controversy–I," p. 25.

102. Rather and Frerichs, "Leibniz-Stahl Controversy–I," p. 28.

103. Schofield, *Mechanism and Materialism,* pp. 117–22.

104. Quoted by Rather and Frerichs, "The Leibniz-Stahl Controversy–I," p. 26.

105. On Trembley see Aram Vartanian, "Trembley's Polyp, La Mettrie, and 18th Century French Materialism," *Journal of the History of Ideas* 11 (1950):

259–86; Virginia Dawson, *Nature's Enigma: The Problem of the Polyp in the Letters of Bonnet, Trembley, and Réaumur* (Philadelphia: American Philosophical Society, 1987).

106. For the crucial role the discussion about monsters played in the battle between preformationists and epigenesists, see Michael Hagner, "Enlightened Monsters," in Clark et al., *The Sciences in Enlightened Europe*, pp. 186–96; "Vom Naturalienkabinett zur Embriologie: Wandlungen des Montrösen und die Ordnung des Lebens," in *Der "falsche" Körper: Beiträge zu einer Geschichte der Monstrositäten*, ed. Michael Hagner (Göttingen: Wallstein, 1995).

107. Terrall, *The Man Who Flattened the Earth*, pp. 206–26, provides a beautiful analysis of how Maupertuis used the highly eroticized language of the salon in his analysis.

108. Buffon, *Histoire naturelle*, vol. 2, p. 164.

109. Roger, *Les sciences de la vie*, p. 481.

110. Roger, *Les sciences de la vie*, p. 481.

111. Buffon, *Histoire naturelle*, vol. 2, p. 164.

112. For Rousseau's debt to Buffon see Mark Hulling, *The Autocritique of Enlightenment: Rousseau and the Philosophes* (Cambridge, Mass.: Harvard University Press, 1994), pp. 172–79. Hulling claims that the *Second Discourse* was intended "to be read as a contribution to Buffon's ongoing and exceptionally popular *Natural History*." For that reason Hulling considers Rousseau to be a "natural historian" (p. 172).

113. Buffon, *Histoire naturelle*, vol. 2, pp. 74, 75.

114. Kästner, a Wolffian, was incensed by Buffon's equation of an argument from a final cause with the argument from sufficient reason. In disdain, he said "that one wouldn't fault him if he admitted that he didn't understand Leibniz, but then why must he make judgments?" (*Historie der Natur*, vol. 2, p. 44).

115. Buffon, *Histoire naturelle*, vol. 2, p. 78.

116. Buffon, *Histoire naturelle*, vol. 2, p. 78.

117. Buffon, *Histoire naturelle*, vol. 2, p. 79.

118. Buffon, *Histoire naturelle*, vol. 2, p. 97.

119. Carlo Ginzburg, "Morelli, Freud and Sherlock Holmes: Clues and Scientific Method," *History Workshop Journal* 9 (1980): 5–36. It is translated by John and Anne C. Tedeschi and reprinted in Ginzburg, *Clues, Myths, and the Historical Method* (Baltimore: Johns Hopkins University Press, 1986).

120. For the rehabilitation of Hippocrates in the eighteenth century see Roy Porter, "Medical Science and Human Science in the Enlightenment," in Fox et al., *Inventing Human Science*, p. 56; Andrew Cunningham, "Medicine to Calm the Mind: Boerhaave's Medical System and Why It Was Adopted in Edinburgh," in *The Medical Enlightenment of the Eighteenth Century*, ed. Andrew Cunningham and Roger French (Cambridge: Cambridge University Press, 1990), pp. 46–47, 54; Jan Golinski, "Barometers of Change: Meteorological Instruments as Machines of Enlightenment," in Clark et al., *The Sciences in Enlightened Europe*," p. 88; Spary, *Utopia's Garden*, p. 151.

121. Larson, *Interpreting Nature*, p. 135.
122. Buffon, *Histoire naturelle*, vol. 2, p. 327.
123. Buffon, *Histoire naturelle*, vol. 2, p. 338.

124. Buffon's enemies recognized the central position of paradox in his work and took him to task for it. Thus, the abbé Joseph Adrien Lelarge de Lignac mounted an attack in 1750 on the *Historie naturelle* in his *Lettres à un Américain sur l'Histoire naturelle, générale et particulière, de M. Buffon*. In these letters he said that Buffon's "way of reasoning is even more revolting than his hypotheses"; he had a "taste for paradox and obscurity." Quoted by Heilbron, *Electricity*, p. 346.

125. Spary does an excellent job showing how Buffon used patronage and his position to advance the career of natural history in France and Europe in her *Utopia's Garden*.

126. Many nineteenth- and twentieth-century commentators have deplored Buffon's style, seeing it as representative of a nonscientific approach to nature. They assumed scientific style had to divest itself of its literary elements. See, for example, Wolf Lepenies, *Das Ende der Naturgeschichte: Wandel kultureller Selbstverständlichkeiten in den Wissenschaften des 18. und 19. Jahrhunderts* (Munich: Hanser Verlag, 1976). However, recent research has called this into question. Spary argues that Buffon's style played a major role in the *Histoire's* success in its "function as a patronage tribute to the king"; *Utopia's Garden*, p. 47. Terrall's work on gendered language in French science can be extended to suggest that the *Histoire's* enormous success may have been due partly to Buffon's ability to mediate between the linguistic spheres of the academy and the salon. See especially her articles "Émilie du Chatelet and the Gendering of Science," *History of Science* 33 (1995): 283–310; and "Gendered Spaces, Gendered Audiences: Inside and Outside the Paris Academy of Sciences," *Configurations* 2 (1995): 207–32.

127. Most modern commentators have emphasized this aspect of Buffon's thought. It was clearly expressed by Philip Sloan in his article "Buffon, German Biology, and the Historical Interpretation of Biological Species," *British Journal for the History of Science* 12 (1979): 109–53, and repeated in many of his other outstanding studies on Buffon including "The Gaze of Natural History." Recently this interpretation has been attacked by John H. Eddy in "Buffon's *Histoire naturelle:* History? A Critique of Recent Interpretations, *Isis* 85 (1994): 644–61. In this article Eddy argues that Buffon "was no more a historicist than he was an evolutionist." He bases this assumption upon his interpretation of how Buffon's concept of primitive design and species functioned. Without going into a long discussion of the article, I believe Eddy misses the core of Sloan's argument. That species are limited by boundaries and reflect a basic design does not mean that Buffon did not believe in dynamic change affecting individuals within species. Eddy's definition of historicism is itself much too constricted and doesn't touch the epistemological issues central to the emergence of historicism, issues clearly present, I believe, in Buffon and in Sloan's discussion of them.

128. Ferguson, *An Essay on the History of Civil Society*, ed. Duncan Forbes (Edinburgh: Edinburgh University Press, 1966), pp. 268–69.
129. Schofield, *Mechanism and Materialism*, p. 191.

2. LEARNING TO "READ THE BOOK OF NATURE"

1. Quoted by Wencelaus Johann Gustav Renger Karsten, *Physische-chemische Abhandlung, durch neuere Schriften von hermetischen Arbeiten und andere neue Untersuchungen veranlaßet*, 2 vols. (Halle, 1786, 1787), vol. 1, pp. 173–74. Bergman repeated this classification in his *An Essay on the Usefulness of Chemistry and Its Application to the Various Occasions of Life* (London, 1763), though he omitted the metaphors of language he had used in the introduction to Scheele's work. Johann Friedrich Gmelin used this same classification of the three major subdivisions in natural science in his textbook *Grundriß der allgemeinen Chemie zum Gebrauch bei Vorlesungen*, 2 vols. (Göttingen, 1789), vol. 1, pp. 2–3.
2. Karsten, *Physische-chemische Abhandlung*, vol. 2, p. 69.
3. Karsten, *Physische-chemische Abhandlung*, vol. 2, p. 69.
4. Johann Samuel Gehler, *Physikalisches Wörterbuch*, 5 vols. (Leipzig, 1787–92), vol. IV, p. 549.
5. Heilbron, who has no great admiration for the turn late eighteenth-century physics took, remarked: "Both Cartesians and Newtonians of earlier generations would have considered the incoherence of physics—not to mention the non-homogeneity of matter—implied by the representation of specific force carriers as unscientific and weak minded"; *Electricity*, p. 68.
6. Hélène Metzger, *Newton, Stahl, Boerhaave et la doctrine chimique* (Paris: Félix Alcan, 1930), p. 143. Also see Westfall, *The Construction of Modern Science*, pp. 72–73; Donovan, "William Cullen and the Research Tradition of Eighteenth-Century Scottish Chemistry," p. 104.
7. See Allen Debus, *The Chemical Dream of the Renaissance* (Cambridge: Heffer, 1968).
8. John Heilbron, *Electricity*, pp. 14–15. This was true for those composed by the Dutch Newtonians,' s'Gravesande and Mussenbroek, the French neo-Cartesian Jean A. Nollet, the English Newtonian Desaguliers, and the Leibnizian Christian Wolff. For Germany see Rudolf Stichweh, *Zur Entstehung des modernen Systems wissenschaftlicher Disziplinen: Physik in Deutschland 1740–1890* (Frankfurt am Main: Suhrkamp, 1984), p. 101.
9. Schofield, *Mechanism and Materialism*, p. 149.
10. Charles Coulston Gillispie, *The Edge of Objectivity: An Essay in the History of Scientific Ideas* (Princeton: Princeton University Press, 1960), p. 246. The remark was made in connection with Gillispie's critique of what he considered "the eighteenth-century philosophy of science," which "prepared the reforming spirit in the Revolution which took" Lavoisier's life. The immediate sentiment leading to Lavoisier's death "erupted rather out of popular romanticism, playing on the sentimental vulgarity which lurks in Baconian utilitarian-

ism, never far beneath the surface." But even beyond this "popular romanticism," this philosophy of science "had dressed out the method of Newtonian physics in the logic of Baconian natural history, which classifies the forms and species of things. Naming . . . it had reached in practice for the naturalist's easy instrument of classification, in preference to the theoretical physicist's exacting instrument of abstraction and mathematicization."

11. Karsten, *Physische-chemische Abhandlung*, vol. 2, pp. 3–4.

12. Bergman, *Usefulness of Chemistry*, p. 7. On the centrality of the concept of simple substances in the reformation of chemistry see Theodore M. Porter, "The Promotion of Mining and the Advancement of Science: The Chemical Revolution of Mineralogy," *Annals of Science* 38 (1981): 543–70.

13. Recent critics of the traditional interpretation of the chemical revolution now speak of an earlier revolution in chemistry, which they call either the "compositional revolution" or the Stahlian Revolution. For a clear and concise statement of this position see Jerry B. Gough, "Lavoisier and the Fulfillment of the Stahlian Revolution," in *The Chemical Revolution: Essays in Reinterpretation*, ed. Arthur Donovan, *Osiris*, 2nd ser., vol. 4 (Chicago: University of Chicago Press, 1988), pp. 15–33. In many ways this revisionist position supports the argument I am trying to make in this volume. However, by limiting the shift to chemistry and attaching it to Stahl, it overlooks the ties this shift had to the larger change in scientific sensibilities that I call Enlightenment Vitalism. It also places too great an emphasis upon a basic continuity uniting Stahl with the so-called Stahlians of the late eighteenth century. This becomes evident in the following observation made by Gough: "That nearly every great chemist of the eighteenth century defined the purpose of the discipline in terms of composition was to a large extent a function of this Stahlian recognition that there existed separate species of matter. For the mechanist chemists who preceded the Stahlian revolution, on the other hand, all matter was homogeneous, and thus composition—at least composition in a Stahlian sense—did not really exist" (p. 22). But when did the Stahlian revolution begin? Certainly not with Stahl, who *preceded* the most famous mechanist chemist, Boerhaave. There is no doubt, as I shall attempt to show, that Stahl served as a symbol for the new way of doing chemistry, but only after his positions were reinterpreted. For another interpretation emphasizing the advances made in chemical thought before Lavoisier to which he was indebted but based on practical concerns see Porter, "The Promotion of Mining," and Anders Lundgren, "The New Chemistry in Sweden: The Debate That Wasn't," in Donovan, *The Chemical Revolution*, pp. 121–45; "The Changing Role of Numbers in 18th Century Chemistry," in Frängsmyr et al., *The Quantifying Spirit in the Eighteenth Century*, pp. 245–66.

14. Many late-eighteenth-century chemists cited natural history as the model they wished to emulate. This was true, for example, for William Cullen, who argued that chemistry and natural history were "necessarily connected together"; quoted by Jan Golinski, *Science as Public Culture: Chemistry and Enlightenment in Britain, 1760–1820* (Cambridge: Cambridge Universit

Press, 1992), p. 20. Evan M. Melhado assumes that most late-eighteenth-century chemists (he excludes Lavoisier) drew their inspiration from Buffon: "[T]he chemists drew their inspiration for investigating attractions from George-Louis Leclerc, Comte de Buffon, a non-mathematical champion of the inverse-square law"; "Chemistry, Physics and the Chemical Revolution," *Isis* 76 (1985), p. 199. As my discussion of Buffon in the preceding chapter tries to make clear, Buffon drew some of his explanatory strategies from nonmechanistic contemporary French chemistry.

15. The characterization of Lavoisier by Karl Hufbauer, *The Formation of the German Chemical Community: 1720–1795* (Berkeley: University of California Press, 1982), p. 3. This is the inherent assumption of Wilda C. Anderson's book *Between the Library and the Laboratory: The Language of Chemistry in Eighteenth-Century France* (Baltimore: Johns Hopkins University Press, 1984). Working from Foucault's characterization of the classical age, she sees Lavoisier's work as the chemical equivalent of the writings of Bopp, Cuvier, and Ricardo in overcoming the *episteme* based on Descartes and unchanging throughout the period. Macquer, Lavoisier's opponent, thus becomes the spokesman for the "dominant" ideas of Stahl: "He is generally recognized as having been one of the last and most important spokesmen for the chemistry of affinities—the phlogiston theory—that dominated chemistry from around the time of Georg Stahl until the major changes brought about by the French chemists led by Lavoisier toward the end of the eighteenth century" (p. 14). With this statement that incorrectly appraises Macquer, the concept of chemical affinities, and Lavoisier's relation to both, Anderson juxtaposes Lavoisier's achievements as the revolutionary experimenter to the conservative philosophic chemists. Lavoisier, for her, not only revolutionized chemistry, but was the representative of a totally new way of thought as well: "In the changes that occur between the philosophical chemistry of Macquer and the positivist chemistry of Lavoisier, more than a chemical revolution has been effected. In a curious way, the philosophical revolution begun by Descartes will have been both finally completed and, as a result, superseded" (p. 13).

16. Metzger, *Newton, Stahl, Boerhaave,* p. 95.

17. Franz Xaver Baader, *Vom Wärmestoff, seine Verteilung, Bindung und Entbindung vorzüglich beim Brennen der Körper* (Vienna and Leipzig, 1786), p. 26, intro. On the late reception of Stahl see Schofield, *Mechanism and Materialism,* pp. 135, 212–14; Jeremy Adler, *"Eine fast magische Anziehungskraft": Goethes Wahlverwandtschaften und die Chemie seiner Zeit* (Munich: Beck, 1987), p. 65; Arthur L. Donovan, *Philosophical Chemistry in the Scottish Enlightenment* (Edinburgh: Edinburgh University Press, 1975), p. 32, and "William Cullen and the Research Tradition of Eighteenth-Century Scottish ⸺try," p. 102; Wilhelm Ostwald's notes to Scheele's *Chemische Abhand-* ⸺ *uft und dem Feuer,* Ostwald's Klassiker der exacten Wis- ⸺g: Engelmann, 1894), p. 109. Ostwald recognized both the general theory of phlogiston and its importance for ⸺logiston verstanden die Chemiker in der zweiten Hälfte

des vorigen Jahrhunderts bekanntlich das Princip der Brennbarkeit, derart, daß bei jeder Verbrennung der Austritt und bei jeder Reduction der Eintritt von Phlogiston angenommen wurde. Das sehr bedeutende Verdienst dieser Lehre lag darin, daß durch sie zum ersten Male die Gesammtheit der Verbrennungserscheinungen unter einen Gesichtspunkt gebracht wurde" (p. 109).

18. Schofield, *Mechanism and Materialism*, p. 212.

19. Recently historians of chemistry have analyzed theory producers in relation to the communities in which they practiced, the audiences they addressed, either in writings, lectures, or public demonstrations, the rhetorical devices they used to convince others, the various functions they ascribed to their work and how they sought to realize them, and finally the general relations of power existing in their society and the political meaning their work expressed either consciously or implied. Simon Schaffer has been instrumental in proposing this new research program, exemplified by a number of crucial essays on eighteenth-century science: "Natural Philosophy and Public Spectacle in the Eighteenth Century," *History of Science* 21 (1983): 1–43; "States of Mind: Enlightenment and Natural Philosophy," in *Languages of the Psyche: Mind and Body in Enlightenment*, ed. George Rousseau (Berkeley: University of California Press, 1990), pp. 253–90; "The Consuming Flame: Electrical Showmen and Tory Mystics in the World of Goods," in *Consumption and the World of Goods*, ed. John Brewer and Roy Porter (London: Routledge, 1993), pp. 489–526; "The Show That Never Ends: Perpetual Motion in the Early Eighteenth Century," *British Journal for the History of Science* 28 (1995), pp. 157–89; "Enlightened Automata," in *The Sciences in Enlightened Europe*, pp. 126–68. Studies influenced by such a research program have helped understand the differences between Scottish, English, French, Swedish, and German chemical practices and assumptions. Thus, Jan Golinski in *Science as Public Culture* has done a wonderful job showing us the social and rhetorical dynamics of eighteenth-century Scottish chemistry shaped by William Cullen, English chemistry embodied in Priestley's vision of a democratic, enlightened chemistry, theoretically open to all, and English chemistry's transformation into a practice and rhetoric of science based upon expert opinion, complex instruments, and authoritarian control, best exemplified by Humphrey Davy. Theodore Porter demonstrated how German and Swedish "chemically-literate mineralogists," working for the state, to improve mining revenue gradually were led to formulate one of the central concepts of the new chemistry, the idea of simple substances; see Porter, "The Promotion of Mining." The vast literature on Lavoisier and the "Chemical Revolution" to which I will refer later in this chapter provides the same insights for France. The most recent attempt to synthesize these has been offered by Arthur Donovan, *Antoine Lavoisier: Science, Administration and Revolution* (Oxford: Blackwell, 1993).

20. In France the shift was most rapid and apparent. It was signaled by the publication of Macquer's *Élemens de chymie-theorique*, which appeared in the same year as the first three volumes of the *Historie naturelle*. Macquer's writings received added support when Diderot chose a Stahlist, Gabriel-François

Venel, to write the chemical articles in the *Encyclopédie*. The Stahlist coup was quick and relatively peaceful. In Great Britain the shift was almost as rapid. Peter Shaw, Boerhaave's and Stahl's translator, led the move from Boerhaave to Stahl, a conversion he announced in 1755. He was not unique. The interest generated by the "new" German doctrines induced British scientists such as William Cullen to study them carefully. In Germany the acceptance of Stahl took longer and then was more difficult to dispel. The reluctance to accept Stahlist views was due in part to the influence of Boerhaave's students in the German academic establishment and to Stahl's Pietist religious convictions. Still, Stahl had a small group of vocal admirers led by Johann Juncker. Though not immediately capturing the academic world, Stahlist doctrines found favor among many practicing chemists, especially within the legion of metallurgists for which Germany was so famous. By 1755 Stahlist chemistry received the imprimatur of the Berlin Academy when it published Johann Eller's Stahlist tract *Essai sur l'origine et la génération des métaux*. By the 1770's Stahlist assumptions had become dominant in Germany and were then defended tenaciously when later criticized by Lavoisier.

21. Quoted by Metzger, *Newton, Stahl, Boerhaave*, p. 102.
22. Schofield, *Mechanism and Materialism*, p. TK.
23. Metzger, *Newton, Stahl, Boerhaave*, pp. 102–6.
24. Quoted by Metzger, *Newton, Stahl, Boerhaave*, p. 118.
25. The four basic elements were air, water, fire, and earth. However, Stahl subdivided earth into three categories, each with its own essence. They were vitrifiable earth, phlogistic earth, and metallic earth. From his explanation of these three subcategories, it is not clear whether they were modifications of an *Ur*-earth or three separate elemental earths.
26. The position was first put forward by Robert Siegfried and Betty Jo Dobbs in "Composition: A Neglected Aspect of the Chemical Revolution," *Annals of Science* 24 (1968): 275–93. Gough develops this argument in his article "Lavoisier and the Fulfillment of the Stahlist Revolution," in Donovan, *Chemical Revolution*, pp. 15–33.
27. This linkage of principle with form has an analogue in Montesquieu's explanation of constitutional form. Each of the basic forms (republic, monarchy, and despotism) is animated by a corresponding principle (virtue, honor, and fear).
28. Pierre Joseph Macquer, *Élemens de chymie théorique* (Paris, 1749), p. 1.
29. Antoine Laurent Lavoisier, *Elements of Chemistry*, trans. Robert Kerr, Great Books of the Western World 45 (Chicago: University of Chicago Press, 1952), p. 17. The enmity between Lavoisier and the older Macquer was made evident in Lavoisier's introduction. There he asserts that he will depart from the usual way of writing "courses of lectures" or of "treatises upon chemistry." These "begin by treating of the elements of matter and by explaining the table of affinities." This was the procedure Macquer followed in his text bearing a similar title. Further, Lavoisier enjoyed mocking those chemists who "have a fondness for reducing all the bodies in nature to three or four elements," which

is what Macquer did. The ultimate affront was that Lavoisier associated this endeavor with the procedures of Greek philosophers who "possessing no facts . . . framed systems." The establishment of four basic elements was characterized as "hypothetical," probably the worst insult one could make at that time. And then, with a final farewell shot at Macquer, Lavoisier remarked, "It is very remarkable that, notwithstanding the number of philosophical chemists who have supported the doctrine of the four elements, there is not one who has not been led by the evidence of facts to admit a greater number of elements into their theory" (pp. 2–3). Despite this critique, Lavoisier's definition of elements or principles does not vary as much as he claims from Macquer's approach.

30. Scheele, *Chemische Abhandlung von der Luft und dem Feuer*, p. 7. Bergman, *Usefulness of Chemistry*, pp. 7–8. For earlier statements of this kind, see Gough, "Lavoisier and the Fulfillment of the Stahlian Revolution," p. 16.

31. For example, Bergman asserted: "In investigating the principles of a body, we must not judge them by a slight agreement with other known bodies, but they must be separated directly by analysis, and that analysis confirmed by synthesis"; quoted by Porter, "The Promotion of Mining," p. 563.

32. Quoted by Eberhard Kessel, *Wilhelm von Humboldt: Idee und Wirklichkeit* (Stuttgart: Koehler, 1967), pp. 71–72.

33. Quoted by E. L. Scott, "Kirwan," in *Dictionary of Scientific Biography*, ed. Charles C. Gillispie, Henry Guerlac, and Julies Mayer (New York: Scribner, 1970–80), vol. 6, p. 388.

34. Schofield's path-breaking book *Mechanism and Materialism* made this distinction between the two ways in which Newton's theories could be interpreted, one positing a void, the other a universe filled with subtle fluids.

35. There was one essential difference between this view and Aristotle's. These new "substantial qualities" were, in fact, made substance; light, heat electricity, magnetism, and the different chemical properties were all to become material.

36. Schofield makes this point when discussing Franklin: "The electrical fluid is an element *sui generis* with no thought of its convertibility. . . . The electrical fluid acts through the characteristics of subtlety and elasticity by its possession of fluid or its lack of it, and both are determined by Franklin's creation of the law of conservation of charge. There is a mark of greatness in this hardly-mathematical quantitative law, a greatness indicated by the fact that, one of the earliest of the conservation laws to be formulated, it still stands essentially unchallenged. But it marks a theory of substance not one of mechanics"; *Mechanism and Materialism*, p. 174.

37. Baader, *Wärmestoff*, pp. 24–25.

38. The number of subtle fluids could grow depending upon the individual researcher. There were, for example, the subtle fluids of electricity (Franklin's single fluid increased by some to two), aether, gravity, magnetism, light, heat, sound, phlogiston, and sometimes even color and smell.

39. Baader, *Wärmestoff*, p. 56.

40. Baader makes this connection clear: "und da man von jedem Körper-

stoffe auf und in unserm Erdball mit Recht voraussezen kann, und wohl auch nothwendig voraussezen muß, daß er wenigst einmal in diesem vom Anfang aneinandergeketteten Perioden der Metamorphose und des stätten Umwandelns aller Bestandtheile der Natur, in Feuer verdampft, oder geschmolzen, d.i. im Wärmematerie aufgelöset ward"; *Wärmestoff,* p. 61.

41. Quoted by Porter, "The Promotion of Mining," p. 546.
42. Baader, *Wärmestoff,* p. 67.
43. Michael Hißmann, "Versuch über das Fundament der Kräfte," *Magazin für die Philosophie und ihre Geschichte: Aus den Jahrbüchern der Akademien angelegt,* vol. VI (Göttingen, 1783), p. 59. The article is in the journal that Hißmann edited. In an anonymous review, which he wrote, in the *Göttingische Gelehrte Anzeigen,* Hißmann suggested that the editor of the journal wrote the article in 1779.
44. Baader, *Wärmestoff,* p. 261.
45. Hißmann's review of his own article, "Ueber das Fundament der Kräfte," *Göttingenische Gelehrte Anzeige,* 1783, p. 1706. Baader makes this clear: "Alle elastische Flüssigkeiten äußern nämlich ein immer wirkendes Bestreben, dorthin sich zu verbreiten, wo ihnen weniger Widerstand entgegensteht, und es bedarf darum gar keine besondern Mediums, das den Wärmestoff aufnimmt, und sich mit ihn, wie man sagt, chemisch verbindet"; *Wärmestoff,* p. 69. In late-eighteenth-century chemical literature, the attribute most frequently used to describe force was striving.
46. Porter, "The Promotion of Mining," p. 563.
47. Quoted by Günther Mensching, *Totalität und Autonomie: Untersuchungen zur philosophischen Gesellschaftstheorie der französischen Materialismus* (Frankfurt: Suhrkamp, 1971), p. 70.
48. Torbern Olof Bergman, *Traité des affinités chymiques ou attractions électives* (Paris, 1788), pp. 2–5.
49. Gehler, *Physikalisches Wörterbuch,* vol. IV, art. "Verwandtschaft, chymische," pp. 481–82.
50. Bergman, *Traité des affinités chymiques ou attractions électives,* p. 4.
51. Bergman, *Traité des affinités chymiques ou attractions électives,* pp. 4–5. In this definition Bergman corroborates the position argued by Siegfried, Dobbs, and Gough concerning the central importance of composition in late-eighteenth-century chemistry.
52. For an excellent contemporary summary of the various types of composed elective affinities see Gehler's article "Verwandtschaft," in *Physikalisches Wörterbuch,* vol. IV, pp. 475–79.
53. Bergman, *Traité des affinités chymiques ou attractions électives,* p. 56.
54. Kapitza, *Theorie der Mischung,* pp. 127–28.
55. It is strange that in the vast literature on the Chemical Revolution, the idea that Lavoisier initiated the turn to gravimetrics has until recently hardly been contested. One of the reasons this opinion carried weight is that few interpreters look to the many German and Swedish chemists and metallurgists who daily used the balance in their investigations. Bergman and Scheele, along with

Black, were experts at quantitative analysis. Bernadette Bensaude-Vincent makes this clear in her excellent article "The Balance between Chemistry and Politics," in *The Chemical Revolution: Context and Practices*, ed. Lissa Roberts, *The Eighteenth Century: Theory and Interpretation* 33 (1992): 217–37: "[G]iven the developments in mining and metallurgy during the eighteenth century, especially in Sweden and Germany, the practice of quantitative analysis was increasingly required and employed" (p. 219). This view is corroborated by Anders Lundgren, "The Changing Role of Numbers in 18th Century Chemistry," in Frängsmyr et al., *The Quantifying Spirit in the Eighteenth Century*, pp. 245–67; and Porter, "The Promotion of Mining." John G. McEvoy makes a similar point when comparing Priestley to Lavoisier in his article "Continuity and Discontinuity in the Chemical Revolution," in Donovan, *The Chemical Revolution*, p. 204.

56. Quoted by Porter, "The Promotion of Mining," p. 564.

57. Baader, *Wärmestoff*, p. 39.

58. Bergman, *Traité affinité*, p. 6. "En 1718, Geoffroy imagina de faire voir au premier coup d'oeil, la série des attractions électives, en disposant les signes chymiques dans un tableau, suivant un certain ordre. Mais cette admirable inventions est louée par quelques-uns, & blamée par d'autres; les premier prétendent que les affinités suivent des loix constantes, les derniers assurent qu'elles sont vagues, & ne dépendent que les seules circonstances."

59. Quoted by Gehler, "Verwandtschaft," p. 478.

60. The use of the term "species" to designate a type of chemical substance was fairly common at the time. Cullen, Black, and Scheele among others used it frequently. Cullen expressed his attempt to join chemistry and natural history as follows: "It may be often useful to refer the productions of chemistry to their proper classes, orders, genera, species, and varieties as is commonly done with respect to the objects of natural history"; quoted by Donovan, *Philosophical Chemistry*, p. 114.

61. Bergman expressed his mediating approach as follows: "Or puisque toutes les óperations de la Chymie consistent dans l'analyse ou la synthèse, & que l'une & l'autre dépendent de l'attraction, il s'en suit qui'il est de la dernière importance de terminer cette dispute. Ne rejettons donc pas toute cette doctrine, pour une ou deux irrégularités, peut-etre mal entendues; examinons au contraire la question avec tout le soin & l'attention possibles: & quand meme nous trouverions enfin que les attractions dépendent uniquement des cirçonstances, ne conclusions pas pour cela, qu'il est inutile de connoitre des différentes conditions qui les favorisent, les empechent ou les troublent. Cette connaissance seroit encore d'une utilité très-étendue: l'on ne voit en effet aucun phénomène dans la nature, qui ne soit telement lié avec certaines conditions, que lorsque'elles viennent à manquer, le phénomène n'a pas lieu, ou varie suivant les cirçonstances. Il est important pour la Science, que les changemens & les combinaisons des causes, soient connus dans chaque óperation, aussi exactement qu'il est possible, & j'espère que dans le courant de cet Ouvrage, l'utilité d'une recherche exacte sur les attractions, sera clairement

démontrée par plusieurs exemples." *Traité des affinités chymiques ou attractions électives*, p. 7.

62. Bergman, *Traité des affinités chymiques ou attractions électives*, pp. 10–56.

63. The following analysis of Berthollet owes much to the following works: Satish C. Kapoor, "Berthollet, Proust and Proportions," *Chymia* 10 (1965) and "Berthollet," in Gillispie et al., *Dictionary of Scientific Biography*, vol. 2, p. 63–82; Jeremy Adler, *"Eine fast magische Anziehungskraft."*

64. For example, Scheele in discussing the attractive relations between saltpeter acid and phlogiston remarked: "Die Saltpetersäure kann das Phlogiston in verschiedener Menge annehmen, sie enthält alsdann bei jeder Proportion auch andere Eigenschaften. a) Wird sie damit gleichsam satuiret, so entsteht ein wahres Feuer, sie wird alsdann gänzlich destruiret. b) Wenn das Principium Inflammabile in einer geringern Menge vorhanden, so wird dieses Acidum in eine Art Luft verwandelt"; *Chemische Abhandlung von der Luft und dem Feuer*, p. 23.

65. Fischer, Berthollet's German translator, evaluated Bergman and Berthollet's achievements as follows: "Die Lehre von der *Wahlverwandtschaft*, die von niemand scharfsinninger als von Bergman bearbeitet worden, ist als der Schlußstein in der bisherigen Theorie der chemischen Verwandtschaft anzusehen. Berthollet zeigt nun in seiner Abhandlung mit Gründen, denen man unmöglich, sobald man sie richtig gefaßt hat, den Beifall versagen kann, daß die bisherige Erklärung der Erscheinungen, welche man der Wahlverwandschaft zuschreibt, ganz unrichtig ist, und das richtige Naturgesetz, daß er an ihrer Statt aufstellt ist folgendes: Wenn auf einen Stoff A, zu gleicher Zeit zwei andere Stoffe B und C wirken, welche Verwandschaftskräfte gegen A haben, so wählt A nicht einen von beiden. Aber das Verhältniss in welchem sich A theilt, ist von so vielerley Umständen abhängig, daß es wenigstens bei der gegenwärtigen Zustand der Theorie so gut als unmöglich ist, dasselbe in jedem Fall durch bestimmte Zahlen *a priori* zu bestimmen"; quoted by Adler, *"Eine fast magische Anziehungskraft,"* pp. 71–72.

66. Quoted by August Thienemann, "Die Stufenfolge der Dinge, der Versuch eines natürlichen Systems der Naturkörper aus dem achtzehnten Jahrhundert: Eine historische Skizza," *Zoologische Annalen: Zeitschrift für Geschichte der Zoologie* III (1909), p. 267.

67. Mi Gyung Kim, "Practice and Representation: Investigative Programs of Chemical Affinity in the Nineteenth Century," Ph.D diss. (University of California, Los Angeles, 1990), p. 13. In her analysis she focuses on practice rather than on theory and argues that the idea of chemical affinity, developed in the eighteenth century as an alternative program to mechanical chemistry, was central to chemical practice in the first half of the nineteenth century.

68. Lavoisier, *Elements of Chemistry*, p. 4, emphasis added.

69. Theodore Porter demonstrates how the search for a new nomenclature was part of the project of late-eighteenth-century Swedish and German mineralogists responding to the practical needs to identify the mineral content of

ores. He describes Bergman's new nomenclature and argues that given the "relation between nomenclature and the analytic definition of simple substances, it is hardly surprising that the move to reform the language of chemistry originated in mineralogy." He also locates this program within the ambit of natural history: "The reform proposals of Cronstadt and even Bergman, were motivated primarily by natural-historical considerations"; "The Promotion of Mining," p. 567.

70. Lavoisier, *Elements of Chemistry*, p. 1.

71. Bergman, *Traité des affinités chymiques ou attractions électives*, p. 10.

72. Metzger, *Newton, Stahl, Boerhaave*, p. 146.

73. Lavoisier's famous statement, "rien ne se creé, rien ne se perd," is typical of this belief. Kiernan claims it was the logical extension of ideas derived from Helmont and Paracelsus; *Enlightenment and Science*, p. 170.

74. Bernadette Bensaude-Vincent, "The Balance between Chemistry and Politics," p. 234.

75. Although Lavoisier supposedly was committed to a static view of nature, he accepted the existence of active forces. He evolved an explanatory model in which active forces disturb an equilibrium, which is then brought back into a new equilibrium: "One can never tire of admiring the system of general liberty that nature seems to have wanted to establish in all that relates to living things. In giving them life, spontaneous movement, an active force *[une force active]*, needs and passions, nature never disallowed her creatures' use of these attributes. She wanted them to be free to abuse them, but ever prudent and wise, she placed regulators everywhere, she made satisfaction follow pleasure"; quoted by Bensaude-Vincent, "The Balance between Chemistry and Politics," p. 227.

76. Baader, *Wärmestoff*, p. 38. To justify this statement, Baader quoted Guyton de Morveau. In an article analyzing French chemical textbooks, Bernadotte Bensaude-Vincent argues that many of Lavoisier's colleagues considered the creation of the new chemistry as "not only a collective enterprise," but that "Guyton was viewed as a leader"; "A View of the Chemical Revolution through Contemporary Textbooks: Lavoisier, Fourcroy and Chaptal," *British Journal for the History of Science* 23 (1990), p. 448.

77. Baader, *Wärmestoff*, p. 52.

78. Baader, *Wärmestoff*, pp. 33, 68.

79. John Elliot, *Physiologische Beobachtungen über die Sinne besonders über das Gesicht und Gehör wie auch über das Brennen und die thierische Wärme nebst Adair Crawfords Versuchen und Beobachtungen über die thierische Wärme* (Leipzig, 1785).

80. Bensaude-Vincent argues that one of the major sources for Lavoisier's concept of regulation was drawn from Buffon: "In any given territory, Buffon stated, population equilibrium is achieved from the oscillation between abundance and scarcity, between a species' capacity and destructive forces such as meteorological conditions, predators, and the quantity of available nourishment"; "The Balance between Chemistry and Politics," p. 236.

81. Horst Thomé, *Roman und Naturwissenschaft: eine Studie zur Vorgeschichte der deutschen Klassik*, Regensburger Beiträge zur deutschen Sprach-und Literaturwissenschaft, Reihe B, vol. 15 (Frankfurt: Peter Lang, 1978), p. 297.

82. For Goethe's physiological works, see my essay "Bildung, Urtyp and Polarity: Goethe and Eighteenth-Century Physiology," in *Goethe Yearbook*, ed. Thomas Saine (Columbia, S.C.: Camden House, 1986), vol. III, pp. 139–48. For his use of chemical ideas, see Adler, "*Eine fast magische Anziehungskraft.*"

83. Johann Wolfgang von Goethe, *Theory of Colours*, trans. Charles Lock Eastlake (Cambridge, Mass.: MIT Press, 1970), pp. xxxviii–xxxix.

84. Scheele, *Chemische Abhandlung von der Luft und dem Feuer*, p. 7.

85. For an excellent discussion of this conflict see Metzger, *Newton, Stahl, Boerhaave*, pp. 209–11, and Gehler, "Wärme," in *Physikalisches Wörterbuch*, vol. V, pp. 533–35. According to Donovan, "Cullen thought of heat as an effect of fire and fire as a chemical substance that enters into reactions governed by elective attractions and repulsions"; "Research Tradition," p. 107.

86. Schofield asserts that it was the most important text on chemistry until Lavoisier's *Elements of Chemistry; Mechanism and Materialism*, p. 147.

87. Introduction to Hermann Boerhaave, *Elements of Chemistry, Being the Annual Lectures of Hermann Boerhaave*, trans. Timothy Dallowe, 2 vols. (London, 1735), vol. 1, p. 18.

88. Both Baader and Gehler pay due respect to Boerhaave for having reintroduced the idea of material heat that Aristotle had already announced. However, while recognizing Boerhaave's contribution, both criticized him for explaining heat generation by mechanical means; Baader, *Wärmestoff*, pp. 3–9; Gehler, "Wärme," pp. 543–44.

89. Gehler gave a fine contemporary summary of this issue in his "Wärme," in *Physikalisches Wörterbuch*, vol. IV, p. 569.

90. Boerhaave's argument runs as follows:

> Hence it appears, that this distribution of Fire is in proportion to the bulk; and that, therefore, when Bodies of the same nature are mixed together, the one hot, and the other cold, the Fire immediately disengages itself from its contact with the Elements of the former, and unites itself with those of the latter, till this becomes as hot as the other. This, then being constantly the case, we see that the common degree of Heat is destroyed, and the difference is then equally distributed through them both. But, now, if the Experiment is made with Mercury, and Water, exactly of the same measure, but different degrees of Heat, and these are in the same manner swiftly mixed together; then the Heat that is produced by this Mixture, will be very different from what has been observed in that just now mentioned.
>
> For if the bulk of the Water, and Mercury to be mixed is exactly equal, but the Water is hotter than the Mercury; then, the Heat

of the Mixture will be always greater than half the difference of their separate Heats. And, on the other hand, if the Mercury is hotter than the Water; then the degree of Heat in the Mixture will be constantly less than half this distance. And this diversity is always found to be the same, as if, in the first case, you had mixed three parts of Cold Water with two of hot. But, now, if the bulk of the Mercury is to that of the Water, as three is to two; then it don't signify at all, whether you heat the Mercury, or the Water: For the mixture will always have a degree of Heat equal to half the difference of their separate Heats, as we found to be the case when we mixed the Water together in equal quantities.

In this experiment, then, we plainly discover the law by which nature distributes Fire through Bodies; which is not in proportion to their densities, but in the same manner as it is diffused through space. For though the specific gravity of Mercury is to that of Water pretty nearly 14 to 1; yet its power of producing Heat when measured by its effect, appears to be only the same, as if Water had been mixed with an equal quantity of Water. But the same thing is abundantly confirmed by every kind of Experiment as I took notice before, when I told you, that I had been convinced by Experiment, that all sorts of Bodies, if they are long enough exposed to the same common temperature acquire exactly the very same Heat, or Fire, without any difference at all except what arises from the different spaces they take up: That, hence, it did not appear from Observation, that any Bodies whatever have a power of attracting Fire, though their greater density makes them capable of retaining it longer when once it is united with them. The Experiments I have just mentioned, were performed for me by the famous Fahrenheit. (Boerhaave, *Elements of Chemistry*, vol. 1, pp. 159–60)

91. Heilbron, *Electricity*, p. 86.
92. Guerlac, "Black," in Gillispie et al., *Dictionary of Scientific Biography*, vol. 1, pp. 173–83. Schofield, *Mechanism and Materialism*, pp. 187–90; Heilbron, *Electricity*, p. 86.
93. Baader, *Wärmestoff*, pp. 41–42.
94. Baader, *Wärmestoff*, p. 119.
95. Donovan, *Philosophical Chemistry*, pp. 246–47.
96. For Black see Donovan, *Philosophical Chemistry* and "Research Tradition"; Schofield, *Mechanism and Materialism*, pp. 188–90; Guerlac, "Black," *DSB*. For Wilcke, see Gehler, "Wärme, specifische," pp. 570–74; Heilbron, *Electricity*, pp. 84–86.
97. Heilbron, *Electricity*, p. 85.
98. Donovan, *Philosophical Chemistry*, p. 227.
99. Venel in his influential article on chemistry in the *Encyclopedia* empha-

sized the distinction between external physical properties and internal, chemical ones; Gough, "The Fulfillment of the Stahlian Revolution," p. 25. Bergman and the Swedish mineralogists concurred (Porter, "The Revolution of Mining"), as did Cullen; Golinski, *Science as Public Culture*, pp. 18–19; Lundgren, "New Chemistry in Sweden," p. 152.

100. Goethe, *Theory of Colours*, p. lix.

101. Guerlac, "Black," p. 178.

102. Donovan, *Philosophical Chemistry*, p. 229. Donovan makes the same point in his article "Research Tradition," where he argues that "the dominant research tradition in Scotland concentrated on heat, not air" (p. 101). Guerlac, in an important article on Black, also confirms by implication the central position of heat research in Black's work; for, though discovering fixed air and realizing that research into airs could lead to many discoveries, Black abruptly turned his attention to his researches on latent and specific heat. Henry Guerlac, "Joseph Black and Fixed Air: A Bicentennary Retrospective, with some New or Little known Material," *Isis* 48 (1957), pp. 449–50.

103. Heilbron, *Electricity*, notes that "one suspects that Black obtained more guidance from the material theory of heat than he allowed"; p. 86, fn. 68.

104. Quoted by Donovan, *Philosophical Chemistry*, p. 229.

105. Lavoisier characterized this process as follows: "It is very remarkable that, notwithstanding the number of philosophical chemists who have supported the doctrine of the four elements, there is not one who has not been led by the evidence of facts to admit a greater number of elements into their theory"; Lavoisier, *Elements of Chemistry*, p. 3. On simple substance see Porter, "The Revolution of Mining."

106. Lavoisier, *Elements of Chemistry*, p. 21.

107. Henry Guerlac, "Lavoisier," in Gillispie et al., *Dictionary of Scientific Biography*, vol. 7, p. 70.

108. Carleton E. Perrin provides a different interpretation. He argued that water remained the basic element until Lavoisier's experiments. "Elemental air had given way to a host of aeriform fluids or gases whose composition was then a moot point. Chemists and mineralogists spoke of four earths rather than one. Fire was separating into distinct matters of heat and of light. Only water remained intact (though not for long)"; "Research Traditions and the Chemical Revolution," p. 77.

109. Quoted and translated by Anderson, *Between the Library and the Laboratory*, p. 171, fn. 132.

110. Scheele, *Abhandlung von Luft und Feuer*, p. 3: "The study of air is now an important part of chemistry. It is this elastic fluid, endowed with so many specific characteristics, that offers to anyone who handles it, much material for new discoveries. Wonderful fire, this product of chemistry, shows us that it cannot be generated without air."

111. Carl Wilhelm Scheele, *The Chemical Essays of Charles William Scheele*, trans. Thomas Beddoes (London, 1786), p. 259.

112. Scheele, *Luft und Feuer*, p. 21.

113. Baader, *Wärmestoff,* pp. 201, 54–55. Baader supports this position by citations from the works of Buffon, Macquer, Christian Ehrenfried Weigel, and Guyton de Morveau.

114. Scheele, *Luft und Feuer,* pp. 65–68.

115. Scheele, *Essays,* p. 260.

116. Scheele, *Luft und Feuer,* p. 57 "It is not unknown to those who work using reason in chemistry that there are a great number of bodies which not only combine with the burnable in more or less amounts, but also that each of these combinations receive different qualities."

117. Scheele, *Luft und Feuer,* p. 57.

118. Scheele, *Luft und Feuer,* p. 57. Or, more simply said, "Das Licht ist kein einfaches Wesen oder Element" (p. 47).

119. Guerlac, "Lavoisier," p. 76.

120. Scheele, *Luft und Feuer,* pp. 93, 97.

121. Gmelin's definition is typical: "Simple substances in chemical usage are those that are not able to be reduced to different parts; with other words, they are named elements"; *Grundriß der Chemie,* vol. I, p. 7.

122. *Wärmestoff,* pp. 283–84.

123. *Wärmestoff,* pp. 53, 33.

124. Donovan, "Introduction," *The Chemical Revolution,* p. 5.

125. Thomas S. Kuhn, *The Structure of Scientific Revolutions* (Chicago: University of Chicago Press, 1970), p. 118.

126. John McEvoy gives an excellent overview of the explanatory strategies that have supported the traditional approach to the chemical revolution, including those of Kuhn and his followers in his article "Continuity and Discontinuity in the Chemical Revolution," in Donovan, *Chemical Revolution,* pp. 195–213.

127. Bensaude-Vincent, "A View of the Chemical Revolution through Contemporary Textbooks," p. 443.

128. Johann Friedrich Blumenbach, another early adherent of Lavoisier, used the same rhetorical strategy, arguing that Lavoisier's explanation for acid formation was very similar to Scheele's: "Hr. Lavoisier über die Natur der Säuren. Das *säurende Principium (le principe acidisant ou oxygine)* sey entweder selbst die reinste (dephlogistisirte) Luft, oder welche doch durch blose Verbindung mit Feuer darein verwandelt (also meist die gleichen Meynungen wie bey Hr. *Scheele*); Blumenbach's review of *Histoire de l'académie royal des Sciences année 1778* in *Medicinische Bibliothek,* I, p. 100.

129. A typical example was the German *Naturphilosoph* Christian Pfaff, who was a classmate of Cuvier's in Tübingen. Cuvier chided him because of his nationalist views concerning chemical theories: "Wie klein Du mir schienst, als Du Experimente bloss deswegen angreiffst, weil sie von Franzosen gemacht worden. Ist denn auch die Natur wie die Landesverfassungen verschieden, dass Du die Chemie in Deutsche, Englische etc. abtheilst; merke Dir dich, Lieber, dass ein ächter Philosoph die Wahrheit überall aufsucht, sie möge herkommen, woher sie wolle"; Cuvier to Pfaff, 18 February 1790, in *Briefe,* p. 137.

130. This tendency, to judge Lavoisier's intentions from what evolved from his work, is present even in those seeking to revise the traditional interpretation of the chemical revolution. For example, Perrin claimed: "Although Lavoisier continued to speak of chemical principles (calling his oxygen the principle of acidity and his caloric the principle of heat), his attack on phlogiston undermined the very foundations of that system"; "Research Traditions," p. 78. This assertion, which Perrin assumes to be self-evident, has meaning only when related to the way in which Lavoisier's system was modernized during the nineteenth century.

131. Quoted by Frederic L. Holmes, "Lavoisier's Conceptual Passage," in Donovan, *Chemical Revolution*, p. 198.

132. Lavoisier, *Elements of Chemistry*, p. 4.

133. Barthez and his followers argued that a *principium vitale* existed in the atmospheric air. See Blumenbach's review of Vrignauld's *Nouvelles recherches sur l'économie animale* (1782) in *Medicinische Bibliothek*, vol. I, p. 336.

134. Lavoisier, *Elements of Chemistry*, p. 22.

135. Lavoisier, *Elements of Chemistry*, p. 3.

136. Lavoisier had difficulty showing how and where nitrogen was active. At best he discerned a retarding activity at work, that is, a negative activity: "It is true that azoytic gas . . . appears to be merely passive during combustion and calcination; but, besides that it retards these operations very considerably, we are not certain but it may even alter their results in some circumstances"; *Elements of Chemistry*, p. 60.

137. Goethe, *Theory of Colours*, p. liv.

138. Lavoisier, *Elements of Chemistry*, pp. 22, 44.

139. Lavoisier, *Elements of Chemistry*, p. 46.

140. Many historians of chemistry who accept the traditional interpretation of the chemical revolution argue that the concept of elective affinity played a minimal role in Lavoisier's thought. Charles Perrin in a critique of Evan Melhado's article "Chemistry, Physics, and the Chemical Revolution," *Isis* 76 (1985): 195–211, argues against this position. According to him, "Lavoisier took . . . chemical affinities for granted in the same manner as other Rouellian chemists. The only way to refute Melhado's contention definitely is to go systematically through Lavoisier's papers to see what use he actually made of these concepts. . . . I have recently made such a study for the case of affinity concepts and found that he made consistent use of them throughout his career, not only in a conventional way but also to inform specific researches"; "Chemistry as a Peer of Physics: A Response to Donovan and Melhado on Lavoisier," *Isis* 81 (1990), p. 266. Bensaude-Vincent has shown that Lavoisier's unfinished plan to compose a new textbook in 1792 to replace the *Traité* "aimed at reintegrating chemistry in eighteenth-century natural philosophy." In so doing, he included "chemical affinity, with Berman's tables of 'elective attractions'"; "A View of the Chemical Revolution through Contemporary Textbooks," p. 568. In Lavoisier's own words, "the science of affinities, or elective attrac-

tions, holds the same place with regard to the other branches of chemistry as the higher or transcendental geometry does with respect to the simpler and elementary part"; *Elements of Chemistry*, p. 3.

141. Lavoisier, *Elements of Chemistry*, p. 46.

142. Lavoisier, *Elements of Chemistry*, p. 41.

143. Lavoisier, *Elements of Chemistry*, pp. 10, 12, 13. This last quotation (p. 10) is the traditional definition of an occult quality employed by people like Buffon, Barthez, and Blumenbach to account for unknowable forces.

144. Lavoisier, *Elements of Chemistry*, pp. 13–14.

145. Baader, who adopted Lavoisier's position, argued that the simple formula that water consists of oxygen and hydrogen was highly misleading. Water was not a gas and therefore could not consist of two gases. Rather, it was a combination of the base of oxygen with the base of hydrogen minus the matter of heat with which both were chemically combined in the gaseous state: "Schon der Ausdruck: *Wasser besteht aus brennbarer und Feuerluft* ist allemal uneigentlich, und giebt allerdings zu Mißverständnißen Anlass. Wasser als solches, ist ja kein *Luft* mehr, und kann also auch aus zween Luftarten nicht zusammengesetzt sein. . . . *Lavoisier* bewies es ja selbst durch unwidersprechliche Erfahrungen und Versuche, daß Luftform eigentlich die Folge einer innigen Verbindung, Auflösung irgend eines Stoffes mit und in Wärmematerie ist, und darum kein obiger Ausdruk auch nur den Sinn haben: *Wasser besteht aus der Basis, dem Grundtheil der Feuerluft, und jenem der Brennbaren*"; *Wärmestoff*, pp. 258–59.

146. Lavoisier, *Elements of Chemistry*, p. 39.

147. "Since this subtle matter penetrates through the pores of all known substances; since there are no vessels through which it cannot escape, and consequently, as there are none which are capable of retaining it, we can only come at the knowledge of its properties by effects which are fleeting and with difficulty ascertainable"; Lavoisier, *Elements of Chemistry*, p. 10.

148. Lavoisier, *Elements of Chemistry*, p. 41.

149. Baader, *Wärmestoff*, p. 21.

150. For the English critique of Lavoisier's reforms, especially those of Priestley and his supporters, see Golinski, *Science as Public Culture*, pp. 130–37.

151. Karl Hufbauer, *The Formation of the German Chemical Community: 1720–1795*, (Berkeley: University of California Press, 1982).

152. *Göttingische Gelehrte Anzeige*, 1785, pp. 1525, 1527.

153. Gmelin, *Grundriss der allgemeinen Chemie zum Gebrauch bei Vorlesungen*, 2 vols. (Göttingen, 1789), pp. xxvii–xxviii.

154. *Göttingische Gelehrte Anzeige*, 1787, p. 355.

155. *Göttingische Gelehrte Anzeige*, 1787, p. 1385.

156. Golinski, *Science as Public Culture*, pp. 148–49.

157. *Göttingsiche Gelehrte Anzeigen*, 1788, p. 395.

158. I make this argument in "Religion, Theology, and the Hermetic Imagination in the Late German Enlightenment: The Case of Johann Salomo Sem-

ler," in *Antike Weisheit und kulturelle Praxis: Hermetismus in der Frühen Neuzeit,* ed. Anne-Charlott Trepp and Hartmut Lehmann (Göttingen: Vandenhoeck & Ruprecht, 2001), pp. 219–34.

159. *Von ächter hermetischer Arznei,* 3 vols. (Leipzig, 1786). Other works of Semler's that dealt with hermetic thought and the primacy of an "inner" secret science were *Briefe an einen Freund in der Schweiz über den Hirtenbrief der unbekanten Obern des Freimaurerordens alten Systems* (Leipzig, 1786), and *Unparteiische Sammlungen zur Historie der Rosenkreuzer,* 4 vols. (Leipzig, 1786–88).

160. *Physische-chemische Abhandlung, durch neuere Schriften von hermetischen Arbeiten und andere neue Untersuchungen veranlasset,* 2 vols. (Halle, 1786, 1787).

161. *Göttingische Gelehrte Anzeige,* 1787, p. 1288.

162. Sergio Moravia, *Beobachtende Vernunft: Philosophie und Anthropologie in der Aufklärung* (Frankfurt: Ullstein, 1977).

163. *Göttingische Gelehrte Anzeigen,* 1787, pp. 1854–55.

164. *Göttingische Gelehrte Anzeigen,* 1787, p. 1856

165. *Göttingische Gelehrte Anzeigen,* 1787, p. 1620.

166. Thomas S. Kuhn, "What Are Scientific Revolutions?" in Lorenz Krüger, Lorraine Daston, and Michael Heidelberger, eds., *The Probabilistic Revolution,* 2 vols. (Cambridge, Mass.: MIT Press, 1987), vol. 1, pp. 7–22. Although Kuhn also dealt with language change in *Scientific Revolutions,* he focused more strongly upon practice, especially upon exempla.

167. Kuhn, "What Are Scientific Revolutions," pp. 19–21.

168. Lundgren, "The New Chemistry in Sweden," p. 168.

3. "WITHIN THE CIRCLE OF ORGANIZED LIFE"

1. I was unable to obtain the French edition, so I used the German translation: *Physiologie des weiblichen Geschlechts,* trans. Christian Friedrich Michaelis (Berlin, 1786).

2. Roussel, *Physiologie des weiblichen Geschlechts,* pp. xiii, xiv, ix–x, 258, and xi, 241, respectively. "All the hypotheses applied to the animal economy based upon a series of movements and mechanical effects . . . remain unsatisfactory as soon as they have to deal with and unite all of the related particulars. This is true because in such a system the most important part, that which should serve as the basis is forgotten. This part is morality, which one must consider the central object when observing organized bodies."

3. Jean Barthez, *Nouveaux Éléments de la science de l'homme,* 2 vols. (Montpellier, 1778), vol. 1, p. xii.

4. Barthez, *Nouveaux Éléments,* vol. 1, pp. xii, xxiv.

5. *Nouveaux Éléments,* vol. 1, p. xxvi.

6. I was unable to find the French edition; therefore I am using the German translation: Charles Louis Dumas, *Anfangsgründe der Physiologie oder Einleitung in eine auf Erfahrung gegründete, philosophische und medicinische*

Kenntniss des lebenden Menschen, trans. Ludwig A. Kra[...] Pickhard, 2 vols. (Göttingen, 1807), vol. 1, p. 97. Accordin[g...] Dumas was the first to have used the term "vitalism" [...] attempt at mediation. In Vartanian's excellent introduct[ion to La Met-] trie's *L'Homme Machine*, he also characterizes La Me[ttrie's attempt at] mediation: "His idea of the 'living machine,' defined hyp[othetically as pur-] posive self-motion, may thus be said to express a 'vitalo-mécanisme u [...] dynamique'"; *L'Homme Machine*, p. 20.

7. This was substantiated by a review written in 1787 by a Göttingen professor of medicine. The reviewer, discussing a German commentary to Cullen's *First Lines of the Practice of Physic*, remarked that "a comparison of Cullen's opinions with others, especially Boerhaave's," is necessary. It "shows the dangerous errors in Boerhaave and his commentator van Swieten and censures and strongly contradicts them. This is still important even in our day because in many German universities the oral instruction in medical practice still follows Boerhaave's *Aphorisms*"; in *Göttingische Gelehrten Anzeigen*, March 1787, p. 862.

8. On Boerhaave's influence in the first half of the eighteenth century see Andrew Cunningham, "Medicine to Calm the Mind: Boerhaave's Medical System, and Why It Was Adopted in Edinburgh," in Cunningham and French, *The Medical Enlightenment of the Eighteenth Century*, pp. 40–66.

9. Christopher Lawrence, "Ornate Physicians and Learned Artisans: Edinburgh Medical Men, 1726–1776," in Bynum and Porter, *William Hunter and the Eighteenth-Century Medical World*, p. 151.

10. Not only was mechanism discredited at Edinburgh, but many able practitioners originally trained in the Boerhaavian tradition abandoned it as well. John Pringle provides an example. Pringle (1707–82) had studied with Boerhaave in the 1720s and was a classmate and close friend of van Swieten. Upon returning to Scotland, he was appointed professor of pneumatics and moral philosophy at Edinburgh in 1734, where he lectured on such topics as the immortality of the soul and Pufendorf's political and social theory. He left Edinburgh in 1742 to pursue a career in medicine, serving first as an army doctor (writing, as a result, the *Observations on the Diseases of the Army* [1764], one of the most important eighteenth-century practical medical tracts) and then as a highly successful private practitioner in London. He served as president of the Royal Society from 1772 to 1778 and was a member of many learned societies. By the late 1740s and early 1750s he came to the conclusion that mechanistic explanations did little to explain the workings of the animal economy and even less to account for the phenomena of sickness and health. He made this clear in a letter to a friend: "I think we are still backward in knowing the laws of the animal economy; for as the common mechanical ones, such as my old master Boerhaave laid such stress upon, they can account for little"; quoted by Blumenbach in a review of *Six Discourses delivered by Sir John Pringle* in *Medicinische Bibliothek*, vol. I, p. 585.

11. For Cullen's critique of Boerhaave's chemistry and his call to base the

chemistry on principles derived from Stahl see Golinski, *Science as Public Culture*, pp. 18–19.

12. Golinski, *Science as Public Culture*, p. 19. "Baconian induction was judged by Cullen 'the best & safest method of reasoning.'" This call for a return to Baconian reasoning ran like a red thread through late Enlightenment thought, culminating in Alexander von Humboldt's efforts to construct a modern form of Baconianism. For Humboldt's appropriation of Baconian ideals see Michael Dettelbach, "Baconianism in Revolutionary Germany," in van der Zande and Popkin, *The Skeptical Tradition around 1800*, pp. 175–86.

13. Lester King, *The Medical World of the Eighteenth Century* (Chicago: University of Chicago Press, 1958), p. 660.

14. Cunningham, "Boerhaave's Medical System," p. 65.

15. Review of Volters, *Gedancken von Psychologischen Curen*, in *Göttingschen Gelerhten Anzeige*, 1751, pp. 955–56. Haller wrote most of the reviews in the *Anzeigen* on medicine, the life sciences, and a host of other topics from its inception until Haller's death. It has been estimated that he composed over twelve thousand reviews.

16. Dumas, *Physiologie*, vol. 1, p. 173.

17. Pierre Jean Georges Cabanis, *Coup d'oeil sur les révolutions et sur la réforme de la médecine* (Paris, 1804), p. 146.

18. Blumenbach was professor in Göttingen from 1775 to 1840. During the last third of the eighteenth century he taught most of Germany's leading life scientists, including Samuel Thomas Sömmerring, Alexander von Humboldt, Carl Friedrich Kielmeyer, Christian Wilhelm Hufeland, Joachim Brandis, Justus Loder, Gottfried Treviranus, and Johann Christian Reil.

19. Blumenbach, *Medicinische Bibliothek*, vol. 2 (1786), p. 396.

20. Although Haller left Göttingen in 1755, he controlled the medical school from afar. He wrote virtually all of the medical reviews in the *Göttingen Gelehrten Anzeige* until his death and was consulted on all of the school's essential decisions.

21. Blumenbach, *Medicinische Bibliothek*, vol. 2, pp. 397, 396. On the relation between Stahl's medical thought and his Pietism see Johanna Geyer-Kordesch, "Georg Ernst Stahl's Radical Pietist Medicine and Its Influence on the German Enlightenment," in Cunningham and French, *The Medical Enlightenment of the Eighteenth Century*, pp. 67–87; *Pietismus, Medizin und Aufklärung in Preußen im 18. Jahrhundert: Das Leben und Werk Georg Ernst Stahls* (Tübingen: Max Niemeyer Verlag, 2000). She basically sees Stahl as an opponent of the Enlightenment, which she interprets in the standard manner as an age dedicated to mechanistic reason. For a different interpretation of Stahl see Richard Mocek, "Der Vitalismus Georg Ernst Stahls: die Ankündigung eines neuen Paradigmas," *Hallesche Physiologie im Werden* (1981): 25–30.

22. Georg Ernst Stahl, "Ueber den Unterschied zwischen Organismus und Mechanismus," in *Georg Ernst Stahl*, Sudhoffs Klassiker der Medizin 36 (Leipzig: Johann Ambrosius Barth, 1961), p. 49.

23. Stahl, "Ueber den Unterschied," p. 52.

24. Stahl, "Ueber den Unterschied," p. 50.
25. Stahl, "Ueber den Unterschied," p. 37.
26. Stahl, "Ueber den Unterschied," p. 26.
27. Stahl, "Ueber den Unterschied," p. 27.
28. Christopher Lawrence, "The Nervous System and Society in the Scottish Enlightenment," in *Natural Order: Historical Studies of Scientific Culture*, ed. Barry Barnes and Steven Shapin (Beverly Hills: Sage Publications, 1979), pp. 19–40.
29. Robert Whytt. *An Essay on the Vital and other Involuntary Motions of Animals*, 2nd ed. (Edinburgh, 1763), p. 2.
30. "The human body, in which there is no mover that can properly be called FIRST, or whose motion depends on something else, is a system far above the power of mechanics"; Whytt, *An Essay*, p. 299.
31. Whytt, *An Essay*, pp. 316, 338. "Upon the whole, there seems to be in man one sentient and intelligent PRINCIPLE, which is equally the source of life, sense and motion, as of reason" (p. 321).
32. Whytt, *An Essay*, pp. 297–99.
33. Whytt, *An Essay*, p. 299.
34. Whytt, *An Essay*, p. 299. "The sympathy, therefore, or consent observed between the nerves of various parts of the body . . . ought to be ascribed to the energy of that sentient BEING, which in a peculiar manner displays its powers in the brain, and by means of nerves, moves, actuates, and enlivens the whole machine" (p. 204).
35. Whytt, *An Essay*, p. 264.
36. Whytt, *An Essay*, p. 268.
37. Haller, *A Dissertation on the Sensible and Irritable Parts of Animals* (London, 1755), introduction by Owsei Temkin, *Bulletin of the Institute of Medicine* 4 (1936): 658–59, 675.
38. Haller, *A Dissertation*, pp. 672–73.
39. Quoted by Alexander von Humboldt, *Aphorismen aus der chemischen Physiologie der Pflanzen*, trans. Gotthelf Fischer (Leipzig, 1794), pp. 44–45.
40. Roger, *Les sciences de la vie*, p. 179.
41. Roger, *Les sciences de la vie*, p. 628.
42. A. von Humboldt, *Physiologie*, vol. 1, p. 183.
43. Quoted by Roger, *Les sciences de la vie*, p. 629.
44. Barthez also pointed to the importance of the epigastric region's influence upon the soul; *Nouveaux Elements*, pp. 227–28.
45. Quoted by Roger, *Les sciences de la vie*, p. 626.
46. Quoted by Roger, *Les sciences de la vie*, p. 623.
47. Quoted by Peter Kapitza, *Die frühromantische Theorie der Mischung*, Münchener Germanistische Beiträge 4, ed. Werner Betz and Hermann Kunisch (Munich: Max Hueber Verlag, 1968), p. 165.
48. Johann Blumenbach, *Handbuch der Naturgeschichte*, 2nd ed., 2 vols. (Göttingen, 1782), vol. 1, p. 10.
49. Many commentators assume that these phrases indicate the machine-

like nature of the thing they designated, that the adjectives animal or living did not directly change the essential quality of the designated entity. Given the manner in which the terms were employed, this, I believe, is a mistaken reading. For many, the terms served as real juxtapositions that graphically announced the vitalist desire to mediate between animism and mechanism by drawing both together into a creative oxymoron. Vartanian suggested this in his insightful reading and interpretation of La Mettrie's *Man the Machine*.

50. A. von Humboldt, *Aphorismen*, p. 3.

51. Dumas, *Physiologie*, vol. 1, pp. 259–60.

52. Linda Orr shows that Michelet was fascinated by Bonnet's ideas in her excellent study *Jules Michelet: Nature, History, and Language* (Ithaca: Cornell University Press, 1976).

53. Charles Bonnet, *Betrachtung über die Natur*, 5th ed., 4 vols. (Leipzig, 1803), vol. 1, pp. 33–34.

54. Bonnet, *Considérations sur les corps organisés, l'on traite de leur origine, de leur développement, de leur réproduction*, 2 vols. (Amsterdam, 1776), pp. xxi–xxii.

55. John E. Lesch, "Systematics and the Geometrical Spirit," in Frängsmyr et al., *The Quantifying Spirit in the Eighteenth Century*, p. 73.

56. Dumas, *Physiologie*, vol. 1, p. 201.

57. Blumenbach, *Elements of Physiology*, trans. Charles Caldwell, 2 vols. (Philadelphia, 1795), vol. 1, p. 45.

58. Quoted by Hugh B. Nisbet, *Goethe and the Scientific Tradition* (London: University of London, 1972), p. 19.

59. Dumas, *Physiologie*, vol. 1, p. 316.

60. Dumas, *Physiologie*, vol. 1, p. 316.

61. The question is raised and answered in Books VI and VII. In the former Rousseau draws a sharp distinction between an aggregation (present society) and a political body or association (the social contract): "c'est, si l'on veut, une agrégation, mais non pas une association; il n'y a là ni bien public, ni corps politique." This distinction leads to the famous central question of the work: "Trouver une forme d'association qui défende et protège de toute la force commune la personne et les biens de chacque associé, et par laquelle chacun, s'unissant à tous, n'obéisse purtant qu'à lui-meme, et reste aussis libre qu'auparavant." This form of association is created through the act of association. "On voit par cette formule que l'acte d'association renferme un engagement récriproque du public avec les particuliers, et que chacque individu, contractant pour ainsi dire avec lui-meme, se trouve engagé sous un double rapport: savoir, comme membre du soverain envers les particuliers, et comme membre de l'État envers le souverain"; Rousseau, *Du Contrat Social*, ed. Edmond Dreyfus-Brisac (Paris: Alcan, 1896), pp. 27, 31, 35.

62. *Ueber das Kantische Prinzip für die Naturgeschichte: ein Versuch diese Wissenschaft philosophisch zu behandeln* (Göttingen: Vandenhoeck & Ruprecht, 1796), p. 2. Girtanner studied medicine in Göttingen from 1780 to 1783

and later chemistry at Edinburgh. As a publicist he published books on syphilis, Brown's system, children's' illnesses, and Erasmus Darwin. He also published a theory of health that was a direct plagiarism of Brown. When it was discovered, he then entered the lists as an opponent of Brown. He also was a political publicist who was a rabid opponent of the French Revolution. The Kantian principles to which the title refers are based upon his reading of Kant's *Critique of Judgment* and his *Anthropology from a Pragmatic Point of View*. The book was dedicated to Blumenbach.

63. Barthez, *Nouveaux éléments*, p. 147.
64. Blumenbach, *Elements of Physiology*, vol. 1, p. 39.
65. Quoted by Duchesneau, *La physiologie des lumières*, p. 397.
66. Barthez, *Nouveaux éléments*, p. 148.
67. Barthez, *Nouveaux éléments*, p. 143.
68. Blumenbach, *Elements of Physiology*, vol. 2, p. 88.
69. Kapitza, *Theorie der Mischung*, p. 59.
70. Duchesneau, "Vitalism in Late Eighteenth-Century Physiology: The Cases of Barthez, Blumenbach and John Hunter," in Bynum and Porter, *William Hunter and the Eighteenth-Century Medical World*, p. 261.
71. Barthez, *Nouveaux éléments*, pp. 245–46.
72. Barthez, *Nouveaux éléments*, p. 246.
73. Barthez acknowledged his debt to earlier Renaissance and ancient theories, yet was also clear in differentiating them from his idea of the *Principe Vital*: "Il est à-peu-près indifferent qu'on au Principe Vital les noms de Nature, d'Archée, d'Ame, etc. Mais se qui est absolument essentiel, c'est qu'on ne rapporte jamais les déterminations de ce Principe, à des affections dérivées des facultés de prévoyance, ou autres qu'on attribute à cette Ame"; *Nouvelle méchanique des mouvements de l'homme et des animaux* (Carcassonne, 1798), pp. ii–iii.
74. Barthez, *Nouveaux éléments*, p. 142.
75. Barthez, thoroughly committed to the monarchy, was not averse to making this analogy. See Alisa Schulweis Reich, "Paul Joseph Barthez and the Impact of Vitalism on Medicine and Psychology," Ph.D diss., University of California, Los Angeles, 1995.
76. *Göttingische Anzeigen von gelehrten Sachen*, 1787, pp. 249–50.
77. *Elements of Physiology*, vol. 1, pp. 32, 210, 33.
78. Blumenbach, *Elements of Physiology*, vol. 1, p. 33.
79. When Blumenbach wrote the *Elements of Physiology* in 1787, most physiologists were reluctant to accord irritability, let alone sensibility to plants. Over time, irritability was increasingly seen as the primordial property of animation, including both plants and animals. Thus, in 1794 Alexander von Humboldt would equate animation with irritability, but not with sensibility: "If I mention animated parts, I understand thereby those which are irritable. Many others have life force *[Lebenskraft]* and irritability but not sensibility. No matter how close the relationship between them (irritability and sensibility) may be, they still appear to be different"; A. von Humboldt, *Aphorismen*, pp. 12–13.

80. Blumenbach, *Elements of Physiology*, vol. 1, p. 33.
81. Blumenbach, *Elements of Physiology*, vol. 1, pp. 33–34.
82. Blumenbach, *Elements of Physiology*, vol. 1, pp. 34–35.
83. Blumenbach, *Elements of Physiology*, vol. 1, pp. 46, 142, 48.
84. Dumas, *Physiologie*, vol. 1, pp. 167–68.
85. Blumenbach *Elements of Physiology*, vol. 1, p. 143.
86. For a fine discussion of how late eighteenth-century psychology sought to account for mind's action see Gary Hatfield, "Remaking the Science of Mind: Psychology as Natural Science," in Fox et al., *Inventing Human Science*, pp. 184–231, especially pp. 196–231.
87. Marcus Herz, *Versuch über den Schwindel* (Berlin, 1788), p. 28. Schiller pleaded for a theory-informed practice to replace a mere pragmatic *Brotstudium* (bread-winning profession). He makes this point in the dedication of his second (accepted) dissertation to Duke Charles of Würtemberg: "But *Your Grace* has raised the Hippocratic art from the narrow sphere of a mechanical, bread-winning science to the higher rank of a philosophical discipline"; "Essay on the Connection between the Animal and the Spiritual Nature of Man," in Kenneth Dewhurst and Nigel Reeves, eds., *Friedrich Schiller: Medicine, Psychology and Literature* (Berkeley: University of California Press, 1978), pp. 254–55.
88. For Barthez's French followers the question of the functions of the nervous system were thought to be part of the larger analysis of *sensibilité*, which they considered one of the basic powers of animal life, spread in degrees of major and minor throughout the body. Hence they spent less time attempting to chart the relations between mind and body than asserting *sensibilité*'s universal validity and its mysterious actions.
89. Blumenbach, *Elements of Physiology*, vol. 1, p. 154.
90. Blumenbach, *Elements of Physiology*, vol. 1, p. 164; Blumenbach, *Handbuch der vergleichende Anatomie* (Göttingen, 1805), p. 319.
91. Blumenbach, *Vergleichende Anatomie*, p. 320.
92. Herz, *Versuch über den Schwindel*, p. 225.
93. John Elliot, *Physiologische Beobachtungen über die Sinne besonders über das Gesicht und Gehör wie auch über das Brennen und die thierische Wärme nebst Adair Crawfords Versuchen und Beobachtungen über die thierische Wärme* (Leipzig, 1785).
94. I have used the German translation of the fifth edition. Charles Bonnet, *Betrachtung über die Natur*, trans. Johann Daniel Titius, 5th ed., 2 vols. (Leipzig, 1803), vol. 1, p. 194.
95. Blumenbach, *Elements of Physiology*, vol. 1, p. 157.
96. Johann Daniel Metzger gives an excellent summary of the various opinions held at that time and also a critique of those with which he disagreed: *Grundriß der Physiologie* (Königsberg, 1783), pp. 86–92.
97. Review of Monro's Nervous System in *Medical Commentaries*, vol. 9 (London, 1785), pp. 15–16.

98. Blumenbach, *Anfangsgründe der Physiologie* (Vienna, 1789), p. 92.
99. Dewhurst and Reeves include the reports of the faculty concerning the dissertation: *Schiller*, pp. 165–68.
100. Schiller, *Philosophy of Physiology* in Dewhurst and Reeves, *Schiller*, p. 154.
101. Schiller, *Philosophy of Physiology*, p. 152.
102. Schiller, *Philosophy of Physiology*, p. 152.
103. Schiller, *Philosophy of Physiology*, p. 155.
104. Herz, *Versuch über den Schwindel*, pp. 2, 4.
105. Herz, *Versuch über den Schwindel*, pp. 206–7.
106. Samuel Thomas Sömmerring, *Ueber das Organ der Seele* (Königsberg, 1796), p. 31.
107. Sömmerring, *Organ der Seele*, pp. 36–37.
108. Rudolf Wagner, *Samuel Thomas von Sömmerrings Leben und Verkehr mit seinen Zeitgenossen*, 2 vols. (Leipzig: Voss, 1844), vol. 1, p. 18: "That class, maybe more than ever, correctly understands its handiwork, which it drives forward with unrelenting rigor, separate from other concerns."
109. Wagner, *Sömmerring Leben und Verkehr*, 28 August 1796, vol. 1, pp. 19–20.
110. Blumenbach, *Elements of Physiology*, vol. 1, p. 156.
111. Blumenbach, *Elements of Physiology*, vol. 1, pp. 157, 156.
112. Alexander von Humboldt, *Aphorismen*, p. 102; Blumenbach, *Elements of Physiology*, vol. 1, p. 41.
113. Christoph Friedrich Michaelis, Roussel's translator, noted the following attempts to expand the number of temperaments: "Herr Dr. Starke in einer Anmerkung zu des Herrn Jadolet's Lehre von der Natur . . . nimmt . . . nachstehend sechs Temperamenten an: 1) das *sanguinische*, welches nach der Meinung des Herrn Roussels, das dem schönen Geschlecht eigne Temperament ist; 2) das *phlegmatische*. 3) Das *cholerische*. 4) Das *melancholische*. 5) Das *sanfte* oder *lenksame*, 6) und das böotische, bäurische oder *Eselstemperament*; *Physiologie des weiblichen Geschlechts*, pp. 41–42.
114. Roussel, *Physiologie des weiblichen Geschlechts*, pp. 45–46.
115. Roussel, *Physiologie des weiblichen Geschlechts*, p. 46.
116. Roussel, *Physiologie des weiblichen Geschlechts*, pp. 46–47.
117. Metzger, *Skizze einer medizinischen Psychologie* (Königsberg, 1787), p. 43.
118. Kant, *Anthropologie in pramatischer Hinsicht, Kants Werke*, Akademie Textausgabe 7 (Berlin: Walter de Gruyter, 1968), p. 292. I thank John Zammito for calling my attention to this.
119. I plan to discuss this in a volume dealing with the interaction between vitalism and the human sciences.
120. Blumenbach, *Elements of Physiology*, vol. 1, pp. 43–44.
121. Blumenbach, *Elements of Physiology*, vol. 1, p. 44.
122. Metzger, *Skizze*, pp. 43–44.

123. Blumenbach, *Elements of Physiology*, vol. 1, p. 44; Metzger, *Skizze*, p. 44.
124. Blumenbach, *Elements of Physiology*, vol. 1, pp. 44–45.
125. Blumenbach, *Elements of Physiology*, vol. 1, p. 45.
126. Larson, *Interpreting Nature*, p. 60.

4. THE METAMORPHOSES OF CHANGE

1. This is one of the major themes of John E. Larson's study *Interpreting Nature*, where he draws a distinction between the founding generation of life scientists who wrote their works at midcentury and the second generation who "made a concerted attempt to make qualitative observations far more exact" (p. 23).
2. "Everything in the system of the universe is in constant movement and activity, is in the process of constant transformation. Nature sustains in the smallest part of matter a constant striving towards movement and activity"; Dumas, *Physiologie*, vol. I, p. 365.
3. Richard Toellner, "Kant und die Evolutionstheorie," *Clio Medica* 3 (1968), p. 244. Larson modifies this position by arguing that late-eighteenth-century naturalists evolved a much more exact methodology, allowing them to investigate subjects with far greater precision than had Buffon, Maupertuis, or Haller. Although I tend to agree with him that the life sciences adopted a much more rigorous approach, I believe no major experimental breakthrough enabled either side to assert its superiority over the other. Thus, at each moment in the discussion the opponents were arguing over the same empirical data.
4. John C. Cook, *The New Theory of Generation according to the Best and Latest Discoveries in Anatomy, Farther improved and fully displayed* (London, 1762), pp. 3–4.
5. Immanuel Kant, *Der einzig mögliche Beweisgrund zu einer Demonstration des Daseins Gottes* (Hamburg: Felix Meiner Verlag, 1963), pp. xx, 59. All the translations are mine.
6. Kant, *Kritik der Urtheilskraft, Kants Werke*, Akademie Textausgabe 5 (Berlin: Walter de Gruyter, 1968), p. 409, my translation.
7. Unlike the first text, Kant discerned two types of teleological explanations for generation modeled upon the philosophical discussion of God's activities. The first, which he called the "occasionalist," was in his opinion contrary to all scientific explanations: "Nach dem ersteren würde die oberste Weltursache ihrer Idee gemäß bei Gelegenheit einer jeden Begattung der in derselben sich mischenden Materie unmittelbar die organische Bildung geben.... Wenn man den Occasionalism der Hervorbringung organisirter Wesen annimmt, so geht alle Natur hierbei gänzlich verloren, mit ihr auch aller Vernunftgebrauch, über die Möglichkeit einer solchen Art Producte zu urtheilen; daher man voraussetzen kann, daß niemand dieses System annehmen wird, dem es irgend um Philosophie zu thun ist." He called the second approach "Preestablishism" *(Prästabilism)*, which he defined as follows: "nach dem zweiten würde sie in die

anfänglichen Produkte dieser ihrer Weisheit nur die Anlage gebracht haben, vermittelst deren ein organisches Wesen seines Gleichen hervorbringt und die Species sich selbst beständig erhält, imgleichen der Abgang der Individuen durch ihre zugleich an ihrer Zerstörung arbeitende Natur continuirlich ersetzt wird." Preformation and epigenesis were two possibilities of the second explanation; Kant, *Kitik der Urtheilskraft*, p. 422.

8. Kant, *Kritik der Urtheilskraft*, p. 424.

9. Shirley A. Roe, *Matter, Life, and Generation: Eighteenth-Century Embryology and the Haller-Wolff Debate* (Cambridge: Cambridge University Press, 1981).

10. Blumenbach, *Über den Bildungstrieb*, 2nd ed. (Göttingen, 1791), pp. 44–45. See Larson, *Interpreting Nature*, pp. 142–59, for a more extensive discussion of Haller's position and Wolff's opposition to it.

11. "It appears very probable to me that the essential parts of the fetus exist formed at all times; not it is true in the way they appear in the adult animal: they are arranged in such a fashion that certain prepared causes, hastening the growth of some of these parts, impeding that of others, changing positions, rendering organs visible that were formerly diaphanous, giving consistency to the fluidity and to the mucosity, form in the end an animal that is very different from the embryo, and yet in which there is no part that did not exist essentially in the embryo"; quoted by Roe, *Matter, Life, and Generation*, p. 41.

12. Quoted by Jacques Roger, *Les sciences de la vie*, pp. 713–14; Charles Bonnet, *Betrachtung über die Nature: mit Anmerkungen und Zusatzen*, ed. Johann Daniel Titius, 5th ed., 2 vols. (Leipzig, 1803), vol. 1, pp. 307, 320.

13. Bonnet, *Betrachtung über die Natur*, vol. 1, pp. 310, 3.

14. Thomas Kuhn, "What Are Scientific Revolutions?" p. 10.

15. Bonnet, *Betrachtung über die Natur*, vol. 1, pp. 5–6, 4, 45.

16. Quoted by Richard W. Burkhardt, Jr., *The Spirit of System: Lamarck and Evolutionary Biology* (Cambridge, Mass.: Harvard University Press, 1977), p. 53. Burkhardt points out that Antoine-Laurent Jussieu also spoke of a chain of being (p. 52).

17. Bonnet, *Betrachtung über die Natur*, vol. 1, p. 46.

18. Bonnet, *Betrachtung über die Natur*, vol. 1, p. 332.

19. Michael Hagner considers the issue of abnormal birth to be an "epistemic instrument," central to the question of explaining generation; "Enlightened Monsters," in Clark et al., *The Sciences in Enlightened Europe*, pp. 175–237, especially pp. 186–96.

20. Bonnet, *Betrachtung über die Natur*, vol. 1, pp. 332–33.

21. Bonnet, *Betrachtung über die Natur*, vol. 1, p. 334.

22. Francesca Rigotti analyzes some of the more renowned proponents of preformation in her excellent article "Biology and Society in the Age of Enlightenment," *Journal of the History of Ideas* 47 (1986): 215–33. In addition to Bonnet, she includes Robinet, De Beaurieu, Delille, and Delisle de Sales. That list could be expanded by adding Antoine-Laurent de Jussieu, Lazzaro Spallanzani, and Jean Senebier.

23. Only recently are scholars now dealing with what is increasingly being referred to as the "medicalization" of late Enlightenment thought. In France, Great Britain, and Germany medically trained men (and in Italy, also women) played important roles in academies, learned societies, secret organizations, clubs and reading circles, and government agencies. For an interesting study on how medical metaphors and thought influenced French political theory see George Armstrong Kelly, *Mortal Politics in Eighteenth-Century France* (Waterloo, Ontario: University of Waterloo Press, 1986). Alain Corbin demonstrates the importance of medical thought in France in his pioneering study *The Foul and the Fragrant: Odor and the French Social Imagination* (Cambridge, Mass.: Harvard University Press, 1986). Roy Porter had mapped out an ambitious research program dealing with the relations between medical thought and social practice in England. For Germany Lothar Müller has eloquently stated the case for looking at the importance of the physician-savant in *Die kranke Seele und das Licht der Erkenntnis: Karl Philipp Mortiz' Anton Reiser* (Frankfurt am Main: Athenäum, 1987).

24. Roussel, *Physiologie*, p. 168.

25. Timothy Lenoir, *The Strategy of Life: Teleology and Mechanics in Nineteenth-Century German Biology* (Dordrecht: Reidel, 1982), p. 19. I have been unable to see the first edition of the *Naturgeschichte;* all subsequent editions replicate Blumenbach's final position on the subject.

26. *Göttingisches Magazin der Wissenschaften und Litteratur*, 1 Jg., 5 St. (1780), pp. 247–66. It was printed as a separate essay in 1781, revised in 1789, and revised again in 1791. Of course, there is no way to prove that Blumenbach had been holding back his critique until Haller's death. But the explanation he gave, namely, that his recent researches into the polyp convinced him of its error, seems a bit strained, especially considering the depth and ferocity of his critique.

27. Blumenbach was extremely careful in his choice of books that he noted or reviewed. It is clear that through the journal he sought to and succeeded in establishing ties to Italy, Great Britain, Bohemia, and Russia (his ambivalence to the French followers of Barthez seemed to be a constant). He also picked some of the most outrageous examples of preformationist arguments to highlight and criticize in the reviews.

28. See Timothy Lenoir's *The Strategy of Life* for a discussion of the relationship between Kant and Blumenbach. Lenoir argues that Kant through his reinterpretation of Blumenbach established a research program, which he calls teleo-mechanism that directed the "development of biology in Germany during the first half of the nineteenth century" (p. 2). Although I agree with the major points of Lenoir's argument, I believe he falls into the trap of assuming that important intellectual or scientific movements are always initiated by leading philosophers. Thus, by some strange form of alchemy, Blumenbach becomes a Kantian teleo-mechanist, where "Blumenbach incorporated Kant's work into the mature formulation of his ideas" (22). I see no movement or change in Blumenbach's position after his initial attack on preformation. In

fact, though he was more than willing to have Kant praise him, Blumenbach along with his fellow Göttingen colleagues Lichtenberg, Kästner, Feder, and his brother-in-law Georg Forster was cool to Kantian philosophy, especially before the publication of the *Critique of Understanding*. I doubt that Blumenbach had read Kant seriously before the appearance of the third Critique and by then his ideas had been formed and changed very little. Kant, however, probably had read everything Blumenbach had written. Blumenbach's position was adopted immediately by Kant's respected colleague Johann Metzger at Königsberg and by many of Kant's correspondents such as Marcus Herz. With respect to the issue of generation, Kant could be called a Blumenbachian. For those concerned with the life sciences, the *Critique of Understanding* seemed to be a legitimatization of positions already established; it also appeared to mark a major shift in Kant's philosophic interests. Natural historians, physiologists, and physical anthropologists who had very little to say about the first two Critiques quoted extensively from the third; yet, their positions could easily have been argued (and often were, as the French analogues attest) without Kant's assistance. For an example of two works that quote Kant extensively yet also affirm positions staked out earlier see Girtanner, *Über das Kantische Princip für die Naturgeschichte* (Göttingen, 1796), and Johann Ith, *Versuch einer Anthropologie oder Philosophie der Menschen nach seinen körperlichen Anlagen* (Bern, 1795). An example of how easily one could misunderstand Kant in this area was demonstrated by Sömmerring's dedication of *Über das Organ der Seele* to Kant. Larson in *Interpreting Nature* also discerns a relationship between Kant and Blumenbach, in which the former shaped the latter's ideas, but he also shows how Kant realized and developed insights first propounded by Buffon. In this larger sense one could almost say both Blumenbach and Kant were Buffonians.

29. Quoted by Roe, *Matter, Life, and Generation*, p. 50.

30. Roe, *Matter, Life, and Generation*, p. 112.

31. Roe, *Matter, Life, and Generation*, p. 146. For a much more positive evaluation of Wolff and his achievement see Larson, *Interpreting Nature*, pp. 143–59. Larson makes an excellent case for Wolff's "observational genius." Still, despite this, I believe Wolff's work did not have the impact upon his contemporaries that Blumenbach's did.

32. On Koelreuter see James Larson, "The Most Confused Knot in the Doctrine of Reproduction," in Frängsmyr et al., *The Quantifying Spirit in the Eighteenth Century*, pp. 267–89; *Interpreting Nature*, pp. 69–78.

33. There may have also been a Cartesian influence present, but his two-fluid theory did not include active powers animating the fluids. Larson claims that in the mid-eighteenth century no one accepted the Cartesian position; *Interpreting Nature*, p. 135. "For the generation of every natural plant, two fluid materials of different types, destined by the creator to unite with each other, are required. One of them is the masculine, the other the feminine semen *(Saame)*. Since these materials are of a different type, or according to their natures differentiated from each other, therefore it is easy to understand that the force of

one must be different from the force of the other. Through the uniting and combination of these two materials, which occurs internally and orderly according to specific relations, arises a third, which is a middle type *(Art)*, and therefore also a mediation, possessing a combined *(zusammengesetzte)* force arising from the two original forces"; *Fortsetzung der vorläufigen Nachricht von einigen des Geschlecht der Pflanzen betreffenden Versuchen und Beobachtungen* (Leipzig, 1763), p. 5.

34. *Zweyte Fortsetzung der vorläufigen Nachricht von einigen des Geschlecht der Pflanzen betreffenden Versuchen und Beobachtungen* (Leipzig, 1764), pp. 4–5, 6–7.

35. Kölreuter, *Vorläufige Nachricht*, p. 40.

36. Blumenbach, *Ueber den Bildungstrieb*, pp. 24–25.

37. Blumenbach, *Ueber den Bildungstrieb*, p. 26.

38. Blumenbach, *Ueber den Bildungstrieb*, pp. 47–48.

39. Blumenbach, *Elements of Physiology*, vol. 1, pp. 176–77.

40. Blumenbach, *Ueber den Bildungstrieb*, pp. 33–34; *Elements of Physiology*, vol. 1, p. 177.

41. Blumenbach, *Elements of Physiology*, pp. 65–66, fn.

42. *Medicinische Bibliothek*, p. 3.

43. Blumenbach, *Handbuch der vergleichende Anatomie* (Göttingen, 1805), pp. 471–72.

44. For a discussion of this concept in France for the same period see Jean Svagelski, *L'idée de compensation en France, 1750–1850* (Lyon: L'Hermès, 1981); see also Lenoir, *Strategies of Life*.

45. Quoted by Wagner in *Sömmerrings Leben*, p. 53.

46. Hagner, "Enlightened Monsters," p. 196.

47. Blumenbach, *Elements of Physiology*, vol. 1, p. 203.

48. Report of his lecture to the Göttingen Academy of Sciences held in 1788 in *Göttingische Anzeigen von gelehrten Sachen*, 8. Stück, 12 January 1789, p. 75.

49. *Medicinische Bibliothek*, vol. 1, 127.

50. Blumenbach, *Ueber den Bildungstrieb*, pp. 79–80.

51. Anon., *Traite des Extremes ou élements de la science de la réalité* (Amsterdam, 1768), pp. 232, 240.

52. This is the major theme of Mendelssohn's *Phädon oder über die Unsterblichkeit der Seele in drei Gesprächen*. For Lessing's and Mendelssohn's ideas about the further development of the spiritual monad see Alexander Altmann, "Lessings Glaube an die Seelenwanderung," in *Die trostvolle Aufklärung: Studien zur Metaphysik und politischen Theorie Moses Mendelssohns* (Stuttgart: Frommann-Holzboog, 1982), 109–34.

53. Hufeland, *Der Scheintod, oder Sammlung der wichtigsten Thatsachen und Bemerkungen darüber in alphabetischer Ordnung* (Berlin, 1808), p. 114.

54. Marcus Herz, *Ueber die frühe Beerdigung der Juden: An die Herausgeber der hebräischen Sammlers*, 2nd ed. (Berlin, 1788), p. 13; Hufeland, *Der Scheintod*; Françoise Thiery, *La vie de l'homme respectée & défendue dans ses*

derniers momens (Paris, 1785). Herz and Hufeland borrowed the concept of a middle state from Thiery.

55. Hufeland, *Scheintod*, p. 275.
56. Hufeland, *Scheintod*, p. 171.
57. Those Hufeland singled out as misleading were (1) the cessation of the heart's beating, (2) the absence of breathing, (3) lack of feeling and the inability to move, (4) total bodily stiffness and the lack of bodily warmth, (5) the absence of flowing blood when an artery is opened, and (6) the total debilitation of the muscles and sinews; *Scheintod*, pp. 290, 292, 293, 294, 295.
58. Hufeland, *Scheintod*, p. 301.
59. *Encyclopedia: or a Dictionary of Arts and Sciences.* (Philadelphia, 1798), vol. 5, pp. 694–95. This paragraph was repeated verbatim under the article "death" in the *Encyclopedia Britannica* (Edinburgh, 1810) and the *London Encyclopedia* (London, 1829); *Encyclopedia Americana* (Philadelphia, 1830), vol. 4, p. 137.
60. A. von Humboldt, "Lebenskraft oder rhodische Genius." Elsewhere he differentiated between dead and living matter as follows: "Träge, unbelebte Materie nennen wir diejenige, deren Bestandtheile nach den Gesetzen der chemischen Verwandschaft gemischt sind; belebte und organisirte Körper hingegen diejenigen, welche, des ununterbrochnen Bestrebens ihre Gestalt zu ändern ungeachtet, durch eine gewisse innere Kraft gehindert werden, ihre erste, ihnen eigenthümliche Form, zu verlassen"; *Aphorismen*, p. 3.
61. Quoted by Hufeland, *Scheintod*, p. 116.
62. John Hunter, *Observations on Certain Parts of the Animal Oeconomy*, 2nd ed. (London, 1786), p. 165.
63. Hunter, *Observations*, p. 167.
64. Herz, *Beerdigung der Juden*, p. 29.
65. Hufeland, *Scheintod*, p. 80.
66. Hufeland, *Scheintod*, pp. 95–97.
67. Mary Shelley, *Frankenstein, or The Modern Prometheus* (New York: Random House, 1993), p. 49.
68. Hunter, *Observations*, pp. 115, 117, 124.
69. Hufeland, *Scheintod*, p. 64. Hunter was unsure about the time allotted for revival. In his analysis of violent deaths, he differentiated between three different kinds. The first applied to drowning: "First, where a stop is only put to the action of life in the animal, but without any irreparable injury to a vital part; which action if not restored in a certain time, will be irrevocably lost. The length of time is subject to considerable variation depending on circumstances with which we are at present unacquainted"; John Hunter, *Observations*, p. 117.
70. *Wilhelm Meisters Wanderjahre, Goethes Werke*, Hamburger Ausgabe 8 (Hamburg, 1961), p. 459.
71. Herz, *Beerdigung Juden*, p. 6.
72. Herz, *Beerdigung Juden*, pp. 7–8.
73. Herz, *Beerdigung Juden*, p. 48. Herz compared the rabbis to medieval

scholastics: "Bekleidet mit dunklen mystischen Ausdrücken, eingehüllt in wortreiche und sinnarme Phrases, schleicht sich ein Gedanke gar sanft in die Köpfe derer, denen reine Wahrheit und deutliche Zergliederung der Begriffe etwas unbekanntes ist."

74. John M. Efron places this controversy within the larger question over who has control of Jewish bodies: "It was with the burial ordinance of 1772 that the German state attempted to wrest control of the Jewish body from the Jews. And as it would turn out, the Haskalah ... was generally able to provide Jewish support for government initiatives"; Efron, "Images of the Jewish Body: Three Medical Views from the Jewish Enlightenment," *Bulletin of the History of Medicine* (1995), p. 366.

75. Samuel T. Sömmerring, "Sur le supplice de la Guillotine: lettre de M. Soemmering á M. Oelsner," in *Magasin encyclopédique* (Paris, 1795), vol. 3, p. 469. Sömmerring contested the proposition that the guillotine is the method of execution that is "plus sure, la plus rapide et la moins douloureuse."

76. Oelsner's statements were printed in *Magasin encyclopédique*, vol. 3 (1795), pp. 463–77, Sue's in *Magasin encyclopédique*, vol. 4 (1795), pp. 170–89.

77. Sömmerring, "Sur le supplice," p. 469.

78. Sömmerring, "Sur le supplice," p. 465.

79. Sömmerring, "Sur le supplice," pp. 473, 469.

80. Oelsner, "Oelsner aux rédacteurs," p. 466.

81. Sue, "Opinion du citoyen Sue sur le supplice de la guillotine," p. 187.

82. Ludmilla Jordanova, "Medical Mediations: Mind, Body and the Guillotine," in *Nature Displayed: Gender, Science and Medicine 1760–1820* (London: Longman, 1999), p. 119.

83. Both Herz and Hufeland were proponents of *Leichenhäuser*. Johann Metzger, a sometimes opponent of Hufeland (he considered *Leichenhäuser* a modern form of purgatory, arguing that *Scheintode* should be kept at home under the watchful eyes of the family), proposed a plan to construct *Rettungsanstalten* all over Germany. Legislation concerning burial customs based on a minimum of a three-day waiting period were passed throughout Germany.

84. Hufeland, "Scheintod," p. 301.

85. Paul B. Salmon, "The Beginnings of Morphology: Linguistic Botanizing in the 18th Century," *Historiographia Linguistica* I, no. 33 (1974), p. 326.

86. Jean Baptiste Robinet, *Vue philosophique de la gradation naturelle des formes d'être, ou les essais de la nature qui apprend a faire l'homme* (Amsterdam, 1768), p. 8.

87. Quoted by Roger, *Sciences de la vie*, pp. 644, 646.

88. Robinet, *Vue philosophique*, pp. 6, 7.

89. *D'Alembert's Dream*, in *Rameau's Nephew and Other Works*, trans. Jacques Barzun and Ralph Bowen (Indianapolis: Bobbs-Merrill, 1964), p. 97

90. *D'Alembert's Dream*, p. 97.

91. *D'Alembert's Dream*, p. 93.

92. *D'Alembert's Dream*, p. 124.

93. *D'Alembert's Dream*, p. 123.

94. *D'Alembert's Dream*, pp. 134–35.
95. *D'Alembert's Dream*, p. 132.
96. *D'Alembert's Dream*, pp. 129–30.
97. Herder, *Ideen zur der Geschichte der Menschheit*, in *Herder's Sämmtliche Werke*, ed. Bernhard Suphan, vols. XIII–XIV (Berlin, 1887–1909), vol. XIV, p. x.
98. There are some authors who have taken Herder's scientific writings seriously, most notably Hugh B. Nisbet in his *Herder and the Philosophy and History of Science*, Modern Humanities Research Association: Dissertation Series 3 (Cambridge: Modern Humanities Research Association, 1970). This was a pioneering work but still tended to place Herder's interests closer to "pseudo-science" than to normal science. Most scholars tend to avoid the scientific side of Herder's thought, focusing instead upon his theories of art, poetry, and language. Usually he receives the most extensive treatment in histories of historicism, where his scientific interests are virtually ignored. For a corrective see Eva Knodt, "Hermeneutics and the End of Science: Herder's Role in the Formation of Natur- and Geisteswissenschaften," in *Johann Gottfried Herder and the Disciplines of Knowledge*, ed. Wulf Koepke (Columbia, S.C.: Camden House, 1996). John Zammito, *Kant, Herder and the Birth of Anthropology* (Chicago: University of Chicago Press, 2001) convincingly brings Herder back into the core of the Enlightenment and points to his command of the scientific literature of the time.
99. Isaiah Berlin, "The Counter-Enlightenment," in *Against the Current: Essays in the History of Ideas,* ed. Henry Hardy (New York: Penguin, 1982), pp. 1–25. Berlin expands upon this theme in his book *Vico and Herder: Two Studies in the History of Ideas* (New York: Viking Press, 1976).
100. A list of some of the people Herder cited provides an insight into his command of this language. They included Buffon, Maupertuis, Needham, Daubenton, Haller, Bonnet, Caspar Friedrich Wolff, Reimarus, Priestley, Monro, Monboddo, Blumenbach, Sömmerring, Camper, Forster, Platner, Metzger, and Pallas. For discussions of Herder's use of science see Hans Dietrich Irmscher, "Aneignung und Kritik naturwissenschaftlicher Vorstellungen bei Herder," in *Texte, Motive und Gestalten der Goethezeit: Festschrift für Hans Reiss,* ed. John L. Hibberd and Hugh B. Nisbet (Tübingen: Max Niemeyer, 1989), pp. 33–63, and his "Beobachtunegn zur Funktion der Analogie im Denken Herders," *Deutsche Vierteljahrschrift für Literaturwissenschaft und Geistesgeschichte* 55 (1981), pp. 64–97, and *Herder and the Philosophy and History of Science.*
101. Herder, *Ideen zur Philosophie der Geschichte der Menschheit* (Berlin and Weimar: Aufbau Verlag, 1965), *Sämmtliche Werke*, vol. 13, p. 276.
102. Herder, *Sämmtliche Werke*, vol. 13, p. 16.
103. Herder, *Sämmtliche Werke*, vol. 13, p. 108.
104. Herder, *Sämmtliche Werke*, vol. 13, p. 167.
105. "Is it eternally determined that from the beginning of creation, the flower should always be a flower, the animal always an animal, all lying

mechanically in preformed germs [Keime]. If so, then good bye [lebe wohl] to the magical expectation of an eternal being! For the present and for no higher existence lay I eternally in a preformed germ: should just the preformed germs of my children spring from me; and if the tree dies does the whole philosophy of the germs die with it?" Herder, *Sämmtliche Werke*, vol. 13, p. 166.

106. Herder, *Sämmtliche Werke*, vol. 13, p. 174.
107. Herder, *Sämmtliche Werke*, vol. 13, p. 177.
108. Herder, *Sämmtliche Werke*, vol. 13, p. 177.
109. Herder, *Sämmtliche Werke*, vol. 13, p. 167.
110. Herder, *Sämmtliche Werke*, vol. 13, p. 177.
111. Herder, *Sämmtliche Werke*, 13, pp. 65–66.
112. Herder, *Sämmtliche Werke*, vol. 13, pp. 65–66.
113. Herder, *Sämmtliche Werke*, vol. 13, pp. 66–67.
114. Herder, *Sämmtliche Werke*, vol. 13, pp. 258, 257.
115. Herder, *Sämmtliche Werke*, vol. 13, p. 173.

116. Roselyne Rey, "La récapitulation chez les physiologists et les naturalistes allemands de la fin du XVIIIe et du début du XIXe siècle," in *Histoire du concept de Récapitulation*, ed. P. Mengel (Paris: Éditions la Découverte, 1993), p. 47.

117. Kielmeyer was trained in the Karlsschule in Stuttgart, where he was a classmate of Cuvier, whom he befriended. After graduating from the Karlsschule, Kielmeyer spent two years at Göttingen, where he studied with Blumenbach and Lichtenberg. Subsequently he traveled widely in Germany, where he met some of the leaders of the German Enlightenment, including Goethe. Upon his return to Stuttgart, he was appointed professor of physiology and chemistry at the Karlsschule. When it was closed, he moved to the university. Kielmeyer did not publish much, but his lectures were distributed throughout Germany and therefore won him great renown. A good example of historians overlooking him is that Ernst Haeckel did not refer to him in his study of the origins of Darwinian thought, though Kielmeyer clearly proposed what Heackel called the basic biological law. Instead Haeckel concentrated on Goethe and Lamarck.

118. The view of Kielmeyer as a Romantic *Naturphilosoph* is partly explained by Schelling's high opinion of him. This direct linkage was enshrined in the 1938 published collection of Kielmeyer's writings: *Carl Friedrich Kielmeyer, Gesammelte Schriften: In Natur und Kraft. Die Lehre von der Entwicklung organische Naturlehre*, ed. Fritz-Heinz Holler (Berlin: Keiper, 1938). It appeared in a series entitled *Schöpferische Romantik*. Lenoir ties Kielmeyer to Kant and Blumenbach (whom he sees as a Kantian) in *The Strategy of Life*. He discusses him as a Romantic in "Generational Factors in the Origin of *Romantische Naturphilosophie*," *Journal of the History of Biology* 11 (1978). He calls Kielmeyer's important essay "Ueber die Verhälniße der organischen Kräfte untereinander in der Reihe der verschiedenen Organizationen: die Gesetze und Folgen dieser Verhältniße" "one of the milestones of the

Romantic era" (p. 164). Dorothea Kuhn, William Coleman, and Nicholas Jardine see Kielmeyer as a transitional figure. They present these views in Dorothea Kuhn, "Uhrwerk oder Organismus: Karl Friedrich Kielmeyers System der organischen Kräfte," in *Nova Acta Leopoldina: Abhandlungen der deutschen Akademie der Naturforscher Leopoldina*, Neue Folge, no. 198, vol. 36 (Leipzig: Johann Ambrosius Barth, 1970), pp. 157–67; William Coleman, "Limits of the Recapitulation Theory: Carl Friedrich Kielmeyer's Critique of the Presumed Parallelism of Earth History, Ontogeny, and the Present Order of Organisms," *Isis* 64 (1973): 341–50; Nicholas Jardine, *The Scenes of Inquiry: On the Reality of Questions in the Sciences*, 2nd ed. (Oxford: Clarendon Press, 2000), pp. 36–37, 51.

119. Kielmeyer, "Geschichte und Theorie der Entwicklung," in *Gesammelte Schriften*, p. 122.

120. Kielmeyer, *Gesammelte Schriften*, p. 228.

121. According to Lenoir, "anyone wishing to understand the biology of this period would do well to examine it carefully"; *Strategy of Life*, p. 44.

122. Kielmeyer, *Verhältniße der organischen Kräfte*, p. 250.

123. Kielmeyer, *Verhältniße der organischen Kräfte*, p. 251. In the "Entwicklungsgeschichte," he characterized it as follows: "und statt die Ursachen solcher Klassen von Erscheinungen angeben zu können, ist man genötigt, den Raum für dieselben einstweilen leer zu lassen, unsere Unbekanntschaft mit ihrem Wesen durch das Wort Kraft und unser weniges Wissen von ihnen auszudrücken, daß wird ihnen die Gesetze der Erscheinungen, sofern sie auch Gesetze der Wirkungweise der Ursache sind, als Attribute beilegen"; *Gesammelte Schriften*, p. 118.

124. Kielmeyer, *Verhältniße der organischen Kräfte*, p. 251.

125. Kielmeyer, *Verhältniße der organischen Kräfte*, p. 254.

126. Kielmeyer, *Verhältniße der organischen Kräfte*, pp. 255, 256, 258, 259.

127. Kielmeyer, *Verhältniße der organischen Kräfte*, p. 253.

128. Kielmeyer, *Verhältniße der organischen Kräfte*, p. 261.

129. Kielmeyer, *Verhältniße der organischen Kräfte*, p. 261.

130. Kielmeyer, *Gesammelte Schriften*, p. 208.

131. Kielmeyer, *Gesammelte Schriften*, p. 209.

132. Kielmeyer, *Gesammelte Schriften*, pp. 263, 209.

133. Lenoir, *Strategy of Life*, p. 50.

134. Richard Burkhardt, Jr., points out the early agreement between Lamarck and Cuvier in "Lamarck and Species," in Atran, *Historie du concept d'espèce dans les sciences de la vie*, p. 173. His excellent study of Lamarck, *The Spirit of System*, makes it clear how Lamarck changed his views from vitalism to a form of biological mechanism in the first decade of the nineteenth century. In this shift Lamarck surrendered the idea of the radical distinction between living and dead matter, took back his critique of the great chain of being, and sought to develop simple mechanical laws explaining species development.

135. Burkhardt, *The Spirit of System*, p. 193.

136. Burkhardt, "Lamarck and Species," p. 166.
137. Quoted by John Hedley Brooke, *Science and Religion: Some Historical Perspectives* (Cambridge: Cambridge University Press, 1991), p. 242.
138. Brooke, *Science and Religion*, p. 242.

5. FROM ENLIGHTENMENT VITALISM
TO ROMANTIC *NATURPHILOSOPHIE*

1. Andrew Bowie sums up this renewed interest in *Naturphilosophie* as follows: "The reasons why his [Schelling's] thought still matters to philosophy relate, then, to the contemporary suspicion, reflected in the growing interest in Nietzsche, Heidegger, Horkheimer and Adorno, that Western rationality has proven to be a narcissistic illusion, which is at the root of 'nihilism,' the 'forgetting of being,' the 'universal context of delusion,' and the ecological crises: in short, of the ills of modernity"; *Schelling and Modern European Philosophy: An Introduction* (London: Routledge, 1993), p. 10. Philip Rehbock also points to the overlapping interests of *Naturphilosophie* and "ecologists and environmentalists of the present day"; *The Philosophic Naturalists: Themes in Early Nineteenth-Century Biology* (Madison: University of Wisconsin Press, 1983), p. 18. This impulse informs the work of Klaus Meyer-Abich. See his *Revolution for Nature: From the Environment to the Connatural World*, trans. Mathew Armstrong (Cambridge: White Horse Press, 1993).
2. Horkheimer, "Reason against Itself," p. 360.
3. See Richard Heckmann's *Vorwort* to the volume he, Hermann Krings, and Rudolf Meyer edited: *Natur und Subjektivität: zur Auseinandersetzung mit der Naturphilosophie des jungen Schelling. Referate, Voten und Protokolle des II. Internationalen Schelling-Tagung Zürich 1983* (Stuttgart: Frommann-Holzboog, 1985), pp. 7–8. Toulmin argues in a similar vein in *Cosmopolis*.
4. Nicholas Jardine, *The Scenes of Inquiry: On the Reality of Questions in the Sciences*, 2nd ed. (Oxford: Clarendon Press, 2000), pp. 51–56. Also see his article "Inner History; or How to End Enlightenment." Although Jardine gives a much more positive spin to *Naturphilosophie*, especially in "Inner History," than I do, I believe our evaluation of the breach separating *Naturphilosophie* from the Enlightenment is very similar.
5. Immanuel Kant, *Metaphysische Anfangsgründe der Naturwissenschaften* (Riga: Johann Friedrich Hartknoch, 1786), p. 48.
6. Henricus Adrianus Marie Snelders, "Atomismus und Dynamismus im Zeitalter der Deutschen Romantischen Naturphilosophie," in *Romantik in Deutschland: ein interdisziplinäres Symposium*, ed. Richard Brinkmann (Stuttgart: Metzlersche Verlagsbuchhandlung, 1978), p. 190.
7. Keilmeyer, *Gesammelte Schriften*, p. 245.
8. Quoted in Hermann Krings, "Natur als Subjekt: ein Grundzug der spekulativen Physik Schellings," in Heckmann et al., *Natur und Subjektivität*, p. 114.
9. In this issue Kant's position still revealed the epistemological modesty

central to the late Enlightenment. As Alexander Gode–von Aesch, an astute commentator on *Naturphilosophie*, remarked, "the characteristic epistemological resignation of the Eighteenth Century . . . reached its philosophical fulfillment in Kant's criticism, with its concise definition of the limits of human understanding. . . . Indeed, the motif of the 'vanity of confidence in opinion,' of the 'brevity and uncertainty of our knowledge,' of the 'falseness of human powers,' of 'the weakness of the human mind'—to put it in phrases gleaned from titles of works in eighteenth- and seventeenth-century literature—can be pursued throughout the Eighteenth Century until it crystallizes in Kant's criticism"; Alexander Gode–von Aesch, *Natural Science in German Romanticism* (New York: Columbia University Press, 1941), pp. 95–96.

10. Kant, *Critique of Judgment*, trans. and introduction by John H. Bernard (New York: Hafner Press, 1951), p. 268; *Kant's Werke*, 9 vols. (Berlin: Walter der Gruyter, 1968), vol. 5, p. 419. I have modified the translation in the first part of the first quotation. Bernard and Meredith both translate *Abenteuer* as "venture." I prefer "adventure," for I believe it better captures the negative connotations of the word for Kant, usually associated by him with romance.

11. Leibniz's position in the German Enlightenment was highly ambivalent. As the supposed source for Wolffian philosophy, he was rejected by most late-eighteenth-century thinkers. They disparaged his seemingly rationalistic and metaphysical stance, a reproach that was strong in a period that witnessed what William Clark and Mary Terrall call the death of metaphysics. At the same time, some authors discovered a "new" Leibniz, the author of the *Nouveau essais*, whose reflections on epistemology they found fascinating. Still, for many late Enlightenment naturalists Leibniz's defense of preformation, which he repeated in the *Nouveau essais*, put him in the opponents' camp. For the rehabilitation of Leibniz after the publication of the *essais* in 1765 see Ernst Cassirer, *The Philosophy of the Enlightenment*, trans. Fritz C. Koelln and James P. Pettegrove (Princeton: Princeton University Press, 1951); John Zammito, *Kant, Herder, and the Birth of Anthropology* (Chicago: University of Chicago Press, 2001).

12. Most modern commentators agree that the *Naturphilosophen* were on top of the latest developments in chemistry, geology, physics—especially electricity and magnetism—and the life sciences. See Dietrich von Engelhardt, "Die organischen Natur und die Lebenswissenschaften in Schellings Naturphilosophie," in Heckman et al., *Natur und Subjektivität*, pp. 39–59.

13. Nicolas Jardine points to the different epistemological concerns separating Enlightenment naturalists (he focuses upon what he calls the Blumenbach-Kant scheme) and the *Naturphilosophen* by contrasting the different questions they posed. After listing the Enlightenment questions, he adds: "On the other hand, a considerable body of fundamental questions is explicitly invalidated, being declared to be in principle beyond the range of evidential considerations. Thus excluded are all questions concerning the relations between God and the natural world, along with questions about the underlying reasons for the apparent harmony between mechanism and purposive for-

mation in living beings, all questions about the inner nature and origin of the vital forces and their immanence in living matter and all questions about the way in which the original organizations themselves came into being"; *Scenes of Inquiry*, pp. 53–54.

14. "Ueber Kant und die Deutsche Naturphilosophie 1807: Schreiben Kielmeyers an Cuvier," in *Gesammelte Schriften*, p. 252.

15. Quoted by Nicolas Jardine in "Naturphilosophen and the Kingdoms of Nature," in Jardine et al., *Cultures of Natural History*, p. 233.

16. Lorenz Oken, *Abriss der Naturphilosophie: Bestimmt zur Grundlage seiner Vorlesungen über Biologie* (Göttingen, 1805), p. vii. Unlike Schelling, who stopped writing about *Naturphilosophie* very quickly after his pathbreaking works appeared, Oken became the central figure for *Naturphilosophic* sciences during the first half of the century, partly because of his writings, partly because of his activities as founder of the journal *Isis* and of the "Gesellschaft deutscher Naturforscher and Aerzte," probably the most important scientific organization in the first half of the century. When *Naturphilosophie* finally reached British shores, it was often through Oken's writings, especially after the 1847 English translation of his *Elements of Physio-Philosophy*. Thus Robert Knox would write, "Since then . . . the doctrines of this worthy and simpleminded enthusiast have been the rage in England, taken up *con furore* on this side of the channel so soon as they had been laid down on the other"; quoted by Philip Rehbock, *The Philosophical Naturalists*, p. 39.

17. They included *Abriss der Naturphilosophie; Abriss des Systems der Biologie: zum Behufe seiner Vorlesungen* (Göttingen, 1805); *Die Zeugung* (Bamberg and Würzburg, 1805); *Ueber Licht und Wärme als das nicht irdische, aber kosmische materiale Element: erste Ideen zur Theorie des Lichts der Finsterniss, der Farben und der Wärme* (Jena, 1808); *Ueber das Universum als Fortsetzung des Sinnensystems: ein pythagoräisches Fragment* (Jena: Friedrich Frommann,1808); *Lehrbuch der Naturphilosophie* (Jena, 1809).

18. Oken, *Abriss der Naturphilosophie*, p. 1.

19. Friedrich Wilhelm Schelling, *Von der Weltseele, eine Hypothese der höheren Physik zur Erklärung des allgemeinen Organismus: nebst einer Abhandlung über das Verhältniß des Realen und Idealen in der Natur oder Entwicklung der ersten Grundsätze der Naturphilosophie an den Principien der Schwere und des Lichts*, 3rd ed. (Hamburg, 1809), p. vi.

20. Schelling, *Erster Entwurf eines Systems der Naturphilosophie: zum Behuf seiner Vorlesungen* (Jena and Leipzig, 1799), p. 29.

21. Nicholas Jardine confronting the incomprehensibility of the *naturphilosophic* formulations remarked: "too few of the questions they addressed are, by our lights, real questions; too few of their beliefs are for us even candidates for truth"; *Scenes of Inquiry*, p. 51

22. For example see Reinhard Löw, "Qualitätenlehre und Materiekonstruktion: zur systematischen Aktualität von Schellings Naturphilosophie,"in Hassler, *Schelling*, pp. 99–106; Hans Poser, "Spekulative Physik und Erfahrung: Zum Verhältnis von Experiment und Theorie in Schellings Naturphilosophie," in

Hassler, *Schelling*, pp. 129–38; Karl E. Rothschuh, "Deutsche Medizin im Zeitalter der Romantik: Vielheit statt Einheit," in Hassler, *Schelling*, pp. 145–51; Dietrich von Engelhardt, "Romantik im Spannugsfeld von Naturgefühl, Naturwissenschaft und Naturphilosophie," in Brinkmann, *Romantik in Deutschland*, pp. 167–74.

23. Quoted by Hans Poser, "Spekulative Physik und Erfahrung," in Hassler, *Schelling*, p. 133.

24. Johann Jakob Wagner, *Theodicee* (Bamberg and Würzburg, 1809), pp. 16–17.

25. Novalis quoted by John Neubauer, *Symbolismus und Symbolische Logik: die Idee der Ars Combinatoria in der Entwicklung der modernen Dichtung* (Munich: Wilhelm Fink Verlag, 1978), p. 83; "preestablished harmony" from Neubauer, "Zwischen Natur und mathematischer Abstraktion: der Potenzbegriff in der Frühromantik," in Brinkmann, *Romantik in Deutschland*, p. 176.

26. Neubauer, *Symbolismus und Symbolische Logik*, p. 67.

27. Wagner, *Theodicee*, p. 31.

28. Schelling, *Von der Weltseele*, p. vi.

29. Schelling, *Erster Entwurf eines Systems der Naturphilosophie*, p. 6.

30. Wagner, *Von der Natur der Dinge* (Leipzig, 1803), pp. xvi–xvii.

31. Wagner, *Theodicee*, p. 19.

32. Wagner, *Theorie der Wärme und des Lichts* (Leipzig, 1802), pp. 3–4.

33. Dietrich Tiedemann, *Geist der spekulativen Philosophie*, 6 vols. (Marburg, 1791–97).

34. Tiedemann, *Philosophie*, vol. 6, p. 417.

35. Neubauer, *Symbolismus und Symbolische Logik*, pp. 42–51.

36. Oken, *Lehrbuch der Naturphilosophie*, pp. 3–4.

37. Oken, *Lehrbuch der Naturphilosophie*, p. 5.

38. Oken, *Lehrbuch der Naturphilosophie*, p. 6.

39. Oken, *Lehrbuch der Naturphilosophie*, pp. 10, 11.

40. Oken, *Lehrbuch der Naturphilosophie*, p. 11.

41. Schelling, *Erster Entwurf eines Systems der Naturphilosophie*, p. 4.

42. Oken, *Lehrbuch der Naturphilosophie*, p. 13.

43. Of course, the term had not yet acquired all of the connotations Hegel would later give it, but it was well on its way. In chemistry it described the merging of different elements to form a new chemical compound. Thus oxygen and hydrogen were *aufgehoben* in water. Schelling is said to have formulated the term in a manner similar to Hegel.

44. Jardine, *Scenes of Inquiry*, p. 44.

45. Oken, *Lehrbuch der Naturphilosophie*, pp. 15–16.

46. Quoted by Neubauer, *Symbolismus und symbolische Logik*, p. 78.

47. Carl von Eschenmayer, *Versuch die scheinbare Magie des thierischen Magnetismus aus physiologischen und psychischen Gesezen zu erklären* (Stuttgart and Tübingen, 1816), p. 4.

48. Wagner, *Von der Natur der Dinge*, p. xi.

49. Quoted by Bowie, *Schelling*, p. 39.

50. Wagner, *Theorie der Wärme und Lichts*, p. 9. There was a radical difference between explanations and constructions. According to Schelling, explanations were trapped in the world of observed reality. A construction leaves empiricism and turns instead to the *absolute* a priori, to the activity where one "deduces the effects from this known, and assumed independent cause.... The concept of an explanation for a natural phenomenon should totally disappear from true natural science. In mathematics one does not explain, one proves. The proof—the construction—is the explanation"; quoted by Poser, "Spekulative Physik und Erfahrung," p. 134.

51. Schelling, quoted by Poser, "Spekulative Physik und Erfahrung," p. 131.

52. Schelling, *Erster Entwurf eines Systems der Naturphilosophie*, p. 10.

53. Schelling, *Von der Weltseele*, pp. 26–27.

54. Dietrich von Engelhardt, *Hegel und die Chemie: Studien zur Philosophie und Wissenschaft der Natur um 1800* (Wiesbaden: Pressler, 1976); Peter Kapitza, *Die frühromantische Theorie der Mischung: über die Zusammenhang von romantischen Dichtungstheorie und zeitgenössichen Chemie* (Munich: M. Hueber, 1968).

55. Schelling, *Erster Entwurf eines Systems der Naturphilosophie*, p. 73.

56. Schelling, *Von der Weltseele*, p. 41.

57. Schelling, *Erster Entwurf Naturphilosophie*, pp. 78–79.

58. Oken, *Universum als Fortsetzung*, p. 17.

59. Schelling, *Erster Entwurf eines Systems der Naturphilosophie*, p. 75.

60. Schelling, *Von der Weltseele*, p. xx.

61. Christian Gottfried Nees von Esenbeck, Carl Gustav Bischof, and Heinrich August Rothe, *Die Entwickelung der Pflanzensubstanz physiologisch, chemisch und mathematisch dargestellt mit combinatorischen Tafeln der möglichen Pflanzenstoffe und den Gesetzen ihrer stöchiometrischen Zusammensetzung* (Erlangen, 1819), p. 8.

62. Schelling, *Von der Weltseele*, p. 165.

63. Schelling, *Von der Weltseele*, p. 169.

64. Oken, *Lehrbuch der Naturphilosophie*, pp. 79–83.

65. Oken, *Universum als Fortsetzung*, pp. 19–20.

66. Schelling, *Von der Weltseele*, p. xlv.

67. Oken, *Universum als Fortsetzung*, p. 7.

68. Jardine provides a vivid example of this type of reaction in his recounting of his first confrontation with Oken's *Lehrbuch der Naturphilosophie*; *Scenes of Inquiry*, p. 1. Jardine, despite his initial confusing confrontation with Oken, provides such an interpretation demonstrating their contribution in "Inner History."

69. Bowie, *Schelling*, p. 45.

70. Schelling, *Erster Entwurf eines Systems der Naturphilosophie*, p. 13.

71. Schelling, *Erster Entwurf eines Systems der Naturphilosophie*, pp. 11, 12. My translation of the last phrase is a clumsy attempt to render what Schelling means by "erscheinend vorüberschwindend."

72. Schelling, *Erster Entwurf eines Systems der Naturphilosophie*, p. 67.
73. Schelling, *Erster Entwurf eines Systems der Naturphilosophie*, p. 5.
74. Schelling, *Erster Entwurf eines Systems der Naturphilosophie*, p. 89.
75. Schelling, *Erster Entwurf eines Systems der Naturphilosophie*, p. 41.
76. Schelling, *Erster Entwurf eines Systems der Naturphilosophie*, p. 59.
77. Engelhardt, "Die organischen Natur und die Lebenswissenschaften," p. 50.
78. Schelling, *Erster Entwurf eines Systems der Naturphilosophie*, p. 35.
79. Eschenmayer, *Die Philosophie in ihrem Uebergang zur Nichtphilosophie* (Erlangen, 1803), p. 84.
80. Oken, *Die Zeugung*, p. 89.
81. Quoted by Jardine, *Scenes of Inquiry*, p. 44.
82. Jardine, *Scenes of Inquiry*, p. 44.
83. Schelling, *Erster Entwurf eines Systems der Naturphilsophie*, p. 134.
84. Schelling, *Erster Entwurf eines Systems der Naturphilosophie*, pp. 89, 48–49.
85. In contrast to Oken, who remained extremely active in propagating *Naturphilosophie* during his very productive lifetime, Schelling virtually abandoned the *naturphilosophic* project in the second decade of the century. Thus, I believe it safe to assume that more educated Germans learned the principles of *Naturphilosophie* from Oken than from Schelling. It is for this reason that he occupies such a prominent role in this analysis.
86. Oken, *Lehrbuch der Naturphilosophie*, p. 31.
87. Oken, *Lehrbuch der Naturphilosophie*, p. 34.
88. Oken, *Lehrbuch der Naturphilosophie*, pp. 35–36.
89. Oken, *Theorie des Lichts*, p. 10.
90. Schelling, *Von der Weltseele*, p. xxxvii.
91. Oken, *Lehrbuch der Naturphilosophie*, p. 17. In Oken's terms, the positive is the "ponirende Idee," the negative, "die ponirte." In my translation I have replaced these terms, which are rather obscure with their equivalents.
92. Oken, *Lehrbuch der Naturphilosophie*, pp. 63, 64.
93. Oken, *Lehrbuch der Naturphilosophie*, p. 70.
94. Oken, *Lehrbuch der Naturphilosophie*, p. 68.
95. Oken, *Lehrbuch der Naturphilosophie*, pp. 73–74.
96. Blumenbach was well aware of Hogarth's definition. It had been popularized in Germany by his teacher and colleague Georg Lichtenberg in his brilliant commentaries on Hogarth, *Georg C. Lichtenberg's ausfürliche Erklärung der Hogarthischen Kupferstiche: mit verkleinerten aber vollständigen Copien derselben* (Göttingen, 1794).
97. Blumenbach, *Ueber den Bildungstrieb*, p. 3.
98. Blumenbach still held the first chair of medicine in Göttingen, had trained two generations of medical men who had received academic positions throughout Germany, and kept his position until his death in 1841. Oken had taught in Göttingen the year he published this work. In *Die Zeugung*, Oken is very careful to praise Blumnebach's contribution, though his whole argument

denies Blumenbach's position. According to Oken, "Dieser Mann [Blumenbach] war der erste und einzige, der sich mit Muth und Geist der rohen Mechanistik, die sich in die Physiologie eingedrungen, entgegenstellt, und ob sie gleich überall feste Wurzel getrieben hatte, doch bis auf den Grund ausrottete." Despite such praise, most of the *Naturphilosphen* hardly employed Blumenbach's categories. This was especially true for the German adherents of Brownian medicine.

99. The choice of an Aristotlean or a Hippocratian version of epigenesis had contradictory gender implications. The same was true if one chose ovist preformation over spermist preformation. One of the reasons that the mid-eighteenth-century natural philosopher Köhlreuter was so opposed to preformation was his belief that preformation in its dominant ovist form had elevated women above men.

100. Thomas Laqueur, *Making Sex: Body and Gender from the Greeks to Freud* (Cambridge, Mass: Harvard University Press, 1990), p. 150.

101. Jordanova, *Sexual Visions*, pp. 50–51.

102. Jordanova, *Sexual Visions*, p. 25.

103. Anne-Charlott Trepp, *Sanfte Männlichkeit und selbstständige Weiblichkeit: Frauen und Männer im Hamburger Bürgertum zwischen 1770 and 1840* (Göttingen: Vandenhoeck & Ruprecht, 1996).

104. Friedrich von Gentz to Rahel Varnhagen in *Rahel Varnhagen im Umgang mit ihren Freunden (Briefe 1793–1808)*, ed. Friedhelm Kemp (Munich: Kosel Verlag, 1967), p. 122.

105. Wilhelm von Humboldt, *Gesammelte Schriften*, ed. Albert Leitzmann, 17 vols. (Berlin: B. Behr's Verlag, 1903–36) vol. 1, pp. 311, 314.

106. W. von Humboldt, *Gesammelte Schriften*, vol. 1, pp. 328–29.

107. Again, I would like to emphasize that there was no hierarchical difference between these two forms of knowledge for Humboldt. In fact, he is considered one of the great early-nineteenth-century theorists of history. For him both history and language were classified "feminine," the two areas where he made his greatest contribution.

108. "Biology of sexual differentiation" from Lacqueur, *Making Sex*, p. 171. For an example of these critics, see Claudia Honegger, *Die Ordnung der Geschlechter: die Wissenschaften vom Menschen und das Weib, 1750–1850* (Frankfurt: Campus, 1991), pp. 182–84.

109. W. von Humboldt, *Gesammelte Schriften*, vol. 1, p. 329.

110. W. von Humboldt, *Gesammelte Schriften*, vol. 1, p. 321.

111. W. von Humboldt, *Gesammelte Schriften*, vol. 1, p. 321. In this reverie Humboldt indulged in sadistic dreams of control and enslavement. Yet it is interesting that the object of this fantasy were physically strong women, not the passive, slave girl model common to such fantasies. In his later life he did indulge in such fantasies.

112. W. von Humboldt, *Gesammelte Schriften*, vol. 1, p. 322.

113. W. von Humboldt, *Briefe an Karl Gustav von Brinckmann*, p. 30.

114. W. von Humboldt, *Gesammelte Schriften*, vol. 15, pp. 451–60.

115. Schiller, probably the most important role model for the young Humboldt, also used the language of hybridity to describe himself. In a letter to Goethe he wrote, "My mind works in a symbolizing way, and so I hover, like a kind of hybrid, between concept and contemplation, between law and feeling"; quoted by Reginald Snell in his introduction to Friedrich Schiller, *On the Aesthetic Education of Man* (New York: Friedrich Ungar, 1954), p. 6.

116. W. von Humboldt, *Gesammelte Schriften,* vol. 1, p. 328.

117. W. von Humboldt, *Gesammelte Schriften,* vol. 1, pp. 333–34.

118. An incident in Oken's personal life might reveal this yearning for more clearly defined gender relations. Oken broke off his first engagement with a very well placed young woman because she did not meet his vision of what a woman's tasks should be. He had visited her and his shirt had been ripped. He expected that she would automatically go upstairs and mend it, which she did not. He considered this a great affront to him and to his honor, which led him to cancel the engagement.

119. As far as I can tell, Laqueur mentions the *Naturphilosophen* only once, and I believe incorrectly characterizes their efforts: "The Naturphilosophen thus seemed to be right in viewing sexual difference as one of the fundamental dichotomies of nature, an unbridgeable chasm born not of Pythagorean opposites but of the reproductive germs themselves and the organs that produced them"; *Making Sex,* p. 172. I would argue that the opposite is true, namely, that they viewed the world in Pythagorean opposites and paid very little attention to the reproductive organs and germs.

120. Schelling, *Erster Entwurf eines Systems der Naturphilosophie,* p. 43.

121. Oken, *Die Zeugung,* p. 110.

122. Oken, *Die Zeugung,* pp. 23, 51. "Es wird sich später zeigen, dass mit dem Acte der Befruchtung d.h. sobald sich das Ei mit dem Samen vereinigt hat, der ganze Embryo mit einem Schlage entsteht, obgleich es wegen seiner Durchsichtigkeit unsichtbar bleibt; daher ist es begreiflich, dass, wie durch Essig, oder unter dem Mikroskop sich etwas zeigt, es schon die ganze Form der Theile des Embryo habe, und nicht erst nach und nach gebildet werde, woraus man mithin nie berechtigt ist, ein Gebildetsein vor der Befruchtung zu behaupten."

123. Oken, *Die Zeugung,* pp. 91, 216.

124. Oken took this idea from Schelling: Schelling, *Von der Weltseele,* p. xlix.

125. Oken, *Die Zeugung,* pp. 112–13.

126. Oken, *Die Zeugung,* p. 13. "Nothing, whether it be magnitude nor matter can change over to its absolute opposite."

127. Oken, *Die Zeugung,* p. 133.

128. Oken, *Die Zeugung,* p. 133.

129. Oken, *Die Zeugung,* p. 166. He also added that these discoveries would go far to save lives. One should not cut the placenta until one is sure the child can breath and if there is any problem providing immediate nourishment to the newborn child, one should cover its nipples with milk.

130. Oken, *Die Zeugung*, pp. 140–42.

131. Carus, born in 1789, became Professor for "Frauenkunde" in Dresden in 1814 and director of its laying-in hospital. He held these positions until 1827, when he was appointed physician to the king. He died in 1869. Carus is often considered the person who coined the term "gynecology" and was certainly the first to use it in a textbook.

132. Carl Gustav Carus, *Natur und Idee, oder das Werdende und sein Gesetz: eine philosophische Grundlage für die specielle Naturwissenchaft* (Vienna, 1861), p. v. "Was nun mich selbst und meine Bestrebungen für philosophisches Erkennen des ewig Werdenden betrifft, so darf ich wohl sagen, daß schon meine frühesten naturwissenschaftlichen Studien, welche in das erste Decennium diese Jahrhunderts fielen, lebhaft den Hauch der Erfrischung und neuer und geistiger Anregung empfanden, welcher namentlich durch Schelling und Oken damals über Alles jener Art sich zu verbreiten begann. Aber ich darf auch hinzufügen, daß selbst in dieser Periode ein richtiges Gefühl, und vielleicht zugleich ein damals namentlich durch E. Platner angeregter und vertheidigter Skepticismus, mich davor bewahrte, in jene Ueberschwenglichkeiten zu verfallen, von denen selbst Oken, trotz seines scharfen, mit reichem Material genährten Geistes sich nicht frei machen konnte."

133. Carl Gustav Carus, *Lehrbuch der Gynäkologie oder systematischen Darstellung der Lehren von Erkenntniß und Behandlung eigenthümlicher gesunder und krankhafter Zustände, sowohl der nicht schwangern, schwangern und gebärenden Frauen, als der Wöchnerinnen und neugebornen Kinder* (Leipzig, 1820), p. 4.

134. Hegel illustrates how the images of the male as animal-like and the female as plantlike or vegetative became commonly accepted by those influenced by *Naturphilosophie*. According to Londa Schiebinger, "Hegel compared the male mind to an animal that acquires knowledge only through struggle and technical exertion. The female mind, by contrast, does not (cannot) rise above its plantlike existence and remains rooted in its an sich experience (*Grundlinien der Philosophie des Rechts* [1821] in his *Werke*, vol. 7, pp. 319–320)"; *The Mind Has No Sex? Women in the Origins of Modern Science* (Cambridge, Mass: Harvard University Press, 1989), p. 241.

135. Carus, *Lehrbuch*, p. 41.
136. Carus, *Lehrbuch*, p. 46.
137. Carus, *Lehrbuch*, pp. 40–48.
138. Carus, *Lehrbuch*, pp. 48–49.
139. Carus, *Lehrbuch*, p. 41.
140. Oken, *Die Zeugung*, p. 1.
141. Jordanova, "Sex and Gender," p. 177.

EPILOGUE

1. Alexander von Humboldt, *Versuch über die gereizte Muskel- und Nervenfaser*, 2 vols. (Berlin, 1797–98). This was quickly translated into French in

1799 by Jean François Jadelot, *Expériences sur le galvanisme et en général sur l'irritation des fibres musculaires et nerveuses* (Paris, 1799).

2. W. von Humboldt to Brinkmann, 18 March 1793, in *Briefe an Karl Gustav von Brinckmann*, pp. 60–61. "Das Studium der physischen Natur nun mit dem der moralischen zu verknüpfen, und in das Universum, wie wir es erkennen, eigentlich erst die wahre Harmonie zu bringen, oder wenn dieß die Kräfte Eines Menschen übersteigen sollte, daß dieser zweite Schritt leicht werde, dazu sage ich, hat mir unter allen Köpfen, die ich historisch und aus eigner Erfahrung in allen Zeiten kenne, nur mein Bruder fähig geschienen."

3. Quoted by Michael Dettelbach, "The Face of Nature: Precise Measurement, Mapping, and Sensibility in the Work of Alexander von Humboldt," *Studies in the History and Philosophy of Biological and the Biomedical Sciences* 30 (1999): 473–504, p. 495.

4. Mary Louise Pratt, *Imperial Eyes: Travel Writing and Transculturation* (London: Routledge, 1992), p. 120.

5. Buffon, *Histoire naturelle*, vol. 1, p. 4.

6. Johann Jacob Wagner, *Von der Natur der Dinge* (Leipzig, 1803) p. xvi; Heinrich Steffens in Hanno Beck, *Gespräche Alexander von Humboldts* (Berlin, 1959), p. 33.

7. My interpretation of Humboldt's relationship with *Naturphilosophie* differs markedly from that of Michael Dettelbach, one of today's finest interpreters of Alexander von Humboldt. Dettelbach considers Humboldt's praise of Schelling sincere, denying any radical breach separating them: "Properly understood, nature-philosophy was an admirable expression of precisely the sensibility Humboldt was attempting to cultivate in 'empirical nature-study': the individual's self-awareness as the product of historical process, natural and social"; "The Face of Nature," p. 503. As should be obvious from my evaluation of *Naturphilosophie* and what follows, I question Humboldt's sincerity and also the degree to which their work reinforced each other's.

8. A. von Humboldt, *Ideen zu Einer Geographie der Pflanzen*, pp. 24–25. Humboldt's complete statement is as follows: "Dem Felde des empirischen Naturforschung getreu, dem mein bisheriges Leben gewidmet gewesen ist, habe ich auch in diesem Werke die mannichfaltigen Erscheinungen mehr neben einander aufgezählt, als, eindringend in die Natur den Dinge, sie in ihrem innern Zusammenwirken geschildert. Dieses Geständniß, welches den Standpunkt bezeichnet, von welchem ich beurtheilt zu werden hoffen darf, soll zugleich auch darauf hinweisen, daß es möglich seyn wird, einst ein Naturgemälde ganz anderer und gleichsam höherer Art naturphilosophisch darzustellen. Eine solche Möglichkeit nämlich, an der ich vor meiner Rückkunft nach Europa fast gezweifelt: eine solche Reduction aller Naturerscheinungen, aller Thätigkeit und Gebilde, auf den nie beendigten Streit entgegengesetzter Grundkräfte der Materie, ist durch das kühne Unternehmen eines der tiefsinnigsten Männer unsers Jahrhunderts begründet worden. Nicht völlig unbekannt mit dem Geiste des Schellingischen Systems, bin ich weit von der Meynung entfernt, als könne das ächte naturphilosophische Studium den empirischen Untersuchungen

schaden, und als sollten ewig Empiriker und Naturphilosophen als streitende Pole sich einander abstoßen. Weniger Physiker haben lauter als ich über das Unbefriedigende der bisherigen Theorien und ihrer Bildersprache geklagt; wenige haben so bestimmt ihren Unglauben an den specifiken Unterschied der sogennanten Grundstoffe geäußert (Versuche über die gereitzt Muskel- und Nervenfaser, B. I, S. 376 und 422; B II, S. 334, 40.) Wer kann daher auch frohern und innigen Antheil, als ich, an einem Systeme nehmen, das, die Atomistik untergrabend, und von der auch von mir einst befolgten einseitige Vorstellungsart, alle Differenz der Materie auf bloße Differenz der Raumerfüllung und Dichtigkeit zurückzuführen, entfernt, helles Licht über Organismus, Wärme, magnetische und elektrische, der bisherigen Naturkunde so umzugängliche, Erscheinungen zu verbreiten verheißt?

9. A. von Humboldt, *Ansichten*, pp. 89–90. "Ich darf mir schmeicheln, daß selbst dem Naturphilosophen, der alle Mannigfaltigkeit der Natur den Elementaractionen Einer Materie zuschreibt, und der den Weltorganismus durch den nie entschiedenen Kampf widerstrebender Kräfte begründet sieht, eine solche Zusammenstellung von Thatsachen wichtig seyn muß. Der Empyriker zählt und mißt, was die Erscheinungen unmittelbar darbieten: der Philosophie der Natur ist es aufbehalten, das allen Gemeinsame aufzufassen und auf Principien zurückzuführen." It should be noted here that Humboldt is talking about real interaction between forces, something the *Naturphilosophen* denied.

10. A. von Humboldt, *Ansichten*, p. 128. "Denn in dem innersten, empfänglichen Sinn spiegelt lebendig und wahr sich die physische Welt."

11. A. von Humboldt, *Ansichten*, p. 181. "Wer demnach die Nature mit *einem* Blicke zu umfassen und von Lokal-Phänomenen zu abstrahieren weiß, der sieht, wie mit Zunahme der belebenden Wärme von den Polen zum Aeqautor hin sich auch allmählich organische Kraft und Lebensfülle vermehren."

12. A. von Humboldt, *Ansichten*, p. 183. I rendered this passage in English in the prologue. "Der Einfluß der physischen Welt auf die moralische, das geheimnisvolle Ineinanderwirken das Sinnlichen und Außersinnlichen gibt dem Naturstudium, wenn man es zu höheren Gesichtspunkten erhebt, einen eigenen, noch zu wenig erkannten Reiz."

13. Alexander von Humboldt to David Friedländer, 11 April 1799, in *Die Jugendbriefe Alexander von Humboldts 1787–1799*, ed. Ilse Jahn and Fritz G. Lange (Berlin: Akademie Verlag, 1973), p. 657. "Mein eigentlicher Zweck ist, das Zusammen- und Ineinander-Weben aller Naturkräfte zu untersuchen."

14. A. von Humboldt, 21 April 1792, *Jugendbriefe*, p. 184. "In jeder Wissenschaft, die keiner reinen Erkenntniß fähig ist, kann nur so viel Gewißheit erlangt werden, als sich Begriffe darin construiren lassen. Jede Naturwissenschaft, auf die sich keine Größenlehre anwenden läßt, fluktuirt."

15. A. von Humboldt, *Ansichten*, p. 116.

16. Dettelbach, "The Face of Nature," p. 481.

17. Dettelbach, "The Face of Nature," p. 481.

18. Quoted by Dettlebach, "'Baconianism' in Revolutionary Germany:

Humboldt's Great 'Instauration,'" in van der Zande and Popkin, *The Skeptical Tradition around 1800*, p. 177.

19. Alexander von Humboldt, *Cosmos: A Sketch of a Physical Description of the Universe*, trans. Elise C. Otté, 2 vols. (Baltimore: Johns Hopkins University Press, 1997), vol. 1, p. xxxvi.

20. Alexander von Humboldt, *Aphorismen aus der chemischen Physiologie der Pflanzen*, trans. Gotthelf Fischer (Leipzig, 1794).

21. Alexander von Humboldt, "Ueber die gereizte Muskelfaser, aus einem Briefe an Herrn Blumenbach," *Neues Journal der Physik* 2 (1795): 127.

22. W. von Humboldt, "Das achtzehnte Jahrhundert," in *Werke*, vol. I, p. 377.

23. Quoted by Eberhard Kessel, *Wilhelm von Humboldt: Idee und Wirklichkeit* (Stuttgart: Koehler, 1967), pp. 71–72.

24. Wilhelm von Humboldt, "On the Historian's Task," in *History and Theory* 6 (1967), p. 59.

25. A. von Humboldt, "Naturgemälde der Tropenländer," in *Ansichten*, pp. 55–56; emphasis added. This paragraph virtually repeats what Humboldt wrote in the *Geographie des Plantes*, with one exception that points to Humboldt's direct critique of the *Naturphilosophen*. In the German text he mentions "the perturbations of supposedly conflicting elements," a direct reference to and denial of the *Naturphilosophen*'s idea of polar confrontation. In the French text he talks of "perturbations and apparent confusion"; A. von Humboldt, *Essai sur la géographie des plantes; accompagné d'un tableau physique des régions équinoxiales* (Paris: Schoell, 1807), p. 43. In the French text there is no need to introduce polar confrontation and then to dismiss it with the term "supposedly." The French text also introduces a similar term, "apparent," but it is directed to a more general question, namely, discerning order when chaos seems dominant.

26. I base this statement upon an unpublished paper by Michael Dettelbach entitled "The Last Universal Man: The Local and the Universal in Humboldt's Science."

27. Dettlebach, "The Face of Nature," p. 490.

28. Daston, *Classical Probability in the Enlightenment*, pp. 271–95.

29. Terrall, "Metaphysics, Mathematics, and the Gendering of Science in Eighteenth-Century France," p. 269. See also Daston, *Classical Probability*; "Rational Individuals versus Laws of Society: From Probability to Statistics," in Krüger et al., *The Probabilistic Revolution*, vol. 1, pp. 295–304; Hahn, "The Laplacean View of Calculation," in Frängsmyr et al., *The Quantifying Spirit in the Eighteenth-Century*, pp. 363–80; "Laplace and the Mechanist Universe."

30. A. von Humboldt, *Ideen einer Geographie der Pflanzen*, p. 24. This was a brave act, for by the time Humboldt published this work, Forster, who had died penniless in Paris in 1798, had been discredited in Germany for his support of the French Revolution. Forster was one of Buffon's strongest supporters in Germany.

31. Georg Forster, "Ein Blick in das Ganze der Natur: Einleitung zu Anfangs-

gründen der Thiergeschichte," in *Georg Forsters Werke,* vol. 8, ed. Siegrfried Scheibe (Berlin: Akademie Verlag, 1991), p. 78. This critique parallels one made by Schiller about physiologists who were only interested in making a living versus those interested in a philosophy of physiology.

32. Dettelbach, "The Face of Nature," p. 486. Humboldt differentiates between the "descriptive" or "systematic botanist" and the *physicien,* which rehearses Buffon's distinction between the *nomenclateur* and *physicien.*

33. Quoted by Dettelbach, "The Face of Nature," p. 482.

34. A. von Humboldt, "Physiognomik der Gewächse, in *Ansichten,* p. 184.

35. *Ideen einer Geographie der Pflanzen,* p. 45; *Essai sur la géographie des plantes,* p. 30. The French version differs slightly from the German. Instead of "fantasy," Humboldt used the term "imagination" and clarified the term "masses" by calling it "the ensemble." "The simple aspect of nature, the view of fields and forests, produces a pleasure that differs essentially from the impression caused by the particular study of the structure of a single organized being. Here it is the detail that interests and excites our curiosity; there, it is the ensemble, the masses, which works on our imagination."

36. The German term *Genuss* as used by Humboldt is very difficult to render in English. It could be called delight and/or pleasure. Certainly for Alexander it had something visceral to it, and therefore I chose pleasure over delight. *Genuss* was also one of Wilhelm's central categories and presents the same problems of translation. For a discussion of the term as used in Germany during the eighteenth century see Wolfgang Binder, "'Genuss' in Dichtung und Philosophie des 17. und 18. Jahrhunderts," *Archiv für Begriffsgeschichte* 17 (1973): 66–92.

37. A. von Humboldt, "Physiognomik der Gewächse," in *Ansichten,* p. 184.

38. A. von Humboldt, "Physiognomik der Gewächse," in *Ansichten,* p. 181.

39. A. von Humboldt, *Ideen einer Geographie der Pflanzen,* p. 35.

40. A. von Humboldt, "Lebenskraft oder rhodische Genius," in *Ansichten,* p. 325. In the "Erläuterung und Zusatz," written later, Humboldt spoke about arranging things systematically according to more or less successfully surmised analogies: "nach mehr oder minder glücklich geahnten Analogien systematisch gruppiert werden."

41. A. von Humboldt, *Cosmos,* vol. 1, p. 54; *Ideen einer Geographie der Pflanzen,* p. 34.

42. Dettelbach, "Introduction" to vol. 2 of *Cosmos,* p. xxx.

43. I have attempted to interpret briefly Wilhelm's thought in the context of Enlightenment Vitalism in two essays: "Science and the Construction of the Cultural Sciences in Late Enlightenment Germany: The Case of Wilhelm von Humboldt," *History and Theory* 33 (October 1994): 346–66; "The Construction of the Social Sciences in Late Eighteenth and Early Nineteenth Century Germany," in *The Rise of the Social Sciences and the Formation of Modernity,* ed. Johan Heilbron et al. (Dordrecht: Kluwer, 1998), pp. 107–40. See also Helmut Müller-Sievers, *Epigenesis: Naturphilosophie im Sprachdenken Wilhelm von Humboldts* (Paderborn: Ferdinand Schöningh, 1993).

44. Alexander von Humboldt, "Bewegende Ursachen der Weltgeschichte," in *Studienausgabe,* ed. Hanno Beck (Darmstadt: Wissenschaftliche Buchgesellschaft, 1989–93), vol. I, p. 573.
45. W. von Humboldt, "On the Historian's Task," p. 66.
46. A. von Humboldt, "Bewegende Ursachen der Weltgeschichte," p. 578.
47. A. von Humboldt, "Bewegende Ursachen der Weltgeschichte," p. 580.
48. A. von Humboldt, "Bewegende Ursachen der Weltgeschichte," p. 572. "Wo ein Krater einstürzt, ein Vulkan sich erhebt, hängt sich Schönheit, oder Erhabenheit um seine Formen; wo eine Nation auftritt, lebt geistige Form, und Phatasie und der Gemüth rührender Ton ihrer Sprache. Drum ist in jedem Untergang Trost, und in jedem Wechsel Ersatz."
49. A. von Humboldt, "Bewegende Ursachen der Weltgeschichte," p. 571.
50. *Essai sur la géographie des plantes,* p. 35.
51. To cite just two examples of these different views: Susan Faye Cannon saw Humboldt as a leader of the "avant-garde" in creating scientific modernism; Susan Faye Cannon, *Science in Culture: The Early Victorian Period* (New York: Dawson and Science History Publications, 1978). For Mary Louis Pratt, Humboldt was simply a German Romantic doing the Romantic thing when writing about South America; *Imperial Eyes,* p. 137.
52. The literature here is immense. The example of Ulrich Muhlack, one of the leading contemporary supporters of the uniqueness of German historicism, should suffice: *Geschichtswissenschaft im Humanismus und in der Aufklärung: die Vorgeschichte des Historismus* (Munich: Beck, 1991). He sees Humboldt as the leader in creating historicism, which he sees as a "paradigm shift," effected at the end of the eighteenth and the beginning of the nineteenth centuries and taking place in Germany (pp. 412–35).
53. For a discussion of this issue see Keith Michael Baker and Peter Hanns Reill, eds., *What's Left of the Enlightenment? A Postmodern Question* (Stanford: Stanford University Press, 2001).
54. Dorinda Outram, "The Enlightenment Our Contemporary," in Clark et al., *The Sciences in Enlightened Europe,"* pp. 32–40, p. 40.
55. Cannon, *Science in Culture,* p. 104.
56. Pratt, *Imperial Eyes,* pp. 137, 138.
57. Michael Dettelbach, "Humboldt zwischen Aufklärung und Romantik," in *Alexander von Humboldt 1799–1999: Aufbruch in die Moderne* (Berlin: Akademie-Verlag, 2001), p. 7. In "The Face of Nature" Dettelbach asserts that Humboldt's work was "not a holistic, teleological theory of the cosmos, but a series of linked cultural practices for manifesting the power and authority of the philosopher. In this sense, there was no 'Humboldtian science,' either in the sense of a cosmic, deterministic science, a positive theoretical understanding, of the causal relations between the phenomena of the cosmos, or in the sense of a cosmic vitalism which understood all the phenomena of the cosmos as the product of a single force or world soul" (pp. 502–3).
58. Muhlack, *Geschichtswissenschaft im Humanismus,* pp. 419, 422–24, 427.

59. Daston, in her closing remarks to the volume *The Sciences in Enlightenment Europe,* reminds us of the distance that separates us from the Enlightenment as did Outram in her opening essay: "The very nature of their accounts [she uses physiocotheology as an example] should compel closer reading by historians alert to the weirdness, the non-self-evidence of the Enlightenment" (p. 504).

Bibliography

PRIMARY SOURCES

Baader, Franz Xaver. *Vom Wärmestoff, seine Verteilung, Bindung und Entbindung vorzüglich beim Brennen der Körper.* Vienna and Leipzig, 1786.
Barthez, Jean. *Nouveaux élements de la science de l'homme.* 2 vols. Montpellier, 1778.
———. *Nouvelle méchanique des mouvements de l'homme et des animaux.* Carcassonne, 1798.
Bergman, Torbern Olof. *An Essay on the Usefulness of Chemistry and Its Application to the Various Occasions of Life.* London, 1783.
———. *Traité des affinités chymiques ou attractions électives.* Paris, 1788.
Bichat, Xaver. *Physiologische Untersuchungen über den Tod* (1800). Edited and translated by Rudolf Boehm. Klassiker der Medizin 16. Leipzig, 1912.
———. *Recherches physiologiques sur la vie et la mort.* Paris, An. VIII (1799–1800).
Blumenbach, Johann Friedrich. *Anfangsgründe der Physiologie.* Vienna, 1789.
———. *The Anthropological Treatises: with Memoirs of Him by Marx and Flourins.* Translated and edited by Thomas Bendyshe. London, 1865.
———. *Elements of Physiology.* Translated by Charles Caldwell. Philadelphia, 1795.
———. *Geschichte und Beschreibung der Knochen des menschlichen Körpers.* 2nd ed. Göttingen, 1807.
———. *Handbuch der Naturgeschichte.* 2nd ed. 2 vols. Göttingen, 1782.
———. *Handbuch der vergleichende Anatomie.* Göttingen, 1805.
———. *Die medicinische Bibliothek.* 3 vols. Göttingen, 1783, 1785, 1788.
———. *Ueber den Bildungstrieb.* Göttingen, 1780.
———. *Ueber den Bildungstrieb.* Göttingen, 1781.
———. *Ueber den Bildungstrieb.* 2nd ed. Göttingen, 1791.
Boerhaave, Hermann. *Elements of Chemistry, Being the Annual Lectures of Hermann Boerhaave, M.D.* Translated by Timothy Dallowe. London, 1735.
Bonnet, Charles. *Betrachtung über die Nature: mit Anmerkungen und Zusatzen.* Edited by Johann Daniel Titius. 5th ed. 2 vols. Leipzig, 1803.

———. *Considérations sur les corps organisés, l'on traite de leur origine, de leur développement, de leur réproduction.* 2 vols. Amsterdam, 1776.
———. *La Palingénésie philosophique, ou idées sur l'état passé et sur l'état futur des entres vivans.* 2 vols. Geneva, 1769.
———. *Werke der natürlichen Geschichte und Philosophie.* 4 vols. Leipzig, 1783–85.
Bordeu, Théophile. *Recherches sur le tissu muqueux ou l'organe cellulaire et sur quelques malades.* Paris, 1791.
Brandis, Joachim Dietrich. *Versuch über die Lebenskraft.* Hannover, 1795.
Brown, John. *The Elements of Medicine.* 2 vols. London, 1795.
———. *John Brown's System der Heilkunde.* Translated by Christoph H. Pfaff. Copenhagen, 1798.
———. *The Works of John Brown.* With a biographical account of Brown by William Cullen Brown. 3 vols. London, 1804.
Buffon, George L. *Allgemeine Historie der Natur.* Translated by Abraham Gotthelf Kästner. 3 vols. Leipzig, 1750.
———. *De la manière d'étudier & de traiter l'Histoire naturelle.* Reprint of original edition. Paris: Bibliothéque Nationale, 1986.
———. *Histoire naturelle, générale et particulière.* 36 vols. Paris: L'Imprimerie royale, 1749–78.
——— "Ueber die Richtung der Gebirge und Ueber die Entstehung der Berge." In *Sammlungen zur Physik und Naturgeschichte von Liebhabern dieser Wissenschaften.* Vol. 1, pp. 738–49. Leipzig, 1779.
Buhle, Johann Gottlieb. *Grundzüge einer allgemeinen Encykolpädie der Wissenschaften.* Lemgo, 1790.
Burnet, James (Lord Monboddo). *Of the Origin and Progress of Language.* 6 vols. Edinburgh, 1773: reprint ed., Hildesheim: Georg Olms, 1974.
Cabanis, Pierre Jean Georges. *Coup d'oeil sur les revolutions et sur la réforme de la médecine.* Paris, 1804.
Camper, Peter. *Sämmtliche kleinere Schriften die Arzney-Wundarzneykunst und Naturgeschichte betreffend.* Translated by J. F. M. Herbell. 3 vols. Leipzig, 1784, 1785, 1788.
———. *Über den natürlichen Unterschied des Gesichtszüge in Menschen verschiedener Gegenden und verschiedenen Alters; über das schöne antiker Bildsäulen und geschnittener Steine; nebst Darstellung einer neuen Art, allerlei Menschenköpfe mit Sicherheit zu zeichen.* Translated by Samuel T. Sömmerring. Berlin, 1792.
Carus, Carl Gustav. *Gelegentliche Betrachtung über den Character des gegenwärtigen Standes der Naturwissenschaften.* Vienna, 1854.
———. *Lehrbuch der Gynäkologie oder systematischen Darstellung der Lehren von Erkenntniß und Behandlung eigenthümlicher gesunder und krankhafter Zustände, sowohl der nicht schwangern, schwangern und gebärenden Frauen, als der Wöchnerinnen und neugebornen Kinder.* Erster Theil. Leipzig, 1820.
———. *Natur und Idee, oder das Werdende und sein Gesetz: eine philosophische Grundlage für die specielle Naturwissenschaft.* Vienna, 1861.
———. *Organon der Erkenntniß der Natur und des Geistes.* Leipzig, 1856.

———. *Die Proportionslehre der menschlichen Gestalt zum ersten Male morphologisch und physiologisch begrundet*. Leipzig, 1854.
———. *Über Begriff und Vorgang des Entstehens* (1859). Edited by Ekkehard Meffert. Stuttgart: Verlag Freies Geistesleben, 1986.
———. *Zwölf Bücher über das Erdleben: als Beigabe: von den Anforderungen eine künftige Bearbeitung der Naturwissenschaften*. Leipzig, 1822.
Cheyne, George. *Philosophical Principles of Religion Natural and Reveal'd*. London, 1715.
Chrestien, Johann A. *Über die iatraleptische Methode oder practische Beobachtungen über die Wirksamkeit der Heilmittel bey deren Anwendung auf dem Wege der Hauptabsorption in der Behandlung mehrerer Krankheiten des äußern und innern Organismus und Beobachtungen über ein neues Heilmittel in der Behandlung der venerischen und lymphatischen Krankheiten*. Göttingen, 1813.
Cook, John C. *The New Theory of Generation according to the Best and Latest Discoveries in Anatomy*. London, 1762.
Cullen, William. *Anfangsgründe der praktischen Arzneywissehschaft nebst einem Anhang in welchen die systematischen Eintheilung der Krankheiten dieses Verfassers befindlich ist*. Translated by Christian Erhard Kapp. 4 vols. Leipzig, 1778, 1780, 1784, 1785.
———. *First Lines of the Practice of Physic*. 3rd ed. 2 vols. Edinburgh, 1781.
———. *Institutions of Medicine. Part I: Physiology*. 3rd. ed. Edinburgh, 1785.
Cuvier, George. *Briefe an Christoph Heinrich Pfaff aus den Jahren 1788 bis 1792*. Edited by Wilhelm Friedrich Behn. Kiel, 1845.
———. *Leçons d'anatomie comparée recueil lies & publies sous ses yeaux*. Paris, An. VIII (1805).
———. *Rapport sur les progrés des sciences physiques depuis 1789*. Paris, 1805.
———. *Le règne animal: distribué d'après son organisation pour servir de base à l'histoire naturelle des animaux et d'introduction à l'anatomie comparée*. Paris, 1817.
Dalberg, Friedrich Hugo Freiherr von. *Blicke eines Tonkünstlers in die Musik der Geister*. Mannheim, 1787.
———. *Untersuchungen über den Ursprung der Harmonie und ihre allmählige Ausbildung*. Erfurt, 1800.
Dalberg, Karl Theodor Anton von. *Grundsätze der Aesthetik deren Anwendung und künftigen Entwicklung*. Erfurt, 1791.
Darwin, Erasmus. *A Plan for the Conduct of Female Education in Boarding Schools* (1797). New York: Johnson Reprint Corporation, 1968.
———. *Zoonomie oder Gesetze des organischen Lebens*. Translated by Joachim D. Brandis. 4 vols. Hannover, 1795.
Döllinger, Ignaz. *Gedächtnißrede von Samuel Thomas Sömmerring*. Munich, 1830.
———. *Von den Fortschritten welche die Physiologie seit Haller gemacht hat*. Munich, 1824.
Donndorff, Johann August. *Über Tod, Scheintod und frühe Beerdigung: ein Buch für Jeder zur Belehrung, zur Warnung, und Verhütung des schreck-

lichsten alle Ereignisse: des Lebendigbegrabens. Quedlinburg and Leipzig, 1823.
Dumas, Charles Louis. *Anfangsgründe der Physiologie oder Einleitung in eine auf Erfahrung gegründete, philosophische und medicinische Kenntniss des lebenden Menschen.* Translated by Ludwig A. Kraus and Christoph J. Pickhard. 2 vols. Göttingen, 1807.

———. *Principes de Physiologie, ou introduction à la science expériméntal, philosophique et médicale de l'homme vivant.* 3 vols. Paris, 1800–1803.
Duncan, Andrew, ed. *Medical Commentaries.* Vol. 9 (1783–84). London, 1785.
Eberhard, Johann August. *Versuch einer Geschichte der Fortschritten der Philosophie.* Halle, 1794.
Elliot, John. *Physiologische Beobachtungen über die Sinne besonders über das Gesicht und Gehör wie auch über das Brennen und die thierische Wärme nebst Adair Crawfords Versuchen und Beobachtungen über die thierische Wärme.* Leipzig, 1785.
Encyclopédie ou dictionnaire raisonné des sciences des artes et des métiers: nouvelle impression en facsimilé de la première édition de 1751–1780. Stuttgart: Frommann-Holzboog, 1966.
Eschenmayer, Carl A. *Der Eremit und der Fremdling: Gespräche über das Heilige und die Geschichte.* Erlangen, 1805.

———. *Die Philosophie in ihrem Übergang zur Nichtphilosophie.* Erlangen, 1803.

———. *Ueber die Enthauptung gegen die Sömmerringische Meinung.* Tübingen, 1797.

———. *Versuch die scheinbare Magie des thiersichen Magnetismus aus physiologishcen und psychischen Gesezen zu erklären.* Stuttgart, 1816.
Esenbeck, Christian Gottfried Nees von, Carl Gustav Bischoff, and Heinrich August Rothe. *Die Entwickelung der Pflanzensubstanz physiologisch, chemisch und mathematisch dargestellt mit combinatorischen Tafeln der möglichen Pflanzenstoffe und den Gesetzen ihrer stöchiometrischen Zusammensetzung.* Erlangen, 1819.
Faust, Bernhard Christian. *Entwurf zu einem Gesundheits-Katechismus für die Kirchen und Schulen des Grafschaft Schaumburg-Lippe.* Bückeburg, 1793.

———. *Die Perioden des menschlichen Lebens.* Berlin, 1794.
Ferguson, Adam. *An Essay on the History of Civil Society.* Edited by Duncan Forbes. Edinburgh: Edinburgh University Press, 1966.

———. *Principles of Moral and Political Science.* 2 vols. Edinburgh, 1792.
Fontenelle, Bernard le Bovier de. *The Eloge of Professor Boerhaave, M.D.* Translated by William Burton. London, 1749.
Forster, Georg. *Forsters Werke.* Edited by Gerhard Steiner. 2 vols. Berlin: Aufbau, 1968.

———. *Forsters Werke.* Edited by Siegrfried Scheibe. Berlin: Akademie Verlag, 1991.

———. *Georg Forsters Briefwechsel mit S. Th. Sömmering.* Edited by Hermann Hettner. Braunschweig, 1877.

Fourier, Jean Baptist. *Analytical Theory of Heat*. Translated by Alexander Freeman. Great Books of the Western World 45. Chicago: University of Chicago Press, 1952.
Gehler, Johann Samuel. *Physikalisches Wörterbuch*. 1st ed. 5 vols. Leipzig, 1789–92.
Geoffroy, Etienne François. *Table des différents rapports observés en chemie entre différentes substances*. Paris, 1718.
Geron, T. F. *Clavicule de la philosophie hermétique, ou les mystéres les plus cachés des anciens & modernes sont misse au jour en faveurs des enfans de l'art, & à la gloire de dieu* (1753). Paris: J. C. Bailly, 1986.
Girtanner, Christoph. *Ausführliche Darstellung des Brownischen Systems der praktischen Heilkunde nebst einer vollständigen Literatur und einer Kritik desselben*. Göttingen, 1797.
———. *Ueber das Kantische Prinzip für die Naturgeschichte: ein Versuch diese Wissenschaft philosophisch zu behandeln*. Göttingen, 1796.
Gmelin, Johann Friedrich. *Geschichte der Chemie: seit dem Wiederaufleben der Wissenschaften bis an das Ende des 18. Jahrhunderts*. 3 vols. Göttingen, 1797. Reprint edition. Hildesheim: Georg Olms, 1965.
———. *Grundris der allgemeinen Chemie zum Gebrauch bei Vorlesungen*. 2 vols. Göttingen, 1789.
Goethe, Johann Wolfgang von. *Theory of Colours*. Translated by Charles Lock Eastlake. Cambridge, Mass.: MIT Press, 1976.
Goldfuss, Georg August. *Ueber die Entwicklungsstufen des Thieres: ein Sendschreiben an Herrn Dr. Nees v. Esenbeck*. Nuremberg, 1817.
Görres, Joseph. *Aphorism über die Oranonomie*. 2 vols. Koblenz, 1803.
———. *Gesammelte Schriften*. Edited by Wilhelm Schellberg. vol. 2. Paderborn: Schöningh, 1934.
———. *Naturwissenschaftliche und Naturphilosophische Schriften: Exposition der Physiologie*. Edited by Robert Stein. Koblenz, 1805.
Göttingische Anzeigen von Gelehrten Sachen. Göttingen, 1753–94.
Göttingische Zeitungen von Gelehrten Sachen. Göttingen, 1751–52.
Haller, Albrecht von. "A Dissertation on the Sensible and Irritable Parts of Animals." Introduction by Owsei Tempkin. *Bulletin of the Institute of Medicine* 4 (1936).
———. *Tagebuch seiner Beobachtungen über Schriftsteller und über sich selbst: zur Karakteristik der Philosophie und Religion dieses Mannes*. 2 vols. Bern, 1787.
———. *Von den empfindlichen und reizbaren Teilen des menschlichen Körpers*. Edited by Karl Sudhoff. Klassiker der Medizin. Leipzig: Johann A. Barth, 1922.
Hardenberg, Friedrich von (Novalis). *Novalis Schriften: die Werke Friedrich von Hardenberg*. Edited by Paul Kluckhohn and Richard Samuel. Vol. 3. Stuttgart: W. Kohlhammer Verlag, 1960.
Heinse, Wilhelm. *Hildegard von Hohenthal*. 3 vols. Berlin, 1795–96.
Helmont, Francis Mercurius van. *The Spirit of Diseases; or, Diseases from the Spirit: Laid open in some Observations concerning Man, and his Diseases.*

Wherein is shewed how much the Mind influenceth the Body in causing and curing Diseases. The Whole Deduced from Certain and Infallible Principles of Natural Reason and Experience (1692). London, 1694.

Herder, Johann Gottfried. *Ideen zur Philosophie der Geschichte der Menschheit. Herders Sämmtliche Werke*, vols. 13 and 14, edited by Berhard Suphan. Berlin: Weidmannsche Buchhandlung, 1887, 1909.

Herdman, John. *An Essay on the Phenomena of Animal Life*. London, 1793.

Herz, Marcus. *Ueber die frühe Beerdigung der Juden: an die Herausgeber der hebräischen Sammlers*. 2nd ed. Berlin, 1788.

———. *Versuch über den Schwindel*. 2nd ed. Berlin, 1788.

Hissmann, Michael. "Versuch über das Fundament der Kräfte." *Magazin für die Philosophie und ihre Geschichte: aus den Jahrbüchern der Akademien angelegt*, vol. VI. Göttingen, 1783.

Hufeland, Christoph Wilhelm. *Bermerkungen über die Brownsche Praxis*. Tübingen, 1799.

———. *Bildniss und Selbstbiographie*. Edited by Johann Michael Lowe. Berlin, 1806.

———. *Geschichte der Gesundheit nebst einer physischen Karakteristik des jetzigen Zeitalters*. Berlin, 1812.

———. *Ideen über Pathogenie und Einfluss der Lebenskraft auf Entstehung und Form der Krankheiten als Einleitung zu pathologische Vorlesungen*. Jena, 1795.

———. *Makrobiotik oder die Kunst des menschliche Leben zu verlängern*. 2 vols. Berlin, 1805.

———. *Pathologie*. 2nd ed. Jena, 1799.

———. *Der Scheintod, oder Sammlung der wichtigsten Thatsachen und Bemerkungen darüber in alphabetischer Ordnung*. Berlin, 1808.

———. *System der practischen Heilkunde: ein Handbuch für academischen Vorlesungen und für den practischen Gerbrauch*. 2 vols. Jena and Leipzig, 1800.

Humboldt, Friedrich Alexander von. *Ansichten der Nature: erster und zweiter Band*. Edited by Hanno Beck. Alexander von Humboldt Studienasugabe 5. Darmstadt: Wissenschaftliche Buchgesellschaft, 1987.

———. *Aphorismen aus der chemischen Physiologie der Pflanzen*. Translated by Gotthelf Fischer. Leipzig, 1794.

———. *Cosmos: A Sketch of a Physical Description of the Universe*. Translated by Elise C. Otté. Baltimore: Johns Hopkins University Press, 1997.

———. *Essai sur la géographie des plantes; accompagné d'un tableau physique des régions équinoxiales*. Paris: Schoell, 1807.

———. *Expériences sur le galvanisme et en général sur l'irritation des fibres musculaires et nerveuses*. Translated by Jean François N. Jadelot. Paris, 1799.

———. *Ideen zu einer Geographie der Pflanzen nebst einem Naturgemälde der Tropengeländer*. Edited by Mauritz Dittrich. Ostwalds Klassiker der Exakten Wissenschaften 248. Leipzig: Akademische Verlagsgesellschaft, 1960.

———. *Ideen zu einer Physiognomik der Gewächse*. Tübingen, 1806.

———. *Die Jugendbriefe Alexander von Humboldt*. Edited by Ilse Jahn and Fritz G. Lange. Berlin: Akademie Verlag, 1973.

———. *Relation historique du voyage aux régions équinoxiales du noveau continent: fait en 1799, 1800, 1801, 1802, et 1804.* Quellen und Forschungen zur Geschichte der Geographie und der Reisen 8. Edited by Hanno Beck. 3 vols. Stuttgart: Brockhaus, 1970.

———. *Studienausgabe.* Edited by Hanno Beck. 7 vols. Darmstadt: Wissenschaftliche Buchgesellschaft, 1989–93.

———. "Ueber die gereizte Muskelfaser, aus einem Briefe an Herrn Blumenbach." *Neues Journal der Physik* 2 (1795): 127.

———. *Versuche über die chemische Zerlegung des Luftkreises und über einige andere Gegenstände der Naturlehre.* Braunschweig, 1799.

———. *Versuch über die gereizte Muskel und Nervenfaser.* 2 vols. Berlin, 1797–98.

Humboldt, Wilhelm von. *Briefe an Christine Reinhard Reimarus.* Edited by Arndt Schreiber. Heidelberg: Lambert Schneider, 1956.

———. "Briefe an John Pickering." Edited by Kurt Müller-Vollmer. In *Universalismus und Wissenschaft in Werk und Wirken des Brüder Humboldts.* Studien zur Philosophie und Literatur des neunzehnten Jahrhunderts 31. Edited by Klaus Hammacher. Frankfurt am Main: Klostermann, 1976.

———. *Briefe an Karl Gustav von Brinckmann.* Bibliothek des Literarischen Vereins in Stuttgart 288. Edited by Albert Leitzmann. Leipzig: Karl Hiersemann, 1939.

———. *Briefe von Wilhelm von Humboldt an Friedrich Heinrich Jacobi.* Edited by Albert Leitzmann. Halle: Max Niemeyer, 1892.

———. *Briefwechsel zwischen Wilhelm von Humboldt und August Wilhelm Schlegel.* Edited by Albert Leitzmann. Halle: Max Niemeyer, 1908.

———. Correspondence with Fabroni. Fabroni Papers, BF 113, American Philosophical Society.

———. *Gesammelte Schriften.* Edited by Albert Leitzmann. 17 vols. Berlin: B. Behr, 1903–36.

———. Letter from Wilhelm von Humboldt to Peter S. du Ponceau and William Smith. American Philosophical Society, du Ponceau Papers 410: D92, Misc. Mss. 403:120.

———. *The Limits of State Action.* Edited by John W. Burrow. Cambridge: Cambridge University Press, 1969.

———. *Neue Briefe Wilhelm von Humboldts an Schiller: 1796–1803.* Edited by Friedrich Clemens Ebrard. Berlin: Paetel, 1911.

———. "On the Historian's Task" *History and Theory* 6 (1967): 57–71.

Hume, David. *The Philosophical Works.* Edited by Thomas Hill Green and Thomas Hodge Grose. 4 vols. London, 1882.

Hunter, John. *Inaugural Disputation on the Varieties of Man.* In Johann Friedrich Blumenbach, *The Anthropological Treatises: with Memoirs of Him by Marx and Flourins.* Translated and edited by Thomas Bendyshe. London, 1865.

———. *Lectures on the Principles of Surgery.* In *The Works of John Hunter, in four volumes,* edited by James F. Palmer, vol. 1, pp. 197–643. London: Longman, 1835–37.

———. *Observations on Certain Parts of the Animal Oeconomy*. 2nd ed. London, 1786.

———. *Observations on Certain Parts of the Animal Oeconomy Inclusive of Several Papers from The Philosophical Transactions*. Edited by Richard Owen. In *The Works of John Hunter, in four volumes*, edited by James F. Palmer, vol. 4. London: Longman, 1835–37.

———. *A Treatise on the Venereal Disease*. In *The Works of John Hunter, in four volumes*, edited by James F. Palmer, vol. 2, pp. 114–488. London: Longman, 1835–37.

———. "Versuche an Thieren und Pflanzen, über die Kräfte Hitze zu erzeugen: vogelesen den 22 Jun. 1775." In *Sammlungen zur Physik und Naturgeschichte von Liebhabern dieser Wissenschaften*, vol. 1. Leipzig, 1778.

Hunter, William. *Two Introductory Lectures delivered by Dr. William Hunter to his last Course of Anatomical Lectures*. London, 1784.

Ith, Johann. "Ueber die Perfectibilität des Menschengeschlechts." *Magazin für die Naturkunde Helvetiens*, vol. 3, edited by Albrecht Höpfner, 1–52. Zurich, 1788.

Kant, Immanuel. *Anthropologie in pragmatischer Hinsicht*. Kants Werke, Akademie Textausgabe VII. Berlin: Walter de Gruyter, 1968.

———. *Critique of Judgment*. Translated and introduction by John H. Bernard. New York: Hafner Press, 1951.

———. *Der einzig mögliche Beweisgrund zu einer Demonstration des Daseins Gottes* (1763). Hamburg: Felix Meiner Verlag, 1963.

———. *Kritik der Urtheilskraft*. Kants Werke, Akademie Textausgabe V. Berlin: Walter de Gruyter, 1968.

———. *Metaphysische Anfangsgründe der Naturwissenschaften*. Riga: Johann Friedrich Hartknoch, 1786.

———. *Von der Macht des Gemüths durch den bloßen Vorsatz seiner krankhaften Gefühle Meister zu sein*. Edited by Christoph W. Hufeland. 5th ed. Leipzig, 1851.

Karsten, Wencelaus Johann Gustav Renger. *Physischechemische Abhandlung, durch neuere Schriften von hermetischen Arbeiten und andere neue Untersuchungen veranlasset*. 2 vols. Halle, 1786, 1787.

Kerner, Justinus. *Geschichten Besessener neuerer Zeit: Beobachtungen aus dem Gebiete kakodämonischmagnetischer Erscheinungen, nebst Reflexionen von Carl A. Eschenmayer über Besessenseyn und Zauber*. Karlsruhe: Braun, 1833.

Kielmeyer, Carl Friedrich. *Gesammelte Schriften: In Natur und Kraft. Die Lehre von der Entwicklung organische Naturlehre*. Edited by Fritz-Heinz Holler. Berlin: Keiper, 1938.

———. "Ueber die Verhältnisse der organischen Kräfte unter einander in der Reihe der verschiedenen Verhältnisse." *Suhoffs Archiv für Geschichte der Medizin* 23, no. 2 (1930): 247–67.

Kölreuter, Joseph Gottlieb. *Fortsetzung der vorläufigen Nachricht von einigen des Geschlecht der Pflanzen betreffenden Versuchen und Beobachtungen*. Leipzig, 1763.

———. *Dritte Fortsetzung der vorläufigen Nachricht von einigen des*

Geschlecht der Pflanzen betreffenden Versuchen und Beobachtungen. Leipzig, 1766.

———. *Vorläufige Nachricht von einigen des Geschlecht der Pflanzen betreffenden Versuchen und Beobachtungen.* Leipzig, 1761.

———. *Zweyte Fortsetzung der vorläufigen Nachricht von einigen des Geschlecht der Pflanzen betreffenden Versuchen und Beobachtungen.* Leipzig, 1764.

Lamarck, Jean Baptist. *Rescherches sur l'organisation des corps vivants: précédé du discours d'ouverture du cours de zoologie donne dans le museum d'historie naturelle.* Paris: Fayard, 1986.

Lambert, Johann Heinrich. *Anlage zur Architectonic, oder Theorie des Einfachen und des Ersten in der philosophischen und mathematischen Erkenntniss.* 2 vols. Riga, 1771. In *Lamberts Philosophische Schriften.* Edited by Hans-Werner Arndt. Hildesheim: Georg Olms, 1965.

———. *Neues Organon oder Gedanken über die Erforschung und Bezeichnung des Wahren und dessen Unterscheidung vom Irrthum und Schein.* 2 vols. Leipzig, 1764. In *Lamberts Philosophische Schriften,* edited by Hans-Werner Arndt. Hildesheim: Georg Olms, 1965.

La Mettrie, Julien Offray de. *L'Homme Machine: A Study in the Origins of an Idea. Critical Edition with an Introductory Monograph and Notes by Aram Vartanian.* Princeton: Princeton University Press, 1960.

Lavater, Johann. *Essays on Physiogonomy Designed to Promote the Knowledge and the Love of Mankind.* Translated by Henry Hunter. 3 vols. London, 1789.

Lavoisier, Antoine Laurent. *Elements of Chemistry.* Translated by Robert Kerr. Great Books of the Western World 45. Chicago: University of Chicago Press, 1952.

Leibniz, Gottfried Wilhelm. "The Leibniz-Stahl Controversy. I. Leibniz' Opening Objections to the *Theorie medica vera.*" Edited by Lelland J. Rather and John B. Frerichs. *Clio Medica* 3 (1968): 21–40.

Lichtenberg, Georg Christoph. *Fragment von Schwänzen: ein Beitrag zu den physiognomischen Fragment.* Göttingen, 1783.

———. *Georg C. Lichtenberg's ausfürliche Erklärung der Hogarthischen Kupferstiche: mit verkleinerten aber vollständigen Copien derselben.* Göttingen, 1794.

———. *Lichtenberg's Briefe an Johann Friedrich Blumenbach.* Edited by Albert Leitzmann. Leipzig: Dietrich, 1921.

———. *Über die Physiognomik: wider die Physiognomen; zur Beförderung der Menschenliebe und Menschenkenntniß.* 2nd ed. Göttingen, 1778.

Macquer, Pierre Joseph. *Élemens de chymie théorique.* Paris 1749.

———. *Élemens de chymie théorique.* 2nd ed. Paris, 1753.

———. *Elements of the Theory and Practice of Chemistry.* 3rd ed. 2 vols. London, 1775.

Marat, Jean Paul. *Entdeckungen über das Licht.* Translated by Christian Weigel. Leipzig, 1783.

———. *An Enquiry into the Nature, Cause and Cure of a Singular Disease of the Eyes.* London, 1776.

Medicus, Friedrich Casimir. *Geschichte der Botanik unserer Zeiten.* Mannheim, 1793.
Meierotto, Johann Heinrich L. *Gedanken über die Entstehung der Baltischen Länder.* Berlin, 1790.
Mendelssohn, Moses. *Kleine philosophische Schriften mit einer Skizze seines Lebens und Charakters von D. Jenisch.* Berlin, 1789.
———. *Ueber die Empfindung.* Berlin, 1755.
Metzger, Johann Daniel. *Aeusserungen über Kant, seinen Charakter und seine Meinungen von einem billigen Verehrer seiner Verdienste.* Königsberg, 1804.
———. *Grundriß der Physiologie.* Königsberg, 1783.
———. *Kurzgefaßtes System der gerichtlichen Arzneiwissenschaft.* Königsberg and Leipzig, 1793.
———. *Skizze einer pragmatischen Literärgeschichte der Medicin.* Königsberg, 1792.
———. *Skizze einer medizinischen Psychologie.* Königsberg, 1787.
———. *Ueber Irritabilität und Sensibilität als Lebensprincipien in der organischen Natur.* Königsberg, 1794.
———. "Ueber Verbesserung der Anstalten zur Rettung der Ertrunkenen." In *gerichtlichmedicinische Abhandlungen: ein Supplement zu seinem kurzgefaßten System der gerichtlichen Arzneiwissenschaft,* vol. 2, p. 14–44. Königsberg, 1804.
———. *Zusätze und Verbesserungen zu seiner Skizze einer pragmatischen Literärgeschichte der Medicin.* Königsberg, 1796.
Millar, John. *Observations on the Asthma, and on the Hooping Cough.* London, 1769.
Monro, Alexander, II. *Vergleichung des Baues und der Physiologie der Fische mit dem Bau des Menschen und der übrigen Thiere: aus dem Englischen übersetzt und mit Zusätzen und Anmerkungen von P. Camper vermittelt durch Johann Gottlob Schneider.* Leipzig, 1787.
Montesquieu, Charles Secondat Baron de. *The Spirit of the Laws.* Translated by Thomas Nugent with an introduction by Franz Neumann. New York: Hafner, 1949.
Müller, Ignatz. *Über den Scheintod.* Edited by G. F. Vend. Würzburg, 1815.
Nieuwentyt, Bernard. *The Religious Philosopher: or the Right Use of Contemplating the Works of the Creator.* Translated by Jean Theophilus Desaguliers. 5th ed. 2 vols. London, 1724.
Oelsner, Conrad Engelbert. "Oelsner aux rédacteurs." *Magasin encyclopédique* 3 (1795): 463–77.
Oken, Lorenz. *Abriss der Naturphilosophie: bestimmt zur Grundlage seiner Vorlesungen über Biologie.* Göttingen, 1805.
———. *Abriss des Systems der Biologie: zum Behufe seiner Vorlesungen.* Göttingen, 1805.
———, ed. *Isis oder Encyclopädische Zeitung.* Jena: Brockhaus, 1817–21.
———. *Lehrbuch der Naturphilosophie.* Jena, 1809.
———. *Lehrbuch der Naturphilosophie.* 2nd ed. Jena, 1831.
———. *Ueber das Universum als Fortsetzung des Sinnensystems: ein pythagoräisches Fragment.* Jena, 1808.

---. *Ueber Licht und Wärme als das nicht irdische, aber kosmische materiale Element: erste Ideen zur Theorie des Lichts der Finsterniss, der Farben und der Wärme.* Jena, 1808.

---. *Die Zeugung.* Bamberg and Würzburg, 1805.

Pallas, Peter S. "Beobachtungen über die Berge, und die Veränderungen der Erdkugel, besonders in Beziehung auf das russische Reich." *Sammlungen zur Physik und Naturgeschichte von Liebhabern dieser Wissenschaften,* 1 Bd., 2 Stück. Leipzig, 1778.

Patrin, L. *Zweifel gegen die Entwicklungstheorie: ein Brief an Herr Senebier.* Translated by Georg Forster. Göttingen, 1788.

Platner, Ernst. *Anthropologie für Aertzte und Weltweise.* Leipzig, 1772.

---. *Neue Anthropologie für Aerzte und Weltweise: mit besonderer Rücksicht auf Physiologie, Pathologie, Moralphilosophie und Aesthetik.* Leipzig, 1790.

---. *Philosophische Aphorismen nebst einigen Anleitungen zur philosophischen Geschichte.* 2 vols. Leipzig, 1793, 1800.

---. *Vorlesungen über Aesthetik: in treuer Auffassung nach Geist und Wort wiedergegeben von dessen dankbarem Schüler M. Moriz Erdmann Engel.* Zittau and Leipzig, 1836.

Previnaire, Pierre Jean Baptiste. *Abhandlung über die Verschiedenen Arten des Scheintodes und über die Mittel, welche die Arzneikunde und Polizei anwenden können, um den gefährlichen Folgen allzufüher Beerdigungen zuvorzukommen: eine von der Akademie der Wissenschaften in Brüssel gekrönte Preisschrift.* Translated by Berhard Gottlob Schreber. Leipzig, 1790.

---. *Traité sur les asphyxies ou: mémoire sur la question suivante proposée en 1784, quels sont les moyensosée en 1784, quels sont les moyens que la médecine et la police pourroient employer pour prévenir les erreurs dangereuses des enterremens préciptes?* Mequignon, 1788.

Pringle, John. *Observations on the Diseases of the Army.* 4th ed. London, 1764.

---. *Six Discourses delivered by Sir John Pringle: to which is prefixed the Life of the Author by Andrew Kippis.* London, 1783.

Rasse, Franz. *Die Unterscheidung der Scheintodes von wirklichen Tode: zur Beruhigung über die Gefahr, lebendig begraben zu werden.* Bonn, 1841.

Reil, Johann Christian. *Entwurf einer allgemeinen Pathologie.* 3 vols. Halle, 1815, 1816, 1816.

---. *Entwurf einer allgemeinen Therapie.* Halle, 1816.

---. *Gesammelte physiologische Schriften, grösstentheils aus dem Lateinischen übersetzt.* 2 vols. Vienna, 1811.

---. *Rhapsodieen über die Anwendung der psychischen Kurmethode auf Geisteszerrüttungen.* Halle, 1818.

---. *Von der Lebenskraft.* Klassiker der Medizin. Edited by Karl Sudhoff. Leipzig: Johann Ambrosius Barth, 1910.

Robinet, Jean Baptiste. *De la nature.* 5 vols. Amsterdam, 1761–68.

---. *Vue philosophique de la gradation naturelle des formes de l'être: ou les essais de la nature.* Amsterdam, 1768.

Röschlaub, Andreas. *Lehrbuch der Nosologie zu seinen Vorlesungen entworfen.* Bamberg and Würzburg, 1801.

———. *Über Medizin ihr Verhältniss zur Chirurgie nebst Materialien zu einem Entwurfe der Polizei der Medizin*. Frankfurt am Main, 1802.

———. *Untersuchungen über Pathogenie oder Einleitung in die Heilkunde*. 3 vols. Frankfurt am Main, 1800–1801.

Rousseau, Jean Jacques. *Du contrat social*. Edited by Edmond Dreyfus-Brisac. Paris: Alcan, 1896.

Roussel, Pierre. *Physiologie des weiblichen Geschlechts*. Translated by Christoph Friedrich Michaelis. Berlin, 1786.

Rudolphi, Karl Asmund. *Beyträge zur Anthropologie und allgemeinen Naturgeschichte*. Berlin, 1812.

Saussure, Horace Bénédict de. *Voyages dans les Alpes, précédés d'un essai sur l'historie naturelle des environs de Geneve*. 4 vols. Geneva, 1779, 1786, 1796. Reprint edition with a life of Saussure by Jean Senebier. Geneva: Editions Slatkine, 1978.

Scheele, Carl Wilhelm. *The Chemical Essays of Charles William Scheele*. Translated by Thomas Beddoes. London, 1786.

———. *Chemische Abhandlung von der Luft und dem Feuer*. Ostwald's Klassiker der exacten Wissenschaften 58. Leipzig, 1894.

———. *Traité chimique de l'air du feu par Charles Guillaume Scheele avec une introduction de Torbern Bergman*. Paris, 1781.

Schelling, Friedrich Wilhelm. *Erster Entwurf eines Systems der Naturphilosophie: zum Behuf seiner Vorlesungen*. Jena and Leipzig, 1799.

———. *Vom Ich als Princip der Philosophie oder über das Unbedingte im menschlichen Wissen*. Tübingen, 1795.

———. *Von der Weltseele, eine Hypothese der höheren Physik zur Erklärung des allgemeinen Organismus nebst einer Abhandlung über das Verhältniß des Realen und Idealen in der Natur oder Entwicklung der ersten Grundsätze der Naturphilosophie an den Principien der Schwere und des Lichts*. 3rd ed. Hamburg, 1809.

Schiller, Friedrich von. *Medicine, Psychology and Literature: With the First English Edition of His Complete Medical and Psychological Writings*. Edited by Kenneth Dewhurst and Nigel Reeves. Berkeley: University of California Press, 1978.

———. *On the Aesthetic Education of Man*. Edited by Reginald Snell. New York: Friedrich Ungar, 1954.

Schlözer, August Ludwig. *Vorstellung seiner Universal-Historie*. Göttingen, 1772.

Semler, Johann Salomo. *Briefe an einen Freund in der Schweiz über den Hirtenbrief der unbekanten Obern des Freimaurerordens alten Systems*. Leipzig, 1786.

———. *Unparteiische Samlungen zur Historie der Rosenkreuzer*. 4 vols. Leipzig, 1786–88.

———. *Verzeichniß der von dem seligen Herrn Doctor und Professor Theologiä Johann Salamo Semler hinterlassenen Bücher*. Halle, 1791.

———. *Von Aechter hermetischer Arznei*. 3 vols. Leipzig, 1786.

Shelley, Mary. *Frankenstein, or The Modern Prometheus*. New York: Random House, 1993.

Sömmerring, Samuel Thomas. *Abbildungen und Beschreibungen einer Misgeburten.* Mainz, 1791.

———. "Sur le supplice de la Guillotine: lettre de M. Soemmering á M. Oelsner." *Magasin encyclopédique* 3 (Paris, 1795): 468–77.

———. *Ueber die körperliche Verschiedenheit des Mohren vom Europäer.* Mainz, 1784.

———. *Ueber die körperliche Verschiedenheit des Negers vom Europäer.* Frankfurt and Mainz, 1785.

———. *Ueber das Organ der Seele.* Königsberg, 1796.

Spallanzani, Lazzaro. *Expériences pour servir a l'historie de la génération des animaux et des plantes avec une ébauche de l'histoire des etres organisés avant leur fécondation par Jean Senebier.* Geneva, 1785.

Stahl, Georg Ernst. *Georg Ernst Stahl: Über den mannigfaltigen Einfluss von Gemütsbewegungen auf den menschlichen Körper (Halle, 1695); Über die Bedeutung des synergischen Prinzips für die Heilkunde (Halle, 1695); Über den Unterschied zwischen Organismus und Mechanismus (1714); Überlegungen zum ärtzlichen Hausbesuch (Halle, 1703).* Edited and translated by Bernward Josef Gottlieb. Sudhoffs Klassiker der Medizin 36. Leipzig: Barth, 1961.

———. "Of the Original of Metallick Veins." In *Pyrotechnical Discourses: being an Experimental Confirmation of Chemical Philosophy by John Kunkel, A short Discourse on the Original of Metallick Veins by Georg Stahl and The Grounds of Pyrotechnical Metallurgy by John Christian Fritschius.* London: B. Bragg, 1705.

Struve, Christian August. *Der Lebensprüfer, oder Anwendung des von mir erfundenen Galvanodesmus zur Bestimmung des wahren von dem Scheintode, um das Lebendiggraben zu verhüten.* Hannover, 1805.

———. *Versuch über die Kunst, Scheintodte zu beleben, und über die Rettung in schnellen Todesgefahren. Ein tabellarisches Taschenbuch.* Hannover, 1797.

Sue, Jean Joseph. *J. J. Sue's Professors der Anatomie zu Paris physiologische Untersuchungen und Erfahrungen über die Vitalität: nebst dessen Abhandlung über den Schmerz nach der Enthauptung, und den Abhandlungen der Bürger Cabanis und Léveillé über denselben Gegenstand.* Translated and annotated by Johann Christian Friedrich Harleß. Nuremberg, 1799.

———. "Opinion du citoyen Sue sur le supplice de la guillotine." *Magasin encyclopédique* 4 (1795): 170–89.

Taberger, Johann Gottfried. *Der Scheintod in seinen Beziehungen auf das Erwachen im Grabe und die verschiedenen Vorschläge zu einer wirksamen und schleunigen Rettung in Fällen dieser Art.* Hannover, 1829.

Thiery, Françoise. *La vie de l'homme respectée & défendue dans ses derniers momens.* Paris, 1785.

Tiedemann, Dietrich. *Geist der spekulativen Philosophie.* 6 vols. Marburg. 1791–97.

Treviranus, Gottfried. *Biologie, oder Philosophie der lebenden Natur für Naturforscher und Ärtze.* Göttingen, 1802.

Varnhagen, Rachel. *Rachel Varnhagen im Umgang wit ihren Freundin: Briefe*

(1793–1833). Lebensläufe: Biographien, Errinnerungen, Briefe. Vol. 10. Munich: Kösel Verlag, 1967.
Varnhagen von Ense, Karl A. *Vermischte Schriften.* 3 vols. Leipzig, 1843.
Vicq d'Azyr, Félix. *Oeuvres de Vicq d'Ayzr.* Edited by Jacques Moreau de la Sarthe. 6 vols. Paris, 1805.
Virey, Julien Joseph. *De la femme sous ses rapports physiologique, moral, et littéraire.* 2nd ed. Brussels, 1826.
Wagner, Johann Jacob. *Theodicee.* Bamberg and Würzburg, 1809.
———. *Theorie der Wärme und des Lichts.* Leipzig, 1802.
———. *Von der Natur der Dinge.* Leipzig, 1803.
Wedekind, Georg. *Ueber die Bestimmung und die Erziehung der Menschheit, oder: Wer, wo, wozu, bin ich, war ich und werde ich sein?* Giessen, 1828.
———. *Ueber die Kachexie im Allgemeinen und über die Hospitalkachexie insbesondere, nebst einer praktischen Einleitung über die Natur des lebendigen Körpers.* Leipzig, 1796.
Werner, Abraham Gottlob. "Geschichte, Karacteristik und kurze chemische Untersuchung des Apatits." In *Bergmännisches Journal,* ed. Alexander Wilhelm Köhler, vol. 1. Freiberg, 1788.
———. "Kurze Classifikation und Beschreibung der verschiedenen Gebirgsarten." In *Abhandlungen der Böhmischen Gesellschaft der Wissenschaften auf das Jahr 1786,* pp. 272–97. Prague and Dresden, 1786.
———. *Neue Theorie von der Entstehung der Gänge mit Anwendung auf den Bergbau.* Freiberg, 1791.
———. *Verzeichnis des Mineralien-Kabinets des weiland kurfürstlich sächischen Berghauptmanns Herrn Eugen Pabst von Ohain.* Freiberg, 1791.
———. "Von den verschiedenen Graden der Festigkeit des Gesteins, als dem Hauptgrunde der Hauptverschiedenkeiten der Hauerarbeiten." In *Bergmännisches Journal,* edited by Alexander Wilhelm Köhler, vol. 1. Freiberg, 1788.
———. "Von den verschiedenerley Mineraliensammlungen, aus denen ein vollständiges Mineralienkabinet bestehen soll." *Sammlungen zur Physik und Naturgeschichte von Liebhabern dieser Wissenschaften,* 1 Bd., 4 Stück. Leipzig, 1778.
Whytt, Robert. *An Essay on the Vital and other Involuntary Motions of Animals.* 2nd ed. Edinburgh, 1763.
Wiedemann, Christian Rudolf Wilhelm. *Anweisung zur Rettung der Ertrunkenen, Erstickten, Erhängten, vom Blitze Erschlagenen, Erfrorenen und Vergifteten nach den neuesten Beobachtungen für Aerzte und Nichtärzte entworfen.* Braunschweig, 1797.

SECONDARY SOURCES

Ackerknecht, Erwin. "George Forster, Alexander von Humboldt and Ethnology." *Isis* 46 (1955): 83–95.
Adler, Jeremy. *"Eine fast magische Anziehungskraft": Goethes Wahlverwandtschaften und die Chemie seiner Zeit.* Munich: Beck, 1987.

Albury, William Randall. "The Logic of Condillac and the Structure of French Chemical and Biological Theory, 1780–1801." Ph.D. diss., Johns Hopkins University, 1972.
Altmann, Alexander. "Lessings Glaube an die Seelenwanderung." In *Die Trostvolle Aufklärung: Studien zur Metaphysik und politischen Theorie Moses Mendelsohns*, pp. 109–34. Stuttgart: Frommann-Holzboog, 1982.
Amrine, Frederick, Francis J. Zucker, and Harvey Wheeler, eds. *Goethe and the Sciences: A Reappraisal*. Dordrecht: Reidel, 1987.
Anderson, Wilda C. *Between the Library and the Laboratory: The Language of Chemistry in Eighteenth-Century France*. Baltimore: Johns Hopkins University Press, 1984.
Ayrault, Roger. *La genèse du romantisme Allemand: situation spirituelle de l'Allemagne dans la deuxième moitié du XVIIIe siècle*. 2 vols. Paris: Aubier, 1961.
Baasner, Rainer. *Abraham Gotthelf Kästner, Aufklärer (1719–1800)*. Tübingen: Max Niemeyer, 1991.
Bachelard, Gaston. *The New Scientific Spirit*. Translated by Arthur Goldhammer. Boston: Beacon Press, 1984.
Baker, Keith Michael. *Condorcet: From Natural Philosophy to Social Mathematics*. Chicago: University of Chicago Press, 1975.
———. "On the Problem of the Ideological Origins of the French Revolution." In *Modern European Intellectual History: Reappraisals and New Perspectives*, edited by Dominick LaCapra and Steven L. Kaplan, pp. 197–21. Ithaca: Cornell University Press, 1982.
Baker, Keith Michael, and Peter Hanns Reill, eds. *What's Left of the Enlightenment? A Postmodern Question*. Stanford: Stanford University Press, 2001.
Balmer, Heinz. "Alexander von Humboldt und Frankreich." *Gesnerus* 33 (1976): 235–52.
Balss, Heinrich. "Kielmeyer als Biologe." *Sudhoffs Archiv für Geschichte der Medizin* 23 (1930): 268–88.
Baumgardt, David. *Franz von Baader und die Philosophische Romantik*. Deutsche Vierteljahrsschrift für Literaturwissenschaft und Geistesgeschichte 10. Halle: Max Niemeyer, 1927.
Beck, Hanno. "Georg Foster und Alexander von Humboldt: zur Polarität ihres geographischen Denkens." In *Der Weltumsegler und seiner Freunde: Georg Foster als gesellschaftlicher Schriftsteller der Goethezeit*, edited by Detlef Rasmussen, pp. 175–88. Tübingen: Gunther Narr Verlag, 1988.
———. *Gespräche Alexander von Humboldts*. Berlin: Akademie Verlag, 1959.
———. "Physikalische Geographie und Philosophie der Nature im Werk Alexander von Humboldt." In *Universalismus und Wissenschaft im Werk und Wirken der Brüder Humboldt*, edited by Klaus Hammacher, pp. 29–33. Studien zur Philosophie und Literatur des neunzehnten Jahrhunderts 31. Frankfurt: Vittorio Klostermann, 1976.
Beck, Richard. "Abraham Gottlob Werner: eine kritischer Würdigung des Begründers der modernen Geologie zu seinem hundertjährigen Todestage."

Jahrbuch für das Berg und Hüttenwesen im Königreich Sachsen 91 (1917): 3–49.
Bensaude-Vincent, Bernadette. "The Balance between Chemistry and Politics." In *The Chemical Revolution: Context and Practices*, edited by Lissa Roberts. *The Eighteenth Century: Theory and Interpretation* 33 (1992): 217–37.

———. "A View of the Chemical Revolution through Contemporary Textbooks: Lavoisier, Fourcroy and Chaptal." *British Journal for the History of Science* 23 (1990): 435–50.
Benz, Ernst. *Les sources mystiques de la philosophie romantique Allemand*. Paris: J. Vrin, 1968.
Berglar, Peter. "Der romantische Aufstand: zur Psycho-Historie des Zeitgeistes." *Saeculum* 27 (1976): 197–210.
Binder, Wolfgang. "'Genuss' in Dichtung und Philosophie des 17. und 18. Jahrhunderts." *Archiv für Begriffsgeschichte* 17 (1973): 66–92.
Blanckaert, Claude. "Buffon and the Natural History of Man: Writing History and the 'Fondational Myth' of Anthropology." *History of the Human Sciences* 6 (1993): 13–50.
Bloch, Ernst. *Das Materialismusproblem, seine Geschichte und Substanz*. In *Ernst Bloch Gesamtausgabe*, vol. 7. Frankfurt am Main: Suhrkamp, 1974.

———. "Natur als organisierendes Prinzip-Materialismus beim frühen Schelling." In *Materialien zu Schellings philosophischen Anfängen*, edited by Manfred Frank and Gerhard Kurz, pp. 292–304. Frankfurt am Main: Suhrkamp, 1975.
Böckmann, Paul. "Goethes naturwissenschaftliches Denken als Bedingung der Symbolik seiner Altersdichtung." In *Literature and Science: International Federation for Modern Languages and Literatures, Proceedings of the Sixth Triennial Congress, Oxford 1954*, pp. 228–36. Oxford: Basil Blackwell, 1955.
Bonjour, Edgar. *Johannes von Müller*. Stuttgart: Benno Schwabe, 1957.
Bonspielen, Wolfgang. "Zu Hegels Auseinandersetzung mit Schellings Naturphilosophie in der 'Pänomenologie des Geistes.'" In *Schelling: seine Bedeutung für eine Geschichte der Natur und der Geschichte*, edited by Ludwig Hasler, pp. 167–72. Stuttgart: Frommann-Holzboog, 1981.
Bowie, Andrew. *Schelling and Modern European Philosophy*. London: Routledge, 1993.
Brady, Ronald D. "Form and Cause in Goethe's Morphology." In *Goethe and the Sciences: A Reappraisal*, edited by Frederick Amrine, Francis Zucker, and Harvey Wheeler, pp. 257–300. Dordrecht: Reidel, 1987.
Bräuning-Oktavio, Hermann. *Oken und Goethe im Lichte Neuer Quellen*. Weimar: Arion Verlag, 1959.

———. *Vom Zwischenkieferknochen zur Idee des Typus: Goethe als Naturforscher in den Jahren 1780–1786*. Nova Acta Leopoldina, Neue Folge 126, vol. 18. Leipzig: Barth, 1956.
Brednow, Walter. "Wilhelm von Humboldt und die Physiognomik." *Clio Medica* 4 (1969): 33–42.
Brinkmann, Richard, ed. *Romantik in Deutschland: ein interdisziplinäres Symposium*. Stuttgart: Metzlersche Verlagsbuchhandlung, 1978.

Brittan, Gorden G., Jr. *Kant's Theory of Science.* Princeton: Princeton University Press, 1978.
Broberg, Gunnar. "The Broken Circle." In *The Quantifying Spirit in the Eighteenth Century,* edited by Tore Frängsmyr, John L. Heilbron, and Robin Rider, pp. 45–72. Berkeley: University of California Press, 1990.
Broman, Thomas H. *The Transformation of German Medicine, 1750–1820.* Cambridge: Cambridge University Press, 1996.
Brooke, John Hedley. *Science and Religion: Some Historical Perspectives.* Cambridge: Cambridge University Press, 1991.
———. "Wöhler's Urea and Its Vital Force? A Verdict from the Chemists." *Ambix* 15 (1968): 84–114.
Brown, Theodore M. "From Mechanism to Vitalism in Eighteenth-Century Physiology." *Journal of the History of Biology* 7 (1974): 179–216.
Browne, Alice. "J. B. van Helmont's Attack on Aristotle." *Annals of Science* 36 (1979): 575–91.
Bruford, Walter H. *The German Tradition of Self-cultivation: 'Bildung' from Humboldt to Thomas Mann.* Cambridge: Cambridge Univeristy Press, 1975.
Buess, Heinrich. "Zur Entstehung der Elementa Physiologiae Albrecht von Hallers (1708)." *Gesnerus* 16 (1959): 17–35.
Burkhardt, Richard W., Jr. "Lamarck and Species." In *Historie du concept d'espèce dans les sciences de la vie,* edited by Scott Atran, pp. 161–80. Paris: Fondation Singer-Polignac, 1985.
———. *The Spirit of System: Lamarck and Evolutionary Biology.* Cambridge, Mass.: Harvard University Press, 1977.
Bynum, William Frederick, and Roy Porter, eds. *William Hunter and the Eighteenth-Century Medical World.* Cambridge: Cambridge University Press, 1985.
Canguilhem, Georges. "The Role of Analogies and Models in Biological Discovery." In *Scientific Change: Historical Studies in the Intellectual, Social and Technical Conditions for Scientific Discovery and Technical Invention, from Antiquity to the Present,* edited by Alistair Cameroon Crombie, pp. 507–21. London: Heineman, 1962.
Cannon, Susan Faye. *Science in Culture: The Early Victorian Period.* New York: Dawson and Science History Publications, 1978.
Cantor, Geoffrey N., and Michael Jonathan Sessions Hodge, eds. *Conceptions of Ether: Studies in the History of Ether Theories 1740–1900.* Cambridge: Cambridge University Press, 1981.
Cantor, Geoffrey N., and Steven Shapin. "Phrenology in Early Nineteenth-Century Edinburgh: An Historiographical Discussion." *Annals of Science* 32 (1975): 195–218.
Cassirer, Ernst. *The Philosophy of the Enlightenment.* Translated by Fritz C. Koelln and James P. Pettegrove. Princeton: Princeton University Press, 1951.
Charlton, D. G. *New Images of the Natural in France: A Study in European Cultural History, 1750–1800.* Cambridge: Cambridge University Press, 1984.

Clark, William. "The Death of Metaphysics in Enlightened Prussia." In *The Sciences in Enlightened Europe*, edited by William Clark, Jan Golinski, and Simon Schaffer, pp. 423–73. Chicago: University of Chicago Press, 1999.
Clark, William, Jan Golinski, and Simon Schaffer, eds. *The Sciences in Enlightened Europe*. Chicago: University of Chicago Press, 1999.
Coleman, William. *Georges Cuvier, Zoologist: A Study in the History of Evolutionary Theory*. Cambridge Mass.: Harvard Univeristy Press, 1964.
———. "Limits of the Recapitulation Theory: Carl Friedrich Kielmeyer's Critique of the Presumed Parallelism of Earth History, Ontogeny, and the Present Order of Organisms." *Isis* 64 (1973): 341–50.
Colvin, Phyliss. "Ontological and Epistemological Commitments and Social Relations in the Sciences: The Case of the Aritmomorphic System of Scientific Production." In *The Social Production of Scientific Knowledge*, edited by Everett Mendelsohn, Peter Weingart, and Richard Whitley, pp. 103–28. Dordrecht: Reidel, 1971.
Corbey, Raymond, and Bert Theunissen, eds. *Ape, Man, Apeman: Changing Views since 1600. Evaluative Proceedings of the Symposium Ape, Man, Apeman: Changing Views since 1600, Leiden, the Netherlands, 28 June–1 July 1993*. Leiden: Department of Prehistory, Leiden University, 1995.
Corbin, Alain. *The Foul and the Fragrant: Odor and the French Social Imagination*. Cambridge, Mass.: Harvard University Press, 1986.
Crombie, Alistair Cameroon. "P. L. Moreau de Maupertuis, F.R.S. (1698–1759): Precurseur du transformisme. *Revue Synthése* 78 (1957): 33–56.
Crosland, Maurice. "The Chemical Revolution of the Eighteenth Century and the Eclipse of Alchemy in the 'Age of Enlightenment.'" In *Alchemy Revisted*, edited by Zweder Rudolf Willem Maria von Martels, pp. 67–80. Leiden: Brill, 1990.
Cowan, Marianne. *Humanist without Portfolio: An Anthology of the Writings of Wilhelm von Humboldt*. Detroit: Wayne State University Press, 1963.
Culotta, Charles. "German Biophysics, Objective Knowledge and Romanticism." *Historical Studies in the Physical Sciences* 4 (1974): 3–33.
Cunningham, Andrew. "Medicine to Calm the Mind: Boerhaave's Medical System and Why It Was Adopted in Edinburgh." In *The Medical Enlightenment of the Eighteenth Century*, edited by Andrew Cunningham and Roger French, pp. 40–66. Cambridge: Cambridge University Press, 1990.
Cunningham, Andrew, and Roger French, eds. *The Medical Enlightenment of the Eighteenth Century*. Cambridge: Cambridge University Press, 1990.
Cunningham, Andrew, and Nicholas Jardine, eds. *Romanticism and the Sciences*. Cambridge: Cambridge University Press, 1990.
Darnton, Robert. *The Forbidden Best-Sellers of Pre-Revolutionary France*. Princeton: Princeton University Press, 1995.
Daston, Lorraine. "Afterword: The Ethos of the Enlightenment." In *The Sciences in Enlightened Europe*, edited by William Clark, Jan Golinski, and Simon Schaffer, pp. 495–505. Chicago: University of Chicago Press, 1999.
———. *Classical Probability in the Enlightenment*. Princeton: Princeton University Press, 1988.

———. "Rational Individuals versus Laws of Society: From Probability to Statistics." In *The Probabilistic Revolution*, edited by Lorenz Krüger, Lorraine Daston, and Michael Heidelberger, vol. 1, pp. 295–304. Cambridge, Mass: MIT Press, 1987.

Dawson, Virginia. *Nature's Enigma: The Problem of the Polyp in the Letters of Bonnet, Trembley, and Réaumur*. Philadelphia: American Philosophical Society, 1987.

Debus, Allen G. *The Chemical Dream of the Renaissance*. Cambridge: Haffner, 1968.

———. "Iatrochemistry and the Chemical Revolution." In *Alchemy Revisted*, edited by Zweder Rudolf Willem Maria von Martels, pp. 51–66. Leiden: Brill, 1990.

Dettelbach, Michael. "Baconisnism in Revolutionary Germany." In *The Skeptical Tradition around 1800*, edited by Johan van der Zande and Richard Popkin, pp. 175–86. Dordrecht: Kluwer, 1998.

———. *Cosmos: A Sketch of a Physical Description of the Universe*. Introduction, vol. II, viixxxix. Translated by E. C. Otté. Baltimore: Johns Hopkins University Press, 1997.

———. "The Face of Nature: Precise Mesaurement, Mapping, and Sensibility in the Work of Alexander von Humboldt." *Studies in the History and Philosophy of Biology and the Biomedical Sciences* 30 (1999): 473–504.

———. "Global Physics and Aesthetic Empire: Humboldt's Physical Portrait of the Tropics." In *Visions of Empire: Voyages, Botany, and Representations of Nature*, edited by David Miller and Peter Hanns Reill, pp. 258–92. Cambridge: Cambridge University Press, 1996.

———. "Humboldtian Science." In *Cultures of Natural History*, edited by Nicholas Jardine, James A. Secord, and Emma C. Spary, pp. 287–304. Cambridge: Cambridge University Press, 1996.

———. "Humboldt zwischen Aufklärung und Romantik." In *Alexander von Humboldt 1799–1999: Aufbruch in die Moderne*, edited by Ottmar Ette. Berlin: Akademie-Verlag, 2001.

Dietzsch, Steffen. "Höhere Nature." In *Schelling: seine Bedeutung für eine Geschichte der Natur und der Geschichte*, edited by Ludwig Hasler, pp. 161–66. Stuttgart: Frommann-Holzboog, 1981.

d'Irsay, Stephan. *Albrecht von Haller: eine Studie zur Geistesgeschichte der Aufklärung*. Arbeiten des Instituts für Medizin an der Universität Leipzig 1. Leipzig: Georg Thieme, 1930.

Dobbs, Betty Jo T. "Newton's Copy of 'Secrets Reveal'd and the Regimens of the Work." *Ambix* 26 (1979): 145–69.

Donovan, Arthur L. *Antoine Lavoisier: Science, Administration and Revolution*. Oxford: Blackwell, 1993.

———, ed. *The Chemical Revolution: Essays in Reinterpretation*. *Osiris*, 2nd series, vol. 4. Chicago: University of Chicago Press, 1988.

———. "Lavoisier and the Origins of Modern Chemistry." In *The Chemical Revolution: Essays in Reinterpretation*, edited by Arthur L. Donovan, pp. 214–31. *Osiris*, 2nd series, vol. 4. Chicago: University of Chicago Press, 1988.

———. *Philosophical Chemistry in the Scottish Enlightenment: The Doctrines and Discoveries of William Cullen and Joseph Black.* Edinburgh: Edinburgh University Press, 1975.

———. "Pneumatic Chemistry and Newtonian Natural Philosophy: William Cullen and Joseph Black." *Isis* 67 (1976): 217–29.

———. "William Cullen and the Research Tradition of Eighteenth-Century Scottish Chemistry." In *The Origins and Nature of the Scottish Enlightenment: Essays,* edited by Roy Hutchinson Campbell and Andrew S. Skinner, pp. 98–114. Edinburgh: John Donald, 1982.

Dougherty, Frank. "Johann Friedrich Blumenbach und Samuel Thomas Sömmerring: eine Auseinandersetzung in anthropologischer Hinsicht?" In *Samuel Thomas Soemmerring und die Gelerhten der Goethezeit,* edited by Gunther Mann and Franz Dumont, pp. 35–56. Stuttgart: Gustav Fischer Verlag, 1985.

Droz, Jacques. *Deutschland und die Französische Revolution.* Wiesbaden: Franz Steiner Verlag, 1955.

Duchesneau, François. *La physiologie des lumières: empirisme, modèles et théories.* International Archives of the History of Ideas 95. The Hague: Martinus Nijhoff, 1982.

———. "Vitalism in Late Eighteenth-Century Physiology: The Cases of Barthez, Blumenbach and John Hunter." In *William Hunter and the Eighteenth-Century Medical World,* edited by William Frederick Bynum and Roy Porter, pp. 259–95. Cambridge: Cambridge University Press, 1985.

Duchet, Michèle. *Anthropologie et histoire au siècle des lumières: Buffon, Voltaire, Rousseau, Helvétius, Diderot.* Paris: Flammarion, 1971.

Dumont, Franz. "Das 'Seelenbündnis': die Freundschaft zwischen Georg Foster und Thomas Sömmerring." In *Der Weltumsegler und seiner Freunde: Georg Foster als gesellschaftlicher Schriftsteller der Goethezeit,* edited by Detlef Rasmussen, pp. 70–100. Tübingen: Gunther Narr Verlag, 1988.

Eddy, John H. "Buffon's *Histoire naturelle:* History? A Critique of Recent Interpretations." *Isis* 85 (1994): 644–61.

Efron, John M. "Images of the Jewish Body: Three Medical Views from the Jewish Enlightenment." *Bulletin of the History of Medicine* 69 (1995): 349–66.

Eich, Wolfgang. *Medizinische Semiotik (1750–1850): Ein Beitrag zur Geschichte des Zeichenbegriffs in der Medizin.* Freiburger Forschungen zur Medizingeschichte, Neue Folge, 13. Freiburg: Hans Ferdinand Schulz, 1986.

Engelhardt, Dietrich von. *Die chemischen Zeitschrift des Lorenz von Crell.* Indices naturwissenschaftlich–medizinischer Periodica bis 1850, 2, edited by Armin Gens. Stuttgart: Anton Heismann, 1974.

———. *Hegel und die Chemie: Studien zur Philosophie und Wissenschaft der Natur um 1800.* Edited by Armin Geus and Guido Pressler. Schriften zur Wissenschaftsgeschichte I. Wiesbaden: Guido Pressler, 1976.

———. "Historical Consciousness in the German Romantic Naturforschung." In *Romanticism and the Sciences,* edited by Andrew Cunningham and Nicholas Jardine, pp. 69–81. Cambridge: Cambridge University Press, 1990.

———. *Historisches Bewußtsein in der Naturwissenschaft von der Aufklärung bis zum Positivismus*. Freiburg: Karl Alber, 1979.

———. "Die Naturwissenschaft der Aufklärung und die romantischidealistische Naturphilosophie." In *Idealismus und Aufklärung: Kontinuität und Kritik der Aufklärung in Philosophie und Poesie um 1800*, edited by Christoph Jamme and Gerhard Kurz, pp. 80–96. Stuttgart: Kletta-Cota, 1988.

———. "Die organischen Natur und die Lebenswissenschaften in Schellings Naturphilosophie." *Natur und Subjektivität: zur Auseinandersetzung mit der Naturphilosophie des jungen Schelling. Referate, Voten und Protokolle des II. Internationalen Schelling-Tagung Zürich 1983*, edited by Reinhard Heckmann, Hermann Krings, and Rudolf W. Meyer, pp. 39–59. Stuttgart: Frommann-Holzboog, 1985.

———. "Prinzipien und Ziele der Naturphilosophie Schellings-Situation um 1800 und spätere Wirkungsgeschichte." In *Schelling: seine Bedeutung für eine Geschichte der Natur und der Geschichte*, edited by Ludwig Hasler, pp. 77–98. Stuttgart: Frommann-Holzboog, 1981.

———. "Romantik im Spannugsfeld von Naturgefühl, Naturwissenschaft und Naturphilosophie." In *Romantik in Deutschland: ein interdisziplinäres Symposium*, edited by Richard Brinkmann, pp. 167–74. Stuttgart: Metzlersche Verlagsbuchhandlung, 1978.

Erman, Wilhelm. *Der tierische Magnetismus in Preussen: vor und nach den Freiheitskriegen*. Beiheft 4 der Historischen Zeitschrift. Munich: Oldenbourg, 1925.

Faivre, Antoine, and Rolf Christian Zimmermann, eds. *Epochen der Naturmystik: Hermetische Tradition im wissenschaftlichen Fortschritt*. Berlin: Erich Schmidt Verlag, 1979.

Farber, Paul Lawrence. "Buffon and Daubenton: Divergent Traditions within the *Histoire naturelle*." *Isis* 66 (1975): 63–74.

Figlio, Karl M. "Theories of Perception and the Psychology of Mind in the Late Eighteenth Century." *History of Science* 13 (1975): 177–212.

Fink, Karl J. *Goethe's History of Science*. Cambridge: Cambridge University Press, 1991.

Foley, Vernard. *The Social Physics of Adam Smith*. West Lafayette, Ind.: Purdue University Press, 1976.

Foucault, Michel. *The Birth of the Clinic: An Archaeology of Medical Perception*. Translated by Alan M. Sheridan Smith. New York: Random House, 1973.

———. *Disicpline and Punish: The Birth of the Prison*. Translated by Alan M. Sheridan. New York: Randon House, 1979.

———. *The Order of Things: An Archaeology of the Human Sciences*. Translated by Alan M. Sheridan. New York: Pantheon Books, 1971.

Fox, Christopher, Roy Porter, and Robert Wokler, eds. *Inventing Human Science: Eighteenth-Century Domains*. Berkeley: University of California Press, 1995.

Frängsmyr, Tore. "The Mathematical Philosophy." In *The Quantifying Spirit in the Eighteenth Century*, edited by Tore Frängsmyr, John L. Heilbron, and Robin Rider, pp. 27–44. Berkeley: University of California Press, 1990.

Frängsmyr, Tore, John L. Heilbron, and Robin Rider, eds. *The Quantifying Spirit in the Eighteenth Century.* Berkeley: University of California Press, 1990.
Frank, Robert G., Jr. *Harvey and the Oxford Physiologists: Scientific Ideas and Social Interaction.* Berkeley: University of California Press, 1980.
Freudenthal, Gideon. *Atom und Individuum im Zeitalter Newtons: zur Genese der mechanistischen Natur und Sozialphilosophie.* Frankfurt am Main: Suhrkamp, 1982.
Funkenstein, Amos. *Theology and the Scientific Imagination from the Middle Ages to the Seventeenth Century.* Princeton: Princeton University Press, 1986.
Geertz, Clifford. *The Interpretation of Cultures: Selected Essays.* New York: Basic Books, 1976.
Gelfand, Toby. *Professionalizing Modern Medicine: Paris Surgeons and Medical Science and Institutions in the Eighteenth Century.* Westport, Conn.: Greenwood Press, 1980.
Geyer-Kordesch, Johanna. "Georg Ernst Stahl's Radical Pietist Medicine and Its Influence on the German Enlightenment." In *The Medical Enlightenment of the Eighteenth Century,* edited by Andrew Cunningham and Roger French, pp. 67–87. Cambridge: Cambridge University Press, 1990.

———. *Pietismus, Medizin und Aufklärung in Preußen im 18. Jahrhundert: das Leben und Werk Georg Ernst Stahls.* Tübingen: Max Niemeyer Verlag, 2000.
Gierl, Martin. "Compilation and the Production of Knowledge in the Early German Enlightenment." In *Wissenschaft als kulturelle Praxis, 1750–1900,* edited by Hans Erich Bödeker, Peter Hanns Reill, and Jürgen Schlumböhm, pp. 69–104. Göttingen: Vandenhoeck & Ruprecht, 1999.

———. *Pietismus und Aufklärung: theologische Polemik und die Kommunikationsreform am Ende des 17. Jahrhunderts.* Göttingen: Vandenhoeck & Ruprecht, 1997.
Gillispie, Charles Coulston. *The Edge of Objectivity: An Essay in the History of Scientific Ideas.* Princeton: Princeton University Press, 1960.

———. "The Encyclopédie and the Jacobin Philosophy of Science: A Study in Ideas and Consequences." In *Critical Problems in the History of Science,* edited by Marshall Clagett, pp. 255–89. Madison: University of Wisconsin Press, 1962.

———. *Science and Polity in France at the End of the Old Regime.* Princeton: Princeton University Press, 1980.
Ginzburg, Carlo. "Morelli, Freud and Sherlock Holmes: Clues and Scientific Method." *History Workshop* 9 (1960): 5–36.
Gode–von Aesch, Alexander. *Natural Science in German Romanticism.* New York: Columbia University Press, 1941.
Goldmann, Lucien. *The Philosophy of the Enlightenment: The Christian Burgess and the Enlightenment.* Translated by Henry Maas. London: Routledge and Kegan Paul, 1973.
Golinski, Jan. "Barometers of Change: Meteorological Instruments as Machines of Enlightenment." In *The Sciences in Enlightened Europe,* edited

by William Clark, Jan Golinski, and Simon Schaffer, pp. 69–125. Chicago: University of Chicago Press, 1999.

———. *Science as Public Culture: Chemistry and Enlightenment, 1760–1820.* Cambridge: Cambridge University Press, 1992.

Gough, Jerry B. "Lavoisier and the Fulfillment of the Stahlian Revolution." In *The Chemical Revolution: Essays in Reinterpretation,* edited by Arthur Donovan, pp. 15–33. *Osiris,* 2nd series, vol. 4. Chicago: University of Chicago Press, 1988.

Gower, Barry. "Speculation in Physics: The History and Practice of Naturphilosophie." *Studies in History and Philosophy of Science* 3 (1973): 301–56.

Gray, Ronald D. *Goethe the Alchemist: A Study of Alchemical Symbolism in Goethe's Literary and Scientific Works.* Cambridge: Cambridge University Press, 1952.

Guerlac, Henry. "Joseph Black." In *Dictionary of Scientific Biography,* edited by Charles C. Gillispie, Henry Guerlac, and Julies Mayer, vol. 1, pp. 173–83. New York: Scribner, 1970–80.

———. "Joseph Black and Fixed Air: A Bicentary Retrospective, with Some New or Little Known Material." *Isis* 48 (1957): 124–51; 433–56.

———. "Antoine Lavoisier." In *Dictionary of Scientific Biography,* ed. Charles C. Gillispie, Henry Guerlac, and Julies Mayer. Vol. 7. New York: Scribner, 1970–80.

Gulyga, Arsenij. *Schelling: Leben und Werk.* Translated by Elke Kirsten. Stuttgart: Deutsche Verlags Anstalt, 1989.

Guntau, Martin, and Hans Jürgen Rösler. "Die Verdienste von Abraham Gottlob Werner auf dem Gebiet der Mineralogie." In *Abraham Gottlob Werner: Gedankschrift aus Anlass der Wiederkehr seines Todestags nach 150 Jahren am 30 Juni 1969,* edited by Karl-Friedrich Lüdemann, pp. 47–82. Leipzig: Deutsche Verlag für Grundstoffindustrie, 1969.

Guyénot, Émil. *Les sciences de la vie aux XVIIe et XVIIIe siécles: l'idée d'evolution.* Paris: Albin Michel, 1957.

Haeckel, Ernst. *Anthropogenie oder Entwicklungsgeschichte des Menschen: gemeinverständliche Vorträge über die Grundzüge der Menschen Keimes und Stammes-Geschichte.* 2nd ed. Leipzig: Verlag Wilhelm Engelmann, 1874.

———. *Natürliche Schöpfugsgeschichte: gemeinverständliche wissenschaftliche Vorträge über die Entwicklungslehre im Allgemeinen und diejenige von Darwin, Goethe und Lamarck in Besonderen.* 5th ed. Berlin: Verlag Georg Reimer, 1874.

Hagner, Michael. "Enlightened Monsters." In *The Sciences in Enlightened Europe,* edited by William Clark, Jan Golinski, and Simon Schaffer, pp. 175–237. Chicago: University of Chicago Press, 1999.

———, ed. *Der "falsche" Körper: Beiträge zu einer Geschichte der Montrositäten.* Göttingen: Wallstein, 1995.

———. "Vom Naturalienkabinett zur Embriologie: Wandlungen des Montrösen und die Ordnung des Lebens." In *Der "falsche" Körper: Beiträge zu einer Geschichte der Montrositäten,* edited by Michael Hagner, pp. 73–107. Göttingen: Wallstein, 1995.

oger. "Laplace and the Mechanistic Universe." In *God and Nature: Historical Essays on the Encounter between Christianity and Science*, edited by David C. Lindberg and Ronald L. Numbers, pp. 256–76. Berkeley: University of California Press, 1986.

———. "The Laplacean View of Calculation." In *The Quantifying Spirit in the Eighteenth Century*, edited by Tore Frängsmyr, John L. Heilbron, and Robin Rider, pp. 363–80. Berkeley: University of California Press, 1990.

Haigh, Elizabeth. "The Roots of the Vitalism of Xavier Bichat." *Bulletin of the History of Medicine* 49 (1975): 72–86.

Hall, Thomas Steele. *Ideas of Life and Matter: Studies in the History of General Physiology, 600 B.C.–A.D. 1900*. 2 vols. Chicago: University of Chicago Press, 1969.

Hansen, Leeann. "From Enlightenment to Naturphilosophie: Marcus Herz, Johann Christian Reil, and the Problem of Border Crossings." *Journal of the History of Biology* 26 (1993): 39–64.

Hankins, Thomas L. "Eighteenth-Century Attempts to Resolve the vis viva Controversy." *Isis* 56 (1965): 281–97.

———. *Science and the Enlightenment*. Cambridge: Cambridge University Press, 1985.

Hasler, Ludwig, ed. *Schelling: seine Bedeutung für eine Philosophie der Natur und der Geschichte: Referate und Kolloquien der Internationalen Schelling-Tagung Zürich 1979*. Stuttgart: Frommann-Holzboog, 1981.

Hatfield, Gary. "Remaking the Science of Mind: Psychology as Natural Science." In *Inventing Human Science: Eighteenth-Century Domains*, edited by Christopher Fox, Roy Porter, and Robert Wokler, pp. 184–231. Berkeley: University of California Press, 1995.

Heckmann, Reinhard, Hermann Krings, and Rudolf W. Meyer, eds. *Natur und Subjektivität: zur Auseinandersetzung mit der Naturphilosophie des jungen Schelling. Referate, Voten und Protokolle des II. Internationalen Schelling-Tagung Zürich 1983*. Stuttgart: Frommann-Holzboog, 1985.

Heilbron, John L. *Electricity in the 17th and 18th Centuries: A Study of Early Modern Physics*. Berkeley: University of California Press, 1979.

———. "The Measure of Enlightenment." In *The Quantifying Spirit in the Eighteenth Century*, edited by Tore Frängsmyr, John L. Heilbron, and Robin Rider, pp. 207–42. Berkeley: University of California Press, 1990.

Henel, Heinrich. "Goethe and Science." In *Literature and Science*, International Federation for Modern Languages and Literatures, Proceedings of the Sixth Triennial Congress, Oxford, pp. 228–36. Oxford: Basil Blackwell, 1955.

Hess, Wilhelm. *Die Entwicklung der Pflanzenkunde in ihren Hauptzügen*. Göttingen: Vandenhoeck & Ruprecht, 1872.

Hill, Christopher. "Science and Magic in Seventeenth-Century England." In *Culture, Ideology and Politics: Essays for Eric Hobsbawm*. History Workshop Series, edited by Raphael S. Samuel and Gareth Stedman Jones, pp. 176–93. London: Routledge and Kegan Paul, 1982.

Hintzsche, Erich "Einige kritische Bemerkungen zur Bio- und Ergographie Albrecht von Hallers." *Gesnerus* 16 (1959): 1–15.

Holmes, Frederick L. "Lavoisier's Conceptual Passage." In *The Chemical Revo-

lution: Essays in Reinterpretation, edited by Arthur Donovan, pp. 82–91. *Osiris,* 2nd series, vol. 4. Chicago: University of Chicago Press, 1988.

Honegger, Claudia. *Die Ordnung der Geschlechter: die Wissenschaften vom Menschen und das Weib, 1750–1850.* Frankfurt: Campus, 1991.

Hoppe, Brigitte. "Polarität, Stufung und Metamorphose in der spekulativen Biologie der Romantik." *Naturwissenschaftliche Rundschau* 20 (1967): 380–83.

Hufbauer, Karl. *The Formation of the German Chemical Community: 1780–1795.* Berkeley: University of California Press, 1982.

Hulling, Mark. *The Autocritique of Enlightenment: Rousseau and the Philosophes.* Cambridge, Mass.: Harvard University Press, 1994.

Iggers, Georg. *The German Conception of History: The National Tradition of Historical Thought from Herder to the Present.* Middeltown, Conn.: Wesleyan University Press, 1968.

Iltis (Merchant), Carolyn. "D'Alembert and the *Vis Viva* Controversy." *Studies in History and Philosophy of Science* 1 (1970): 135–44.

———. "The Decline of Cartesianism in Mechanics: The Leibnizian-Cartesian Debates." *Isis* 64 (1973): 356–73.

———. "The Leibnizian-Newtonian Debates: Natural Philosophy and Social Psychology." *British Journal for the History of Science* 6 (1973): 343–77.

———. "Madam du Chatelet's Metaphysics and Mechanics." *Studies in History and Philsophy of Science* 8 (1977): 29–48.

Irmscher, Hans Dietrich. "Aneignung und Kritik naturwissenschaftlicher Vorstellungen bei Herder." In *Texte, Motive und Gestalten der Goethezeit: Festschrift für Hans Reiss,* edited by John L. Hibberd and Hugh B. Nisbet, pp. 33–63. Tübingen: Max Niemeyer, 1989.

———."Beobachtunegn zur Funktion der Analogie im Denken Herders." *Deutsche Vierteljahrschrift für Literaturwissenschaft und Geistesgeschichte* 55 (1981): 64–97.

Israel, Jonathan. *Radical Enlightenment: Philosophy and the Making of Modernity.* Oxford: Oxford University Press, 2002.

Jacob, Margaret C. "Christianity and the Newtonian World View." In *God and Nature: Historical Essays on the Encounter between Christianity and Science,* edited by David C. Lindberg and Ronald L. Numbers, pp. 238–55. Berkeley: University of California Press, 1986.

———. *Living the Enlightenment: Freemasonry and Politics in Eighteenth-Century Europe.* New York: Oxford University Press, 1991.

———. *The Radical Enlightenment: Pantheists, Freemasons, and Republicans.* London: George Allen and Unwin, 1981.

Jacobs, Wilhelm G. *Zwischen Revolution und Orthodoxie? Schelling und seine Freunde im Stift und an der Universität Tübingen. Texte und Untersuchungen.* Stuttgart: Frommann-Holzboog, 1989.

Jaeckle, Erwin. *Vom Sichtbaren Geist: Naturphilosophie.* Stuttgart: Klett-Cotta, 1984.

Jahn, Ilse. "Die anatomischen Studien der Brüder Humboldt unter Justus Christian Loder in Jena." *Beiträge zur Geschichte der Universität Erfurt* 14 (1968–69): 91–97.

Jardine, Nicholas. "Inner History: or How to End the Enlightenment." In *The Sciences in Enlightened Europe*, edited by William Clark, Jan Golinski, and Simon Schaffer, pp. 477–95. Chicago: University of Chicago Press, 1999.

———. "Naturphilosophen and the Kingdoms of Nature." In *Cultures of Natural History*, edited by Nicholas Jardine, James A. Secord, and Emma Spary, pp. 230–45. Cambridge: Cambridge University Press, 1996.

Jardine, Nicholas, James A. Secord, and Emma Spary, eds. *Cultures of Natural History*. Cambridge: Cambridge University Press, 1996.

———. *The Scenes of Inquiry: On the Reality of Questions in the Sciences*. 2nd ed. Oxford: Clarendon Press, 2000.

Jaynes, Julian, and William Woodward. "In the Shadow of the Enlightenment: I. Reimarus against the Epicureans." *Journal of the History of the Behavioral Sciences* 10 (1974): 3–15.

———. "In the Shadow of the Enlightenment: II. Reimarus and His Theory of Drives." *Journal of the History of the Behavioral Sciences* 10 (1974): 144–59.

Jones, Colin. "Montpellier Medical Students and the Medicalisation of 18th-Century France." In *Problems and Methods in the History of Medicine*, edited by Roy Porter and Andrew Wear, pp. 57–80. London: Croom Helm, 1987.

Jordanova, Ludmilla. *Languages of Nature: Critical Essays on Science and Literature*. London: Free Association Books, 1986.

———. "Medical Mediations: Mind, Body and the Guillotine." In *Nature Displayed: Gender, Science and Medicine 1760–1820*, pp. 118–30. London: Longman, 1999.

———. "Sex and Gender." In *Inventing Human Science: Eighteenth-Century Domains*, edited by Christopher Fox, Roy Porter, and Robert Wokler, pp. 152–83. Berkeley: University of California Press, 1995.

———. *Sexual Visions: Images of Gender in Science and Medicine between the Eighteenth and Twentieth Centuries*. New York: Harvester Wheatsheaf, 1989.

Jordanova, Ludmilla, and Roy Porter, eds. *Images of the Earth: Essays in the History of the Environmental Sciences*. British Society for the History of Science Monographs 1. Chalfont St. Giles: British Society for the History of Science, 1981.

Kaehler, Siegfried A. *Wilhelm von Humboldt und der Staat: ein Beitrag zur Geschichte deutscher Lebensgestaltung um 1800*. 2nd ed. Göttingen: Vandenhoeck & Ruprecht, 1963.

Kapitza, Peter. *Die frühromantische Theorie der Mischung*. Münchener Germanistische Beiträge. Edited by Werner Betz and Hermann Kunisch. Munich: Max Hueber Verlag, 1968.

Kapoor, Satish. "Berthollet, Proust, and Proportions." *Chymia* 10 (1965): 53–110.

Karcher, Johannes. "Die animalistische Theorie Georg Ernst Stahls im Aspekt der pietistischen Bewegung an der Universität zu Halle an der Saale im zu Ende gehenden 17. und beginnenden 18. Jahrhundert." *Gesnerus* 15 (1958): 1–16.

Käuser, Andreas. *Physiognomik und Roman im 18. Jahrhundert*. Forschungen zur Literatur und Kulturgeschichte 24. Edited by Helmut Kreuzer and Karl Riha. Frankfurt am Main: Peter Lang, 1989.

Keller, Evelyn Fox. *Reflections on Gender and Science*. New Haven: Yale University Press, 1985.

Kelly, George Armstrong. *Mortal Politics in Eighteenth-Century France*. Waterloo, Ontario: University of Waterloo Press, 1986.

Kerker, Milton. "Hermann Boerhaave and the Development of Pneumatic Chemistry." *Isis* 46 (1955): 36–49.

Kessel, Eberhard. *Wilhelm von Humboldt: Idee und Wirklichkeit*. Stuttgart: Koehler, 1967.

Kiernan, Colm. "Additional Reflections on Diderot and Science." *Diderot Studies* 14 (1971): 113–42.

———. *The Enlightenment and Science in Eighteenth-Century France*. Studies on Voltaire and the Eighteenth Century, edited by Theodore Besterman. Oxfordshire: Voltaire Foundation, 1973.

Kiesewetter, Carl. *Geschichte des neueren Occultismus: geheimwissenschaftliche Systeme von Agrippa bis zu Carl du Prel*. Leipzig, 1891.

Kim, Mi Gyung. "Practice and Representation: Investigative Programs of Chemical Affinity in the Nineteenth Century." Ph.D diss., University of California, Los Angeles, 1990.

King, Lester. *The Medical World of the Eighteenth Century*. Chicago: University of Chicago Press, 1958.

Kleinsorge, John Arnold. "Beiträge zur Geschichte der Lehre vom Parallelismus der Individual und der Gesamtentwicklung." Diss., Jena, 1900.

Knight, David. "Romanticism and the Sciences." In *Romanticism and the Sciences*, edited by Andrew Cunningham and Nicholas Jardine, pp. 13–24. Cambridge: Cambridge University Press, 1990.

Knodt, Eva. "Hermeneutics and the End of Science: Herder's Role in the Formation of Natur and Geisteswissenschaften." In *Johann Gottfried Herder and the Disciplines of Knowledge*, edited by Wulf Koepke, pp. 1–12. Columbia, S.C.: Camden House, 1996.

Koelbing, Huldrych M. "Georg Joseph Beer's 'Lehre von den Augenkrankheiten' (Wien 1813–1817) im Zusammenahng mit der Medizin der Zeit." *Clio Medica* 5 (1970): 225–48.

Koerner, Lisbet. "Daedalus Hyperboreus: Baltic Natural History and Mineralogy in Enlightened Prussia." In *The Sciences in Enlightened Europe*, edited by William Clark, Jan Golinski, and Simon Schaffer, pp. 389–422. Chicago: University of Chicago Press, 1999.

———. *Linnaeus: Nature and Nation*. Cambridge, Mass.: Harvard University Press, 1999.

———. "Purposes of Linnaean Travel: A Preliminary Report." In *Visions of Empire: Voyages, Botany, and Representations of Nature*, edited by David Philip Miller and Peter Hanns Reill, pp. 117–52. Cambridge: Cambridge University Press, 1996.

Kopp, Hermann. *Die Alchemie in Aelterer und neuerer Zeit: ein Beitrag zur Kulturgeschichte*. Reprint ed., 1886. Hildesheim: Georg Olms, 1962.

Krings, Hermann. "Vorbermerkungen zu Schellings Naturphilosophie." In *Schelling: seine Bedeutung für eine Geschichte der Natur und der Geschichte*, edited by Ludwig Hasler, pp. 73–76. Stuttgart: Frommann-Holzboog, 1981.

———. "Vobermerkungen zu Schellings Naturphilosophie." In *Schelling: seine Bedeutung für eine Geschichte der Natur und der Geschichte*, edited by Ludwig Hasler, pp. 73–76. Stuttgart: Frommann-Holzboog, 1981.

Krohn, Wolfgang, and Günther Küppers. "Die natürlichen Ursachen der Zwecke: Kants Ansätze der Selbstorganisation." *Selbstorganisation: Jahrbuch für Komplexität in den Natur-, Sozial- und Geisteswissenschaften* 3 (1992): 7–15.

Kuczynski, Jürgen, and Wolfgang Heise. *Bild und Begriff: Studien über die Beziehungen zwischen Kunst und Wissenschaft.* Berlin: Aufbau Verlag, 1975.

Kuhn, Dorothea. "Goethe's Relationship to the Theories of Development of His Time." In *Goethe and the Sciences: A Reappraisal*, edited by Frederick Amrine, Francis J. Zucker, and Harvey Wheeler, pp. 3–17. Dordrecht: Reidel, 1987.

———. "Uhrwerk oder Organismus: Karl Friedrich Kielmeyers System der organischen Kräfte." In *Nova Acta Leopoldina: Abhandlungen der deutschen Akademie der Naturforscher Leopoldina*, Neue Folge 198, vol. 36, pp. 157–67. Leipzig: Johann Ambrosius Barth, 1970.

Kuhn, Thomas. "The Caloric Theory of Adiabatic Compression." *Isis* 49 (1958): 132–40.

———. *The Structure of Scientific Revolutions.* Chicago: University of Chicago Press, 1970.

———. "What Are Scientific Revolutions?" In *The Probabilistic Revolution,* edited by Lorenz Krüger, Lorrain Daston, and Michael Heidelberger, vol. 1, pp. 7–22. Cambridge, Mass.: MIT Press, 1987.

Lacqueur, Thomas. *Making Sex: Body and Gender from the Greeks to Freud.* Cambridge, Mass.: Harvard University Press, 1990.

Langthaler, Rudolf. *Organismus und Umwelt: die biologische Umweltlehre im Spiegel traditioneller Naturphilosophie.* Hildesheim: Georg Olms, 1992.

Larson, James. *Interpreting Nature: The Science of Living Form from Linnaeus to Kant.* Baltimore: Johns Hopkins University Press, 1994.

———. "The Most Confused Knot in the Doctrine of Reproduction." In *The Quantifying Spirit in the Eighteenth Century,* edited by Tore Frängsmyr, John L. Heilbron, and Robin Rider, pp. 267–90. Berkeley: University of California Press, 1990.

Laurent, Goulven."La notion d'espèce chez les paléontologistes français du XIX ème siécle." In *Historie du concept d'espèce dans les sciences de la vie,* edited by Scott Atran, pp. 141–59. Paris: Fondation Singer-Polignac, 1985.

Lawrence, Christopher. "The Nervous System and Society in the Scottish Enlightenment." In *Natural Order: Historical Studies of Scientific Culture,* edited by Barry Barnes and Steven Shapin, pp. 19–40. Beverly Hills: Sage Publications, 1979.

———. "Ornate Physicians and Learned Artisans: Edinburgh Medical Men, 1726–1776." In *William Hunter and the Eighteenth-Century Medical World*, edited by William Frederick Bynum and Roy Porter, pp. 153–76. Cambridge: Cambridge University Press, 1985.

Lemoine, Albert. *Le vitalisme et l'animisme de Stahl*. Paris: Germer Bailliére, 1864.

Lenoir, Timothy. "The Eternal Laws of Form: Morphotypes and the Conditions of Existence in Goethe's Biological Thought." In *Goethe and the Sciences: A Reappraisal*, edited by Frederick Amrine, Francis J. Zucker, and Harvey Wheeler, pp. 17–29. Dordrecht: Reidel, 1987.

———. "Generational Factors in the Origin of *Romantische Naturphilosophie*," *Journal of the History of Biology* 11 (1978): 57–100.

———. "Morphotypes and the Historicalgenetic Method in Romantic Biology." In *Romanticism and the Sciences*, edited by Andrew Cunningham and Nicholas Jardine, pp. 119–29. Cambridge: Cambridge University Press, 1990.

———. *The Strategy of Life: Teleology and Mechanics in Nineteenth-Century German Biology*. Dordrecht: Reidel, 1982.

Lepenies, Wolf. *Das Ende der Naturgeschichte: Wandel kultureller Selbstverständlichkeiten in den Wissenschaften des 18. und 19. Jahrhunderts*. Munich: Hanser Verlag, 1976.

———. "Linnaeus's *Nemesis divina* and the Concept of Divine Retaliation." *Isis* 73 (1982): 11–27.

Lesch, John E. "Systematics and the Geometrical Spirit." In *The Quantifying Spirit in the Eighteenth Century*, edited by Tore Frängsmyr, John L. Heilbron, and Robin Rider, pp. 73–112. Berkeley: University of California Press, 1990.

Lessky, Erna. "Albrecht von Haller, Gerard van Swieten und Boerhaavens Erbe." *Gesnerus* 16 (1959): 120–40.

———. "Albrecht von Haller und Anton de Haen im Streit um die Lehre von der Sensibilität." *Gesnerus* 16 (1959): 16–46.

Levere, Trevor H. "Lavoisier: Language, Instruments, and the Chemical Revolution." In *Nature, Experiment and the Sciences*, edited by Trevor H. Levere and William R. Shea, pp. 207–33. Dordrecht: Kluwer, 1990.

Lindeboom, Gerrit Arie. "Boerhaave's Concept of the Basic Structure of the Body." *Clio Medica* 5 (1970): 203–8.

Löw, Reinhard. "Qualitätenlehre und Materiekonstruktion: zur systematischen Aktulität von Schellings Naturphilosophie." In *Schelling: seine Bedeutung für eine Geschichte der Natur und der Geschichte*, edited by Ludwig Hasler, pp. 99–106. Stuttgart: Frommann-Holzboog, 1981.

Lundgren, Anders. "The Changing Role of Numbers in 18th Century Chemistry." In *The Quantifying Spirit in the Eighteenth Century*, edited by Tore Frängsmyr, John L. Heilbron, and Robin Rider, pp. 245–67. Berkeley: University of California Press, 1990.

———. "The New Chemistry in Sweden: The Debate That Wasn't." In *The Chemical Revolution: Essays in Reinterpretation*, edited by Arthur Donovan, pp. 121–45. *Osiris*, 2nd ser., vol. 4. Chicago: University of Chicago Press, 1988.

Mann, Gunther, and Franz Dumont, eds. *The Natur des Menschen: Probleme der physischen Anthropologie und Rassenkunde (1750–1850).* Stuttgart: Gustav Fischer Verlag, 1990.

———. *Samuel Thomas Sömmerring und die Gelehrten der Goethezeit.* Sömmerring Forschung: Beiträge zur Naturwissenschaft und Medizin der Neuzeit 1. Stuttgart: Gustav Fischer Verlag, 1985.

Marks, Ralph. *Differenz der Konzeption einer dynamischen Naturphilosophie bei Schelling und Eschenmayer.* Diss., University of Munich, 1983.

Martels, Zweder Rudolf Willem Maria von, ed. *Alchemy Revisted.* Collection de Travaux de l'Académie Internationale d'Histoire des Sciences 33. Edited by John D. North. Leiden: Brill, 1990.

Matussek, Peter, ed. *Goethe und die Verzeitlichung der Natur.* Munich: Beck, 1998.

Mayer, Peter. *Christoph Wilhelm Hufeland und der Brownianismus.* Diss., University of Mainz, 1993.

McEvoy, John G. "Continuity and Discontinuity in the Chemical Revolution." In *The Chemical Revolution: Essays in Reinterpretation,* edited by Arthur Donovan, pp. 195–213. *Osiris,* 2nd ser., vol. 4. Chicago: University of Chicago Press, 1988.

McIntosh, Christopher. "The Alchemy of the Gold und Rosenkreuz." In *Alchemy Revisted,* edited by Zweder Rudolf Willem Maria von Martels, pp. 245–49. Leiden: Brill, 1990.

McLaughlin, Peter. "Die Welt als Maschine: zur Genese des neuzeitlichen Naturbegriffs." In *Macrocosmos in Microcosmo: die Welt in der Stube. Zur Geschichte des Sammelns 1450–1800,* edited by Andreas Grote, pp. 439–51. Opladen: Leske and Burdich.

Meijer, Miriam. *Race and Aesthetics in the Anthropology of Petrus Camper, 1772–1789.* Amsterdam: Rodopi, 1999.

Melhado, Evan M. "Chemistry, Physics and the Chemical Revolution." *Isis* 76 (1985): 195–211.

———. "Metzger, Kuhn, and Eighteenth-Century Disciplinary History." In *Études sur Hélène Metzger,* edited by Gad Freudenthal, pp. 111–34. Paris: Fayard, 1989.

———. "Toward an Understanding of the Chemical Revolution." In *Knowledge and Society: Studies in the Sociology of Science Past and Present,* vol. VIII, edited by Robert A. Jones, Andrew Pickering, and Lowell Hargens, pp. 123–37. Grenwich, Conn.: JAI Press, 1989.

Mendelsohn, Everett. *Heat and Life: The Development of the Theory of Animal Heat.* Cambridge, Mass.: Harvard Press, 1964.

Mensching, Günther. *Totalität und Autonomie: Untersuchungen zur philosophischen Gesellschaftstheorie der französischen Materialismus.* Frankfurt am Main: Suhrkamp, 1971.

Merleau Ponty, Maurice. "Der Naturbegriff." In *Materialien zu Schellings philosophischen Anfängen,* edited by Manfred Frank and Gerhard Kurz, pp. 280–90. Frankfurt am Main: Suhrkamp, 1975.

Metzger, Hélène. *Newton, Stahl, Boerhaave et la doctrine chimique.* Paris: Félix Alcan, 1930.

Meyer-Abich, Klaus. *Revolution for Nature: From the Environment to the Connatural World*. Translated by Mathew Armstrong. Cambridge: White Horse Press, 1993.

Mocek, Reinhard. *Johann Christian Reil (1759–1813): das Problem des Uebergangs von der Spätaufklärung zur Romantik in der Biologie und Medizin in Deutschland*. Philosophie und Geschichte der Wissenschaften: Studien und Quellen 28. Edited by Hans Jörg Sandkühler. Frankfurt am Main: Peter Lang, 1995.

———. "Uebergänge: Aufregende Wissenschaftsgeschichte oder wie ein nüchterner Arzt zum Romantiker wurde." In *Wissenschaftskolleg Jahrbuch 1993/94*, pp. 113–18. Berlin: Nicolaische Verlagsbuchhandlung, 1995.

———. "Der Vitalismus Georg Ernst Stahls: die Ankündigung eines neuen Paradigmas." In *Hallesche Physiologie im Werden: Hallesches Symposium 1981*, edited by Wolfram Kaiser and Hans Hübner, pp. 25–30. Halle: Martin Luther University Halle-Wittenberg, 1981.

Moiso, Francesco. "Zur Quellenforschung der Schellingschen Naturphilosophie." In *Schelling: seine Bedeutung für eine Geschichte der Natur und der Geschichte*, edited by Ludwig Hasler, pp. 153–59. Stuttgart: Frommann-Holzboog, 1981.

Moore, James R., ed. *History, Humanity and Evolution: Essays for John C. Greene*. Cambridge: Cambridge University Press, 1989.

Moran, Bruce. *The Alchemical World of the German Court: Occult Philosophy and Chemical Medicine in the Circle of Moritz of Hessen (1572–1632)*. Sudhoffs Archiv: Zeitschrift für Wissenschaftsgeschichte, Beiheft 29. Stuttgart: Franz Steiner, 1991.

Moravia, Sergio. *Beobachtende Vernunft: Philosophie und Anthropologie in der Aufklärung*. Translated by Elizabeth Piras. Frankfurt: Ullstein, 1977.

———. "From *Homme Machine* to *Homme Sensible*: Changing Eighteenth-Century Models of Man's Image." *Journal of the History of Ideas* 39 (1978): 45–60.

Morgan, S. R. "Schelling and the Origins of his *Naturphilosophie*." In *Romanticism and the Sciences*, edited by Andrew Cunningham and Nicholas Jardine, pp. 25–37. Cambridge: Cambridge University Press, 1990.

Mornet, Daniel. "Les enseignements des bibliothèques privées (1750–1780)." *Revue d'Histoire Littéraire de la France* 17 (1910): 449–96.

Mortier, Roland. *Diderot in Deutschland: 1750–1850*. Stuttgart: Metzler, 1972.

Muhlack, Ulrich. *Geschichtswissenschaft im Humanismus und in der Aufklärung: die Vorgeschichte des Historismus*. Munich: Beck, 1991.

Mühlfriedel, W., and Martin Guntau. "Abraham Gottlob Werner's Wirken für die Wissenschaft und sein Verhältnis zu den geistigen Strömungen des 18. Jahrhunderts." In *Abraham Gottlob Werner: Gedankschrift aus Anlass der Wiederkehr seines Todestags nach 150 Jahren am 30 Juni 1969*, edited by Karl Friedrich Lüdemann, pp. 9–46. Leipzig: Deutsche Verlag für Grundstoffindustrie, 1967.

Müller, Lothar. *Die kranke Seele und das Licht der Erkenntnis: Karl Philipp Mortiz' Anton Reiser*. Frankfurt am Main: Athenäum, 1987.

Müller-Sievers, Helmut. *Epigenesis: Naturphilosophie im Sprachdenken Wilhelm von Humboldts*. Paderborn: Ferdinand Schöningh, 1993.
Mutschler, Hans Dieter. *Spekulative und empirische Physik: Akualität und Grenzen der Naturphilosophie Schellings*. Münchener Philosophische Studien 5. Stuttgart: Kohlhammer, 1990.
Neubauer, John. *Symbolismus und Symbolische Logik: die Idee der Ars Combinatoria in der Entwicklung der modernen Dichtung*. Munich: Wilhelm Fink Verlag, 1978.
———. "Zwischen Natur und mathematischer Abstraktion: der Potenzbegriff in der Frühromantik." In *Romantik in Deutschland: ein interdisziplinäres Symposium*, edited by Richard Brinkmann, pp. 175–86. Stuttgart: Metzlersche Verlagsbuchhandlung, 1978.
Nisbet, Hugh B. *Goethe and the Scientific Tradition*. London: University of London, 1972.
———. *Herder and the Philosophy and History of Science*. Modern Humanities Research Association, Dissertation Series 3. Cambridge, Mass.: Modern Humanities Research Association, 1970.
Oldenburg, Dieter. *Romantische Naturphilosophie und Arzneimittellehre 1800–1840*. Diss., Technische Universität Braunschweig, 1979.
Orr, Linda. *Jules Michelet: Nature, History, and Language*. Ithaca: Cornell University Press, 1976.
Outram, Dorinda. *The Body and the French Revolution: Sex, Class, and Political Culture*. New Haven: Yale University Press, 1989.
———. *The Enlightenment*. New Approaches to European History 6. Cambridge: Cambridge University Press, 1995.
———. "The Enlightenment Our Contemporary." In *The Sciences in Enlightened Europe*, edited by William Clark, Jan Golinski, and Simon Schaffer, pp. 32–40. Chicago: University of Chicago Press, 1999.
Papineau, David. "The Vis Viva Controversy: Do Meanings Matter?" *Studies in History and Philosophy of Science* 8 (1977): 111–42.
Partington, James Riddick. *A Short History of Chemistry*. 3rd ed. New York: Harper and Row, 1960.
Perrin, Carleton E. "The Chemical Revolution: Shifts in Guiding Assumptions." In *Scrutinizing Science: Empirical Studies of Scientific Change*, edited by Arthur Donovan, Larry Laudan, and Rachel Laudan, pp. 105–24. Dordrecht: Kluwer, 1988.
———. "Chemistry as Peer of Physics: A Response to Donovan and Melhado on Lavosier." *Isis* 81 (1990): 259–70.
———. "Lavoisier's Thoughts on Calcination and Combustion, 1772–1773." *Isis* 77 (1986): 647–66.
———. "Research Traditions, Lavoisier and the Chemical Revolution." In *The Chemical Revolution: Essays in Reinterpretation*, edited by Arthur Donovan, pp. 53–81. *Osiris*, 2nd series, vol. 4. Chicago: University of Chicago Press, 1988.
———. "Revolution or Reform? The Chemical Revolution and Eighteenth-Century Views of Scientific Change." *History of Science* 25 (1987): 395–423.

———. "The Triumph of the Antiphlogistians." In *The Analytic Spirit: Essays in the History of Science in Honor of Henry Guerlac,* edited by Harry Woolf, pp. 40–63. Ithaca: Cornell University Press, 1981.

Peter, Jean Pierre. "Malades et maladies à la fin du XVIIIe siècle." In *Médecins, climat et épidémies aux XVIIIe siécle,* edited by Jean-Paul Desaive et al., pp. 138–70. Paris: Mouton, 1972.

Philipp, Wolfgang. *Das Werden der Aufklärung in theologiegeschichtlicher Sicht.* Forschungen zur systematischen Theologie und Religionsphilosophie 3. Göttingen: Vandenhoeck & Ruprecht, 1957.

Pinch, Trevor J. "What Does a Proof Do if It Does Not Prove? A Study of the Social Conditions and Metaphysical Divisions Leading to David Bohm and John von Neumann Failing to Communicate in Quantum Physics." In *The Social Production of Scientific Knowledge,* edited by Everett Mendelsohn, Peter Weingart, and Richard Whitley, pp. 171–215. Dordrecht: Reidel, 1977.

Pinto-Correia, Clara. *The Ovary of Eve: Egg and Sperm Preformation.* Chicago: University of Chicago Press, 1997.

Porter, Roy S., ed. *The Cambridge History of Science. Volume 4: The Eighteenth Century.* Cambridge: Cambridge University Press, 2002.

———. "Medical Science and Human Science in the Enlightenment." In *Inventing Human Science: Eighteenth-Century Domains,* edited by Christopher Fox, Roy Porter, and Robert Wokler, pp. 53–87. Berkeley: University of California Press, 1995.

———. *Mind-Forged Manacles: A History of Madness in England from the Restoration to the Regency.* London: Penguin Books, 1987.

———. "Science, Provincial Culture and Public Opinion in Enlightenment England." *British Journal for Eighteenth-Century Studies* 3 (1980): 20–46.

Porter, Roy S., and Dorothy Porter, eds. *Patient's Progress: Doctors and Doctoring in Eighteenth-Century England.* Cambridge: Polity Press, 1989.

Porter, Roy S., and Mikulas Teich, eds. *The Scientific Revolution in National Context.* Cambridge: Cambridge University Press, 1992.

Porter, Theodore M. "The Promotion of Mining and the Advancement of Science: The Chemical Revolution of Mineralogy." *Annals of Science* 38 (1981): 543–70.

Portman, Adolf. "Goethe and the Concept of Metamorphosis." In *Goethe and the Sciences: A Reappraisal,* edited by Frederick Amrine, Francis J. Zucker, and Harvey Wheeler, pp. 133–46. Dordrecht: Reidel, 1987.

Poser, Hans. "Spekulative Physik und Erfahrung: zum Verhältnis von Experiment und Theorie in Schellings Naturphilosophie." In *Schelling: seine Bedeutung für eine Geschichte der Natur und der Geschichte,* edited by Ludwig Hasler, pp. 129–38. Stuttgart: Frommann-Holzboog, 1981.

Pratt, Mary Louise. *Imperial Eyes: Travel Writing and Transculturation.* London: Routledge, 1992.

Priesner, Claus. "Defensor Alchymiae: Gabriel Clauder versus Athanasius Kircher. Defence Strategies of Alchemists in the Seventeenth and Eighteenth Century." In *Alchemy Revisted,* edited by Zweder Rudolf Willem Maria von Martels, pp. 229–30. Leiden: Brill, 1990.

Querner, Hans. "Ordnungsprinzipien und Ordnungsmethoden in der Naturgeschichte der Romantik." In *Romantik in Deutschland: ein interdisziplinäres Symposium*, edited by Richard Brinkmann, pp. 214–25. Stuttgart: Metzlersche Verlagsbuchhandlung, 1978.

———. "Das Phänomen der Zweigeschlechtlichkeit im System der Naturphilosophie von Schelling." In *Schelling: seine Bedeutung für eine Geschichte der Natur und der Geschichte*, edited by Ludwig Hasler, pp. 139–43. Stuttgart: Frommann-Holzboog.

Quinlan, Sean W. "Apparent Death in Eighteenth-Century France and England." *French History* 9 (1995): 27–47.

Rasmussen, Detlef, ed. *Der Weltumsegler und seiner Freunde: Georg Foster als gesellschaftlicher Schriftsteller der Goethezeit*. Tübingen: Gunther Narr Verlag, 1988.

———. "Georg Foster, Wilhelm von Humboldt und die Idee der Freiheit." In *Der Weltumsegler und seiner Freunde: Georg Foster als gesellschaftlicher Schriftsteller der Goethezeit*, edited by Detlef Rasmussen, pp. 133–75. Tübingen: Gunther Narr Verlag, 1988.

Rather, Lelland J. "G. E. Stahl's Psychological Physiology." *Bulletin for the History of Medicine* 35 (1961): 37–49.

Rehbock, Philip. *The Philosophical Naturalists: Themes in Early Nineteenth-Century British Biology*. Madison: University of Wisconsin Press, 1983.

———. "Transcendental Anatomy." In *Romanticism and the Sciences*, edited by Andrew Cunningham and Nicholas Jardine, pp. 144–60. Cambridge: Cambridge University Press, 1990.

Reich, Alisa Schulweis. "Paul Joseph Barthez and the Impact of Vitalism on Medicine and Psychology." Ph.D diss., University of California, Los Angeles, 1995.

Reill, Peter Hanns. "Anthropology, Nature and History in the Late Enlightenment: The Case of Friedrich Schiller." In *Schiller als Historiker*, edited by Otto Dann, Norbert Oellers, and Ernst Osterkamp, pp. 243–66. Stuttgart: Metzler, 1995.

———. "Bildung, Urtyp and Polarity: Goethe and Eighteenth-Century Physiology." In *Goethe Yearbook*, edited by Thomas Saine, vol. III, pp. 139–48. Columbia, S.C.: Camden House, 1986.

———. "Between Mechanism and Hermeticism: Nature and Science in the Late Enlightenment." In *Frühe Neuzeit Frühe Modern? Forschungen zur Vielschichtigkeit von Übergangsprozessen*, edited by Rudolf Vierhaus, pp. 393–421. Göttingen: Vandenhoeck & Ruprecht, 1992.

———. "The Construction of the Social Sciences in Late Eighteenth and Early Nineteenth Century Germany." In *The Rise of the Social Sciences and the Formation of Modernity: Conceptual Change in Context, 1750–1850*, edited by Björn Wittock, Johan Heilbron, and Lars Magnusson, pp. 107–40. Dordrecht: Kluwer, 1998.

———. "Death, Dying and Resurrection in Late Enlightenment Science and *Wissenschaft als kulturelle Praxis, 1750–1900*, edited by Hans ‹er, Peter Hanns Reill, and Jürgen Schlumbohm, pp. 255–74. Vandenhoeck & Ruprecht, 1999.

———. *The German Enlightenment and the Rise of Historicism.* Berkeley: University of California Press, 1975.
———. "Religion, Theology and the Hermetic Imagination in the Late German Enlightenment: The Case of Johann Salomo Semler." In *Antike Weisheit und kulturelle Praxis: Hermetismus in der Frühen Neuzeit,* edited by Anne-Charlott Trepp and Hartmut Lehmann, pp. 219–34. Göttingen: Vandenhoeck & Ruprecht, 2001.
———."Science and the Construction of the Cultural Sciences in Late Enlightenment Germany: The Case of Wilhelm von Humboldt." *History and Theory* 33 (October 1994): 346–66.
Rey, Roselyne. *History of Pain.* Translated by Louise Elliott Wallace, J. A. Cadden, and S. W. Cadden. Paris: Éditions la Découverte, 1993.
———. *Naissance de développenment du vitalisme en France de la deuxiéme siècle à la fin du premier empire.* 2 vols. Thèse d'état, University of Paris, 1987.
———. "La récapitulation chez les physiologists et les naturalistes allemands de la fin du XVIIIe et du début du XIXe siécle." In *Histoire du concept de récapitulation,* edited by Paul Mengal, pp. 39–53. Paris: Masson, 1993.
Richards, Evelleen. "'Metaphorical Mystifications': The Romantic Gestation of Nature in British Biology." In *Romanticism and the Sciences,* edited by Andrew Cunningham and Nicholas Jardine, pp. 130–43. Cambridge: Cambridge University Press, 1990.
Rigotti, Francesca. "Biology and Society in the Age of Enlightenment." *Journal of the History of Ideas* 47 (1986): 215–33.
Roberts, Lissa, ed. *The Chemical Revolution: Context and Practices. The Eighteenth Century: Theory and Interpretation* 33 (1992).
———. "Condillac, Lavoisier, and the Instrumentalization of Science." In *The Chemical Revolution: Context and Practices,* edited by Lissa Roberts. *The Eighteenth Century: Theory and Interpretation* 33 (1992): 252–71.
———. "Going Dutch: Situating Science in the Dutch Enlightenment." In *The Sciences in Enlightened Europe,* edited by William Clark, Jan Golinski, and Simon Schaffer, pp. 389–422. Chicago: University of Chicago Press, 1999.
Roe, Shirley A. *Matter, Life, and Generation: Eighteenth-Century Embryology and the Haller-Wolff Debate.* Cambridge: Cambridge University Press, 1981.
Roger, Jacques. *Buffon: A Life in Natural History.* Translated by Sarah Lucille Bonnefoi. Ithaca: Cornell University Press, 1997.
———. *The Life Sciences in Eighteenth-Century French Thought.* Edited by Keith Benson and translated by Robert Ellrich. Stanford: Stanford University Press, 1997.
———. "The Mechanistic Conception of Life." In *God and Nature: Historical Essays on the Encounter between Christianity and Science,* edited by David C. Lindberg and Ronald L. Numbers, pp. 277–95. Berkeley: University of California Press, 1986.
———. *Les sciences de la vie dans la pensée francaise du XVIIIe siècle.* Paris: Armand Colin, 1971.

Rothschuh, Karl E. "Deutsche Medizin im Zeitalter der Romantic: Vielheit statt Einheit." In *Schelling: seine Bedeutung für eine Geschichte der Natur und der Geschichte*, edited by Ludwig Hasler, pp. 145–51. Stuttgart: Frommann-Holzboog, 1981.

———. "Naturphilsophische Konzepte der Medizin aus der Zeit der deutschen Romantik." In *Romantik in Deutschland: ein interdisziplinäres Symposium*, edited by Richard Brinkmann, pp. 243–66. Stuttgart: Metzlersche Verlagsbuchhandlung.

Rousseau, George S., ed. *The Languages of Psyche: Mind and Body in Enlightenment Thought*. Berkeley: University of California Press, 1990.

Rousseau, George S., and Porter, Roy, eds. *The Ferment of Knowledge: Studies in the Historiography of Eighteenth-Century Science*. Cambridge: Cambridge University Press, 1980.

Rupke, Nicholas A. "Caves, Fossils and the History of the Earth." In *Romanticism and the Sciences*, edited by Andrew Cunningham and Nicholas Jardine, pp. 241–59. Cambridge: Cambridge University Press, 1990.

Salmon, Paul B. "The Beginnings of Morphology: Linguistic Botanizing in the 18th Century." *Historiographia Linguistica* 1, no. 33 (1974): 313–39.

Sauder, Gerhard. *Empfindsamkeit*. Vols. 1 and 3. Stuttgart: Metzler, 1974, 1980.

Schaffer, Simon. "The Consuming Flame: Electrical Showmen and Tory Mystics in the World of Goods." In *Consumption and the World of Goods*, edited by John Brewer and Roy Porter, pp. 498–526. London: Routledge, 1993.

———. "Enlightened Automata." In *The Sciences in Enlightened Europe*, edited by William Clark, Jan Golinski, and Simon Schaffer, pp. 126–65. Chicago: University of Chicago Press, 1999.

———. "Genius in Romantic Natural Philosophy." In *Romanticism and the Sciences*, edited by Andrew Cunningham and Nicholas Jardine, pp. 82–100. Cambridge: Cambridge University Press, 1990.

———. "Natural Philosophy and Public Spectacle in the Eighteenth Century." *History of Science* 21 (1983): 1–43.

———. "The Show That Never Ends: Perpetual Motion in the Early Eighteenth Century." *British Journal for the History of Science* 28 (1995): 157–89.

———. "States of Mind: Enlightenment and Natural Philosophy." In *Languages of the Psyche: Mind and Body in Enlightenment*, edited by George Rousseau, pp. 253–90. Berkeley: University of California Press, 1990.

Scheibe, Erhard. "Der Zeitbegriff in der Physik: ein Beitrag zum Gespräch zwischen den Natur und Geisteswissenschaften." *Saeculum* 23 (1972): 236–51.

Schiebinger, Londa. *The Mind Has No Sex? Women in the Origins of Modern Science*. Cambridge, Mass: Harvard University Press, 1989.

———. *Nature's Body: Gender in the Making of Modern Science*. Boston: Beacon Press, 1993.

Schiller, Joseph. "Physiology's Struggle for Independence in the First Half of the Nineteenth Century." *History of Science* 7 (1968): 64–89.

———. "Queries, Answers and Unsolved Problems in Eighteenth Century Biology." *History of Science* 12 (1974): 184–99.

Schipperges, Heinrich, "Krankwerden und Gesundsein bei Novalis." In *Romantik in Deutschland: ein interdisziplinäres Symposium*, edited by Richard Brinkmann, pp. 226-42. Stuttgart: Metzlersche Verlagsbuchhandlung, 1978.

Schofield, Robert. *Mechanism and Materialism: British Natural Philosophy in the Age of Reason*. Princeton: Princeton University Press, 1970.

Schon, Donald A. *Displacement of Concepts*. London: Tavistock, 1963.

Schönfeld, Nicolas. *Beiträge zum ideengeschichtlichen Hintergrund der "Makrobiotik" von Christoph Wilhelm Hufeland*. Diss., Free University Berlin, 1988.

Scott, E. L. "Kirwan." In *Dictionary of Scientific Biography*, edited by Charles C. Gillispie, Henry Guerlac, and Julies Mayer, vol. 6, p. 388. New York: Scribner, 1970-80.

Segebrecht, Wulf. "Krankheit und Gesellschaft: Zu E. T. A. Hoffmanns Rezeption der Bamberger Medizin." In *Romantik in Deutschland: ein interdisziplinäres Symposium*, edited by Richard Brinkmann, pp. 267-90. Stuttgart: Metzlersche Verlagsbuchhandlung, 1978.

Sepper, Dennis L. "Goethe, Colour and the Science of Seeing." In *Romanticism and the Sciences*, edited by Andrew Cunningham and Nicholas Jardine, pp. 189-98. Cambridge: Cambridge University Press, 1990.

Shaffer, Elinor S. "Romantic Philosophy and the Organization of Disciplines: The Founding of the Humboldt University of Berlin." In *Romanticism and the Sciences*, edited by Andrew Cunningham and Nicholas Jardine, pp. 38-54. Cambridge: Cambridge University Press, 1990.

Shklar, Judith. "Virtue in a Bad Climate: Good Men and Good Citizens in Montesquieu's *L'Esprit des lois*." In *Enlightenment Studies in Honour of Lester G. Crocker*, edited by Alfred Bingham and Virgil Topazio, pp. 315-28. Oxford: Voltaire Foundation, 1979.

Siegfried, Robert. "The Chemical Revolution in the History of Chemistry." In *The Chemical Revolution: Essays in Reinterpretation*, edited by Arthur Donovan, pp. 34-52. *Osiris*, 2nd series, vol. 4. Chicago: University of Chicago Press, 1988.

——— and Dobbs. Betty Jo. "Composition: A Neglected Aspect of the Chemical Revolution." *Annals of Science* 24 (1968): 275-93.

Sloan, Philip R. "The Buffon-Linnaeus Controversy." *Isis* 67 (1976): 356-75.

———. "From Logical Universals to Historical Individuals: Buffon's Idea of Biological Species." In *Histoire de concept d'espèce dans les science de la vie*, edited by Scott Atran, pp. 101-40. Paris: Fondation Singer-Polignac, 1987.

———. "The Gaze of Natural History." In *Inventing Human Science: Eighteenth-Century Domains*, edited by Christopher Fox, Roy Porter, and Robert Wokler, pp. 112-51. Berkeley: University of California Press, 1995.

Smith, Pamela. "Consumption and Credit: The Place of Alchemy in Johann Joachim Becher's Political Economy." In *Alchemy Revisted*, edited by Zweder Rudolf Willem Maria von Martels, pp. 215-21. Leiden: Brill, 1990.

Snelders, Henricus Adrianus Marie. "Atomismus und Dynamismus im Zeitalter der Deutschen Romantischen Naturphilosophie." In *Romantik in Deutschland: ein interdisziplinäres Symposium*, edited by Richard

Brinkmann, pp. 187–201. Stuttgart: Metzlersche Verlagsbuchhandlung, 1978.

Spary, Emma C. "Codes of Passion: Natural History Specimens as a Polite Language in Late Eighteenth-Century France." In *Wissenschaft als kulturelle Praxis, 1750–1900*, edited by Hans Erich Bödeker, Peter Hanns Reill, and Jürgen Schlumbohm, pp. 105–35. Göttingen: Vandenhoeck & Ruprecht, 1999.

———. "The 'Nature' of the Enlightenment." In *The Sciences in Enlightened Europe*, edited by William Clark, Jan Golinski, and Simon Schaffer, pp. 272–304. Chicago: University of Chicago Press, 1999.

———. "Political, Natural and Bodily Economies." In *Cultures of Natural History*, edited by Nicholas Jardine, James A. Secord, and Emma Spary, pp. 178–96. Cambridge: Cambridge University Press, 1996.

———. *Utopia's Garden: French Natural History from Old Regime to Revolution*. Chicago: University of Chicago Press, 2000.

Stafford, Barbara Maria. *Body Criticism: Imaging the Unseen in Enlightenment Art and Medicine*. Cambridge, Mass.: MIT Press, 1991.

Stichweh, Rudolf. *Zur Entstehung des modernen Systems wissenschaftlicher Disziplinen: Physik in Deutschland 1740–1890*. Frankfurt am Main: Suhrkamp, 1984.

Svagelski, Jean. *L'idee de compensation en France, 1750–1850*. Lyon: Éditions L'Hermes, 1981.

Sweet, Paul Robinson. *Wilhelm von Humboldt: A Biography*. 2 vols. Columbus: Ohio State University Press, 1978, 1980.

Teich, Mikulas. "J. J. Becher and Alchemy." In *Alchemy Revisted*, edited by Zweder Rudolf Willem Maria von Martels, pp. 222–28. Leiden: Brill, 1990.

Terrall, Mary. "The Culture of Science in Frederick the Great's Berlin." *History of Science* 28 (1990): 333–64.

———. "Émilie du Chatelet and the Gendering of Science." *History of Science* 33 (1995): 283–310.

———. *The Man Who Flattened the Earth: Maupertuis and the Sciences of the Enlightenment*. Chicago: University of Chicago Press, 2002.

———. "Metaphysics, Mathematics, and the Gendering of Science in Eighteenth-Century France." In *The Sciences in Enlightened Europe*, edited by William Clark, Jan Golinski, and Simon Schaffer, pp. 246–71. Chicago: University of Chicago Press, 1999.

———. "Representing the Earth's Shape: The Polemics Surrounding Maupertuis's Expedition to Lapland." *Isis* 83 (1992): 218–37.

———. "Salon, Academy and Boudoir: Generation and Desire in Maupertuis's Science of Life." *Isis* 87 (1996): 217–29.

Thienemann, August. "Die Stufenfolge der Dinge, der Versuch eines natürlichen Systems der Naturkörper aus dem achtzehnten Jahrhundert: Eine historische Skizza." *Zoologische Annalen: Zeitschrift für Geschichte der Zoologie* 3 (1909).

Thomé, Horst. *Roman und Naturwissenschaft: eine Studie zur Vorgeschichte der deutschen Klassik*. Regensburger Beiträge zur deutschen Sprache und Literaturwissenschaft, Reihe B, vol. 15. Frankfurt: Peter Lang, 1978.

Toellner, Richard. "Kant und die Evolutionstheorie." *Clio Medica* 3 (1968): 243–49.

———. "Randbemerkungen zu Schellings Konzeption der Medizin als Wissenschaft." In *Schelling: seine Bedeutung für eine Geschichte der Natur und der Geschichte*, edited by Ludwig Hasler, pp. 117–28. Stuttgart: Frommann-Holzboog, 1981.

Tonelli, Giorgio. "The Philosophy of d'Alembert: A Sceptic beyond Sceptism." *Kant Studien* 67 (1976): 353–71.

———. "The 'Weakness' of Reason in the Age of the Enlightenment." *Diderot Studies* 14 (1971): 217–44.

Toulmin, Stephen Edelson. *Cosmopolis: The Hidden Agenda of Modernity.* New York: Free Press, 1990.

Trepp, Anne Charlott. *Sanfte Männlichkeit und selbstständige Weiblichkeit: Frauen und Männer im Hamburger Bürgertum zwischen 1770 and 1840.* Göttingen: Vandenhoeck & Ruprecht, 1996.

Tsouyopoulos, Nelly. "Doctors contra Clysters and Feudalism: The Consequences of a Romantic Revolution." In *Romanticism and the Sciences,* edited by Andrew Cunningham and Nicholas Jardine, pp. 101–18. Cambridge: Cambridge University Press, 1990.

———. "Schellings Konzeption der Medizin als Wissenschaft und die 'Wissenschaftlichkeit' der Modernen Medizin." In *Schelling: seine Bedeutung für eine Geschichte der Natur und der Geschichte,* edited by Ludwig Hasler, pp. 107–16. Stuttgart: Frommann-Holzboog, 1981.

Vartanian, Aram. "Trembley's Polyp, La Mettrie, and 18th Century French Materialism." *Journal of the History of Ideas* 11 (1950): 259–86.

Wagenbreth, Oscar. "Abraham Gottlob Werners System der Geologie, Petrographie und Lagenstättenlehre." In *Abraham Gottlob Werner: Gedankschrift aus Anlass der Wiederkehr seines Todestags nach 150 Jahren am 30 Juni 1969,* edited by Karl-Friedrich Lüdemann, pp. 83–148. Leipzig: Deutsche Verlag für Grundstoffindustrie, 1967.

Wagner, Rudolf. *Samuel Thomas von Sömmerrings Leben und Verkehr mit seinen Zeitgenossen.* 2 vols. Leipzig: Voss, 1844.

Webster, Charles. *From Paracelsus to Newton: Magic and the Making of Modern Science.* Eddington Memorial Lectures. Cambridge: Cambridge University Press, 1982.

———. *The Great Instauration: Science, Medicine and Reform 1626–1660.* London: Duckworth, 1975.

Westfall, Richard S. *The Construction of Modern Science: Mechanisms and Mechanics.* Cambridge: Cambridge University Press, 1977.

Wetzels, Walter D. "Johann Wilhelm Ritter: Romantic Physics in Germany." In *Romanticism and the Sciences,* edited by Andrew Cunningham and Nicholas Jardine, pp. 199–212. Cambridge: Cambridge University Press, 1990.

White, Alan. *Schelling: An Introduction to the System of Freedom.* New Haven: Yale University Press, 1983.

Wieland, Wolfgang. "Die Anfänge der Philosophie Schellings und die Frage nach der Natur." In *Materialien zu Schellings philosophischen Anfängen,* edited by Manfred Frank and Gerhard Kurz, pp. 237–79. Frankfurt am Main: Suhrkamp, 1975.

Wokler, Robert. "From l'homme physique to l'homme moral and Back: Towards a History of Enlightenment Anthropology." *History of the Human Sciences* 6 (1993): 121–38.

Yolton, John W. *Thinking Matter: Materialism in Eighteenth-Century Britain.* Minneapolis: University of Minnesota Press, 1983.

Zammito, John. *Kant, Herder and the Birth of Anthropology.* Chicago: University of Chicago Press, 2001.

Zaunick, Rudolph, ed. *Lorenz Oken und die Universität Frieburg i. Br.* Leipzig: J. A. Barth, 1938.

Zimmermann, Rolf Christian. *Das Weltbild des Jungen Goethe: Studien zur Hermetischen Tradition des Deutschen 18. Jahrhunderts.* 2 vols. Munich: Fink, 1969, 1979.

Index

Abriss der Naturphilosophie (Oken), 203
absolutism, 59–60, 144
acidification, 103, 105–8, 291n128
active energy/force: 103, 105–8; animal economy and, 128, 129, 130–31; animal generation and, 67; Blumenbach and, 144–47; *faculté generatrice*, 165–66; Lavoisier and, 287n75; life sciences and, 143; matter and, 201; and organized body, 142, 143–44, 192–93; reintroduction of, 9
Adorno, Theodor, 2, 4, 251, 267n38
aesthetics, 20, 243–44, 248–49
aether, universal, 79, 93, 219, 283n34
affinity, 21, 36, 56, 62, 69, 135, 141, 143, 153, 154, 157, 159
affinity, elective *(Wahlverwandschaft)*: animal economy and, 135, 141, 143; caloric and, 109–11; causes of, 84–85, 284n51; and classification, 154; constancy of, 85–86; gravity vs., 82; influence of, 286n67; intensity of, 77, 83–85; Lavoisier and, 103, 108–11, 292–93n140; *rapport* and, 272n52; and saturation levels, 86–87, 285–86n61; in Stahlian chemistry, 76–77; suspension of, and putrefaction, 174; sympathy as analogue to, 141; tables of, 83–84; and temperaments, 157
affirmation (mathematical function), 207–9
aggregation: animal economy and, 135; body and, 121; mechanism and, 138; vital principle and, 142
air, as element, 98, 290n110
alchemy, 113, 168, 183
Aldrovanus, 39
Alembert, Jean Le Rond d', 5, 6, 41, 184, 185, 252, 271n37
ambiguity, 25–28, 44, 182, 236
Americana Encyclopedia, 174
analogical reasoning: Buffon and, 55–56; centrality of, Enlightenment Vitalism and, 195; comparative analysis and, 8; discursive logic vs., 55–56; elective affinity and, 77; Herder and, 189, 191; Humboldt (Alexander) and, 248; Kielmeyer and, 192
Analyse chimique et concordance des trois règnes (Sage), 117
analysis: a priori, 201, 210, 316n50; causal, 52, 189; chemistry and, 80; comparative, 8; mathematical, 8, 41; mechanism and, 36; poetics and, 243–44; quantitative, 284–85n55; synthesis vs., 201; systematic, 47–48

Index

Anderson, Wilda C., 280n15
androgyny, 223–28
Anfangsgründe der Physiologie (Blumenbach), 144–45
animal economy: Barthez and, 143–44; Bordeu and, 131–33; definition of, 136; as dynamic equilibrium, 144; Haller and, 130–31; irritability and, 299n79; political metaphor of, 133; sense organs and, 148–50; Stahlian theory and, 125, 127–28; and temperaments, 157; vital principle and, 143–44; Whytt and, 128–30. *See also* nature, economy of
animal generation. *See* generation
animaliculism, 58
animal motion, 128
animal reproduction. *See* reproduction
animism, 61, 81; interconnection in, 139–40; mechanism vs., 81–82, 131, 136; physiological revolution and, 120, 121, 123; *solidistes* and, 119–20; and temperaments, 154
animus, 81
Anschauung. See intuition
Ansichten der Natur (A. von Humboldt), 21, 239, 241
Anthropologie (Kant), 156
antimechanism: Baader and, 102–3; Lavoisier and, 102, 112; in life sciences, 120–21, 264–66n34, 295n10; in natural history, 264–66n34; political implications of, 266n35; skepticism and, 5–7, 37–38, 74; Stahl and, 123–28; and temperaments, 154–55
anti-Newtonianism, 266n35
aphorism, 243
Aphorismi de cognoscendi et curendis (Boerhaave), 121–22, 295n7
a priori analysis, 201, 210, 316n50
archaeus, 44, 81, 143, 183
Aristotle/Aristotelianism: Boerhaave and, 93; Buffon and, 39, 42, 48, 64–65, 66; divine preformation vs., 57; and epigenesis, 64–65, 318n99; and generation, 222; Herder and, 187; and material heat, 288n88;

mechanism vs., 34; revival of, 79, 91, 92, 123, 125
Arrais, Duarte Madeira, 273n59
art, creation of, 225
atomism, 44, 201, 240, 321–22n8
attraction, 135–36; chemical, 83–84; *Naturphilosophie* and, 219
Augustine, Saint, 58
azoyte, 107–8, 292n136

Baader, Franz von: Boerhaave and, 288n88; Chemical Revolution and, 102–3; on fluidity, 80, 283–84n40; on heat distribution, 94; Lavoisier and, 102, 110, 112, 293n145; on love and elective affinity, 84–85; on matter and power, 82, 284n45; and matter of heat, 79–80, 102; on nature as active force, 89–90; and Stahlian chemistry, 74; on "virgin" elements, 101
Bachelard, Gaston, 44
Bacon, Francis, 122, 124, 187, 243, 278–79n10; influence of, 296n12
Baker, Keith, 271n37
Band, 212–13, 218
Barry, Martin, 14
Barthez, Paul-Joseph: and "biological" histories, 255; Blumenbach and, 304n27; and *faites-principes*, 137; influences on, 299n73; Kielmeyer and, 192; as monarchist, 144, 299n75; and occult force, 293n143; and physiology, renewal of, 119, 120; and sympathetic reactions, 140–42; and synergy, 139, 140; and vital principle, 106, 143–44, 259n20, 292n133, 299n73
bastardization. *See* hybridization
Beaurieu, Gaspard Guillard de, 303n22
Bensaude-Vincent, Bernadette, 89, 102, 284–85n55, 287n76, 287n80, 292n140
Bergman, Torbern Olof: and chemical method, 78; and elective affinity, 83–84, 86, 87, 157, 284n51, 285–86n61; and language of chem-

istry, 88; Lavoisier and, 102; and natural philosophy, forms of, 71, 73, 278n1; and quantitative analysis, 284–85n55
Bergson, Henri, 12
Berlin Academy, 282n20
Berlin, Isaiah, 29, 186
Berthollet, Claude Louis, 86–88, 89, 113–14, 157, 245
Beseke, Johann Melchoir, 116
Bildersprache, 18, 88, 240
Bildungstrieb, 23, 24, 222–23; and gender differentiation, 222–23; and generation, 146–47, 166, 168–70; and mass/motion dichotomy, 24; pleasures of, 220–21; Schelling's usage of, 214–15
binary systems, 25, 189, 263n26
biology, vitalization of, 268n4
Black, Joseph: and "fixed air," 98; and heat distribution, 93, 94–95; and heat measurement, 96; as heat theorist, 92, 97, 290n102; Lavoisier and, 102; and quantitative analysis, 284–85n55; and species as chemical substance, 285n60
Bloch, Ernst, 229
Blumenbach, Johann Friedrich: and active energies, 144–47, 299n79; and "biological" histories, 255; epigenesis, conversion to, 166; and functional systems, 147; and gender, 220–21, 222–23, 231; Haller and, 304n26; and Hogarth, 220, 317n96; Humboldt (Alexander) and, 237; Humboldt (Wilhelm) and, 225; influence of, 296n18, 304n27; on interconnection in organized body, 137–38, 139; Kant and, 304–5n28; Kielmeyer and, 191, 192, 310n118; Lavoisier and, 112; and occult force, 293n143; Oken and, 317–18n98; on organized body, transformation of, 134; preformation critiqued by, 168–70; rhetorical strategy of, 291n128; and sense organs, 148–49; on Stahl, 124; on sympathy as affinity, 141; and temperaments, 156–58. See also *Bildungstrieb*
body: functions of, 128; interconnection and, 136; mechanistic view of, 121; political metaphor of, 133; rational soul and, 125–27; system vs., 125
body, organized: active energies in, 144–47, 174, 192–93; and conjunction, 297n30; definition of, 134, 139; functional systems within, 147; interconnection in, 137–39; and morality, 155–56; nervous system and, 128–30, 147–54; opposed powers in, 130–31; sympathetic reactions in, 139–42, 297n34; and temperaments, 154–58; transformation in, 183; vital principle and, 143–44
Boerhaave, Hermann: and chemistry, 72; Haller and, 130; and heat distribution, 93–94, 288–89n90; and heat, reconceptualization of, 92–93, 288n88; influence of, 121–22, 295n7, 295n10; as mechanist, 34; Stahl and, 282n20
Bohemia, Blumenbach's influence in, 304n27
Bonnet, Charles: and animal reproduction, 164–65; Blumenbach's critique of, 168; and *emboîtment,* 168; epigenesis critiqued by, 161, 162–65; Kölreuter and, 167–68; Michelet and, 298n52; on sensations, 149; and spirit of systems, 31; and universal interconnection, 136, 137
Bopp, Franz, 280n15
Bordeu, Théophile, 31, 131–34, 135, 145, 185–86
Bowie, Andrew, 312n1
Boyle, Robert, 11–12, 34, 59
Brandis, Joachim, 112, 296n18
Broberg, Gunnar, 270n9
Buffon, Georges-Louis Leclerc, comte de: Cabanis and, 124; and Cartesian dualism, 39, 43, 271n25, 272n45; and chemistry, 67, 70, 280n14; and Classical *episteme,* 268–69n7; con-

Buffon, (*continued*)
temporary criticism of, 277n124, 277n126; contemporary significance of, 10, 68–70, 268n3, 277n127; critique of mechanism, 38–42; Cullen and, 122; Diderot and, 183–84; on elective affinity, 67–68, 85–86; epigenesis revived by, 159, 162; epistemology of, 53–54; and equilibrium, 287n80; and generation, 61–68, 164–65, 276n114; Herder and, 187, 190; on historical knowledge, 249; Humboldt (Alexander) and, 30, 238–39, 248–49; impact on Enlightenment Vitalism, 31, 67; Kant on, 161; Kästner on, 276n114; language of nature, 33–34, 38–39; Lavoisier and, 287n80; Leibniz and, 272–73n53; and life sciences, organization of, 158; literary style of, 69, 277n126; and mathematics, 39–41, 271n30, 271n37; *moule intérieur*, 46–47, 50, 51–52, 100, 161; and natural history, 33, 41–42, 47, 52–53, 75, 120; natural philosophy of, 38–42, 198, 238, 271n30; new science of, 52–56, 273n63; and occult force, 46–47, 67–68, 293n143; organic matter, redefinition of, 42–47; and paradox, 277n124; as "proto-Romantic," 199; reproduction law of, 195; as "Romantic," 254; scientific system of, 47–52, 87–88, 137, 247; as skeptical critic, 5; "sleeper" analogy of, 54–55; and species classification, 27, 182, 277n127; Vico and, 52–53. See also *Histoire naturelle*
burial: Jewish practices, controversy over, 176, 177–78, 181, 307–8n73, 308n74; premature, fear of, 172, 175, 178, 180, 308n83
Burkhardt, Richard, Jr., 311n134
burnable substance, 113–14. See also phlogiston

Cabanis, Pierre Jean Georges, 124
calcination, 76, 103, 111. See also oxidation
calculus, 204, 272n40
caloric, theory of, 103, 109–11
Calvinism, 59, 130
Cannon, Susan Faye, 253–54, 325n51
Carbonniéres, Ramond de, 245
Carpenter, William, 14
Cartesian dualism: Buffon and, 39, 43–44, 271n25, 272n45; harmonic mediation and, 7, 148; Herder and, 188; mechanism and, 36, 270n12; political/religious adaptations of, 37; substantialized force and, 150–52
Cartesian science, 278n5, 305–6n33
Carus, Carl Gustav, 200, 232–35, 320nn131, 132
catalysts, 83
Catholicism, 59
causation: analysis of, 189; animal economy and, 129; Buffon and, 51–52; Enlightenment Vitalism and, 7–8, 15; final, 64, 163, 276n114; Hume and, 38; inner forces and, 51–52; mechanism and, 35; in *Naturphilosophie*, 208; physiological activities and, 135
Cavendish, Henry, 98
cellular organ, 132–33
change: continuous, 95–96, 146, 170–71, 182–86; discontinuous, 188, 195–96; linear, 216, 217. See also development, diachronic
Chateaubriand, François Auguste René, Vicomte de, 254
Chatelet, Gabrielle Émilie Le Tonnelier de Breteuil, marquise du, 60
Chemical Dictionary (Macquer), 85
chemical reactions: Berthollet and, 89; fluidity of matter and, 80–81; Lavoisier and, 105–11, 147; nature's activities as, 185
Chemical Revolution: Baader and, 102–3; Lavoisier and, 74, 101–4, 111, 118, 292n130; origins of, 93, 97, 287n76; Stahlian Revolution and, 279n13
chemistry: Buffon and, 67, 70, 280n14; inner vs. outer, 115–16; and matter, concept of, 10–11; mechanistic

views of, 77; nationalism and, 291n129; natural historical approach to, 86–88, 285n60; and natural philosophy, forms of, 71; *Naturphilosophie* and, 206, 211; operational definition of, 77–78; Paracelsian, 26; philosophical, 210–12; premechanistic, 115–16; as professional discipline, 113; rejected writings in, 114–17; reproduction and, 67; Stahlian Revolution in, 73–74, 76, 279n13. *See also* affinity, elective; chemical reactions; elements; heat; phlogiston
chemistry, language of: development of, 71–75, 88–89, 113–14, 279n13, 286–87n69; grammar of, 78–79, 96–97; natural history and, 279–80n14; scientific revolution and, 118; significance of, 91; three-stage pattern of, 75–77. *See also* nature, language of
Cheyne, George, 57
Chimborazo, Mount (Ecuador), 20–21, 26–27, 238
Clark, William, 313n11
classification: Cuvier on, 274n69; Linnean, 158; natural, 87–88, 104; plant, 27; systematics and, 137
Coleman, William, 311n118
colonialism, 2
combustion, 76, 103, 105–6, 111
compensation, law of, 169–70, 193
"compositional revolution," 73–74, 279n13
compounds: Scheele and, 100; in Stahlian chemistry, 81–82
Condorcet, Marie-Jean-Antoine Caritat, marquis de, 5, 6, 41, 252, 271n37
conformity, 186
conjunction: animal economy and, 134; as attribute of matter, 43–44; Buffon and, 49; and individuality, 138; organic, 128, 297n30; vital economy and, 10
consensus, 133, 135, 136, 140, 145, 190, 213. *See also* sympathy
conservatism, 12

Constant, Benjamin, 12–13
Contemplation de la nature (Bonnet), 164
contingency, 53, 169, 220
continuity, theory of, 182–86
contractibility, 145
Contrat social (Rousseau), 138, 298n61
Cook, James, 30, 254
Cook, John C., 160
Corbin, Alain, 304n23
Corday, Charlotte, 179
Cosmos (A. von Humboldt), 18, 238, 243
"Counter-Enlightenment," 15, 29, 186, 199, 255
Coup d'oeil sur les revolutions et sur la réforme de la médecine (Cabanis), 124
Critique of Judgment (Kant), 161, 201
Critique of Understanding (Kant), 305n28
Cudworth, Ralph, 44
Cullen, William: as antimechanist, 122–23; Boerhaave and, 295n7; and chemistry/natural history interrelation, 279n14; and species as chemical substance, 285n60; and spirit of systems, 31; and Stahlian chemistry, 281n19, 282n20
Cupola, 212–13
Cuvier, George: and discontinuous change, 195–96; on Humboldt (Alexander), 237–38, 248; Lamarck and, 196–98, 311n134; and language of nature, 198; Lavoisier and, 280n15; and *Naturphilosophie*, 200–201; Pfaff and, 291n129; St. Hilaire vs., 259n25; on species classification, 274n69

Dacheröden, Caroline, 227
D'Alembert, Jean Le Rond. *See* Alembert, Jean Le Rond d'
D'Alembert's Dream (Diderot), 133, 184–86
Daston, Lorraine, 41, 257n7, 260n31, 326n59

Daubenton, Louis-Jean-Marie, 197, 246
Davy, Humphrey, 281n19
death: apparent *(Scheintod)*, 172, 174–76, 182, 307n57, 308n83; by decapitation, 178–80, 308n75; dictionary/encyclopedia articles on, 173–74; discourse of, practical applications of, 180–82; evidence of, 174–75, 181; inducement of, 108; mechanist vs. vitalist definitions of, 171–74; resurrection from, 172, 175–77, 180, 307n69. *See also* burial
degeneration, 63, 169, 182, 190, 248; and degenerate organisms, 50
De generatione animalium (Harvey), 57
de Graaf, Regnier, 58, 66, 68
Delille, Jacques, 303n22
Delisle de Sales, Jean Baptiste, 303n22
Descartes, René: Buffon's critique of, 38, 54, 66, 68; La Mettrie and, 268n4; and matter as *agens*, 81; as mechanist, 34, 36; *Naturphilosophie* and, 236; vortices, theory of, 116. *See also* Cartesian dualism; Cartesian science
design: argument from, 59; primitive, 51, 182–83, 277n127
determinism, 9, 250
Dettelbach, Michael, 242, 246, 249, 254, 321n7, 325n57
development, diachronic, 134: *Bildungstrieb* and, 169–70; and death/dying, 172–81; and generation, 159–61, 302n2; Kielmeyer and, 194–95; and language of nature, 158; in *Naturphilosophie*, 208; and organization, 159; and progress, 190–91; and reproduction, 161–65
dialectical reasoning, 25
Dialectic of Enlightenment (Adorno and Horkheimer), 2
Diderot, Denis: and animal economy, 133; and diachronic development, 183–86; as Enlightenment vitalist, 12, 273n63; as "Romantic," 254; as

skeptical critic, 5; Stahlian chemistry and, 281–82n20
Discours de la méthode (Descartes), 38
Disquitio de attractionibus (Bergman), 86
Dissertation on Air and Fire, A (Scheele), 71
divination, 9, 36, 42, 55, 56, 69. 88
Dobbs, Betty Jo, 76
Donovan, Arthur L., 290n102
Driesch, Hans, 12
drowning, resurrection from, 176–77, 307n69
duality: law of, 214; of nature, 215; in spirit, 210–11; in trias, 235. *See also* Cartesian dualism; polarity
Dumas, Charles Louis: on Bordeu, 131; and functional systems, 147; on nature as dynamic, 302n2; and nervous system, 131; and physiology, revolutionizing of, 120; and Stahlian science, 124; and universal interconnection, 137, 138; and vitalism, origin of term, 294–95n6
Dumeril, André-Marie-Constant, 14
dying, 172. *See also* death

earth, as element, 98, 282n25
ecology, *Naturphilosophie* and, 312n1
Eddy, John H., 277n127
Edinburgh (Scotland), 9–10, 122–24, 295n10
Efron, John M., 308n74
Egypt, Berthollet's experiments in, 87
Einzig mögliche Beweisgrund zu einer Demonstration des Daseyn Gottes, Der (Kant), 160
electricity, and fluidity, 283n36
Élemens (Macquer), 85
elements: active, 105–8, 292n136; definition of, 107; mechanism and, 91–92; "peripatetic" definition of, 91, 97–98, 103, 290n105; redefinition of, 98, 100–101. *See also* heat
Elements of Chemistry, The (Boerhaave), 92

Eller, Johann, 282n20
Elliot, John, 90, 149
empiricism: Buffon and, 39; Humboldt (Alexander) and, 239–40, 243, 251; *Naturphilosophie* and, 209; and quantification, 269–70n9; Stahl and, 126
encasement *(emboîtment)*, 164, 168
Encyclopedia (Philadelphia, 1798), 174
Encyclopédie (Diderot and d'Alembert), 33
Engelhard, Dietrich von, 214
Enlightenment: aesthetics of, 249; critiques of, 2–3, 199, 251–52, 257n7, 257–58n8; definition of, 28–29, 251–55; epistemology of, 201, 245, 312–13n9, 313–14n13; historiography and, 266–67n38; internal periodization of, 258n13; Jewish *(Haskala)*, 177–78; Jewish, 308n74; Kant and, 252, 312–13n9; knowledge factory of, 13; Leibniz and, 313n11; mechanism and, 28–31, 264–66n34; medicalization of, 165, 304n23; nature and, 2–3; non-self-evidence of, 16, 260n31, 326n59; opposing, 4, 30, 267n38; religion vs., 177–78; Stahl as opponent of, 296n21; vitalism of, 12–13
"Enlightenment project," 2–3, 15, 199, 251–52
Enlightenment Vitalism: and analogical reasoning, 249; Buffon's impact on, 67, 68–70; as coherent movement, 15, 255–56; core elements of, 158, 159, 253; current relevance of, 15–16, 256; decline of, 13–14, 248; definition of, 11–13; and elective affinity, 84; epistemology of, 8–9, 15–16, 255–56; experimental/explanatory procedures of, 110; formulation of, 31, 127–28; and gender, scientific construction of, 220–29; and heat as element, 93; Herder and, 186–87; as language of nature, 9–10, 13, 235–36; life as organizational circle in, 154; and mechanism vs. animism, 81–82; mediating imperative of. *see* harmonic mediation; and modernity, 253; natural philosophy of, 6–8, 9; *Naturphilosophie* vs., 13–14, 198, 199–203, 209, 220–21, 253; and nervous system, 148; and occult force, 138, 150; and sensation, 150; and species differences, 49–50; Stahlian Revolution and, 279n13; structural difficulties of, 152–53; as synthetic category, 9–10, 14–15; and temperaments, 127; and universal interconnection, 137–38. *See also specific philosophers*
Enquiry Concerning Human Nature (Hume), 38
Entwurf eines Systems der transcendental Chemie (Beseke), 116
environmentalism, *Naturphilosophie* and, 312n1
epigenesis: acceptance of, 165–66, 170; Buffon and, 64–65, 68; and continuity, theory of, 184, 185–86; critique of, 161–65; definition of, 8; divine preformation vs., 57–58, 159–65, 221, 318n99; as explanatory strategy, 7–8; and gender differentiation, 318n99; Kant and, 259n21, 302–3n7; and life, definition of, 172; Oken and, 229–30; origin of term, 57; revival of, 62
episteme, 251, 252–53; Classical, 43, 236, 268–69n7, 280n15
epistemology: of Buffon, 53–54; of Enlightenment, 201, 245, 312–13n9, 313–14n13; of Enlightenment Vitalism, 8–9, 15–16, 255–56; of mechanism, 34, 36, 53; of *Naturphilosophie*, 200, 205, 209–14, 313–14n13, 316n50
equilibrium, 89–90, 194, 249, 287n75
Erxleben, Johann Christian Polykarp, 88
Eschenmayer, Carl von, 200, 209–10, 215
Esenbeck, Nees von, 212
Esprit des lois, L' (Montesquieu), 33

Essai de statique chemique (Berthollet), 87
Essai sur la géographie des plantes (A. von Humboldt), 20–21, 239–40, 244, 246
Essay on the Vital and other Involuntary Motions of Animals, An (Whytt), 128
Euler, Leonard, 272n40
extended middle, 79, 107, 116, 152. *See also* harmonic mediation
extinctions, 198

faculté generatrice, 165–66
Fahrenheit, Gabriel Daniel, 93–94
faites-principes, 137
Faivre, Antoine, 29
Feder, Johann Heinrich Georg, 305n28
femininity, 223–28, 236
feminism, critiques of Enlightenment, 2
Ferguson, Adam, 40, 48, 69–70, 97
Ferment of Knowledge (ed. Shapin), 3, 266–67n38
fertilization, 168
Fichte, Johann Gottlieb, 200
fire acid, 117
fire, as element. *See* heat
First Lines of the Practice of Physics (Cullen), 122
fluidity: generation and, 305–6n33; of matter, 79–81, 283n36, 283–84n40, 307n60
Fontenelle, Bernard de, 92–93
force: essential, 167–68; matter and, 79–82, 201, 284n45; mechanistic definition of, 8; and striving, 284n45; substantialized, 89, 103–4, 146, 150–52, 198, 201; vital, 21–25, 195, 222. *See also* active energy/force; *Bildungstrieb*; free play of forces, occult force; *vis*
Forster, Georg: as Enlightenment vitalist, 12, 31; Humboldt (Alexander) and, 237, 245–46, 323n30; Humboldt (Wilhelm) and, 30; Kant and, 305n28; Lavoisier and, 112; as

"Romantic," 254; and spirit of systems, 31
fossil evidence, and transformation, 196, 197
Foucault, Michel: and binary logic, 25, 263n26; and Buffon, 268–69n7; "Classical Age" defined by, 26, 43, 263n26, 268–69n7, 280n15; Enlightenment portrayed by, 252–53; and *episteme* shift, 14, 236, 252–53; knowledge/power dyad, 181; and *Naturphilosophie*, 14; and opposing Enlightenments, 4, 267n38; on universal *mathesis*, 35
Fourcroy, Antoine François de, 81–82, 113
France: capital punishment in, 179; Cartesian dualism and monarchy in, 37; Enlightenment medicalized in, 304n23; Hippocrates revived in, 165; *Naturphilosophie* in, 198; physiology revolutionized in, 120; quantification vs. mathematics in, 206; Stahlian chemistry in, 9–10, 281n19, 281–82n20
Frankenstein (Shelley), 175–76
Franklin, Benjamin, 283n36
freedom, 9, 22, 24, 25, 28, 69, 138, 139, 151, 188, 208, 233, 236, 249, 250
free play of forces, 20, 21, 238, 242, 244, 250, 256
French Revolution: failure of, and *Naturphilosophie*, 202, 217, 229, 236; and guillotine, controversy over, 176, 179; Lavoisier and, 278–79n10; and premature burial, 175

Galen, 154
Galileo Galilei, 35
Gassendi, Pierre, 34
Gehler, Johann Samuel, 72, 112, 288n88
Geist der spekulative Philosophie (Tiedemann), 206
Geisteswissenschaften. See humanistic sciences

gender discrimination, Enlightenment critics and, 2
gender, scientific construction of: in Enlightenment Vitalism, 220–29; and gender relations, 223–25, 320n134; generation and, 221–23, 225–27, 229–32; in *Naturphilosophie*, 220–21, 229–36; sexuality and, 222–23
generation: abnormal birth and, 303n19; animal, 56, 61–68; Blumenbach and, 168–71; Buffon and, 61–68; causes of, 146, 305–6n33; Dumas on, 302n2; and epigenesis/preformation debate, 159–61; and gender, 221–23, 229–32; occasionalist vs. preestablishist, 302–3n7; political/religious metaphors for, 221; principles of, 103; spontaneous, 62, 197, 229–30. See also *Bildungstrieb*; epigenesis; preformation, divine
Gentz, Friedrich, 224–25, 260n1
Geoffrey, Etienne François, 85, 272n52
German Enlightenment and the Rise of Historicism, The (Reill), 1
Germany: antimechanism in, 29; Boerhaave's influence in, 295n7; chemical nomenclature in, 286–87n69; Enlightenment medicalized in, 304n23; epigenesis accepted in, 166; French classicism, rebellion against, 223; gender relations in, 223–25; Jewish burial practices, controversy over, 176, 177–78, 181, 307–8n73, 308n74; Lavoisier's critical reception in, 111–14; *Leichenhäuser* in, 308n83; *Naturphilosophie* formulated in, 198; physiology revolutionized in, 120; Stahlian chemistry in, 281n19, 282n20
germes (seeds), 56–61, 183
Gesellschaft deutscher Naturforscher und Aerzte, 314n16
Geyer-Kordesh, Johanna, 296n21
Gierl, Martin, 13, 259n29

Gillispie, Charles, 73, 266n35, 278–79n10
Ginzburg, Carlo, 65–66
Girtanner, Christoph, 139, 298–99n62
Gmelin, Johann Friedrich, 112–15, 116–17, 278n1
Gode-von Aesch, Alexander, 312–13n9
Goethe, Johann Wolfgang von: and harmonic mediation, 90–91; Humboldt (Alexander) and, 237, 239, 249; on organized system, 138; and primitive design, 51; on resurrection, 176–77; Schelling and, 239; and semiotics, 96; and soul as organ, 153; and *Urtyp*, 100, 246; and vitalism vs. organicism, 259n25
Golinski, Jan, 114, 266n35, 281n19
Goodsir, John, 14
Göttingen Gelehrte Anzeige, 113, 166, 296n15, 296n20
Gough, Jerry B., 76, 279n13
gradation, 182–83, 194, 214
gravimetrics, 284–85n55
gravitation, universal, 272n40
gravity: elective affinity vs., 82; as occult force, 43, 46
Great Britain: Blumenbach's influence in, 304n27; Enlightenment medicalized in, 304n23; Hippocrates revived in, 165; *Naturphilosophie* in, 198, 314n16; physiology revolutionized in, 120; Stahlian chemistry in, 281n19, 282n20
Great Chain of Being: Blumenbach and, 170; Bonnet and, 162, 163–64; Buffon and, 49; and continuity, theory of, 183; fluidity of matter and, 80; harmonic mediation and, 90; Herder and, 188; Lamarck and, 196–97, 311n134; latent heat and, 95; *Naturphilosophie* and, 216; and temperaments, 157
Greek history, 63–64
Greene, Robert, 61
Grew, Nehemiah, 44
Grundriss der Chemie (Gmelin), 113
Guerlac, Henry, 290n102

guillotine, controversy over, 176, 178–80, 308n75
Guyénot, Émil, 275n91
Guyton de Morveau, Louis Bernard, 113, 287n76
gynecology, 233, 320n132

habit, 38, 127, 222
Haeckel, Ernst, 189, 310n117
Hagner, Michael, 303n19
Hahn, Roger, 272n40
Haller, Albrecht von: as antimechanist, 130–31; Blumenbach and, 304n26; epigenesis critiqued by, 161–64; impact on Enlightenment Vitalism, 133–34; influence of, 145, 296n20; Kölreuter's critique of, 167–68; membrane-continuity theory, 162, 163, 303n11; reviews written by, 123–24, 296n15; Schiller and, 150; and Stahlian chemistry, 123–24; Wolff's critique of, 166–67
Handbuch der Naturgeschichte (Blumenbach), 166
Handbuch der vergleichende Anatomie (Blumenbach), 144
harmonic mediation: ambiguity and, 25–28; of animism and mechanism, 297–98n49; Bergman on, 285–86n61; *Bildungstrieb* and, 169, 223; Buffon and, 44; Diderot and, 184; difficulties of, 152–53; as Enlightenment vitalist discursive practice, 9, 90, 181–82, 253, 255–56; and gender differentiation, 225, 228, 236; Goethe and, 90–91; Humboldt (Alexander) and, 25–27; Humboldt (Wilhelm) and, 20, 25, 27–28, 228; La Mettrie and, 295n6; in nervous system, 148; and organized body, 193; universal interconnection and, 137–39
harmony, 9, 20, 24, 25, 28, 89, 90, 95, 133, 139, 179, 193, 204, 210, 228, 237; death and, 179–80; Great Chain of Being and, 163–64; Herder and, 189–91; between man and nature, 241, 322n11; as metaphor, 12; and middle realm, 189–91; preestablished, 60–61, 81, 270n12; Stahl and, 126
Harvey, William, 57, 66, 68, 187
Haskala (Jewish Enlightenment), 177–78, 308n74
Hauptformen, 27, 189, 247–48
Haupttypus, 9, 189, 194, 214–15, 246
heat: as active agent, 97; and chemical reactions, 80; distribution of, 93–95, 288–89n90; latent, 95–96; matter of *(Wärmestoff)*, 79–80, 98–101, 105, 109, 110, 290n108; measurement of, 96–97; phlogiston and, 105; reconceptualization of, 91–97, 288n88; research in, 97–98
Hegel, G. W. F., 200, 315n43, 320n134
Heilbron, John, 269–70n9, 278n5
Helmont, Jan Baptista van: as animist, 81; and *archaeus*, 44; and elective affinity, 76–77; revival of, 91, 120, 122–23, 131, 132, 145
Herder, Johann Gottfried von, 194; and harmony, 189–90; *Haupttypus*, 9, 189, 194, 214–15, 246; Humboldt (Alexander) and, 248; influences on, 309n98; and language of nature, 186–87, 186–87, 309n98; and organization, 187–91; as post-Enlightenment figure, 15, 186, 199; and primitive design, 51; recapitulation theory of, 188–89; scientific writings of, 186, 309n98
heredity, 185
hermeticism, 34; Buffon and, 39, 42; divine preformation vs., 57; Humboldt brothers and, 26; mechanism vs., 29, 34; revival of, 115–16
Herz, Henriette, 224, 227
Herz, Marcus: and experiential psychology as science, 148; Hufeland and, 173; and Jewish burial customs, 307–8n73; Kant and, 305n28; and *Leichenhäuser*, 308n83; on premature burial, 175, 177; and sensation, 149; and substantialized matter, 150, 151–52
Heyne, Christian Gottlob, 115

Heyne, Therese, 224, 227
Hippocrates, 165, 167; Buffon and, 39, 65–66; fertilization theory of, 168; and gender differentiation, 318n99; and generation, 222; Herder and, 187; revival of, 123, 165; Stahl and, 123, 124, 125
Hißmann, Michael, 82
Histoire naturelle (Buffon): contemporary significance of, 268n3; and elective affinity, 85–86; harmonic mediation in, 44; and language of nature, 31, 38; literary style of, 69, 277n126; on *moule intérieur*, 51; Rousseau and, 276n112; significance of, 31, 33–34, 68–69
historical knowledge, 1, 40–42, 48–49, 54, 62–64, 187, 226, 249–50
historicism:, 1, 2; Buffon and, 69, 277n127; Enlightenment vs. Romantic, 1; Humboldt (Wilhelm) as founder of, 17, 29, 251, 254–55, 264n33, 325n52; *Naturphilosophie* and, 214, 220; rise of, 17
history, human, 187–88, 249–50
Hogarth, William, 220, 317n96
Holbach, Paul Henri d', 82
homme machine, 268n4
Horen, Das (journal), 21, 225
Horkheimer, Max: and Enlightenment, political/religious adaptations of, 4, 251, 267n38; on inner logic of science, 9; on mechanism, 5; on *Naturphilosophie*, 199; postmodern Enlightenment critiques and, 2
Hufbauer, Karl, 112
Hufeland, Christian: Blumenbach and, 296n18; and death, resurrection from, 176; and *Leichenhäuser*, 308n83; and *Naturphilosophie*, 200; and *Scheintod*, 173–74, 175, 307n57
Hulling, Mark, 276n112
humanism, 39
humanistic sciences *(Geisteswissenschaften)*: Buffon and, 271n25; Enlightenment and, 1–2; German historicism and, 1; natural sciences separate from, 2, 14, 17, 18

human nature, 23, 33, 148, 256; interconnection and, 137–38
Humboldt, Alexander von, 14–15; and ambiguity, 25–28; on animation and irritability, 299n79; assumptions held by, 22–23; and Baconianism, 296n12; Blumenbach and, 296n18; Buffon and, 30, 238–39, 246, 248–49; career of, 17–18; on dead vs. living matter, 307n60; decline of, 249; Forster and, 245–46, 323n30; "general physics" of, 245–48, 324n32, 324n35, 324n36; Humboldt (Wilhelm) on, 237, 321n2; impact on Enlightenment Vitalism, 250–51; language of nature, 18, 20–23, 28–30, 88, 238, 242; Lavoisier and, 112; as liberal, 13; and life forces, 21–25, 174; and matter/motion dichotomy, 23–25; natural philosophy of, 238, 240–44; and *Naturphilosophie*, 200, 239–45, 321n7, 321–22n8, 322n9, 323n25; and observation, 237–38, 241–42, 243; and philosophy, 254, 325n57; as post-Enlightenment figure, 251, 253–54, 325n51; post-expedition dilemma of, 237–39; and primitive design, 51; Schelling and, 321n7; significance of, 17
"Humboldtian science," 253–54
Humboldt University (Berlin), 17
Humboldt, Wilhelm von, 14–15; and ambiguity, 25–28; assumptions held by, 23; career of, 17–18; and chemical method, 78; and gender differentiation, 224, 225, 227–28, 318n107, 318n111; and gender, reconstruction of, 228–29; and generation, 225–27; on Humboldt (Alexander), 237, 321n2; impact on Enlightenment Vitalism, 250; intellectual character of, 19, 260n1; language of nature, 18–20, 28–30, 242; and language of science, 56, 274–75n88; Lavoisier and, 112; as liberal, 13; and life forces, 23–25; and matter/motion dichotomy, 23–25; and middle

Humboldt, Wilhelm von, *(continued)*
    realm, 190, 274–75n88; natural philosophy of, 241, 243–44; and *Naturphilosophie*, 200; as post-Enlightenment figure, 29, 251, 254–55, 264n33, 325n52; significance of, 17; and world-historical physics, 249–50
Hume, David, 5–6, 37–38, 41
Hunter, John, 174–75, 176, 255, 307n69
Hunter, William, 255
hybridization, 164, 168, 169–70

ideal types, concept of, 214–15
Ideen zur Philosophie der Geschichte der Menschheit (Herder), 186, 188
identity, 38, 54–55, 83, 203–4
idiosyncratic systemization, 115, 117
Iggers, Georg, 264n33
impulsion, 135
individuality: Buffon and, 45, 69; conjunction and, 138, 213–14; and Enlightenment vitalist natural philosophy, 9, 80, 138, 145; In Humboldt, 213; in *Naturphilosophie*, 207–8, 213
induction, Baconian, 296n12
innate ideas, 54
inner/outer topos, 126
Institutiones medicae (Boerhaave), 121
instrumentalism, 84
interconnection: Great Chain of Being and, 163–64; life sciences and, 143; metaphors for, 159; organic, 159, 302n1; in organized body, 137–39; reciprocal, 139, 143; and sympathy, 139–42; universal, 136–37, 182, 184–85. *See also* harmonic mediation
intuition *(Anschauung)*, 9, 20, 36, 55–56, 88, 116, 136–37. *See also* divination
irritability: animation and, 299n79; and gender differentiation, 222; and organized body, 130–31, 132–33,
    145, 192–93; sensibility vs., 141; sympathy and, 142; and temperaments, 154
Irvine, William, 92
Isis (journal), 314n16
Italy, 120, 304n27

Jacob, Margaret, 37, 266n35
Jacoby, Friedrich, 237
Jardine, Nicholas, 200, 311n118, 313–14n13, 314n21, 316n68
Jefferson, Thomas, 50
Jena, University of, 239
Jordanova, Ludmilla, 9, 25, 29, 180, 222, 236
Judaism: burial practices, 176, 177–78, 181, 307–8n73, 308n74; Enlightenment *(Haskala)*, 177–78, 308n74; Kabbala, 204
Juncker, Johann, 282n20
Jussieu, Antoine-Laurent de, 164, 303n22
juxtaposition, 56, 68, 96, 297–98n49

Kabbala, 204
Kant, Immanuel: and "basic types," 246; as Enlightenment symbol, 252; and epigenesis, 166, 259n21; epistemology of, 312–13n9; and generation, 160–61, 302–3n7; Herder and, 187; Humboldt (Wilhelm) and, 228; Kielmeyer and, 310n118; and mediating imperative, 152–53; and *Naturphilosophie*, 200–201; and polarity, 116; Sömmering and, 152–53; and teleo-mechanism, 304–5n28; and temperaments, 156
Karsten, Wencelaus Johann, 71–72, 73, 116
Kästner, Abraham Gotthelf: on Buffon and Leibniz, 276n114; as Buffon's translator, 46, 272n45, 272–73n53; influence of, 113; Kant and, 305n28
Kielmeyer, Carl Friedrich: Blumenbach and, 191, 296n18; career of, 310n117; as Enlightenment vitalist, 191–92; Herder and, 191; on inter-

acting forces, 311n123; and language of nature, 198; and *Naturphilosophie*, 200–202, 310–11n118; and ontogenesis, 191–95
Kim Mi Gyung, 88, 286n67
King, Lester, 122
Kleine Schriften (Forster), 246
knowledge: chemical, 84; historical, 40–42, 62–64, 249; self-evident, and reason, 54. *See also* epistemology
Knox, Robert, 14, 314n16
Kölreuter, Joseph Gottlieb, 166, 167–68, 318n99
Kuhn, Dorothea, 311n118
Kuhn, Thomas, 101–2, 110

Lagrange, Joseph-Louis, comte de, 6, 245
Lamarck, Jean-Baptiste, 195, 196–98, 311n134
Lambert, Johann Heinrich, 187
La Mettrie, Julien Offroy de, 61–62, 113, 268n4, 295n6
Laplace, Pierre-Simon, 6, 107, 113, 237, 245, 252
Laqueur, Thomas, 222, 229, 231, 319n119
Larson, John E., 158, 302n1, 305n31, 305–6n33
Lavater, Johann, 158
Lavoisier, Antoine Laurent: and active elements, 105–11, 292n136; Baader and, 293n145; Buffon and, 287n80; caloric, theory of, 103, 109–11; and chemical reactions, 147; Chemical Revolution and, 74, 101–4, 111, 118, 292n130; and Classical *episteme*, 280n15; critical reception of, 104, 111–14; and elective affinity, 87, 108–9, 292–93n140; and element definition, 107, 290n105, 290n108; and equilibrium, 287n75; and gravimetrics, 284n55; influence of, 292n130; and language of chemistry, 74, 75, 88, 103, 105–6, 108; Macquer and, 282–83n29; *Naturphilosophen* critique of, 206, 211;
and oxygen, 106–7; and phlogiston, 104–5, 280n15; and water as compound, 98
Lawrence, Christopher, 122
Leclerc, Georges-Louis, comte de Buffon. *See* Buffon, Georges-Louis Leclerc, comte de
Leeuwenhoeck, Antoni von, 58
Lehrbuch der Gynäkologie (Carus), 233
Lehrbuch der Naturphilosophie (Oken), 206–9, 217, 316n68
Leibniz, Gottfried Wilhelm: and analogy, 191; Buffon and, 272–73n53; and Cartesian dualism, 36, 270n12; and divine power, 150, 160; and final causes through sufficient reason, 64; and German Enlightenment, 313n11; harmonic ideal of, 126; and matter, activity of, 34–35, 81; *Naturphilosophie* and, 202, 204–5, 236; Newton vs., 60; and preestablished harmony, 60–61; Tiedemann on, 206; universal vision of, 202
Leichenhäuser, 180–81, 308n83
Leiden school, 121–22
Lelarge de Lignac, Joseph Adrien, 277n124
Lenoir, Timothy, 12, 304–5n28, 310–11n118
Lesch, John E., 137
Lessing, Gotthold Ephraim, 171
Le Vaillant, François, 254
liberalism, 12–13
Lichtenberg, Georg, 112, 113, 141, 237, 305n28, 317n96
life, definition of, 15, 19, 21–24, 43, 57, 65, 90, 92, 101, 120, 131, 133–34, 135–36, 138, 143–47, 154, 172, 179, 211, 225
"Life Force or the Rhodian Genius" (A. von Humboldt), 23, 174
life-saving associations, 180–81
life sciences: Buffon and, 70; and chemistry, 75; and Hippocrates, 66, 123; and language of nature, 10, 143, 158; mechanism and, 121, 241,

life sciences (*continued*)
  264–66n34; revolutionizing of, 119–21, 158, 169–70, 294n2, 295n10; and Stahl, 123; vitalization of, 6–7, 268n4, 273n63. *See also* physiology
Linneaus, Carolus, 27, 34, 48
Locke, John, 54, 273n63
Loder, Justus, 296n18
logical predisposition, 60–61
Louis XIV (king of France), 37
love, 84–85, 223
Lundgren, Anders, 118
Lyonet, Pierre, 170

McEvoy, John, 291n126
Macquer, Pierre-Joseph: and catalysts, 83; on chemical method, 77–78; and elective affinity, 85; and elementary earth, 98; Gmelin on, 113; on heat as element, 98; and identity attraction, 83; Lavoisier and, 282–83n29; Stahlian chemistry and, 281–82n20
magnetism, 46, 67, 90, 212, 240, 247, 273n59
Maillet, Benoit de, 268n4
Malebranche, Nicolas, 58
Malpighi, Marcello, 58, 66, 68
Man the Machine (La Mettrie), 61–62
Marx, Karl, 257n7
masculinity, 223–28, 236
materialism, 120, 161, 184, 186
mathematics: analysis, 8, 41; Buffon and, 39–41, 271n30, 271n37; definition of, 204; essence of, 207; as language of mechanistic natural philosophy, 35–36, 39–41, 269–70n9; and nature, 6; in *Naturphilosophie*, 203–9; quantification vs., 205–6
mathematization, vs. quantification, 269n9
mathesis, 35, 41, 203–9, 236
matter: as *agens*, 81, 89–91; Buffon's redefinition of, 42–47, 272n45; chemistry and, 10–11; convertibility of, 184–85; dead vs. living, 195, 307n60, 311n134; definition of, 201;

divisibility of, 71–72; Enlightenment Vitalism and, 6–8; first forms of, 212–13; fluidity of, 79–81, 283n36, 283–84n40, 307n60; and force, 79–82, 201, 284n45; inner/outer relationship, 43; mechanistic definition of, 5, 6, 34–35, 42, 75–76; motion vs., 23–25; *Naturphilosophie* and, 200, 212–13; non-homogeneity of, 278n5; and spirit, identity between, 203–4; Stahl and, 75–76. *See also* Cartesian dualism; force, substantialized; heat, matter of
Maupertuis, Pierre-Louis Moreau de: as antimechanist, 268n4; Buffon and, 273n55; epigenesis revived by, 62, 159; and generation, 56, 66; Kant on, 161; least action, law of, 160, 161, 273n55; as skeptical critic, 5; and spirit of systems, 31
mechanism: animism vs., 81–82, 131, 136; *Bildungstrieb* and, 169; and chemical reactions, 77; death in, 171; decline of, 119; and divine preformation, 56–61; and elements, 91–92; Enlightenment and, 2, 28–31, 264–66n34; Enlightenment Vitalist critique of, 6–7, 9; epistemology of, 34, 36, 53; Gmelin and, 113; goals of, 34; and heat, 92, 93–94; Herder and, 186–87; Humboldt (Alexander) and, 241; interconnection in, 139–40; Kant and, 201; and language of chemistry, 73–74; and life sciences, 241; mathematics and, 35–36, 39–41; matter/spirit dichotomy in, 25; natural philosophy of, 5, 34–37, 42, 269–70n9; noncontradiction, principle of, 40–41; organicism vs., 203; organization vs., 135, 297–98n49; physiological revolution and, 120–21; political/religious adaptations of, 5, 29, 35–36, 37, 59–60, 266n35; and sensation, 150; skeptical critique of, 5–7, 37–38, 74; *solidistes* and, 119–20; Stahl and,

75–76. *See also* antimechanism; *specific philosophers*
mediation. *See* harmonic mediation
medicine, 10, 70, 304n23
Medicinische Bibliothek, Die, 166
meditation, 237–38
Melhado, Evan M., 280n14, 292n140
membrane-continuity theory, 162, 163, 168, 303n11
Mendelssohn, Moses, 171, 177
Mersenne, Marin, 41
metaphors: of animal economy, 133; chemical, 67, 77; of Enlightenment Vitalism, 12; of generation, 221; of harmony, 228; life sciences and, 143; mechanistic, 29, 36–37; of organic interconnection, 159; of organized body, 174, 297–98n49; political, 133, 221; sexual, 67; sympathy and, 141, 159; wheel of life, 216
Metzger, Hélène, 88–89, 157
Metzger, Johann, 174, 305n28
Meyer, Johann F., 100
Michaelis, Caroline, 224
Michaelis, Christoph Friedrich, 301n113
Michelet, Jules, 298n52
mind: energy of, 128–29; nature as, 210. *See also* Cartesian dualism
mineralogy, chemical nomenclature and, 286–87n69
modernity: Enlightenment and, 251–52; Enlightenment Vitalism and, 253; *Naturphilosophie* and, 199, 214, 312n1
monads, spiritual, 171
Monas, 207–8, 235
Monro, Alexander, 122
monstrosities (abnormal births), 164, 169–70, 303n19
Montesquieu, Charles Louis de Secondat, baron de la Brede de: as antimechanist, 268n4; and constitutional form, 52, 282n27; and language of nature, 33; political principles of, analogies to, 100, 215; and spirit of systems, 31

Montpellier (France): Hippocratic medicine in, 131; medical mechanism critiqued in, 122, 124; neo-Stahlians in, 155; Stahlian chemistry in, 9–10; vitalism in, 273n63
morality, organized body and, 155–56
moral regeneration, 120
Moravia, Sergio, 116
morgue, institution of, 181
moule intérieur, 46–47, 50, 51–52, 100, 161
mucous membrane, 132–33
Muhlack, Ulrich, 254
Müller, Lothar, 304n23
muscles: and active energy, 129; contraction of, 128; and irritability, 130, 132–33, 145

Napoleonic Wars, 175, 229
nationalism, 291n129
Natron, Lake (Egypt), Berthollet's experiments at, 87
natural history: Baconian, 278–79n10; Buffon and, 33, 41–42, 47, 52–53, 75, 120; chemistry and, 74, 86–88, 97, 104, 279–80n14, 285n60; contemporary significance of, 268n3; historicization of, 195–97; and human history, 186, 249; and language of nature, 10; Linnean, 71; mechanism and, 73–74, 119, 264–66n34; and physical sciences, 137; Rousseau and, 276n112
naturalism, 39
natural law, 19–20
natural magic, 34
natural philosophy: and animal generation, 63; of Buffon, 38–42, 198, 238, 271n30; of Enlightenment Vitalism, 6–8, 9; history of, 63; of Humboldt (Alexander), 238, 240–44; of Humboldt (Wilhelm), 241, 243–44; as language, 38; of mechanism, 5, 34–37, 42, 269–70n9; organic matter, redefinition of, 42–47; reordering of, 71–75, 278n1; and scientific system, 47–52; and

natural philosophy (continued)
  systematic analysis, 47–48. See also
  chemistry; natural history; physics
natural sciences (Naturwissenschaften), 1–2, 14, 17, 18
nature: ambiguity of, 25–28; and analogy, 191; as dynamic, 69–70, 82, 90, 92, 95–96, 170–71, 183–86, 188, 214, 244; forces in, 7, 23–24, 46–47, 82, 84–85, 122, 125–27, 141, 146; and freedom and determinism, 9, 207–8, historicization of, 6, 10–11, 69–70, 252; human connection to, 22–23, 25, 52, 63, 84–85, 209, 225, 237, 238, 241–42, 249–51, 322n11; and identity with mind, 210–11; and interconnection, 44, 75–76, 78, 133, 137; mechanism and, 3, 5, 35–37, 58; observation of, 202–3; opposition in, 23–25, 90–91, 229–30; primordial (Ur) beginnings, 19–23, 217–20; representation of, 21–23, 39–42, 44–45, 52–53, 54, 55–56, 88, 108, 241–45, 246–48; skeptical view of, 6, 38; as unity in diversity, 8–9, 25, 137, 146, 193, 211–12; unity of, 203–4, 210–11, 213–17; and universal mathesis, 203
nature, economy of: and active force, 89–91; as dynamic, 95–96, 103–4; interconnection and, 159; as teleological, 125–26; transformation in, 182–86. See also animal economy
nature, language of: Buffon and, 31, 33–34, 38–39; controversy over, 161; core elements of, 158; decline of, 13; and diachronic development, 162–63; Enlightenment and, 28–31, 235–36; Enlightenment Vitalism as, 9–10; Geoffrey and, 85; Herder and, 186–87; Humboldt (Alexander) and, 238, 242, 245; Humboldt brothers and, 18–23, 28–30; Lavoisier and, 103, 105–6; of mechanism, 34–37; natural philosophy as, 38; Naturphilosophie and, 200, 208–9,
211–12, 220; organized matter and, 143; quantification and, 242, 245; structure of, 143; sympathy and, 154. See also chemistry, language of
Naturphilosophie, 25; and atomism, 240, 321–22n8; current relevance of, 199, 312n1; Enlightenment Vitalism vs., 13–14, 198, 199–203, 209, 220–21, 253, 313–14n13; epistemology of, 200, 205, 209–14, 313–14n13, 316n50; formulation of, 198; and gender, scientific construction of, 220–36; Humboldt (Alexander) and, 239–45, 321n7, 321–22n8, 322n9, 323n25; incomprehensibility of, 203–4, 314n21; Kielmeyer and, 310–11n118; and language of nature, 208–9, 211–12, 220; and mathematics, 203–9; and modernity, 312n1; observation and, 202–3; Oken and, 314n16, 317n85; origins of, 199; and polarity, 323n25; and process, 214–20, 315n43, 316n68; Schelling and, 314n16, 317n85
Naturwissenschaften. See natural sciences
Needham, John Turberville, 62, 162, 268n4
negation (mathematical function), 207–9
neomechanism, 6, 252
neo-Stahlians, 155–56
nervous system: animal economy and, 129, 131; definition of, 148; as functional system, 147–54; and irritability, 132–33; and Nervenkraft, 150; opposed powers in, 130–31; and organized body, 128; and sensibility, 300n88
Neubauer, John, 204–5
Newtonian science: anti-Newtonianism, 266n35; Buffon and, 67; mechanism and, 5, 29; Oken and, 219; penetrating power, 67; and physics, 278n5; 278–79n10, and planetary

motion, 42; radical politics and, 266n35
Newton, Isaac: and analogy, 191; and divine power, 150, 160; and gravity, 46; Leibniz vs., 60; mechanism and, 34; motion, laws of, 272n40; Stahl and, 124; and universal aether, 79, 93, 219, 283n34
Nieuwentyt, Bernard, 57
Nisbet, Hugh B., 309n98
nisus formativus. See *Bildungstrieb*
nomina propria, 38
noncontradiction, principle of, 40–41
Normaltypus, 169
nosology, 154
Nouveau essais (Leibniz), 313n11
Nouveaux éléments de la science de l'homme (Barthez), 119, 140
Novalis, 112, 200, 204, 206
nutrition, 169, 186

observation, 202–3, 237–38, 241–42, 243
occult force, 8; *Bildungstrieb* as, 169; Buffon and, 43, 46–47, 56, 67–68; chemical attraction and, 84; definition of, 109, 273n59, 293n143; gravity as, 43, 46; Leibniz and, 60–61; sympathy and, 140; universal interconnection and, 138; vital principle as, 142
Oelsner (physician), 178–79
Oken, Lorenz: Blumenbach and, 317–18n98; and gender, scientific construction of, 229–32, 319n118, 319n122, 319n129; Goethe and, 239; and language of nature, 13; Lavoisier and, 112; and mathematics, definition of, 204; and *Naturphilosophie,* 13, 200, 314n16, 317n85; on observation in science, 202–3; and organic process, 217–20, 316n68; solar theory of, 218–20; and universal *mathesis,* 203, 206–9
one-sidedness, 190, 228
"On Kant and German *Naturphilosophie*" (Kielmeyer), 201

"On the Historian's Task" (W. von Humboldt), 18, 243–44, 249–50, 254–55
On the Limits of State Action (W. von Humboldt), 18
ontogeny, 10, 188–89, 191–95, 197–98
opposition. See polarity
Optics (Newton), 79
Order of Things, The (Foucault), 252
organicism, 11, 203, 259n25
organic molecules, 44–45
organic process, *Naturphilosophie* and, 208–9, 214–20, 315n43, 316n68
organization: and development, 158; diachronic development and, 159; Enlightenment Vitalism and, 159; human history and, 187–88; ladders of, 164, 188–89, 190–91, 197; and language of nature, 143; living system as, 134; mechanism vs., 135, 297–98n49; and mechanism vs. animism, 136; vital economy and, 10; vitalism and, 135–37, 154. See also body, organized
Organ of the Soul (Sömmering), 152–53
Orr, Linda, 298n52
Ostwald, Wilhelm, 280–81n17
Outram, Dorinda, 260n31, 326n59
ovism, 56–57, 58, 162, 318n99
Owen, Richard, 14
oxidation, 110, 211
oxygen: as acidifying agent, 103, 106–7, 113–14; discovery of, 102

Paligénése philosophique (Bonnet), 165
palingenesis, 164
Pallas, Peter Simon, 158
pan-spermism, 230, 231–32
Paracelsus: as animist, 81; and elective affinity, 76–77; Humboldt brothers and, 26; *Naturphilosophie* and, 204; revival of, 91, 92, 122–23, 125
paradox, 26–27, 44, 47, 182, 236, 277n124
passions, 127

penetrability, 80
Perrin, Carleton E., 290n108, 292n130, 292n140
Pfaff, Christian H., 200–201, 274n69, 291n129
phenomenology, 84
Philosophy of Physiology, The (Schiller), 150
phlogiston: caloric and, 109; controversy over, 101–2, 113–14, 118; definition of, 104–5; and elective affinity, 286n64; elemental earth as, 116; hydrogen and, 98; Lavoisier and, 104–5, 280n15; matter of heat as, 99–100; *Naturphilosophie* and, 211; and phlogistication, 211; Stahlian chemistry and, 74, 76, 280–81n17
phylogeny, 10, 188–89, 191, 193–95
physician-savant, 304n23
physicotheology, 160, 162–63
physics: Humboldt (Alexander) and, 245–48, 324nn32, 35, 36; Humboldt (Wilhelm) and, 249–51; incoherence of, 278n5; and natural philosophy, forms of, 71, 73; Newtonian, 278–79n10
Physikalisches Wörterbuch (Gehler), 72, 112
physiognomy, 247–48
physiology: and causation, 135; and interdisciplinary connections, 249; and nervous system, 148; origins of, 138; "philosophical," 148, 300n87; renewal of, 119–21; synergy in, 259n20. *See also* animal economy; body, organized; generation; nervous system; reproduction
Pietism: and divine preformation, 59; Kant and, 156; secularization of, and *Naturphilosophie*, 223; Stahl and, 106, 124–25, 127, 282n20; and "voluntarism," 127
planetary motion, 42
Plato, 63–64, 202, 204, 206
Pliny, 39, 48
Plotinus, 202, 204, 206
Pluche, Abbé, 59

poetry/poetics, 20, 225, 243
polarity: Buffon and, 67; and elements, definition of, 107–8; and generation, 230–32; Goethe and, 90–91, 108; harmonic mediation of, 89–91, 127; Humboldt (Alexander) and, 23–25, 240, 323n25; Kant and, 116; *Naturphilosophie* and, 210–13, 218–20, 323n25; in organized body, 130–31; Schelling and, 210–11; *Ur*-polarity, 210–11. *See also* harmonic mediation
Porter, Roy, 3, 304n23
Porter, Theodore, 281n19, 286–87n69
positivism, 14, 245–46
postmodernism: critiques of Enlightenment, 2, 199, 251–52, 253; Enlightenment Vitalism and, 15–16, 256
postpyrrhonist tradition, 41
Pratt, Mary Louise, 238, 254, 325n51
preformation, divine, 56–61; Blumenbach's critique of, 168–70, 304n27; Bonnet and, 161, 162–65; Buffon's critique of, 61–68; definition of, 56–57; epigenesis vs., 57–58, 159–65, 221, 318n99; Haller and, 130, 161–64; Herder and, 188; Kant and, 302–3n7; Kölreuter and, 167–68; Leibniz and, 313n11; Oken and, 229–30; proponents of, 303n22; Roger on, 275n91
premechanistic reasoning, revival of, 115–16, 121. *See also* animism; hermeticism; *specific premechanistic philosopher*
Premier discourse (Buffon), 39
Priestley, Joseph, 12, 98, 102, 114, 281n19
primitive design, 51, 182–83, 277n127
Primus Motor, 116
Principes de physiologie (Dumas), 120
principe vital. *See* vital principle
Pringle, John, 295n10
process. *See* organic process
progress, 183, 190–91
Protestantism, 115. *See also* Pietism

"proto-Romanticism," 12, 199, 255, 259n27
prototype, 9, 182–83, 189, 214–15
Prussia, defeat of, 229
psychology, 148, 249, 300n87
public health, 181
putrefaction, as evidence of death, 174, 181
Pythagoras, 63–64, 202, 204–5, 206, 217

quantification, 27, 35, 205–6, 242, 245, 269–70n9, 271n37
quantitative analysis, 284–85n55

race discrimination, 2
radical force, 142
radius, 217
Ranke, Leopold von, 1
rapport: Buffon and, 45, 51–52, 272n52; conjunction and, 134; organism constituted through, 213; Stahl and, 76–77; violent death and, 179–80. *See also* affinity, elective; sympathy
rationalism, 28–29, 126, 151
reason: Kant and, 201; mathematics and, 35; *Naturphilosophie* as corrective to, 199, 201–3; poetic act and, 20; self-evident knowledge and, 54; skepticism and, 252; teleological, 64; sufficient, argument from, 64, 190, 276n114; unknown and, 37–38. *See also* analogical reasoning
recapitulation, theory of, 184, 188–89
Recherches sur les lois d'affinité (Berthollet), 87
Redi, Francesco, 58
Rehbock, Philip, 312n1
Reil, Johann Christian, 296n18
Reill, Peter Hanns, 1
Religious Philosopher, The (Nieuwentyt), 57
reproduction, 161–65, 169, 192–93, 195
resemblance, 54–55, 56, 77, 164
resurrection, 172, 175–77, 180, 307n69

Rey, Roselyn, 191, 295n6
Ricardo, David, 280n15
Rigotti, Francesca, 303n22
Robinet, Jean-Baptiste: Diderot and, 184; and generation, 182–83; Herder and, 188; Humboldt (Alexander) and, 248; Lamarck and, 197; as preformationist, 182, 303n22; and primitive design, 51, 246
Roger, Jacques, 273n63; on Buffon, 44, 48, 50, 259n25; and opposing Enlightenments, 3; on preformationism, 275n91
Roget, Peter Mark, 14
Romanticism, 9, 251, 254, 325n51; "proto-Romanticism," 12, 199, 255, 259n27. *See also Naturphilosophie*
romanticism, popular, 278–79n10
Röschlaub, Andreas, 200
Rosicrucians, 115
Rouelle, Guillaume-François, 113
Rousseau, Jean Jacques: on aggregate as social body, 138, 298n61; Buffon and, 63; as Enlightenment symbol, 252; as Enlightenment vitalist, 12; Herder and, 187; as natural historian, 63, 276n112
Roussel, Pierre: and *faculté generatrice*, 165–66; and life sciences, revolutionizing of, 119, 120, 294n2; on Stahl, 124; and temperaments, 155
Russia, Blumenbach's influence in, 304n27

St. Hilaire, Étienne Geoffrey, 14, 259n25
St. Jean-de-Luz (Spain), 19–20, 23, 27, 30, 228
St. Pierre, Bernardin de, 254
salt: universal, 116; and salification, 108
saturation, 86–87, 285–86n61
Saussure, Benedict, 30
Schaffer, Simon, 3, 258n8, 281n19
Scheele, Carl Wilhelm, 71; and air, study of, 99, 290n110; and chemical method, 78; and elective affinity, 87;

Scheele, Carl Wilhelm (*continued*)
and elements, definition of, 91, 98, 100–101; Lavoisier and, 102; and matter of heat, 99–100; and phlogiston, 109; and quantitative analysis, 284–85n55; rhetorical strategy of, 291n128; and species as chemical substance, 285n60
Scheintod (apparent death), 172, 174–76, 182, 307n57, 308n83
Schelling, Friedrich: and *aufgehoben*, 315n43; on explanations, 316n50; and gender differentiation, 229–30; Goethe and, 239; Humboldt (Alexander) and, 321n7; Kielmeyer and, 310n118; and language of nature, 13; Lavoisier and, 112; and *Naturphilosophie*, 200, 205, 314n16, 317n85; and organic process, 214–15, 216–17; and philosophical chemistry, 210–12
Schiebinger, Londa, 320n134
Schiller, Friedrich von, 21; and active force, 150–51; and experiential psychology as science, 148, 300n87; and gender differentiation, 228, 319n115; as "Romantic," 254
Schlegel, August Wilhelm, 134, 229
Schlegel, Friedrich, 112, 229, 260n1
Schlözer, Dorothea, 224
Schneider, Carl, 117
Schofield, Robert, 3, 70, 79, 283n34, 283n36
science. *See* natural philosophy
Sciences in Enlightened Europe, The, 4, 257n7, 257–58n8, 266–67n38
scientific revolution, characteristics of, 117–18
Scotland: antimechanism in, 295n10; heat research in, 290n102; physiology revolutionized in, 120; Stahlian chemistry in, 9–10, 281n19
secretion, 192
semen, 164–65
semiotics: Buffon and, 56; and heat measurement, 96–97; Humboldt brothers and, 25–26, 243; and language of chemistry, 88–89; life sciences and, 143; mechanism and, 36; *Naturphilosophie* and, 204; reintroduction of, 8; scientific revolution and, 118
Semler, Johann Salomo, 115–16
Senebier, Jean, 161, 303n22
sensation, 128–29, 132, 149–50, 178–79, 186
sense organs, operation of, 148–50
sensibility: irritability vs., 141; nervous system and, 147–48, 300n88; and organized body, 130, 131–33, 145, 192–93
sensorium commune, 153–54
sentiments, theory of, 157
series, process and, 216–17
Serre, Michel, 89
Serres, Étienne, 14
sexuality, 222–23, 230–31
Shapin, Steven, 3–4, 30
Shaw, Peter, 282n20
Shelley, Mary, 175–76
Siegfried, Robert, 76
skepticism: and antimechanism, 5–7, 37–38, 74; and Enlightenment, distrust of, 257n7; impact on Enlightenment Vitalism, 252; *Naturphilosophie* and, 209
Sloan, Philip, 3, 41, 48, 52, 271n25, 273n63
Smith, Adam, 141
solar system, and organic process, 218–20
solidistes, 119–20, 143, 144, 145, 150
solubility, 80
Sömmering, Samuel Thomas, 301n108; Blumenbach and, 296n18; and guillotine, controversy over, 178–80, 308n75; Kant and, 152–53; Lavoisier and, 112
Sonderweg, 29
soul: body and, 125–27, 270n12; conscious, 140; as organ, 152–53; rational, 125–26, 128. *See also* active energy/force; Cartesian dualism

Spallanzani, Lazzaro, 161, 168, 303n22
Spary, Emma, 33, 268n3, 277n126
species: *Bildungstrieb* and, 223; chemistry and, 87–88, 285n60; classification of, 27, 49–50, 54–55, 182, 274n69; continuity within, 157, 184, 194–95; fixity of, 195–96; normal type/schemata of, 169; unity in diversity, 223; variation within, 146–47, 277n127
spermism, 56–57, 58, 230, 231–32
sphere, as complete natural form, 217
Spinoza, Baruch, 35
spirit: duality in, 210–11; as essence of reality, 202; and matter, dichotomy between, 25; and matter, identity between, 203–4; of systems, 31, 202, 252
spiritualism, 120
spiritual monads, 171
spontaneous generation, 62, 197, 229–30
Staël, Madame de, 224, 227
Stahl, Georg: and animal motion, 128; as animist, 81; as anti-Enlightenment, 296n21; Blumenbach on, 124; and body/soul relationship, 125–27; and chemistry, language of, 75–77, 78–79; and elective affinity, 83; and elementary earth, 98, 282n25; Herder and, 187; Leibniz on, 36, 60; and mind/matter relationship, 270n12; and phlogiston, 104–5; as Pietist, 106, 124–25, 127, 282n20; revival of, 91, 123–28, 131; and synergy, 259n20; and temperaments, 126–27, 154–56; and vitalism, 9–10
Stahlian Revolution, 73–74, 76, 279n13
Stahlian science: Chemical Revolution and, 101–2; compounds in, 81–82; phlogiston and, 74, 280–81n17; physiology and, 120; regional adoption of, 281n19, 281–82n20
Stedman, John Gabriel, 254
Steffens, Heinrich, 239
stimulus/response, 131

Stufengang, 216
Sturm und Drang, 223
succession, language of, 218
Sue, Jean Joseph, 178–79
sufficient reason, argument from, 64, 190, 276n114
Swammerdam, Jan, 58
Sweden, 281n19, 286–87n69
Swieten, Gerhard van, 121, 295n7
sympathy: elective affinity as analogue for, 141; interconnection and, 139–42; and language of nature, 154; as metaphor, 159; organism constituted through, 213; sensation and, 149; Stahl and, 76–77; types of, 141–42; vital economy and, 10. *See also* consensus
synergy, 7, 126, 139, 140, 159, 259n20
synthesis, 80, 243
system: Buffon and, 47–52, 87–88, 137, 247; definition of, 137; functional, 147; interconnection and, 136–37; spirit of, 31, 202, 252; universal, 136
Systême physique et moral de la femme (Roussel), 119

Tableaux de la nature (A. von Humboldt), 237
teleology: *Bildungstrieb* and, 169; Bonnet and, 163; Buffon and, 64, 276n114; as explanatory strategy, 15; and final ends, 64, 163; Humboldt brothers and, 23; and natural history, 196; progressive development and, 183; redefinition of, 170–71; Stahl and, 125; vital economy and, 125
teleo-mechanism, 304–5n28
temperaments, 126–27, 154–58, 222, 301n113
temperature, 96, 247
Terrall, Mary, 277n126, 313n11
Tetens, Johann Nicolas, 187
Theory of Colors (Goethe), 90–91
theosophy, 206
Thomé, Horst, 90

Tiedemann, Dietrich, 206
totalitarianism, 2
Toulmin, Stephen, 2–3, 7
Traité des affinités chymiques (Bergman), 83–84
transmutation, 168
Trembly, Abraham, 62
Trepp, Anne-Charlott, 224
Treviranus, Gottfried, 296n18
trias, duality in, 212–13, 218, 235
Turgot, Anne-Marie-Robert, 106, 271n37
"two seeds" theory, 66, 68

Über den Bildungstrieb (Blumenbach), 166, 220–21, 222–23
Ueber die Verhältniße der organische Kräfte unter einander (Kielmeyer), 192
Ur-line, radius as, 217
Ur-surface, sphere as, 217
Urtyp, 9, 100, 214–15

vaporization, 95
Varnhagen, Rachel, 224–25
Vartanian, Aram, 268n4, 295n6, 297–98n49
Veit, Brendel, 224
Venel, Gabriel-François, 281–82n20, 289–90n99
Vénus physique (Maupertuis), 62
Versuch über den Schwindel (Herz), 151–52
Vico, Giambattista, 53–54, 132
vis: cellulosa, 145; *essentiales*, 166–67; *nervea*, 145, 150
vis viva controversy, 6
vital economy. *See* nature, economy of
vital forces, 21–25, 195, 222
vitalism, 9–10, 11–13; organicism vs., 11, 259n25; and organization, 135–37; origin of term, 294–95n6; physiology and, 120. *See also* Enlightenment Vitalism
vital principle: Barthez and, 106, 143–44, 292n133, 299n73; definition of, 143; interconnection and, 140; as occult force, 142; and organized body, 134
vita maxima vs. *vita minima*, 172
vita propria (specific life), 145–47
Volney, Constantin François Chasseboeuf Boisgirais, Comte de, 254
Voltaire, 252
voluntarism, 127
Von ächter hermetischer Arznei (Semler), 115
vortices, theory of, 116
Vue philosophique de la gradation naturelle des formes d'être (Robinet), 182–83

Wagner, Johann Jakob, 200, 204, 205, 210, 217, 239
Wahlverwandschaft. *See* affinity, elective
Wärmestoff. *See* heat, matter of
warmth, 99
water: as *Cupola*, 213; as element, 98, 290n108; experiments with, 113; generation of, 108
Weber, Max, 214
Werner, Abraham Gottlob, 250
Whytt, Robert: and animal economy, 135; impact on Enlightenment Vitalism, 133–34; influence of, 145; and medical mechanism, 122; and nervous system, 131; and organized body, 128–30, 297n30, 297n34; and spirit of systems, 31
Wilcke, Johan, 92, 93, 94–95, 96, 102
Wilhelm Meisters Wanderjahre (Goethe), 176–77
Wissenschaft, Humboldt brothers and, 17
Wolff, Caspar Friedrich, 166–67, 186, 305n31, 313n11
Wolff, Christian, 64
world machine, 36–37, 130
world organism, 22, 241

zero, nonmateriality of, 206–9
Zeugung, Die (Oken), 220, 229–32
Zimmerman, Rolf Christian, 29

Compositor:	Sheridan Books, Inc.
Text:	Aldus 10/13
Display:	Aldus
Printer and binder:	Sheridan Books, Inc.